DISABILITY MANAGEMENT
THEORY, STRATEGY & INDUSTRY PRACTICE

Fourth Edition

Dianne E.G. Dyck
RN, BN, MSc, COHN(C), COHN-S, CRSP

with contributions by

Heidi Börner, RN, BN, MN, COHN(C), Cert. Professional Supervision
Sharon Chadwick, RN, BScN, COHN(C), COHN-S
Michelle Forgues, B.Comm, B. SocSc
Jane Hall, RN, MPA, CCM
Bonnie Rogers, Dr. PH, BN, MSc, FAAN
Tony Roithmayr, MA, President, BA, MEd, Performance by Design
Kristine Robidoux, LL.B, QC, Gowling, Lafleur, Henderson
Kelly Williams-Whitt, RN, MBA, PhD, University of Lethbridge

LexisNexis®

Disability Management: Theory, Strategy & Industry Practice, Fourth Edition

© LexisNexis 2009
October 2009

Members of the LexisNexis Group worldwide

Canada	LexisNexis Canada Inc, 123 Commerce Valley Dr. E. Suite 700, MARKHAM, Ontario
Australia	Butterworths, a Division of Reed International Books Australia Pry Ltd, CHATSWOOD, New South Wales
Austria	ARD Betriebsdienst and Verlag Orac, VIENNA
Czech Republic	Orac, sro, PRAGUE
France	Éditions du Juris-Classeur SA, PARIS
Hong Kong	Butterworths Asia (Hong Kong), HONG KONG
Hungary	Hvg Orac, BUDAPEST
India	Butterworths India, NEW DELHI
Ireland	Butterworths (Ireland) Ltd, DUBLIN
Italy	Giuffré, MILAN
Malaysia	Malayan Law Journal Sdn Bhd, KUALA LUMPUR
New Zealand	Butterworths of New Zealand, WELLINGTON
Poland	Wydawnictwa Prawnicze PWN, WARSAW
Singapore	Butterworths Asia, SINGAPORE
South Africa	Butterworth Publishers (Pty) Ltd, DURBAN
Switzerland	Stämpfli Verlag AG, BERNE
United Kingdom	Butterworths Tolley, a Division of Reed Elsevier (UK), LONDON, WC2A
USA	LexisNexis, DAYTON, Ohio

Library and Archives Canada Cataloguing in Publication

Dyck, Dianne E. G.
  Disability management: theory, strategy & industry
practice/Dianne E.G. Dyck; with contributions by Heidi
Börner ... [et al.]. — 4th ed.

Includes index.
ISBN 978-0-433-45995-8

  1. Disability insurance claims — Canada — Management.
2. Handicapped — Employment — Canada. 3. Industrial hygiene.
4. Employee health promotion. I. Title.

HD7255.D92 2006   658.3'8   C2006-900985-6

Printed and bound in Canada.

This book is dedicated to all the Canadian Occupational Health Nurses and WorkSafeBC personnel who assisted in the preparation of the Disability Management Nursing Best Practices and a model on the effective management of disability claims that involve over-riding psychosocial components.

About the Author

Dianne Dyck is an Occupational Health & Safety (OH&S) specialist who has extensive experience in developing and managing OH&S programs. Her areas of specialization include the development and implementation of OH&S, Disability Management and Occupational Health services; auditing of OH&S-related programs, benefit programs, Disability Management programs, ergonomic programs, health data information systems, employee wellness programs, and employee assistance programs; and design and implementation of computerized occupational/health information systems. She has worked for private and public-funded agencies.

Dianne has authored numerous articles and text books in the area of disability management and occupational health and safety. For the past two years, she has been the editor of the WHMIS Compliance Manual published by Thomson-Carswell, Scarborough, ON.

In terms of academic and business achievements, Dianne has a Master's Degree in Science with a focus on Community Health Science; certification as a Canadian Occupational Health Nurse; certification as an Occupational Health Nursing Specialist in the United States; and the designation as a Canadian Registered Safety Professional. Over the years, Dianne has functioned as a Public Health Nurse, Community Health Nurse, Occupational Health Nurse, OH&S Specialist and Consultant; and Director OH&S for a Canadian electrical utility.

Her greatest interests lie in the area of workplace illness and injury prevention. Dianne has worked in collaboration with a number of OH&S and Human Resources professionals to develop innovative ways to create supportive work environments that support worker health and safety. As well, she actively participates in the development and delivery of Disability Management and Occupational Health & Safety educational programs and courses.

Preface

The growth of disability management services in Canada is an exciting area; however, as with any emerging field of practice, it brings with it uncertainty as well as many opportunities. For disability management services to be practiced in a responsible manner, the related structure, process, and outcome elements need to be in place. The intent of this text is to offer insight and guidance into these areas. To that end, this book was written to provide some general guidelines on the creation and management of a quality Disability Management Program.

I would like to acknowledge the contributions made by Heidi Börner, Sharon Chadwick, Michelle Forgues, Joyce Gravelle, Jane Hall, Dr. Bonnie Rogers, Tony Roithmayr, Barbara Roberts, Kristine Robidoux, Dr. Martin Shain, Dr. Kelly Williams-Whitt, WorkSafeBC, and the Canadian Occupational Health Nurses who attended the 2009 National Nurses Conference in Vancouver, BC, May 13 and 14th. Without the support of these knowledgeable professionals, the authoring of this resource would not have been possible.

When writing about such a dynamic subject, the process can be somewhat daunting. It is a challenge to provide the most recent and relevant information for readers. My hope is that the *Disability Management: Theory, Strategy & Industry Practice*, 4th *Edition*, will meet your professional and business needs, and that it will prove to be a useful resource as you make your contributions towards advancing the field of Disability Management in Canada.

The first three editions of *Disability Management: Theory, Strategy & Industry Practice* have contributed towards the development of a framework for Disability Management in Canada. This fourth edition offers an added component — the development of the skills needed by Disability Management professionals/practitioners.

I thank the many readers, scholars, and media personnel for their interest and valuable feedback over the years. Your contributions have enhanced the quality of this work.

Dianne Dyck
September 2009

Table of Contents

Chapter 9 — Workplace Attendance Support and Assistance

Section 2: Disability Management: Other Considerations

Chapter 19 — Disability Management: Ethical Practice

Section 3: Disability Management: Glossary

Disability Management Strategy and Theory

INTRODUCTION

Disability management is still a relatively new field. For years, disability management was practised within the occupational health nursing domain. As employer and union interest in getting employees back to work grew, other health care practitioners entered the disability management field. In essence, what evolved in Canada was a largely unregulated practice born out of the occupational health arena and governed by the case law associated with the human rights (duty to accommodate) legislation. Other influences in the field of disability management were Occupational Health & Safety legislation, provincial Workers' Compensation Acts, various professional practice standards, and the privacy legislation.

Today, the field of disability management is deemed to be a valuable asset to employees, employers, and unions. It has been generally identified as being "required for legislative compliance", "a good business practice", and "the right thing to do". However, as with any new field, there remains some confusion as to the scope, intent, best practices, and measurement techniques. As well, most of the industry practices in disability management came into being by "trial and error", as opposed to being clinically researched, and were dependent on the organizational setting in which they originated. Likewise, the human rights case law continues to emerge and impact the field of disability management and the related practices. The result is that disability management best practices are still evolving and are in a state of flux.

CHALLENGES

Many challenges exist in the field of disability management. They stem from the evolving legislation, differences in the interpretation of the legislative decisions, gaps between employer activities and insurance benefit plan responses, recognition of new "hot illnesses",[1] various ethical considerations, the lack of accreditation and case management standards, and poorly understood methods for program evaluation.

---

[1] Many illnesses, which in the past were not compensable, have now, become recognized as being compensable under employee benefit plan coverage. The result is that employees can be off work with illnesses that are ill defined and poorly understood in terms of case management

This textbook is designed to present the applicable legislation along with how employers can effectively implement a sound Disability Management Program and manage employee absence and disability. It outlines the current disability management "best practices".

INTENDED AUDIENCE

My intention in writing this book is to create a resource for the various players in the workplace disability management field. The readers who may find this book relevant to their practice or areas of work are:

- Occupational health nurses and physicians
- Human resources professionals
- Occupational therapists
- Safety practitioners
- Employee Assistance Program counsellors
- Return-to-work Coordinators
- Claims administrators
- Case managers
- Rehabilitation specialists
- Union leaders
- Management personnel
- Insurance carrier staff
- Legal counsellors

In Canada, few books have been written on this topic. The books that do exist tend to focus on the reasons for disability management initiatives, the related costs, and some of the relevant principles. However, little has been done to describe how to implement disability management, who should be involved, what each player should do, the legalities involved, how to market such a program, the relationship with Occupational Health & Safety and Wellness Programs, and how success or failure can be measured. As well, none address the skills required for disability management professionals/practitioners to practice competently in this field of endeavour.

As a result, care has been taken to craft the contents of the fourth edition of this book so that it can be widely understood and applied. As with any rapidly changing field, what is written today may quickly become dated. However the principles remain unchanged.

FORMAT

There are three sections to this textbook. Section 1 addresses the fundamentals of disability management. Section 2 covers the other considerations — topics like ethics, the legal aspects, the impact of cultural diversity, the impact of four

---

techniques. Some examples are chronic fatigue syndrome, fibromyalgia, multiple chemical sensitivities and Epstein-Barr syndrome.

generations in the workplace, outsourcing disability management services, career development for disability management professionals/practitioners, internal and external consulting skills, and the future challenges in the field of disability management. Section 3 provides a glossary of terms used in the field of disability management.

Section 1 — Disability Management Theory, Strategy and Industry Practices

Chapter 1 provides an overview of disability management. It describes what disability management is, why it is important, the current models in place, and the value that a Disability Management Program can offer various stakeholders. As with any business function, a Disability Management Program must add value to an organization. Chapter 1 discusses how to demonstrate that value to senior management and union leaders to garner their support and endorsement.

The importance of joint labour-management support and involvement in a Disability Management Program, the reasons this level of support and involvement is essential, what is involved, and how successful results can be achieved, are addressed in Chapter 2. Some of the potential pitfalls that can be encountered are also discussed.

Chapter 3 describes the need for a supportive infrastructure for a Disability Management Program. Successful Disability Management Programs need three components: structure, process, and recognizable outcomes. The type of infrastructure required for a Disability Management Program is fully described. As well, examples of the recommended elements are included. To make this chapter even more useful to readers, an industry example of selected aspects of a Disability Management Program policy and procedure manual has been crafted. The intent is to assist the reader in exploring some of the areas that should be addressed by a Disability Management Program manual.

The roles and responsibilities of the various stakeholders in a Disability Management Program are defined in Chapter 4. As people become involved in disability management, role confusion occurs. Questions like: "Who does what?"; "Where do my responsibilities start and stop?"; "How can we work successfully together to deal with all the relevant issues involved?"; "Who should take charge of coordinating the disability?"; and many more loom. Chapter 4 attempts to deal with many of these questions. However, one *caveat* is that each organization has different stakeholders and players. Their exact roles and responsibilities in a Disability Management Program will vary depending on the available organization resources and internal/external expertise. These variations are to be expected — the key is to clarify in each situation who will be doing what, when, and how.

To explain the requisite principles and elements involved in a Disability Management Program, an illustration of a Disability Management Program that was industry-developed and successfully implemented is provided in Chapter 5. Questions like: "What is a Disability Management Program?"; "Why is it important and who benefits?"; "What is the purpose?"; "How can it be implemented?"; and "How to amass and measure program outcomes?" are addressed. Disability management measurement techniques are also provided.

Although Chapter 5 addresses outcome measures for a Disability Management Program, Chapter 6 deals with other measurement techniques that can be used to quantify and present the benefits of a Disability Management Program. The importance of program evaluation, data collection, and program evaluation techniques are described.

Chapter 7, "The Role of Employee Assistance Programs in Disability Management" is presented because the service linkage to assistance programs is so critical. For a Disability Management Program to be successful, ill or injured employees and their families need support. As well, by facilitating a successful re-entry into the workplace, the duration of workplace absence can be reduced. The Employee Assistance Program can also help organizations to be proactive in management style, and prevent disabilities before they occur.

Chapter 8 is a case study of how employees experiencing a "hot illness", like chronic fatigue syndrome, can be assisted through the recovery process and brought back into the workplace. This case study defines chronic fatigue syndrome, identifies challenges in diagnosing it, outlines its prevalence, and illustrates how to manage employees experiencing the syndrome. The secret is to use a multi-disciplinary approach. Although this clinical research was done in 1995, the approach remains relevant today.

In any successful Disability Management Program, a critical element is an Attendance Support & Assistance Program. The best way to prevent disability situations is to be proactive and to deal with a potential employee absence before it happens. Chapter 9 presents the various aspects of employee absenteeism, the costs, and the importance of supporting employee work. A model for an Attendance Support & Assistance Program is described and presented for reader use.

Chapter 10 outlines what disability management standards of practice should contain. Four topics — disability claim management, disability case management, confidentiality, and documentation — are addressed as separate practice standards.

The prevention of employee illness and injury is addressed in Chapter 11. By examining the potential roles between the Disability Management Program and other company programs such as the Occupational Health and Safety Programs, Employee Assistance Programs, Workplace Wellness Programs, and human resources management practices, opportunities for prevention are identified. Examples of possible synergies are provided, along with a sample industry-developed workplace wellness model.

Chapter 12 examines the impact that management practices can have on employee health and wellness. The term "toxic workplace" is used to depict those workplaces in which a high number of organizational stressors exist — a place where employee performance is compromised. The outcome is poor employee morale, increased employee absenteeism, high staff turnover, and reduced productivity. This chapter was co-authored with Tony Roithmayr, President, Performance by Design and specialist in helping organizations to develop high performance cultures (available online at: <http://www.performance–bydesign.com>).

Once a disability management program is developed, it is important to "tell and sell" the benefits of the Disability Management Program to stakeholders. Chapter 13 addresses program communication and marketing techniques.

Chapter 14 is dedicated to disability management education and how disability management professionals/practitioners can enable employers to design and deliver effective Disability Management Education Programs or educational sessions.

The concept of the Social Capital Theory and its application in managing workplace disabilities is explained in Chapter 15 by Dr. Kelly Williams-Whitt RN, MBA, PhD, University of Lethbridge. A valuable perspective, the Social Capital Theory helps to explain why the disability situations that fail to resolve in terms of a return to work, are often those claims in which the employee is not socially accepted within the workplace. In essence, it is not the medical reasons that delay/prevent the return to work; rather it is the social aspects.

Chapter 16 discusses the effective management of disability claims that encompass strong psychosocial aspects. These are the most difficult claims to resolve, taking up more than 85 per cent of a Disability Case Manager's time and resources. The theory and internationally recognized approaches to identify and address psychosocial claims are provided. Readers will benefit from the work undertaken by WorkSafeBC Occupational Health Nurses, May 2009.

Over the years, there has been increased interest in the current best practices in the field of disability management, which are summarized in Chapter 17. Concepts such as using an integrated approach to disability management, centralizing responsibility for the program, providing disability management education and training, implementing disability data management processes, recognizing the need for good communication strategies, establishing functional linkages with other organizational programs, standardizing case and claims management practices, protecting any collected employee medical data from inappropriate disclosure, using measurement to monitor and improve the program, developing a supportive infrastructure, having graduated return-to-work opportunities, and ensuring that early intervention is one of the cornerstones for the program are discussed. Best practices for each topic are provided.

As with the disability management best practices, so are there disability management nursing best practices. Chapter 18 presents the 18 disability management nursing best practices as defined by the Canadian Occupational Health Nurses in attendance at the May 2009 WorkSafeBC Occupational Health Nurses' Conference, Vancouver, BC.

Section 2 — Disability Management: Other Considerations

In addition to the disability management principles and practices, there are a number of other considerations of which disability management professionals/ practitioners should be aware. These are covered in Section 2.

Disability management is based on relationships and trust. Inevitably when dealing with people and organizational issues, ethical considerations need to be addressed. In Chapter 19, Dr. Bonnie Rogers, Dr PH, BN, MSc, FAAN begins by discussing the key ethical theories and their implications for disability management. Jane Hall, RN, MPA, CCM then addresses ethics and case management. The topics of ethical decision-making and conflicting goals in disability management are also presented.

All stakeholders in the disability management process must be aware of the relevant legislation that may impact on the disability management processes. Chapter 20 addresses the legal aspects of disability management, including the duty to accommodate and privacy legislation. As well, Sharon Chadwick, RN, BScN, COHN(C), COHN-S and Kristine Robidoux, LL.B., QC address the impact of changing legislation on the field of disability management. Work accommodation and its effective application in the workplace rounds off the contents of this chapter.

Chapter 21 covers the impact of cultural diversity on the management of disability claims. Today's workplaces are culturally diverse, with each culture possessing its own unique values, beliefs, needs, and expectations on life and work. Disability management professionals/practitioners must have a working knowledge of the features of the various cultures as well as be culturally competent in assisting employees from different cultures to successfully cope with an illness/injury and return to work.

Carrying on with the same concepts, Chapter 22 addresses the impact of four generations in the workplace on the management of disability situations. This is a recent phenomenon: one with which workplaces have never had to deal. It influences how management, unions, human resources, occupational health & safety and disability management professionals/practitioners should deal with employees, employee relationships, work practices, and work motivators. To successfully interact with the four generations, disability management professionals/practitioners are encouraged to familiarize themselves with the unique influencers, features, and preferences of each of the generational groups. This will assist them greatly in terms of working with employees to effectively manage a medical absence, disability and return to work.

Chapter 23 offers information on outsourcing disability management services and how this approach to disability management servicing can be achieved. It explores issues like: reasons for outsourcing; what internal preparation is required; conducting a market search; establishing performance measures and contract development; and vendor management. This is a more recent aspect of disability management programming and an area that remains poorly understood.

Chapters 24 and 25 focus on two skills that the disability management professionals/practitioners must have in their "Disability Management Tool Kit", namely, career development and internal/external consulting skills. These topics have been included as little information exists on how disability management professionals/practitioners can effectively manage their careers, as well as attain the important skill of consulting.

The last chapter, Chapter 26, provides a discussion on some of the future challenges in the field of disability management, namely:

- "Professionalism: How does the Field of Disability Management 'Stack up'?";
- "Educational Preparation of Disability Management Practitioners/ Professionals";
- The "Canadian Approach to Disability Management Advanced Education"; and
- "Disability Management: The International Scene".

The intent of this chapter is to foster thought about the future of disability management in Canada, and how to effectively address these critical issues.

Section 3 — Disability Management: Glossary of Terms

Section 3 provides an extensive glossary of terms related to the field of disability management. Throughout this book, terms highlighted using the bolding technique, are included in the book's glossary.

The purpose of providing a glossary is that with any emerging field, confusion can exist in regards to the terms and definitions people use. By defining these terms, disability management terms can be clarified.

SUMMARY

This disability management resource has been designed for front-line use. The author's hope is that readers will find the information useful and readily applicable to their practice areas. As well, if this book can, in any way, clarify the cloudy topic of disability management, then this author's chief aim has been achieved.

Section 1:

Disability Management Theory, Strategy and Industry Practices

Chapter 1

Disability Management: Overview

WHAT IS DISABILITY MANAGEMENT?

The term "disability management" means different things to different people. For example, "disability management" has been defined as:

> ... a collaborative partnership that involves employers, employees, unions, health care providers, and vocational rehabilitation professionals for the goal of minimizing the impact of injury or disability on an employee's capacity to perform his or her job.[1]

"Disability management" is also described as:

> ... a workplace program that uses prevention, early intervention, and proactive return to work interventions to reduce the impact of injury and disability, as well as to accommodate those employees who experience functional work limitations.[2]

For the purposes of this text, **disability management** is a systematic, goal-oriented process of actively minimizing the impact of impairment on the individual's capacity to participate competitively in the work environment, and maximizing the health of employees to prevent disability, or reducing the risk of further deterioration when a disability exists.[3]

Hence, a **Disability Management Program** is a workplace program designed to facilitate the employment of persons with a disability through a coordinated effort that addresses individual needs, workplace conditions, and legal responsibilities.[4] Ideally, Disability Management Programs are proactive in nature and incorporate stakeholder involvement and accountability. Most Disability Management Programs are designed to control the human and

---

[1] A. Ahrens & K. Mulholland, "Vocational Rehabilitation and the Evolution of Disability Management: An Organizational Case Study" (2000) 15 Journal of Vocational Rehabilitation 39 at 39-46.

[2] D. Rosenthal, N. Hursh, J. Lui, R. Isom & J. Sasson, "A Survey of Current Disability Management Practice: Emerging Trends and Implications for Certification" (2007) 50 Rehabilitation Counselling Bulletin 76 at 76-86.

[3] D.G. Tate, R.V. Habeck & D.E. Galvin, "Disability Management: Origins, Concepts and Principles for Practice" (1986) 17:3 Journal of Applied Rehabilitation Counselling 5.

[4] National Institute of Disability Management and Research (NIDMAR), *Code of Practice for Disability Management* (Port Alberni, BC: NIDMAR, 2000) at 5.

economic costs of employee injury or illness, to convey a message that employees are valued, and to demonstrate compliance with the relevant legislation.

An **Integrated Disability Management Program** is a planned and coordinated approach to facilitate and manage employee health and productivity. It is a human resource risk management and risk communication approach designed to integrate all organizational/company programs and resources to minimize or reduce the losses and costs associated with employee medical absence regardless of the nature of those disabilities. It is aimed at:

- assisting ill/injured employees and employees experiencing diminished work capacities;
- providing early intervention and support measures;
- facilitating a collaborative approach to managing employee disabilities;
- restoring the disabled employee's work/functional capacities to an optimal level;
- maximizing the disabled employee's capabilities;
- integrating the organization's/company's employee support programs;
- measuring program performance and outcomes in human and business terms;
- evaluating the organization's/company's various disability management efforts and performance with a focus on continuous improvement; and
- attaining a healthy workforce through injury/illness prevention.

Operationally, an Integrated Disability Management Program includes eight key elements (Figure 1.1):

1. MANAGEMENT-LABOUR COMMITMENT AND SUPPORTIVE POLICIES

This element compels management and labour to:

- be sensitive to the impact of disability on employees, families, work units, and the organization as a whole;
- be aware of the relevant pieces of legislation and the duty to comply (due diligence);
- promote the development of supportive policies and employee services;
- strive to create a people-oriented work culture that values employees when they are ill/injured;
- develop management-labour agreements that protect worker employability;
- design employee benefit plans that reward a safe and timely return to work;
- support the development of flexible and creative return-to-work options;
- work together towards reducing employee absenteeism through the development of a people-oriented work culture that includes Occupational Health & Safety leadership, due diligence, and the integration of the Disability Management Program, Occupational Health & Safety Program, Employee Assistance Program, and Workplace Wellness Program;

- commit adequate financial and personnel resources towards the Integrated Disability Management Program; and
- be cognizant of the potential effect of management practices on worker well-being.

Figure 1.1: The Umbrella of an Integrated Disability Management Program

2. STAKEHOLDER EDUCATION AND INVOLVEMENT

This element obligates management and labour to:

- establish common goals for an Integrated Disability Management Program;
- develop an Integrated Disability Management Program;
- define stakeholder roles, responsibilities, and accountabilities;
- provide stakeholder education;
- promote stakeholder sensitivity to the physical, psychological, social, and vocational consequences of disability;
- reward stakeholder participation;
- promote employee/supervisor understanding of the Integrated Disability Management Program and their respective roles, responsibilities, and accountabilities to reduce and mitigate employee absenteeism; and
- motivate employees/supervisors to participate in the Integrated Disability Management Program as well as in wellness and prevention activities aimed at illness/injury protection and prevention.

3. SUPPORTIVE BENEFIT PROGRAMS

This element addresses the need for management and labour to:

*   develop employee benefit plans that support employee work attendance and that encourage a safe and timely return to work by ill/injured employees;
*   implement plans that promote and accommodate workplace rehabilitation; and
*   provide Employee Assistance Program (EAP) support that includes employee and family counselling.

4. A COORDINATED APPROACH TO INJURY/ILLNESS MANAGEMENT

This element requires the need for management to ensure the following actions occur:

*   implementation of effective claim management processes (defined in Chapter 10, "Disability Management Practice Standards");
*   implementation of effective case management practices (defined in Chapter 10, "Disability Management Practice Standards");
*   initiation of early intervention post employee injury/illness — intervention that is viewed as considerate and caring in nature;
*   provision of employee guidance towards access and use of responsible health care services (case management);
*   implementation and use of medical/vocational fitness-to-work evaluations (*i.e.*, medical forms, job demands analyses, functional capacity assessment referrals, *etc.*);
*   implementation of multi-disciplinary interventions into the disability management process;
*   development of alliances/linkages with external resources (*i.e.*, health care providers, Employee Assistance Programs (EAPs), vocational rehabilitation, insurers, *etc.*);
*   use of early rehabilitation/retraining for the recovering employee;
*   collection injury/illness data using disability management information systems; and
*   regular evaluation of the claim and case management processes with a view to continuous improvement.

5. A COMMUNICATION STRATEGY

This element deals with the need for management to ensure that:

*   the needs of the key stakeholders are identified;
*   the benefits of an Integrated Disability Management Program for the key stakeholders are identified;
*   a communication plan for the Integrated Disability Management Program that includes a marketing component is developed;

- the Integrated Disability Management Program marketing strategy clearly identifies the benefits that the program can offer to stakeholders;
- the company's available communication vehicles are used to reach all the key stakeholders;
- a Disability Management Program communication strategy and action plan that encourages a free-flow of information to and from the key stakeholders is built; and
- the effectiveness of the implemented communication strategy and marketing plans is evaluated.

6. GRADUATED RETURN-TO-WORK

This element involves management ensuring that:

- the available return-to-work options are regularly offered;[5]
- flexible and creative return-to-work options are used;
- a system of employee/union/line identification of modified/alternate work options is in place;
- workplace accommodations are promoted and facilitated;
- safe and timely return-to-work practices are instituted and monitored;
- the return-to-work opportunity does not disadvantage supervisors or co-workers;[6]
- supervisor and co-worker understanding and support for the Integrated Disability Management Program are promoted;
- supervisors are prepared to facilitate, implement, and support a timely and safe return to work;[7] and
- insurer support and participation is sought and maximized.

7. PERFORMANCE MEASUREMENT

This element requires management to ensure that:

- suitable performance measures for the Integrated Disability Management Program are established;
- strategies for measuring the desired performances/outcomes are developed;
- a plan of action for performance measurement is in place, implemented, monitored, and evaluated;
- the performance of the Integrated Disability Management Program is evaluated as planned; and

---

[5] Institute for Work & Health, "Seven 'Principles' for Successful Return to Work", Institute for Work & Health, Toronto (March 2007) at 2, available online at:<http://www.iwh.on.ca/seven-principles-for-rtw>.

[6] *Ibid.*

[7] *Ibid.*

- the return on investment realized by the Integrated Disability Management Program is determined.

8. WORKPLACE WELLNESS

This element deals with the need for management to ensure that:

- disability data are analyzed;
- the jobs/positions that experience an increased incidence of injuries/illness are identified and evaluated;
- the patterns of injury/illness are identified;
- prevention strategies (*i.e.*, workplace safety, ergonomic, positive employee-employer relationships, cultural, *etc.*) are developed and implemented;
- incident-prevention practices are actively promoted;
- employee wellness is recognized and rewarded; and
- employee/union involvement in the workplace to increase employee job satisfaction is promoted and supported.

WHY EARLY INTERVENTION?

Early intervention is defined as an employer-initiated response aimed at keeping the ill/injured employee connected with the workplace; and potentially, preventing the medical absence in the first place. Early intervention tends to occur following the onset of the illness/injury. It also includes the actions taken to assist employees who are experiencing diminished functional or work capacities.

The intent of early intervention is to facilitate appropriate and timely treatment and rehabilitation, as well as a safe and timely return to work. Through the use of early intervention, organizations are able to shorten the employee's absence duration[8] and to mitigate the potential losses associated with the disability, as well as reduce the overall human and financial costs.[9]

With any employee work absence, research and industry experiences support the importance of early intervention. Delays in recovery tend to be associated with the development of psychosocial problems that in turn, require psychological support and treatment.[10] The longer the employee is away from work, the less likely he or she will ever return.[11] The window of opportunity for successfully bringing the employee back into the workplace appears to be within

---

[8] *Ibid.*

[9] P. Reed, "Recent Ruling on ADA and the Value of Interventions" (2002) 27:2 Employee Benefits Journal 3.

[10] H. Harder & L. Scott, *Comprehensive Disability Management* (Elsevier, Churchill Livingstone, Toronto: 2005) at 7.

[11] J. Curtis & L. Scott, "Integrating Disability Management into Strategic Plans: Creating Healthy Organizations" (2004) 52:7 AAOHN Journal 298; L. Gates, Y. Taler & S. Akabas, "Optimizing Return to Work Among Newly Disabled Workers: A New Approach to Cost Containment" (1989) 5:2 Benefits Quarterly 19.

the first 30 days following the absence onset. By facilitating appropriate and timely treatments and rehabilitation, employers can assist employees to regain their health, thereby enabling them to return to work in a shorter time frame. This approach benefits the employee, family, and organization.

Informally, many organizations report more success with returning the recovering employee to the workplace if the intervention begins at, or soon after, the time of illness or injury. Typically, early intervention involves contacting the ill or injured employee and initiating case management if warranted. Companies demonstrating the best results in disability management outcomes begin early intervention by day three or five of a non-occupational medical absence, and by day one of an occupationally related medical absence.

Early intervention can:

- open the lines of communication between the employee/family and the workplace;
- enhance the employee's expectations for recovery — a factor that is strongly associated with successful rehabilitation and a timely return to work;[12]
- avoid delays in the employee obtaining appropriate health/rehabilitation services;
- ease the process of coping and adjustment for the employee/family;
- help the employee and family with the physical, psychological, vocational, social, and financial implications of a disability situation;[13]
- encourage family members to provide positive reinforcement and support to the recovering employee;
- assist the employee and family to re-establish a sense of control;
- reduce the negative effects of physical and psychological de-conditioning;
- prevent a break in the **occupational bond** — the mutually beneficial relationship between the employee and the employer.[14]
- enhance employee motivation to return to work;
- address both the business and human aspects for a timely recovery and safe return to work;
- minimize the separation and loss of support from co-workers;[15]

---

[12] D. Gross & M. Battié, "Work-related Recovery Expectations and the Prognosis of Chronic Low Back Pain Within a Workers Compensation Setting" (2005) 47 Journal of Occupational and Environmental Medicine 428, available online at: <http://www.rtwknowledge.org/browse.php?article_id=92&view_type=research>.

[13] T. Riggar, D. Maki & A. Wolf, *Applied Rehabilitation Counselling* (New York: Springer Publishing Co., 1986).

[14] D. Shrey, *Principles and Practices of Disability Management in Industry* (Winter Park, FL: GR Press Inc., 1995).

[15] T. Michalak, "Disability Management: An Assessment of Psychological Factors and Early Intervention" (2007) 6:1 International Journal of Disability, Community & Rehabilitation, available online at: <http://www.ijdcr.ca/VOL06_01_CAN/articles/michalak.shtml>.

- decrease/prevent feelings of loneliness and abandonment that reduce the employee's motivation to get well;
- help prevent the development of psychological problems, such as the adoption of the "**sick role**"[16] and related secondary gains;
- increase the likelihood of a successful rehabilitation outcome; and
- prove to be cost-effective. Research has shown a 47 per cent return to work rate among workers referred for rehabilitation services within three months post-injury. This led to a 71 per cent cost savings.[17] In contrast, only 33 per cent of those referred for rehabilitation services later at the four to six-month post-injury period returned to work, and the cost savings dropped to 61 per cent.[18]

Ill/injured employees tend to fall into one of the following three categories:

1. those with strong resilience who respond well to treatment;
2. those who are more vulnerable and prone to emotional reactions in response to an illness/injury or to being away from work; or
3. those who are physically and/or emotionally fragile and become disabled as a result of the illness/injury or workplace stressors.[19]

For Disability Management Case Managers, the challenge is to identify which category the employee falls into, and then with the employee's consent, contact the treating physician to gain support for the development and implementation of a treatment plan focused on a safe and timely return to work.

DISABILITY MANAGEMENT MODELS

There are a number of models or paradigms for disability management in today's work and marketplaces. Four examples are:

1. *Traditional Model* — This is a model in which the care plan, authorized leave, and return-to-work process are medically directed. The employer relies on the treating practitioners (primarily the employee's attending physician) to validate the illness and to help the employee to return to work. This model is often the starting point in disability management for many organizations, as well as for insurer disability management models.
2. *Job Matching Model* — This is a model which involves a fitness assessment of the injured or ill employee and an analysis of the physical/psychological

---

[16] The "**sick role**" is a societal-sanctioned role that an ill or injured person assumes once he or she becomes ill or injured.

[17] R. Rundle, "Move Fast if You Want to Rehabilitate the Worker" (1983) 17:18 Business Insurance 10.

[18] G.C. Pati, "Economics of Rehabilitation in the Workplace" (1985) 51:4 Journal of Rehabilitation 22.

[19] J. Regan, cited in D. Thompson, "In Support of STD", *Benefits Canada* (2001), available online at: <http://www.benefitscanada.com/content/legacy/Content/2001/11-01/std.html>.

demands of the employee's job. The intent is to determine if there is a "match" or "mismatch" in terms of a safe return to work for the employee.

3. *Managed Care Model* — In a managed care model, the employee's diagnosis is referenced against standardized care plans, procedures and diagnostic testing guidelines to determine if treatment and the physician's suggested leave duration are appropriate. This model, like the traditional model, tends to be medically driven.

4. *Direct Case Management Model* — This employee-employer approach to dealing with the employee's reduced work capacity and the employer's business needs/resources uses some of the elements of the first three models. However, it is the employee and employer who decide, based on their respective needs, the terms of the medical absence and the return-to-work plan.[20]

Although each of these four models were developed in response to different drivers, they all offer valuable contributions to the disability management process. In fact, most Disability Management Programs use some elements of each model. Typically, the Traditional Model is the starting point for a Disability Management Program,[21] and elements of the other models are then added as required, or as the Disability Management Program evolves.

From experience as a disability management professional, and from auditing existing Disability Management Programs within various organizations, I have learned that the best approach to disability management is one that focuses on maintaining a strong employee-employer relationship. Effective programs, such as the one depicted in the model developed by the National Institute for Disability Management and Research (Figure 1.2), maintain the employee-employer relationship, focus on the employee's capabilities versus disabilities, and are supported by a variety of technical specialists and case management approaches.

Supporting the employee and family through an illness or injury period usually promotes a "win-win" situation for all parties and related stakeholders. It also reduces the resistance to claims and case interventions and encourages a successful return to work.

---

[20] A. Clarke, "Disability Case Management Models" (Presented at the Disability Case Management Forum, Vancouver, March 24-26, 1997) [unpublished].

[21] *Ibid.*

Figure 1.2: Employee-Employer Disability Management Model[22]

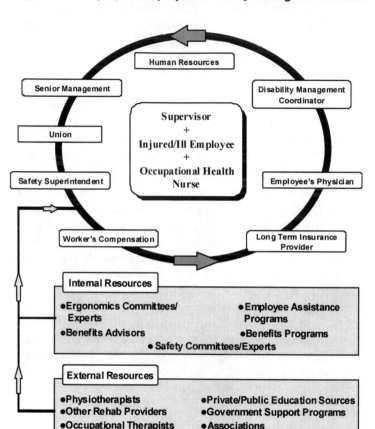

[22]   Adapted with permission from: National Institute of Disability Management and Research (NIDMAR), *Disability Management in the Workplace: A Guide to Establishing a Joint Workplace Program* (Port Alberni, BC: NIDMAR, 1995).

AN INTEGRATED DISABILITY MANAGEMENT PROGRAM: VALUE TO STAKEHOLDERS

To market and sell the merits of an Integrated Disability Management Program, one must consider the interests and values of the key stakeholders.

For the Corporation

In 2007, Canadian workers missed 10.2 workdays[23] for approximately 113 million lost workdays due to illness/disability and personal or family responsibilities.[24] This cost the Canadian economy about $24.4 billion[25] in direct employee earnings.[26] This represents a dramatic increase in employee lost time due to injury and illness since 1998,[27] when workers missed 7.8 workdays for a total of 72 million lost work hours; and over the absence outcomes for 2004 when workers missed 9.2 days for a total of 102 million lost workdays.[28]

For Canadian employers, the average cost per employee for workplace absence equates to $1,707.89 in lost productivity as measured in terms of employee earnings per year.[29] For a company of 1,000 employees, this translates to a minimum of $1,707,890 in lost productivity costs (direct costs) alone. According to the Hewitt Disability Absence Index 2007 Report, the total direct and indirect disability absence costs for 1,000 employees would range from $3,500,000 to $3,675,000.[30]

In the United States, employee absences take a hefty toll on the corporate bottom line as well. An estimated 69 million workers reported missing workdays

---

[23] Statistics Canada, *Work Absence Rates, 2007*, Cat. No. 71-211-XWE (Ottawa: Statistics Canada, May 2008).

[24] *Ibid.*

[25] Calculated by multiplying the number of lost-time workdays in 2007 (142,918,000 lost workdays) by the average daily wage for full-time Canadian employees as of November 2007 ($167.44 per day). Data obtained from Statistics Canada, *Work Absence Rates, 2007*, Cat. No. 71-211-XWE (Ottawa: Statistics Canada, May 2008) and Statistics Canada, *Average Hourly Wages of Employees by Selected Characteristics*, available online at: <http://www40.statcan.ca/101/cst01/labr69a-eng.htm>.

[26] Marsh Risk Consulting, *Workforce Risk: Fourth Annual Marsh Mercer Survey of Employers' Time-Off and Disability Programs* (2003), available online at: <http://www.marshriskconsulting.com/>.

[27] E. Akyeampong, *Work Absence Rates, 1987 to 1998*, Cat. No. 71-535-MPB, No. 10 (Ottawa: Statistics Canada, 1999).

[28] D. Dyck, *Disability Management: Theory, Strategy and Industry Practice*, 3rd ed. (Markham, ON: LexisNexis Canada, 2006) at 14.

[29] Calculated by determining the daily wage from the average daily wage for full-time Canadian employees as of November 2007 ($167.44 per day), and multiplying that value by the average number of lost time days per Canadian worker (10.2 days). Data obtained from Statistics Canada, *Work Absence Rates, 2007*, Cat. No. 71-211-XWE (Ottawa: Statistics Canada, May 2008); and Statistics Canada, *Average Hourly Wages of Employees by Selected Characteristics*, available online at: <http://www40.statcan.ca/101/cst01/labr69a-eng.htm>.

[30] Hewitt Associates, *Disability Absence Index Survey 2007* (2007), available online at: <http://www.hewittassociates.com/Intl/NA/en-CA/KnowledgeCenter/ArticlesReports/DAIS_highlights.aspx>.

due to illness in 2003, for a total of 407 million lost workdays and $48 billion in lost economic output.[31] This translates to an overall average cost of $660 per employee per year.[32] The annual worker absence costs can range from $60,000 for small employers[33] to more than $760,000 per year in direct payroll costs for large employers.[34] These costs are even more when lowered productivity, lost revenue, service interruptions, customer dissatisfaction, and the effects of poor employee morale are considered.

Employee absence rates and costs are escalating.[35] New illnesses, an aging workforce, increased medical costs, decreased government support, and the lack of understanding of the total costs related to disabilities, all continue to contribute to the financial burden borne by employers. Add to this, the impact of **employee presenteeism** which is estimated to cost employers nine times the organization's/company's work absence costs.[36] **Employee presenteeism** is defined as the phenomenon of employees being at work, but because of wasted time, failure to concentrate, sleep deprivation, distractions, poor health, and/or lack of training, they may not be working at all.

Through an Integrated Disability Management Program, employers can identify injury or illness causes, reduce the risk of injuries, promote employee well-being, and contain the health care and disability-related costs. The estimated saving is a 30-50 per cent reduction in lost time and related costs.[37] The net result can be a healthier workforce, reduced absenteeism, solid productivity, lowered disability costs, lower insurance premiums and rates, and Workers' Compensation discounts and/or rebates. As well, by helping the employee to overcome an illness/injury and to successfully return to work, the employer retains a valuable employee while decreasing disability costs and meeting legislative obligations.

---

[31] M. Mahon, "Lost Labor Time Costs U.S. $260 Billion Each Year" in *Newsroom, The Commonwealth Fund* (August 31, 2005), available online at: <http://www.cmwf.org/newsroom/ newsroom_ show.htm?.doc_id=294188>.

[32] CCH Incorporated, *2007 CCH Unscheduled Absence Survey* (Riverwoods, IL: CCH Incorporated, 2007).

[33] CCH Incorporated, "Unscheduled Employee Absenteeism Rises to Five Year High" in *2004 CCH Unscheduled Absence Survey* (Riverwoods, IL: CCH Incorporated, 2004), available online at: <http://www.cch.com/press/news/2004/20041007h.asp>.

[34] CCH Incorporated, "Unscheduled Employee Absenteeism Rises to Five Year High" in *2007 CCH Unscheduled Absence Survey* (Riverwoods, IL: CCH Incorporated, 2007), available online at: <http://www.cch.com/press/news/2007/20071010h.asp>.

[35] Hewitt Associates, *Disability Absence Index Survey 2007* (2007), available online at: <http://www. hewittassociates.com/Intl/NA/en-CA/KnowledgeCenter/ArticlesReports/DAIS_highlights.aspx>.

[36] S. Aldana, *Top Five Strategies to Enhance the ROI of Worksite Wellness Programs*, Wellness Council of America (February 2009), available online at: <http://www.welcoa.org/freeresources/ pdf/top_5_strategies.pdf>.

[37] NIDMAR, *Occupational Standards in Disability Management: Executive Summary* (Port Alberni, BC: NIDMAR, 2000) at 2.

For the Union

Unions, like management and employees, have a legal responsibility to help ill or injured employees (their members) return to work.[38] Through support and participation in an Integrated Disability Management Program, union leaders can demonstrate their level of commitment and compliance to the Canadian human rights legislation. As well, an Integrated Disability Management Program affords unions the opportunity to:

* promote member (employee) well-being;
* maintain labour rights and principles;
* demonstrate value of the program to union members by protecting the employability of its members;
* interact and build relationships;
* problem-solve in addressing areas of mutual interest and concern; and
* contribute to the company's profitability and competitiveness.

For the Employee

The benefits of an Integrated Disability Management Program to the employee and family during a vulnerable period in their lives are numerous and invaluable. Some of these benefits include:

* the promotion of a speedy rehabilitation;
* the ability to maintain a sense of self-identity, self-worth and self-respect;
* the opportunity to stay in contact with, and to gain support from, co-workers;
* the ability to remain current in their field; and
* less disruption in their normal family and workplace lives and relationships.

    Graduated return-to-work (modified work) opportunities allow employees to:

* concentrate on recovery;
* keep a regular routine;
* maintain a sense of self-worth;
* make a contribution to the company;
* work at regular duties for as many hours as possible;
* keep work contacts;
* remain current with the changing work skill sets, duties, and responsibilities;
* remain current with changing technology;
* gradually adjust to full-time work; and
* return to work without upgrading.

---

[38] B. Armstrong & S. Greckol, "Accommodation Guidelines" in *Illness and Disability Claims in the Unionized Workplace* (Winnipeg: Centre for Labour-Management Development, 1999).

In summary, an Integrated Disability Management Program and the associated graduated return-to-work opportunities can be a "win-win" situation for everyone involved. They can promote human savings as well as financial ones. For example, the reported effects of disability on British Columbia's economy were $3.6 billion per year, or eight cents on every dollar earned in the province. This translates to 35 per cent of the disability costs being borne by employers, 27 per cent borne by disabled individuals and families, and the rest (38 per cent) through government programs.[39] By reducing, and/or mitigating the impact of workplace disabilities, all parties "win".

AN INTEGRATED DISABILITY MANAGEMENT PROGRAM: HYPE OR GOOD BUSINESS PRACTICE[40]

An Integrated Disability Management Program is like any other business function. For it to survive, it must make good business sense, and offer a financial return on the resources invested. To demonstrate the impact an Integrated Disability Management Program can have on the organization's "bottom line", first determine the costs associated with disability and the required Disability Management Program resources.

Secondly, determine the outcomes realized by other existing Integrated Disability Management Programs, better known as **benchmarking**.[41] Fortunately, many companies report their program results at conferences and in print. For example:

- The City of Winnipeg realized a $2.7 million saving since introducing their Disability Management Program.[42]
- Weyerhaeuser was able to reduce their Workers' Compensation Board costs by 51 per cent over six years through disability management efforts. They also noted an average reduction in cost per claim of 18 per cent.[43]
- Petro-Canada, through the Managed Rehabilitation Care Program saved $1.33 million in 1996. They reduced their long-term disability premium

---

[39] Editor, "Disabilities Draining the B.C. Economy" (1997) 1:7 Back to Work 1.

[40] D. Dyck. Excerpts reprinted with permission from *Stating Your Case* (Ottawa: Benefits Canada, 1998) at 55-59.

[41] **Benchmarking** is defined as a continual and collaborative discipline that involves measuring and comparing the results of the key process with "best performers" or with one's own previous achievements.

[42] National Institute of Disability Management and Research (NIDMAR), *Disability Management in the Workplace: A Guide to Establishing a Joint Workplace Program* (Port Alberni, BC: NIDMAR, 1995).

[43] Weyerhaeuser, "Transitional Return-to-Work at Weyerhaeuser Company" (Presented at the National Conference on Disability and Work: Solutions for Canadians, Sheraton Centre, Toronto, Ontario, 7-9 October 1996) [unpublished].

rates to 4.8/1,000 (1996), and enjoyed long-term disability plan premium holidays[44] each year since 1991.[45]

- Canada Post saved $54.6 million per year by introducing early return-to-work initiatives. They also experienced a drop in employee absenteeism from 20 to 9.93 days per employee per year.[46]

- The University of Calgary had 71 per cent of employees indicate satisfaction with the Attendance Support Program that the University of Calgary has in place. This is an integrated program that combines occupational health nursing and Employee Assistance Program counselling services to promote an early return to work. The University's annual report indicated that 73.1 per cent of the cases that were closed in 1996 resulted in a return to work by employees.[47]

- The Toronto Transit Commission, through management of soft tissue injuries, reduced the length of their Workers' Compensation claims by 17 per cent, their Workers' Compensation medical aid costs by 27 per cent, the length of the short-term disability claims by 19 per cent, and the number of employees on long-term disability by 11 per cent.[48]

- MacMillan Bloedel Ltd., Port Alberni, British Columbia, saved $1.25 million in disability costs in one year; reduced the number of long-term disability claims by 37 per cent from 1995 to 1996; and decreased the number of lost time days due to occupational illness or injury from 20 days to 4 days through the establishment of a Disability Management Program.

- BC Hydro (1994) introduced a Disability Management Program that lowered the employee sick days from 2,732 in 1995, to 2,573 in 1996 (5.8 per cent decrease). The days off for long-term disability decreased from 1,083 to 934 for that same period. As well, Workers' Compensation premiums were reduced by $700,000, and the number of employee absences of 10 or more days in duration were lowered from 83 to 51 cases.[49]

---

[44] A **premium holiday** is the period of time that a client or employee is not required to pay insurance plan premiums because the plan is over-funded.

[45] Petro-Canada, "Managed Rehabilitation Care Program" (Presented at the CPBI Conference, Calgary, Alberta, 1996) [unpublished].

[46] Canada Post, "Building a Business Case for Disability Management: Proving the Value of a Return to Work Program at Canada Post" (Presented at the National Conference on Disability and Work: Solutions for Canadians, Sheraton Centre, Toronto, Ontario, 7-9 October 1996) [unpublished].

[47] University of Calgary, *Annual Report* (Calgary: University of Calgary, 1996).

[48] L. Stellini, "Preferred Provider Network for Integrated Management of Soft Tissue Injuries" (Presented at the Conference on Developing Effective Return-to-Work Programs, Toronto, Ontario, 24-25 October 1996) [unpublished].

[49] S. Lebrun, "Employers Take Notice of Disability Costs: Management of Injury and Illness Can Save Millions" (1997) 29 December *C.H.R.R.*

- A major airline implemented a total absence management program for a net saving of more than 14 per cent of the total costs over five years.[50]
- An integrated disability management program can reduce a company's benefit costs by 15 per cent to 35 per cent, depending on the benefits offered and how they are managed.[51]

Further support for the added value of Integrated Disability Management Programs comes from studies done on the practice of early intervention following an illness or injury. For example, the American International Group (AIG) Claim Survey to 300 companies reported that by implementing case management procedures immediately after the occurrence of a Workers' Compensation claim, costs were reduced by as much as 40 per cent.[52]

According to the 2005 Watson Wyatt Staying@Work[TM] Survey, 81 per cent of the 94 participating companies reported that they perceived documented return-to-work plans to be a key factor for managing disability-related costs, and for improving employee health, employee satisfaction and productivity.[53]

The Alberta Workers' Compensation Board (2005) reported that employers who instituted post-injury reduction services lowered their 2004 injury claim costs by 20 per cent as compared to non-participants.[54] This is a 3 per cent increase in savings over 10 years ago when the saving was 17 per cent.[55] In short, managing occupational injuries makes good business sense for many Alberta companies.

Watson-Wyatt, in the 2007 Staying@Work Survey, determined that the most effective cost-reducing health management practices include the use of:

- disability case management with illness/injury claims;
- documented modified work plans;
- return-to-work plans for mental health illness; and
- supervisor/manager involvement in absence management.[56]

---

[50]   Aon Consulting, "The Case for Absence Management", *Aon Workforce Strategies, 2003*, available online at: <http://www.aon.com>.
[51]   N. Vimadalal & J. Wozniak, "Best Practices to Help Employers Capture the Benefits of Integrated Disability Management", *Employee Benefits News* (March 1, 2008), online: <http://ebn. benefitnews.com/asset/article/548491/best-practices-help-employers-capture-benefits.html?pg=>.
[52]   AIG Claims Services Inc., "Early Intervention Cuts Workers' Compensation Costs" (*Aon Commentary*, June 17, 1996).
[53]   Watson Wyatt Worldwide, *Staying@Work Report 2005* (Canada 2005), available online at: <http://www.watsonwyatt.com/research/resrender.asp?id=w-860&page=1>.
[54]   Workers' Compensation Board Alberta, *2004 Annual Report* (Edmonton: Workers' Compensation Board Alberta, 2005) at 18, available online at: <http://www.wcb.ab.ca/pdfs/public/annual_report_2004.pdf>.
[55]   J. Cowell, "Serving Albertans Through Effective Injury Prevention and Disability Management" (Presented at the National Conference on Disability and Work: Solutions for Canadians, Sheraton Centre, Toronto, Ontario, October 7-9, 1996).
[56]   Watson-Wyatt, *Staying @Work: Effective Presence at Work* (2007), at 10, available online at: <https://www.watsonwyatt.com>.

Lastly, the challenge is to present the merits of the Integrated Disability Management Program in business language. A critical part of that language includes a cost/benefit analysis of launching such a program, the potential influence on the company's bottom-line, and the anticipated return on investment. The findings that can support these endeavours include:

- Since 1996, the number of companies that have implemented integrated disability management programs has increased from 25 per cent to 51 per cent (2004). The reason is simple: it is a cost-effective approach to managing worker absence and mitigating the associated costs. According to a recent Watson Wyatt Worldwide survey, savings of 0.25-1 per cent of payroll can be realized.[57]
- Shell Oil Company, Houston, Texas, implemented an "in-house" Disability Management Program to reduce non-occupational absences. The program was administered by full-time certified, corporate-based case managers and nine manufacturing location nurses. This program resulted in a 10 per cent reduction in total absence days per employee (6.9 to 6.2 days) as compared with the previous year. Business units not using this Disability Management Program had an 8 per cent increase in absence days per employee (5.5 to 5.9 days). The return on investment equalled more than a four to one return on investment based on direct expenditures and cost savings in terms of reduced absence days.[58]
- The direct costs of work absence and the related costs equates to between 5 per cent and 6 per cent of payroll (estimated to be 5.31 per cent by Watson Wyatt, 2007[59]). Taking steps to address and lower worker absence just makes good business sense.
- Employers who implement at least three disability and absence management techniques experience 74 per cent lower employee absence rates.[60]

HOW TO SELL AN INTEGRATED DISABILITY MANAGEMENT PROGRAM TO SENIOR MANAGEMENT

Many human resources and occupational health professionals/practitioners attend seminars, conferences, and industry focus groups on the topic of

---

[57] Watson Wyatt Worldwide, *Managing Health Care Costs in a New Era: 10th Annual National Business Group on Health/Watson Wyatt Survey Report 2005*, Executive Summary available online at: <http://www.watsonwyatt.com/research/resrender.asp?id=w-821&page=1>.

[58] Shell Oil Company, Houston, "Impact of a Disability Management Program on Employee Productivity in a Petrochemical Company" (2006) 48:5 Journal of Occupational and Environmental Medicine 497.

[59] Watson-Wyatt, *Staying@Work: Effective Presence at Work* (2007), at 6, available online at: <https://www.watsonwyatt.com>.

[60] Washington Business Group on Health, *Fifth Annual Washington Business Group on Health/Watson Wyatt Worldwide Survey on Disability Management* (Watson Wyatt Worldwide, 2004), available online at: <http://www.watsonwyatt.com>.

disability management. They leave these sessions convinced that an Integrated Disability Management Program would be of value to their company or organization — however, they are unsure of how they can sell their ideas to senior management.

Perceived Barriers

One of the perceived barriers around initiating an Integrated Disability Management Program is the myth that workplace accommodations are expensive. Workplace accommodation includes changes in, or reassignment of, parts of a job so that the recovering employee can return to work. This could translate into modifying existing job duties, offering transitional work, arranging for a training opportunity, providing an alternate job placement, or any combination of these.

A study by Alan Cantor[61] demonstrated that the majority of the workplace accommodations cost under $500, with 31 per cent of the workplace accommodations occurring at no added cost to the employer. In fact, Cantor reported that only 5 per cent of the workplace accommodations cost the company more than $5,000.

This finding is supported by the Job Accommodation Network. Their research indicates that work accommodations usually cost nothing. Of those accommodations that do cost, the typical expenditure is around $500.[62] The employers who participated in this study indicated that the benefits of making workplace accommodations far outweighed the costs. On average, the return on investment on work accommodation was $10 for every dollar spent. Hence, work accommodations make good business sense.[63]

A second perceived barrier is the belief that there are limited modified work positions available within an organization for the recovering employee. This perception needs to be challenged. If all stakeholders are committed to making disability management work, modified work opportunities seem to materialize. From past experience, this author has come to appreciate that the employee population and union leaders are very resourceful at unearthing modified work positions. For example, the individuals within a workgroup can band together to alter their jobs so that a recovering workmate can do tasks within his or her reduced work capabilities. In one instance, a company without truck driving positions was able to call on its partner company to provide the prescribed modified duties for a recovering employee. The point is that, "where there is a will, there is a way".

---

[61] A. Cantor, "The Future of Workplace Accommodations: Containing Costs and Maximizing Effectiveness" (Presented at the National Conference on Disability and Work: Solutions for Canadians, Sheraton Centre, Toronto, Ontario, October 7-9, 1996) [unpublished.]

[62] Job Accommodation Network, *Workplace Accommodations: Low Cost, High Impact, 2007*, at 2, available online at: <http://www.jan.wvu.edu/media/LowCostHighImpact.doc>.

[63] *Ibid.*, at 3.

A third perceived barrier is that the existing employee group benefit plans may be unsupportive of modified work. For example, plans that promote absence with pay, or that allow the employee to earn more income by staying at home than doing modified work, lack incentives for the employee to return to the workplace. This barrier may be real. For this reason, companies should examine their employee group benefit plans and determine the impact that each has on the employee return-to-work outcomes.

A fourth barrier is disability policies and procedures that focus on employee disability rather than capabilities. This approach promotes a "disability mindset", not an "ability mindset" for managers, human resources professionals, union leaders and employees. This is one area that can negatively impact the corporate culture and that warrants serious introspection by a company.

The fifth barrier centres around the belief held by some human resources managers that disability management has become so complex that the practice should be abandoned. This mindset tends to be reactive and akin to "throwing in the towel". Although the recent privacy legislation has made it unacceptable to access to employee medical information, it has not removed the legal obligation of the employee to provide the workplace with the nature of the absence (work-related or non-work-related); the expected duration of absence; work limitations, if any; and a realistic return-to-work date. By providing human resources and the operations with relevant information on the employee's fitness to work in a timely manner, Disability Management Coordinators can overcome this barrier.

The sixth barrier is getting "stakeholder buy-in". Involving stakeholders, from the onset, in the design, development, and implementation of an Integrated Disability Management Program can eliminate this barrier. Being part of the solution to a problem reduces the later need to market the Disability Management Program.

The last barrier is gaining access to consolidated data that can be used to build a business case for an Integrated Disability Management Program. Many companies do not have accurate disability data, or information on their efforts to mitigate the losses associated with those disabilities. Producing historical disability data is equally impossible. Without that type of information, it is difficult for a company to identify its current situation, or to even envision what an ideal state for an Integrated Disability Management Program would look like. This is an area where human resources and occupational health professionals/ practitioners can take a lead role in collecting, analyzing, and interpreting the impact of a company's disabilities and disability management initiatives.

How to Move Forward

STEP 1: ANALYZE YOUR SITUATION

One way to analyze the company/organization's situation is to identify the barriers and the drivers for an Integrated Disability Management Program. Using a tool like Lewin's Force Field Analysis (Figure 1.3),[64] determine the various ways to decrease the barriers for implementing an Integrated Disability Management Program, while increasing the drivers for the program.

Figure 1.3: Lewin's Force Field for an Integrated Disability Management Program

Driving Forces	Restraining Forces (Barriers)
Rising costs of disability ➔	← Lack of company/union awareness and "buy-in"
Disability management reduces ➔ costs	← No early intervention
Available internal resources ➔	← Some non-supportive disability benefit plans
Employees requesting to return ➔ to work from a disability	← Lack of disability-related data
Employee Assistance Program ➔ available	← Fear of workplace accommodation costs
Some supportive policies ➔ available	← Perception of few graduated return-to-work opportunities
Claim management ➔	← Lack of rehabilitation resources
Case management ➔	← Lack of formal accountability for employee absence
Attendance Support & Attendance ➔ Program in place	← Mismanagement of medical claims

This Force Field Analysis helps individuals select the targets for change. By focusing on the restraining forces and looking for ways to reduce their effect, or ways to change them into driving forces, one can identify the real underlying factors preventing the implementation of an Integrated Disability Management Program and the potential solution.

STEP 2: GATHER SUPPORTIVE DISABILITY DATA

By using research outcome findings, one can project the potential savings for the company/organization. This includes using recent survey data and the identified trends in disability costs. It also means the inclusion of any hidden costs of disability such as:

---

[64]   M. Brassard & D. Ritter, *The Memory Jogger: Tools for Continuous Improvement and Effective Planning* (Methuen, MA: GOAL/PC, 1994).

- the overtime paid for the remaining workers who assume a heavier workload while the ill or injured employee is absent;
- hiring replacement workers;
- training costs for replacement workers;
- lowered productivity due to the work-flow disruption;
- customer service disruptions;
- customer dissatisfaction;
- missed business opportunities;
- costs of employee benefits/services provided during the disability; and
- increased insurance premiums.

Also, the potential costs of "doing nothing" to manage illness/injury costs should be considered and taken into account.

STEP 3: DEMONSTRATE THE VALUE

Lastly, demonstrate the outcomes of whatever disability management efforts are in place, or are planned. This can be achieved by using the following principles:

- Consider the structure, process and outcomes of the Integrated Disability Management Program as per the established performance measures.
- Address the value that the Integrated Disability Management Program offers to the organization. Is the program justified from a business standpoint? What is the potential return on investment?
- Consider whether some of the Integrated Disability Management Program performance measures should be valued higher than others. That is, is the impact on injury/illness severity more important than the injury/illness frequency of occurrence?
- Measure disability management data such as the frequency of claims; duration of claims; type and nature of claims; the number of long-term disability claims avoided; the return-to-work statistics; the cost of interventions; the cost of replacement workers; the degree of cost-avoidance through the graduated return-to-work opportunities; the Workers' Compensation Board costs; and any identified trends.

EVOLUTION OF AN INTEGRATED DISABILITY MANAGEMENT PROGRAM

Most organizations/companies become interested in disability management and establishing an Integrated Disability Management Program as a result of increasing disability claim rates and costs. Initial Disability Management Programs tend to very reactive in nature, and then slowly evolve towards an integrated approach to disability management (Figure 1.4).

Figure 1.4: Evolution of An Integrated Disability Management Program

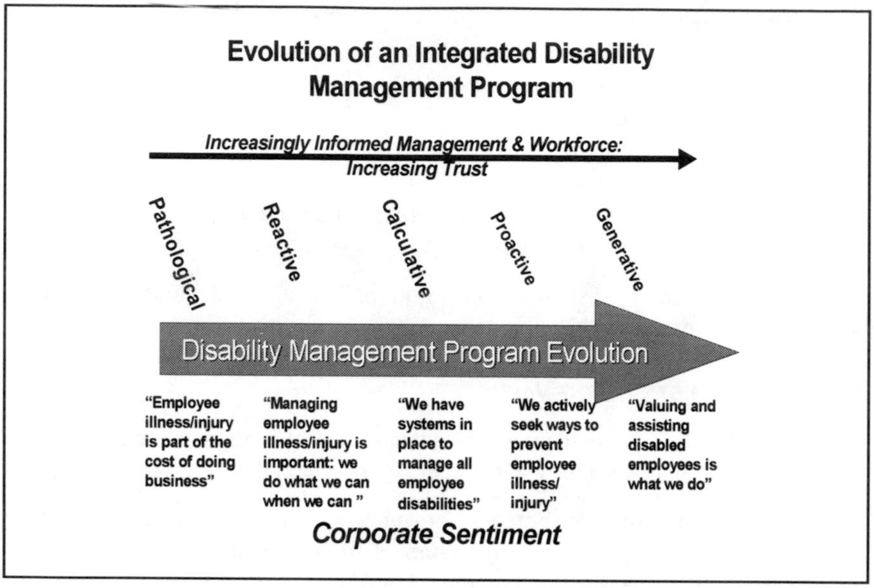

The *Pathological Stage* is where the organization/company fails to recognize that employee injury and illness are preventable occurrences. Rather, the organization/company believes that: "Employee illness and injury are part of the normal costs of doing business. After all, we are working with people. What do you expect?"

The *Reactive Stage* is typified by a realization that employee illness and injury events are costly in human and financial terms, and should be addressed. "One-off attempts" at disability management are informally undertaken. The sentiment is: "Managing employee illness/injury is important: we do what we can when we can." There is limited to no investment in disability management. Hence, none of the elements of a Disability Management Program exist, only a general awareness of the need to address employee illness and injury events as best they can.

The *Calculative Stage* signals a dawning of a formal Disability Management Program. The organization/company establishes a formal Disability Management Program with the necessary infrastructure, policies, procedures, and data management systems. This is the onset of a formalized business function. Success with the "easy" disability claims is realized and encourages the organization/company to observe that: "We have systems in place to manage all employee disabilities." However, at this stage, many organizations/companies segregate their disability management efforts; that is, they may manage only the occupational illness/injuries, but not the non-occupational disabilities. Alternatively, they may manage disabilities in the short-term phases, but not the longer term disability situations.

The *Proactive Stage* is a higher order of Disability Management Program operation. The organization/company "[takes] stock of the issues and pressures unique to each organization, and [comes] up with one co-ordinated approach to facilitate and maximize continued employee contribution to the success of the organization, and to minimize or reduce the costs associated with employee absence."[65] Occupational and non-occupational disability claims, whether in the short- or long-term stages, are treated in a coordinated manner. Disability data is tracked. Performance of the Disability Management Program is measured with a view to continuous improvement. Illness/injury prevention becomes the goal. The sentiment is: "We actively seek ways to prevent employee illness/injury." The outcome is a "win-win" situation for employees and the employer.

The final stage, the *Generative Stage*, is a true integration of the Disability Management Program with other organization/company business functions — the Human Resources function, Attendance Assistance & Support Program, Occupational Health & Safety Program, ergonomics initiatives, Wellness Program, *etc*. The intent is to maximize the efforts of all these various functions/programs so as to best meet the organization's/company's needs. With today's climate of complex and interrelated disability claim conditions, a holistic approach to disability management is required. Likewise the organization/ company requires the same integrated approach to help it deal with increased business demands and complexities. The overriding goal becomes continual improvement of the organization by increasing employee satisfaction, lowering costs, and improving return-to-work times for employees on disability claims. The focus shifts from individual disability claims management to enhancing the organization such that employee disabilities are prevented. The message is then: "Valuing and assisting disabled employees is what we do."

SUMMARY

Employee illness and injury are costly to everyone involved. In Canada, employer and union efforts to manage disability and return employees have advanced to the point where in 2005, 82 per cent of employers reported that they have, at a minimum, return-to-work practices in place.[66] This is encouraging because in 1999, only 23.1 per cent of Canadian employers had any disability

---

[65] Watson-Wyatt Worldwide, reported in G. Shell, "Hands On: An Introduction to Integrated Disability Management" (2003), available online at: <http://www.hrpao.org/HRPA/HRResourceCentre/KnowledgeCentre/newscluster3/An+Introduction+to+Integrated+Disability+Management.htm>.

[66] Watson Wyatt Worldwide, *Staying@Work Report 2005* (Canada 2005), available online at: <http://www.watsonwyatt.com>.

management services.[67] Today, 52 per cent of American respondents have Integrated Disability Management Programs in place; while, of organizations that do not yet have an Integrated Disability Management Program, 61 per cent plan to implement one within the next two years.[68]

Going forward, employers and unions need to continue to proactively manage employee disabilities. Occupational health or human resources professionals can assist with this effort by demonstrating that disability management is good business practice, with immense possibilities for significant returns on the investment made. The remaining chapters of this book are dedicated to helping the reader appreciate this premise.

CHAPTER REFERENCES

A. Ahrens & K. Mulholland, "Vocational Rehabilitation and the Evolution of Disability Management: An Organizational Case Study" (2000) 15 Journal of Vocational Rehabilitation 39.

AIG Claims Services Inc., "Early Intervention Cuts Workers' Compensation Costs" (*Aon Commentary*, 17 June 1996).

E. Akyeampong, *Work Absence Rates, 1987 to 1998*, Cat. No. 71-535-MPB, No. 10 (Ottawa: Statistics Canada, 1999).

S. Aldana, *Top Five Strategies to Enhance the ROI of Worksite Wellness Programs*, Wellness Council of America (February 2009); available online at: <http://www.welcoa.org/freeresources/pdf/top_5_strategies.pdf>.

Aon Consulting, "The Case for Absence Management", *Aon Workforce Strategies, 2003*, available online at: <http://www.aon.com>.

B. Armstrong & S. Greckol, "Accommodation Guidelines" in *Illness and Disability Claims in the Unionized Workplace* (Winnipeg: Centre for Labour-Management Development, 1999).

M. Brassard & D. Ritter, *The Memory Jogger: Tools for Continuous Improvement and Effective Planning* (Methuen, MA: GOAL/PC, 1994).

Canada Post, "Building a Business Case for Disability Management: Proving the Value of a Return to Work Program at Canada Post" (Presented at the National Conference on Disability and Work: Solutions for Canadians, Sheraton Centre, Toronto, Ontario, 7-9 October 1996) [unpublished].

---

[67] Conference Board of Canada, *Supporting Workplace Health: An Exploratory Study of Stakeholder Groups* (Ottawa: Conference Board of Canada, 1999). Unpublished study reported in K. Bachmann's *More Than Just Hard Hats and Safety Boots* (Ottawa: Conference Board of Canada, 2000) at 33.

[68] N. Vimadalal & J. Wozniak, "Best Practices to Help Employers Capture the Benefits of Integrated Disability Management", *Employee Benefits News* (March 1, 2008), available online at: <http://ebn.benefitnews.com/asset/article/548491/best-practices-help-employers-capture-benefits.html?pg=>.

A. Cantor, "The Future of Workplace Accommodations: Containing Costs and Maximizing Effectiveness" (Presented at the National Conference on Disability and Work: Solutions for Canadians, Sheraton Centre, Toronto, Ontario, 7-9 October 1996) [unpublished].

CCH Incorporated, *2007 CCH Unscheduled Absence Survey* (Riverwoods, IL: CCH Incorporated, 2007).

CCH Incorporated, "Unscheduled Employee Absenteeism Rises to Five Year High", in *2004 CCH Unscheduled Absence Survey* (Riverwoods, IL: CCH Incorporated, 2004), available online at: <http://www.cch.com/press/news/2004/ 20041007h. asp>.

A. Clarke, "Disability Case Management Models" (Presented at the Disability Case Management Forum, Vancouver, British Columbia, 24-26 March 1997) [unpublished].

Conference Board of Canada, *Supporting Workplace Health: An Exploratory Study of Stakeholder Groups* (Ottawa, ON: Conference Board of Canada, 1999). Unpublished study reported in K. Bachmann's *More Than Just Hard Hats and Safety Boots* (Ottawa: Conference Board of Canada, 2000) at 33.

J. Cowell, "Serving Albertans Through Effective Injury Prevention and Disability Management" (Presented at the National Conference on Disability and Work: Solutions for Canadians, Sheraton Centre, Toronto, Ontario, 7-9 October 1996).

J. Curtis & L. Scott, "Integrating Disability Management into Strategic Plans: Creating Healthy Organizations" *AAOHN Journal* 298.

D. Dyck, *Disability Management: Theory, Strategy and Industry Practice*, 3rd ed. (Markham, ON: LexisNexis Canada, 2006) at 14.

D. Dyck, *Stating Your Case* (Ottawa: Benefits Canada, 1998) at 55-59.

Editor, "Disabilities Draining the B.C. Economy" (1997) 1:7 *Back to Work* 1.

L. Gates, Y. Taler & S. Akabas, "Optimizing Return to Work Among Newly Disabled Workers: A New Approach to Cost Containment" (1989) 5:2 Benefits Quarterly 19.

D. Gross & M. Battié, "Work-related Recovery Expectations and the Prognosis of Chronic Low Back Pain Within a Workers Compensation Setting" (2005) 47 *Journal of Occupational and Environmental Medicine* 428. Available online at: <http://www.rtwknowledge.org/browse.php?article_id= 92& view_type=research>.

H. Harder & L. Scott, *Comprehensive Disability Management* (Toronto: Elsevier, Churchill Livingstone, 2005).

Hewitt Associates, *Disability Absence Index Survey 2007* (2007), available online at: <http: www.hewittassociates.com/Intl/NA/en-CA/KnowledgeCenter/ ArticlesReports/DAIS_highlights.aspx>.

Institute for Work & Health, "Seven 'Principles' for Successful Return to Work", *Institute for Work & Health*, Toronto (March 2007) at 2, available online at: <http://www. iwh.on.ca/seven_principles_for_rtw>.

Job Accommodation Network, *Workplace Accommodations: Low Cost, High Impact, 2007*, at 2, available online at: <http://www.jan.wvu.edu/media/LowCostHighImpact.doc>.

S. Lebrun, "Employers Take Notice of Disability Costs: Management of Injury and Illness Can Save Millions" (1997) 29 December *C.H.R.R.*

M. Mahon, "Lost Labor Time Costs U.S. $260 Billion Each Year" in *Newsroom, The Commonwealth Fund*, (August 31, 2005), available online at: <http://www.cmwf.org/newsroom/newsroom_show.htm?doc-id=294188>.

Marsh Risk Consulting, *Workforce Risk: Fourth Annual Marsh Mercer Survey of Employers' Time-Off and Disability Programs* (2003), available online at: <http://www.marshriskconsulting.com/>.

T. Michalak, "Disability Management: An Assessment of Psychological Factors and Early Intervention" (2007) 6:1 International Journal of Disability, Community & Rehabilitation, available online at: <http://www. ijdcr.ca/VOL06_01_CAN/articles/michalak.shtml>.

National Institute of Disability Management and Research (NIDMAR), *Disability Management in the Workplace: A Guide to Establishing a Joint Workplace Program* (Port Alberni, BC: NIDMAR, 1995).

National Institute of Disability Management and Research (NIDMAR), *Code of Practice for Disability Management* (Port Alberni, BC: NIDMAR, 2000) at 5.

National Institute of Disability Management and Research (NIDMAR), *Occupational Standards in Disability Management: Executive Summary* (Port Alberni, BC: NIDMAR, 2000) at 2.

G.C. Pati, "Economics of Rehabilitation in the Workplace" (1985) 51:4 Journal of Rehabilitation 22.

Petro-Canada, "Managed Rehabilitation Care Program" (Presented at the CPBI Conference, Calgary, Alberta, 1996) [unpublished].

P. Reed, "Recent Ruling on ADA and the Value of Interventions" (2002) 27:2 Employee Benefits Journal 3.

J. Regan, cited in D. Thompson, "In Support of STD", *Benefits Canada*, (2001), available online at: <http://www.benefitscanada.com/content/legacy/Content/2001/11-01/std.html/>.

T. Riggar, D. Maki & A. Wolf, *Applied Rehabilitation Counselling* (New York: Springer Publishing Co., 1986).

D. Rosenthal, N. Hursh, J. Lui, R. Isom & J. Sasson, "A Survey of Current Disability Management Practice: Emerging Trends and Implications for Certification" (2007) 50 Rehabilitation Counselling Bulletin 76.

R. Rundle, "Move Fast if you Want to Rehabilitate the Worker" (1983) 17:18 Business Insurance 10.

Shell Oil Company, Houston, "Impact of a Disability Management Program on Employee Productivity in a Petrochemical Company" (2006) 48:5 Journal of Occupational and Environmental Medicine 497.

D. Shrey, *Principles and Practices of Disability Management in Industry* (Winter Park, FL: GR Press Inc., 1995).

Statistics Canada, *Work Absence Rates, 2007*, Cat. No. 71-211-XWE (Ottawa: Statistics Canada, May 2008).

Statistics Canada, *Average Hourly Wages of Employees by Selected Characteristics*, available online at: <http://www40.statcan.gc.ca/l01/cst01/labr69a-eng.htm>.

L. Stellini, "Preferred Provider Network for Integrated Management of Soft Tissue Injuries" (Presented at the Conference on Developing Effective Return-to-Work Programs, Toronto, Ontario, 24-25 October 1996) [unpublished].

D.G. Tate, R.V. Habeck & D.E. Galvin, "Disability Management: Origins, Concepts and Principles for Practice" (1986) 17 Journal of Applied Rehabilitation Counselling 5.

University of Calgary, *Annual Report* (Calgary: University of Calgary, 1996).

N. Vimadalal & J. Wozniak, "Best Practices to Help Employers Capture the Benefits of Integrated Disability Management" *Employee Benefits News* (March 1, 2008), available online at: <http://ebn.benefitnews.com/asset/article/548491/best-practices-help-employers-capture-benefits.html?pg=>.

Washington Business Group on Health, *Fifth Annual Washington Business Group Health/Watson Wyatt Worldwide Survey on Disability Management* (Watson Wyatt Worldwide, 2004), available online at <http://www.watsonwyatt.com>.

Watson Wyatt Worldwide, *Managing Health Care Costs in a New Era: 10th Annual National Business Group on Health/Watson Wyatt Survey Report, 2005*, available online at: <http://www.watsonwyatt.com>.

Watson-Wyatt, *Staying@Work: Effective Presence at Work (2007)* at 10, available online at: <https://www.watsonwyatt.com/>.

Watson Wyatt Worldwide, *Staying@Work, Report 2005* (Canada 2005) at 5, available online at <http://www.watsonwyatt.com/research/resrender.asp?id=w-860&page=1>.

Watson-Wyatt Worldwide, reported in G. Shell, "Hands On: An Introduction to Integrated Disability Management" (2003), available online at: <http://www.hrpao.org/HRPA/HRResourceCentre/KnowledgeCentre/newscluster3/An+Introduction+to+Integrated+Disability+Management.htm>.

Weyerhaeuser, "Transitional Return-to-Work at Weyerhaeuser Company" (Presented at the National Conference on Disability and Work: Solutions for Canadians, Sheraton Centre, Toronto, Ontario, 7-9 October 1996) [unpublished].

Workers' Compensation Board Alberta, *2004 Annual Report* (Edmonton: Workers' Compensation Board Alberta, 2005), available online at: <http://www.wcb.ab.ca/pdfs/public/annual_report_2004.pdf>.

Chapter 2

Joint Labour-Management Support and Involvement

IMPORTANCE

For an Integrated Disability Management Program to be successful, joint labour-management endorsement, support, and involvement is essential. This belief, although widely upheld by researchers in the field,[1] is less likely to be explored or implemented by industry. This is an unfortunate situation because:

- employers can enhance an Integrated Disability Management Program's success by involving unions in the planning, implementation, and evaluation of Integrated Disability Management Programs, and in coordinating gradual return-to-work initiatives;[2] and
- unionized employees, in Canada and the United States, have traditionally missed significantly more workdays each year when compared to their non-unionized counterparts.[3]

This chapter is dedicated to a discussion on the rationale for joint-labour involvement, what that entails, what is required from each player, and how this partnership can be successfully achieved.

CANADIAN LABOUR UNIONS: HISTORY AND ROLE

History

The history of the trade union movement in Canada started in Montreal with the registration of a union among boot and shoe workers in 1827.[4] However, given the lack of legal support for unions in Canada at that time, it was not until 1872

---

[1] National Institute of Disability Management and Research (NIDMAR), *Disability Management in the Workplace: A Guide to Establishing a Joint Workplace Program* (Port Alberni, BC: NIDMAR, 1995). See also S. Jodoin & H. Harder, "Strategies to Enhance Labour-Management Cooperation in the Development of Disability Management Programs" (2004) 3:4 International Journal of Disability, Community & Rehabilitation 1, available online at: <http://www.ijdcr.ca/VOL03_04_CAN/articles/jodoin.shtml>.

[2] S. Jodoin & H. Harder, *ibid.*

[3] See Chapter 17, "Disability Management Best Practices". See also Mercer Inc., *The Total Financial Impact of Employee Absences — Survey Highlights* (October 2008), available online at: <http://www.kronos.com/absenceanonymous/media/Mercer-Survey-Highlights.pdf>.

[4] S. Applebaum, M.D. Beckman, L. Boone & D. Kurz, *Contemporary Canadian Business*, 3rd ed. (Toronto: Holt, Rinehart & Winston of Canada, 1987) at 257.

when the John A. Macdonald government introduced the *Trade Unions Act*, that workers had the right to band together to seek better working conditions. In 1907, the enactment of the *Industrial Disputes Investigation Act* introduced the principle of compulsory delay in work stoppages. This Act also made provisions for the investigation and conciliation of labour disputes by a tripartite board — a board with the legal power to investigate the situation, to compel testimony, to determine the root causes of the issues at hand, and to recommend labour settlements.

Prior to 1919, the Canadian labour movement appeared to have a bright future. It had played a significant role in improving the working conditions and benefits for Canadian workers. However, the years between 1919 and 1949 became a time of upheaval and change. Unions were "beset by crisis after crisis, catastrophe upon catastrophe".[5] Abella recounts that Canadian unions were attacked on all fronts — by business, by governments, and by their own respective memberships. There were times during those years when the very survival of an organized labour movement in Canada seemed in jeopardy. Yet by the 1950s, trade unions emerged triumphant and successful as a powerful political and economic force.

Role

Trade unions are organizations of employees who have joined together to obtain a stronger voice in decisions affecting their wages, benefits, working conditions, and other employment aspects. Through the process of collective bargaining, union leaders negotiate with management collective agreements that spell out the terms and conditions of employment. These collective agreements provide structure, process, and the expected outcomes that help to define the nature of the working relationship between labour and management.

The formation of a union is "an attempt to adjust a power imbalance and to make the employee as strong as the employer by acting as a single united group".[6] The right to strike remains the union's basic weapon. However, a strike is only successful if production can be shut down, and if the employer is willing to concede due to the withdrawal of services and related costs.

Today, the Canadian labour movement is strong. Over the years, labour demands for improving inhumane working conditions have been met. Now the focus is on job security and employee benefits. In fact, many unions have become actively involved in employee benefit programs such as Employee Assistance Programs, Disability Management Programs, and gradual return-to-work activities.

For example, the labour movement played an instrumental role in assisting the British Columbia Workers' Compensation Board to undertake research and

---

[5]   I. Abella, *On Strike: Six Key Labour Struggles in Canada 1919-1949* (Toronto: James Lorimer & Co., 1975).

[6]   *Ibid.*

program development in the area of disability management. The National Institute for Disability Management and Research (NIDMAR), in Port Alberni, BC, is but one example of their efforts.

Since 1994, NIDMAR has been recognized as an organization committed to reducing the human, social, and economic costs of disability in Canada. The Institute has developed a recognized educational program for Canadian disability coordinators, offered educational sessions, produced resource materials, undertaken valuable research on disability management in Canada, promoted workplace solutions to reducing disability rates and costs, and supported companies, unions and other players in their efforts to develop successful Disability Management Programs. Some of NIDMAR's notable contributions are:

- Development of a recognized disability management educational curriculum.
- Presentation and sponsorship of numerous seminars on disability management.
- Research on the cost of disability in British Columbia and published in *The Effects of Disability on B.C.'s Economy.*[7]
- Development of a disability database — REHADAT, which provides data on the relevant legislation, best practice case studies, and other available resources for successful disability management.
- Development of a disability management audit tool and process — Consensus Based Disability Management Audit™.[8]
- Publication of numerous resource materials such as:

  - *Industrial Disability Management: An Effective Economic and Human Resource Strategy;*[9]
  - *Disability Management in the Workplace: A Guide to Establishing a Joint Workplace Program;*[10]
  - *Strategies for Success: Disability Management in the Workplace;*[11]
  - *Disability Management Success: A Global Corporate Perspective;*[12]

---

[7]   National Institute of Disability Management and Research (NIDMAR), *The Effects of Disability on B.C.'s Economy* (Port Alberni, BC: NIDMAR 1995), available online at: <http://www.nidmar.ca/products/products_details.asp?id=15>.

[8]   National Institute of Disability Management and Research (NIDMAR). *Consensus Based Disability Management Audit™*. Further information is available online at: <http://www.nidmar.ca>.

[9]   National Institute of Disability Management and Research (NIDMAR), *Industrial Disability Management: An Effective Economic and Human Resource Strategy* (Port Alberni, BC: NIDMAR, 1992), available online at: <http://www.nidmar.ca>.

[10]   National Institute of Disability and Research (NIDMAR), *Disability Management in the Workplace: A Guide to Establishing A Joint Workplace Program* (Port Alberni, BC: NIDMAR, 1995).

[11]   National Institute of Disability Management and Research (NIDMAR), *Strategies for Success: Disability Management in the Workplace* (Port Alberni, BC: NIDMAR, 1997), available online at: <http://www.nidmar.ca>.

[12]   National Institute of Disability Management and Research (NIDMAR), *Disability Management Success: A Global Corporate Perspective* (Port Alberni, BC: NIDMAR, 2005), available online at: <http://www.nidmar.ca>.

- *Code of Practice for Disability Management: Describing Effective Benchmarks for the Creation of Workplace-Based Disability Management Programs*;[13]
- *Code of Practice for Disability Management*, 2nd edition;[14]
- *Occupational Standards in Disability Management: Establishing Criteria for Excellence In Canada*;[15]
- *Effective Re-Integration Strategies for the '90s: The Role of Employers, Union, Government, and Consumers in Partnership*;[16] and
- *Challenges in Disability Management: A Resource Manual for Return to Work Practitioners*.[17]

- Production of videos[18] such as *Disability in the Workplace*; *The Final Step: The Case for Getting Disabled Workers Back on the Job*; *The Challenge to Lead: The Rewards of Disability Management*; and *Every 12 Seconds*.
- Development of Canadian standards and a certification process for certified return-to-work coordinators and certified disability management professionals.[19]
- In consort with the Canadian government, business and labour leaders, the establishment of National Awards of Excellence in Disability Management (1999).[20]

Through efforts like these, Canadian trade unions continue to demonstrate their concern about the needs and well-being of their members — particularly those members with disabilities. As well, in industry settings, they have provided sponsorship and support for employee benefit programs such as Employee Assistance and Integrated Disability Management Programs.

---

[13] National Institute of Disability Management and Research (NIDMAR), *Code of Practice for Disability Management: Describing Effective Benchmarks for the Creation of Workplace-Based Disability Management Programs* (Port Alberni, BC: NIDMAR 2000), available online at: <http://www.nidmar.ca>.

[14] National Institute of Disability Management and Research (NIDMAR), *Code of Practice for Disability Management*, 2nd ed. (Port Alberni, BC: NIDMAR, 2004), available online at: <http://www.nidmar.ca>.

[15] National Institute of Disability Management and Research (NIDMAR), *Occupational Standards in Disability Management: Establishing Criteria for Excellence In Canada* (Port Alberni, BC: NIDMAR, 1999), available online at: <http://www.nidmar.ca>.

[16] National Institute of Disability Management and Research (NIDMAR), *Effective Re-Integration Strategies for the '90s: The Role of Employers, Union, Government, and Consumers in Partnership* (Port Alberni, BC: NIDMAR, 1991), available online at: <http://www.nidmar.ca>.

[17] National Institute of Disability Management and Research (NIDMAR), *Challenges in Disability Management: A Resource Manual for Return to Work Practitioners* (Port Alberni, BC: NIDMAR, 1992), available online at: <http://www.nidmar.ca>.

[18] For more information, refer to <http://www.nidmar.ca/products/products.asp?cat=5>.

[19] C. Moser, "Canada's Occupational Standards Outline Two Certification Possibilities" (1999) 3:7 Back to Work 1.

[20] NIDMAR Launches First National Awards of Excellence in Disability Management, information available online at: <http://www.nidmar.ca/awards/awards_background/background_info.asp>.

MANAGEMENT: BACKGROUND AND ROLE

Management is defined as the achievement of organizational objectives through people and other resources. The challenge is to combine human and technical resources in the best possible way to attain the desired objectives.

Various levels of management within an organization make up a management pyramid. Senior management, the highest level of management on the pyramid, is composed of the president and senior executives or vice-presidents. Middle management, which includes a level of executives such as plant managers, department heads and assistant vice-presidents, is involved in developing detailed operational plans and procedures to implement the business strategies developed by senior management. Line management, the pyramid base, are the individuals who are directly responsible for assigning workers to specific jobs and evaluating their daily work performances.[21]

To be successful at any level, managers need technical, business, and relationship skills. The technical skills involve the ability to understand and use the techniques, knowledge and tools specific to the industry or one's area of expertise. Business skills include planning, organizing, directing, and controlling the business aspects of the organization. This includes the ability to conceptualize — better known as being able to "see the big picture".

Relationship skills are commonly termed "people skills". They involve the ability to work with and to motivate people to get the work done. The ability for a manager to be able to communicate, lead and motivate people is crucial. So is the ability to listen, empathize, care for and support employees in a constructive manner. As well, attention to the development of a work environment conducive to top performance by employees is key.

The term **labour relations** describes "all the interactions between labour and management in which employees are represented by a trade union".[22] In non-unionized settings, this relationship is termed as **employee relations**.

Many managers believe that an organization is less flexible and effective when a union represents all or some of their employees. This belief stems from the perception that wages are above competitive levels, inefficient work practices rule, and lower work output occurs due to strikes in unionized workplaces. However, research has shown that unions can increase organizational effectiveness by reducing staff turnover and by inducing management to adopt more efficient policies and practices.[23] Another study found evidence of productivity gains in unionized firms.[24]

---

[21] S. Applebaum, M.D. Beckman, L. Boone & D. Kurz, *Contemporary Canadian Business*, 3rd ed. (Toronto: Holt, Rinehart & Winston of Canada, 1987) at 257.

[22] T. Stone & N. Meltz, *Human Resources Management in Canada*, 2nd ed. (Toronto: Holt, Rinehart & Winston of Canada, 1988) at 540.

[23] R.B. Freeman & J.L. Medoff, *What Do Unions Do?* (New York: Basic Books, 1984) at 166.

[24] K.B. Clark, "The Impact of Unionized Productivity: A Case Study" (1980) 33:4 Industrial Labour Relations Review 451.

The effects of unionization on organizational effectiveness depend both on the development of an effective working relationship between labour and management and on management's ability to make efficient use of labour, capital and technology. "According to an old saying, 'Management *usually gets the union it deserves'*".[25]

With many Canadian employers interested in managing employee medical absences and disabilities, illness and disability claims and case management in the unionized workplace has become a topic of interest. The remainder of this chapter deals specifically with this topic.

DISABILITY MANAGEMENT: JOINT LABOUR-MANAGEMENT SUPPORT

Disability management is based on relationships and is founded on trust, open and honest communication, and mutual respect by and for all stakeholders. For an Integrated Disability Management Program to be successful, a level of trust and commitment among the stakeholders must be attained. *These programs also depend on stakeholders taking ownership of their problems, and working together to develop workable solutions.* As well, the strategies adopted for disability management must fully address stakeholder interests, needs and goals in a way that benefits all parties. For these and numerous other reasons, which will now be discussed, joint labour-management support and involvement is required.

* *In order to understand the negative impacts of employee absenteeism and disability and the positive aspects afforded through a Disability Management Program in terms of support to the employee, family and work group, joint labour-management support is required.*

Disability brings with it sizable human and financial costs to the employee, family, work group, organization, and society in general. One widely received estimate in Canada is that disability-related costs are 1 per cent to 3 per cent of payroll for the direct costs of short-term disability and 0.5 per cent to 1.5 per cent for the direct costs of long-term disability.[26] The indirect costs are estimated to be three to seven times that amount. In the U.S.A., the direct costs of short-term disability, workers' compensation absences and long-term disabilities equal

---

[25]   S. Applebaum, M.D. Beckman, L. Boone & D. Kurz, *Contemporary Canadian Business*, 3rd ed. (Toronto: Holt, Rinehart & Winston of Canada, 1987) at 547.

[26]   See K. Nagel, "Total Organizational Health Costs: What Are They? What Can Organizations Do About Them?" (Presented at the Strategic Leadership Forum '99, Toronto, Ontario, 20 October 1999) [unpublished]; and B. Anderson, "Disability Management" (Seminar presented in Calgary, Alberta, 1990) [unpublished].

4.0 per cent of payroll with the associated indirect costs being an additional 5.2 per cent of payroll for a total of 9.2 per cent of payroll.[27]

Apart from the dollar aspects, disability brings with it a plethora of negative impacts for the employee, family, and workgroup that range from economic hardships, to biological, psychological, social, and vocational suffering. The bottom line is that the true cost of disability in Canada remains unknown. Suffice it to say that it is far more than what people "guesstimate" it to be.

By working together, labour and management can identify the true impact and costs for their own organization. This can create a joint awareness of the magnitude of the problem, and the degree of investment required by both parties to own and address the situation.

Integrated Disability Management Programs have shown that employees/ union members, families, and work groups can be supported through periods of illness/injury; that effective return-to-work outcomes can be achieved; that illness/injury prevention can be accomplished; and that cost-avoidance in terms of disability costs can be realized.

- *Joint labour-management involvement and support is required in order to promote a broad understanding of the Integrated Disability Management Program, including the barriers and drivers for a successful return to work by the recovering employee.*

According to the Honourable Lawrence MacAulay, former Minister of Labour for Canada:

> Employers, employees and unions must work together in order to ensure that policies and programs that effectively address the situation of persons with disabilities are introduced into the workplace. Consultation and collaboration are important in addressing questions of accommodation and in raising awareness generally.[28]

Part of this process is to identify the specific barriers and drivers for successful disability management and graduated return-to-work processes within the organization. By working together, employers and unions (if unionized), or employers and employees (if not unionized), can make a significant contribution toward getting a "true picture" of the issues at hand and toward finding workable solutions.

- *Labour and management must work together to address the corporate cultural issues that impact employee attendance and attitudes towards an*

---

[27] Mercer Inc., *The Total Financial Impact of Employee Absences — Survey Highlights* (October 2008), at 4, available online at: <http://www.kronos.com/absenceanonymous/media/Mercer-Survey-Highlights.pdf>.

[28] National Institute of Disability Management and Research (NIDMAR), *Strategies for Success: Disability Management in the Workplace* (Port Alberni, BC: NIDMAR, 1997) at 13, available online at: <http://www.nidmar.ca/products/products_details.asp?id=7>.

Integrated Disability Management Program, and toward helping ill/injured employees to successfully return to work.

Corporate culture can be defined as the system of shared beliefs and values that develops within an organization and guides the behaviour of its members. It is "the way things are done" within an organization.

Corporate culture exerts a major influence on employee work attendance and employee/management attitude towards the disability management processes. Organizations that send a clear message that:

- work attendance is important;
- employees are valued; and
- the contribution made by each stakeholder is vital to company success;

are more likely to have employees that are receptive to regular work attendance, and that are also receptive to helping fellow employees get back to work following illness/injury. To develop a positive corporate culture, joint labour-management support and involvement are required. All parties must believe that they are involved, and that they are a part of an exciting and vibrant place to work.

- *Joint labour-management support and involvement will result in a trusting and positive environment in which disability management practices can successfully function.*

Trust, as already mentioned, is a critical component to the development of a functional relationship. Disability management is highly dependent on good working relationships. To build a trusting and positive environment in which disability management practices can successfully operate, labour and management have to constantly work at relationship building and maintenance. Labour-management leaders are also advised to act as role models to demonstrate how these positive working relationships should function within their specific organization. Followers learn more from their leader's actions, as opposed to their words.

"Labour-management collaboration can improve labour relations, improve union and employee buy-in for the program, and reduce the human and financial costs of disability."[29] In a recent Institute for Work and Health study, it was determined that strong union support for disability management intervention resulted in shorter disability claim absences and lower costs.[30]

---

[29] S. Jodoin & H. Harder, "Strategies to Enhance Labour-Management Cooperation in the Development of Disability Management Programs" (2004) 3:4 International Journal of Disability, Community & Rehabilitation 1, available online at: <http://www.ijdcr.ca/VOL03_04_CAN/articles/jodoin.shtml>.

[30] Institute for Work & Health, "Seven 'Principles' for Successful Return to Work". Institute for Work & Health Toronto (March 2007) at 2, available online at: <http://www.iwh.on.ca/seven-principles-for-rtw>.

- *For decision-making regarding employee welfare, group benefits and vocational future, joint labour-management support and involvement is required.*

Collaboration with unions is the only option for Canadian and American employers seeking to develop an Integrated Disability Management Program.[31] In a disability situation, issues emerge regarding the employee's welfare, vocational future, and available group benefits. In the unionized workplace, these are the issues that labour and management tend to address as part of labour relations. Therefore, it is imperative for both parties to play a role in the disability management of the ill/injured employee.

In terms of legalities, management is obliged to work with union leaders to offer effective disability management, return-to-work, and rehabilitation services. The rationale behind this arrangement is that the union is the certified bargaining agent for the employee. The premise is based on the fact that the individual gives up his or her individual bargaining position on behalf of a stronger voice with the union. In return, the union has a legal obligation to review decisions made between the employer and employee. If they fail to do so, the union can be sued by the employee.[32]

The union, on the other hand, has the responsibility to fairly represent its member when a complaint comes forward about the employee's work capacity, or likelihood of risk due to health conditions. The employer and the union have the duty to accommodate the ill or injured worker, and that worker has the right to be accommodated unless there is a **Bona Fide Occupational Requirement**[33] that cannot be met, or if the accommodation is to the point of undue hardship on the employer and union's part.

Thus, in dealing with employee welfare and vocational issues, all parties need to be involved. Hence, it is advisable for management and unions to consider, as part of the collective bargaining process, issues like:

- What is the goal of the organization's/company's Integrated Disability Management Program?

---

[31] S. Jodoin & H. Harder, "Strategies to Enhance Labour-Management Cooperation in the Development of Disability Management Programs" (2004) 3:4 International Journal of Disability, Community & Rehabilitation 1, available online at: <http://www.ijdcr.ca/VOL03_04_CAN/articles/jodoin.shtml>.

[32] D.B. Mercer, "Roles and Responsibilities in Job Modification and Accommodation" (Seminars in Occupational Health and Medicine, Faculty of Medicine, Continuing Education, University of Calgary, 3 February 1999) [unpublished].

[33] **Bona Fide Occupational Requirement (BFOR)** is defined as a standard or rule that is integral to carrying out the functions of a specific position. For a standard to be considered a BFOR, an employer has to establish that any accommodation or changes to the standard would create an undue hardship. For example, an airline pilot must have very good eyesight. This standard is integral to carrying out the duties of a pilot's job. Source: Canadian Human Rights Commission. Overview, CHRC Home Page, available online at: <http://www.chrc-ccdp.ca/preventing_discrimination/page4-en.asp>.

- Is the Integrated Disability Management Program consistent with the organization's/company's/union's philosophies and values?
- How is the Integrated Disability Management Program administered? Is it management operated, or joint labour-management run?
- How does the Integrated Disability Management Program function? Who is involved?
- What are the entry and exiting criteria for the Integrated Disability Management Program?
- What impact could the Integrated Disability Management Program and related policies, and/or processes/practices have on the wording of the collective agreement?
- How does the dispute resolution read?
- How does employee seniority factor into the Integrated Disability Management Program and processes?
- How will modified work and alternate work be defined? How will those jobs be identified?
- Will there be instances when modified/alternate work offers will include crossing union jurisdictions?
- How will the Integrated Disability Management Program's performance be evaluated? Who will have access to the results?
- How will management and labour be involved in the continuous improvements of the Integrated Disability Management Program?

- *Labour and management can build creative solutions for supporting employee medical absence, vocational challenges, workplace accommodations, and return-to-work practices.*

"For a unionized Canadian employer with reasonable working relationship with the union, a joint disability management initiative is more likely to produce practical and innovative solutions."[34] By all stakeholders taking ownership for the problems and challenges, and by working together, they can develop workable solutions that benefit all parties. Historically, unions have improved the working conditions and benefits for Canadian workers, unionized or not.[35] As well, union advocacy has positively impacted a variety of pieces of legislation applicable to the workplace.[36]

---

[34] National Institute of Disability Management and Research (NIDMAR), *Strategies for Success: Disability Management in the Workplace* (Port Alberni, BC: NIDMAR, 1997), at 100, available online at: <http://www.nidmar.ca/products/products_details.asp?id=7>.

[35] D. Miles, "Building Joint Labor-management Initiatives for Worksite Disability Management", in D. Shrey & M. Lacerte, eds., *Principles and Practices of Disability Management in Industry* (Winter Park, FL: GR Press, 1995) 225.

[36] S. Shurman, D. Well, P. Landsbergis & B. Israel, "The Role of Unions and Collective Bargaining in Preventing Work-related Disability", in T. Thomason, J.F. Burton, Jr. & D.E. Hyatt, eds., *New Approaches to Disability in the Workplace* (Madison, WI: Industrial Relations Research Association, 1998) 121.

- *Labour and management must be in compliance with the applicable legislation: Occupational Health and Safety Acts, privacy legislation, and Canadian Human Rights and Duty to Accommodate legislation.*

The various provincial Occupational Health and Safety Acts and pieces of privacy legislation in Canada address the issue of collection of employee personal health data. Employee personal health information is not to be collected indiscriminately. Only the personal health information relevant to the disability management process and relevant to the purposes for which it is to be used should be collected. This means that the knowledge and consent of the employee are required for the collection and disclosure of personal health data relevant to disability management. Both labour and management require an appreciation of this regulation and respect the parameters involved.

According to the *Canadian Human Rights Act*,[37] disabled employees must be accommodated within the workplace up to the point of "undue hardship" on the person accommodating the disabled employee's needs. This is a tripartite responsibility:

1. the employer must accommodate up to the point of undue hardship;
2. the union must support the employee's return to work and the accommodation process up to the point of undue hardship; and
3. the employee must seek and sustain a workable solution to accommodate his or her disability, and the employee must also provide the necessary information from the physician, and advise the employer of the effectiveness of the modified work measures.[38]

To achieve these legal obligations, all three of the stakeholder groups must work together.

The Model Code for the Protection of Personal Information defines "**consent**" as "the voluntary agreement with what is being done or proposed".[39] While consent may be expressed or implied, organizations should seek express consent where information is of a sensitive nature. Implicit in this act, is that the person providing consent is doing so in an informed manner. Consent of the individual must be obtained unless legal, medical, security, or other reasons make it impossible or impractical. Obtaining consent for the release of personal health information is a common practice in disability management. It therefore behoves labour and management to adopt a consistent approach for the consent forms and the practices used.

---

[37] R.S.C. 1985, c. H-6, s. 15(2).

[38] Centre for Labour-Management Development, "Accommodation Guidelines" (Presented at the Illness and Disability Claims in the Unionized Workplace Seminar, February 10-11, 1999) [unpublished].

[39] Canadian Standards Association (CSA), *Model Code for the Protection of Personal Information* (Can/C.S.A. — Q830-96) (Ottawa: CSA, 1996).

As for the various pieces of privacy legislation, which are discussed further in Chapter 20, "Disability Management: Legal Aspects", employers and unions are advised to be aware of the issues around seeking personal health information from employees and maintaining the collected information in a confidential manner.

By working together, labour and management can develop disability management policies, procedures and processes that are compliant with the relevant pieces of Canadian legislation.

- *Labour and management must be familiar with collective agreements and their impact on disability management initiatives.*

Many unions have included provisions for disability management within their collective agreements. These documents provide the governance for workplace labour practices and therefore, impact disability management initiatives within an organization. Thus, both parties need to ensure that the organization and union's disability management practices are in alignment with the applicable collective agreements. By working together, this can be achieved in the planning and implementation phases of an Integrated Disability Management Program.

- *Labour and management should work together on health and management issues that tend to co-exist in disability management situations and are difficult to resolve.*

Employee disability brings with it a myriad of issues and situations. Some issues are clearly health-related, while other issues are a mixture of health, workplace, and performance situations. Difficult disability cases tend to involve performance problems, labour relations issues, and/or workplace discord. Each of these situations can be challenging in their own right. They become even more challenging when health problems exist and information is kept confidential.

In successful Integrated Disability Management Programs, labour and management work together with the Disability Case Manager, often an occupational health nurse, to tease apart the health and management issues. Once identified, each issue can be addressed accordingly.

Without working together, labour and management will experience problems when the recovered employee is deemed fit to return to work in some capacity, but the non-medical reasons associated with the disability can prevent a return to work. By working together, non-medical issues can be addressed in combination with the medical issues so that, hopefully, all issues will be at the same state of preparedness for the person to return to work in a safe and timely manner.

- *Labour and management need to participate in developing prevention strategies required to lower the incidence of employee illness or injury.*

Illness or injury prevention strategies, which are part of a comprehensive Integrated Disability Management Program, are highly dependent on stakeholder support and involvement. In order to develop prevention strategies, all parties must understand the importance of pro-activity and prevention as means to reduce employee illness/injury, and must be willing to participate fully in the process. To garner such support from the organization, labour and management leaders need to act as role models and demonstrate their commitment and involvement in illness/injury prevention.

- *Labour and management involvement and support can enhance the Integrated Disability Management Program's communication capabilities of the organization.*

Open communication is a vital component of any successful Integrated Disability Management Program. For stakeholders to support the program, they need to know what the program is about, how it works, and what the expected and actual outcomes are. They also need to know "what is in it for them" and why they should even care to support such an initiative within their workplace.

In terms of disability case management, good information flow among the parties involved is essential to keep everyone "on track" and focused on the goal at hand - a safe and timely return-to-work for the employee, or rehabilitation to an optimal level of functioning.

By working together to develop an Integrated Disability Management Program communication strategy/plan, labour and management can set the stage for good communication around disability management. They can also prepare an Integrated Disability Management Program marketing plan.

- *Labour and management promote the marketing of the Integrated Disability Management Program.*

For any Integrated Disability Management Program to be recognized, a marketing and communication plan is required. However, joint labour-management involvement and support is required to develop, implement and evaluate the marketing plan. To successfully market a program, all the relevant stakeholders must be identified along with their interests and issues concerning the proposed program. As well, a joint effort is required to determine suitable marketing strategies, messages, communication vehicles and evaluation processes. By working together, labour and management can better undertake this important process.

HOW IS JOINT LABOUR-MANAGEMENT SUPPORT AND INVOLVEMENT ACHIEVED?

To achieve joint labour-management support and involvement, the prime element is to develop a positive working relationship based on mutual respect, trust, and confidence in each other's integrity, and a willingness to work together to develop a functional and effective Integrated Disability Management Program.

This is not an easy task, especially in settings where labour-management relations are strained. However, successful relations can be achieved by:

- identifying program champions from both labour and management to spearhead the movement towards program development;
- ensuring that the key decision-makers are "at the table";
- having equal representation from both parties;
- providing disability management education to all participants so that everyone has the same level of knowledge in the area and hence, power;
- identifying the current and desired state of disability management initiatives within the organization and the gaps between the two (gap analysis);
- determining which strategies for reducing/eliminating those gaps will be used, and according to what time frames;
- deciding on the proposed Integrated Disability Management Program's vision, goals, objectives, and desired outcomes;
- identifying and clarifying stakeholder roles, responsibilities, and accountabilities within the proposed Integrated Disability Management Program;
- deciding how the Integrated Disability Management Program and processes will be managed within the organization;
- identifying individual roles within the proposed Integrated Disability Management Program through the use of an organizational chart;
- developing supportive linkages between the Disability Management Program and other employee resources such as the Occupational Health & Safety Program, Human Resources Program and services, Employee Assistance Program, employee benefit plans, and Workplace Wellness Program;
- deciding how dispute resolution will be handled within the organization;
- developing evaluation criteria and success indicators for the proposed Integrated Disability Management Program;
- establishing evaluation measurement techniques and schedules;
- building a business case for the Integrated Disability Management Program;
- developing a communication strategy and marketing plan for the Disability Management Program;
- seeking funding and resources for the proposed Integrated Disability Management Program;
- working together to adopt and implement the Integrated Disability Management Program as designed; and
- establishing an ongoing forum for dealing with disability management issues.

The development of a joint labour-management steering committee for the Integrated Disability Management Program allows for joint involvement in the program design, infrastructure development, implementation (*i.e.*, marketing, communication, education and training, dispute resolution, *etc.*), evaluation, and continuous improvement.

The functions that a Joint Labour-Management Steering Committee assumes are:

- establishing a program vision and philosophy for the Integrated Disability Management Program;
- setting the Integrated Disability Management Program's goals and objectives;
- developing a Disability Management Program design/model;
- reviewing the various organizational/company policies that impact the Integrated Disability Management Program with a view to ensuring that they are supportive to program success;
- mapping out the process flow for the Integrated Disability Management Program processes;
- developing the Integrated Disability Management Program's policies and procedures;
- determining the skills required for a central figure such as a Disability Management Coordinator;
- articulating the role, responsibilities and accountabilities of the various stakeholder groups;
- identifying available gradual return-to-work options;
- educating management, union leaders and employees;
- exploring the needs of the various stakeholders;
- increasing the general awareness of the Integrated Disability Management Program's goals, benefits and outcomes throughout the organization;
- overseeing the implementation and continuous improvement of the Integrated Disability Management Program;
- serving as a dispute resolution forum;
- participating in the Integrated Disability Management Program evaluation process;
- recommending to the senior management/board/executive leadership team the needed support systems and the identified continuous improvement opportunities; and
- encouraging preventative strategies such as an Attendance Support & Assistance Program, Employee Assistance Program intervention, Occupational Health & Safety actions and Workplace Wellness initiatives.[40]

This steering committee advises and consults with all levels of stakeholders and receives advice and suggestions for the Disability Management Program. As part of assessing the overall effectiveness of the Disability Management

---

[40] National Institute of Disability and Research (NIDMAR), *Disability Management in the Workplace: A Guide to Establishing A Joint Workplace Program* (Port Alberni, BC: NIDMAR, 1995).

Program, the committee receives reports on the utilization rate of the Disability Management Program. The information provided to the committee is population, or aggregate, data so that individual employees are not identified.

The resources available to this steering committee could include the Disability Management Coordinator (possibly an occupational health nurse), occupational safety personnel, human resources personnel, employee assistance professionals or liaison, and internal/external consultants.

OTHER JOINT LABOUR-MANAGEMENT ACTIVITIES

Unions can be involved in many aspects of the functioning of an Integrated Disability Management Program, from the planning and design, to the implementation, evaluation and continuous improvement activities. For example:

1. *Planning and Design* — Participation of the Joint Labour-Management Integrated Disability Management Program Steering Committee has been discussed. To successfully meet their mandate, committee members should be offered, and avail themselves of, disability management educational opportunities. Without this education, they will be ill prepared to meet the challenges of the committee's mandate and the tasks they are assuming.

2. *Implementation* — Labour and management can collaboratively undertake the following Integrated Disability Management Program activities:

    *   play an instrumental role in the selection of a Disability Management Coordinator;
    *   develop modified work and alternate work job banks;
    *   participate on Return-to-Work Committees designed to facilitate a safe and timely return to work for ill/injured employees;
    *   assist in the design of suitable Integrated Disability Management Program forms and communication tools;
    *   promote the Integrated Disability Management Program communication and marketing efforts; and
    *   work to facilitate crossing union jurisdictional lines if required.

3. *Program Evaluation* — When evaluating the Integrated Disability Management Program, labour and management can play an instrumental role in:

    *   providing feedback on the program, its infrastructure, processes and outcomes;
    *   analyzing and interpreting the evaluation results; and
    *   recommending continuous improvement actions.

4. *Continuous Improvement of the Integrated Disability Management Program* — Both parties must work together to arrive at workable solutions, recognizing that Integrated Disability Management Programs are continually changing, and evolving.

INDUSTRY APPLICATION

One Canadian organization developed a joint labour-management steering committee to address the issue of enhancing employee attendance and disability management practices within their organization. Their first step was to establish a working relationship for the new team. By developing an operating charter, the members established a vision, mission, purpose, values, goals, and objectives, roles and ground rules for the steering committee. This approach set the parameters for a functional working relationship, and provided an opportunity for labour and management to work together on a project and earn each other's trust.

Step two involved providing educational sessions on attendance and disability management and program strategy preparation to all the committee members. The educational sessions were intended to provide all players with similar information, and enable them to apply attendance support and disability management theories to their particular workplace setting and issues.

Step three involved the development of a customized disability management strategy for the organization. The process for strategy development that had been discussed in the educational sessions was followed. The outcome was a vision, a goal, program objectives, and a series of proposed actions for a disability management plan. In essence, the strategy development moved from a preparation model to an actual plan for action.

This step took considerable time to complete. Although a generic template for a Disability Management Program plan was used, adapting it to suit the organization's specific needs was challenging. Revisiting the various aspects of the plan design as new issues came to light was time-consuming. For example, with multiple collective agreements in place, the organization identified a number of conflicts between the proposed disability management plan document and the wording of some of the governing collective agreements. These issues had to be addressed and resolved.

Another test that the joint labour-management steering committee used for the proposed Disability Management Program plan design was to assess its functionality in terms of how well it would have worked in dealing with past disability situations. By going through some of the known disability management scenarios that the organization had faced in the past, other issues warranting review were identified.

The biggest challenge for the joint labour-management steering committee was to develop a plan that could address issues such as:

- defining terms such as "modified work" and "alternate work";
- dealing with cross-jurisdictional return-to-work placements;
- budgeting — global versus departmental budgeting;
- employee replacement costs — who assumes the cost;
- re-training costs for permanent placements (alternate work situations); and
- dispute resolution.

Step four resulted in the development of illness/injury prevention strategies. Collaboratively, the joint labour-management steering committee identified opportunities for linking the proposed Disability Management Program with the Occupational Health and Safety Program, Employee Assistance Program, and Attendance Support and Assistance Program. The intent was to integrate all these programs into a comprehensive approach to managing employee illness/injury.

Step five involved the development of a business case for the Disability Management Program. Baseline data was used to establish the current and desired states for the organization's disability costs. Targets were set for years one and two of the Disability Management Program.

Step six was to develop a communication strategy. Labour and management worked together to decide who the relevant stakeholders were, what information they would need to have, how best to deliver the information, and when and who should conduct the sessions. The strength of this process came from joint participation. By working together, they were able to identify all the relevant stakeholders, the messages each group would hear, and how to conduct educational and marketing activities. Their plan was to roll out the program using joint labour-management presenters wherever possible.

The last step was to devise a marketing strategy. Here again, the benefits of a joint labour-management approach were evident. The organization had a number of communication vehicles, from newsletters to cheque inserts, email, bulletin boards, departmental or union meetings, and employee orientation sessions. The intent was to use all these available means to market the Disability Management Program.

This organization moved from a situation in which labour and management were at odds with each other, to one where they were working together towards a cause that both believed could be successfully addressed. The program was successfully developed, but even more importantly, labour-management relations were improved.

POTENTIAL PITFALLS

Not all joint labour-management relationships prove to be as effective as the one described above. "Why not?", you may ask. There can be a great number of reasons for ineffective labour-management relationships. The list that follows is not meant to be inclusive, but rather is a smattering of the more common problems that can negatively impact joint labour-management working relationships.

Union-Management Culture Mismatch

Unions, like organizations, have their own culture. Depending on the nature of that culture, the union may or may not be amenable to collaborating with management to develop an Integrated Disability Management Program. This is particularly evident with a union culture that perceives its role as always defending their members against management. Likewise, some management cultures are innately suspicious of union involvement.

Of the labour-management cultures that have been able to mesh, and to form a collaborative approach to disability management, unions and management both have demonstrated a willingness to assist ill/injured employees to successfully return to work.

Hidden Agendas

When players come together for reasons other than to work together towards a common goal or good, their ulterior motives can erode the trust that is needed to allow successful program development to occur.

Loss of Respect

If, during the course of the Integrated Disability Management Program development, committee members lose respect for each other, the success of the project can be jeopardized. Loss of respect tends to come primarily from a violation of trust developed between the members. Some common causes are irregular attendance to meetings, failing to take responsibility for assigned duties, divulging information meant to be kept within the committee setting, usurping another member's authority, failing to meet scheduled activities/plans, or blaming others for one's own shortcomings.

Introduction of New Committee Members

The introduction of new committee members, who are not adequately oriented to the joint labour-management approach and the project-at-hand, can undermine the progress made by the committee. Any change in committee members should be carefully handled. Prospective committee members, if they are to successfully integrate into the group, need to be fully briefed on the project, the relevant background materials and all the elements involved in the program development.

Change in Labour Relations

A decay in the labour relations within an organization can put program development or project management on hold. This is especially true in the development of an Integrated Disability Management Program, the basic ingredient of which is trust.

Breakdown in Communication

As already mentioned, open, honest communication is key to successful project management and program development. If a communication breakdown occurs, the project can be jeopardized. Likewise, communication should be timely and tailored to the informational needs of the stakeholders group.

INDUSTRY EXAMPLES

Industry examples of joint labour-management support and involvement in disability management have been reported at conferences and in print. Some notable examples are:

- MacMillian Bloedel Limited and its unions (CEP/IWA) developed a workplace-based Disability Management Program, one of the first in Canada, that was modelled on the NIDMAR approach to disability management. The outcome was a long-standing program in which injured/ill employees were successfully able to return to work. The outcome produced significant human and financial savings.[41]
- Bowater Pulp and Paper Mill, through the joint efforts of labour and management, set up its Disability Management Program in 1992. This Return-to-Work Program was built on a collaborative model: "The multi-stakeholder team fosters a strong sense of co-operation among union and management representatives."[42] The outcome was a program based on good communication and stakeholder education about available return-to-work options, and a financial success. Today, this program is still operational and seeking ways to continually improve its processes.[43]
- Weyerhaeuser (1996) reported the development of a Return-to-Work Program sponsored jointly by labour and management. They used a partnership approach, and were able to put in a Return-to-Work Program that saved them a considerable amount of money and demonstrated that Weyerhaeuser valued its people. The results have already been reported in Chapter 1, "Disability Management: Overview".[44]
- In 1996, the City of Sault Ste. Marie reported that it built a Disability Management Program founded on labour and management ownership. Their program focused on early intervention, rehabilitation, and return-to-work opportunities. They have enjoyed success and openly promote the continuation of the program through stakeholder education.[45]
- The Industrial, Wood and Allied Workers of Canada (IWA) adopted the Canadian National Return to Work Policy (1996) which outlined both the Union's commitment to a safe, voluntary return to meaningful work for its

---

[41]   *Ibid.*, at iii.

[42]   Editor, "Avenor's Unions Part of Day-to-day RTW Options" (1997) 1:6 Back to Work 4.

[43]   Editor, "Disability Reviews: How Bowater Keeps Getting Better" (1999) 3:7 Back to Work 4.

[44]   Weyerhaeuser, "Transitional Return-to-Work at Weyerhaeuser Company" (Presented at the National Conference on Disability and Work: Solutions for Canadians, Sheraton Centre, Toronto, Ontario, October 7-9, 1996) [unpublished].

[45]   Sault Ste. Marie (City of), "Introduction to E.R.P." (Presented at the National Conference on Disability and Work, October 1996) [unpublished].

members post-injury/illness and the basic protocol by which this return-to-work initiative would be implemented. This policy set the stage for the introduction of a Joint Disability Management Committee and the adoption of an accommodation paradigm that focused on worker ability, not disability. Today, there are Joint Disability Management Committees in most large sawmills throughout British Columbia, and the resultant Disability Management Programs show positive results for IWA members by providing the required supports when worker disabilities warrant accommodation. The outcome is that many IWA members have been able to return to full-time employment with their pre-disability employers.[46]

These are but a few examples of many successful Integrated Disability Management Programs that have been based on labour-management involvement and support. These systems are the product of evolution and an environment where the employer can see the financial payback realized through joint disability management. The direct ties between effective joint disability management programming, improved return to work outcomes, and the positive impact those programs have on health and welfare costs have helped to sell these initiatives at the bargaining table.

UNION INVOLVEMENT: CURRENT PRACTICES IN CANADA AND THE UNITED STATES

By Michelle Forgues

Many unions in Canada and the United states are proactively addressing issues concerning accommodation of employees with disabilities regardless of the cause. Efforts by unions to eliminate workplace hazards and to support a safe and timely return to work, enhanced by legislative requirements, encourage union and management to collaborate jointly in the development and implementation of disability management policies and procedures as well as workplace health and safety initiatives. Supported by research and literature, the importance of the joint commitment, support, and active participation of union and management is an essential feature of a successful Integrated Disability Management Program.[47]

The following is a review of how unions contribute meaningfully to the disability management process; how unions have proactively addressed and influenced legislation regarding accommodation of employees with disabilities;

---

[46] Industrial, Wood and Allied Workers of Canada (IWA), "Disability Management West Coast Model", on the United Steel Workers (USW) Canada Website. Prepared by the Ex-IWA-FI Benefits Trusts and available online at: <http://www.usw.ca/program/content/3176.php>.

[47] A.-S. Brooker *et al.*, "Effective Disability Management and Return to Work Practices: What Can We Learn from Low Back Pain?", available online at: <http://www.qp.gov.bc.ca/rcwc/research/brooker-disability.pdf>.

and what unions in both Canada and the United States are doing to contribute to the disability management initiative.

Disability Management and Labour Unions Involvement

Unions should have a meaningful involvement in the disability management process, because they understand the workplace conditions and represent the interests and protect the rights of their bargaining employees. Therefore, they are keen to collaborate in the return of injured/ill employees to the workplace. As employee advocates, labour unions play a critical role in Integrated Disability Management Programs because they can help identify and coordinate other employment opportunities that lead to a successful return to work as well as identify and minimize the risk of further disability. Not only can unions contribute to higher employee engagement in the return-to-work process but they can also influence greater accountability for recovery by setting return-to-work expectations with their membership.

Union involvement in the planning and implementation of an Integrated Disability Management Program can improve labour relations and improve employee "buy-in" for the program. By promoting early intervention and soliciting member involvement, unions are instrumental in the disability management process.

Organized labour plays a large role in prevention, which is part of disability management. Unions can help the organization identify strengths and weaknesses in the production process that may lead to accidents. They can also help identify unique patterns of injury in members and can analyze jobs that create injuries in order to develop ergonomic modifications to prevent future work disabilities. Unions take a positive and active role in promoting prevention. They educate their members on injury prevention and promote workplace safety. The unions' prevention efforts contribute greatly to workplace wellness and allow the organization to better manage their workforce and reduce injuries.

The central goal of managing disability is to return the injured worker to his or her job as early and as safely as possible. Unions play a key role in a graduated return-to-work program which is a key element of an Integrated Disability Management Program.

Unions can facilitate the return-to-work process by providing clear and precise job descriptions. They can also help provide important information regarding the physical job demands. This type of information is crucial to the return-to-work process as it ensures that the employee's job demands do not exceed his or her physical abilities. In situations where accommodation is required to safely return an injured/ill worker to the workplace, unions can support the development of flexible and creative work transition options and provide possible work site accommodation solutions. As every work site is different, the union is in a better position to assess the actual work site to determine the injured employee's needs for accommodation. By identifying and providing suitable modified duties and following up after the accommodation is implemented, the union actively contributes to the employee's rehabilitation; which is another key point in the disability management process. The union can also assist with the assessment of whether the accommodation is working or not, and help address any of the associated issues.

Many unions work together in order to share best practices and information related to various occupational illnesses and prevention strategies. By pooling their knowledge, they are able to effectively return their members to work. Unions strive for better health, safety, disability prevention, and return-to-work programs in the workplace.

The Institute for Work & Health reviewed quantitative and qualitative literature regarding return-to-work interventions. This research suggested that when unions and labour representatives are committed and participate fully in the return-to-work process, that the involvement is very beneficial.[48] Furthermore, successful graduated return-to-work outcomes depend on a cooperative and collaborative approach between employee, union, and management.

Unions have important knowledge on work site issues and can contribute meaningfully to the development of policies to support prevention, return to work and rehabilitation. Their efforts should not be overlooked by management because the union can impact the disability management process either negatively or positively depending on the degree to which management involves them in the Integrated Disability Management Program.

Effective disability management strategies and intervention can be jointly developed and implemented by labour and management. Cooperation between labour and management is critical to avoid the development of adversarial relationships between worker and employer. Together labour and management can develop appropriate policies and procedures and address workplace issues that contribute to workplace injury and disability. Based on their research, the Institute for Work & Health recommends that increased attention be given to labour-management relations, as their cooperation is associated with shorter work disability duration.[49]

Both labour and management have a vested interest in controlling the personal and economic costs of injury and disability. Labour unions want to protect the employability and safety of the workers they represent. Management wants to retain productive, reliable, and experienced employees. When managers are genuinely concerned about employees' well-being, and demonstrate that concern, mutual trust and respect are often established. This involves fair treatment and communication going above and beyond the requirements of the collective agreement. Forming labour/management

---

[48]   Institute for Work & Health, *Workplace-based Return-to-Work Interventions: A Systematic Review of the Quantitative and Qualitative Literature* (Toronto: Institute for Work & Health, 2004).

[49]   *Ibid.*

committees to investigate and resolve complex issues can lead to innovative and creative solutions as well as a better relationship.

The National Institute of Disability Management and Research (NIDMAR) advocates that the collaborative approach in disability management is achieved through the creation of joint labour management committees within the organization. These committees oversee the development and implementation of all facets of the Integrated Disability Management Program.[50] The union's role on these committees is to ensure that their members' rights are equally represented and protected and that together with management they can significantly reduce the impact of disability in the workplace.

Many large public sector employers and some private sector employers use joint labour-management committees as the means by which their unions participate fully in the Disability Management Program. Examples of large private sector employers that successfully developed collaborative approaches include MacMillan Bloedel, Bowater Pulp & Paper, and Weyerhaeuser. In British Colombia (BC), the Disability Management Program operated by the province and involving the BC Public Service has a joint labour management committee made up of Ministry representatives and the union.[51]

Chrysler Canada recognizes that the success of their workplace Disability Management Program was made possible by management and union's efforts to work together on workplace health and safety issues. Worker education at all levels about safe work and modified duties as well as the redesign of certain jobs produced a 35 per cent drop in the absentee rate in 1996-1997 and an 18 per cent drop in the injury frequency rate.[52]

Many companies have achieved best practices in disability management by collaborating with labour and working together to jointly develop effective strategies to facilitate the safe and timely return to work of ill/injured employees. In fact, some union workplace representatives have suggested that in workplaces where management's focus is on direct cost savings versus the creation of optimal return-to-work programs, recurrences in injury are more frequent, income support for subsequent time loss is lower, and termination of employment is more likely.[53] Therefore, cooperation and strong communication amongst all parties — injured workers, employer, and labour union — is imperative for a successful return-to-work outcome and injury/illness prevention, which are key elements of the disability management process.

---

[50]   *Supra* note 1.

[51]   British Columbia Public Service Agency, *Disability Case Management*, available online: <http://www.bcpublicservice.ca/dismgmt/>.

[52]   A. Silversides, "Disability Management Efforts Can Reduce the Number of Injuries, Improve Bottom Line" (1998) 159 CMAJ 268.

[53]   A.-S. Brooker *et al.*, "Effective Disability Management and Return to Work Practices: What Can We Learn from Low Back Pain?", available online at: <http://www.qp.gov.bc.ca/rcwc/research/brooker-disability.pdf>.

Influencing and Addressing Legislation

In Canada and the United States, the labour movement has been in the forefront of groups seeking to secure better wages and working conditions. Unions in both countries play a large role in preventing occupational injuries and illnesses and in offering help and support to their members in the aftermath of injury or illness.

Unions are also involved in discussing disability-related issues at the global level. The International Labour Organization (ILO) is a tripartite group of labour, employer, and government representatives under the auspices of the United Nations that provides guidance on managing disability in the workplace.

According to the International Labour Organization, labour unions are partly responsible for the increased recognition by companies to treat employees with disabilities equitably and the need to maintain a healthy workplace.[54] Unions lend their workplace expertise to these organizations in order to develop programs that will help all people with disabilities re-enter the workforce.

In Canada, labour was instrumental in founding the National Institute of Disability Management and Research (NIDMAR). Today, NIDMAR is supported by employers, unions, and the federal and provincial governments. NIDMAR's focus continues to be on workplace-based reintegration which aims to reduce the human and economic cost of disability to workers, employers, and society, through education, training, and research.[55]

In their quest to meet the needs of workers with disabilities, unions have been helped by favourable government legislation which promotes accommodation in the workplace for people with disabilities. For example, in the United States (U.S.) the *Americans with Disabilities Act (ADA)* prohibits discrimination against people with disabilities in work and community life. The *Americans with Disabilities Act* also requires that employers make reasonable efforts to accommodate disabled workers. The enactment and implementation of this Act was promoted by U.S.-based labour unions. Prior to the passage of this Act, many members from The American Federation of Labor and Congress of Industrial Organizations (AFL-CIO) were already involved in training their membership on disability rights and awareness.[56]

In Canada, the *Canadian Human Rights Act (CHRA)* clearly outlines the roles and responsibilities of the employer, union, and employee regarding accommodation within the workplace. Both the *Americans with Disabilities Act* and the *Canadian Human Rights Act* along with occupational health and safety

---

[54] International Labour Organization (ILO), "Rights and Duties: Workers' Perspective" (1998) 1 Disability and Work 17.1.

[55] Canadian Labour Congress, *MORE We Get Together: Disability Rights and Collective Bargaining Manual* (Ottawa: Canadian Labour Congress, 2003), available online at: <http://canadianlabour.ca/updir/manual.pdf>.

[56] American Federation of Labor and Congress of Industrial Organizations (AFL-CIO). For more details, refer to: <http://www.aflcio.org/>.

laws force labour and management to assume responsibility for disabled employees' needs.

In Canada, there have been Human Rights tribunal and court decisions that have stimulated changes to union collective agreements. These decisions have caused employers and unions to rethink the terms and wording of their collective agreements. For instance, with the decision of the *Meiorin*[57] court case, both employers and unions were forced to become proactive in their accommodation efforts.[58] This decision also broadened the interpretation of the *Canadian Human Rights Act* and clarified that the employer must proactively eliminate discrimination in its policies and practices.

As a result of legislation and a number of other court decisions, unions have proactively taken measures to protect the rights of disabled workers. It is becoming commonplace for collective agreements to expressly incorporate provisions for the protection of disabled workers. When this occurs, members of the bargaining unit can enforce their rights through grievances or arbitration procedures rather than make a complaint through human rights or other legislation.

Union action impacts non-unionized employees as well. Many unions play a constructive role in policing the enforcement of employee rights, and therefore help standardize human resource policies and practices for all workers.

Labour unions can advocate rights for workers with disabilities on a broad scale by promoting, monitoring, and supporting relevant legislative initiatives. In the workplace, unions can work with management to develop policies and actions that remove barriers to employment for disabled workers.

Current Practices in Canada and the United States

Current practices in Canada and in the United States suggest that labour unions play an important role in the development of Integrated Disability Management Programs and their support is crucial for quality outcomes. For example, in the United States (U.S.), the National Business & Disability Council is a group of national corporations and labour unions committed to employing individuals with disabilities. United States-based unions have produced publications and videos, and organized training programs, and workshops to further educate union members on effective management of disability in the workplace.

The American Federation of Labor and Congress of Industrial Organizations and other labour union representatives carefully monitor the implementation of the *Americans with Disabilities Act*, including litigation and alternative dispute resolution processes in order to support the rights of workers with disabilities and to ensure that their interests and the rights of all workers are fully considered.

---

[57] *British Columbia (Public Service Employee Relations Commission) v. British Columbia Government and Service Employees' Union (B.C.G.S.E.U.) (Meiorin Grievance)*, [1999] S.C.J. No. 46, [1999] 3 S.C.R. 3 (S.C.C.).

[58] Public Service Alliance of Canada, *Duty to Accommodate*, available online at: <http://www.psac.com/what/humanrights/Duty_to_accommodate-e.shtml>.

In Canada, unions continue to negotiate favourable contract language that reduces the impact of disability in the workplace. They also promote initiatives that protect the employability of persons with disabilities.

The Public Service Alliance of Canada is committed to ensuring that workplaces are equitable. They have devised a duty to accommodate guide for local representatives and have included in their regulations provisions to protect disabled members employment.[59]

The United Steelworkers' Union has developed a policy on disability rights. The steelworkers union has been involved in national and international projects to identify the core elements of an effective workplace program for accommodating workers with disabilities, in particular the International Labour Organization's code of practice on managing disability in the workplace and NIDMAR's Canadian Code of Practice. The United Steelworkers' Union is committed to employment of people with disabilities and has adopted that all collective agreements should include directives on accommodation of employees with disabilities regardless of the cause. They also advocate the consensus-based approach suggested by the International Labour Organization and NIDMAR.[60]

Most recently in Ottawa, the Canadian Union of Public Employees, the city's largest union, and the Amalgamated Transit Union, filed a Canadian Human Rights complaint against the city. Together, the unions represented 9,000 city employees. The unions launched the complaint as they believed that the city of Ottawa was systematically discriminating against disabled employees by using employee assistance programs and other methods to punish and fire employees.[61] It seems that the city had a Disability Management Program, but had failed to involve the union, or had not been able to secure union "buy-in" of the program. This had resulted in poor labour relations, employee dissatisfaction, and two complaints filed with the Canadian Human Rights Commission. In unionized workplaces, the relationship between management and the union is an essential component of an Integrated Disability Management Program.

Unions are aggressively looking to support the needs of their disabled workers whether it is through education, participation in national or international forums or by lodging human rights complaints. Unions are actively involved directly or indirectly in one or more of disability management's key elements.

Conclusion

Integrated Disability Management Programs must be built on the principle of employee advocacy, with the idea that what is good for the employee is good for

---

[59] *Ibid.*

[60] See the United Steel Workers website, online at: <http://www.uswa.ca>.

[61] J. Rupert, "City targets disabled, union says; Workers being pushed out of jobs, complaint states" *Ottawa Citizen* (12 May, 2007) F1.

the company.[62] Unions are in a unique position to use their leverage as representatives to ensure that they minimize the impact of disablement on their members by promoting workplace health and safety, and actively participating in Integrated Disability Management Programs.

Unions are a key participant in disability management as they promote integration of persons with disabilities and work with employers to reduce barriers to employment. Labour unions support member rights related to job protection, early intervention in the provision of rehabilitative services, and sound disability management practices.

Through their activities in the workplace and their advocacy of favourable disability legislation, unions have improved the quality of life and maximized the opportunities for all workers. As unions promote healthy and productive workplaces, their contribution to disability management goes a long way in returning injured workers to the workplace and in advancing the rights of people with disabilities.

FUTURE INTEGRATED DISABILITY MANAGEMENT PROGRAMS: UNION IMPACT

At the 2002 Canadian Labour Congress Convention, a national coordinated bargaining strategy that focuses on providing workers with disabilities and disability-related issues with a higher profile during collective bargaining, union organizing, workplace committee work and government lobbying, was proposed. Operationalized in *Building a Stronger Movement at the Workplace*, the intent is to push for better wording around disability rights and work accommodation.

Going forward, bargaining objectives should include:

- anti-discrimination, anti-harassment, pay equity, and employment equity for disabled workers;
- the right to transfer or train the worker for another job regardless of whether or not the disability injury/illness was work-related;
- a move to increase employer payment and benefit coverage for long-term disability plans;
- employee extended health benefits that include employer-paid prescription drug coverage;
- obtaining employee counselling services, health services, fitness facilities, job rotation and workplace health and safety committees;
- a return-to-work policy that covers all types of injuries/illness, and defines the available resources and supports;
- paid sick leave;

---

[62]   A.-S. Brooker *et al.*, "Effective Disability Management and Return to Work Practices: What Can We Learn from Low Back Pain?", available online at: <http://www.qp.gov.bc.ca/rcwc/research/brooker-disability.pdf>.

- provisions by the employer to maintain personal health information confidentiality; and
- the existence of ergonomic programs.[63]

The Canadian Auto Workers (CAW) has been equally proactive towards returning ill or injured employees back into the workplace. At the 2002 Collective Bargaining Convention, Canadian Auto Workers proposed to ensure that injured and disabled workers would be accommodated in the workplace, and that jobs are changed so that the potential for re-injury is eliminated.[64]

In essence, we are witnessing a more proactive approach by Canadian unions to promote disability management and set into motion a return-to-work effort that can support their ill or injured members.

SUMMARY

The purpose of this chapter was to demonstrate the importance of joint labour-management involvement in the development and operation of an Integrated Disability Management Program. This concept is continually reinforced in upcoming chapters.

CHAPTER REFERENCES

I Abella, *On Strike: Six Key Labour Struggles in Canada 1919-1949* (Toronto: James Lorimer & Co., 1975).

American Federation of Labor and Congress of Industrial Organizations (AFL-CIO), online at: <http://www.aflcio.org/>.

B. Anderson, "Disability Management" (Seminar Presented in Calgary, Alberta, 1990).

S. Applebaum, M.D. Beckman, L. Boone & D. Kurz, *Contemporary Canadian Business*, 3rd ed. (Toronto: Holt, Rinehart & Winston of Canada, 1987) at 257, 547.

British Columbia Public Service Agency, *Disability Case Management*, available online at: <http://www.bcpublicservice.ca/dismgmt/>.

British Columbia (Public Service Employee Relations Commission) v. British Columbia Government and Service Employees' Union (B.C.G.S.E.U.) (Meiorin Grievance), [1999] S.C.J. No. 46, [1999] 3 S.C.R. 3 (S.C.C.).

A.-S. Brooker *et al.*, "Effective Disability Management and Return to Work Practices: What Can We Learn from Low Back Pain?", available online at: <http://www.qp.gov.bc.ca/rcwc/research/brooker-disability.pdf>.

---

[63] Canadian Labour Congress, *Building a Stronger Movement at the Workplace* (Presented at the 23rd Constitutional Convention, June 10-14, 2002) [unpublished].

[64] Canadian Auto Workers, "Report on the 2002 Collective Bargaining Convention" (2002) 10:3 CAW Health, Safety and Environment Newsletter, available online at: <http://www.caw.ca>.

Canadian Labour Congress, *MORE We Get Together: Disability Rights and Collective Bargaining Manual* (Ottawa: Canadian Labour Congress, 2003), available online at: <http://canadianlabour.ca/updir/manual.pdf>.

Canadian Auto Workers, "Report on the 2002 Collective Bargaining Convention" (2003) 10:3 CAW Health, Safety and Environment Newsletter, available online at: <http://www.caw.ca>.

Canadian Human Rights Act, R.S.C. 1985, c. H-6.

Canadian Human Rights Commission, *Overview*, CHRC Home Page, available online at: <http://www.chrc-ccdp.ca/preventing_discrimination/page4-en.asp>.

Canadian Labour Congress, *Building a Stronger Movement at the Workplace* (Presented at the 23rd Constitutional Convention, June 10-14, 2002) [unpublished].

Canadian Standards Association (CSA), *Model Code for the Protection of Personal Information* (Can/C.S.A. — Q830-96) (Ottawa: CSA, 1996).

Centre for Labour-Management Development, "Accommodation Guidelines" (Presented at the Illness and Disability Claims in the Unionized Workplace Seminar, Edmonton, Alberta, February 10-11, 1999) [unpublished].

K.B. Clark, "The Impact of Unionized Productivity: A Case Study" (1980) 33:4 Industrial Labour Relations Review 451.

Editor, "Avenor's Unions Part of Day-to-Day RTW Options" (1997) 1:6 Back to Work 4.

Editor, "Disability Reviews: How Bowater Keeps Getting Better" (1999) 3:7 Back to Work 4.

R.B. Freeman & J.L. Medoff, *What do Unions Do?* (New York: Basic Books, 1984) at 166.

Industrial, Wood and Allied Workers of Canada (IWA), "Disability Management West Coast Model", on the United Steel Workers (USW) Canada Website. Prepared by the Ex-IWA-FI Benefits Trusts and available online at: <http://www.usw.ca/program/content/3176.php>.

Institute for Work & Health, *Workplace-based Return-to-Work Interventions: A Systematic Review of the Quantitative and Qualitative Literature* (Toronto: Institute for Work & Health, 2004).

Institute for Work & Health, "Seven 'Principles' for Successful Return to Work". Institute for Work & Health, Toronto (March 2007) at 2, available online at: <http://www.iwh.on.ca/seven-principles-for-rtw>.

International Labour Organization (ILO), "Rights and Duties: Workers' Perspective" (1998) 1 Disability and Work 17.1.

S. Jodoin & H. Harder, "Strategies to Enhance Labour-Management Cooperation in the Development of Disability Management Programs" (2004) 3:4 International Journal of Disability, Community & Rehabilitation 1, available online at: <http://www.ijdcr.ca/VOL03_04_CAN/articles/jodoin.shtml>.

D.B. Mercer, "Roles and Responsibilities in Job Modification and Accommodation" (Seminars in Occupational Health and Medicine, Faculty of Medicine, Continuing Education, University of Calgary, February 3, 1999) [unpublished].

Mercer Inc., *The Total Financial Impact of Employee Absences — Survey Highlights* (October 2008), available online at: <http://www.kronos.com/absenceanonymous/media/Mercer-Survey-Highlights.pdf>.

D. Miles, "Building Joint Labor-management Initiatives for Worksite Disability Management", in D. Shrey & M. Lacerte, eds., *Principles and Practices of Disability Management in Industry* (Winter Park, FL: GR Press, 1995) 225.

C. Moser, "Canada's Occupational Standards Outline Two Certification Possibilities" (1999) 3:7 Back to Work 1.

K. Nagel, "Total Organizational Health Costs: What Are They? What Can Organizations Do About Them?" (Presented at the Strategic Leadership Forum '99, Toronto, Ontario, October 20, 1999) [unpublished].

National Institute of Disability Management and Research (NIDMAR), *Challenges in Disability Management. A Resource Manual for Return to Work Practitioners* (Port Alberni, BC: NIDMAR, 2004), available online at: <http://www.nidmar.ca>.

National Institute of Disability Management and Research (NIDMAR), *Code of Practice for Disability Management*, 2nd ed. (Port Alberni, BC: NIDMAR, 2004), available online at: <http://www.nidmar.ca>.

National Institute of Disability Management and Research (NIDMAR), *Code of Practice for Disability Management: Describing Effective Benchmarks for the Creation of Workplace-Based Disability Management Programs* (Port Alberni, BC: NIDMAR 2000), available online at: <http://www.nidmar.ca>.

National Institute of Disability Management and Research (NIDMAR), *Consensus Based Disability Management Audit™*. Further information is available online at: <http://www.nidmar.ca>.

National Institute of Disability Management and Research (NIDMAR), *Disability Management in the Workplace: A Guide to Establishing a Joint Workplace Program* (Port Alberni, BC: NIDMAR, 1995).

National Institute of Disability Management and Research (NIDMAR), *Disability Management Success: A Global Corporate Perspective* (Port Alberni, BC: NIDMAR, 2005), available online at: <http://www.nidmar.ca>.

National Institute of Disability Management and Research (NIDMAR), *Effective Re-Integration Strategies for the '90s: The Role of Employers, Union, Government, and Consumers in Partnership* (Port Alberni, BC: NIDMAR, 1991), available online at: <http://www.nidmar.ca>.

National Institute of Disability Management and Research (NIDMAR), *Industrial Disability Management: An Effective Economic and Human Resource Strategy* (Port Alberni, BC: NIDMAR, 1992), available online at: <http://www.nidmar.ca>.

National Institute of Disability Management and Research (NIDMAR), *Occupational Standards in Disability Management: Establishing Criteria for Excellence In Canada* (Port Alberni, BC: NIDMAR, 1999), available online at: <http://www.nidmar.ca>.

National Institute of Disability Management and Research (NIDMAR), *Strategies for Success: Disability Management in the Workplace* (Port Alberni, BC: NIDMAR, 1997), available online at: <http://www.nidmar.ca>.

National Institute of Disability Management and Research (NIDMAR), *The Effects of Disability on B.C.'s Economy* (Port Alberni, BC: NIDMAR, 1995), available online at: <http://www.nidmar.ca/products/products_details.asp?id=15>.

NIDMAR Launches First National Awards of Excellence in Disability Management, information available online at: <http://www.nidmar.ca/awards/awards_background/background_info.asp>.

Public Service Alliance of Canada, *Duty to Accommodate*, available online at: <http://www.psac.com/documents/what/duty_to_accommodate2007-e.pdf>.

J. Rupert, "City targets disabled, union says; Workers being pushed out of jobs, complaint states" *Ottawa Citizen* (12 May, 2007) F1.

Sault Ste. Marie (City of), "Introduction to E.R.P." (Presented at the National Conference on Disability and Work, Sault Ste. Marie, October 1996) [unpublished].

A. Silversides, "Disability Management Efforts Can Reduce the Number of Injuries, Improve Bottom Line" (1998) 159 CMAJ 268.

S. Shurman, D. Well, P. Landsbergis & B. Israel, "The Role of Unions and Collective Bargaining in Preventing Work-related Disability", in T. Thomason, J.F. Burton, Jr. & D.E. Hyatt, eds., *New Approaches to Disability in the Workplace* (Madison, WI: Industrial Relations Research Association, 1998) 121.

T. Stone & N. Meltz, *Human Resources Management in Canada*, 2nd ed. (Toronto: Holt, Rinehart & Winston of Canada, 1988) at 540.

Weyerhaeuser, "Transitional Return to work at Weyerhaeuser Company" (Presented at the National Conference on Disability and Work: Solutions for Canadians, Sheraton Centre, Toronto, Ontario, October 7-9, 1996) [unpublished].

Chapter 3

The Supportive Infrastructure for an Integrated Disability Management Program

THE INTEGRATED DISABILITY MANAGEMENT PROGRAM: WHAT IS AN INFRASTRUCTURE?

The Integrated Disability Management Program infrastructure is the system and environment within which an Integrated Disability Management Program can operate. It encompasses the corporate culture, the disability-related policies and procedures, a policy and procedure manual, the disability benefit plans, and the linkages between the Integrated Disability Management Program and other company resources. This chapter deals with these five infrastructure components and offers an industry example of how to develop an Integrated Disability Management Program manual.

Corporate Culture

The **corporate culture** embodies the learned values, assumptions, and behaviours that convey a sense of identity for employees and management.[1] It acts to encourage employee commitment and organizational stability as desired behaviours.[2]

Depending on the nature of the corporate culture, employees, unions and management may, or may not, be receptive to:

- helping each other to find innovative ways to accommodate recovering employees back into the workplace;
- taking risks on certain workplace rehabilitation approaches; and
- implementing employee benefit plans that encourage a return to employability for the ill/injured employee.

As well, the corporate culture dictates what type of disability management model will be adopted. For instance, a paternalistic culture tends to adopt a model that is more company-operated and directed. Here, the onus is on the

---

[1]   V. McNeil & M.A. Garcia, "Enhancing Program Management Through Cultural Organizational Assessment" (1991) 4:6 AAOHN Update Series 1.
[2]   L. Smircich, "Concepts of Culture and Organizational Analysis" (1983) 28 Administrative Science Quarterly 339.

company for the person's successful return to work. This is typical of the traditional model of disability management described in Chapter 1, "Disability Management: Overview". On the other hand, a democratic culture tends to encourage employee responsibility for absence and successful return-to-work. In this model, the company works with the employee to effect a successful rehabilitation plan leaving the employee ultimately in control of his or her situation. The direct case management model for disability management discussed in Chapter 1 exemplifies this.

In a more subtle fashion, the corporate culture affects employer-employee occupational bonding. **Occupational bonding** is a mutually beneficial relationship between the employee and the employer.[3] When companies have a corporate culture that promotes pride in belonging to the organization and adheres to a strong work ethic, employees are more likely to see personal value in belonging to the social group and in working for the company. They are less likely to be absent except for valid reasons, and they are more likely to return to work as soon as possible. A successful occupational bond is difficult to break.

However, the reverse can also be true. When employees do not experience corporate pride, a sense of belonging, or feel that they add value to the corporation, the occupational bond is easily broken and remaining off work on disability is more likely.

For an Integrated Disability Management Program to be successful, the corporate culture should value the employee and convey the message that all employees are valuable contributors, and that absence from the workplace is a matter of great concern.

Disability Management Policies and Procedures

Corporate policies and procedures reflect management's attitude regarding disability management, establish the parameters for the disability management practice, and promote equal treatment of all employees. They are designed to facilitate the achievement of established program goals.

Management develops **policies** as guides for employees in the course of their employment activities. Ideally, they are consistent with the company's vision, goals and business strategies. One of their purposes is to prevent, or help to resolve problems. For that reason, policies should be comprehensive in their scope, clear in their intent, fair to all, documented, and readily available.

Procedures are defined actions that serve to standardize the Integrated Disability Management Program. They provide a basis for stakeholder education, clarify the process, and facilitate smooth functioning of the Integrated Disability Management Program.

Disability management policies and procedures need to be current and appropriate for the organization. For this reason, a periodic review of their

---

[3]   D. Shrey, *Principles and Practices of Disability Management in Industry* (Winter Park, FL: GR Press Inc., 1995).

applicability is critical to any Integrated Disability Management Program's success.

Many aspects of disability management tend to be open to interpretation. Employer-employee trust and relationship issues can often cloud actions that are taken during the management of a disability situation. For this reason, the existence of clear disability management policies and procedures is critical.

The following sections of this chapter address the various components of a typical Disability Management Program policy and procedure manual. Illustrations are provided in an attempt to clarify the concepts presented.

Policy and Procedure Manual Components

THE MISSION STATEMENT

A **mission statement** on disability management describes the labour-management commitment to the Integrated Disability Management Program. It presents the high-level program objectives and describes the values and beliefs of the workplace towards minimizing the impact of illness or injury on the stakeholders. The commitment to allocate resources to the Integrated Disability Management Program's design and implementation is stated.

A well-composed mission statement emphasizes a collaborative approach to returning recovering employees to work. This means that all the stakeholders have a responsibility in the early return-to-work process and that they are held accountable for their respective roles.

Lastly, the mission statement acknowledges and explains the impact of the Integrated Disability Management Program on the collective agreements, grievance procedures or other internal programs such as the Occupational Health and Safety Program and the Employee Assistance Program.

An example of a mission statement is as follows:

Company XYZ's Integrated Disability Management Program is designed to attain the best performance in both human and financial terms regarding disability management and workplace health. The program includes case management for sick leave, short-term, long-term disability and workers' compensation illness and injury; fitness to work assessments; health surveillance; emergency response; education and data management. The aim is to ensure the employee's health through active health and workplace management resulting in increased productivity and profitability and decreased absenteeism.

The Integrated Disability Management Program will:
- ensure employees have access to the best available health care services;
- manage absences and intervene at the onset of illness or injury;
- facilitate the rehabilitation of employees and expedite an early return to work or modified work;

- follow confidentiality guidelines;
- respond to the corporate vision of providing employees with a safe and healthy workplace; and convey the message that employees are valued;
- contribute to employee and community morale by conveying the message that employees are valued; and
- demonstrate compliance with legislation and regulations (*e.g.*, workers' compensation and accommodation for disabled workers).

PROGRAM GOALS AND OBJECTIVES

Program goals are the broad statements central to the disability management process. Objectives are the specific aims for the Integrated Disability Management Program. They state the desired outcomes in a manner that is meaningful, relevant, realistic, actionable, sustainable, useful, measurable, and results-oriented.

Each objective should be written so that it:

- is measurable;
- measures only one thing;
- is attainable, but challenging;
- is time-oriented; and
- addresses an observable behaviour.

For the successful functioning of the Integrated Disability Management Program, the program objectives should be mutually agreed upon by management and labour. By accepting these objectives, both parties agree to follow the same path.

An example of a program goal is as follows:

- *To develop an integrated and comprehensive Integrated Disability Management Program.*

Examples of program objectives are:

- *To obtain management support for the Integrated Disability Management Program as evidenced by a Disability Management mission statement and the provision of adequate program resources.*
- *To increase stakeholder knowledge and use of disability management concepts, programs and services through the development of an Integrated Disability Management Program communication strategy and marketing plan.*
- *To reduce disability claim duration and cost through the consistent application of disability claim and case management practices.*

DISPUTE RESOLUTION POLICY

An inevitable part of any collaborative process is a disagreement between the parties involved. To facilitate effective conflict resolution, it is advisable to have a dispute resolution policy in place to assist with the process.

An example of a dispute resolution policy is as follows:

The Company XYZ maintains an open-door policy. All employees will be treated fairly, justly and equitably. Company XYZ will act immediately should problems occur. All employees are encouraged to bring forward to management any complaints or recommendations dealing with the Integrated Disability Management Program without fear of reprisal. Any disputes, controversies, or suggestions must first be handled between the employee and supervisor.

An employee who has not obtained a solution within five business days of the circumstances has the right to bring the situation to the attention of the supervisor's immediate superior or human resources representative. That person will review the circumstances within five business days. Complaints should be documented and include all the relevant facts. The employee and supervisor will receive a response within five more business days.

If the employee remains dissatisfied with the outcome, he or she has the right to discuss the problem with senior management. If the problem cannot be resolved at this level, then the matter can be submitted in writing to the board of directors. Their decision will be final.

ADMINISTRATION OF THE INTEGRATED DISABILITY MANAGEMENT PROGRAM

This section includes the formal duties of the people (committee members or individuals) responsible for the administration of the Integrated Disability Management Program. It includes the by-laws (rules) and the lines of responsibility and accountability. The frequency and purpose of the Integrated Disability Management Program committee meetings are also defined.

The specific policies and procedures related to disability management are also presented. Relevant policies and procedures form the standards for case management, confidentiality, documentation of personal health information, retention, and storage of personal health information, and access to confidential information. These are described at length in Chapter 10, "Disability Management Practice Standards".

STAKEHOLDER ROLES AND RESPONSIBILITIES

The policy and procedures manual identifies the primary stakeholders in the Integrated Disability Management Program. These include management, supervisors, employees, unions, occupational health nurses, attending physicians and human resources professionals.

The roles for each stakeholder are described, as well as specific lines of communication and reporting. An effective method of describing roles and lines of communication involves using a simple organization chart, like Figure 3.1, or a more complex flow diagram, like Figure 3.2.

Figure 3.1: Organizational Structure for the Integrated Disability Management Service within an Organization: An Industry Example

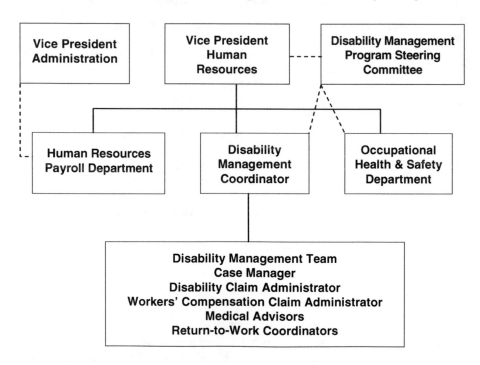

Figure 3.2: Integrated Disability Management Program Process

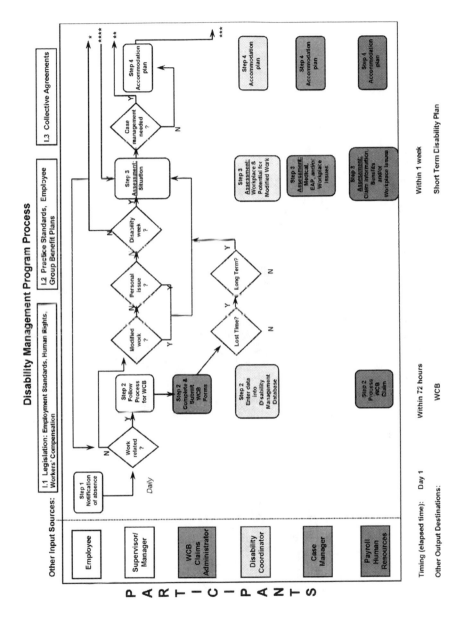

Figure 3.2: Integrated Disability Management Program Process (cont'd.)

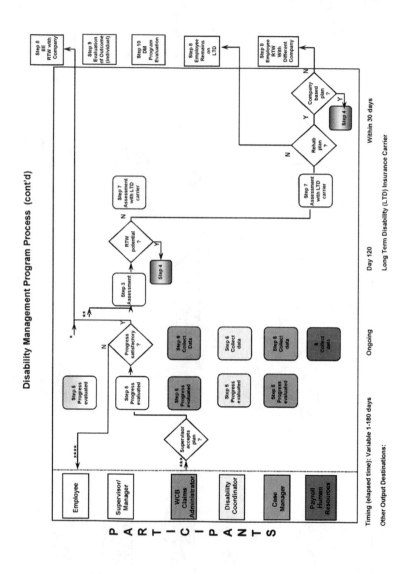

ELIGIBILITY CRITERIA

This section defines who is to be assisted by the Integrated Disability Management Program. The general exit requirements and re-entry points are also described. Figure 3.3 provides a simple decision tree that indicates when and how an employee may return to work.

Figure 3.3: Disability Case Management Flow Chart Decision Tree

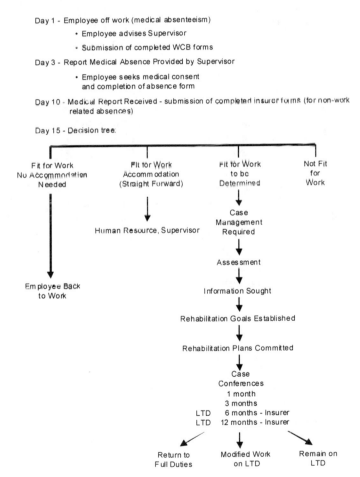

Day 1 - Employee off work (medical absenteeism)
  • Employee advises Supervisor
  • Submission of completed WCB forms

Day 3 - Report Medical Absence Provided by Supervisor
  • Employee seeks medical consent
  and completion of absence form

Day 10 - Medical Report Received - submission of completed insurer forms (for non-work related absences)

Day 15 - Decision tree:

Fit for Work No Accommodation Needed	Fit for Work Accommodation (Straight Forward)	Fit for Work to be Determined	Not Fit for Work

Human Resource, Supervisor

Case Management Required

Assessment

Information Sought

Rehabilitation Goals Established

Rehabilitation Plans Committed

Case Conferences
1 month
3 months
LTD   6 months - Insurer
LTD   12 months - Insurer

Employee Back to Work

Return to Full Duties   Modified Work on LTD   Remain on LTD

IMPLEMENTATION STRATEGIES

Disability management implementation strategies define the methods of assessment, the referral points, intervention options, potential job accommodations, and alternative jobs.

In Chapter 5, "An Integrated Disability Management Program: The Managed Rehabilitative Care Program", the assessment phase of the managed rehabilitative care program is presented as an example of an implementation strategy. It includes an assessment model that examines the personal, vocational, medical, psychological, performance, physical, educational, and financial factors that impact a disability (Figure 5.2). As well, the nature of the employee's job is determined (Figures 5.3 and 5.4). The assessment phase is intended to examine the current and proposed person-job fit.

Referral points occur during the case management for a disability management case when the employee is referred for various forms of medical assessment, physical therapy, rehabilitation, or vocational assistance. Graphic presentations can be very useful in depicting referral points. For example, Figure 3.4 depicts the management of the employee with a health concern, and Figure 3.5 depicts the management of the employee with a personal issue or problem. Each denotes the appropriate times for initiating referrals.

Implementation strategies also involve gathering information about the various services and resources available to support the Integrated Disability Management Program. These include Employee Assistance Programs, Occupational Health & Safety Programs, Human Resources Programs and services, union services, local caregivers (*i.e.*, physicians, hospitals, rehabilitation specialists, *etc.*), government or municipal agencies, insurer (government and private) benefits, in-house training programs, *etc.*

Re-entry for the ill or injured employee back into the workplace often involves accommodating the employee or developing alternative jobs. The usual sequence is:

1. returning the employee to his or her own job with job modifications;
2. returning the employee to his or her own job with reduced hours;
3. undertaking alternate duties full or reduced time; and
4. working with another agency/company.

Figure 3.4: Management of Employees with Health Problems

MANAGEMENT OF EMPLOYEES WITH HEALTH PROBLEMS

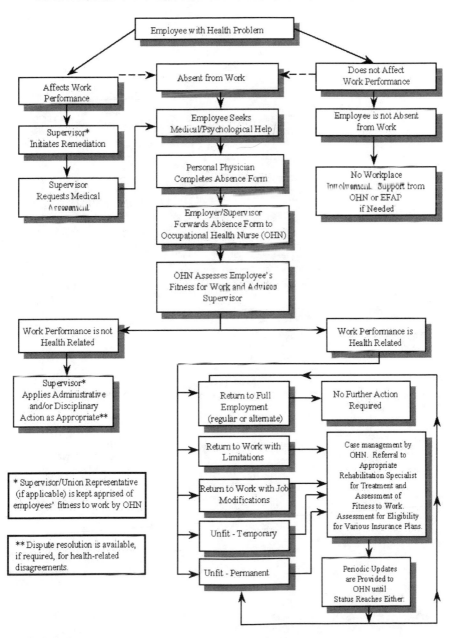

Figure 3.5: Employee and Family Assistance Program

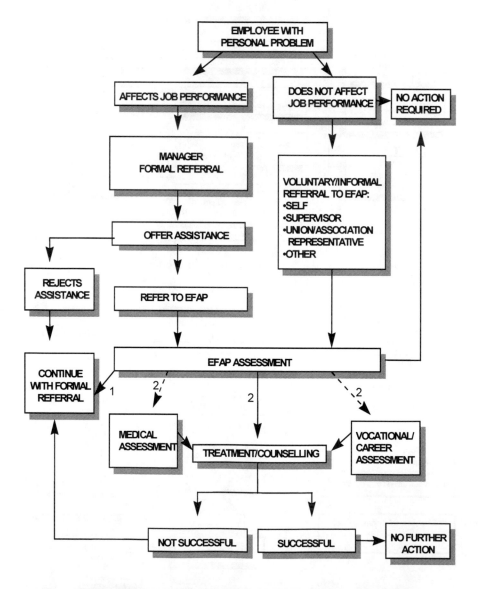

EMPLOYEE AND FAMILY ASSISTANCE PROGRAM
FLOWCHART

NOTE: 1) REJECTS EFAP RECOMMENDATIONS, CONTINUE WITH FORMAL REFERRAL STEPS
       2) SUPERVISOR KEPT INFORMED OF APPROPRIATE INFORMATION (E.G., EMPLOYEE
          FOLLOWING PROGRAM) BUT NOT GIVEN DIAGNOSTIC OR PERSONAL INFORMATION

Job modifications can include adjustments or a redesign of the employee's workstation, use of adaptive devices (*e.g.*, ergonomically designed tools), use of work aids (*e.g.*, enlarged font on the computer for visually impaired employees), and/or telecommuting. The techniques used depend on the nature of the work done by the company and the resources available to facilitate job modifications. Job modification also involves a job-demands analysis and the development of a job inventory. A **Job Demands Analysis (JDA)** (also known as Position Demands Analysis (PDA)) is an examination of the various components of a job or position. For example, what are the sitting, standing, lifting, carrying, pushing, pulling, climbing, finger dexterity, vision, hearing, writing, speech, and/or problem-solving requirements for the job? What are the stress factors and travelling demands? Each element should be quantified and qualified whenever possible. A sample Job Demands Analysis form is provided in Chapter 5, Figure 5.4.

A **job inventory** is a listing of the available jobs for employees on an early return to work or modified work program. The key element is that these jobs are meaningful ones: that is, if recovering employees were not available to complete the work, then it would have to be contracted out or assigned to in-house employees. Having gainful employment available to the recovering worker is a key element for any Disability Management Program.

Job finding is the process of finding suitable alternate employment for the disabled employee. This action is taken as a last resort as it usually involves work external to the company.

Lastly, the establishment of a database to collect information on the Integrated Disability Management Program is required. This database can be manual or electronic. The key aspect is that the data on employee medical absence are maintained. The nature of the data and the types of analyses that can be executed are described in Chapter 5, "An Integrated Disability Management Program: The Managed Rehabilitative Care Program" and Chapter 6, "Integrated Disability Management Program: Outcome Measurements".

PROGRAM EVALUATION

Many people question the value of evaluating a program. Program evaluation is critical because you cannot manage what has not been measured. This section of the manual should define methods of measuring performance, and the expected outcomes of the Integrated Disability Management Program. Chapter 6, "Integrated Disability Management Program: Outcome Measurements" discusses program evaluation in detail.

PROGRAM PROMOTION

In the policy and procedures manual, it is important to describe the lines of communication for the Integrated Disability Management Program. The "who, what, when, how and where" of promotion should be described in the manual. For example:

Policy
The Integrated Disability Management Program should be accessible and made easy for employees to identify their need for assistance, or for supervisors to refer employees when required.

Procedures
i.   The Integrated Disability Management Program should be promoted no less than three times per year at all worksites. Promotion may be accomplished through the distribution of promotional materials, information sessions, e-mail announcements, and/or posters.
ii.   There should be some form of targeted promotional material made available to eligible employees at least every twelve months.
iii. All employees who go on to disability benefits are to receive an informational package that outlines their responsibilities, provides them with the required forms, and articulates their return-to-work options.
iv.   Educational sessions on the Integrated Disability Management Program are to be presented as a component of the standard employee orientation and supervisory training packages.
v.   Key disability management education/training is to be provided to human resources professionals, occupational health and safety personnel, joint health and safety committee members, union representatives and similar personnel.

This section also explains the strategies that have been developed to inform the internal and external stakeholders of the Integrated Disability Management Program and of any changes that may develop.

Lastly, the policy section creates and maintains an awareness of the benefits of the workplace disability management model. This can involve regular feedback on nature of disabilities, modified work initiatives used, program outcomes, and goals of the future Integrated Disability Management Program. For example, the use of graphic representations of the Integrated Disability Management Program outcomes can be very effective (Figure 3.6). For more details on program marketing, please refer to Chapter 13, "Marketing Disability Management Programs and Communicating the Results".

Figure 3.6: Reasons for Medical Absence: 2008

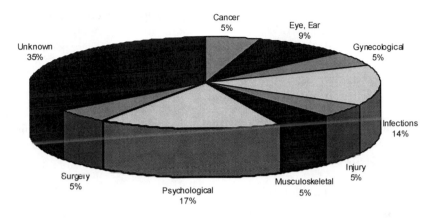

Disability Benefit Plans

A third infrastructure component is the various employee benefit plans that provide income continuance to the ill or injured employee during the disability period. It is important for all stakeholders to understand the terms and lengths of coverage for each plan, and how these plans interrelate. For example, a Disability Case Manager needs to understand the nuances of each type of plan and how they can impact a graduated return-to-work opportunity. Although the principles of the graduated return-to-work process remain the same, the operation of these principles differ. The following is a brief description of the typical disability benefit plans found in the workplace.

SHORT-TERM DISABILITY PLANS

Short-term disability insurance coverage can take on a variety of forms from weekly indemnity (or accumulated sick leave plan) to self-insured short-term disability coverage. The various plans are all designed to provide income replacement for the employee during a period of non-occupationally related injury or illness. The following is a brief description of each type of disability coverage:

Weekly Indemnity

Weekly indemnity is an insurance arrangement that usually begins payments on the first day of a non-occupational accident or absence requiring hospitalization, and on the fourth or eighth day for other illnesses. The percentage of salary continuance paid depends on issues such as the taxation of benefits and corporate philosophy.

Accumulated Sick Leave Plan

For this type of benefit plan, the eligibility of sick leave coverage is directly tied to the employee's length of service. For example, for every month of service, the employee is entitled to a set number of sick leave days. These sick days are "banked" and are used for medical absences during the long-term disability-qualifying period.

This type of plan is popular with public sector organizations. In some instances, employees are able to accumulate sick leave days without a ceiling, or maximum number. In others, employees not only accumulate an unlimited number of sick leave days, but also are entitled to a "payout" for the unused portion at the time of retirement.

Short-term Disability Plan

Typically, this type of disability coverage provides the employee with a percentage of salary, usually 75 per cent to 100 per cent depending on years of service, for a set period of time (17 to 26 weeks, or longer). Eligibility can vary, but typically an employee is disabled if he or she cannot do either 100 per cent, or the essential duties of the job. This type of plan has traditionally been implemented for salaried personnel or management staff.

LONG-TERM DISABILITY

Long-term Disability (LTD) insurance plans provide benefits to employees who are disabled and have exhausted their short-term benefit supports. These plans vary greatly in the following ways:

- *Insurance Arrangement* — Is the employer self-insuring the disability period, or is a third party insurance arrangement in place?
- *Length of Time for the Qualifying Period* — The initial period of time when the employee receives short-term coverage.
- *Definition of "Disability"* — Is the employee disabled because the employee cannot do 60 per cent of his or her pre-disability job, or essential duties of his or her regular position?
- *Replacement Ratios* — The proportion of the employee's net earnings that will be paid out if the employee meets the disability definition. For some plans it is 65 per cent of the pre-disability earnings. For others, the plan may pay 66 2/3 per cent of the first $2,500 of monthly earnings and then a lower percentage for the remaining amount to a monthly maximum benefit.
- *Tax Arrangement* — Is the benefit taxable or non-taxable? Employer-paid plans are taxable, whereas the employee-paid ones tend to be non-taxable.

WORKERS' COMPENSATION

The provincial **Workers' Compensation Board** is the government or state operated "no fault" insurance agreement between employers and workers that requires employers to be responsible for occupational injuries and/or illness. Under this legislated insurance arrangement, employers pay all the premiums and compensation in exchange for the legally binding agreement that workers who make Workers' Compensation benefit claims forfeit their right to take legal action against the employer.

The types of benefits provided under the Workers' Compensation insurance are:

- *Cash Benefits* — This includes both impairment and disability benefits relative to the impairment and the wage loss.
- *Medical Benefits* — Workers' Compensation pays for the medical assessments and treatments, along with the related prescription drug costs and prosthetic devices.
- *Rehabilitation Benefits* — This includes both medical and vocational rehabilitation. Retraining costs may be part of this benefit.
- *Job Searches* — For workers with permanent work restrictions who are ready to re-enter the job market, job search services may be provided to help them find employment or gain job search skills that will help them be competitive in the job market. According to the Alberta Workers' Compensation Board, these services may include help with resume writing, employment leads, and job search and employment skills counselling (employment search techniques, interview skills, presenting a business-like appearance, *etc.*).

Linkages Between the Disability Management Program and Other Company Resources

A Disability Management Program is part of the overall business system functioning within a company. It operates with, and is affected by, other system components such as employee pension and compensation, employee benefits, Workers' Compensation Board claims management, human resources support and programs, labour union/association support, business operations, Employee Assistance Program, employee fitness facilities, Occupational Health & Safety Programs, corporate counsel support, *etc.* The Disability Management Program needs to be aligned with these business systems and operate according to the general system rules in place within the organization.

In many companies, however, the Disability Management Program works in isolation from the other business activities and from the other employee supports. At times, this isolation ("the silo-effect") can result in programs that work in opposition to each other, rather than in a synergistic fashion. One way to deal with this is to use a flow chart to map out the disability management processes and to identify all the players involved and their optimal time of involvement (Figure 3.2 or 3.3).

One natural linkage is the Disability Management Program with the Employee Assistance Program. Chapter 7, "The Role of the Employee

Assistance Program in Disability Management", emphasizes the importance of a linkage between a Disability Management Program and the Employee Assistance Program. By aligning the efforts of both programs, employees, and employers are served in the most effective and efficient manner.

Integration of the Disability Management Program with other company programs is the most effective approach — an approach that maximizes company resources and enhances the benefits realized. For more information on an Integrated Disability Management Program refer to Chapter 11, "Prevention of Workplace Illness and Injury".

INTEGRATED DISABILITY MANAGEMENT PROGRAM MANUAL DEVELOPMENT: AN INDUSTRY EXAMPLE

For an Integrated Disability Management Program to be successfully operated, it requires a number of policies and procedures. As already mentioned, they function to treat employees fairly and equitably, to communicate the rules and regulations that are in place, and to facilitate the functioning of the disability management process. The pages that follow provide some examples of the issues and concerns that a company, like Company XYZ, needs to consider when developing its disability management policies and procedures. Appendix 1 contains an actual example for the reader to observe. The format used is that of a typical policy and procedure manual.

Preliminary Concerns

The following policies are only useful to a company if they are accepted, endorsed and supported by senior management, union leaders and all employees. To create acceptance, we recommend that a company:

- have a committee review and modify the policies to meet stakeholder needs;
- communicate the policies to all employees;
- implement the policies in a unified manner to all employees;
- evaluate their impact; and
- modify and readjust the policies as required.

Development and Maintenance of the Policy Manual

Senior management, human resources professionals/practitioners and union leaders, if applicable, must be directly involved in the development of company policies and their presentation to employees. This is one way to get "buy-in" on the success of the total process. Management, human resources and union involvement ensures greater understanding of the policy by those required to interpret and to administer it, provides insight into employee concerns, and promotes employer-employee communication.

Where practical, a committee should be selected from employees, union representatives, and from middle to senior management. The size of the committee varies depending on management's willingness to broaden the process. Broader representation brings different viewpoints and perspectives to the discussions and helps to develop a better set of policies. The involvement of senior management ensures that the corporate philosophies regarding business, production and employee satisfaction are found within the manual. Chapter 4, "Disability Management Program: Stakeholder Roles", contains specifics on the role of a Disability Management Program Committee.

Some suggestions that the Disability Management Program Committee may choose to consider when developing the policy manual are:

- Meet with senior management and union leaders to delineate what is to be accomplished by the guidelines.
- Select a person on the committee to coordinate the development of the Integrated Disability Management Program manual.
- Determine which of the company's current policies are to be included in the manual and whether or not they need to be revised.
- Have supervisors/managers and union representatives respond to a checklist of tentative policies and an outline of instructions for implementing policies.
- Set deadlines for completion of the manual.

Another important responsibility of the committee is a training session to introduce the Integrated Disability Management Program manual to all employees. One option is to consider an employee-orientation meeting during which:

- management and union comment on the importance of the manual and its purposes;
- one or more of the committee members involved in developing the manual presents a brief discussion of its organization, each of its policies and the reasons for including them in the manual; and
- time is allotted for questions and comments from the employees.

If the company has made revisions to any of its current policies, or is adding a few new policies, a more informal meeting may be appropriate.

Note: An important part of the process, prior to introducing the manual to employees, is to have a lawyer specializing in human resources, and labour and employment law review the contents.

The manual's publication does not complete the project. As the company grows and its workforce becomes larger and more diverse, new issues need to be faced and new policies developed to address them. Similarly, changes in laws, regulations, employee benefits and other areas necessitate revisions. Plans for periodic reviews of the developed policy and procedure manual should be made and documented for due diligence purposes.

Formatting the Manual

There are several formats available for organizing a Disability Management Program policy and procedure manual. When customizing the guidelines, the following questions should be considered:

- What image does the company want to portray to employees?
- Will the manual be presented in hardcopy or electronic format?
- How often are major revisions to the manual anticipated?
- What will be the maintenance method for the manual? Will manuals be returned to one location for updating, or distributed to employees who will be expected to maintain their own manuals, or will it be electronically updated and presented?

Here are some general points to consider when developing the content of the manual policies and procedures:

- keep in mind who the policies are written for;
- organize each policy in a logical operational sequence;
- stay on the subject;
- make the sentences and paragraphs brief and succinct;
- avoid rigid formality unless that degree of strictness is desired;
- check for user understanding. Try to be flexible and to avoid vague, unclear or indirect statements; and
- establish the terminology for key words such as gender, organization, location, department, division, and positions. These should be used consistently throughout the manual.

If you choose the loose-leaf binder format for the manual, the company name or logo should be prominently presented on each page. The section name and policy title on each page helps in organizing and referencing the manual. The use of "page ___ of ___ pages" makes it easy for everyone to determine if he or she has the complete policy in their version of the manual. The use of "issue effective date" and "revision date" assists in researching the history and changes to each policy. The inclusion of "Approved by" legitimizes the policy and signifies that senior management has reviewed the manual.

SUMMARY

Having a functional infrastructure for an Integrated Disability Management Program ensures that the program continues to operate despite changes in personnel responsible for the program, that all employees are treated fairly and equitably, that outcome measures are identified and that the program's success can be measured and reported.

Appendix 1

Disability Management Program Policy and Procedure Manual: An Industry Example

The remainder of this chapter has been used to illustrate a Disability Management Program manual template.

Integrated Disability Management Program Manual
Company XYZ[4]
September 1, 2009

Table of Contents

---

[4]   Adapted from: *Policies and Procedures Manual* (Toronto: Aon Consulting, 1990).

INTRODUCTION

This policy and procedure manual is designed to clearly state the policies and procedures that balance employee and employer rights and expectations at Company XYZ (XYZ).

COMPANY XYZ: INTEGRATED DISABILITY MANAGEMENT PROGRAM POLICY

Company XYZ will make every effort to promote workplace safety and employee well-being through various practices including the Occupational Health & Safety, and Attendance Support and Assistance Policies. However in the event that illness/injury occurs, the Integrated Disability Management Program provides a forum for:

- managing absences due to illness or injury;
- conveying the message that employees are valued;
- intervening early at the onset of an illness/injury;
- facilitating the rehabilitation of employees while expediting a safe return-to-work through an early return-to-work plan;
- following confidentiality guidelines;
- responding to the corporate/union vision of providing employees with a safe and healthy workplace;
- focusing on illness/injury prevention;
- promoting the image of a caring and responsible employer/union while contributing to employee and community morale; and
- demonstrating compliance with legislation and regulations (*e.g.*, *Workers' Compensation Act*, Duty to Accommodate, and Collective Agreements).

The Integrated Disability Management Program is designed to attain the best performance in managing employee medical absences in both human and financial terms. The aim is to promote employee health and recovery through active claims and case management, and safe return-to-work opportunities.

President and CEO
XYZ Company
September 1, 2009

CONFIDENTIALITY OF EMPLOYEE MEDICAL INFORMATION

Applicable to:	**All Employees**
Issue Date:	**September 1, 2009**
Revision Date:	
Approved by:	

Company XYZ has established a policy for the confidential management of employee medical information.

Background Information

Employees have a legal right to privacy in relation to personal health information collected by the Company or designates.

Definitions

Confidentiality is the maintenance of trust expressed by an individual verbally, or in writing, and the avoidance of an invasion of privacy through accurate reporting and authorized communication.

Personal Health Information is an accumulation of data relevant to the past, present and future health status of an individual that includes all that Occupational Health Services staff learn while exercising their responsibilities.

Privacy is the claim of individuals, groups or institutions to determine for themselves when, how, and to what extent information about them is communicated to others.

Designated Representative is any individual (or organization) to whom an employee gives written authorization to exercise a right to access.

Policy

Company XYZ requires that all persons who collect, maintain, handle, and use health information protect the confidentiality of the information related to employees.

Procedure

- Personal health information is to be treated as confidential and distributed only on a "need-to-know" basis.

- Personal health information is restricted to Occupational Health Services staff who sign a Pledge of Confidentiality and are subject to a recognized professional code of ethics.
- Personal health information related to the management of an occupational illness/injury and a disability claim can be shared **in privacy** between the Occupational Health & Safety and Disability Management professionals and caregivers employed by Company XYZ to enhance the continuity of care and a coordinated injury management approach.
- Documented health information is the property of Company XYZ entrusted to Occupational Health Services staff for safeguarding and protection of confidentiality.
- Information will not be released without the written consent of the employee.
- Employees have the right to access all information regarding his or her health and fitness.
- Disclosure of all other employee personal health information will be considered a breach of confidentiality and will be reported to the Director, Human Resources, and may result in disciplinary action including immediate termination of employment **with cause**.
- All health information is to be stored separately from other employee information.
- All computerized health information is to be secured using passwords and access codes.
- Management Disclosure is having health information released to management and is limited to the following:
    - report of employee fitness to work;
    - determination that a medical condition exists and that the employee is under medical care;
    - time that the employee has been or is expected to be off work; and
    - medical limitation/restrictions, if any, to carry out work in a safe and timely manner.
- Should disclosure be necessary because of a clear danger to the employee, the co-workers, the workplace or the public, and:
    - the employee concerned consistently refuses to give consent; and
    - a second opinion is obtained from the employee's personal physician when the concern is for the health of the employee or to fellow employees, or from the Medical Officer of Health when the risk is to the public;
- The Occupational Health Services may make the disclosure to the appropriate manager after giving notice in writing to the employee, indicating that confidential information will be disclosed.
- Destruction of records will render them completely and permanently unidentifiable through destruction by burning, shredding, or automated erasure.

- The Director, Human Resources is responsible for ensuring that the Company XYZ staff involved in disability management are aware of and have signed the Pledge of Confidentiality.

INDEPENDENT MEDICAL EXAMINATION

Applicable to:	**All Employees**
Issue Date:	**September 1, 2009**
Revision Date:	
Approved by:	

Company XYZ has established a step-by-step process for requesting a secondary medical assessment of an employee for an absence due to illness or disability.

Background Information

Company XYZ, as the employer, has the right to ensure that its short-term disability plan is being well run. Part of that process is to ensure that the adjudication of disability claims proceeds so that only those employees who match the pre-defined criteria are eligible for benefits. Independent Medical Examinations can be an integral part of the adjudication process.

Definition

Independent Medical Examinations (IMEs) are third party medical examinations of employees who are presently receiving or have applied for disability benefits. Their purpose is to determine the employee's level of disability and length of disability, and to make recommendations regarding possible rehabilitation and modified work programs.

Policy

An employee may be required to attend a medical assessment under the following circumstances:

(i)   to determine the employee's medical status;
(ii)   to obtain a second medical opinion;
(iii)   to determine the employee's fitness for work;
(iv)   to determine the length of time the employee may be absent from work in order to allow for adequate replacement resources;
(v)   to determine the employee's restrictions and/or limitations;
(vi)   to develop a rehabilitation strategy, if necessary;

(vii) to ensure that the employee can return to work safely and productively fit;

(viii) if the disabling condition claimed for is not usually totally disabling;

(ix)   if the actual or estimated period of disability is longer than usual for the identified disabling condition;

(x)   if the physician's diagnosis or symptoms are vague rather than a firm diagnosis;

(xi)   if the return-to-work date cannot be provided by the physician or is shown as unknown or indefinite; and

(xii) if benefits are applied for when it is convenient not to be at work (lay-offs, strikes, holidays).

Upon receipt of the completed medical assessment, the case manager for disability will advise the supervisor if the employee is fit to return to work and the date of the return.

Costs associated with this type of assessment will be paid by Company XYZ. This does not include the cost of medicals required for insurance purposes.

GRADUATED RETURN-TO-WORK POLICY

Applicable to:	**All Employees**
Issue Date:	**September 1, 2009**
Revision Date:	
Approved by:	

Company XYZ is committed to helping its disabled employees return to productive work in a safe and timely manner. Company XYZ strives to assist its disabled employees to return to work as soon as they are physically capable. Company XYZ adheres to the general duty to accommodate disabled employees up to the point of undue hardship. Company XYZ has created its modified return-to-work policy to help employees with the transition from being disabled to being fully employed.

Background Information

The goal of a Graduated Return-to-Work Program is to return the injured employee back to work in a safe and timely manner which is cost-effective and accommodates the employee's identified work limitations whenever possible. Rehabilitation following an illness/injury encompasses many things including: social, physical, and psychological well-being. Ideally, a Graduated Return-to-Work Program is considered as part of an overall rehabilitation plan.

Some of the benefits of a Graduated Return-to-Work Program are:

1. increased productivity, as skilled workers stay at work or return to work more quickly after their injury;
2. financial independence for the employee and enhanced feelings of self-worth;
3. greater commitment to health and safety issues from both the employer and the employee;
4. decreased lost time per Workers' Compensation claim and a corresponding decrease in Workers' Compensation costs; and
5. a decrease in Short-term Disability and Long-term Disability costs.

The organizations with successful Graduated Return-to-Work Programs:

- recognize the potential of the injured employee;
- recognize that it is good business practice to have modified work (MW) and alternate work (AW) options available; and
- seek and receive support from all areas of management, union, and employee representation.

Program Manager

Critical for the success of a Graduated Return-to-Work Program, is for the company to choose one person to manage the process — a program champion. This person should have the following characteristics:

- be accepted by both management, union/bargaining group, and employees;
- be knowledgeable about the various jobs available within the company;
- be able to speak to groups of employers and managers to convince them of the importance of a Graduated Return-to-Work Program; and
- be able to liaise with managers, union representatives, physicians, and rehabilitation specialists.

Policy

To provide a fair and consistent policy for recovering employees who have been ill/injured, Company XYZ recognizes the benefits of a Graduated Return-to-Work Program.

Company XYZ therefore undertakes to provide meaningful employment for both permanently and temporarily disabled employees, thereby returning valuable Human Resources benefits, and productivity into Company XYZ.

Steps

1. DEVELOP AN ACCIDENT HISTORY

This includes:

a)   the annual number of accidents over the past five years;
b)   trends in the number of reported accidents or in the type of work done by accident victims;
c)   statistics on repeat accidents; and
d)   the nature of reported injuries and the circumstances under which they occur.

This information is used to improve Company XYZ's Occupational Health & Safety record, and to determine the most common types of physical restrictions that the Graduated Return-to-Work Program will have to accommodate.

2. IDENTIFY JOBS SUITABLE FOR A GRADUATED RETURN-TO-WORK PROGRAM

After determining the most common types of physical restrictions faced by injured employees, the process of identifying jobs that can accommodate common workplace restrictions begins.

A list of potential suitable jobs or tasks from each department or line supervisor is requested. These can be jobs or tasks that are done regularly, on a full-time or part-time basis. The work should be both meaningful and productive. In other words, it contributes to Company operations and provides the employee with a goal-oriented job and rehabilitation opportunity.

Although it is easiest and most preferable to have an injured employee return to his or her own department for modified work, this is not always possible. Therefore, a cross-reference to other possible modified/alternate jobs by physical demands needs to be made.

3. COMPLETE A PHYSICAL DEMANDS ANALYSIS

A basic physical and psychological demands analysis on each job will be done so that person/job matching can be done.

The results of the Physical Demands Analysis can then be compared to the relevant data on reported injuries in Company XYZ's work site accident profile. From this comparison, the jobs that can best accommodate the most common types of physical restriction faced by injured employees are identified.

4. DEVELOP AN INDIVIDUAL PROGRAM FOR THE EMPLOYEE

Since every injured employee has different requirements for modified/alternate work, individual programs have to be developed. This is the responsibility of the supervisor, union representative and employee with input from the Occupational Health Nurse, third party Claims Manager, Human Resources, and Program Manager.

a. establish the physical capabilities of the employee;
b. determine the duration of the program;
c. select appropriate work;
d. decide what workplace modifications/accommodations are needed; and
e. create a new job, if necessary.

a. ESTABLISH PHYSICAL CAPABILITIES OF THE EMPLOYEE

In consultation with the employee, the Occupational Health Nurse, the third party claims manager, and supervisor must establish what physical restrictions the returning employee will face.

b. DETERMINE THE DURATION OF THE PROGRAM

On the basis of discussions with the employee and relevant personnel, the supervisor should determine whether short- or long-term accommodation is required. Generally, a program of 90 days or less is considered short-term.

c. SELECT APPROPRIATE WORK

Once the duration of the program has been decided, appropriate work must be found. The best solution is to return the employee to his or her pre-accident job, with whatever modifications are needed. This option is preferable so that the employee can perform the job safely and without risk of re-injury or danger to others.

If the employee cannot be accommodated in his or her original job, the supervisor and employee, with help from the Occupational Health Nurse, should select from the list of available jobs, a position best suited to the employee's capabilities.

d. DECIDE WHAT MODIFICATIONS ARE NEEDED

After a job has been selected, the supervisor and employee, with help from the Occupational Health Nurse, must determine what, if any, workplace modifications are required. Modifications may be administrative; for example, changes in work-rest periods, short scheduling or work sequencing. Modifications may be physical; for example, the addition of specialized equipment, such as reaching assists or moving controls or changes made to the layout of the workplace. Modifications may be psychological; for example, movement to a less mentally demanding position with greater emphasis on routine and manual tasks.

e. CREATE AN ALTERNATE POSITION, IF NECESSARY

If there is no suitable position in Company XYZ for the returning employee, a third solution is the creation of an alternate position. This requires a sound understanding of the employee's abilities and vocational aptitudes. The Occupational Health Nurse and/or third party insurer claims manager may, therefore, ask the employee to undergo vocational testing.

It is important that the alternate work position be productive, and, if possible, in the employee's pre-accident work department so that he or she can be in a familiar environment, among familiar people.

An alternate work position can be created by combining the duties of various part-time jobs that already exist. Alternatively, a new job may be created on the advice of management to cover residual tasks from other jobs. Again, a Physical Demands Analysis should be done on each task to ensure that it is suitable for the employee. If the employee cannot eventually return to a regular job, Company XYZ will decide if the newly created position should be maintained; that is, the creation of a permanent alternate work position.

5. SET GRADUATED RETURN-TO-WORK PROGRAM GOALS

As soon as suitable work is found, the supervisor and employee should meet to:

- discuss the job duties;
- set a date for the start of modified/alternate work arrangement;
- decide how long the employee will require the modified job; and
- establish the ultimate goal of the program; in most cases, a return to the pre-accident job.

6. MONITOR THE GRADUATED RETURN-TO-WORK OPPORTUNITY

The supervisor should monitor the employee's progress closely to evaluate the program's success and to make additional modifications (if required) to the job. Through the monitoring process, the supervisor can also help the employee adapt to the new job.

7. ESTABLISH PLAN FOR THE EMPLOYEE WHO CANNOT RETURN TO WORK

The injured employee may not be able to return to employment with Company XYZ. If so, Company XYZ should still take an active role in the individual's rehabilitation, particularly since it may be bearing the cost until the employee is financially self-sufficient. Usually an Occupational Health Nurse will be invited to case manage the disability.

The Program Manager should ensure that the employee's entitlement to a Workers' Compensation temporary partial disability pension, or long-term disability insurance through a private carrier is in place. The Program Manager should also ensure that a rehabilitation professional is available to the employee and should meet with both parties to establish a course of action including a program of evaluation, training and/or education, and job placement.

REHABILITATION POLICY

Applicable to:	**All Employees**
Issue Date:	**September 1, 2009**
Revision Date:	
Approved by:	

Company XYZ supports the rehabilitation of disabled employees. Disabled employees are actively encouraged to return to work as soon as they are medically fit. Company XYZ will support all reasonable efforts to return an employee to work that meets the guidelines listed below.

Background Information

Rehabilitation may be defined as the restoration of an employee who has been disabled by an injury, disease, or congenital abnormality to an optional level of vocational, medical, social, and psychological functioning. The ultimate goal of rehabilitation is the return of the disabled employee to the workplace with the maximal use of his or her capacities.

Rehabilitation, to be successful, has to be a managed process with mutual understanding and commitment between the supervisor, the employee and the rehabilitation specialists. In practical terms, this means a written rehabilitation plan agreed upon by all parties. The plan must identify a job goal and the therapy, training and job modification needed to achieve this goal. As well, a reasonable schedule against which to measure progress must be established.

Policy

The Company recognizes that rehabilitation:

1. is a cost effective way of supporting disability management;
2. improves employee productivity because experienced workers are returned to work more quickly;
3. reduces absenteeism and lost time frequency; and
4. may improve employee morale because the organization is demonstrating to its employees that it is concerned with their welfare and their prompt return to work.

Note: Management might want to consider that in the short-term, a supervisor's main goal is productivity and a disabled employee's is income maintenance. Management has to examine the current initiative systems, such as the employee's pay while absent and the supervisor's need for fully productive employees, to ensure that both parties are encouraged to work within the policy.
Some common disincentives to implementing rehabilitation are:

1. *Benefits under sick leave are usually paid from a corporate account. Savings from returning an employee to work are credited to the corporate account. Rehabilitation and workstation modification are often paid from department cost, effectively making the supervisor pay for rehabilitation.*
2. *Often restraints are put on staffing levels. Therefore, an employee who can only work half days, but who is counted as a full employee, reduces the supervisor's incentive to return the employee to work.*
3. *In many instances, employees are unaware that they are expected to return to work if they can perform some aspects of their duties. All employees should understand that Company XYZ offers rehabilitation programs. Then, if the employees become injured, they know they will be supported in their efforts to return to the job.*

WORKPLACE WELLNESS POLICY

Applicable to:	**All Employees**
Issue Date:	**September 1, 2009**
Revision Date:	
Approved by:	

Company XYZ is committed to maintaining a comprehensive Workplace Wellness policy encompassing the physical, emotional and social needs of employees.

Background Information

Wellness in the workplace means that employees are educated and the organization is empowered to manage the challenges facing them. For employees, this workplace support translates to managing both the psychological and physical issues in response to environmental stress. For the organization, it is managing both business functioning and employee well-being in a manner that allows the organization to be more resistant to environmental pressures. It is a valuable adjunct to maintaining employee "fitness to work".

The benefits of a Workplace Wellness program are:

1. It encourages employees to take more responsibility for their health and well-being.
2. It focuses attention on "high risk" workers through health risk assessments that measure such things as blood pressure, cholesterol level, and fitness levels. Thus, the organization can help employees take preventive measures to minimize the risk of disability of these workers.
3. It improves employee productivity because workers feel physically stronger, are better able to handle stress, and are less tired at work.
4. It helps make Company XYZ an attractive company to work for.

The purpose of a Workplace Wellness policy is to minimize medical and disability costs to the organization while maximizing the physical, social, and emotional well-being of employees. The benefits of individual wellness should be communicated to employees and they should be encouraged to participate in the program regardless of whether they are considered high health risks or not.

Policy

Company XYZ believes that the health and well-being of its employees is key to its process as a company.

How to Establish A Workplace Wellness Policy

1. The goals of a Workplace Wellness program are:
    *   healthier employees;
    *   increased productivity;
    *   reduced employee absenteeism; and
    *   sound control of health care costs.
2. Seek employee input:
    *   Ask employees what they want from a Workplace Wellness program.
3. Address problems:
    *   Tailor the Workplace Wellness policy to address the health needs of the workforce.

4. Utilize Employee Assistance Program resources:

    •   If the organization has an Employee Assistance Program, it can be used to provide organizational and employee wellness support. For employees, this can include education on change management, stress management, smoking cessation, nutrition, and other wellness issues.

5. Reinforce efforts:

    •   Create incentives for the employee to participate in the various Workplace Wellness program offerings.

6. Monitor the program's progress:

    •   Evaluate the effectiveness of the policy both quantitatively and qualitatively (*i.e.*, changes in the number of disability claims, absentee rates, safety records, and program participation rates). This will help to determine if the policy is meeting its objectives.

7. Communicate the program to the workforce.

The long-term success of the Workplace Wellness policy requires wellness to become part of the organization's culture and fabric. It must be a stated priority. The promotion of a healthy workforce has the potential to provide the organization with considerable medical and disability cost savings.

CHAPTER REFERENCES

Aon Consulting, *Policies and Procedures Manual* (Toronto: Aon Consulting, 1990).

V. McNeil & M.A. Garcia, "Enhancing Program Management Through Cultural Organizational Assessment" (1991) 4:6 AAOHN Update Series 1.

D. Shrey, *Principles and Practices of Disability Management in Industry* (Winter Park, FL: GR Press Inc., 1995).

L. Smircich, "Concepts of Culture and Organizational Analysis" (1983) 28 Administrative Science Quarterly 339.

Chapter 4

Integrated Disability Management Program: Stakeholder Roles

WHY STAKEHOLDERS NEED TO BE KNOWLEDGEABLE ABOUT THE INTEGRATED DISABILITY MANAGEMENT PROGRAM

The Integrated Disability Management Program involves all employees at various levels of the organization. To give their endorsement and support, these stakeholders need to understand the Disability Management Program goals, objectives, benefits and desired outcomes. Only by understanding the magnitude of the issues within their workplace, can stakeholders provide their support and input towards a common solution.

Clarity of stakeholder roles is an essential element towards garnering stakeholder support and to ensuring a successful Integrated Disability Management Program. This chapter focuses on the roles of the specific personnel involved in the disability management process. In Chapter 5, "An Integrated Disability Management Program: The Managed Rehabilitative Care Program", the roles of senior management, supervisors, employees, unions, and family physicians are discussed within the context of an industry graduated return-to-work application.

ROLES OF THE DISABILITY MANAGEMENT PERSONNEL

Role of the Disability Management Program Committee

The Disability Management Program Committee is a joint labour-management committee that acts as a steering committee for a Disability Management Program. The Disability Management Program Committee is the foundation of the Integrated Disability Management Program and provides support for the Disability Management Coordinator and the program.

RESPONSIBILITIES

The Disability Management Program Committee is responsible for:

* understanding the business, people and legislative drivers for having an Integrated Disability Management Program in place;
* being cognizant of their legal responsibilities related to returning ill/injured employees to work;

- establishing the Integrated Disability Management Program vision and philosophy;
- setting the program objectives;
- developing a program design/model, perhaps like the NIDMAR model for disability management (Chapter 1, "Disability Management: Overview", Figure 1.2);
- mapping out the process flow for the disability management process like the example provided in Chapter 3, "The Supportive Infrastructure for an Integrated Disability Management Program", Figures 3.2 and 3.3;
- developing policies and procedures;
- developing and approving the skill sets required for a Disability Management Coordinator position;
- communicating the roles and responsibilities of the various corporate stakeholders;
- supporting the efforts to identify return-to-work options;
- exploring the needs of the various corporate stakeholders;
- increasing the general awareness of the Integrated Disability Management Program goals, benefits, and outcomes throughout the company;
- overseeing the implementation of the Integrated Disability Management Program;
- providing a dispute resolution forum;
- participating with the Disability Management Coordinator to monitor and evaluate the program's effectiveness;
- recommending to management the support systems and any identified program needs; and
- considering preventative strategies such as an Attendance Support & Assistance Program.[1]

This steering committee advises and consults with management, and receives concerns, advice, and suggestions for the Integrated Disability Management Program from the various stakeholders. The committee also receives reports regarding the usage of the Integrated Disability Management Program to assist in assessing its overall effectiveness. The information provided to the committee and to management is population, or aggregate, data. Individual clients are not identified.

The Disability Management Program Committee membership has representatives from labour and management. The chairperson is elected by the committee for a set term. The resources that could be available to this steering committee are the Disability Management Coordinator, the Employee Assistance Program Administrator or Representative, and internal or external consultants as required.

---

[1]   **Attendance Support & Assistance Program** — a term coined by The City of Medicine Hat personnel to describe an attendance management program as described in Chapter 9, "Workplace Attendance Support & Assistance".

Role of the Disability Management Coordinator

The Disability Management Coordinator is accountable for the overall management of all disabilities. This includes acting as a liaison with all stakeholders, including the third party insurers, being an active supporter of the ill or injured employee and family members, and functioning as a catalyst for facilitating the reintegration of the disabled worker back into the workplace.

RESPONSIBILITIES

The Disability Management Coordinator oversees the coordination of employee medical absences from the onset of illness or injury to the return to full-time work. This involves the overall management of the illness or injuries in the short-term and long-term disability periods. This means that the Disability Management Coordinator is ultimately responsible for overseeing both the claim and case management, and the vocational rehabilitation activities.

Working with management, unions, employee groups, human resources professionals, insurers, and internal/external health care service providers, the Disability Management Coordinator leads the disability management team, which:

- assists managers/supervisors in communicating with the employee on the first day of illness/injury;
- manages the claim administration processes;
- assists supervisors in identifying the potential candidates for early intervention;
- works with employee, supervisor and union to establish recovery and rehabilitation goals and objectives;
- oversees the support provided to the employee and family members if required;
- determines if and when outside professional help is needed;
- establishes a liaison with outside professionals, insurers and Workers' Compensation Board, on behalf of employers and employees;
- helps supervisors to establish individual early return-to-work plans;
- maintains confidentiality of medical information;
- works with supervisors and the union leaders to determine modified work opportunities;
- respects the terms of the governing collective agreements in relation to early return-to-work initiatives;
- arranges for workplace modifications or job restructuring when needed and facilitates regular, open communication between stakeholders to ensure a smooth, seamless transition from short-term disability to long-term disability, when required;
- develops strategic alliances with community and internal groups;
- collects and evaluates the disability management data;

- reports the disability management outcomes to the appropriate stakeholders; and
- educates management, supervisors and employees with respect to disability management.

SCOPE AND DIMENSIONS

The scope of this position includes the management of people, functions and disability costs. The Disability Management Coordinator:

- is accountable for the Integrated Disability Management Program function and the disability management services (Chapter 3, Figure 3.1);
- establishes communication plans regarding the Integrated Disability Management Program;
- provides focus to cost-avoidance goals and objectives by evaluating injury and illness statistics and trends, identifying opportunities to prevent disabilities and absences, developing approaches and strategies to minimize the impact of employee absence due to disability, and facilitating or negotiating modified work opportunities;
- assists in the monitoring of employee disability benefits and conducts cost-benefit analysis on the impact of disability management on employee benefit costs;
- partners externally with insurers and third party service providers, and internally with management, human resources department (*i.e.*, benefits, payroll, labour relations), occupational health and safety, unions, and the Disability Management Program Committee to continually improve policies and procedures, to contain absenteeism costs and to meet legislative requirements;
- works with people and groups in crisis situations serving as a facilitator and offering innovative approaches towards resolutions that best serve the company and employees;
- develops and conducts an evaluation process of the program that considers client satisfaction, processes, outcomes and cost-effectiveness;
- is accountable for all disability management services, program communications, programs, and prevention;
- safeguards confidentiality of employee personal health and disability information and records;
- identifies researchable problems with a view to disability prevention; and
- assumes accountability for personal and staff professional development and continuing education.

GENERAL DIRECTION

Program direction is generally provided to the Disability Management Coordinator through the Disability Management Program Committee, whereas the general and functional direction may come from a set department such as the occupational health or human resources department. Figure 3.1 provides a graphic example of how this could be organized. For the Disability Management Coordinator, authority should be delegated within established limits for programming, financial, personnel and material management matters.

INFORMATION ACCESS

The Disability Management Coordinator has access to confidential medical information, and is consulted in advance on employee terminations, performance issues and grievances that involve disability-related issues.

REQUIRED SKILLS AND ABILITIES

The Disability Management Coordinator must have the requisite skills and abilities to do the job. Typically the eligible candidate possesses:

- A university degree with additional certification in occupational health, and/or disability management.
- Experience of eight to 10 years in the fields of occupational health and/or disability management with evidence of progressive scope and responsibility. If this role is to include the management of the occupational health function, then a strong background in occupational health is essential.
- Knowledge of human resources functions. A certificate, degree, or experience in human resources management would be a definite asset.

A full description of the skills required for this senior professional position is provided in Appendix 1. In summary, the key skills include:

- high-level technical skills;
- leadership;
- high-level communication skills;
- strong interpersonal skills;
- networking skills;
- negotiating skills;
- process facilitation;
- crisis management;
- coaching skills;
- consulting skills;
- project management;
- risk management; and
- change management.

CHALLENGES

This position involves many challenges, including:

- Managing disability costs and ensuring a quality Integrated Disability Management Program by balancing cost-containment within the company and escalating external health care costs.
- Ensuring a consistent high quality Integrated Disability Management Program and service delivery. This involves achieving the expected results, identifying problems and issues, recommending corrective actions and monitoring solutions.
- Minimizing the illness/injury costs and the disruptions for the employees and company operations through effective disability management.
- Balancing the conflicting needs of the company to meet its service and "due diligence" requirements, and of the employees' health concerns.
- Consulting with management, supervisors, employees, health professionals, and human resources professionals on fitness-to-work and workplace accommodation when there are complicating medical, psychological, and personnel or labour relation issues.
- Influencing and co-managing issues with insurance organizations (private insurers and Workers' Compensation Board), medical professionals, and industry organizations to best serve the company and its employees.
- Being an effective risk manager regarding disability issues.
- Coordinating disability management efforts with the company's strategic business plan.
- Working across organizational boundaries anticipating and proactively planning for major changes that would impact the company's operations, the employees and the Integrated Disability Management Program. The intent is to continually improve the disability management process and methods used.
- Planning, designing, implementing and evaluating information systems so that disability management data can be collected and analyzed, and the composite findings interpreted to management in an accurate, timely and meaningful manner.
- Scanning the rapidly changing external environment for provincial and federal legislation on disability management and human rights. The purpose is to identify trends and issues, to assess the potential impact, and to design appropriate strategies of response that "best fit" the company's culture and commitment to employee health and well-being.

Role of the Disability Case Manager

Many organizations confuse the roles of the Disability Claim Manager and Disability Case Manager. The two functions are entirely different. **Disability case management** is a collaborative process for assessing, planning, implementing, coordinating, monitoring, and evaluating the options and services available to meet an individual's health needs through communication and accessible resources.[2] The intent is to promote high quality, cost-effective outcomes to disability management.

Disability claim management is the service provided in administering income loss claims through employee benefit plans such as short-term disability, Workers' Compensation, and long-term disability. This activity includes the determination of eligibility to receive benefits according to the definition of eligibility contained in the plan contract, the facilitation of income loss replacement and the processing of the claim towards a resolution or termination.

The Disability Case Manager is an occupational health professional[3] who practices within an occupational setting to assist ill and injured workers in reaching maximum health and productivity. The Disability Case Manager is also responsible for the coordination of employee health care services across multiple environmental systems from the onset of injury or illness to a safe return to work or an optimal alternative. The Disability Case Manager is determined to achieve quality care delivered in a cost-effective manner. Using a unique knowledge of employees, their families and the work environment, the Disability Case Manager assesses, plans, implements, coordinates, monitors and evaluates care for clients in the Integrated Disability Management Program.

FUNCTION

The Disability Case Manager:

- assesses the broad spectrum of client needs, including physical and psychosocial factors, using data from employees and families, other health care providers, health records, *etc.*;
- identifies client (employee and employer) goals, objectives and actions in a comprehensive case management plan to achieve desired outcomes within designated time frames;
- identifies the need for vocational rehabilitation when appropriate;
- is accountable for the progression of a disability claim/case;
- establishes communication plans involving internal and external parties, as appropriate;
- implements interventions to achieve client goals and objectives;
- identifies qualifications and expectations for, and monitors and evaluates outcomes and quality of services delivered by, health care providers and vendors in the treatment outcomes;

---

[2]   Case Management Society of America (CMSA), *Standards for Practice of Case Management* (Little Rock, AR: CMSA, 1995).

[3]   The Disability Case Manager is often an Occupational Health Nurse whose role is described fully in Chapter 5, "An Integrated Disability Management Program: The Managed Rehabilitative Care Program".

- identifies needed community resources and coordinates referrals as appropriate;
- assists with the Integrated Disability Management Program evaluation process regarding client satisfaction, processes, outcomes and cost effectiveness;
- supports claim processing with insurance and third party representatives;
- generates consistent documentation of the case management aspects of the program;
- contributes to the assessment of Integrated Disability Management Program using company, insurance and other health data;
- acts as a professional occupational health resource for the company's management in planning and maintaining the Integrated Disability Management Program;
- assists with the development of primary, secondary and tertiary prevention and health promotion strategies to optimize employee health and prevent injuries/illness;
- assists with the establishment of criteria to identify employees for inclusion in the Integrated Disability Management Program;
- assists with the development of processes for identifying situations that require early intervention to maximize the desired outcomes;
- supports the vocational rehabilitation efforts implemented by the Vocational Rehabilitation Specialist;
- maintains and safeguards confidentiality of employee personal health, and disability information and records;
- develops and conducts educational programs to enhance case management for health care providers, management and employees;
- identifies researchable problems and participates in studies and projects according to research skills; and
- assumes responsibility for his or her own professional development and continuing education.

QUALIFICATIONS

The qualifications for the Disability Case Manager depend on the breadth and scope of the position. Typically, a Disability Case Manager should possess:

- a current licence to practise as an occupational health professional;
- five or more years of occupational health nursing experience or equivalency;
- experience in occupational health nursing, case management, disability management and rehabilitation services;
- experience in coordinating services, working with multiple organizational groups and acting as a team member to make practice judgments;
- current knowledge of laws and regulations governing worker and occupational safety and health;

- the ability to organize work and manage time effectively;
- the ability to express ideas clearly in oral and written forms; and
- a university degree in nursing, or a related health discipline, and certification in occupational health.

Role of the Disability Claim Administrator

Keeping the definition of claim management in mind, the Disability Claim Administrator is responsible for the administration of the claim adjudication process for medical absences, including follow-up procedures for the various employee benefit plans such as short-term disability and long-term disability.

In smaller companies, the Disability Claim Administrator also processes all Workers' Compensation claims. For the purpose of clarity, the roles of Disability Claim Administrator and Workers' Compensation Claim Administrator have been described separately.

FUNCTION

The Disability Claim Administrator:

- acts as resource and contact person with respect to the claim management for non-occupationally-related medical absences;
- coordinates all the related medical absence claims;
- calculates benefits payable under the long-term disability plan with consideration for any offsets, if applicable;
- prepares cheque requisitions, long-term disability cheques and employee information forms, if required;
- assists in the administration (oral and written) and interpretation of company policies to staff and supervisors;
- consults with the Disability Case Manager, Vocational Rehabilitation Specialist, medical advisor, attending physicians, human resources, claimants, and departments to establish and coordinate claim follow-up;
- maintains liaison with claimants, departments, insurance agencies and legal representatives regarding claim management;
- maintains a computerized database of non-occupational medical absences;
- participates in claim appeals;
- acts as secretary to committee meetings in preparation of agenda, minutes and follow-up action as required;
- provides clerical support for the Disability Management Coordinator, Medical Advisor, Case Manager and Vocational Rehabilitation Specialist, and composes non-routine correspondence;
- assists in special projects assigned by the Disability Management Coordinator;
- prepares monthly long-term disability claim reports for budget and planning purposes;
- performs related duties as assigned; and
- supports the Workers' Compensation Claim Administrator when required.

QUALIFICATIONS

To function effectively as a Disability Claim Administrator, the candidate should possess:

- two to three years claim management experience;
- claim management training;
- experience in coordinating activities, working with professionals, and acting as a team member to make claim process judgments;
- current knowledge of the related disability benefit plans and policies, along with other related employee benefits;
- strong computer skills in word processing, database management, report generation, and systems;
- the ability to organize work and time effectively; and
- the ability to express ideas clearly in oral and written forms.

Role of the Workers' Compensation Claim Administrator

The Workers' Compensation Claim Administrator is responsible for the administration and implementation of the Workers' Compensation Claims. The Workers' Compensation Claim Administrator advises the company of the appropriate process and procedure relating to Workers' Compensation; provides interpretation, advice and guidance to employees on how to proceed with Workers' Compensation claims; and is the contact and liaison for Workers' Compensation matters for the employees and departments.

FUNCTION

The Workers' Compensation Claim Administrator:

- processes any Workers' Compensation claims generated by employees;
- assists with the completion of forms and explains the claim submission process;
- advises employees as to their responsibilities and benefits;
- monitors progress of claims;
- keeps the departments, employees and Workers' Compensation updated on any changes to a claim;
- identifies trends (*e.g.*, repetitive injuries, needle punctures, *etc.*) in specific areas or by specific individuals;
- processes Workers' Compensation payments through payroll, making sure that dates and amounts are correct;
- verifies monthly statement of cost for the company;
- assesses the validity of all claims;
- handles the required internal processes for Workers' Compensation benefit payments;

- initiates appeals when warranted. This involves evaluating Workers' Compensation's acceptance or denial, investigating and assembling information to protest a Workers' Compensation decision;
- follows up on the claimant's recovery by:

  1. confirming that proper treatment plans are complied with until the claimant returns to work;
  2. recommending modified work to departments and Workers' Compensation, if applicable;
  3. advising the Disability Management Team of any candidates that may need assistance in securing rehabilitation employment so that they may coordinate with Workers' Compensation rehabilitation; and
  4. ensuring the proper financial arrangements are met.

- maintains a computerized database on Workers' Compensation claims and status;
- represents the company in meetings with the Workers' Compensation Board;
- makes presentations to departments and employees regarding the current Workers' Compensation regulations and benefits; and
- supports the position of Disability Claim Administrator as required.

QUALIFICATIONS

- Minimum of a post-secondary diploma in business, health sciences or social sciences with three to five years in a Workers' Compensation-related position.
- Thorough knowledge of the applicable Workers' Compensation regulations, and of the company's long-term disability plan regulations and policies.
- Workers' Compensation claim cost-avoidance training.

Role of the Vocational Rehabilitation Specialist

Some organizations employ or contract internal rehabilitation specialists. In the model proposed in this chapter, the Vocational Rehabilitation Specialist is responsible for the coordination of the vocational rehabilitation of ill or injured employees. The Vocational Rehabilitation Specialist coordinates rehabilitation efforts across multiple environmental systems as part of the disability management team and facilitates a return to employability.

Rehabilitation is coordinated with a focus on achieving quality service in a cost-effective manner. Drawing from vocational rehabilitation knowledge, research and experience, the Vocational Rehabilitation Specialist assesses, plans, implements, coordinates, monitors and evaluates the rehabilitation care for clients in the Integrated Disability Management Program.

FUNCTION

The Vocational Rehabilitation Specialist:

- assists ill/injured employees in reaching their optimal level of vocational functioning;
- as part of a Disability Management Team, assesses the barriers to a successful return to work, including physical and psychosocial factors, using data from clients and families, other health care providers, health records, *etc.*;
- assists the client in addressing the barriers to returning to work;
- identifies client goals, objectives and actions in a comprehensive vocational rehabilitation plan to achieve desired outcomes within designated time frames;
- maintains open communication involving internal and external parties, as appropriate;
- assists with the development of processes for identifying situations that require early vocational rehabilitation interventions to maximize the desired rehabilitation outcomes;
- facilitates the development of a network that works toward placing disabled employees back to work and toward developing a supportive network for employee assessment;
- implements interventions to achieve client goals and objectives;
- identifies qualifications and expectations for, and monitors and evaluates outcomes and quality of services delivered by, rehabilitation care service providers and vendors in the treatment and rehabilitation outcomes;
- identifies needed community resources and coordinates referrals as appropriate;
- contributes to the assessment of the rehabilitation aspects of the Integrated Disability Management Program using company, insurance, and other rehabilitation outcome data;
- acts as a professional rehabilitation resource for the company's management in planning and maintaining the Integrated Disability Management Program;
- assists with the establishment of criteria to identify employees for vocational rehabilitation under the company's Integrated Disability Management Program;
- assists supervisors and employees with return-to-work issues including modified scheduling and job accommodations;
- conducts job demands analyses of company positions as appropriate;
- contributes to the prevention of workplace injuries through the appropriate implementation of ergonomic measures;
- maintains and safeguards confidentiality of employee rehabilitation information and records;
- identifies researchable rehabilitation problems and participates in studies and projects according to research skills; and
- assumes the responsibility for his or her own professional development and continuing education.

QUALIFICATIONS

The requisite qualifications for the Vocational Rehabilitation Specialist typically include:

- current registration in a vocational rehabilitation association;
- five or more years vocational rehabilitation experience;
- experience in coordinating services, working with various organizational groups and acting as a team member to make practice judgments;
- the ability to counsel and facilitate conflict resolution;
- the ability to organize work and manage time effectively;
- the ability to express ideas clearly in oral and written forms; and
- a university degree in a vocational rehabilitation discipline.

Role of the Return-to-Work Coordinator

The Return-to-Work Coordinator is accountable for working with the other team members to facilitate the safe and timely return to work by the recovering employee. This includes acting as a liaison between the Integrated Disability Management Program team and the workgroups, employee groups and unions.

FUNCTION

The Return-to-Work Coordinator:

- identifies the available return-to-work opportunities (modified work, or alternate work);
- works with the Disability Management Program team to evaluate the person-job fit for the potential placement;
- coaches the returning employee, as required;
- monitors the return-to-work placement;
- collects, analyzes and interprets data on various return-to-work placements; and
- prepares reports on the return-to-work placement outcomes.

QUALIFICATIONS

- in-depth Disability Management Program training and knowledge, ideally certified as a Return-to-Work Coordinator (Certification available through NIDMAR, Port Alberni, British Columbia);
- knowledge of the workplace; and
- respect and trust of the stakeholders.

SUMMARY

Each stakeholder has a role to play in the disability management process. The Disability Management Program Committee, Disability Management Coordinator, Disability Case Manager, Disability Claim Manager, Workers' Compensation Claim Administrator, Vocational Rehabilitation Specialist and Return-to-Work Coordinator have been described in this chapter. These are the Disability Management Program players. Their roles will vary with the size of the organization, the industry and geographic location. The roles of the employee, management, union and other key stakeholders are described in Chapter 5, "An Integrated Disability Management Program: The Managed Rehabilitative Care Program".

The communication of these roles to all involved is of prime importance. How this is accomplished will vary. Some organizations choose to design, or have designed, their own educational sessions, and to deliver them to all stakeholders. Others will use community educational programs to transmit the required information. Others will rely on case-by-case experience to explain disability management to the organization.

In general, the best approach is to clearly articulate what the Integrated Disability Management Program is, who is involved, what their role is, and how those roles will be enacted. Without that information, the program will be misinterpreted and will not succeed as designed.

Appendix 1

Required Skills for the Disability Management Coordinator

The Disability Management Coordinator requires the following skill sets:

1. Core Management/Business Skills
2. Relationship Skills
3. Technical/Specialist Skills

Core Management/Business Skills are the skills required to effectively manage people and business functions. They include planning and organization, decision-making, problem-solving, leadership, financial/business perspective, negotiating, information systems, internal consulting, process facilitation, performance management, employee development, training, change management, presentation making, and risk communications.

Relationship Skills are otherwise known as "people skills" and include communication, interpersonal skills, team-building/team-work, mentoring, negotiating, and reputation management.

Technical/Specialist Skills are the skills required for disability management and encompass counselling, health promotion, professional networking, fitness-to-work evaluation, human factor analysis, work site evaluation, risk assessment, quality assurance, regulatory compliance, technical communication, case management, auditing, program evaluation, social marketing, and strategic issues management.

The remainder of this appendix fully defines each of these skills.

1. CORE MANAGEMENT/BUSINESS SKILLS

Planning and Organization

The ability to set appropriate goals and objectives, to predetermine a realistic course of action, and to negotiate correctly and allocate the resources required to complete a project.

WHAT IS INVOLVED? THE ABILITY TO:

- consider the potential problems and opportunities that may arise from the implementation of actions to prevent problems and maximize opportunities;
- formulate a desired outcome and assign resources to effectively achieve that outcome;
- visualize goals and objectives, and implement activities directed toward goal-attainment while regularly monitoring and managing the process;

- evaluate the project goals, objectives and outcomes; and
- implement necessary changes.

Decision-making

The ability to objectively analyze a range of possible alternatives and to apply judgment in selecting the most appropriate course of action.

WHAT IS INVOLVED? THE ABILITY TO:

- establish requirements for the decision;
- create a range of possible alternatives;
- assess and compare alternatives based on requirements; and
- assess and minimize the risk factors.

Problem-solving

The ability to apply rational and creative approaches for analyzing and solving problems.

WHAT IS INVOLVED? THE ABILITY TO:

- identify the problem;
- determine true cause(s);
- consider possible solutions;
- isolate the solution which effectively addresses the cause of the problem; and
- implement the solution.

Leadership

The ability to influence the activity of another individual, or a group, in an effort to accomplish desired goals and objectives.

WHAT IS INVOLVED? THE ABILITY TO:

- formulate a vision and direction and translate it into goals and objectives;
- use the appropriate style of leadership considering the people involved, the task at hand, and the results to be achieved;
- lead and motivate others toward the desired results when one has formal authority to do so through position; and
- influence and motivate others toward the desired results when one has no formal authority to direct them.

Financial/Business Perspective

The ability to understand and to apply basic financial concepts (*i.e.*, profit/loss, loss control, variance, *etc.*) to the management and stewardship of the company's operations, and to understand the relevance of a specific job activity or function to the company operations and objectives as a whole.

WHAT IS INVOLVED? THE ABILITY TO:

* assess any implications, problems, decisions, plans and results from a financial viewpoint through a basic understanding and application of financial principles;
* understand the relevance of jobs, activities or functions, both internally and externally (*i.e.*, to the industry, economy and political environment), in which operations take place;
* develop priorities and work plans based on the company objectives; and
* participate in interdepartmental task forces or committees working on loss control/risk management concerns.

Negotiating

The ability to interact with internal and external parties, with a view to making joint decisions when the involved parties have different preferences.

WHAT IS INVOLVED? THE ABILITY TO:

* negotiate wisely on the issues, and diplomatically with the people involved. The discussions are two-way and designed to reach an agreement where both parties have some interests that are shared, and others that are opposed; and
* quickly understand and/or calculate the implications of proposed actions and decisions prior to agreements, and utilize this technique to improve the company's position.

Information Systems

The ability to access computer systems for daily activities and familiarity with the application of computer technology related to disability management functioning.

WHAT IS INVOLVED? THE ABILITY TO:

* use existing computer technology (*e.g.*, electronic mail, employee health monitoring systems, loss control management systems, electronic spread sheets, *etc.*) in daily work situations; and
* apply the understanding of computer technology to develop or enhance the current disability management functioning.

Consulting

The ability to provide temporary professional help to assist a client in addressing current or potential problems, or opportunities.

WHAT IS INVOLVED? THE ABILITY TO:

- help the client discover problems and to facilitate the assessment of the client's needs and willingness to change;
- ensure clarity of roles, responsibilities and resources through formal, and/or informal, contracting with the client;
- gather and present facts, observations, opinions and feelings that assist the client to define problems;
- coordinate the implementation of one or more interventions (*i.e.*, resource, expert or process) which successfully and productively address the defined problems in a manner that is fully supported by the client;
- evaluate the effectiveness of the intervention and identify any further actions required;
- develop self-sufficiency in the client-system in order to minimize dependence on the consultant, and to ensure a minimum of stress during disengagement; and
- assume any of the varying roles of a consultant as an advocate, technical specialist, trainer or educator, collaborator in problem-solving, identifier of alternatives, fact-finder, process specialist or reflector.

Process Facilitation

The ability to introduce and steward a process to assist a client or group to achieve the desired results in an effective, collaborative manner.

WHAT IS INVOLVED? THE ABILITY TO:

- develop methods for groups to use to examine, discuss, problem-solve, evaluate and/or come to agreements within time constraints and with available resources;
- use techniques (*e.g.*, brainstorming) that will encourage involvement of group members, yielding more information, ideas and better solutions to problems;
- create a climate in which group members feel free to express their opinions and beliefs, and will respect the opinions and beliefs of others;
- build a sense of teamwork among group members which can carry over to other work situations; and
- manage conflict so that a "win-win" resolution occurs.

Performance Management

The ability to plan, monitor and evaluate the individual performance and development of the employees reporting to the position of the Disability Management Coordinator.

WHAT IS INVOLVED? THE ABILITY TO:

- plan the work to be accomplished and set performance standards jointly with employees;
- provide ongoing coaching and feedback to improve performance; and
- objectively review accomplishments.

Employee Development

The ability to define the developmental experiences required to enhance an employee's job performance, and to prepare the employee for future responsibilities.

WHAT IS INVOLVED? THE ABILITY TO:

- assist employees to examine personal career interests;
- identify and initiate with employees the appropriate developmental activities (*e.g.*, special assignments, projects, on-the-job coaching) to achieve their personal developmental goals; and
- establish with employees a plan to achieve developmental goals based on realistic opportunities for development within the company.

Education

The ability to effectively instruct clients on various topics.

WHAT IS INVOLVED? THE ABILITY TO:

- determine the learning needs of the target audience;
- identify the desired level of learning to be attained through the educational experience;
- establish the educational objectives and targets;
- design an educational approach that will suit the client's needs;
- prepare for the educational session;
- implement the educational session;
- evaluate the educational objectives and targets; and
- institute changes if warranted.

Training

The ability to provide clients with the skills and attitudes required to accomplish a task, and to remain current regarding future changes.

WHAT IS INVOLVED? THE ABILITY TO:

- analyze and define the client's needs so that the training is relevant and useful;
- design training that will suit the client's needs, and to know existing training tools and modify them accordingly;
- apply appropriate training techniques to ensure that participants gain the required competency and/or knowledge levels;
- evaluate the training objectives; and
- institute changes if warranted.

Change Management

The ability to anticipate and to plan proactively for major changes impacting the company's operations.

WHAT IS INVOLVED? THE ABILITY TO:

- redirect goals and objectives with flexibility and with minimal disruption to ongoing company operations; and
- provide the appropriate leadership to those affected by major changes so that performance and productivity are maintained or enhanced.

Presentation Skills

The ability to orally convey facts, concepts and reasoning to a group, and to receive feedback from that group.

WHAT IS INVOLVED? THE ABILITY TO:

- communicate orally in a clear and concise manner in order to generate understanding by others;
- use various audio-visual aids (*i.e.*, slides, overheads, video programs, *etc.*) to enhance the communication process; and
- listen effectively to facts, feelings and intentions generated by the group, and coherently summarize group reactions.

Risk Communications

The exchange of information among interested parties about the nature, magnitude, significance or control of a risk. Interested parties include individual citizens or communities, unions, scientists, government or industry associations.

WHAT IS INVOLVED? THE ABILITY TO:

- have an in-depth knowledge of risk communication research;
- have an in-depth understanding of the knowledge, attitudes and perceptions of the target audience;

- develop trust and credibility with audience;
- organize content meaningfully and interpret risks;
- present facts and figures effectively, and organize comprehensible arguments to be acted upon; and
- respond effectively to difficult health, safety or environmental questions.

2. RELATIONSHIP SKILLS

Communication

The ability to convey facts, concepts or reasoning clearly to others, and to receive and understand the communication of others.

WHAT IS INVOLVED? THE ABILITY TO:

- communicate in a clear and concise manner to facilitate comprehension of the message;
- understand communication of others through careful listening for facts, feelings and intentions; and
- apply communication skills effectively in meetings, presentations, discussions and in writing.

Interpersonal Skills

The ability to form and to maintain effective working relationships with individuals or groups.

WHAT IS INVOLVED? THE ABILITY TO:

- resolve situations effectively where the feelings and attitudes of others may threaten individual or group performance;
- demonstrate an awareness of and understanding of people and their feelings;
- apply a practical and effective method of coping with interpersonal differences; and
- listen effectively and be willing to consider other points of view.

Team-building

The ability to plan steps designed to gather and analyze data on group functioning and to implement changes to increase group effectiveness.

WHAT IS INVOLVED? THE ABILITY TO:

- identify whether a problem exists;
- gather information on the level of group functioning in regards to task and relationship behaviours;

- analyze and interpret the data;
- decide on a plan of action;
- implement plans to move the group towards a mature stage of decision-making and performance; and
- evaluate the results.

Teamwork

Teamwork involves a group of people working together to pool their skills, talents and knowledge to address specific problems and arrive at solutions.

WHAT IS INVOLVED? THE ABILITY TO:

- develop a foundation of mutual respect, cooperation, open communication and flexible ties in an employee group; and
- collectively use this foundation to problem-solve, make decisions and achieve quality results and continuous improvement.

Mentoring

The process of coaching employees/other Disability Management professionals/practitioners to learn a new role.

WHAT IS INVOLVED? THE ABILITY TO:

- guide employees towards career development both within and outside the organizational group;
- provide a supportive work experience and challenging perspectives; and
- empower employees to achieve their career goals.

Reputation Management

The process of establishing and maintaining the esteem of the internal and external public regarding the company's disability management responsibility.

WHAT IS INVOLVED? THE ABILITY TO:

- maintain high standards for the Disability Management Program;
- support internal and external groups in their endeavours to safely function in business;
- be an active member of corporate, community and professional groups involved in disability management and occupational health and safety practices/issues; and
- support Canadian research and other efforts towards improving disability management practices.

3. TECHNICAL/SPECIALIST SKILLS

Counselling

The process of helping employees (clients) manage health and psychosocial problems.

WHAT IS INVOLVED? THE ABILITY TO:

- develop a healthy client relationship based on mutual trust and respect;
- assist the client in exploring and clarifying problem situations or opportunities for involvement;
- help the client to interpret and understand experiences, behaviour and feelings; explore consequences of behaviour; and move to action;
- contract with the client to commit to specific goals;
- provide challenging and supportive feedback to the client; and
- identify and refer the client to appropriate professional experts to enhance skill and knowledge development.

Health Promotion

The process of enabling individuals and groups to control and to improve their health.

WHAT IS INVOLVED? THE ABILITY TO:

- effectively counsel individuals to make decisions and take actions in the interest of their own health;
- motivate behavioural changes and elicit social support through effective group presentations;
- network and negotiate with external resources, as well as to analyze health and research findings in an effort to identify healthy approaches to behavioural and organizational change;
- plan, develop, implement and evaluate programs so that they become effective, efficient and quality-assured; and
- create an organizational climate which effectively responds to major health challenges through consultations, partnerships and healthy public policy development.

Professional Networking

The process of establishing relationships with community professionals to best serve the needs of employees and the organization.

WHAT IS INVOLVED? THE ABILITY TO:

- identify and maintain health-related resource lists which include agencies, organizations, professionals, self-help groups, and the ability to appropriately refer employees;
- develop working relationships with the employees' physicians to ensure that fitness-for-work standards are met;
- select and designate through agreement, or contract, specialists and specialist functions (*i.e.*, service providers, rehabilitation units, treatment centres, clinics, *etc.*) to serve the needs of the company; and
- assess the quality of services provided to the company, and to monitor the fee-for-service costs.

Fitness-to-Work Evaluation

The ability to determine suitability of an individual or group's health in relation to the job and work environment.

WHAT IS INVOLVED? THE ABILITY TO:

- evaluate physical and psychosocial health of individuals or groups;
- understand the physical, chemical, biological and psychological impact of a job on individuals and groups;
- network with internal and external resources to communicate and resolve issues;
- effectively advise individuals and managers by providing expert information, defining limitations and producing alternative approaches; and
- maintain privacy and confidentiality of medical information.

Human Factor Analysis

The process of analyzing the relationship between people, technology and organizational systems to optimize organizational goals and human health.

WHAT IS INVOLVED? THE ABILITY TO:

- assess the impact of psychological and psychosocial stressors, technology and organizational systems on human health;
- recognize the health needs of a diverse employee population, and to utilize this information when adapting workplace technology and systems to optimize human performance;
- identify individual and group health concerns, and to recommend appropriate ergonomic, organizational and system changes; and
- communicate and teach about the relationship between humans and work systems and the potential related health impacts.

Worksite Evaluation

The ability to assess worksites for physical, chemical, biological, safety and psychosocial hazards, and to recommend corrective activities.

WHAT IS INVOLVED? THE ABILITY TO:

- analyze worksites effectively for the purpose of identification and evaluation of places, processes and products potentially detrimental to health;
- understand legal, political and organizational parameters which can impact health, safety and environmental issues and solutions; and
- consult and negotiate with internal and external resources to ensure corrective actions.

Risk Assessment

The ability to evaluate environment, health and safety risks to employees and the public that may arise from company operations.

WHAT IS INVOLVED? THE ABILITY TO:

- identify and characterize risk;
- assess the risk of current or potential operations quantitatively by evaluating research and by using risk-management models;
- critically evaluate risk assessment done by regulators and other outside parties, and to determine whether appropriate theories and models have been used in their assessment of risk; and
- communicate risks and uncertainties to management, government and the public in a manner that the audience understands, and that allows for informed decision-making.

Quality Assurance

The ability to assure a high level of excellence in Disability Management Programs and servicing.

WHAT IS INVOLVED? THE ABILITY TO:

- set standards for programs and professional practices;
- monitor/audit programs, practices and results;
- interpret and evaluate data collected;
- recommend and ensure corrective action; and
- recommend and communicate positive practices.

Regulatory Compliance

The process of managing the company's statutory obligations regarding disability management.

WHAT IS INVOLVED? THE ABILITY TO:

- assess and forecast areas of regulatory concerns and their potential impact;
- negotiate with government agencies directly, or through industry associations, to address regulatory issues; and
- recommend specific actions in environmental, health and safety areas for addressing present and future operational compliance.

Technical Communication

The ability to research, analyze, transform and present technical data into a format understandable by targeted groups.

WHAT IS INVOLVED? THE ABILITY TO:

- research and analyze technical data from numerous sources;
- recognize the characteristics of risk perception to identify concerns and account for typical reactions of client groups;
- transform technical information accurately into the appropriate communication format (*i.e.*, oral or written forums); and
- communicate the data in a format understandable to targeted sub-groups (*i.e.*, unions, employees, management, community and government) and to address their questions, concerns and issues.

Case Management

The planned coordination of activities to maintain, or rehabilitate, an employee to an optimal level of functioning and gainful employment without risk to the health of the employee or fellow workers.

WHAT IS INVOLVED? THE ABILITY TO:

- identify at an early stage the employees who may require a managed, coordinated return-to-work rehabilitation effort;
- assess physical, medical, psychological and job factors, and to develop a proactive intervention approach;
- assist employees and managers with re-entry to the workplace and with accommodation strategies while monitoring the impact on their health;
- coordinate activities with community and human resources systems to effectively manage re-employment with minimal organizational disruptions; and

- collect and to provide population data reports on incidence rates and trends while identifying system issues and providing recommended solutions.

Auditing

The process to systematically examine the Disability Management Program performance for the purposes of evaluating and reporting on company operations and of being compliant with company standards and regulatory requirements.

WHAT IS INVOLVED? THE ABILITY TO:

- evaluate management systems and processes objectively in order to determine the level of risk that exists for the company;
- compare analytical results with standard requirements;
- anticipate potential risks and to recommend proactive plans to address them; and
- communicate the audit results to appropriate parties effectively, and to take effective action on audit feedback.

Program Evaluation

The examination of whether a program has met its objectives, of other consequences that have occurred because of the program, and of whether the program's structure and activities are relevant and appropriate in terms of the program, company and government goals and changing conditions.

WHAT IS INVOLVED? THE ABILITY TO:

- use research-based examination techniques to demonstrate program accountability;
- analyze findings to improve, amend, replace or dispense with an element of the program;
- estimate the consequences of program changes;
- allocate, or reallocate resources; and
- monitor the program costs.

Social Marketing

The process of applying organizational analysis, planning and control to problems associated with social change in order to persuade different groups to accept the recommended ideas, concepts and actions.

WHAT IS INVOLVED? THE ABILITY TO:

- analyze situations through the use of quantitative research (*i.e.*, survey, polls, *etc.*) and qualitative research (*i.e.*, in-depth interviews, focus groups, *etc.*) to assess the competition and to review the current situation;
- develop communication strategies for target groups. This requires consideration of the group's psychological, demographic and health characteristics;
- position information, through the use of marketing tools (*i.e.*, public relations, promotions, distribution and response channels, *etc.*), so that it is heard; and
- measure the effectiveness of the implemented strategies on health and social change within the population groups.

Strategic Issues Management

Disability Management Strategic Issues Management links major health and safety issues to the corporate strategic business plans.

WHAT IS INVOLVED? THE ABILITY TO:

- understand the complex state of health issues and their potential opportunities and risks for the corporation;
- use an array of relationship skills (*i.e.*, consult, negotiate, interact, *etc.*) to incorporate a strategy that addresses the environmental, health and safety issues into the corporation's business direction; and
- report systematically the company's progress on the implementation of recommended programs.

CHAPTER REFERENCES

Case Management Society of America (CMSA), *Standards for Practice of Case Management* (Little Rock, AR: CMSA, 1995).

The City of Medicine Hat personnel coined a term to describe an attendance management program as described in Chapter 9, "Workplace Attendance Support and Assistance".

Chapter 5

An Integrated Disability Management Program: The Managed Rehabilitative Care Program[1]

This chapter describes the functioning of an Integrated Disability Management Program. In 1989, Marilyn Walker, BScN, coined the phrase "Managed Rehabilitative Care". "Managed" indicates that the process is monitored and controlled. The word "Rehabilitative" denotes the nature and the intent of the program. "Care" symbolizes the overall sentiment and objective for the program. In this chapter, the term, "Managed Rehabilitative Care", is used to denote an Integrated Disability Management Program.

WHAT IS MANAGED REHABILITATIVE CARE?

Managed Rehabilitative Care is a comprehensive approach towards accommodating ill or injured employees back into the workplace as soon as they are medically fit to function without harm to themselves or others. Goal-oriented and gainful work is offered to eligible employees in the form of modified/ alternate work on a temporary basis, or alternate work on a permanent basis.

The key objectives of an integrated disability management program are to:

- deliver consistent recovery support and return-to-work assistance to ill/ injured employees in a safe and timely manner;
- prevent the human costs associated with disability;
- support business and operational interests for a safe and timely return to work by the employee;
- reduce the lost work time and related disability costs;
- attain employee, company, and union satisfaction with the program and processes; and
- comply with the applicable legislation.

[1] Excerpts taken from: D. Dyck, "Managed Rehabilitative Care: Overview for Occupational Health Nurses" (1996) 44:1 AAOHN Journal 18. Reprinted with permission from the AAOHN Journal.

WHY IS IT IMPORTANT?

There are many warning signs that may alert a company to problems associated with the management of short-term disability, long-term disability and Workers' Compensation Board programs, such as:

- significant numbers of employees taking advantage of the short-term disability plan with minimal or non-existent use of rehabilitation;
- unquestioned acceptance of report of absence claims signed by personal physicians and submitted by employees as proof of qualification for short-term disability;
- increasing short-term disability and long-term disability plan costs;
- rising prescription drug and supplementary health care utilization and costs;
- a shift in the employee absence reasons to include an increasing number of stress claims;
- concern that there is minimal integration, or monitoring, between the short-term disability and long-term disability plans; and
- receipt of employee personal health information without a mechanism for confidential data management.

Organizations should be prepared to provide rehabilitative care to ill or injured employees in an effective, efficient and managed approach, namely via a Disability Management Program.

WHO DOES MANAGED REHABILITATIVE CARE BENEFIT?

A Managed Rehabilitative Care Program benefits the employee, the company, the union, and both the provincial Workers' Compensation Boards and third party private insurance carriers. In Chapter 1, "Disability Management: Overview", the value of an Integrated Disability Management Program to stakeholders was discussed. As was indicated, both the employer and employee benefit from getting employees back to work in a safe and timely fashion. Insurers recognize this, and over the past 18 years they have been actively endorsing early intervention and graduated return-to-work programs.

BACKGROUND HISTORY

Current Statistics: Canada and the United States

In 2007, 8.8 per cent of full-time Canadian workers missed time from work.[2] This equates to a loss of 4.1 per cent of the scheduled workweek and a total of 113 million workdays by full-time workers.[3]

---

[2] Statistics Canada, *Work Absence Rates, 2007*, Cat. No. 71-211-XWE (Ottawa: Statistics Canada, May 2008).

[3] *Ibid.*

Historically in Canada, 1991, the related disability costs in Canada were approximately $1,112 per employee per annum.[4] Today, based on an eight-hour day and the average daily earning of $167.44,[5] the average direct disability costs for the Canadian workforce are approximately $1,708 per full time worker.[6] In the United States, employers paid $4,581 per employee as total disability costs and $2,685 in medical costs.[7]

In 1991, 63 per cent of the Canadian workforce was between the ages of 20 and 62 years.[8] By 2001, Canada's working-age population was made up of a higher number of older workers. The number of workers aged 45-64 years of age had increased by 35.8 per cent and the median age of Canadian workers reached an all-time high of 37.6 years.[9] As of 2008, the average age of Canadian workers was 41 years of age,[10] with the median age group being between 45-49 years.[11]

Not surprisingly the number of lost time workdays increased as well, with older workers experiencing more lost days due to illness than did their younger co-workers. In 2001, older workers missed more workdays than did workers in any other age category.[12] Workers aged 55-64 years missed an average of 11.1 days, while younger workers (15-19 years) missed an average of 5.2 days.[13] Today, this phenomenon continues, with workers aged 55-64 years missing an

---

[4]   Peat, Marwick, Stevenson & Kellogg, *Data Produced on 1991 Employee Benefit Costs in Canada* (1993) [unpublished].

[5]   Statistics Canada, *Average Hourly Wages of Employees by Selected Characteristics*, available online at: <http://www40.statcan.ca/l01/cst01/labr69a-eng.htm>.

[6]   Calculated by multiplying the average number of missed workdays per full-time employee (10.2 lost days) by the average daily wage for full-time Canadian employees as of November 2007 ($167.44 per day). Data obtained from: Statistics Canada, *Work Absence Rates, 2007*, Cat. No. 71-211-XWE (Ottawa: Statistics Canada, May 2008); and Statistics Canada, *Average Hourly Wages of Employees by Selected Characteristics*, *ibid.*

[7]   Work Loss Data Institute, *Disability Benchmarks by Major Diagnostic Category* (Corpus Christi, TX: Work Loss Data Institute, 2002).

[8]   Peat, Marwick, Stevenson & Kellogg, Data Produced on 1991 Employee Benefit Costs in Canada (1993) [unpublished].

[9]   Statistics Canada, 2001 *Census, Release 2 — July 16, 2002* (Ottawa: Statistics Canada 2002), available online at: <http://www12.statcan.ca/english/census01/release/age_sex.cfm>.

[10] Canadian Centre for Occupational Health & Safety, *Aging Workers* (2002), available online at: <http://www.ccohs.ca/oshanswers/psychosocial/aging_workers.html>.

[11] Statistics Canada, *Population by Sex and Age Group*, available online at: <http://www40.statcan.ca/l01/cst01/demo10a-eng.htm>; and Statistics Canada, 2006 Census Data, *Generation Status (4), Age Groups (9) and Sex (3) for the Population 15 Years and Over of Canada, Provinces and Territories, 1971, 2001 and 2006 Censuses - 20% Sample Data*, available online at: <http://www12.statcan.ca/english/census06/data/topics/Index.cfm?Temporal=2006&APATH=7&FREE=0&FL=G>.

[12] Peat, Marwick, Stevenson & Kellogg, Data Produced on 1991 Employee Benefit Costs in Canada (1993) [unpublished].

[13] Statistics Canada, *Average Hourly Wages of Employees by Selected Characteristics*, available online at: <http://www40.statcan.ca/l01/cst01/labr69a-eng.htm>.

average of 11.4 days, while younger workers (15-19 years) missed an average of 5.9 days.[14]

Work Absence Costs

Work absence costs stem from occupational illness and injury, non-occupational illness and injury, and unscheduled absence costs. In this chapter, only the first two types of work absence costs will be addressed — the unscheduled absence costs are addressed in Chapter 9, "Workplace Attendance Support & Assistance".

In a time of shrinking profits and tough market competition, the rising costs of disability and Workers' Compensation Board rates tend to tax company budgets. A review of the Workers' Compensation Premium Assessment Rates indicates that on average, Canadian employers pay $1.98 per $100 of payroll for WCB coverage.[15] For a company with an average payroll of $46M, this would equate to $896,069 in Workers' Compensation premium per year. The total WCB assessment premiums paid by Canadian employers in 2007, equates to $5.1B for insurance coverage against occupational disability costs.[16]

Add to the above the costs for non-occupational illness/injury, which tend to be more numerous and lengthy in nature. The estimated cost to Canadian employers of occupational and non-occupational (short- and long-term) disabilities, and unscheduled absences is 5.31 per cent of payroll.[17] In the United States, the current estimate is that the direct and indirect absence costs associated with sick leave, short-term, long-term, and workers' compensation disabilities total 9.2 per cent of payroll.[18]

To provide a picture of what work absence costs could look like, Nagel[19] estimated the direct financial or productivity costs for employee absences per full-time employee. Using the 2007 Canadian worker absence data and Nagel's model (Figure 5.1), the cost of absence for companies of various sizes would be as follows:

Number of employees × Days Absent × Wage per day = Lost Time Cost

---

[14]   Statistics Canada, *Work Absence Rates, 2007*, Cat. No. 71-211-XWE (Ottawa: Statistics Canada, May 2008).

[15]   Association of Workers' Compensation Boards of Canada, *Key Statistical Measures for 2007* (December 2008), available online at: <http://www.awcbc.org/common/assets/ksms/2007ksms.pdf>.

[16]   *Ibid.*

[17]   Watson-Wyatt, *Staying@Work: Effective Presence at Work* (2007), at 6, available online at: <https://www.watsonwyatt.com>.

[18]   Mercer Inc., *The Total Financial Impact of Employee Absences — Survey Highlights* (October 2008), at 4, available online at: <http://www.kronos.com/absenceanonymous/media/Mercer-Survey-Highlights.pdf>.

[19]   K. Nagel, "Total Organizational Health Costs: What Are They? What Can Organizations Do About Them?" (Presented at the Strategic Leadership Forum '99, Toronto, Ontario, 20 October 1999) [unpublished].

Figure 5.1: Productivity Costs for Employee Absence

Number of employees	Days Absent (Average/ employee[20])	Wage/Day (8 hr) (Two ranges**)	Estimated Lost Time Cost for Each Wage Scenario (Two ranges***)
1 - 99	10.2 days	$160 – $240	$161,568 – $242,352
100 - 199	10.2 days	$160 – $240	$324,768 – $487,152
500 – 1,999	10.2 days	**$160 – $240**	$3,262,368 – $4,893,552
2,000 – 4,999	10.2 days	**$160 – $240**	$8,158,368 – $12,237,552
5,000 – 10,000	10.2 days	**$160 – $240**	$16,320,000 – $24,480,000

** Based on an earnings range of $20 – $30 per hour
*** Based on an end point for the range

It is important for employers to remember that disability dollars are "after tax dollars", which means that organizations have to produce a certain quantity of product, or provide a certain amount of services, to pay for their disability costs. Clearly worker absence is expensive and the reality is that short-term disability, long-term disability, and Workers' Compensation Board costs are expected to continue to escalate primarily due to an aging population and the increased cost of health care.

Source of Disability Costs

The costs associated with illness or injury-related absences may arise from:

- paid employee sick leave, weekly indemnity, and/or short-term disability insurance costs;
- salary for replacement workers;
- health care benefits;
- extended supplementary health care benefits;
- rising provincial Workers' Compensation Board rates;
- long-term disability insurance premium rates and costs;
- supervisory time to reschedule work;
- supervisory time to work with the disabled employee;
- disability claim and case management time and costs;
- recruitment and training of replacement workers;
- lowered employee morale;
- lowered productivity; and
- lost business opportunities.

---

[20] Statistics Canada, *Average Hourly Wages of Employees by Selected Characteristics*, available online at: <http://www40.statcan.ca/l01/cst01/labr69a-eng.htm>.

The number of long-term disability insurance claims has been increasing due to the impact of an aging workforce and the following seven factors:

1. *Difficult economic conditions* — Experience has shown that, with a downturn in the economy, more employees opt for long-term disability. Employees with disabilities, who have been balancing work and health issues, tend to apply for long-term disability as opposed to continuing to struggle to work.

2. *Dual income families* — Some families can manage financially on long-term disability benefits if at least one steady full-time income continues to be earned.

3. *Changing disabilities* — New categories of disability, "hot illnesses", have been accepted as valid reasons for long-term disability. These "hot illnesses" include conditions such as stress, sick building syndrome, chronic fatigue syndrome, multiple chemical sensitivities and repetitive strain injuries.

4. *Change in work ethics* — Long-term disability insurance coverage is now more socially acceptable to apply for and receive than it used to be. [21]

5. *Changing worker demographics in the workplace* — Having, for the first time, four generations in the workplace brings with it increased worker medical absences and disabilities. The impact of this phenomenon is discussed in more depth in Chapter 22, "Disability Management: Impact of Four Generations in the Workplace".

6. *Increased work demands and pressures* — Employees who could return to work doing a "basic" level of work are challenged to work at a higher level and greater work pace. In some instances, cross-functional activities are required. For these reasons, employees are unable to remain in the changing world of work.

7. *Increased number of Illness/Injuries with Strong Psychological Overtones* — The most difficult disability situations to manage and successfully resolve are the ones in which significant psychological overtones negatively impact the employee's ability to return to work. Successful management of this type of disability claim is described in Chapters 7, 8, 9, 15, 16, and 17.

In this day and age, the issues of early intervention and effective rehabilitation of injured/ill employees should be of concern to all companies. The degree of commitment that a company has in managing employee absence can, and does, directly affect the company's disability costs and Workers' Compensation Board rates. The good news is that companies can take an

---

[21]   Great West Life, "Coordinated Disability Care" (Presentation to Petro-Canada, Calgary, Alberta, 1993) [unpublished].

"upstream"[22] approach to the problem; that is, they can be proactive in managing employee medical absences and can realize significant cost savings. The alternative to proactive management is a cycle of steadily increasing absence and disability costs that can erode company profits. **"Downstream"**[23] approaches to remedy the situation always take more time and money.

MANAGED REHABILITATIVE CARE PROGRAM: PURPOSE

An Integrated Disability Management Program, like the Managed Rehabilitative Care Program, is designed to maintain the health of employees and the integrity of corporate short-term disability, long-term disability, and Workers' Compensation Board plans. The Managed Rehabilitative Care Program is an effective method of returning healthy employees to work while contributing to cost-containment.

The development, introduction and implementation of a Managed Rehabilitative Care framework for the organization have broader and possibly more significant implications for companies. It can:

- institute an effective administrative process for managing absences due to illness/injury;
- facilitate the rehabilitation of employees to an optimal level of health and capability through modified/alternate work and a process of **work hardening** thereby expediting a graduated return to work;
- convey a sense of concern for employees, and ultimately convey the message that employees are valued;
- promote the image of a caring and responsible employer while contributing to employee and community morale;
- respond to the corporate vision of providing employees with a safe and healthy workplace, and uphold a company's social and moral obligations; and
- provide a forum in which management and unions can work together towards a common goal, the rehabilitation of ill/injured employees and the prevention of similar illnesses and injuries.

More specifically, an Integrated Disability Management Program such as the Managed Rehabilitative Care Program can help demonstrate compliance with the "duty to accommodate" legislation which is law in all Canadian provinces.[24] As well, with the recent changes in the Canadian Workers' Compensation Board

---

[22] In business, the term "upstream" refers to the product/service research, development, production, and refinement activities. In terms of disability management, upstream activities are all the activities that occur to prevent employee illness/injury.

[23] In business, the term "downstream" relates to the product/service marketing, retail, transportation, handling, storage, use, and disposal activities. In terms of disability management, downstream activities are all the activities that occur once an illness/injury has occurred.

[24] Ontario Human Rights Commission, *Guidelines for Assessing Accommodation Requirements for Persons with Disabilities* (Toronto: Ontario Human Rights Commission, 1990).

and human rights legislation, new pressures for workplace accommodation of the disabled worker are being placed on organizations. Accommodation to the point of "undue hardship" can mean workplace, and/or work-duty modifications, or even necessitate the creation of alternate positions.[25]

GENERAL FACTS

An overwhelming majority (80 per cent to 85 per cent) of injured, ill or disabled employees return to work without any difficulty.[26] However, for approximately 15 per cent to 20 per cent of employees on short-term disability, long-term disability, or Workers' Compensation, their disability provokes a constellation of personal, emotional, and work-related issues that may delay their return to work.[27] The existence of person-job mismatch, workplace discord, and performance problems are the best indicators of a prolonged absence from work due to illness or injury.

Some of the factors associated with a delay in an employee's return to work are:

- the absence of graduated return-to-work opportunities;
- time lags in obtaining medical care or other forms of therapy;
- lack of knowledge on the part of the community practitioner about the workplace and what accommodations can be made for the disabled employee;
- disability insurance plans that promote a "reward" for being disabled;[28]
- unreliable methods for tracking the ill or injured worker;
- employee fear of losing disability income if he or she attempts an unsuccessful return to work;[29]
- physical/psychological pain;
- employee fear of relapse or re-injury;[30]
- employee anxiety concerning poor job performance due to disability;
- decreased self-confidence;[31]
- a work situation perceived as intolerable by the employee;
- a negative industrial relations climate;
- layoffs due to "downsizing";
- cultural differences in illness/injury response;

---

[25] L. Steeves & R. Smithies, "Foresight is Your Best Defence" (1996) 4:2 Group Health Care Management 29.

[26] Petro-Canada Inc., *Managed Rehabilitative Care Program, Occupational Health* (Calgary: Petro-Canada, 1990).

[27] *Ibid.*

[28] P. Booth, *Employee Absenteeism: Strategies for Promoting an Attendance-Oriented Corporate Culture* (Ottawa: The Conference Board of Canada, 1993) at 2.

[29] L. Gross, "Managing Your Escalating Health and Safety Costs" (Presented to the Petroleum Industry's Annual Safety Seminar, Alberta, May 1993) [unpublished].

[30] *Ibid.*

[31] *Ibid.*

- few or limited social credits and supports (refer to Chapter 15, "Disability Management: The Social-Capital Theory-Perspective for Managing Disability Claims", for details on social credits);
- a breakdown in communication between the employee and employer; and
- lack of understanding by all stakeholders of the real costs associated with disability.

Since there are many reasons for the existence of these barriers to returning to work, it takes a concerted effort by employers, unions, employees, and health care professionals to overcome them.

In comparison, the factors associated with a timely return to work are:

- job satisfaction;
- mutual respect for the employee/supervisor;
- open communication between the supervisor and employee;
- strong social acceptance and credits;
- existence of graduated return-to-work opportunities; and
- the use of a team approach (*i.e.*, employee, supervisor, union, insurance company, human resource professionals, personal physician, occupational health professionals, *etc.*) towards a graduated return to work with the employee being the key player.

The objective of an Integrated Disability Management Program, such as the Managed Rehabilitative Care Program, is to promote a safe and timely return to work. The challenge is to reinforce the drivers to return to work, and to mitigate barriers standing in their way.

Occupational health professionals have the expertise and, with management/ union approval, can be given the responsibility to provide a planned approach to minimize barriers so that employees can return to work in a timely fashion without risk to their health, or to the health of others.

TERMINOLOGY

Disability is the loss or reduction of functional ability and activity consequent to impairment.[32] This is the reduction of the ability to "do things" such as performing movements or tasks.

Integrated Disability Management Program is a planned and coordinated approach to facilitate and manage employee health and productivity. It is a human resource risk management and risk communication approach designed to integrate all organizational/company programs and resources to minimize or reduce the losses and costs associated with employee medical absence regardless of the nature of those disabilities.

---

[32] World Health Organization, *International Classification of Impairment, Disabilities and Handicaps* (Geneva: World Health Organization, 1980).

Managed Rehabilitative Care is an approach towards accommodating ill or injured employees back into the workplace. Goal-oriented and gainful work is offered to eligible employees in the form of modified or alternate work. The aspects of the Managed Rehabilitative Care Program include:

- liaison between the workplace, management, union, employees, community, health care services and third party insurance carriers;
- client advocacy;
- provision of graduated return-to-work opportunities; and
- claims management and case management.

Early intervention is an employer-initiated response to a worker's medical absence that occurs within three to five days from the onset of the illness/injury. The intent is to facilitate appropriate and timely treatment, rehabilitation and return to work. In Chapter 1, "Disability Management: Overview", the rationale for early intervention was discussed.

Liaison is the position, or responsibility, within an organization for maintaining communication links with external individuals, agencies or organizations.

Client advocacy is the activity associated with pleading or representing an employee's cause to management, or to external individuals or agencies.[33]

Accommodation is the process and implementation of changes to a job which enable a disabled person to perform the job productively and/or to the environment in which the job is accomplished.[34]

Modified/Alternate work is the change of work duties or time to accommodate the individual currently off because of illness or injury. It is any job, task or function, or combination of functions that a worker who suffers from a diminished capacity may safely perform without risk to self or to others, which would not normally be done by that worker. The key ingredient is that the work be gainful with rehabilitation as the ultimate goal.

Modified work is interim work offered to recovering employees, or those experiencing a diminished capacity when it is medically foreseen that the employee will return to his or her own occupation. It includes:

- changing the existing "own" occupation conditions (*i.e.*, hours, duties, responsibilities, *etc.*);
- accommodating workplace restrictions (*i.e.*, lifting, sitting, bending, climbing, driving, *etc.*);
- providing transitional work;
- providing different duties within another occupation/work site;

---

[33]   J. White, "The Evolving Role of Nursing in Patient Advocacy" (May 1992) Canadian Nursing Management 6.

[34]   National Institute of Disability Management and Research (NIDMAR), *Code of Practice for Disability Management* (Port Alberni, BC: NIDMAR, 2000), at 4.

- providing a training opportunity;
- all, or any combination of the above.[35]

Alternate work is a permanent placement offered to recovering employees, or those with diminished capacity, when it is medically determined that the employee will not return to his or her own occupation. It includes:

- changing existing "own" occupation conditions (hours/duties/responsibilities);
- providing different duties within another occupation/worksite; and/or
- providing retraining or job search assistance for movement to a new occupation.[36]

Case management is a collaborative process for assessing, planning, implementing, coordinating, monitoring and evaluating the options and services available to meet an individual's health needs through communication and accessible resources. The intent is to promote quality, cost-effective outcomes to disability management.[37] To rehabilitate an employee to the optimal level of functioning without risk to personal or fellow workers' health, involves specific goals, case coordination and evaluation.

Case management has been used in the fields of nursing and social work to coordinate and develop the use of resources and services. The same process applies to coordinating employment issues for disabled employees. Case management promotes return-to-work efforts, early identification of disability claims for services, and coordination of services, such as: early intervention, maintaining contact with disabled employees, developing modified/alternate work opportunities, monitoring modified/alternate work, coordinating issues with the insurer, and establishing vocational rehabilitation if required.

Claim management is the service provided in administering income loss claims through employee benefit insurance plans such as short-term disability, Workers' Compensation, and long-term disability. This activity includes the determination of eligibility to receive a benefit according to the definition of eligibility contained in the plan contract, the facilitation of income loss replacement, and the processing of the claim towards a resolution or termination.

Rehabilitation is the process of assisting medically disabled employees to adjust to their disabled condition, and to recognize and maximize their financial, occupational, and social goals.[38]

---

[35] Term defined by City of Medicine Hat Disability Management Program Steering Committee (April 1999).

[36] *Ibid.*

[37] Case Management Society of America (CMSA), *Standards for Practice of Case Management* (Little Rock, AR: CMSA, 1995).

[38] B. Anderson, "Disability Claims Management" (Seminar presented by M. Mercier at Westin Hotel, Calgary, Alberta, February 1992) [unpublished].

MANAGED REHABILITATIVE CARE IMPLEMENTATION

Key Stakeholders and Their Roles

A Managed Rehabilitative Care program is a company-wide effort that involves cooperation by employees, supervisors, human resources personnel, and occupational health professionals. Support of the program by senior management and union leaders is essential if program credibility and acceptance is to be established.

SENIOR MANAGEMENT

Management's role in establishing a Managed Rehabilitative Care Program is to endorse, support, and be actively involved in the initiative. Once the decision has been made to develop a Managed Rehabilitative Care Program, the following key steps should be taken:

- involve the workforce and union leaders in the development of the Managed Rehabilitative Care Program and obtain its commitment to the program;
- develop a company policy on Managed Rehabilitative Care and modified/alternate work;
- determine the operational relationship of modified/alternate work with short-term disability, long-term disability, and Workers' Compensation insurance plans;
- reach a formal understanding with unions;
- publicize the program;
- promote the identification of jobs within the organization that would be suitable for modified/alternate work;
- support the development of Managed Rehabilitative Care protocols;
- ensure that middle management and supervisors receive adequate education and training on the effective management of employees, both when they are healthy and when they are ill/injured;
- insist on the establishment of rehabilitation plans for employees unable to return to their own jobs;
- build compliance with the Managed Rehabilitative Care Program into the system for performance appraisals; and
- actively seek "upstream measures" for preventing employee illness/injury.

Broad-based support for the program is important. Experience has shown that the most successful companies have taken the following measures to:

- recognize the capabilities and potential contributions that the injured employee can make to the company;
- recognize that it is good business to have an Integrated Disability Management Program that includes claim management, case management, and graduated return-to-work opportunities;

- involve the employee in his or her rehabilitation process from the onset of illness or injury;
- enlist the cooperation of their unions as early as possible;
- obtain endorsement, support and involvement from all stakeholders;
- reinforce compliance with the Managed Rehabilitative Care Program through performance rewards; and/or
- find ways to prevent/mitigate employee illness/injury.

It is critical for Senior Management to recognize that disability management is a risk management approach, designed to mitigate failures in the organization's Human Resource and Occupational Health & Safety systems. Research indicates that in an organization where a people-oriented work culture exists, and Occupational Health & Safety due diligence and leadership are evident, there are fewer disability claims and lower related costs.[39]

THE UNION

Union support of a Managed Rehabilitative Care Program is crucial. Meetings between senior management and union representatives should occur early so that an understanding about the program objectives and requirements can be reached by both parties. Issues like modified/alternate work and employee benefits while employees are on modified/alternate work are of concern to unions. Likewise, many national unions have developed and gained industry experience with disability management initiatives.

THE EMPLOYEE

The injured or ill employee plays a key role in a successful Managed Rehabilitative Care Program with the chief responsibilities being:

- advise the supervisor of an injury/illness as soon as possible;
- have a report of absence form of some kind completed by his or her treating physician;
- maintain regular contact with the occupational health nurse or company liaison working with the external insurer;
- communicate medical, social, and psychological concerns that may impact the safe and timely return to work;
- take an active role in initiating and developing a modified/alternate work opportunity with the supervisor;
- obtain medical clearance for modified/alternate work;
- communicate any concerns about the functionality of the modified/alternate work experience so that potential problems can be quickly resolved; and

---

[39] R. Williams *et al.*, *A Survey of Disability Management Approaches in Ontario Workplaces*, (Toronto: McMaster University and WSIB Ontario, 2005), at 2, available online at: <http://www.wsib.ca/wsib/wsibsite.nsf/Public/researchresultssurveydisabilitymgnt>.

- when possible, schedule other activities (*i.e.*, physiotherapy, doctor's appointments, *etc.*) so they do not interfere with the modified/alternate work experience.

MIDDLE MANAGEMENT AND SUPERVISORS

The full support of middle management and supervisors is paramount if a Managed Rehabilitative Care Program is to be successful. In essence, this level of management will have the greatest impact on the timely and safe return to work by the employee. For this reason, they need to be well informed about disability management principles, graduated return-to-work practices, the economic benefits of a Managed Rehabilitative Care Program and its positive impacts on employee morale and productivity. Typically, this requirement is met by providing middle management and supervisors with disability management education, thereby enabling them to apply the disability management concepts, principles, and practices. Ongoing coaching and mentoring can be used to reinforce this working knowledge.

The key roles and responsibilities of middle management and supervisors are:

- generating a formal report of absence form when an employee is absent. This form should indicate the nature of the disability (*i.e.*, illness or injury, occupational/non-occupational); prognosis (anticipated return-to-work date and workplace limitations, if any); treatment plan (if the employee is under an appropriate treatment and compliant); and suggested workplace support (*i.e.*, accommodation needs). Sample of forms that could be used for this purpose are provided in Chapter 10, "Disability Management Practice Standards", Appendix 3, Form 2a and Form 2b. Form 2a is designed to be submitted to occupational health services, because it requests confidential medical information. On the other hand, Form 2b is applicable to work settings that are without occupational health support and are limited to specific pieces of information as outlined above;
- participating to provide modified/alternate work opportunities when required;
- supporting employees working modified/alternate work;
- helping the occupational health nurse, or company liaison for an external insurer, to monitor the progress of workers on modified/alternate work; and
- providing feedback on the Managed Rehabilitative Care Program's processes and outcomes.

DISABILITY MANAGEMENT COORDINATORS

Ideally, one person is responsible for the overall program management and the daily operations of a Managed Rehabilitative Care Program.[40] Continuity and consistency are the keys to success of such a program.

---

[40] R. Berresford, J. Farmery & D. Mitchell, *Modified/Alternate Work Guidelines* (Toronto: Aon Consulting, 1993) at 4.

In many companies, this role of Disability Management Coordinator is assumed by an occupational health nurse. The Disability Management Coordinator becomes the first-line contact with the ill or injured employee. Liaison with the employee, workplace and external professionals, client advocacy, case management and program evaluation are roles that occupational health nurses regularly assume.

The Disability Management Coordinator's responsibilities in Integrated Disability Management Programs, such as the Managed Rehabilitative Care Program, include:

- communicating with the employee as soon as possible after the injury or illness onset;
- working with the employee and supervisor to establish recovery and rehabilitation goals and objectives;
- determining what outside professional help is needed, if any;
- liaising with outside professionals and the Workers' Compensation Board, if applicable, on the employee's behalf;
- establishing individual programs for workers with help from other professionals;
- advising the supervisor of an employee's expected return-to-work date, physical capabilities, and work restrictions that may apply;
- if applicable, working with supervisor or management to determine if modified/alternate work opportunities are available;
- respecting the terms of an existent collective agreement in relation to modified/alternate work, if they apply;
- monitoring the progress of employees on modified/alternate work;
- collecting and evaluating Managed Rehabilitative Care Program data; and
- reporting the Managed Rehabilitative Care Program outcomes to management.

Companies that do not have an occupational health nurse employed can purchase similar disability management services from the marketplace. However, these companies still require an internal Disability Management Program and a graduated return-to-work process for the contracted services to be successfully implemented. Often these are managed by human resource professionals/practitioners with advanced education in the field of Disability Management.

HUMAN RESOURCES PROFESSIONALS/PRACTITIONERS

Developing the Managed Rehabilitative Care Program policy and procedures, and employee benefit plans are typically the responsibility of the human resources professionals/practitioners. However, the depth and breadth of their role is much greater than that. Ideally, it includes:

- advertising the intent and goals of the Managed Rehabilitative Care Program;
- communicating the roles and responsibilities of all the key players;
- developing the protocols required to implement the program;
- coaching middle management and supervisors on modified/alternate work possibilities and opportunities;
- developing contractual agreements associated with modified/alternate work; and
- helping with the management of returning workers when performance issues and other workplace issues impede a graduated return to work.

ATTENDING PHYSICIAN

The attending physician is an important link between the employee, the company and the Workers' Compensation Board, if involved. This professional can provide the necessary information regarding the employee's expected return-to-work date, the limitations that may apply and the prognosis of the illness or injury. Ongoing communication between the treating physician and the occupational health nurse, disability management service provider, or external insurer is essential. This helps to prevent misunderstandings among the stakeholders and prolonged employee absences.

Management of Health Care and Personal Problems

Most Disability Management Coordinators and Occupational Health Nurses recognize that employees would rather be at work, productive, and earning a living, instead of being at home collecting disability benefits. Likewise, most employers want their ill/injured employees to return to productive work.[41] The challenge for Disability Management Coordinators and Occupational Health Nurses is to broker a "win-win" outcome for both parties. A collaborative approach between the employee, manager/supervisor, union representative (where applicable), and occupational health nurse is required to successfully manage employee health problems.

When job performance appears to be affected by employee health or personal problems, the manager/supervisor can address them by:

- identifying corporate expectations for the employee's level of performance;
- reviewing the employee's actual performance or conduct;
- explaining the consequences of performance deficiencies and attempting to identify any personal or job barriers to corrective action;

---

[41] E. Quick, "Disability Management that Works" (January/February 2007) Benefit Solutions Magazine 44, available online at: <http://old.bcsolutionsmag.com/archives.asp>.

- referring the employee for help if a health problem is suspected or admitted (see Chapter 3, "The Supportive Infrastructure for an Integrated Disability Management Program", Figure 3.4); and
- referring the employee for Employee Assistance Program help if a personal or work-related problem is suspected or admitted (see Chapter 3, Figure 3.5).

The *supervisor or union representative*, if applicable, should not attempt to diagnose the problem. They do not have the right to know the details of the employee's medical and/or personal problems. However, the supervisor or union representative needs to know:

- if the illness/injury is work-related;
- the expected return-to-work date;
- the employee's capabilities and work limitations; and
- the expected duration of any work limitations following the employee's return to work.

The *employee* is obliged to:

- provide the employer with a reasonable explanation for absence from work;
- provide the required information from a physician or other health care provider;
- seek and sustain a workable return-to-work opportunity; and
- advise the supervisor or union representative and/or Occupational Health Nurse of the effectiveness of the return-to-work opportunity.

> *In accordance with the Canadian human rights legislation (duty to accommodate) an employee is obliged to maintain open communication with the workplace, to provide adequate medical documentation supporting the absence and to participate in safe and timely return-to-work opportunities.*

The *Disability Management Coordinator* or *Occupational Health Nurse* is the health advisor specializing in providing information to managers/supervisors on employee fitness to work, disability case management, and suitable return-to-work accommodations.

Clinical case management that is undertaken by occupational health nurses is recognized as an effective means to reduce the financial losses associated with disability.[42] Managed Rehabilitative Care guidelines were designed to be applied to the case management of the 15 per cent to 20 per cent of employees having

---

[42] Watson-Wyatt, *Staying@Work: Effective Presence at Work* (2007), at 10, available online at: <https://www.watsonwyatt.com>.

difficulty returning to work from medical disability, whether on short-term disability, long-term disability, or Workers' Compensation.

Managed Rehabilitative Care Guidelines

The Disability Management Coordinator or Occupational Health Nurse, in accordance with recognized professional practice standards, evaluates illness or injury situations with a view to a safe and timely return to work. This includes assessments of the employee and workplace situation; development of a rehabilitation plan; goal setting and coordination of the case; and return-to-work opportunities.

EARLY IDENTIFICATION OF CASES

The criteria for the early identification of employees who require case management coordination include:

- expected duration of disability exceeding one month;
- hospitalization greater than one week;
- Workers' Compensation Board claims that go on longer than one week;
- an employee aged 50 years or older;
- "stress" as the medical diagnosis;
- diagnoses of cardiovascular, cancer, digestive, skeletal, neurological, or psychological conditions;
- multiple diagnoses;
- employee expectations that are out of proportion with the nature of the injury;
- cases which fail just before the expected return-to-work date;
- frequent changes in health caregivers;
- employees with limited social acceptance and support;
- job dissatisfaction;
- presence of labour relations problems;
- presence of performance problems;
- presence of pending litigation associated with the illness or injury;
- an injured or ill employee with a high rate of absenteeism; and
- any multiple of the above.

ASSESSMENT

An early initial contact with the employee is carried out to determine the potential for the illness or injury to become chronic, and to establish whether help is necessary. Some of the factors to be assessed include:

Physical factors, such as the:

- employee's physical capabilities;
- job demands, pace and stressors;

- potential for job modification;
- potential for use of adaptive devices; and
- potential for worksite/environmental modifications.

Personal factors, such as:

- changes in the family prior to and since the onset of the illness or injury;
- the presence of a personal crisis compounding the disability (*i.e.*, legal, domestic problems, job insecurity, *etc.*);
- the cultural orientation to illness/injury and disability management;
- the health status of other family members; and
- how the family dynamics impact the current disability situation.

Vocational factors, such as the:

- degree of job satisfaction;
- occurrence of recent changes at work (*i.e.*, hours, assignment, performance, availability of work, change in management/supervisor, labour unrest, lay offs/restructuring, *etc.*);
- employee's previous work activities and other marketable skills;
- employee's vocational interests and aptitudes; and
- supervisor's and human resource professional's promotion of a graduated return-to-work.

Medical factors, such as:

- diagnosis;
- prognosis;
- treatment plan;
- expected return-to-work date;
- employee confidence and satisfaction with medical treatment;
- potential residual limitations;
- presence of pain and coping skills;
- presence of other health problems; and
- presence of support from an independent practitioner, of nutritional guidance, of adaptive devices, of aids to daily living, of home help, and/or of home care services, *etc.*

Psychological factors, such as:

- the employee's reaction to illness/injury;
- the employee's thoughts and feelings, level of self-esteem, outlook, locus of control, and degree of personal power;
- cultural factors;
- the employee's interests and attitude about work and the illness or injury;
- the employee's reliance on alcohol and/or drugs;
- stress management needs; and
- the employee's willingness to try modified work/alternate work duties.

Performance issues, such as the:

- quality of the relationship between the employee and his or her supervisor;
- quality of relationships with co-workers;
- level of social acceptance and credibility;
- employee's past and recent work performance; and
- past history of absenteeism.

Educational factors, such as the employee's:

- level of formal education; and
- any specialized training.

Financial factors, such as:

- available employee benefits;
- current income;
- financial assets/liabilities; and
- treatment/rehabilitation expenses.

Organizational factors, such as the company's:

- willingness to host case management conferences to expedite a successful graduated return-to-work plan; and
- available resources to meet the employee's rehabilitation needs.

A Rehabilitation Assessment can be done for each short-term disability and Workers' Compensation Board case and recorded on a form such as the one provided in Figure 5.2.

DEVELOPMENT OF REHABILITATION PLAN

Once the rehabilitation assessment is complete, the occupational health nurse develops a specific rehabilitation plan with the assistance of the employee, supervisor, union representative (if applicable) and human resources personnel (if required), for each employee who can benefit from proactive case management. A variety of tools, as described below, are used in this process.

Job Analysis

Using a standard Job Analysis Form (Figure 5.3),[43] the physical demands for the job can be used to identify the employee's capabilities, as well as his or her limitations. Comparisons are then made between the job demands and the employee's capabilities and limitations, to determine fitness to work and appropriate early return-to-work options.

---

[43] R. Berresford, J. Farmery & D. Mitchell, *Modified/Alternate Work Guidelines* (Toronto: Aon Consulting, 1993) at 4.

The "Physical Abilities" section examines the physical demands of the job. For each area, bending, walking, sitting, lifting, standing and hand-eye coordination, the user notes whether or not the activity occurs and records the data indicating how often, for how long, or how much, each activity is done. Using the guidelines provided, a value from one to four is assigned to each activity. The "Language Skills" section also converts data to numerical values. These forms can be adapted to meet the needs of many industries.

Another option is to have Job Demands Analysis for each position within a company (Figure 5.4), dealing with both the physical and psychological demands of a job.

Linkage with the Attending Physician or Health Care Provider

The purpose of the Managed Rehabilitative Care Program is to work as a team to benefit the employee. The Occupational Health Nurse liaises with the attending health care providers to explain the benefits and supports available to employees. Examples of the types of assistance offered by some companies are:

- occupational health services that offer ergonomic assistance and manage the confidentiality of employee health information;
- job or worksite modifications, such as a temporarily reduced work schedule, change of work duties, physical changes to the worksite, and/or use of specialized tools, or adaptive devices;
- availability of an Employee Assistance Program to help with work stress, personal issues and any mental health component of the existent medical condition(s);
- coordination with a specialist, when warranted, to obtain a timely appointment for the employee; and
- third party functional capacity assessment with reports going to the family physician if the employee consents to the communication.

Job Modifications

Job changes, or the reassignment of parts of a job, are considered so that the employee can return to work in a safe and timely manner. Once the employee's capabilities have been identified by an occupational health professional, the supervisor, union representative, Return-to-Work Coordinator, and human resources personnel are usually the leaders of a modified/alternate work opportunity.

Adaptive Devices

Special clothing, devices or equipment that allows adaptation of the work to the employee's limitations are considered where possible. From the beginning, the disabled employee and supervisor are involved in selecting and learning how to use any device that assists in the workplace accommodation of the returning employee. This is one area where occupational hygiene professionals can be an excellent team resource.

Independent Medical Examination

Independent, "third party" medical examinations can be used to determine the employee's level of disability, the length of duration of disability and possible recommendations for rehabilitation and successful return to work. The independent medical examination is not disciplinary in nature, nor is it intended to determine the employee's eligibility for benefit plan coverage.

An independent medical examination may be arranged for one or more of the following circumstances:

1. To determine the employee's medical status and fitness for work.
2. To determine the length of time the employee may be absent from work in order to allow for adequate replacement resources.
3. To determine the employee's work restrictions and/or limitations.
4. To assist with the development of a rehabilitation strategy, if necessary.
5. To ensure that the employee can return to work safely and productively.
6. If the disabling condition is not usually "totally disabling".
7. If the actual or estimated period of disability is longer than usual for the disabling condition.
8. If there is no definitive diagnosis.
9. If the return-to-work date cannot be provided by the physician, or is shown as "unknown" or "indefinite".
10. To obtain a second medical opinion and/or case management guidance.

Figure 5.2: Rehabilitation Assessment Form

EMPLOYEE: _____   EMPLOYEE #: _____
WORK LOCATION: _____   TEL #: _____
OCCUPATION: _____
DIAGNOSIS: _____   PHYSICIAN: _____

FACTOR	(Check if appropriate)	COMMENTS
A. PHYSICAL	Physical capabilities	_____
	Job demands	_____
	Job modification potential	_____
	Need for adaptive devices	_____
	Worksite modification	_____
B. PERSONAL	Change in family dynamics	_____
	Personal crisis	_____
	Health of family members	_____
	Impact of disability on family	_____
C. VOCATIONAL	Level of Job satisfaction	_____
	Work changes	_____
	General employment skills	_____
	Vocational interests/aptitudes	_____
	Supervisory support for MW	_____
D. MEDICAL	Diagnosis	_____
	Prognosis	_____
	Treatment plan	_____
	Expected RTW date	_____
	Employee's confidence/ Satisfaction with treatment	_____
	Potential residual limitations	_____
	Pain and coping skills	_____
	Other Health Problems	_____
	Other Health care supports	_____
E. PSYCHOLOGICAL	Employee's reaction	_____
	Employee outlook/self-esteem	_____
	Cultural factors	_____
	Employee treatment goals	_____
	Use of alcohol, drugs	_____
	Stress management needs	_____
	Willingness to work MW	_____
F. PERFORMANCE	Relationship with supervisor	_____
	Relations with co-workers	_____
	Work performance	_____
	Past absenteeism rate	_____
G. EDUCATIONAL	Formal education	_____
	Specialized training	_____
H. FINANCIAL	Available group benefits	_____
	Income	_____
	Financial assets/liabilities	_____
	Treatment costs	_____
I. ORGANIZATIONAL	Use of case conferences	_____
	Available rehabilitation resources	_____

REHABILITATION GOAL: OWN JOB ☐   OTHER JOB ☐
Return to Work Date _____   _____

Figure 5.3: Standard Job Analysis Form

Worker's Name: _____ Job: _____

Date of Evaluation: _____ Completed by: _____

Address: _____ Phone: _____

Physical Abilities

						Comments
Bending	At waist	1	2	3	4	_____
	Stooping	1	2	3	4	_____
	Kneeling	1	2	3	4	_____
	Crouching	1	2	3	4	_____
	Crawling	1	2	3	4	_____
Walking	Level Surface	1	2	3	4	_____
	Rough Ground	1	2	3	4	_____
	Stairs	1	2	3	4	_____
	Ladders	1	2	3	4	_____
Sitting	Chair	1	2	3	4	_____
	Stool	1	2	3	4	_____
	Vehicle Seat	1	2	3	4	_____
Lifting	From Ground	1	2	3	4	_____
	From Bench	1	2	3	4	_____
	From Shoulder	1	2	3	4	_____
	Over Head	1	2	3	4	_____
	Carrying	1	2	3	4	_____
	Pushing	1	2	3	4	_____
	Pulling	1	2	3	4	_____
Standing	Inside	1	2	3	4	_____
	Outside	1	2	3	4	_____
Hand-Eye Coordination		1	2	3	4	_____

Language Skills

		Yes	No=1	Minimal=2	Average=3	Fluent=4
English	Spoken	❑	❑	❑	❑	❑
	Written	❑	❑	❑	❑	❑
French	Spoken	❑	❑	❑	❑	❑
	Written	❑	❑	❑	❑	❑
Other	Spoken	❑	❑	❑	❑	❑
	Written	❑	❑	❑	❑	❑

Clerical Skills

Required: Yes ❑   No ❑   Specify: _____

Figure 5.4: Job Demands Analysis

Company XYZ **Job Demands Analysis**

Date:		Hours in Shift:		Business Unit:	
Job Title:		Occupation:		Location:	

	Job Demands	Category	Frequency 0	1	2	3	Essential Duty Yes / No	Description
S T R E N G T H	Lifts:	Usual weight						
		Max. weight						
	Lifting:	Floor to waist						
		Waist & higher						
	Carrying:	Usual weight						
		Max. weight						
	Carrying:	Single arm						
		Double arm						
	Handling:	Right						
		Left						
	Reaching: Shoulder	Above						
	height	Below						
	Gripping:	Minimum						
		Moderate						
		Maximum						
	Finger Movements:	Right						
		Left						
M O B I L I T Y	Sitting							
	Standing							
	Walking							
	Climbing							
	Stooping							
	Crouching							
	Kneeling							
	Crawling							
	Twisting							
P E R C E P T I O N	Hearing:	Conversation						
		Other Sounds						
	Smelling							
	Vision:	Far						
		Near						
		Colour						
		Depth						
	Reading/Writing							
	Speech							
W O R K E N V I R O N M E N T	Inside Work (% of time)							
	Outside Work (% of time)							
	Noise Exposed Worker							
	Exposure to Extreme Heat ($>26°C$)							
	Exposure to Extreme Cold ($<-7°C$)							
	Exposure to Vibration Sources							
	Exposure to Chemicals							
	Exposure to Hazardous Materials							
	Exposure to Radiation							
	Exposure to Biological Hazards							
	Exposure to Electrical Hazards							
	Exposure to Dust							
	Exposure to Welding Fumes							
	Works With Moving Objects							
	Operates a Vehicle or Mobile equipment							
	Operates Hazardous Machines/Equipment							
	Works With Sharp Tools							
	Works on Uneven/Slippery Terrain/Surfaces							
	Exposed to Confined Spaces							
	Use of Respiratory Equipment							
	Works at Heights (> 2.4 meters high)							
	Repetitive Motion							
	Video Display Terminal Use							
G E N E R A L	Air Travel							
	Vehicle Travel							
	Interaction With Public							
	Overtime							
	On-call Responsibilities							
	Emergency Response Duties							
P S Y C H O L O G I C A L	Work Demands/Pressures							
	Work Pace							
	Supervisory/ Managerial Duties							
	Control of Work							
	Span of Control							
	Irregular Hours/Fatigue							

Job Specific Comments:

Job Finding

Whenever there is the likelihood that the employee will not be able to return to his or her own job, the human resource professionals are advised. Then, the challenge of finding the employee an alternate job suitable to his or her capabilities begins. By early placement of a permanently disabled employee into a suitable job, long-term disability can be avoided.

Employee Education

Resources can be used to help the employee understand and cope with his or her disability. Education is important when trying to encourage a positive attitude towards illness or injury management. The employee needs to feel a sense of control over his or her life to cope successfully with the situation.

GOAL SETTING

Specific goals with time frames are developed and communicated to the team of which the employee is the key player. A Rehabilitation Action Plan, which can be used to document rehabilitation goals, is provided in Figure 5.5.

Figure 5.5: Rehabilitation Action Plan
(designed to be attached to the Rehabilitation Assessment Form, Figure 5.2)

Health	Date	Completed
Vocational (human resources, supervisor)	Date	Completed
Benefit/Insurance	Date	Completed

Key Decision-makers (telephone numbers)

1._____   4._____
2._____   5._____
3._____   6._____

Other Comments   Date
_____
_____
_____

_____   _____
Signature   Date

CASE COORDINATION

Occupational health professionals advocate and negotiate on the company and employee's behalf with all the professionals involved. Employees become better consumers of health care and are provided with support to enhance compliance with treatment regimens.

The Managed Rehabilitative Care process chart (Chapter 3, Figure 3.3) is used by all members of the team.

GRADUATED RETURN TO WORK

Graduated return-to-work opportunities are intended to assist recovering employees in safely returning to the workplace and, ultimately, to regular full-time employment. This practice is associated with effective improvement of employee health, enhancement of employee satisfaction, reduction of disability claim costs and increased productivity.[44]

Gradual return-to-work and work accommodation are viewed as a "core element of disability management, leading to favourable outcomes".[45] The challenge is to attain a sound "employee/job fit". Ideally, employees should be returned to their own job — a position they know, and in which they can benefit from co-worker support.[46] In addition to this requirement, consideration should be given to a potential need for an ergonomic assessment to ensure a functional person-job fit. [47]

Return-to-work planning is viewed as a "socially fragile process",[48] in which the returning employee, supervisor and co-workers face the development of new work and duties relationships. If the return to work plan disadvantages the supervisor/co-workers, resentment can result. This outcome, in turn, can sabotage the return-to-work efforts. Hence, return-to-work plans must anticipate and avoid negatively impacting supervisors and co-workers.

Many individuals can facilitate the gradual return-to-work process — the supervisor, the Disability Management Coordinator, a Return-to-Work Coordinator, *etc*. However, regardless of who is involved, a successful graduated return-to-work outcome depends on a cooperative and collaborative approach between the employee, direct supervisor, union representative, management, and co-workers.

Objectives of the Graduated Return-to-Work Plan

A return-to-work plan is designed to achieve the following objectives:

1. ensure fair and consistent treatment for all employees who are returning to work;
2. promote shared responsibility for effective return-to-work plans and placements among ill/injured employees, supervisors, union representatives, and Disability Management Coordinator;
3. provide coordinated claims and case management services for the ill/injured employee;
4. respect the rights and relationships present in the workplace;
5. engage all parties in assisting the ill/injured worker to successfully return to work; and
6. mitigate medical absence costs associated with disability claims.

---

[44]   Watson-Wyatt, *Staying@Work: Effective Presence at Work* (2007), at 10, available online at: <https://www.watsonwyatt.com>.

[45]   Institute for Work & Health, "Seven 'Principles' for Successful Return to Work", *Institute for Work & Health*, Toronto (March 2007), available online at: <http://www.iwh.on.ca/seven-principles-for-rtw>.

[46]   *Ibid.*

[47]   *Ibid.*

[48]   *Ibid.*, at 3.

Graduated return-to-work opportunities are intended to assist recovering employees in safely returning to the workplace and, ultimately, to regular full-time employment. Often, a Return-to-Work Coordinator is involved to facilitate this process. However, regardless of who is involved, a successful return-to-work outcome depends on the use of a cooperative and collaborative approach between the employee, union representative and management.

Principles of a Graduated Return-to-Work Plan

A graduated return-to-work plan is based on a number of principles. Some examples are as follows:

1. *A safe and timely return to work is in the best interest of the ill or injured employee and the organization.* The employee benefits from having meaningful employment, gradual work conditioning and the social supports associated with being at work, when deemed appropriate. The organization is able to mitigate the costs associated with lost production, hiring and training replacement workers, and rescheduling of other workers. Supporting the recovering employee to return to productive work minimizes the direct and indirect costs associated with disability.

2. *Early intervention is critical to achieving a positive return-to-work experience.* It can:

    - help the employee to receive appropriate and timely care;
    - help with the physical, social, psychological, vocational, and financial implications of illness/injury;
    - increase the likelihood of successful rehabilitation;
    - facilitate the process of coping and adjustment for the employee, family, and work group;
    - build social credibility for the returning employee with the supervisor and workgroup;
    - promote a safe, timely and successful return to work; and
    - be cost-effective for the employee, family, and employer.

3. *A positive approach to disability is advantageous.* This means focusing on the person's capabilities and the contributions that he or she can make to the workplace. By bringing ill or injured employees back into the workplace, the organization and unions can demonstrate the belief that each employee, regardless of disability, has abilities that can be valuable. This approach can enhance employee morale.

4. *Return-to-work plans should include meaningful, goal-oriented work that matches the employee's capabilities.* Work accommodations consider the type of work to be performed and the hours to be worked. Supervisors should be educated in the principles of disability management and involved in the return-to-work planning, implementation, monitoring, and evaluation.

5. *Employees should be compensated in accordance with the work performed.*

6. *Crossing union jurisdictional issues must be addressed and resolved for a graduated return-to-work opportunity to function successfully.*

7. *A return-to-work plan must recognize the employee's diminished capability and not compromise the employee's recovery or safety.*

8. *A return-to-work plan must benefit all the involved parties — the employee, employer, supervisor, and co-workers.*

9. *A return-to-work plan must ensure that the general workplace safety is not compromised.*

10. *The return-to-work plan is not a disciplinary tool.* Performance issues are to be resolved through the appropriate administrative processes and collective agreements.

11. *A return-to-work plan may include a return to*:

- the employee's own job with reduced hours;
- a portion of the employee's own job duties with full-time or part-time hours;
- a different job within the employee's department on a full-time or part-time basis;
- an unrelated job in another department on a full-time or part-time basis; and/or
- a new job outside of the organization on a full-time or part-time basis.

The Hierarchy of Return-to-Work Options is provided in Figure 5.6.

Figure 5.6: Hierarchy of Return-to-Work Options

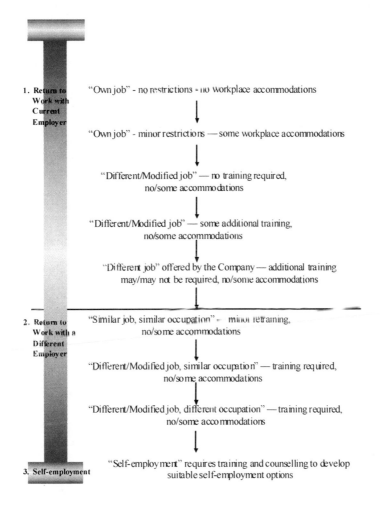

1. Return to Work with Current Employer

"Own job" - no restrictions - no workplace accommodations

↓

"Own job" - minor restrictions — some workplace accommodations

↓

"Different/Modified job" — no training required, no/some accommodations

↓

"Different/Modified job" — some additional training, no/some accommodations

↓

"Different job" offered by the Company — additional training may/may not be required, no/some accommodations

↓

2. Return to Work with a Different Employer

"Similar job, similar occupation" — minor retraining, no/some accommodations

↓

"Different/Modified job, similar occupation" — training required, no/some accommodations

↓

"Different/Modified job, different occupation" — training required, no/some accommodations

↓

3. Self-employment

"Self-employment" requires training and counselling to develop suitable self-employment options

In essence, an Integrated Disability Management Program such as the Managed Rehabilitative Care Program can help companies cope with rising disability costs, the challenges of an aging and changing workforce, the effects of uncertain economic times on disability costs, the intricacies of a complex health care system, and the administration of disability cases.

MANAGED REHABILITATIVE CARE OUTCOME MEASURES

What benefits can be realized through the implementation of a Managed Rehabilitative Care Program? Realistically, one can expect a decline in casual absence, sick leave, short-term disability, long-term disability; and Workers' Compensation Board insurance rates and costs. Additionally, the information gathered through the Managed Rehabilitative Care Program can help identify emerging problems, or the development of trends that warrant further investigation.

Measuring Success

The evaluation process can occur at many levels. At the individual case level, the process and results are continually reviewed throughout the course of the disability and improvements are sought. At the program level, program results, costs, system concerns and recommendations are analyzed and reported periodically to local management. Confidentiality of individual information is maintained in accordance with medical or nursing confidentiality codes of practice. At the process level, auditing of the Managed Rehabilitative Care Program is recommended.

An example of a spreadsheet for setting up a Managed Rehabilitative Care Program database is provided in Figure 5.7.

Figure 5.7: Managed Rehabilitative Care Spreadsheet

Total Claims = 25 Short-term Disability (STD) Claims

Name/ Claim #	STD Start	STD End	STD Length (days)	Cause	MWP (Y/N)	Days Saved (days)
X	05.08.06	05.09.20	32	Cancer	N	0
A	05.08.12	05.10.01	35	N.O.A	N	0
C	05.08.26	06.01.10	92	N.O.I	Y	41
B	05.09.03	06.03.03	124	N.O.I.	Y	66
D	05.09.03	06.03.03	124	R.S.I.	N	0
I	05.07.02	05.11.13	90	R.S.I.	Y	52
Y	05.09.16	05.10.25	29	Stress	Y	10
M	05.09.09	06.02.03	119	Stress	Y	72
J	05.08.01	05.08.23	15	N.O.I.	N	0
N	05.09.12	05.09.20	7	Flu	N	0
T	05.09.03	05.10.15	30	Surgery	Y	15
U	05.09.03	05.09.13	9	N.O.I.	N	0
W	05.09.24	05.11.22	42	E.T.O.H.	N	0
O	05.09.18	05.09.25	6	Surgery	N	0
P	05.09.19	05.10.07	11	Surgery	Y	5
L	05.09.12	05.11.01	36	Surgery	Y	5
V	05.10.22	06.04.20	124	Deg. C.	Y	38
E	05.10.22	05.12.02	29	Back	Y	19
F	05.10.07	06.04.07	125	Back	Y	78
H	05.10.15	05.10.25	9	Flu	N	0
K	05.10.16	06.03.11	100	Stress	Y	97
Q	05.10.30	05.11.22	17	Surgery	Y	5
R	05.11.05	05.11.15	8	Cardiac	N	0
S	05.10.28	06.01.02	43	Stress	N	0
G	05.11.10	05.11.18	8	Surgery	N	0
25 Employees			1264 Days		13 Employees	503 Days

Legend:
N.O.A. = Non-occupational Accident; N.O.I. = Non-occupational Injury; E.T.O.H. = Alcohol Abuse; R.S.I. = Repetitive Strain Injury; Deg. C. = Degenerative Condition; MWP = Modified Work Program.

This table indicates that 25 employees were on short-term disability for a total of 1,264 days at an average of 50.5 workdays per claim. At a rate of $233 per day, the total cost of the short-term disability was $294,512, an average of $11,766.50 per claim. As well, 13 (52 per cent) of the employees returned to modified/alternate work for a total of 503 workdays. The cost-avoidance, or dollar savings, realized through the modified/alternate work initiatives was

$117,199. By subtracting the "days saved" from the total short-term disability days, the "time lost" is calculated. In this scenario, that equals 761 days at a total cost of $117,313. The cost/benefit ratio of the Managed Rehabilitative Care Program can be calculated by dividing the potential program costs by the actual program costs; hence, 2.5 in this scenario.

Using Managed Rehabilitative Care data, many types of reports can be generated. Figure 5.8 is an example of an annual report.

Figure 5.8: Annual Report of the Managed Rehabilitative Care Program: Summary Statistics — Short-term Disability, 2008

2008 Short-term Disability Results		
Number of employees on Short-term Disability (STD)	103 employees	
Program Measures	**Days**	**Cost/Savings**
Total potential STD claim days	3309 days	$ 770,997*
Total actual STD claims time	1927 days	$ 448,991
Absence days avoided (saved) — MWP	1382 days	$ 322,006
Average potential STD claim duration	32 days	$ 7,456
Average actual STD claim duration	21 days	$ 4,893
Average actual days saved per claim	11 days	$ 2,563
Percentage of claimants on MWP**	44%	

* Short-term disability Cost = $770,997, or $233 per day absent
** MWP = Modified/alternate Work Program

In 2008, the cost to have 103 employees on short-term disability was $770,997. The average potential absence time was 32 days. This meant a potential average of $7,456 per claim. By placing 44 per cent of the recovering employees on modified/alternate work (MWP), 1382 absence days were avoided — a saving of $322,006. Thus, the total actual short-term disability claims time equalled 1,927 days at a cost of $448,991. The average duration of a short-term disability claim dropped from 32 days to 21 days — an 11-day saving.

This report might conclude by stating that, "Through the support for the Managed Rehabilitative Care Program from management, unions, employees and co-workers, these positive results have been made possible. Going forward, this continued endorsement and support can enable Company XYZ to mitigate the human and financial losses associated with employee disability."

Other Measurement Techniques

There are other ways to evaluate success. The following are a few techniques that can be used.

1. *Determine the "difference" that a Managed Rehabilitative Care Program has made:*

   • Calculate the total number of employees on each of the disability programs before the program began and after it had been operational for one year. Compare the differences.
   • Quarterly and annual comparisons can also be made as shown in the example in Figure 5.9.

Figure 5.9: Comparison of the Managed Rehabilitative Care Program Results:
Four Operational Quarters, 2008
Short-term Disability (STD)

Performance Measures	1st Q	2nd Q	3rd Q	4th Q
Number of employees on STD	30	31	50	41
Total STD days	882	823	955	960
Average STD time (days)	29.4	26.5	19.1	23.6
% on MWP*	20%	48%	64%	58%
Absence days avoided	204	318	414	429

* MWP = Modified/alternate Work Program

2. *Calculate the cost of the total sick-time:*

   • Establish the total number of days on short-term disability and then multiply that number by the average, or actual employee salary including the burden factor. Some companies use a set cost, such as an average salary of $233 per day as the "sick leave cost" (Figure 5.10). This is increased to $633 per day if a replacement worker is required for that period of time. In this scenario, the "replacement cost" is $400 per day.

Figure 5.10: **Quarterly Report on Managed Rehabilitative Care Program**
Short-term Disability (STD)
2009.04.01 – 2009.06.30

Number of employees on STD**	30 claims
Total STD claim days	882 days
Average STD time per claim	29.4 days
Total STD claim costs	$ 205,506*
Average STD cost per claim	$ 6,850.20
STD claim costs per month	$ 68,502

* Total short-term disability costs = Sick-Leave Cost ($233 per day) × Total short-term disability days
** Includes only absences of 5 or more days

3. *Calculate the total "days-saved":*

   - This can be done two ways, or by combining both:

      a) determine the difference between the predicted and actual return-to-work time, or,
      b) determine the number of days each employee is on modified/alternate work.
         Either of these methods yields the "days saved" by the Managed Rehabilitative Care Program.

   - To place a dollar-savings on this figure, multiply the number of "days saved" by the "sick leave cost", with or without the "replacement cost", as the actual case might be.

4. *Calculate the causes of the claims:*

   - Determine the cause for each claim, short-term disability, long-term disability or Workers' Compensation, whichever is of interest. Broad categories like occupational illness, occupational injury, non-occupational illness or non-occupational injury could be used. Other possible classifications include surgery, stress, degenerative conditions, infections, *etc.* (Figure 5.11).

Figure 5.11: Causes of Short-term Disability

Total Number of STDs = 99 claims

Cause of Short-term Disability (STD)	Percent
Surgery	37%
Infections	17%
Non-occupational injuries	10%
Stress	9%
Pregnancy disorders	5%
Degenerative conditions	5%
Back disorders	3%
Cardiac conditions	3%
Immune disorders	3%
Neurological disorders	2%
Cancer	2%
Others	3%

5. *Calculate the cost of each cause to the company:*

• This involves determining the "time-lost" for each category of causes and assigning a dollar figure to the cause (Figure 5.12).

**Figure 5.12: Causes of Short-term Disability,
Percent of Total Short-term Disability Days (3,208 days)**

Cause of Short-term Disability (STD)	Number of STD Days	Percent of Total STD
Surgery	1050	33%
Non-occupational injuries	603	19%
Degenerative conditions	320	10%
Infections	252	8%
Stress	232	7%
Back disorders	177	6%
Cancer	168	5%
Immune disorders	146	4%
Pregnancy disorders	127	4%
Cardiac conditions	61	2%
Neurological disorders	10	0.3%
Others	62	2%

6. *Calculate the success of modified/alternate work initiatives:*

    •   Examine the data on all the short-term disability claims that went into modified/alternate work. Subdivide the group by the disability causes. Total the number of "days saved" for each claim in each disability subgroup and then, add a dollar figure to the "days saved" for each. This will indicate where the biggest differences were made by modified/alternate work (Figure 5.13).

Figure 5.13: Savings Realized by Modified/Alternate Work Initiatives

Total number = 48 modified/alternate work opportunities

Condition	Employees Returned to Work	Average Days Saved	Savings per STD Claim
Back	3/3	51	$ 11,883
Non-Occupational Injuries	7/11	46	$ 10,718
Pregnancy Disorders	3/5	28	$ 6,524
Degenerative Conditions	2/5	24	$ 5,592
Infections	8/16	21	$ 4,893
Stress	6/9	20.5	$ 4,777
Surgery	16/37	10	$ 2,330
Immune Disorders	1/3	93	$ 21,669
Others	1/3	43	$ 10,019
Cancer	1/2	24	$ 5,592

    •   Figure 5.13 shows that all the employees with back disabilities went to modified/alternate work and an average of 51 days were saved for each claim. This translates to a savings of $11,883 per claim. In comparison, only 16 out of 37 of the surgery claims returned early to modified/ alternate work. An average of 10 days per claim was saved, $2,330 per claim.

    •   This type of data helps occupational health professionals to decide where and how they can make the biggest difference to the company's "bottom line".

7. *Determine the impact of treatment interventions on the duration of short-term disability claims*

    •   By identifying the treatment interventions ("medical specialist intervention", "work accommodation", "work accommodation and medical specialist", and "no intervention"), one can determine the impact of each treatment modality on the duration of short-term disability claims. This was demonstrated by Dr. A. Clark (1999) and he determined that the "work accommodation with medical specialist intervention" modality was the most effective, resulting in almost half the absence days of the "no intervention" modality. However, the "modified work intervention" modality was almost as effective. The "medical specialist intervention alone" modality was the least effective (Figure 5.14).

Figure 5.14 Impact of Treatment Interventions on Short Term Disability Duration[49]

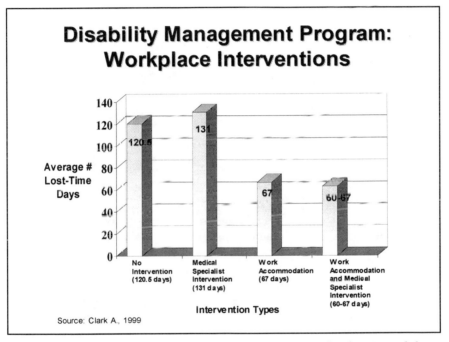

Disability Management Program: Workplace Interventions

Source: Clark A., 1999

8. *Determine the impact of workplace interventions on the duration of short-term disability claims*

- By examining the short-term disability claim durations associated with the outcomes of the workplace interventions used ("Modified work", "Modified work and EAP intervention", "EAP intervention alone", "No intervention"), one can determine the impact of each intervention on the duration of short-term disability claims (Figure 5.15). For example, what was the average duration of short-term disability claims in which employees availed themselves of "Modified work", "Modified work and EAP intervention", "EAP intervention alone", or "No intervention"?

---

[49] A. Clark, "Impact of Treatment Interventions on Short Term Disability Duration" (1999) (Presented at the Disability Management in the Workplace Conference, Toronto, June 2000) [unpublished].

Figure 5.15: Disability Management: Workplace Interventions[50]

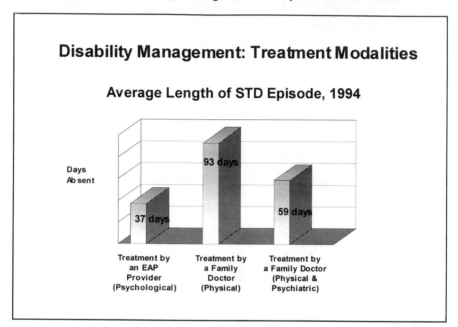

- The differences in the average claim duration for each workplace intervention would be a measure of the impact of those interventions.

8. *Determine short-term disability outcomes:*

- The outcome of each short-term disability claim can be established to determine how many short-term disability claims progressed to long-term disability, and if there are some common factors associated with that outcome. For example, of the short-term disability claims, establish how many progressed to long-term disability status. Examine each claim to find out what the determining factors were, *e.g.*, the nature of the illness/injury; limited/no modified or alternate work opportunities available; employees with few transferable skills; employees with few social supports/social credits, *etc.*

9. *Determine the workplace accommodations made:*

- List each disability claim that resulted in any type of workplace accommodation by occupation, nature of disability and the type of accommodation offered. This serves as a record of the company's "duty

---

50   D.J. Conti, "The Management of Psychiatric Short-term Disability" (Presented at the American Psychiatric Association Annual Meeting, Miami, FL, 21 May 1996) [unpublished].

to accommodate" (Figure 5.16) performance, as well as a measure of the level of compliance with government employment equity programs.

Figure 5.16: Workplace Accommodations (2008)

Occupation	Disability	Accommodation Description
Driver	Wrist dysfunction: inability to drive safely	Computer work within the distribution terminal
Office worker	Heart disease	Given a rest area to use at noon hour so work can be tolerated
Computer Operator	Repetitive strain injury	Bilateral articulating arms for computer work station
Computer Operator	Eye disease	Job modified to half day, optic shield on computer screen to reduce glare
Computer Operator	Eye degeneration	Optic shield on computer
Field Operator Maintenance	Heart disease	Alternate work on eight-hour days
Maintenance Supervisor	Deteriorating spine	Permanent office work organizing maintenance
Millwright	Heart disease	Permanent position in tool crib

11. *Other outcome measures* — Additional operational information can be obtained through review and analysis of the Managed Rehabilitative Care data. For instance:

   - By knowing the causes of disability claims, a proactive approach to prevent injury or illness occurrence can be recommended for implementation by the company. For example, if the main cause of disability is "non-occupational injuries", an Off-the-Job Safety Program may be warranted. Or, if the major reason for disability is associated with back injuries, a back-care program or a fitness program may prove cost-effective. If degenerative diseases are top on the list of disability causes, proactive lifestyle practices could be promoted.

   - By comparing the disability claims of the company's various divisions, a standard for performance can be set. A comparison of the business, occupational health & safety practices, or modified work rates/practices between the "best" and "worst" performers may provide insight into ways to lower the company's disability claim rates and costs.

- An effective way of evaluating a Managed Rehabilitative Care Program is to audit the program. Auditing will be covered in more detail in Chapter 6, "Integrated Disability Management Program: Outcome Measurements". However it is presented here as a measurement technique.

Auditing can be done in many ways. Primarily the aim is to determine whether the program is meeting its objectives or not, and the degree to which this is being done. Some examples of auditing questions are provided in Figure 5.17.

Figure 5.17: Managed Rehabilitative Care Audit Questions

Audit Questions	Comments
Does the employee receive the right service at the right time?	
How often is the Case Manager notified of an absence by day five?	
Is the standardized case management approach used in all claims?	
Who are the usual members of the Managed Rehabilitative Care management team?	
How often is modified/alternate work usually available?	
Is the modified/alternate work "gainful employment"?	
Are supervisors proactive in the Managed Rehabilitative Care Program?	
How does senior management demonstrate support for the Managed Rehabilitative Care Program?	
How do union leaders demonstrate support for the Managed Rehabilitative Care Program?	
What percentage of employees return to work within one month? Within three months? Within six months?	
How many short-term disability claims move to long-term disability?	
How many Workers' Compensation claims move to long-term disability?	
What types of workplace accommodations are made?	

SUMMARY

The incentives for instituting an Integrated Disability Management Program, such as the Managed Rehabilitative Care Program, are:

- a complex health care system;
- rising disability costs;
- an aging workforce;

- past experience of companies using Managed Rehabilitative Care to make a difference in their claims experience;
- pressures to recognize the "human element" in the workplace;
- pending legislation forcing employers to accommodate disabled employees in the workplace;
- the reality of a "tight" labour market; and
- a highly competitive marketplace and economy.

Integrated Disability Management Programs can help companies cope with the rising disability costs, the challenges of an aging and changing workforce, the effects of uncertain economic times on disability costs, the intricacies of a complex health care system, and the administration of disability claims.

By working with employees, their medical practitioners, Employee Assistance Plan counsellors, human resources professionals, and community agencies, Disability Management professionals/practitioners can help to rehabilitate employees thereby getting them back to work earlier. In short, an Integrated Disability Management Program can be a very effective means of maintaining the integrity of a disability program, while minimizing the costs in human and financial terms.

CHAPTER REFERENCES

B. Anderson, "Disability Claims Management" (Seminar presented by M. Mercier at Westin Hotel, Calgary, Alberta, February 1992) [unpublished].

Association of Workers' Compensation Boards of Canada, *Key Statistical Measures for 2007* (December 2008), available online at: <http://www. awcbc.org/common/assets/ksms/2007ksms.pdf>.

R. Berresford, J. Farmery & D. Mitchell, *Modified/alternate Work Guidelines* (Toronto: Aon Consulting, 1993).

P. Booth, *Employee Absenteeism: Strategies for Promoting an Attendance-Oriented Corporate Culture* (Ottawa: The Conference Board of Canada, 1993) at 2.

Canadian Centre for Occupational Health & Safety, *Aging Workers* (2002), available online at: <http://www.ccohs.ca/oshanswers/psychosocial/aging_ workers.html>.

Case Management Society of America (CMSA), *Standards for Practice of Case Management* (Little Rock, AR: CMSA, 1995).

City of Medicine Hat Disability Management Program Steering Committee (April 1999).

A. Clark, "Impact of Treatment Interventions on Short Term Disability Duration", (1999) (Presented at the Disability Management in the Workplace Conference, Toronto, June 2000) [unpublished].

D.J. Conti, "The Management of Psychiatric Short-term Disability" (Presented at the American Psychiatric Association Annual Meeting, Miami, FL, 21 May 1996) [unpublished].

D. Dyck, "Managed Rehabilitative Care: Overview for Occupational Health Nurses" (1996) 44:1 AAOHN Journal 18.

Great West Life, "Coordinated Disability Care" (Presentation to Petro-Canada. Calgary, Alberta, 1993) [unpublished].

L. Gross, "Managing Your Escalating Health and Safety Costs" (Presented to the Petroleum Industry's Annual Safety Seminar, Alberta, May 1993) [unpublished].

Institute for Work & Health, "Seven 'Principles' for Successful Return to Work". *Institute for Work & Health*, Toronto (March 2007), available online at: <http://www.iwh.on.ca/seven-principles-for-rtw>.

Mercer Inc., *The Total Financial Impact of Employee Absences — Survey Highlights* (October 2008), at 4, available online at: <http://www.kronos.com/absenceanonymous/media/Mercer-Survey-Highlights.pdf>.

K. Nagel, "Total Organizational Health Costs: What Are They? What Can Organizations Do About Them?" (Presented at the Strategic Leadership Forum '99, Toronto, Ontario, 20 October 1999) [unpublished].

National Institute of Disability Management (NIDMAR), *Code of Practice for Disability Management* (Port Alberni, BC: NIDMAR, 2000), at 4.

Ontario Human Rights Commission, *Guidelines for Assessing Accommodation Requirements for Persons with Disabilities* (Toronto: Ontario Human Rights Commission, 1990).

Peat, Marwick, Stevenson & Kellogg, *Statistical Data on 1991 Employee Benefit Costs in Canada* (1993) [unpublished].

Petro-Canada Inc., *Managed Rehabilitative Care Program Occupational Health* (Calgary: Petro-Canada, 1990).

E. Quick, "Disability Management that Works" (January/February 2007) Benefit Solutions Magazine 44, available online at: <http://old.bcsolutionsmag.com/archives.asp>.

Statistics Canada, *Work Absence Rates, 2007*, Cat. No. 71-211-XWE (Ottawa: Statistics Canada, May 2008).

Statistics Canada, *Average Hourly Wages of Employees by Selected Characteristics*, available online at: <http://www40.statcan.ca/l01/cst01/labr69a-eng.htm>.

Statistics Canada, *Population by Sex and Age Group*, available online at: <http://www40.statcan.ca/l01/cst01/demo10a-eng.htm>.

Statistics Canada, *2001 Census — Release 2 — July 16, 2002*, "Age and Sex" (Ottawa: Statistics Canada, 2002), available online at: <http://www12.statcan.ca/english/census01/release/age_sex.cfm>.

Statistics Canada, *2006 Census Data, Generation Status (4), Age Groups (9) and Sex (3) for the Population 15 Years and Over of Canada, Provinces and Territories, 1971, 2001 and 2006 Censuses - 20% Sample Data*, available online at: <http://www12.statcan.ca/english/census06/data/topics/Index.cfm?Temporal=2006&APATH=7&FREE=0&FL=G>.

L. Steeves & R. Smithies, "Foresight is Your Best Defence" (1996) 4:2 Group Health Care Management 29.

Watson-Wyatt, *Staying@Work: Effective Presence at Work (2007)*, available online at: <https://www.watsonwyatt.com>.

J. White, "The Evolving Role of Nursing in Patient Advocacy" (May 1992) Canadian Nursing Management 6.

R. Williams *et al.*, *A Survey of Disability Management Approaches in Ontario Workplaces* (Toronto: McMaster University and WSIB Ontario, 2005) at 2, available online at: <http://www.wsib.ca/wsib/wsibsite.nsf/Public/researchresultssurveydisabilitymgnt>.

World Health Organization, *International Classification of Impairment, Disabilities and Handicaps* (Geneva: World Health Organization, 1980).

Work Loss Data Institute, *Disability Benchmarks by Major Diagnostic Category* (Corpus Christi, TX: Work Loss Data Institute, 2002).

Chapter 6

Integrated Disability Management Program:
Outcome Measurements

INTRODUCTION

To measure the productivity and effectiveness of an Integrated Disability Management Program, various types of data must be collected and documented. Canadian and American employers recognize that the costs associated with employee unscheduled work absence and disability-related absences are significant. For example, the current estimate is that the direct disability-related absences cost Canadian employers between $1,598.95[1] to $1,756 per employee per year.[2] For a company of 1,000 employees, this cost would be between $1.6 to $1.8 million.

These direct absence costs (measured as employee earnings) are conservative values. If the indirect costs associated with employee medical absences were to be included, that amount alone would be 3-7 times the direct absence costs. However, despite evidence of increasing employee medical absenteeism rates and costs, most employers are not measuring employee unscheduled absence and disability rates and outcomes.[3] Nor are they measuring the effectiveness of their Integrated Disability Management Programs.[4] This is unfortunate given that an Integrated Disability Management Program can reduce an organization's disability management costs by 19 per cent to 25 per cent[5] and employee group

---

[1]   Calculated by multiplying the average number of missed workdays per full-time employee (10.2 lost days) by the average daily wage for full-time Canadian employees as of November 2007 ($156.76 per day). Data obtained from: Statistics Canada, *Work Absence Rates, 2007*, Cat. No. 71-211-XWE (Ottawa: Statistics Canada, May 2008); and Statistics Canada, *Average Hourly Wages of Employees by Selected Characteristics*, available online at: <http://www40.statcan.ca/101/cst01/labr69a.htm>.

[2]   Hewitt Associates, Press Release, "Ignoring Employee Absences May Prove Costly for Canadian Organizations, According to Hewitt" (15 June 2005), available online at: <http://www.hewittassociates.com/Intl/NA/en-CA/Default.aspx>.

[3]   Hewitt Associates, *Disability Absence Index Survey 2007* (2007), at 4, available online at: <http://www.hewittassociates.com/Intl/NA/en-CA/KnowledgeCenter/ArticlesReports/DAIS_highlights.aspx>.

[4]   *Ibid.*

[5]   Watson Wyatt, *Staying@Work 2004* (2004), available online at: <https://www.watsonwyatt.com>.

benefits by 15 to 35 per cent.[6] Integration also enables the organization to better address the benefit needs of ill/injured employees.

Disability Management experts believe that, "You can't manage what you can't measure. What you can't measure, you can't control." Program evaluation can reveal to management the hidden costs of disability, and the added costs of lost productivity, staff replacement, and worker retraining.

PROGRAM EVALUATION

Before proceeding with the topic of Integrated Disability Management Program evaluation, the concept of program evaluation must be addressed. In essence, **program evaluation** identifies the gaps between *the current state* and *the desired state* of a program, indicates whether the program goals/objectives are met or not, and enables improvements both along the way and periodically.

Structure, Process, and Outcome: Evaluation

Inherent to program evaluation is the establishment of a program that has an infrastructure which includes the elements of structure, processes, and outcome. In terms of an Integrated Disability Management Program (Figure 6.1), the structure would include the makeup of the Disability Management Team, its position within the organization, its functions, the qualifications and career paths of the Integrated Disability Management Program professionals/practitioners, the Integrated Disability Management Program Manual that houses the Disability Management Program standards, the Integrated Disability Management Program forms and other tools, the Integrated Disability Management Program Communication Plan, and the Integrated Disability Management Program communication tools (*e.g.*, webpage, brochures, promotional items, posters, newsletter articles, *etc.*).

---

[6]   N. Vimadalal & J. Wozniak, "Best Practices to Help Employers Capture the Benefits of Integrated Disability Management", *Employee Benefits News* (March 1, 2008), available online at: <http://ebn.benefitnews.com/asset/article/548491/best-practices-help-employers-capture-benefits.html?pg=>.

Figure 6.1: The Anatomy of an Integrated Disability Management Program

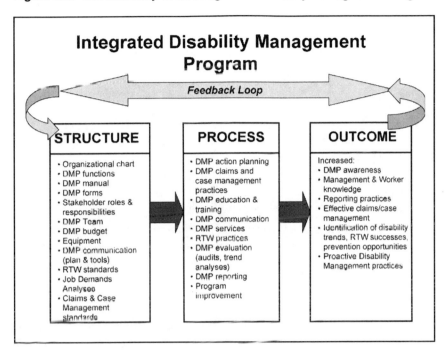

The Integrated Disability Management Program processes involve illness/injury reporting; claim management; case management; Disability Management Program education and training; Disability Management Program communication and marketing; Disability Management Program services and activities; Disability Management Program data management; Disability Management Program reporting; audits; satisfaction surveys; trend analyses; and other analyses of the Disability Management Program outcomes.

The Integrated Disability Management Program outcomes comprise the Disability Management Program performance measures. In this model, the Disability Management Program structure contributes to the processes, and both result in the nature and quality of the achieved program outcomes.

In addition to these elements, the system must include a feedback mechanism for continuous improvement of the individual components — the structure, process, and outcome.

Program Goals, Objectives and Targets: Evaluation

Integrated Disability Management Programs require program goals, objectives, and targets. These are the elements that are examined during a program evaluation. A **goal** is a broad statement about something to be accomplished.

An **objective** is a specific aim set to achieve a desired goal. When developing objectives, it is important to be "*SMART*": that is, they must be:

- *S*pecific — Should be clearly defined.
- *M*easurable — Can be measured.
- *A*ttainable — Within one's power to do and something people want to do.
- *R*ealistic — Can be achieved.
- *T*ime-specific — Attainable within a specific period of time.

Targets are levels of performance that the company wishes to attain. Typically, a company will set their targets as improvements of 5-10 per cent over the previous year's results. To garner continued support for the Disability Management Program, it is important to set realistic and attainable targets, thereby demonstrating continuous improvement in effectively managing worker illness/injury.

Sample goals for an Integrated Disability Management Program might be:

1. *To promote a safe and healthy workplace through illness/injury prevention.*
2. *To minimize the personal and economic losses and costs of injury and disability.*

Based on the above sample goals, the Integrated Disability Management Program objectives might be:

1. *To have an effective Integrated Disability Management Program in place as evidenced by meeting or exceeding 100 per cent of the program targets in 2010.*
2. *To promote illness/injury mitigation and prevention as evidenced by the achievement of the delivery of 90 per cent of the Disability Management Education Schedule in 2010.*
3. *To minimize the personal and economic costs of illness/injury and disability as evidenced by a reduction of 30 per cent of the disability claim costs in 2010.*

A typical program evaluation plan for an Integrated Disability Management Program (Figure 6.2) could include:

1. *Establish the Integrated Disability Management Program goal(s).*
2. *Set the Disability Management Programs objectives.*
3. *Determine the Disability Management Program targets.*
4. *Plan a schedule/action plan for the achievement of the objectives and targets, and for the measurement of each.*
5. *Implement the plan.*
6. *Check progress.*
7. *Determine the results.*
8. *Analyze the results.*
9. *Interpret the findings.*
10. *Draw conclusions.*
11. *Develop recommendations.*
12. *Communicate the findings and recommendations.*

Figure 6.2: Program Evaluation: Evaluation Plan

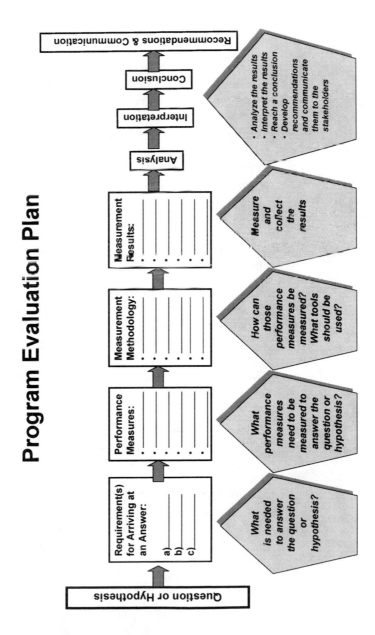

Program Evaluation Plan

Question or Hypothesis

Requirement(s) for Arriving at an Answer:
a)
b)
c)

Performance Measures:
. . . . .

Measurement Methodology:
. . . . .

Measurement Results:
. . . . .

Analysis

Interpretation

Conclusion

Recommendations & Communication

What is needed to answer the question or hypothesis?

What performance measures need to be measured to answer the question or hypothesis?

How can those performance measures be measured? What tools should be used?

Measure and collect the results

• Analyze the results
• Interpret the results
• Reach a conclusion
• Develop recommendations and communicate them to the stakeholders

Summative and Formative Evaluation

Three other evaluation terms and techniques that are commonly used include:

- **Needs Assessment** which is a form of gap analysis. In essence, it is the systematic exploration of the way things are (the *current state*) and the way they should be (the *desired state*). The intent is to define the need — that is the gap(s) between the current and desired states with a view to reducing or eliminating those identified gaps.

- **Summative Evaluation** provides information on a program's efficacy, that is, the ability to do what it was designed to do.[7] For example, did the supervisors learn what they were supposed to learn from a disability management educational session? In a sense, it lets the participant and the educator measure "how they did". More importantly, looking at the participant's level of achievement enables the educator to determine if the educational session teaches what it is designed to teach.

  Summative evaluation is typically quantitative in nature. It uses numeric scores or letter grades to assess learner achievement. It is usually conducted after a certain period of time (*e.g.*, the first year, third year) to determine if the program has met established standards, goals, objectives or targets. The findings and reports can be distributed internally or externally.

- **Formative Evaluation** is a little more complex. It is done during the development, delivery, or improvement of a program/product/educational session.[8] Typically, it is conducted with small groups of people who are asked to evaluate, or "test run", various aspects of a program/product/ training course or materials. For example, a Disability Management professional/ practitioner might ask a group of workers to comment on a Disability Management form, or the contents of a Disability Management Program brochure prior to its publication and use in the workplace. At times, feedback from a target audience might be sought. For example, when developing content for a Disability Management Program webpage, comments should be sought from the stakeholders for whom the webpage content is being designed.

  The purpose of formative evaluation is to validate or ensure that the goals of the program/product/training course are being achieved and to make improvements, if necessary, by means of identification and subsequent remediation of problematic aspects.[9] Other distinguishing

---

[7]   M. Scriven, *Evaluation Thesaurus*, 4th ed. (Newbury Park, CA: Sage Publications, 1991).

[8]   *Ibid.*

[9]   C. Weston, L. McAlpine & T. Bordonaro, "A Model for Understanding Formative Evaluation in Instructional Design" (1995) 43:3 Educational Technology Research and Development 29.

features are that a formative evaluation tends to be conducted repeatedly with a view to improvement, and the findings/reports are intended for internal use.

Impact Evaluation

An **impact evaluation** measures the degree of change in the behaviours/well-being/attitudes of workers, workgroups, business units, or organizations that can be attributed to a particular Disability Management policy, program initiative, or process. The central impact evaluation question is: "What would have happened to those receiving the intervention if they had not in fact experienced the disability management policy, program initiative, or process?"

Since evaluation of workers/workgroups/business units/organizations with and without an intervention is not possible, the use of a control group is adopted for comparison purposes. A **control group** is a group which is as similar as possible (in observable and unobservable dimensions) to those receiving the intervention (the study group). This comparison allows for the establishment of **definitive causality**, *i.e.*, attributing observed changes to the program, while removing confounding factors.

Impact evaluation is aimed at providing feedback to help improve the design of Disability Management Programs and policies In addition to providing for improved accountability, impact evaluations are a tool for dynamic learning, allowing policymakers to improve ongoing Disability Management Programs and ultimately better allocate resources and funds.

Table 6.1 provides a summary of the evaluation types, the techniques that are typically used and the level of resources required to conduct the evaluation. Note that the presentation of this table is arranged so that each level is expected to include the evaluation technique described at lower levels in ascending program evaluations in addition to those described at the higher level.

Table 6.1: Program Evaluation: Types, Resources, and Techniques

Program Evaluation: Types, Resources and Techniques			
Evaluation Types	**Resources: Minimal**	**Resources: Modest**	**Resources: Substantial**
Structure	• Document review • Comparison against a standard	Audit	Comparison against "best disability management practices"
Process	Record keeping (*e.g.*, monitoring activity timetables)	Program checklist (*e.g.*, review of adherence to Disability Management Program plans)	Management audit (*e.g.*, external management review of Disability Management Program activities)
Outcome	Activity assessments (*e.g.*, numbers of disability claims open and managed as well as the outcomes realized)	Progress in attaining Disability Management Program objectives	Assessment of target audience for knowledge gain (*e.g.*, level of employee awareness of the Disability Management Program)
Summative	Disability statistics	Trend analysis	Performance comparisons between groups, between years, or between industry groups

Program Evaluation: Types, Resources and Techniques			
Evaluation Types	**Resources: Minimal**	**Resources: Modest**	**Resources: Substantial**
Formative	Readability/ "eyeballing" or use of the "snicker test"	• Central location • Participant interviews	• Focus groups • Individual in-depth interviews
Impact	Print media review (*e.g.*, monitoring of management & union agreements; review of company policies)	Employee surveys (*e.g.*, perception survey about the Disability Management Program and its processes – SERVQUAL Tool)	Studies of employee/supervisor behaviour/ health change (*e.g.*, knowledge or practice changes regarding disability management practices)

WHY MEASURE AN INTEGRATED DISABILITY MANAGEMENT PROGRAM'S PERFORMANCE?

One question that is always raised is: "Why continuously monitor and check the Integrated Disability Management Program performance results?" The answer is to:

- Determine whether the Integrated Disability Management Program has been successful and/or effective in achieving its stated goals, objectives and targets.
- Determine whether the Integrated Disability Management Program reached the target population(s).
- Determine the cost of the Integrated Disability Management Program and the related return on investment.
- Justify past and future costs and challenges faced by the Integrated Disability Management Program.
- Justify continuation, continuation with modifications, or termination of the Integrated Disability Management Program.
- Contribute to the field of Disability Management knowledge-base.
- Determine the strengths and weaknesses of the Integrated Disability Management Program elements for continuous improvement actions.

- Demonstrate that the Integrated Disability Management Program is meeting the organization's expectations and aligns with the overall business strategies.
- Promote confidence in the quality, value and benefits of the Integrated Disability Management Program.
- Assess and comment on the current governance, accountability and performance measurement systems within the organization.

The value obtained from conducting an evaluation of an Integrated Disability Management Program is that it:

- Creates greater stakeholder awareness of the Integrated Disability Management Program, its goals, elements, functions and outcomes.
- Identifies opportunities for Integrated Disability Management Program improvement(s).
- Provides direction for enhancement of the Integrated Disability Management Program's elements, standards and procedures.
- Increases stakeholder appreciation that "upstream" company practices and behaviours (**leading indicators**) can positively impact "downstream" outcomes (**lagging indicators**), which are typically noted by the Integrated Disability Management Program.
- Promotes greater focus on inducing long-term behavioural and organizational cultural change.
- Can be used as a performance measurement for organizational incentive programs.
- Provides "real" data for organizational marketing initiatives; for enhancing the organization's image as a responsible player in occupational health & safety; for leveraging system/program improvements; and for worker training programs.
- Demonstrates corporate due diligence in terms of managing employee disabilities.

Ideally when developing a Disability Management Program, the organization establishes the desired performance measures. However, this is rarely achieved for a number of reasons.[10] Instead, Disability Management Programs are implemented with little forethought of what success would look like.

Once a Disability Management Program is established, the next step is to measure its actual performance by comparing the results against established Disability Management Program standards. For example, NIDMAR has established Disability Management Program standards; as well, there are industry Disability Management best practices that can be used as practice guidelines. The effectiveness of the Disability Management Program can also be

---

[10]   H. Harder & L. Scott, *Comprehensive Disability Management* (Toronto: Elsevier, Churchill Livingstone, 2005).

demonstrated in terms of the achievement of stated goals, objectives, and targets.

Analyzing the data provides a measure of the Disability Management Program's cost-effectiveness, which in turn directly impacts the company's bottom line. Data collection and analysis also provides reports demonstrating compliance with Canadian duty to accommodate legislation, and supports the legal concept of due diligence.

DATA COLLECTION TECHNIQUES

Data collection techniques range from being manual to electronic in nature. The main issue is to identify the relevant variables on which to collect disability management data. In Chapter 5, "An Integrated Disability Management Program: The Managed Rehabilitative Care Program", a number of data collection techniques were described. However, these techniques are by no means all encompassing. As more data on disability is being collected and linked with other databases, more ways to evaluate Integrated Disability Management Programs emerge.

Typically, Integrated Disability Management Program evaluation involves:

- determining the differences made by the Integrated Disability Management Program;
- calculating the causes and costs of disability claims;
- calculating the number of employees who work modified/alternate work and the resulting cost-avoidance;
- documenting the number and nature of workplace accommodations;
- noting trends in the disability experience; and
- auditing the program outcomes against the expectations/industry standards for an Integrated Disability Management Program.

The types of data variables collected often include the:

- nature of the disability (*i.e.*, severity, functional impairments, prognosis, *etc.*);
- course of medical management used (*i.e.*, treatments, therapies, independent medical examinations, *etc.*);
- number and cost of "lost time" hours;
- age of the ill/injured employee;
- length of service with the company;
- type of disability benefit coverage;
- history of employee's disability claims;
- presence/absence of labour relations issues;
- employee's performance ratings;
- level of employee job satisfaction;
- level of employer satisfaction with the employee;
- psychological aspects of the disability;

- marital/family status;
- presence/absence of secondary health problems or conditions; and
- type of return-to-work option used.

Using these data, along with information from other databases, disability patterns can be identified. These patterns may include seasonal variations, off-the-job injuries versus workplace injuries, psychological illnesses associated with specific work units, increased injuries in high-risk occupations, disabilities due to lifestyle versus workplace injuries, and so on.

The information required to determine disability patterns are:

- rates of disability by job (high and low risk jobs);
- lost time hours/days by work unit;
- age-group patterns;
- ergonomic job modification needs;
- types of injuries/illness by age, gender, work units and jobs;
- body parts affected;
- causes of injury;
- rate of recurrent claims; and
- other absenteeism or lost time patterns such as seasonal differences, effect of job insecurity or labour relation problems.

DISABILITY MANAGEMENT MEASUREMENT METRICS

The field of Disability Management uses a number of measurement metrics, namely:

- **Disability Frequency Rate** — Determined by dividing the total number of disability claims multiplied by 200,000 by the total number of hours worked.

$$\text{Disability Frequency Rate} = \frac{\text{Total claims} \times 200,000}{\text{Total hours worked}}$$

This metric provides the incidence rate of disabilities per 100 workers and is similar to the Injury Frequency Rate used in the field of Occupational Health & Safety. It can also be termed the "Claim Incidence". For consistency, it is advisable to use calendar days when determining the total hours worked.

- **Disability Severity Rate** — Determined by dividing the total number of disability days lost multiplied by 200,000 by the total number of hours worked.

$$\text{Disability Severity Rate} = \frac{\text{Total hours lost} \times 200,000}{\text{Total hours worked}}$$

This metric provides the severity rate of disabilities per 100 workers and is similar to the Injury Severity Rate used in the field of Occupational Health & Safety. It can also be termed the "Morbidity Rate". For consistency, it is advisable to use calendar days when determining the lost work hours and number of total hours worked.

- **Claims per Employee** — Determined by dividing the total number of claims for a given period of time by the total number of employees for that same period of time.

- **Average Disability Claim Cost** — Determined by dividing the number of total disability claim costs by the number of claims for a particular period of time.

$$\text{Average claim cost} = \frac{\text{Total claims costs}}{\text{Total number of claims}}$$

Companies use this metric to calculate the average costs of their occupational claims (short-term disability and long-term disability plan claims), or their non-occupational claims (Workers' Compensation insurance claims), or a combination of both (all disability claims).

- **Costs per Employee** — Determined by dividing the total claim costs for a given period of time by the total number of employees for that same period of time.[11]

- **Cost-benefit Analysis** — Determined by dividing the potential cost for a program for a given period of time by the actual costs for that same time period.

$$\text{Program Cost/Benefit Analysis} = \frac{\text{Potential Cost}}{\text{Actual Cost}} = \frac{(\text{Potential hours off work} \times \text{hourly salary}) + \text{Average LTD debt/case}}{(\text{Actual hours off work on STD}) + (\text{Program Costs per case})}$$

- **Return on Investment** — Determined by dividing the total savings realized through a program/intervention (*e.g.*, Disability Management Program, case management, return-to-work initiative, *etc.*) by the total cost of the program/intervention for that same time period. Taking an individual disability management claim or case, the formula to calculate the return on investment is as follows:

$$\text{ROI} = \frac{\text{Savings realized through modified/alternate work} + \text{Program intervention savings} + \text{Unused LTD reserve}}{\text{Total Costs for the Case}}$$

---

[11] Washington Business Group on Health (2004), available online at: <http://www.wbgh.org>.

In this formula, the:

Total Costs for the Case = (STD/LTD Costs) + (Assessment, treatment, rehabilitation & accommodation costs)

To interpret the ROI, a positive value indicates that for every dollar spent on the program/intervention, the organization saved that amount of money up to the amount spent. So an ROI = +$2 indicates a saving of $2 for every dollar spent. A negative value signals an investment loss, *e.g.* an ROI = -$0.25 denotes that the company lost 25 cents for every dollar that it spent on its investment (the Disability Management Program or a particular intervention).

• **Payout Ratio** — Determined by dividing the total dollars saved through the efforts of a Disability Management Program, initiative, gradual return-to-work program by the total dollars paid for the cost of the Disability Management Program, initiative, gradual return-to-work program for that same time period.

Payout Ratio = <u>Dollars Saved through the Disability Management Program</u>
Cost of the Disability Management Program

This is the ratio of employee work hours and productivity saved (expressed as dollars saved or cost-avoided) divided by the investment dollars required to realize that saving. If this ratio is >1, the payout realized was greater than what was spent. If it is <1, then it cost more to operate the program, or to bring the person back to work than the financial benefit realized.

COMPUTERIZED DATA MANAGEMENT

Computerized disability data management software programs tend to collect the employee demographic data such as employee name, home address, date of birth, marital status, work details, job details, hours of work, salary and relevant medical history or work restrictions. This information is then used to assist with the data analysis and interpretation for all Disability Management Program data.

In terms of individual medical absence, information on the nature of the absence (*i.e.*, illness or injury, occupational or non-occupational, *etc.*), date and time of the absence, expected length of absence, modified/alternate work activity and the actual return to work should be collected. Using this data, most software programs are able to determine the hours lost and the cost; the hours and the cost avoided on modified/alternate work; and the costs associated with the nature of the absence. This data is usually available by work location, department and supervisor. In this way, the Disability Management Program Manager/Coordinator can establish the costs, and cost-avoidance opportunities, associated with the disability management activities. This is one way to demonstrate the value of the Integrated Disability Management Program to the company.

Some software programs deal with strictly Workers' Compensation Board absences while others address all employee absences. Some programs use a linear approach to data analysis, while others use an integrated approach. The linear approach deals with the absence data only. However, the integrated approach allows the user to examine absence data in relation to demographic data, workplace descriptors, industrial hygiene data, Employee Assistance Program information, and occupational or non-occupational absence data.

This latter approach is by far the more powerful of the two options because many disabilities are the end result of other factors such as management styles, labour disputes, organizational change, an economic downturn, and/or changing societal beliefs and values. By linking the variables and outcomes from a number of occupational areas or databases, trends, and associations can be established.

EVALUATION OF A DISABILITY MANAGEMENT PROGRAM

There are a number of ways to evaluate the functionality and effectiveness of a Disability Management Program:

- **Auditing** — using this measurement technique, the current Disability Management Program is measured against the organization's Disability Management Program goals, objectives, and targets, and/or against an established or pre-determined protocol or standard. Auditing involves documentation reviews, interviews and observations to verify the existence and functionality of various programs, policies and procedures. The goal is to identify the gaps between the current and "ideal" state of the program. Typically, the audit process includes recommendations for reaching the "ideal" state.

  NIDMAR has developed a Consensus Based Disability Management Audit™ (CBDMA™) that can be used for benchmarking purposes. The CBDMA is designed to set the minimum acceptable criteria for disability management programs, identify improvement opportunities, and promote the use of "best practices" in disability management.[12]

- **Benchmarking** — benchmarking is a continual and collaborative discipline that involves measuring and comparing the results of the key process with "best performers", or with one's own previous achievements. Internally, benchmarking can be used to compare the Disability Management Program results against previous performance results. This can be done in terms of

---

[12] National Institute of Disability Management and Research (NIDMAR), *Consensus Based Disability Management Audit*™ (CBDMA™) (Port Alberni, BC: NIDMAR, 2004), available online at: <http://www.nidmar.ca/audit/audit_synopsis.asp>.

the whole company, or among the various divisions within the company. Externally, benchmarking involves comparing an organization's Disability Management Program and/or the results against those of another organization. Typically, benchmarking is undertaken to improve the quality of the service or product, address an identified problem, learn "best practices", or, in response to increased pressures, to improve performance. It is not an exact science, but rather a methodology designed to determine the best way to do things.

In terms of benchmarking Disability Management Programs, the process would be to:

1. determine the desired information, that is, the questions to be asked (Table 6.2);

Table 6.2: Benchmarking: Typical Questions

	Question
1.	Is your Disability Management Program an "inhouse" or outsourced service?
2.	Does your organization have a formalized Disability Management Program?
3.	Who administers your Disability Management Program?
4.	Who manages your Disability Management Program?
5.	Is the Disability Management Program managed by certified disability management specialists equipped with the education and experience to handle difficult disability situations?
6.	How does your Disability Management Program operate from onset of a disability to its resolution?
7.	Do you have graduated return-to-work initiatives? How do they work?
8.	How is employee absence and return to work funded — by the home department or through a global funding?
9.	Are the organization's labour and management leaders committed and actively involved in the Disability Management Program?
10.	Is the Disability Management Program linked with other company programs such as the Attendance Support & Assistance Program, Occuaptional Health & Safety Program, Employee Assistance Program, Human Resources Program, Workplace Wellness Program, Ergonomic Program, *etc.*?
11.	How does the organization collect and track its disability data?
12.	How is the information about the Disability Management Program reported and communicated?

Table 6.2: Benchmarking: Typical Questions (cont'd)

	Question
13.	Have benefits been noted as a result of having a Disability Management Program? Please explain.
14.	Does the organization have a communication strategy? Is it effective?
15.	How often is the Disability Management Program evaluated — informally and formally? How is that achieved?

2. plan what and who to benchmark;
3. collect and analyze relevant data;
4. integrate the findings into the organization's/company's frame of reference;
5. determine what will and will not work; and
6. develop an action plan that would implement, monitor and evaluate the changes made.

- **Cost Effectiveness and Cost-Benefit Analysis** — evaluation of the Disability Management Program often includes some measurement of cost. This may range from a requirement to demonstrate the cost effectiveness of the Disability Management Program to analyzing the cost benefit of a specific aspect of the program, such as employee awareness of the program, the average duration of a short-term disability claim, the number of short-term disability claims that move on to long-term disability, *etc.*

Cost containment refers to keeping costs to a minimum. **Cost effectiveness** is demonstrating the results of the Disability Management Program from a financial perspective. **Cost benefit** is weighing costs of the Disability Management Program against the benefits provided.

One formula that can be used for determining the cost-benefit of a Disability Management Program is:

$$\text{Program Cost/Benefit Analysis} = \frac{\text{Potential Cost}}{\text{Actual Cost}} = \frac{(\text{Potential hours off work} \times \text{hourly salary}) + \text{Average LTD debt/case}}{(\text{Actual hours off work on STD}) + (\text{Program Costs per case})}$$

This formula can be applied to calculate the cost per benefit of individual cases, and a mean value can be derived for the entire program.

Effective analysis of costs requires planning, data collection and the appropriate analysis tools. The first step is to decide what is to be measured. The second step is to decide what data is required to provide the information, and how the data will be collected and analyzed.

Data to demonstrate cost effectiveness usually needs to be collected over time, both to provide meaningful information for analysis and to provide the necessary information for measurement of improvement.

- **Cost-benefit Analysis Projection** — involves establishing the causal relationship between the Disability Management Program and the benefits realized (Figure 6.3); categorizing the costs and benefits as short-term versus long-term, and fixed versus variable; quantifying the benefits and costs through direct or indirect projections; and comparing the benefits and costs (Figure 6.4).

Figure 6.3: Causal Relationship Between the Disability Management Program and the Benefits Realized[13]

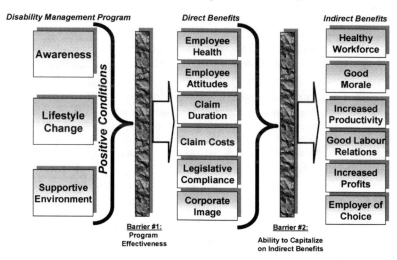

Adapted from: O'Donnell (1984) and Watson-Wyatt (2007)

---

[13]   M.P. O'Donnell & T.H. Ainsworth, eds., *Health Promotion in the Workplace* (New York: John Wiley & Sons, 1984); and Watson-Wyatt, *Staying@Work: Effective Presence at Work* (2007), available online at: <https://www.watsonwyatt.com/research/resrender.asp?id=2007-US-0166&page=1>.

Figure 6.4: Framework for Cost-Benefit Analysis Projection[14]

Disability Management Program: Causal Relationship between Program and Benefits

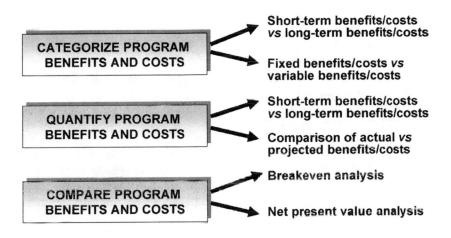

Adapted from O'Donnell, 1984

- **Return On Investment (ROI)** — for having a sound Disability Management Program (DMP), the formula is:

$$\textbf{ROI} = \frac{(\text{Costs without a DMP}) - (\text{Costs with a DMP})}{\text{Cost of developing/operating the DMP}} = \text{Savings}$$

This measurement technique can be applied at an individual, group, or program level. Basically, the process involves determining the costs, benefits, and savings realized by the disability management services and/or activities. The return on investment is calculated by dividing the savings by the costs required by a company to realize those savings.

A model, like the one presented in Figure 6.5, can be used to determine both the costs/benefits of a Disability Management Program and the return on investment. The model operates by determining the company costs with and without a Disability Management Program. The model calculates the saving realized by having a Disability Management Program in place. To

---

[14]   M.P. O'Donnell & T.H. Ainsworth, *ibid.*

determine the return on investment, the established saving value is divided by the amount invested to realize this saving. Models like this function with the use of assumptions; the key factor is to ensure that the assumptions used are valid.

Typically, the return on investment for having a sound Disability Management Program in place is $3 for every $1 spent on Disability Management.[15] When determining ROI, companies tend to deal with direct safety costs.[16] However, if the data elements (*e.g.*, number of short-term disability claims within a specific workgroup, or occupational injury frequency rates for a specific workgroup) and indirect costs[17] of Disability Management are included, the ROI increases 3-5 fold.[18]

In addition, the non-financial returns can include the provision of a healthy and safe work environment, compliance with regulations, reduction in work-related injuries/illness, healthier workforce, good employee morale, retention of workers, and reputation and corporate image management.

---

[15]   Liberty Mutual, reported in "Proving the Return on Investment on Safety" (2001) 1:2 Safety Compliance Insider 15.

[16]   **Direct Disability Management costs** are the costs directly identifiable in terms of disability management such as disability claim costs, Workers' Compensation Administrative costs, work accommodation costs, replacement worker costs, and the associated Disability Management Program costs.

[17]   **Indirect Disability Management costs** include the "hidden" costs such as the management time and effort to facilitate a safe and timely return to work, scheduling costs, worker re-training costs, data management time and costs, *etc.*

[18]   *Ibid.*

Figure 6.5: Estimated Return on Investment for Company XYZ'S Disability Management Program

ASSUMES

- 15% reduction in Sick Leave through DMP;
- Company XYZ employs 800 employees at an average salary of $45,000;
- 14.23% WCB discount (rebate);
- 7% incidence rate for LTD each year; and
- LTD reserve per claimant to be $95,000.

COSTS WITHOUT DMP

A	Cost of Sick Leave	$800,000
B	Cost of WCB Assessment	$277,200
C	WCB Rebates (Discounts)	14.23%
D	PIR Incentive Discount (5%)	$13,860
E	Net WCB Costs (B – D)	$263,340
F	LTD Rates (Assumes a 7% LTD rate or 2- 3 LTD cases per year)	$2,391,025
G	Total Costs (A + E + F)	$3,454,365

COSTS WITH DMP

H	Cost of Sick Leave (assumes a 15% reduction)	$680,000
I	Cost of WCB Assessment (assumes a 5% improvement)	$262,800
J	WCB Rebate (Discount) – 5% increase	19.23%
K	PIR Incentive Discount (5 + 5%)	$26,280
L	Net WCB Costs (B-D)	$236,520
M	LTD Rates (assumes a reduction of 5 claims and lowered reserves – 5 x $95,000 = $475,000 reduction)	$1,916,025
N	Total Costs with the DMP (H + L + M)	$2,832,545
O	Total Price for the DMP	$80,000

SAVINGS WITH DMP

P	(G-N)	$3,454,365-$2,832,545	$621,820

RETURN ON INVESTMENT

Q	(P ÷ O)	$621,820 + $80,000	7.77

- **Perception Surveys** — measurement of worker experience and perception of the quality and effectiveness of the Disability Management Program can be achieved through the use of a perception survey. Employees are well-positioned to provide feedback on the quality and effectiveness of the Disability Management Program, as well as the individual components of the program (such as claim management, case management, return-to-work efforts, *etc.*).

  An example of this measurement technique is provided in the section of this chapter entitled "Gap Analysis of a Managed Rehabilitative Care Program". It enables a gap analysis of the current Disability Management Program in comparison with the desired state for the Disability Management Program. From there, gaps can be identified and an action plan to eliminate or reduce the identified gaps, developed. The strength of the perception surveys (SERVQUAL tool) is that it identifies what continuous improvement actions employees perceive as valuable for the organization to pursue.[19]

- **Client Satisfaction Surveys** — typically ask those employees who participated in the Disability Management Program for their impressions of the service, caregivers, Disability Management professionals/ practitioners, and outcomes. The questions that are usually asked are designed to measure specific elements of the program such as timeliness, accessibility, appropriateness, and universality of the program. The last section of this chapter describes in detail a client satisfaction survey technique that not only elicits responses about the service, but also identifies the techniques for dealing with any gaps in service that are identified.

- **Efficiency Measurement** — determines the timing of the return by the ill/injured worker to full time work by type of return-to-work modality,[20] or by treatment regimen, or some similar factor. Unlike the other evaluation techniques mentioned so far, this is an intervention outcome measure designed to determine the efficiency of various return-to-work opportunities or treatment modalities. For example, one could examine the length of time workers are off work on disability claim and unable to return to their regular jobs by the treatment modalities received such as psychological treatment by an EAP counsellor, physical treatment by a family physician, or treatment by a family physican and psychiatrist. The intent would be to try to establish if one treatment modality is more effective than the other in getting workers back to their regular jobs. This was done by D. Conti who determined that disability duration was greater when workers received

---

[19] D. Dyck, "Gap Analysis of Health Services: Client Satisfaction Surveys" (1996) 44 AOHNA Journal 541.

[20] H. Harder & L. Scott, *Comprehensive Disability Management* (Toronto: Elsevier, Churchill Livingstone, 2005) at 15.

"physical treatment from the family physican alone" (93 days) as opposed to "physical and psychiatric treatment" (59 days), or "psychological treatment" (37 days).[21]

Another example, would be to address the efficiency or return-to-work modalities. In this instance, the evaluation process includes this question: "For the claims handled within a period of time, what were the claim durations for each of the following return-to-work modalities:

- those claimants who returned to work;
- those claimants who returned to modified work;
- those claimants who returned to alternate work; and
- those claimants who returned to work outside of the organization?"

This approach enables examiners to determine if one return-to-work modality is more efficient than another. They also must recognize and note the potential variables that could confound the findings, such as workforce demographics, nature of work, geographic differences, legislative restrictions and organizational factors, to name but a few.[22]

PROGRAM IMPROVEMENT STRATEGIES

To improve the Disability Management Program's results, there are a few recommended strategies that organizations can choose to adopt:

- be clear on the vision, goals, objectives and targets for the Disability Management Program;
- regularly monitor and measure them;
- use an integrated bottom-line approach. That is, link the Disability Management Program results with the Occuaptional Health & Safety Program, Attendance Management Progam, Employee Assistance Program, and Human Resources (*e.g.*, staff turnover) data;
- learn from the results;
- be persistent and diligent in the selected program evaluation approach;
- let go of "what is not working";
- recognize, communicate and celebrate the achieved progress and successes;
- learn from the experts; and
- aim for continuous improvement.

---

[21] D.J. Conti, "The Management of Psychiatric Short-term Disability" (Presented at the American Psychiatric Association Annual Meeting, Miami, FL, 21 May 1996) [unpublished] and represented at the Psychological Disabilities in the Workplace: Prevention, Rehabilitation and Cost Control Conference, Toronto, June 10-11, 1996) [unpublished].

[22] H. Harder & L. Scott, *Comprehensive Disability Management* (Toronto: Elsevier, Churchill Livingstone, 2005) at 15.

With any program, there are barriers or challenges that can prevent the attainment of desired Disability Management results. They include:

- being afraid to dream or "think outside the box";
- adoption of the "It didn't work before" attitude. That may be so, but with time and change, the proposed approach may now work;
- discomfort with looking at results. "The Ostrich Approach" (*i.e.*, denial and fear) is ineffective: Face the results and determine how to address them;
- an established Integrated Disability Management Program goal that was not a priority, and hence, was not addressed;
- loss of focus;
- seeing only "problems and roadblocks", not ways to reaching workable solutions;
- choosing someone else's goals. To attain a goal, it requires ownership of that goal, as well as the passion to go after that goal;
- reluctance to ask for help;
- not keeping commitments that were made; and
- the presence of competing work demands, pressures, and stressors.

Knowing these possible detractors, Disability Management Program designers can build drivers into their program that effectively counter these potential barriers.

GAP ANALYSIS OF A MANAGED REHABILITATIVE CARE PROGRAM[23]

The first part of this section explains the Gap Analysis process and the SERVQUAL instrument, which is a survey tool used to measure client satisfaction in regards to a service.[24] The last part demonstrates how the instrument can be used to measure client satisfaction with an entire Integrated Disability Management Program, or its parts, like the Managed Rehabilitative Care Program or graduated return-to-work initiatives.

Introduction

There is an oriental saying "The customer is God".[25] However, few occupational health services focus on client satisfaction. Traditionally, the emphasis has been on evaluating the quality of care given believing that the client's knowledge of expert care is limited. However, with the increased level of client knowledge about health care and the rise in consumerism, occupational health services

---

[23] Preprinted with permission from the AAOHN Journal, D. Dyck, "Gap Analysis of Health Services: Client Satisfaction Surveys" (1996) 44 AAOHN Journal 541.

[24] V. Zeithaml, A. Parasuraman & L. Berry, *Delivering Quality Service* (Toronto: The Free Press, 1990).

[25] M. Youngblood, *Eating the Chocolate Elephant: Take Charge of Change Through Total Process Management* (Richardson, TX: Micrografx Inc., 1994).

should pay attention to client satisfaction. **Client satisfaction** can be defined as the client being aware of receiving care in a timely and responsible manner, and of the many variables in the environment that contribute to his or her successful recovery.[26]

Successful companies know that concentrating on client satisfaction is essential and, by knowing their clients' expectations, they are able to formulate their fundamental business structure. As well, client-focused companies recognize that client perceptions are formed as a result of every contact with the company. For this reason, it is important to determine the degree of harmony between client expectations and the service quality that service providers believe they are delivering.

This section defines service quality, identifies the causes of service quality problems, and outlines what occupational health services can do to solve these problems.

Service Quality

Service quality can be defined as the extent of discrepancy between client expectations, or desires, and their perceptions (Figure 6.6). The key to good service quality is meeting or exceeding client expectations of the service.[27] The motto is "under-promise" and "over-deliver".

Service quality is important because we live in a highly competitive service economy. Efficient servicing can be a source of superiority for an agency. "Excellent service pays off because it creates true customers" and "true customers are like annuities".[28]

Excellent service also differentiates service providers from otherwise similar competitors. Companies that provide excellent service perform better on the bottom line because they perform better for their clients. Clients respond to these companies because they perceive more value. Value is the client's "overall assessment of the utility of a product [or service] based on perceptions of what is received and what is given".[29] The concept of value helps to explain why companies with strong service reputations are able to charge higher prices than their competitors. Clients are willing to pay more to have confidence in the service and product.

---

[26] E. Sullivan & P. Decker, *Effective Management in Nursing*, 2nd ed. (Menlo Park, CA: Addison-Wesley Publishing, 1988).

[27] V. Zeithaml, A. Parasuraman & L. Berry, *Delivering Quality Service* (Toronto: The Free Press, 1990).

[28] *Ibid.*

[29] V. Zeithaml, "Consumer Perceptions of Price, Quality and Value: A Means-End Model and Synthesis of Evidence" (1988) 52:3 Journal of Marketing 2 at 14.

Figure 6.6: Components of Service Quality

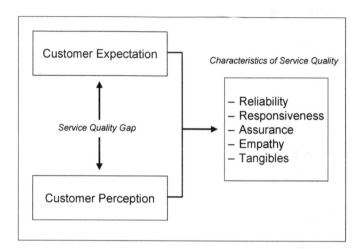

Services are more difficult to evaluate than products. First, services are intangible, "when what is being sold is purely performance, the criteria customers use to evaluate it may be complex and difficult to capture precisely".[30] Second, services are heterogeneous — performance often varies from provider to provider, from client to client and from day to day.[31] Third, the production and consumption of many services are inseparable: "quality in services often occurs during the service delivery, usually in an interaction between the client and the provider, rather than being engineered at the manufacturing plant and delivered intact to the client".[32]

The factors that influence client expectations are word of mouth communications, personal needs of the clients, past experience with a service, and external communications from service providers about the service.[33] Their relationship to expected service is depicted in Figure 6.7.

Clients judge service quality by the following criteria:

---

[30]   V. Zeithaml, A. Parasuraman & L. Berry, *Delivering Quality Service* (Toronto: The Free Press, 1990).

[31]   *Ibid.*

[32]   *Ibid.*

[33]   *Ibid.*

Figure 6.7: Dimensions of Service Quality

Dimension of Service Quality	Definition	Examples
Tangibles	Appearance of physical facilities, equipment, personnel and communication materials.	Are the OHS facilities attractive? Are the EAP Advisors dressed appropriately? Is communication to clients easy to understand (*i.e.*, correspondence letters, memos, presentations, *etc.*)?
Reliability	Ability to perform the promised service dependably and accurately.	Are the service records free of error? Is a client's concern addressed properly the first time?
Responsiveness	Willingness to help clients and provide prompt service.	Do we give clients a specific time when we will see them? How long do clients have to wait for an appointment?
Assurance	Competence Possession of required skills and knowledge to perform the service.	Can we process client needs without fumbling around? Are we able to answer client questions upon request?
	Courtesy Politeness, respect, consideration and friendliness.	Do we have a friendly attitude? Do we act like clients are interrupting us when they ask a question?
	Credibility Trustworthiness, believability, honesty of the service provider.	Does the department have a good reputation? Are our service costs consistent with the services provided?
	Security Freedom from danger, risk or doubt.	Is client confidentiality trusted? Can clients be confident that the prescribed treatment/modification is safe for use?
Empathy	Access Approachability and ease of contact.	How easy is it for clients to talk to a caregiver when they have a problem? Is the service open at hours that a client can get help?
	Communication Keeping clients informed and listening to them.	When clients call the department, are we willing to listen to them? Can we explain clearly all the various details of the client's circumstance?
	Understand the client Making the effort to know clients and their needs.	Do we recognize clients after their initial visit? Are we willing to be flexible enough to accommodate the client's schedule?

Gap Analysis

The service gap analysis methodology integrates the concepts, ideas and findings that emerged from a study of service quality which started in 1983. Research sponsored by the Marketing Science Institute in Cambridge, Massachusetts[34] resulted in the conceptual models of service quality discussed below and a methodology for measuring client perceptions of service quality — the Gap Analysis.

If the key to ensuring good service is meeting or exceeding what clients expect from the service, judgements of high and low service quality depend on how clients perceive the actual service performance in the context of what they expected (Figure 6.6).

The clients' perception of service quality is altered when there are gaps between:

- the clients' expectations and the service provider's perception of those expectations (Gap 1);
- the service provider's perception of client expectations and the specifications of service quality under which the services are governed (Gap 2);
- the specifications of service quality and the actual service that is delivered (Gap 3);
- the actual service that is delivered and what the service organization communicates to the clients about what it will deliver (Gap 4); or
- the clients' expected level of service quality and their perception of what level of service quality they actually received (Gap 5).

The nature of these gaps is explained further below.

GAP 1 — GAP BETWEEN THE CLIENTS' EXPECTATIONS AND THE SERVICE PROVIDER'S PERCEPTION OF THOSE EXPECTATIONS

Knowing what clients expect is the first and most critical step in delivering quality service. This gap sometimes occurs because companies miss the mark by thinking "inside-out". That is, they operate based on what they believe clients should want and deliver it accordingly. When this happens, services do not match clients' expectations, important features are left out and the levels of performance on features that are provided are inadequate.

The contributing factors that account for this gap include insufficient market research, inadequate use of market research findings and insufficient communication between client and service provider.

The first step in improving the quality of service is for service providers to acquire accurate information about client expectations.

---

[34]   A. Parasuraman, V. Zeithaml & L. Berry, "SERVQUAL: A Multiple-Item Scale for Measuring Consumer Perceptions of Service Quality" (1988) 64:1 Journal of Retailing 12.

GAP 2 — GAP BETWEEN THE SERVICE PROVIDER'S PERCEPTION OF CLIENT EXPECTATIONS AND THE SPECIFICATIONS OF SERVICE QUALITY UNDER WHICH THE SERVICES ARE GOVERNED

Correct perceptions of client expectations are necessary. Once service providers accurately understand what clients expect, they face a second critical challenge: using this knowledge to set appropriate service quality standards.

The contributing factors that may account for this gap include inadequate commitment to service quality, perception of unfeasibility, inadequate standardization of tasks and absence of goal setting.

Another prerequisite for providing high service quality is the presence of performance standards.

GAP 3 — GAP BETWEEN THE SPECIFICATIONS OF SERVICE QUALITY AND THE ACTUAL SERVICE THAT IS DELIVERED

In some cases, although service providers may understand client expectations and set appropriate specifications (either formally or informally), the service delivered by the organization still falls short of the expectations of the client or clients.

The primary factor in the cause of a service-performance gap is the possibility that employees are unable and/or unwilling to perform the service at the desired level. This may be a result of an inadequate understanding of his or her role; role conflict; poor employee-job fit; poor employee-technology fit; inappropriate measurement/reward systems; lack of empowerment; and/or lack of team-work.

GAP 4 — GAP BETWEEN THE ACTUAL SERVICE THAT IS DELIVERED AND WHAT THE SERVICE ORGANIZATION COMMUNICATES TO THE CLIENTS ABOUT WHAT IT WILL DELIVER

Promises made by a service group serve as the standard against which clients assess service quality. A discrepancy between actual service and promised service may have an adverse effect on client perceptions of service quality if the service has been over-promised.

GAP 5 — GAP BETWEEN THE CLIENTS' EXPECTED LEVEL OF SERVICE QUALITY AND THEIR PERCEPTION OF WHAT LEVEL OF SERVICE QUALITY THEY ACTUALLY RECEIVED

A gap in any one of the four areas listed above will cause a gap between what clients expect to receive and their perception of the level of service quality actually received. The key to closing this last gap is to close Gaps 1 through 4 and to keep them closed. Figure 6.8 is a summary of the reasons these gaps exist and the areas to investigate when closing the gaps.

Gaps 1 and 2 are managerial gaps. Gap 1 stems from a manager's lack of understanding of customer expectations while Gap 2 represents a manager's failure to set appropriate service qualifications.

Gaps 3 and 4 are front-line gaps. Front-line employees' service-delivery performance may fall short of service specifications (Gap 3) and fail to fulfil promises made through external communications (Gap 4).

Figure 6.8: Reasons for Gaps and Areas to Investigate

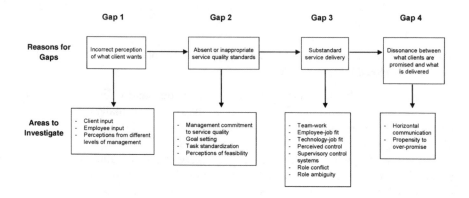

Addressing Service Quality Gaps

The major benefit of the SERVQUAL tool is that it not only identifies the gaps that exist, but also offers recommendations for addressing the problems. Figure 6.9 provides an overview of the potential causes of service quality gaps. The following discussion on each gap provides suggestions for narrowing or eliminating the gaps.

Figure 6.9: Potential Causes of Service Quality Shortfalls

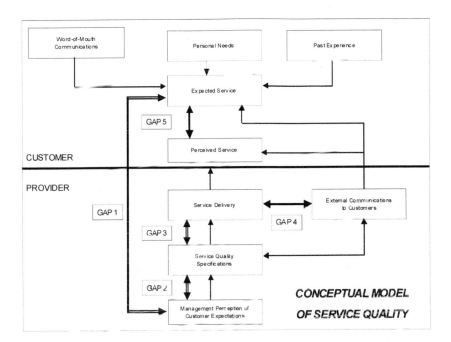

GAP 1 — CLIENT EXPECTATIONS AND MANAGEMENT PERCEPTIONS

Management may be unaware of the characteristics or service features that are valued by clients. When this happens, companies provide services that do not match client expectations. Thus, they may make decisions and resource allocations resulting in client perceptions of poor service quality. The necessary first step in improving service quality is for management to obtain accurate information about client expectations. The key contributing factors that make up Gap 1, as well as ways to close Gap 1 are provided in Figure 6.10.

Figure 6.10: Factors Contributing to Gap 1

Problem	Ways to Close Gap 1
Insufficient market research	Research client expectations Use complaints strategically Research clients' expectations of similar services Research intermediate clients such as contact professionals/staff Conduct key client studies Track client satisfaction with individual servicing Engage in comprehensive client expectation studies
Inadequate use of market research findings	Use market research findings effectively
Lack of interaction between management and clients	Increase management-client interaction
Insufficient upward communication from contact personnel to management	Improve upward communication from contact professionals/staff
Too many levels between contact personnel/staff and management	Flatten the organizational structure

GAP 2 — MANAGEMENT PERCEPTION AND SERVICE QUALITY SPECIFICATIONS

Once management understands client expectations, the next challenge is using this knowledge to set service quality standards. However, management may not be willing or able to meet these expectations or the actual specifications established for service delivery. The causes of Gap 2 are provided in Figure 6.11.

Figure 6.11: Factors Contributing to Gap 2

Problem	Ways to Close Gap 2
Inadequate management commitment to service quality	Commit to quality and ensure middle management commitment to service quality Develop performance standards that mirror management's perception of client expectations
Perception of unfeasibility	Create possibilities
Inadequate standardization of tasks	Standardize tasks with hard technology (*i.e.*, databases, systems) and with soft technology (*i.e.*, policies, procedures, changed work processes, *etc.*)
Lack of goal setting	Set service quality goals

GAP 3 — SERVICE QUALITY SPECIFICATIONS AND SERVICE DELIVERY

Both clients and providers experience and respond to each other's mannerisms, attitudes, competencies, moods and language. Maintaining service quality depends on maintaining a workforce willing and able to perform at specified levels.

The factors contributing to Gap 3 are included in Figure 6.12.

Figure 6.12: Factors Contributing to Gap 3

Problem	Ways to Close Gap 3
Employee-job fit Technology-job fit	Improve employee/technology-job fit
Employee role ambiguity	Provide role clarity
Role conflict	Eliminate role conflict
Lack of perceived control	Empower service providers
Inappropriate supervisory control systems	Measure and reward service performance
Lack of teamwork	Nurture teamwork Actively build teamwork

GAP 4 — SERVICE DELIVERY AND EXTERNAL COMMUNICATIONS TO CLIENTS

A discrepancy between actual and promised service reflects an underlying breakdown in coordination between those responsible for delivering the service and those charged with describing or promising the service.

Marketing can influence client expectations by informing clients of all the behind-the-scenes activities performed in order to protect them. By making clients aware of the commitment to quality service, improvements in client service perceptions are realized. Service perceptions can be enhanced by educating clients to be better consumers and service users. The factors contributing to Gap 4 are provided in Figure 6.13. By closing Gaps 1 through 4, Gap 5 is eliminated.

Figure 6.13: Factors Contributing to Gap 4

Problem	Ways to Close Gap 4
Inadequate horizontal communication	Open channels of communication between those marketing the service and those providing the service
Avoid over-promising	Develop appropriate and effective communications about the service
Differing policies and procedures	Provide consistent servicing throughout the agency/company

Instrument Reliability and Validity

The SERVQUAL instrument[35] was designed to help companies better understand service expectations and perceptions of their clients. It is a multi-item scale with good reliability and validity. A complete discussion of the instrument's reliability and validity can be found in the research sponsored by the Marketing Science Institute.[36]

This instrument can be used in a number of companies or services and the developers acknowledge that it can be adapted to meet the individual needs of a company.[37]

In addition to computing service quality gaps, SERVQUAL can also be used to:

---

[35] V. Zeithaml, A. Parasuraman & L. Berry, *Delivering Quality Service* (Toronto: The Free Press, 1990).

[36] A. Parasuraman, V. Zeithaml & L. Berry, "SERVQUAL: A Multiple-item Scale for Measuring Consumer Perceptions of Service Quality" (1988) 64:1 Journal of Retailing 12.

[37] *Ibid.*

- identify trends in client expectations and perceptions over time;
- compare a company's or service's SERVQUAL scores against those of competitors;
- examine client segments with differing quality perceptions; and
- assess quality perceptions of internal customers.

Industry Application

At one large Canadian company, as part of total quality management, client satisfaction surveys were conducted by many service departments in an effort to continually improve service quality and delivery. Occupational health services joined this effort and chose the Gap Analysis method to evaluate its early Return-to-Work Program and Managed Rehabilitative Care program.

Since SERVQUAL was designed to evaluate business servicing, changes had to be made to adapt the questions for a disability management service. Care was taken to ensure that the service qualities continued to be measured as originally developed. Also, all the questions were left in their order of presentation. Comment sections were included to augment the standardized questions and to elicit responses not dealt with by the questions. The result was two survey tools designed for this type of service evaluation using the Gap Analysis technique.

Survey Methodology

The Managed Rehabilitation Care surveys were distributed to all employees on modified/alternate work plans while on short-term disability or long-term disability between January 1, 1994 and September 30, 1994. For each client on a modified/alternate work plan, a corresponding manager was included. These client-participant and client-manager survey numbers are distinguished with the suffixes P and M, respectively. In addition, all relevant disability management professionals involved with the Managed Rehabilitation Care program were surveyed.

The assessment of gaps in service quality was performed through the use of two questionnaires: one questionnaire was sent to the clients of the service (Appendix 1); the other to caregivers, management and staff (Appendix 2).

The client questionnaire focused on priorities, expectations for service quality and perceptions of the quality of service clients are receiving. The caregiver questionnaire focused on measuring:

- the caregiver's understanding of client expectations;
- whether service quality standards are formalized within the service group;
- whether the actual service delivery meets service quality standards; and
- the degree to which the service delivers what is promised to clients.

It was recognized that problems would occur in attempting to use a business tool to evaluate health services. Some issues encountered were:

- awkwardly worded questions which were difficult for clients to interpret and understand;
- redundant or leading questions;
- respondents who reported that they were too inexperienced with the service to answer the questions posed;
- too much focus on quantitative measures, as opposed to qualitative measures; and
- the dimensions of service quality (*i.e.*, tangibles, reliability, responsiveness, assurance, empathy, *etc.*) were measured at a macro-level, which proved difficult for clients to understand. This resulted in a very general questionnaire, which did not deal with why individual cases were successes or failures.

If these services are to be surveyed again, the questionnaires used would have to focus more on human concerns than on business concerns.

MANAGED REHABILITATION CARE SERVICE SURVEY RESULTS

Out of the 67 surveys sent out to Managed Rehabilitation Care service clients, 51 responded (76 per cent), 48 (72 per cent) were used for analysis and three were incomplete and could not be used.

Figure 6.14: MRC Client Expectations versus Perceptions — Gap 5

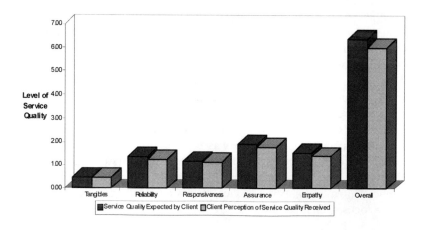

FINDINGS

1. Managed Rehabilitation Care caregivers do not have a clear understanding of what service qualities are most important to clients. Client-participants indicate that the most important service quality is assurance. Client-managers indicate that the most important service quality is reliability. Caregivers think that the most important service qualities are reliability and empathy.

   Result: More attention could be given to assurance.

2. Managed Rehabilitation Care caregivers may understand that reliability is important to client-managers, however they do not seem to understand how important other service qualities are to clients. Client-participants rate assurance much higher in importance than caregivers do. Client-managers rate reliability much higher in importance than caregivers do.

   Result: More attention could be given to assurance and reliability.

3. Managed Rehabilitation Care caregivers generally understand and meet both client groups' expectations, however the client-participant group has a higher expectation of Managed Rehabilitation Care assurance than they perceive they get. The client-manager group has a higher expectation of Managed Rehabilitation Care reliability than they perceive they get.

4. If Managed Rehabilitation Care service desires to increase the understanding of the service qualities important to clients, suggested improvement activities would include:

   (a) Increase market research (*i.e.*, track satisfaction with individual transactions, use complaints strategically, *etc.*).
   (b) Assess performance measurement/reward systems to ensure caregivers are rewarded for quality service provided.

OVERALL RESULTS

Service quality assessments indicated that the clients perceive the service quality as relatively high, and that only small gaps were revealed in the survey. However, there were opportunities for improvement and this information came from the client commentaries.

Positive Client Feedback

- Reliable and quick responses are appreciated by employees.
- Security is vital: confidentiality of employee health information remains paramount and constant vigilance is required to uphold this confidentiality.
- Professional competence is important.
- Courtesy is important.
- Empathy is essential.

- Credible counselling and care is valued.

Issues to Address

- Market the available services better.
- Educate managers/supervisors on the use of Managed Rehabilitation Care as supports for employees.
- Educate stakeholders about their roles and responsibilities concerning Managed Rehabilitation Care.
- Increase communication with all involved in Managed Rehabilitation Care to ensure efficient business functioning and effective employee participation occurs.
- Pay more attention to the case management of employees off on Workers' Compensation.
- Be proactive regarding ergonomics, indoor air quality, employee wellness, mental/social health and balancing work and family life.

RESEARCH CONCLUSION

To remain competitive in this economic market, client satisfaction is key to successful servicing. Gap analysis can be a powerful method for evaluating client satisfaction. The strengths of the SERVQUAL instrument are that it identifies service quality gaps, provides suggestions for closing those gaps and allows for service quality analysis. It has been well researched, clinically tested and demonstrates reliability and validity. Its limitations are that it does not provide opportunity for client commentary and tends to focus more on the business aspects and less on the human aspects of servicing. However, by adding in comment sections, as was done in the above industry application, the elicited client responses proved valuable in understanding the nature of the gaps identified.

SUMMARY

Outcome measurements are vital to any program, especially one in which the participation of a number of stakeholders is critical for program success and longevity. For stakeholders to continue to support a program, they must have data to demonstrate the value that the program adds to the organization as a whole, and to specific individuals. The bottom line is: "What is in it for me and how can I recognize the benefits that the program is offering?"

Appendix 1[38]

Client Survey Tool
Managed Rehabilitation Care
Service Client Service Quality
Survey

Client Name: _____

Department: _____

Directions — Part 1

Based on your experiences as a consumer of a Managed Rehabilitation Care service, please think about the kind of Managed Rehabilitation Care services that would deliver excellent quality of service and with which you would be pleased to work. Please show the extent to which you think such a Managed Rehabilitation Care service would possess the feature described by each statement.

If you feel a feature is *not at all essential* for excellent Managed Rehabilitation Care services, circle the number 1. If you feel a feature is *absolutely essential*, circle 7. If your feelings are less strong, circle one of the numbers in the middle. There are no right or wrong answers — all we are interested in is a number that truly reflects your feelings regarding services that would deliver excellent quality of service.

	Strongly Disagree						**Strongly Agree**
1. An excellent Managed Rehabilitation Care service will be housed in modern looking facilities.	1	2	3	4	5	6	7
2. The physical facilities will be visually appealing.	1	2	3	4	5	6	7

---

[38] D. Dyck, "Gap Analysis of Health Services: Client Satisfaction Surveys" (1996) 44 AOHNA Journal 541.

		Strongly Disagree						Strongly Agree
3.	Employees involved with an excellent Managed Rehabilitation Care service will be professional in their appearance.	1	2	3	4	5	6	7
4.	The materials associated with the service (*i.e.*, notices, memos, forms, educational materials, *etc.*) will have a professional appearance in an excellent Managed Re-habilitation Care service.	1	2	3	4	5	6	7
5.	When an excellent Managed Rehabilitation Care service promises to do something by a certain time, it does so.	1	2	3	4	5	6	7
6.	When a client has a problem, an excellent Managed Rehabilitation Care service will show a sincere interest in dealing with it.	1	2	3	4	5	6	7
7.	An excellent Managed Rehabilitation Care service will perform the service right the first time.	1	2	3	4	5	6	7
8.	An excellent Managed Rehabilitation Care service will provide services at the promised time.	1	2	3	4	5	6	7
9.	An excellent Managed Rehabilitation Care service will insist on error-free records.	1	2	3	4	5	6	7

	Strongly Disagree						Strongly Agree

10. Employees involved with an excellent Managed Rehabilitation Care service will tell clients when the services will be performed.

    1   2   3   4   5   6   7

11. Employees involved with an excellent Managed Rehabilitation Care service will give prompt service to clients.

    1   2   3   4   5   6   7

12. Employees involved with an excellent Managed Rehabilitation Care service will always be willing to help clients.

    1   2   3   4   5   6   7

13. Employees involved with an excellent Managed Rehabilitation Care service will never be too busy to respond to client requests.

    1   2   3   4   5   6   7

14. The behaviour of employees involved with an excellent Managed Rehabilitation Care service will instil confidence in clients.

    1   2   3   4   5   6   7

15. Clients of an excellent Managed Rehabilitation Care service will feel safe in their interactions.

    1   2   3   4   5   6   7

16. Employees involved with an excellent Managed Rehabilitation Care service will be consistently courteous to clients.

    1   2   3   4   5   6   7

	Strongly Disagree						Strongly Agree
17. Employees involved with an excellent Managed Rehabilitation Care service will have the knowledge or resources to answer client questions.	1	2	3	4	5	6	7
18. An excellent Managed Rehabilitation Care service will give clients individual attention.	1	2	3	4	5	6	7
19. An excellent Managed Rehabilitation Care service will have operating hours convenient to all clients.	1	2	3	4	5	6	7
20. An excellent Managed Rehabilitation Care service will have employees who give clients personal attention.	1	2	3	4	5	6	7
21. An excellent Managed Rehabilitation Care service will have the client's best interests at heart.	1	2	3	4	5	6	7
22. The employees involved with an excellent Managed Rehabilitation Care service will understand the specific needs of their clients.	1	2	3	4	5	6	7

Directions — Part 2

Listed below are five features pertaining to Managed Rehabilitation Care services and the services they offer. We would like to know how important each of these features is to you when you evaluate the service quality of Managed Rehabilitation Care services.

Please allocate a total of 100 points among the five features *according to how important each feature is to you* — the more important a feature is to you, the more points you should allocate to it. *Please ensure that the points you allocate to the five features add up to 100.*

1. The appearance of the Managed Rehabilitation Care service's physical facilities, equipment, personnel and communication materials. _____ points

2. The Managed Rehabilitation Care service's ability to perform the promised service dependably and accurately. _____ points

3. The Managed Rehabilitation Care service's willingness to help clients and provide prompt service. _____ points

4. The knowledge and courtesy of the Managed Rehabilitation Care service employees and their ability to convey trust and confidence. _____ points

5. The caring, individualized attention the Managed Rehabilitation Care service provides clients. _____ points

    TOTAL points allocated   **100   points**

Which *one* feature among the above five is *most important* to you? (please enter the feature's number)   _____

Which feature is *second most important* to you?   _____

Which feature is *least important* to you?   _____

Directions — Part 3

The following set of statements relate to your feelings about Company XYZ's inhouse Managed Rehabilitation Care service. *For each statement, please show the extent to which you believe Company XYZ's Managed Rehabilitation Care service has the feature described by the statement.*

Circling 1 means that you strongly disagree that Company XYZ's Managed Rehabilitation Care service has that feature, and circling 7 means that you strongly agree. You may circle any of the numbers in the middle that show how strong your feelings are. There are no right or wrong answers — all we are interested in is a number that best shows your perceptions about Company XYZ's Managed Rehabilitation Care service.

		Strongly Disagree					Strongly Agree	
1.	Company XYZ's Managed Rehabilitation Care service is housed in a modern looking facility.	1	2	3	4	5	6	7
2.	The Company XYZ Managed Rehabilitation Care service's physical facilities are visually appealing.	1	2	3	4	5	6	7
3.	Company XYZ's Managed Rehabilitation Care service employees are professional looking in their appearance.	1	2	3	4	5	6	7
4.	The materials associated with Company XYZ's Managed Rehabilitation Care service (*i.e.*, notices, memos, forms, educational materials, *etc.*) are professional looking.	1	2	3	4	5	6	7
5.	When Company XYZ's Managed Rehabilitation Care service promises to do something by a certain time, it does so.	1	2	3	4	5	6	7
6.	When you have a problem, Company XYZ's Managed Rehabilitation Care service shows a sincere interest in dealing with it.	1	2	3	4	5	6	7
7.	Company XYZ's Managed Rehabilitation Care service performs the service right the first time.	1	2	3	4	5	6	7

	Strongly Disagree					**Strongly Agree**	

8. Company XYZ's Managed Rehabilitation Care service provides its services at the promised time.

   1   2   3   4   5   6   7

9. Company XYZ's Managed Rehabilitation Care service insists on error-free records.

   1   2   3   4   5   6   7

10. Employees involved with Company XYZ's Managed Rehabilitation Care service tell you exactly when services will be performed.

   1   2   3   4   5   6   7

11. Employees involved with Company XYZ's Managed Rehabilitation Care service give you prompt service.

   1   2   3   4   5   6   7

12. Employees involved with Company XYZ's Managed Rehabilitation Care service are always willing to help you.

   1   2   3   4   5   6   7

13. Employees involved with Company XYZ's Managed Rehabilitation Care service are never too busy to respond to your requests.

   1   2   3   4   5   6   7

14. The behaviour of employees involved with Company XYZ's Managed Rehabilitation Care service instils confidence in you.

   1   2   3   4   5   6   7

15. You feel safe in your interactions with Company XYZ's Managed Rehabilitation Care service (*e.g.*, information is kept confidential).

   1   2   3   4   5   6   7

	Strongly Disagree					Strongly Agree	
16. Employees involved with Company XYZ's Managed Rehabilitation Care service are consistently courteous with you.	1	2	3	4	5	6	7
17. Employees involved with Company XYZ's Managed Rehabilitation Care service have the knowledge to answer your questions.	1	2	3	4	5	6	7
18. Company XYZ's Managed Rehabilitation Care service gives you individual attention.	1	2	3	4	5	6	7
19. Company XYZ's Managed Rehabilitation Care service is readily accessible.	1	2	3	4	5	6	7
20. Company XYZ's Managed Rehabilitation Care service has employees who give you personal attention.	1	2	3	4	5	6	7
21. Company XYZ's Managed Rehabilitation Care service has your best interests at heart.	1	2	3	4	5	6	7
22. The employees of Company XYZ's Managed Rehabilitation Care service understand your specific needs.	1	2	3	4	5	6	7

Part 4

Your comments and suggestions concerning Company XYZ's Managed Rehabilitation Care Program are helpful to us. Please feel free to address any issue surrounding the health services, modified work, interaction with insurance carriers, *etc.*

_____
_____
_____

_____
_____
_____
_____
_____
_____

Part 5

	Strongly Disagree					**Strongly Agree**

Do you believe that this questionnaire
is a valid way to assess a Managed
Rehabilitation Care service?   1   2   3   4   5   6   7

Comments:

_____
_____
_____
_____
_____
_____
_____
_____
_____
_____
_____
_____
_____
_____
_____
_____

Appendix 2[39]

Caregiver Survey Tool

MANAGED REHABILITATION CARE SERVICES
EMPLOYEE SERVICE QUALITY SURVEY
Directions — Part 1

This portion of the survey deals with *how you think your clients feel* about a Managed Rehabilitation Care service, that *in their view*, delivers an excellent quality of service. *Please indicate the extent to which your clients feel that an excellent Managed Rehabilitation Care service would possess the feature described by each statement.*

If *your clients* are likely to feel a feature is *not at all essential* for excellent Managed Rehabilitation Care service, circle 1. If *your clients* are likely to feel a feature is *absolutely essential*, circle 7. If *your clients* are likely to feel less strongly about an issue, circle one of the numbers in the middle. Remember, there are no right or wrong answers — we are interested in what you think your clients' feelings are regarding Managed Rehabilitation Care services that would deliver excellent quality of service.

	Our Clients Would Strongly Disagree					Our Clients Would Strongly Agree
1. An excellent Managed Rehabilitation Care service will be housed in modern looking facilities.	1	2	3	4	5	6	7
2. The physical facilities will be visually appealing.	1	2	3	4	5	6	7

---

[39]   D. Dyck, "Gap Analysis of Health Services: Client Satisfaction Surveys" (1996) 44 AOHNA Journal 541.

	Our Clients Would Strongly Disagree					Our Clients Would Strongly Agree	
3. Employees involved with an excellent Managed Rehabilitation Care service will present as professionals.	1	2	3	4	5	6	7
4. The materials associated with the service (*i.e.*, notices, memos, forms, educational materials, *etc.*) will have a professional appearance in an excellent Managed Rehabilitation Care service.	1	2	3	4	5	6	7
5. When an excellent Managed Rehabilitation Care service promises to do something by a certain time, it does so.	1	2	3	4	5	6	7
6. When a client has a problem, an excellent Managed Rehabilitation Care service will show sincere interest in dealing with it.	1	2	3	4	5	6	7
7. An excellent Managed Rehabilitation Care service will perform the service right the first time.	1	2	3	4	5	6	7
8. An excellent Managed Rehabilitation Care service will provide services at the promised time.	1	2	3	4	5	6	7

	Our Clients Would Strongly Disagree						Our Clients Would Strongly Agree
9. An excellent Managed Rehabilitation Care service will insist on error-free records.	1	2	3	4	5	6	7
10. Employees involved with an excellent Managed Rehabilitation Care service will give prompt service to clients.	1	2	3	4	5	6	7
11. Employees involved with an excellent Managed Rehabilitation Care service will always be willing to help clients.	1	2	3	4	5	6	7
12. Employees involved with an excellent Managed Rehabilitation Care service will never be too busy to respond to client requests.	1	2	3	4	5	6	7
13. The behaviour of employees involved with an excellent Managed Rehabilitation Care service will instil confidence in clients.	1	2	3	4	5	6	7
14. Clients of an excellent Managed Rehabilitation Care service will feel safe in their interactions.	1	2	3	4	5	6	7

	Our Clients Would Strongly Disagree						Our Clients Would Strongly Agree
15. Employees involved with an excellent Managed Rehabilitation Care service will be consistently courteous to clients.	1	2	3	4	5	6	7
16. Employees involved with an excellent Managed Rehabilitation Care service will have the knowledge or resources to answer client questions.	1	2	3	4	5	6	7
17. An excellent Managed Rehabilitation Care service will give clients individual attention.	1	2	3	4	5	6	7
18. An excellent Managed Rehabilitation Care service will have operating hours convenient to all their clients.	1	2	3	4	5	6	7
19. An excellent Managed Rehabilitation Care service will have employees who give clients personal attention.	1	2	3	4	5	6	7
20. An excellent Managed Rehabilitation Care service will have the client's best interests at heart.	1	2	3	4	5	6	7

	Our Clients Would Strongly Disagree					Our Clients Would Strongly Agree	

21. The employees involved with an excellent Managed Rehabilitation Care service will understand the specific needs of their clients.

                    1   2   3   4   5   6   7

Directions — Part 2

Listed below are five features pertaining to Managed Rehabilitation Care services and the services they offer. We would like to know how important each of these features is to *your clients* when they evaluate a Managed Rehabilitation Care service's quality of service.

    Please allocate a total of *100 points among the five features according to how important each feature is to your clients* — the more important a feature is likely to be to your clients, the more points you should allocate to it. *Please ensure that the points you allocate to the five features add up to 100.*

1. The appearance of the Managed Rehabilitation Care service's physical facilities, equipment, personnel and communication materials.   _____ points

2. The Managed Rehabilitation Care service's ability to perform the promised service dependably and accurately.   _____ points

3. The Managed Rehabilitation Care service's willingness to help clients and provide prompt service.   _____ points

4. The knowledge and courtesy of the Managed Rehabilitation Care service employees and their ability to convey trust and confidence.   _____ points

5. The caring, individualized attention the Managed Rehabilitation Care service provides its clients.   _____ points

        TOTAL points allocated   **100   points**

Which *one* feature among the above five is *most important to your clients*? (please enter the feature's number)   _____

Which feature is likely to be *second most important to* _____
your clients?

Which feature is likely to be *least important to your clients?* _____

Directions — Part 3

Service quality performance standards in companies can be *formal* — written, explicit, and communicated to employees. They can also be *informal* — oral, implicit, and assumed to be understood by employees.

For each of the following features, circle the number that best describes the extent to which service quality performance standards are formalized in your department. If there are no standards in your department, check the appropriate box.

	Informal Standards				Formal Standards		No Standards Exist
1. The appearance of the Company XYZ Managed Rehabilitation Care service's physical facilities, equipment, personnel and communication materials.	1 2	3	4	5	6	7	[ ]
2. The ability of the Company XYZ Managed Rehabilitation Care service to perform the promised service dependably and accurately.	1 2	3	4	5	6	7	[ ]
3. The willingness of the Company XYZ Managed Rehabilitation Care service to help clients and provide prompt service.	1 2	3	4	5	6	7	[ ]

		Informal Standards				Formal Standards		No Standards Exist	
4.	The knowledge and courtesy of the Company XYZ Managed Rehabilitation Care service employees and their ability to convey trust and confidence.	1 2 3 4				5 6		7 [ ]	
5.	The caring, individualized attention the Company XYZ Managed Rehabilitation Care service provides its clients.	1 2 3 4				5 6		7 [ ]	

Directions — Part 4

Listed below are the same five features as in Part 3. Employees and units sometimes experience difficulty in achieving the service quality standards established for them.

For each feature below, circle the number that best represents the degree to which your department and its staff are able to meet the formal service quality performance standards established.

Remember, there are no right or wrong answers — we need your candid assessments for this question to be helpful.

		Unable to Meet Standards Consistently				Able to Meet Standards Consistently		No Standards Exist	
1.	The appearance of the Company XYZ Managed Rehabilitation Care service's physical facilities, equipment, personnel and communication materials.	1 2 3			4 5 6			7 [ ]	

	Unable to Meet Standards Consistently			Able to Meet Standards Consistently		No Standards Exist		
2. The ability of Company XYZ's Managed Rehabilitation Care service to perform the promised service dependably and accurately.	1	2	3	4	5	6	7	[ ]
3. The willingness of Company XYZ's Managed Rehabilitation Care service to help clients and provide prompt service.	1	2	3	4	5	6	7	[ ]
4. The knowledge and courtesy of Company XYZ's Managed Rehabilitation Care service employees and their ability to convey trust and confidence.	1	2	3	4	5	6	7	[ ]
5. The caring, individ-ualized attention Company XYZ's Managed Rehabilitation Care service provides its clients.	1	2	3	4	5	6	7	[ ]

Directions — Part 5

Often, promises are made about the level of service a group will deliver. Sometimes, it is not possible to fulfil these promises.

For each feature below, we want to know the extent to which you believe that your department and its staff deliver the level of service promised to clients. Circle the number that best describes your perception.

		Unable to Meet Promises Consistently						**Able to Meet Promises Consistently**
1.	The appearance of the Company XYZ Managed Rehabilitation Care service's physical facilities, equipment, personnel and communication materials.	1	2	3	4	5	6	7
2.	The ability of Company XYZ's Managed Rehabilitation Care service to perform the promised service dependably and accurately.	1	2	3	4	5	6	7
3.	The willingness of Company XYZ's Managed Rehabilitation Care service to help clients and provide prompt service.	1	2	3	4	5	6	7
4.	The knowledge and courtesy of the Company XYZ Managed Rehabilitation Care service employees and their ability to convey trust and confidence.	1	2	3	4	5	6	7

	Unable to Meet Promises Consistently						Able to Meet Promises Consistently

5. The caring, individualized attention Company XYZ's Managed Rehabilitation Care service provides its clients.

        1   2   3   4   5   6   7

Directions — Part 6

Listed below are a number of statements intended to measure your perceptions about your department and its operations.

Please indicate the extent to which you disagree or agree with each statement by circling one of the seven numbers next to each statement.

If you strongly disagree, circle 1. If you strongly agree, circle 7. If your feelings are not strong, circle one of the numbers in the middle. There are no right or wrong answers. Please tell us honestly how you feel.

PLEASE READ THE QUESTIONS CAREFULLY

	Strongly Disagree						Strongly Agree

1. We regularly collect information about the needs of our Managed Rehabilitation Care clients.

        1   2   3   4   5   6   7

2. We rarely use marketing research information that is collected about our Managed Rehabilitation Care clients.

        1   2   3   4   5   6   7

3. We regularly collect information about the service-quality expectations of our Managed Rehabilitation Care clients.

        1   2   3   4   5   6   7

4. The Director of our Managed Rehabilitation Care service rarely interacts with clients.

        1   2   3   4   5   6   7

		Strongly Disagree					**Strongly Agree**	
5.	The front-line employees involved with our Managed Rehabilitation Care service frequently communicate with the Director.	1	2	3	4	5	6	7
6.	The Director in our Managed Rehabilitation Care service rarely seeks suggestions about serving Managed Rehabilitation Care clients from front-line employees.	1	2	3	4	5	6	7
7.	The Director in our Managed Rehabilitation Care service frequently has face-to-face interactions with front-line employees.	1	2	3	4	5	6	7
8.	The primary means of communication in our Managed Rehabilitation Care service between front-line employees and the Director is through memos.	1	2	3	4	5	6	7
9.	Our Managed Rehabilitation Care service has too many levels of management between front-line employees and the Director.	1	2	3	4	5	6	7
10.	Our Managed Rehabilitation Care service does not commit the necessary resources for service quality.	1	2	3	4	5	6	7
11.	Our Managed Rehabilitation Care service has internal programs for improving the quality of service to Managed Rehabilitation Care clients.	1	2	3	4	5	6	7

	Strongly Disagree						Strongly Agree
12. In the occupational health group, the Advisor who improves service quality is more likely to be rewarded than other Advisors in the company.	1	2	3	4	5	6	7
13. Our Managed Rehabilitation Care service group emphasizes service marketing as much as, or more, than it emphasizes serving Managed Rehabilitation Care clients.	1	2	3	4	5	6	7
14. Our Managed Rehabilitation Care service group has a formal process for setting service quality goals for employees.	1	2	3	4	5	6	7
15. In our Managed Rehabilitation Care service group, we try to set specific quality of service goals.	1	2	3	4	5	6	7
16. Our Managed Rehabilitation Care service group effectively uses automation to achieve consistency in serving Managed Rehabilitation Care clients.	1	2	3	4	5	6	7
17. Programs are in place in our Managed Rehabilitation Care service group to improve operating procedures so as to provide consistent service.	1	2	3	4	5	6	7
18. Our Managed Rehabilitation Care service has the necessary capabilities to meet client requirements for service.	1	2	3	4	5	6	7

	Strongly Disagree					Strongly Agree	

19. If we gave our Managed Rehabilitation Care clients the level of service they really want, Company XYZ would go broke.

    1   2   3   4   5   6   7

20. Our Managed Rehabilitation Care service has the operating systems to deliver the level of service that clients demand.

    1   2   3   4   5   6   7

Directions — Part 7

Listed below are a number of statements intended to measure your perceptions about your department and its operations.

Please indicate the extent to which you disagree or agree with each statement by circling one of the seven numbers next to each statement.

If you strongly disagree, circle 1. If you strongly agree, circle 7. If your feelings are not strong, circle one of the numbers in the middle. There are no right or wrong answers. Please tell us honestly how you feel.

PLEASE READ THE QUESTIONS CAREFULLY

	Strongly Disagree					Strongly Agree	

1. I feel that I am part of a team providing Company XYZ's Managed Rehabilitation Care service.

    1   2   3   4   5   6   7

2. Everyone in Company XYZ occupational health service contributes to a team effort in servicing Managed Rehabilitation Care clients.

    1   2   3   4   5   6   7

3. I feel a sense of responsibility to help my fellow employees do their jobs well.

    1   2   3   4   5   6   7

4. My fellow employees and I cooperate more often than we compete.

    1   2   3   4   5   6   7

		Strongly Disagree						Strongly Agree
5.	I feel that I am an important member of this Managed Rehabilitation Care service group.	1	2	3	4	5	6	7
6.	I feel comfortable in my job in the sense that I am able to perform the job well.	1	2	3	4	5	6	7
7.	Company XYZ's occupational health service hires people who are qualified to do Managed Rehabilitation Care as part of their jobs.	1	2	3	4	5	6	7
8.	Company XYZ's occupational health services gives me the tools and equipment that I need to perform the Managed Rehabilitation Care portion of my job well.	1	2	3	4	5	6	7
9.	I spend a lot of time in my job trying to resolve problems over which I have little control.	1	2	3	4	5	6	7
10.	I have the freedom in my job to truly satisfy my Managed Rehabilitation Care clients' needs.	1	2	3	4	5	6	7
11.	I sometimes feel a lack of control over my job because too many Managed Rehabilitation Care clients demand service at the same time.	1	2	3	4	5	6	7

	Strongly Disagree					**Strongly Agree**

12. One of my frustrations on the job is that I sometimes have to depend on other employees involved with serving my Managed Rehabilitation Care clients.

   1   2   3   4   5   6   7

13. My supervisor's appraisal of my job performance includes how well I interact with Managed Rehabilitation Care clients.

   1   2   3   4   5   6   7

14. At Company XYZ, making a special effort to serve Managed Rehabilitation Care clients well does not result in more pay or in more recognition.

   1   2   3   4   5   6   7

15. At Company XYZ, employees who do the best job serving their Managed Rehabilitation Care clients are more likely to be rewarded than other employees.

   1   2   3   4   5   6   7

16. The amount of paperwork in my job makes it hard for me to effectively serve my Managed Rehabilitation Care clients.

   1   2   3   4   5   6   7

17. The Managed Rehabilitation Care service group places so much emphasis on marketing to clients that it is difficult to serve our clients properly.

   1   2   3   4   5   6   7

	Strongly Disagree						Strongly Agree
18. What my Managed Rehabilitation Care clients want me to do and what the Director wants me to do are usually the same thing.	1	2	3	4	5	6	7
19. The Managed Rehabilitation Care service group and I have the same ideas about how the Managed Rehabilitation Care portion of my job should be performed.	1	2	3	4	5	6	7
20. I receive a sufficient amount of information from the Director concerning what I am supposed to do in the Managed Rehabilitation Care portion of my job.	1	2	3	4	5	6	7
21. I often feel that I do not understand the services offered by Company XYZ's Managed Rehabilitation Care service.	1	2	3	4	5	6	7
22. I am able to keep up with changes in the occupational health service group that affect the Managed Rehabilitation Care portion of my job.	1	2	3	4	5	6	7
23. I am not sure which aspects of my job my supervisor will stress most in my evaluation.	1	2	3	4	5	6	7

	Strongly Disagree					Strongly Agree
24. The people who develop our Managed Rehabilitation Care marketing presentations consult employees like me about the realism of promises made in those presentations.	1	2	3	4	5	6	7
25. I am often not aware in advance of the promises made in the Managed Rehabilitation Care service marketing presentations.	1	2	3	4	5	6	7
26. Employees like me interact with other operations people to discuss the level of service Company XYZ's Managed Rehabilitation Care services can deliver to clients.	1	2	3	4	5	6	7
27. Our Company XYZ Managed Rehabilitation Care service policies on serving clients are consistent for everyone in the group that services clients.	1	2	3	4	5	6	7
28. Intense competition from external occupational health vendors is creating more pressure inside this group to generate new ideas and ways of managing rehabilitative care.	1	2	3	4	5	6	7
29. Our key occupational health service competitors make promises in Managed Rehabilitation Care they cannot possibly keep in an effort to gain new clients.	1	2	3	4	5	6	7

Part 8

Your comments and suggestions concerning Company XYZ's Managed Rehabilitation Care program are helpful to us. Please feel free to address any issue surrounding the health services, modified work, contact with insurance carriers or Workers' Compensation.

_____

_____

_____

_____

_____

_____

_____

Part 9

	Strongly Disagree						**Strongly Agree**

Do you believe that this questionnaire is a valid way to assess a Managed Rehabilitution Care service?

    1   2   3   4   5   6   7

Comments:

_____

_____

_____

_____

_____

_____

_____

_____

_____

CHAPTER REFERENCES

D.J. Conti, "The Management of Psychiatric Short-term Disability" (Presented at the American Psychiatric Association Annual Meeting, Miami, FL, 21 May 1996) [unpublished] and (re-presented at the Psychological Disabilities in the Workplace: Prevention, Rehabilitation and Cost Control Conference, Toronto, 10-11 June 1996) [unpublished].

D. Dyck, "Gap Analysis of Health Services: Client Satisfaction Surveys" (1996) 44 AOHNA Journal 541.

H. Harder & L. Scott, *Comprehensive Disability Management* (Toronto: Elsevier, Churchill Livingstone, 2005).

Hewitt Associates, *Disability Absence Index Survey 2007* (2007), at 4, available online at: <http://www.hewittassociates.com/Intl/NA/en-CA/KnowledgeCenter/ArticlesReports/DAIS_highlights.aspx>.

Hewitt Associates, Press Release, "Ignoring Employee Absences May Prove Costly for Canadian Organizations, According to Hewitt" (15 June 2005), available online at: <http://www.hewittassociates.com/Intl/NA/en-CA/Default.aspx>.

National Institute of Disability Management and Research (NIDMAR), *Consensus Based Disability Management Audit* (Port Alberni, BC: NIDMAR, 2004), available online at: <http://www.nidmar.ca/audit/audit_synopsis.asp>.

M.P. O'Donnell & T.H. Ainsworth, eds., *Health Promotion in the Workplace* (New York: John Wiley & Sons, 1984).

A. Parasuraman, V. Zeithaml & L. Berry, "SERVQUAL: A Multiple-Item Scale for Measuring Consumer Perceptions of Service Quality" (1988) 64:1 Journal of Retailing 12.

M. Scriven, *Evaluation Thesaurus*, 4th ed. (Newbury Park, CA: Sage Publications, 1991).

Statistics Canada, *Work Absence Rates, 2007*, Cat. No. 71-211-XWE (Ottawa: Statistics Canada, May 2008).

Statistics Canada, *Average Hourly Wages of Employees by Selected Characteristics*, available online at: <http://www40.statcan.ca/l01/cst01/labr69a.htm>.

E. Sullivan & P. Decker, *Effective Management in Nursing*, 2nd ed. (Menlo Park, CA: Addison-Wesley Publishing, 1988).

N. Vimadalal & J. Wozniak, "Best Practices to Help Employers Capture the Benefits of Integrated Disability Management", *Employee Benefits News* (March 1, 2008), available online at: <http://ebn.benefitnews.com/asset/article/548491/best-practices-help-employers-capture-benefits.html?pg=>.

Washington Business Group on Health (2004), available online at: <http://www.wbgh.org>.

Watson-Wyatt, *Staying@Work: Effective Presence at Work* (2007). Available online at: <https://www.watsonwyatt.com/research/resrender.asp?id=2007-US-0166&page=1>.

Watson Wyatt, *Staying@Work 2004* (2004), available online at: <https://www.watsonwyatt.com>.

C. Weston, L. McAlpine & T. Bordonaro, "A Model for Understanding Formative Evaluation in Instructional Design" (1995) 43:3 Educational Technology Research and Development 29.

M. Youngblood, *Eating the Chocolate Elephant: Take Charge of Change through Total Process Management* (Richardson, TX: Micrografx Inc., 1994).

V. Zeithaml, "Consumer Perceptions of Price, Quality and Value: A Means-End Model and Synthesis of Evidence" (1988) 52:3 Journal of Marketing 2.

V. Zeithaml, A. Parasuraman & L. Berry, *Delivering Quality Service* (Toronto: The Free Press, 1990).

Chapter 7

The Role of Employee Assistance Programs in Disability Management[1]

INTRODUCTION

Canadian employees missed an average of 10.2 workdays in 2007, of which 2.1 days were due to personal or family demands.[2] Mental illness is estimated to result in 35 million lost workdays at a cost to Canadian employers of $51 billion in lowered productivity, lost workdays, disability, and medical costs.[3]

In the United States, the picture is similar. Workers reported stress, family reasons, and personal needs as the key reasons for 53 per cent of the unscheduled absences in 2007.[4] This was a 2 per cent increase over the 2005 results and a 7 per cent increase over the 1995 findings.[5]

According to the American Institute of Stress, job stress costs the American industry $300 billion annually in absenteeism, diminished work productivity, staff turnover, and direct medical, legal and insurance fees.[6] The problem employee was estimated to cost an average of 25 per cent of annual salary per year.[7] As well, for the American society at large, the cost of serious mental illness is estimated to be at least $193 billion a year in lost earnings.[8]

[1] Adapted from D. Dyck, "Directions in Disability Management" (1997) 44:2 EAP Digest 16. Reprinted with permission.

[2] Statistics Canada, *Work Absence Rates, 2007*, Cat. No. 71-211-X (Ottawa: Statistics Canada, 2008), available online at: <http://www.statcan.gc.ca/pub/71-211-x/71-211-x2008000-eng.htm>.

[3] Mercer & The Canadian Alliance on Mental Illness and Mental Health (CAMIMH), *2008 Mental Health in the Workplace Survey* (2008), available online at: <http://www.mercer.ca/referencecontent.htm?idContent=1313070>.

[4] CCH, *CCH 2007 Unscheduled Absence Survey* (October 2007), available online at: <http://www. cch.com/press/news/2007/20071010h.asp>.

[5] CCH, "Unscheduled Absenteeism Rises to a Five-year High", (2004) 592 *Human Resources Management: Ideas & Trends* 145.

[6] The American Institute of Stress, Stress in the Workplace (2004), available online at: <http://www. stress.org/topic-workplace.htm>.

[7] Concern: EAP, *Cost Effectiveness* (2005), available online at: <http://www.concern-eap.com/html/bc-cost-effective.htm>.

[8] National Institute of Mental Health, *News Release* (May 7, 2008) "Mental Disorders Cost Society Billions in Unearned Income", available online at: <http://www.nimh.nih.gov/science-news/2008/mental-disorders-cost-society-billions-in-unearned-income.shtml>.

In short, mental health issues are steadily rising in Canada and the United States, and remain costly. According to the World Health Organization, by 2020, mental illness will be the second leading cause of disability worldwide.[9]

BACKGROUND INFORMATION

Absenteeism costs are often symptomatic of serious workplace problems. The changing dynamics in the modern workplace have been linked with numerous health problems.[10] For example, job insecurity, unequal power distribution, role conflicts, and antagonistic labour-management relations have been associated with physiological changes, somatic complaints, and psychological distress.[11] Fatigue, chronic infections and digestive disturbances have been linked with the increased pace of work.[12] Increased work demands have been connected with family discord, alcoholism and psychological disturbances.[13] Unreasonable demands and deadlines, withholding important information, lack of recognition for work done and failing to allow employee discretion in conducting work and work priorities leads to high stress and ill health.[14] Lack of social supports at work, job demands and unfair treatment by supervisors are risk factors for mental illness.[15] Economic and workplace restructuring can have damaging effects on employee and family health and well-being (Figure 7.1).

---

[9] World Health Organization (WHO) reported in Watson Wyatt Worldwide, "Addressing Mental Health in the Workplace" (June 2003), available online at: <http://www.watsonwyatt.com>.

[10] K. Blair, "Probing the Links Between Work and Health" (April 7, 1997) *Canadian Human Resource Reporter* 6; R. Csiernik, "From EAP to Wellness: Program Evolution and Service Provider Selection" (Presented at the Psychological Disabilities in the Workplace: Prevention, Rehabilitation and Cost Control Conference, Toronto, June 10-11, 1996) [unpublished].

[11] J. Eakin, "Psychological Aspects of Workplace Health" (April 1992) Canadian Centre for Occupational Health and Safety (April 1992) 8; S. Klitzman, J. House, B. Israel & R. Mero, "Work Stress, Nonwork Stress and Health" (1990) 13:3 Journal of Behavioural Medicine 221; and R. Karasek & T. Theorell, *Healthy Work: Stress, Productivity and Reconstruction of Working Life* (New York: Basic Books, 1990).

[12] L. Lewis, "Employers Place More Emphasis on Managing Employee Stress" (1993) 11:2 Business & Health 46; M. Ross, "Psychiatric Disability Management" (Presentation at The Disability Management Conference, Toronto, May 27-28, 1996) [unpublished]; S.T. Maier, L.R. Watkins & M. Fleshner, "Psychoneuroimmunology: The Interface Between Behaviour, Brain and Immunity" (1994) 40 American Psychologist 771.

[13] J. Eakin, "Psychological Aspects of Workplace Health" (April 1992) Canadian Centre for Occupational Health and Safety 8; S. Klitzman, J. House, B. Israel & R. Mero, "Work Stress, Nonwork Stress and Health" (1990) 13:3 Journal of Behavioural Medicine 221; and R. Karasek & T. Theorell, *Healthy Work: Stress, Productivity and Reconstruction of Working Life* (New York: Basic Books, 1990).

[14] W. Weeks, "Stressing Prevention", *Benefits Canada* (May 2004) 54, available online at: <http://www.benefitscanada.com/content/legacy/Content/2004/05-04/benefits.pdf>.

[15] A. Nicoll, "Time for Action: Managing Mental Health in the Workplace" (September 29, 2008), available online at: <http://www.mercer.ca/referencecontent.htm?idContent=1322990>.

Figure 7.1: Related Statistics

FACTS

- In any workforce, 20% of the employees are "troubled".[16]
- 20% of Canadians will experience a mental health problem in their lives.[17]
- 8% of Canadian employees take drugs for mental illness.[18]
- Stress-related issues account for 20% loss in productivity.[19]
- Stress-related illnesses alone, cost the Canadian economy approximately $5 billion per year.[20]
- 50% of disability cases have a psychological component — cases which are considered the most difficult to handle.[21]
- The largest number of psychological claims occurred with women, the teaching profession and people aged 30 to 39 years old.[22]
- Mental illness and addictions account for 60-65% of all insurance claims among selected Canadian and American employers.[23]
- Depression has a significant negative impact on workplace productivity and profitability.[24]
- Mental and nervous conditions are, respectively, the primary and secondary causes of 55-60% of disability claims.[25]
- Disability and the related costs for mental illness have been estimated to cost companies up to 14% of their net annual profits.[26]
- Psychological conditions are the leading cause of short-term disability (STD) claims, and the leading cause of long-term disability (LTD) claims.[27]
- The percentage of casual absences has doubled since 1995.[28]
- Disability claims attributable to mental illness are the fastest growing category of disability costs in Canada.[29]

[16] C. Sherman, "Who is the Problem Employee?", *Human Resources Management in Canada* (February 1989) at 70, 507-70, 508.

[17] Canadian Mental Health Association, "Fast Facts: Mental Health/Mental Illness", available online at: <http://www.cmha.ca/bins/content_page.asp?cid=6-20-23-43>.

[18] Ipsos Reid, "Mental Health in the Workplace Study" (November 2007), available online at <http://www.ipsos.ca>.

[19] A. Bierbrier, "Opening Remarks" (Presented at the Psychological Disabilities in the Workplace: Prevention, Rehabilitation and Cost Control Conference, Toronto, June 10-11, 1996) [unpublished].

[20] J. Kranc, "Fact Check", *Benefits Canada* (March 2004) 70.

[21] R.W. Francis, "Medcan Health Management" (Presentation at The Disability Management Conference, Toronto, May 27-28, 1996) [unpublished].

[22] H. Minuk, "The Mercantile and General Disability Claims Survey, 1994" (Presented at the Psychological Disabilities in the Workplace: Prevention, Rehabilitation and Cost Control Conference, Toronto, June 10-11, 1996) [unpublished].

As of 1993, it was noted that 26 per cent of workplace absenteeism was related to stress.[30] In 1994, the Mercantile and General Claims Survey discovered that mental and nervous claims accounted for 19 per cent of the group long-term disability claims, and 15 per cent of the individual portfolio long-term disability claims.[31] They also noted that mental and nervous claims were alarmingly high for the professional and academic occupations, for those aged 30 to 39 years and for women.

The *Ontario Health Survey, Mental Health Supplement, 1994* indicated that 5.7 per cent of the Canadian population 15 years and older reported a major depressive episode within the last 12 months. Of those aged 15 to 24 years, 25 per cent reported one or more mental disorders within the last 12 months.[32]

The Canadian Institute of Actuaries (CIA, 1997) identified that psychological disorders account for 23.8 per cent of long-term disability claims in Canada per year.[33] By 2006, this rate increased to 60-65 per cent of all disability insurance claims among selected Canadian and American employers.[34] Stress and mental health problems account for 82 per cent of short-term disabilities and 72 per cent of the long-term disability claims.[35]

There are occupational variances in this rate. For example, the teaching or academic occupations experience 44 per cent of all psychological disorders,

---

[23] *Out of the Shadows at Last*, Final Report of The Standing Senate Committee on Social Affairs, Science and Technology, Senator Kirby, May 2006, available online at: <http://www.parl.gc.ca/ 39/1/parlbus/commbus/senate/Com-e/SOCI-E/rep-e/pdf/rep02may06part1-e.pdf>.

[24] Mental Health Roundtable, *Employers Getting Started: On the Road to Mental Health and Productivity* (March 28, 2006), available online at: <http://www.mentalhealthroundtable.ca/ 20060328/part4module3.pdf>.

[25] W. Weeks, "Stressing Prevention", *Benefits Canada* (May 2004) 54, available online at: <http://www.benefitscanada.com/content/legacy/Content/2004/05-04/benefits.pdf>.

[26] J. Kranc, "Fact Check", *Benefits Canada* (March 2004) 70.

[27] Watson Wyatt Worldwide, "Addressing Mental Health in the Workplace" (June 2003), available online at: <http://www.watsonwyatt.com>.

[28] Refer to Chapter 9, "Workplace Attendance Support & Assistance", Figure 9.2.

[29] *Out of the Shadows at Last*, Final Report of The Standing Senate Committee on Social Affairs, Science and Technology, Senator Kirby, May 2006, available online at: <http://www.parl.gc.ca/ 39/1/parlbus/commbus/senate/Com-e/SOCI-E/rep-e/pdf/rep02may06part1-e.pdf>.

[30] Ontario Ministry of Labour, "Counting the Cost of Absenteeism" (1993) 1:1 Group Healthcare Management 9.

[31] H. Minuk, "The Mercantile and General Disability Claims Survey, 1994" (Presented at the Psychological Disabilities in the Workplace: Prevention, Rehabilitation and Cost Control Conference, Toronto, June 10-11, 1996) [unpublished].

[32] Ibid.

[33] Canadian Institute of Actuaries (CIA), *Long-term Disability Causes* (Ottawa: CIA Group Experience Committee, 1997).

[34] *Out of the Shadows at Last*, Final Report of The Standing Senate Committee on Social Affairs, Science and Technology, Senator Kirby, May 2006, available online at: <http://www.parl.gc.ca/ 39/1/parlbus/commbus/senate/Com-e/SOCI-E/rep-e/pdf/rep02may06part1-e.pdf>.

[35] Ipsos Reid, "Mental Health in the Workplace Study" (November 2007), available online at: <http://www.ipsos.ca>.

white collar occupations experience 36 per cent, service workers 28 per cent, and blue collar occupations 16 per cent[36] of all psychological disorders.

DRIVERS OF STRESS-RELATED CLAIMS

There appear to be three main drivers for an increase in the number of stress-related claims. First, there are the work-related drivers that include:

- increased job uncertainty;
- increased stress at work due to increased performance expectations, limited resources, and/or working too hard;[37]
- lack of social acceptance and supports at work;[38]
- abusive co-workers[39] or supervisors;[40]
- perceived lack of control in the workplace — *i.e.*, unreasonable demands, urgent deadlines, lack of recognition for work performed, lack of discretion on how to do the work, inability to set own work priorities;[41]
- increased work hours resulting in problems balancing work and family life[42] and feeling overwhelmed;[43]
- increased workload which contributes to an increased prevalence of the "I can't wait to retire" attitude, the desire to leave the job, and a decreased capacity for creativity and innovation;[44]
- the "Do it at any cost" approach to management;
- constant technological advancements mean that employees are in a continuous learning mode, which is tiring;

---

[36] Canadian Institute of Actuaries (CIA), *Long term Disability Causes* (Ottawa: CIA Group Experience Committee, 1997).

[37] Ipsos Reid, "Mental Health in the Workplace Study" (November 2007), available online at: <http://www.ipsos.ca>.

[38] A. Nicoll, "Time for Action: Managing Mental Health in the Workplace" (September 29, 2008), available online at: <http://www.mercer.ca/referencecontent.htm?idContent=1322990>.

[39] Ipsos Reid, "Mental Health in the Workplace Study" (November 2007), available online at: <http://www.ipsos.ca>.

[40] A. Nicoll, "Time for Action: Managing Mental Health in the Workplace" (September 29, 2008), available online at: <http://www.mercer.ca/referencecontent.htm?idContent=1322990>.

[41] K. Blair, "Probing the Links Between Work and Health" (April 7, 1997) Canadian Human Resource Reporter 6; R. Csiernik, "From EAP to Wellness: Program Evolution and Service Provider Selection" (Presented at the Psychological Disabilities in the Workplace: Prevention, Rehabilitation and Cost Control Conference, Toronto, June 10-11, 1996) [unpublished]. W. Weeks, "Stressing Prevention" *Benefits Canada* (May 2004) 54, available online at: <http://www.benefitscanada.com/ content/legacy/Content/2004/05-04/benefits.pdf>.

[42] A. Bierbrier, "Opening Remarks" (Presented at the Psychological Disabilities in the Workplace: Prevention, Rehabilitation and Cost Control Conference, Toronto, June 10-11, 1996) [unpublished]. See also L. Duxbury, C. Higgins & K. Johnson, *An Examination of the Implications and Costs of Work-life Conflict in Canada* (Ottawa: Health Canada, 1999).

[43] J. MacBride-King, "Wrestling with Workload: Organizational Strategies for Success" *Conference Board of Canada Report* (Ottawa: Conference Board of Canada, 2005) at 1.

[44] *Ibid.*, at 3.

- limited management response to signs and symptoms of employee distress;
- employees have to expend energy to adapt to stressful workplace situations;
- multi-tasking, for example, talking on the telephone while reading or responding to mail; and
- information overload — the estimate is that the average employee receives and sends 190 messages per day (voice mail, email, fax), and is interrupted on average, six times per hour.[45]

In short, in North America, "we are our jobs". We tend to measure our self-esteem by our job and position in an organization. When job issues or pressures loom or the employer-employee relationship is in jeopardy, employees react negatively. In many instances, this can lead to physical or psychological ailments and in some cases a disability claim.

Second, there are societal drivers that contribute to an increase in stress-related disability claims. They include:

- a general increase in the prevalence of depression and anxiety disorders;[46]
- failure to recognize mental health issues until the employee becomes severely ill;[47]
- fear of seeking help;[48]
- increased perception of entitlement to compensation for psychological disorders;
- greater societal acceptance of mental health problems;
- many dual income families;
- the responsibilities and stressors of the so-called "sandwich generation", those caught between the demands of their children and their parents. Eldercare is on the increase and those responsible for this care report a lack of sleep, decreased personal time and more health problems;[49]
- increased economic and financial pressures;
- a society that is 44 per cent more difficult than 30 years ago according to the Likert Scale for measuring stress to societies.[50] For example, in 1999

---

[45] Conference Board of Canada, *News Release*, "Workplace Solutions for Stressed Out Workers" (September 7, 1999).

[46] B. Wilkerson, "Perspective on Mental Health in the Workplace," reported in Watson Wyatt Worldwide, *Staying@Work Report, 2005* (Canada 2005) at 9, available online at: <http://www.watsonwyatt.com>. Ipsos Reid, "Mental Health in the Workplace Study" (November 2007), available online at: <http://www.ipsos.ca>.

[47] Ibid.

[48] Institut de sante publique du Quebec, reported in "Taboos and Prejudices" (2008), available online at: <http://www.fondationdesmaladiesmentales.org/en/p/help-a-person/our-assistance-programs/managers-and-employees/mental-illness/taboos-and-prejudice>.

[49] J. MacBride-King, "Caring about Caregiving: The Eldercare Responsibilities of Canadian Workers and the Impact on Employers" (Ottawa: The Conference Board of Canada, 1999).

[50] B.A. Cryer, "Neutralizing Workplace Stress: The Physiology of Human Performance and Organizational Effectiveness" (Presented at the Psychological Disabilities in the Workplace: Prevention, Rehabilitation and Cost Control Conference, Toronto, June 10-11, 1996) [unpublished].

twice as many Canadian workers reported moderate to high stress levels due to problems balancing work and family life as opposed to 10 years ago (46.2 per cent in 1999 versus 26.7 per cent in 1989).[51] Those experiencing a high degree of perceived stress also said they missed twice as much work as those reporting lower stress levels;[52] and

- a tendency to adapt to dysfunctional situations, making it impossible to detect the negative effects of stress until it is too late.

The third driver is the medicalization of social and/or employment problems. Our society is poorly prepared to support people with interpersonal difficulties such as marital problems, relationship breakdowns, and identity crises. As a result, the "troubled employee" tends to seek medical advice to deal with such issues. Society expects physicians to identify and cure ailments. Thus, employees tend to end up with a diagnosis of burn-out, anxiety attacks, sleep disorders, or migraines for marital, interpersonal and personal crises. This is also true for over-extended lifestyles and traumatic life events such as death, victimization, harassment or grievance. Recently, these diagnoses have become compensable, resulting in new reasons for workplace absences. The outcome has been a steady increase in new types of disability claims.

DISABILITY MANAGEMENT

Disability management, to reiterate, is a systematic, goal-oriented process of actively minimizing the impact of impairment in the individual's capacity to participate competitively in the work environment, and maximizing the health of employees to prevent disability, or further deterioration when a disability exists.[53] It means being proactive, demonstrating joint responsibility and promoting illness and injury prevention. It involves joint labour-management support, supportive policies and procedures, education, a modified work program, and data collection and analysis.

However, just assisting employees to get well does not translate into them overcoming their vocational problems, nor regaining their vocational capacity. Employees who were poor performers before getting ill/injured do not turn into "shining stars" after a course of rehabilitation. The acquisition of new life and job skills is required along with the opportunity and the encouragement to practice the new skills in a safe environment. Likewise, many employees who experience mental illness try to work through their condition, often damaging

---

[51] H. Minuk, "The Mercantile and General Disability Claims Survey, 1994" (Presented at the Psychological Disabilities in the Workplace: Prevention, Rehabilitation and Cost Control Conference, Toronto, June 10-11, 1996) [unpublished].

[52] Conference Board of Canada, "Survey of Canadian Workers on Work-Life Balance" (Ottawa: Conference Board of Canada, 1999).

[53] D.G. Tate, R.V. Habeck & D.F. Galvin, "Disability Management: Origins, Concepts and Principles for Practice" (1986) 17:3 Journal of Applied Rehabilitation Counselling 5.

workplace relationships. Mending these relationships is part of the road to a successful recovery.

The good news is that employees who receive disability management support are more likely to achieve vocational success. When these support services are continuous and well coordinated, vocational achievement is even more probable.

EMPLOYEE ASSISTANCE PROGRAM

An Employee Assistance Program provides confidential, professional assistance to employees and their families to help them resolve problems affecting their personal lives and, in some cases, their job performance.

Historically, Employee Assistance Programs were introduced to deal with employee alcohol and drug abuse (Figure 7.2). However, over time and with a changing marketplace, most Employee Assistance Programs began to provide services such as:

- crisis management;
- financial counselling;
- legal counselling;
- career/vocational counselling;
- stress management counselling/seminars;
- time management counselling/seminars;
- change management counselling/seminars; and
- alternative therapies.

Figure 7.2: Scope of Employee Assistance Programs

In the future, the face of Canadian EAPs will change again, moving away from the traditional short-term counselling model, and towards an organizational approach of mental health protection and illness prevention, intervention, and recovery support.[54] Responding to the changing demographic, economic, and work scenes, EAPs are introducing:

- new service technologies such as online services (websites, interactive assessments, self-directed health promotion tools, *etc.*);
- tele-counselling;
- business linkages between Disability Management and EAP initiatives with insurers;
- new programs aimed at stress management, gambling and Internet addiction management, the relationship between physical and mental health and well-being, and the development of an increased workplace awareness of depression and other mental health issues;
- strategies that control/reduce health care costs; and
- better measurement of EAP program outcomes.

EMPLOYEE ASSISTANCE PROGRAMS: EFFECTIVENESS

In Canada, as early as 1997, approximately 80 per cent of companies with 500 or more employees had EAPs available for their employees and families.[55] The current market penetration is estimated to be 71 per cent of the mid- to large-sized companies offer EAP services.[56]

EAPs work for employers of any size and the range of savings that can be realized are exciting. For example,

- Ninety percent of workers benefit from using EAP services.[57]
- At McDonnell Douglas, employees treated for alcohol and drug dependency missed 29 per cent fewer days absent, experienced 42 per cent fewer terminations, and incurred $7,150 less in medical costs and $14,728 less in dependent medical costs.[58]
- Black & Decker experienced a decrease in behavioural health claims and a 60 per cent decrease in behavioural health benefit costs.

---

[54] K. Seward, "Employee Benefits — The State of EAPs in Canada, Benefits and Pensions Monitor" (June 2005) 21, available online at: <http://www.bpmmagazine.com>.

[55] Conference Board of Canada, *Compensation Planning Outlook* (Ottawa: Conference Board of Canada, 1997).

[56] Buffett & Company Workside Wellness Ltd., "National Wellness Survey Report 2006" (2006), available online at: <http://www.buffettandcompany.com/NWS2009/Buffett_Company_NWS2006.pdf>.

[57] EAP, "Why Your Company Needs an EAP" (2005), available online at: <http://www.eap4u.com/ cms/need>.

[58] P. Stuart, "How McDonnell Douglas Cost-justified Its EAP, *Personnel Journal* (February 1993) 72:2 at 48, available online at: http://www.workforce.com/archive/feature/22/21/86/223227.php>.

- Abbott Labs realized a $2,000 per employee savings on their medical claim costs because of employee use of the EAP.[59]
- Many companies report that EAPs are very effective for improving employee health and satisfaction and moderately effective in contributing to lower absenteeism costs and higher work productivity.[60]
- Buffett, Taylor & Associates Ltd. reports its EAP reduced employee absenteeism to less than two days a year per employee. The cost avoidance realized is $100,000, with only 30 people.[61]
- Research indicates that employers save $4 to $17 per dollar invested.[62]

From an employee perspective, EAPs have been reported to be used by employees to enhance their work performance. For example, one client satisfaction survey reports that as a result of EAP counselling:

- 70.3 per cent of the respondents noted improvement in their ability to concentrate at work;
- 67 per cent of the respondents reported an improvement in their ability to cope with job demands;
- 58 per cent of the respondents said they were able to avoid missing work;
- 52 per cent of the respondents experienced improved relationships with their supervisor and co-workers; and
- 75 per cent of the respondents believed that without counselling help, their health would have been affected.[63]

EMPLOYEE ASSISTANCE PROGRAMS AND DISABILITY MANAGEMENT

Employee Assistance Program counsellors and services have a significant role to play in disability management (Figure 7.3). They can be involved before the disability occurs, during the disability period, in the return-to-work process and as part of the follow-up process.

---

[59]   J. Prohofsky, "Speaking to Your CEO About EAPs: Three Strategies that Can Make EAP Believers Out of CEO Skeptics", *EAP Digest* (May 2005).

[60]   Watson Wyatt Worldwide, *Staying@Work 2005* (Canada 2005), available online at: <http://www.watsonwyatt.com>.

[61]   E. Buffett, quoted in S. Overman, "Measuring the Success of EAPs", Employee Benefit News Canada (2006), available online at: <http://www.accessmylibrary.com/coms2/summary_0286-13897917_ITM>.

[62]   K. Seward, "Employee Benefits — The State of EAPs in Canada" (December 2006) 21, available online at: <http://www.hrac.org>; Conference Board of Canada, "Survey of Canadian Workers on Work-Life Balance" (Ottawa: Conference board of Canada, 1999).

[63]   FGI, "One Workplace, Four Generations: Managing their Conflicting Needs" (September 2004) 7 Working Well for Managers, available online at: <http://www.mta.ca/hr/managers/workingwell_sept2004.pdf>.

Figure 7.3: Levels of Prevention for Employee Assistance Program Intervention

Level of Primary Prevention[64] (Before problems exist)	Level of Secondary Prevention[65] (Dealing with identified problems)	Level of Tertiary Prevention[66] (Keeping chronic situations from worsening)
Change Management (group/individual)	Counselling	Counselling
Stress Management (group/individual)	Counselling	Counselling
Crisis Management - policies	Trauma Counselling (group/individual)	Counselling
Career counselling - retirement planning	Counselling	Counselling
Harassment - education	Counselling	Counselling
Substance abuse in workplace - education	Counselling Support for employee and work group	Substance abuse therapy sessions Support for employee and workplace

Primary prevention involves Employee Assistance Program counsellors conducting seminars on change management, stress management, crisis management, career counselling, substance abuse awareness, workplace harassment, and balancing work and family life. These seminars address people and work issues before they become serious health conditions. Their effectiveness in reducing employee stress was recently demonstrated in a study on rising health care costs. The indication was that 66 per cent of the employer respondents felt that their EAP reduced employee stress and 50 per cent noted that the EAP helped to lower employee absenteeism.[67]

During the disability and the return-to-work process (secondary prevention), Employee Assistance Program counsellors can assist the disabled employee in

---

[64] **Primary prevention** deals with preventing problems before they exist, such as health education on heart health, smoking cessation, cancer awareness, nutrition, and off-the-job safety.

[65] **Secondary prevention** deals with the early detection of disease and the initiation of early treatment programs such as screening for vision disorders, cholesterol, diabetes, tuberculosis, and lung disorders.

[66] **Tertiary prevention** deals with the correction of disease and/or prevention of further health deterioration as a result of disease such as rehabilitation and restoration with chronic diseases and conditions (substance abuse).

[67] K. Bachmann, "Workplace Solutions for Stressed-Out Workers" (Ottawa: Conference Board of Canada, 1999).

dealing with identified problems. This may involve individual counselling, group therapy, and referrals to self-help groups and/or treatment centres. The idea is to assist employees and families in acquiring the coping skills necessary for successful recovery.

As part of the follow-up process (tertiary prevention), Employee Assistance Program counselling and support can help employees keep chronic disabilities from worsening. Employee Assistance Program support for the employee, family members and the workplace can prevent recurrences and promote optimal functioning.

Case Scenarios

The following case scenarios are some real-life examples of how Employee Assistance Program support can assist Case Managers and employees with disability management:

CASE A

James, a 32-year-old analyst, experienced a recurrent episode of depression and anxiety. He was still working, but he was fearful, indecisive and visibly anxious, had insomnia, and was unable to focus on issues. He had been part of a team that was involved in an intense project, working 70 hours a week for the past eight months.

James had many family and community responsibilities. He also had good family, workplace and peer support. He had a history of three major depressions and was aware of his need for help. As a result, he sought Employee Assistance Program help and was referred to the occupational health centre for disability management.

A multi-disciplinary intervention ensued. The Case Manager worked with the Employee Assistance Program counsellor to:

- coordinate care between James, his wife and his attending physician;
- educate the couple about chronic depression and the need for treatment;
- help James maximize his capabilities;
- assist James in setting personal boundaries and in increasing his coping skills;
- encourage James to set priorities in his life; and
- promote a graduated return to work.

This approach included assessing and preparing the workplace and James' co-workers for his return to work. Without Employee Assistance Program support, this successful return to work could not have occurred, nor would James have been likely to remain healthy.

Depression will affect one in ten Canadians in any given year.[68] However, people need help to understand the nature of this disorder and the acceptable forms of treatment. Also, people need assistance in realistically setting limits on their capabilities and being comfortable with those limits. Employee Assistance Programs can provide support in both these areas.

CASE B

Sally was absent and produced a medical note stating, "Off for six weeks due to stress". The Case Manager interviewed Sally to assess the biopsychosocial aspects of her disability situation. The real issue was job dissatisfaction, but Sally lacked the insight and skills to deal with her unhappiness.

The Case Manager referred Sally to the Employee Assistance Program counsellor. Using a Stress Map,[69] Sally and the Employee Assistance Program counsellor were able to identify the stressors in her life. As well, they addressed Sally's vocational and personal likes and dislikes.

The outcome was that Sally decided that her job was not meeting growth needs. The Employee Assistance Program counsellor then assisted Sally in identifying some career options to pursue. Sally returned to work within two weeks and then made plans to leave her job and enrol in university.

Many people who have complex life and vocational decisions to make get stuck and are unable to complete the process. They know they are unhappy, but do not know what to do to rectify the situation. In a number of cases, like this one, they become ill and need help to move on. Employee Assistance Program counsellors are well-equipped to assist employees and their dependants in addressing such challenges.

CASE C

Janet, a 36-year-old woman, had been with a company for 15 years. During that time she averaged 27 days off per year. Each absence was for a different medically substantiated reason. Janet's attendance was monitored several times but her high rate of absenteeism continued.

The Case Manager, in reviewing a recent absence, decided to refer Janet to the Employee Assistance Program for a thorough assessment. The assessment revealed that Janet had been suffering from anorexia and bulimia since the age of 15 and the numerous ailments were secondary events to these major health problems.

---

[68] Canadian Mental Health Association, "Canadian Mental Health Association (CMHA): Depression in the Workplace" (Presented at the Psychological Disabilities in the Workplace: Prevention, Rehabilitation and Cost Control Conference, Toronto, June 10-11, 1996) [unpublished].

[69] Essi Systems, *Stress Map: A Personal Exploration* (Collingwood: Essi Systems, 1987).

Janet was then referred to an eating disorder clinic. The treatment focused on an examination of the family, the origin of the issues and the development of self-esteem.

Janet's personal growth was amazing. She began to realize the impact of her illness on her job, her marriage and her family. As well, she recognized the drivers for her behaviour and decided to disclose her secret to her family and work group. She was tired of the secrecy and wanted to enlist support to help her to make the changes she wanted. The Case Manager and Employee Assistance Program counsellor were instrumental in helping Janet with her plan of action. The work group was astounded, and, once they understood the nature of the disorder, they were quick to rally to Janet's side.

Personal growth for the employee and work group was achieved, and the disability that had been a source of work group dissension became the seed of work group unity and support. Janet remains well and after six years of treatment and peer support, she is enjoying a much better quality of life and work.

In summary, the complex disability cases are made up of 10 per cent medical components and 90 per cent other factors. There is no quick approach to rehabilitation of ill or injured workers. People's lives are complicated and illnesses or injuries make things more complex. A multi-faceted, multi-disciplinary approach to rehabilitation is essential.

THE VALUE OF EMPLOYEE ASSISTANCE PROGRAMS IN DISABILITY MANAGEMENT

Much work has been done in determining the cost-benefits of an Employee Assistance Program.[70] The "value-addedness" of an Employee Assistance Program can be measured in the disability management arena. Research has shown that employees were absent fewer short-term disability days when treated by Employee Assistance Program services versus medical practitioners. Also, Employee Assistance Program management of psychiatric short-term disability claims led to a decrease in the average duration of illness.[71] In general, Employee Assistance Programs are reported to yield five dollars of savings and three dollars of productivity gains for every one dollar invested in Employee Assistance Program services to manage and prevent disabilities.[72]

---

[70]   R. Csiernik, "From Employee Assistance Program to Wellness: Program Evolution and Service Provider Selection" (Presented at the Psychological Disabilities in the Workplace: Prevention, Rehabilitation and Cost Control Conference, Toronto, June 10-11, 1996) [unpublished].

[71]   D.J. Conti, "The Management of Psychiatric Short-term Disability" (Presented at the American Psychiatric Association Annual Meeting, Miami, FL, May 21, 1996) [unpublished].

[72]   R.J. Price, "Absenteeism and Disability" (1995) *The ACPM Reporter*, at 34-37.

Conclusion

The workplace is a powerful determinant of employee wellness. It can also be a strong support to ill or injured employees and to their families. Through disability management, which is integrated with the Employee Assistance Program and other corporate resources (*i.e.*, human resources, occupational safety, industrial hygiene, *etc.*), a multi-faceted, multi-disciplinary approach involving the employee and line management can be achieved. Organizations that have used this approach have been successful at containing both the human and financial costs of disability. In essence, it allows for a holistic approach that is tailored to the employee, the disability and the workplace, so that an optimal level of functioning can be regained.

THE FUTURE CHALLENGES FOR AN EMPLOYEE ASSISTANCE PROGRAM SERVICE PROVIDER

There are a number of future challenges for workplaces that Employee Assistance Program service providers can address. The discussion below will cover five of these future challenges, along with some suggestions for involvement by the Employee Assistance Program service provider.

ISSUE 1

People today seem to be locked into a "fight or flight" mode. Responses to daily pressures and demands tend to be edgy, with a readiness to react. Instead of being a useful reaction, the "fight or flight" response can become dysfunctional. For example, increased heart rate, elevated blood pressure and increased respirations can be helpful when fleeing from an enemy. However, these symptoms can be dysfunctional when they are reactions to stress, and they can cause incapacitating anxiety attacks.

The challenge for the Employee Assistance Program service is to:

- understand the employee's physical responses to events, both functional and dysfunctional;
- teach and encourage coping skills; and
- promote the value and existence of social support (*i.e.*, group or teamwork).

ISSUE 2

According to Cryer, individuals tend to experience problems with perception of situations and therefore can have negative reactions. This can lead to distress:

"Unmanaged reactions to stressful events in life create a chain reaction that inhibits our learning ability and clouds our perception on life."[73]

The challenge for the Employee Assistance Program is to help people to recognize their perceptions and reactions. In that way, they can learn and cope with life events successfully.

ISSUE 3

Emotional intelligence (EQ) is the ability to motivate oneself and persist despite frustrations; to control impulse and delay gratification; to regulate one's moods; and to empathize and to hope. It has been identified as the key to a better integration of an individual's physical, mental and emotional resources. People who possess a high EQ tend to be the most successful in their life endeavours. Likewise, companies or organizations that demonstrate a high EQ are the most successful at attaining business goals.[74]

The challenge for the Employee Assistance Program is to help employees and organizations foster and master the skills associated with high EQ for their benefit.

ISSUE 4

Many organizations exhibit the net effect of emotional mismanagement, better known as being under the state of an emotional virus. The symptoms of this emotional virus include caustic humour; defeatism; "us versus them" mentality; judgmental approaches to life; constant complaints; resentment; suspiciousness; and chronic anxiety, fear, intolerance, resignation, antagonism and despair. Many popular cartoons depict this virus well. This virus can be very infectious and deadly to company morale. If left unchecked, it can infect an entire workforce. However, it can be neutralized.

The challenge for the Employee Assistance Program is to assist both individuals and organizations. For employees, the Employee Assistance Program can assist in developing and maintaining credible supports, in the development of insight and self-esteem, and in the development of motivation. For the organization, the Employee Assistance Program can help management and employers identify the emotional virus and neutralize it. This involves applying internal self-management, creating a people-focused culture, applying heart intelligence and providing good communication.

---

[73] B.A. Cryer, "Neutralizing Workplace Stress: The Physiology of Human Performance and Organizational Effectiveness" (Presented at the Psychological Disabilities in the Workplace: Prevention, Rehabilitation and Cost Control Conference, Toronto, June 10-11, 1996) [unpublished].

[74] D. Goleman, Emotional Intelligence: Why it Can Matter More Than IQ (New York: Bantam Books, 1995).

ISSUE 5

Many organizations exhibit maladaptive and dysfunctional behaviour. These can be symptomatic of severe management problems.

The challenge for an Employee Assistance Program is to assist the organization in establishing or regaining balance in its level of functioning. Balance comes from equal value and attention being placed on five areas (Figure 7.4):

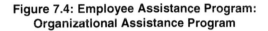

**Figure 7.4: Employee Assistance Program:
Organizational Assistance Program**

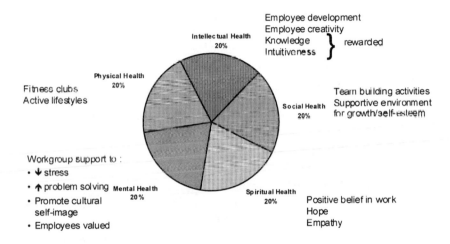

- *Intellectual Health* — Focus on employee development, and reward or compensate creativity, knowledge and intuitiveness.
- *Social Health* — Promote a supportive environment and team-building activities.
- *Spiritual Health* — Maintain a positive belief in what is right and in the value of work, hope and empathy.
- *Mental Health* — Promote work group support to reduce stress, address problem solving, shape a cultural self-image and demonstrate that employees are valued.
- *Physical Health* — Support employee physical well-being through the promotion of healthy lifestyles.

SUMMARY

Management is legally responsible to provide a safe and healthy workplace for workers. This includes worker physical and psychological safety. Chapter 11, "Prevention of Workplace Illness and Injury" and Chapter 15, "Disability Management: The Social Capital Theory Perspective for Managing Disability

Claims" address some of the effective methods for promoting employee physical and psychological safety. Employee Assistance Programs have traditionally been involved in reactive approaches to dealing with employee personal and workplace problems. However, by addressing issues at the source, employee and organizational well-being can be enhanced.

CHAPTER REFERENCES

The American Institute of Stress, "Stress in the Workplace" (2004). available online at: <http://www.stress.org/topic-workplace.htm>.

K. Bachmann, "Workplace Solutions for Stressed-Out Workers" (Ottawa: Conference Board of Canada, 1999).

A. Bierbrier, "Opening Remarks" (Presented at the Psychological Disabilities in the Workplace: Prevention, Rehabilitation and Cost Control Conference, Toronto, June 10-11, 1996) [unpublished].

K. Blair, "Probing the Links Between Work and Health" (April 7, 1997) Canadian Human Resource Report 6.

Buffett & Company Workside Wellness Ltd., "National Wellness Survey Report 2006" (2006), available online at: <http://www.buffettandcompany.com/ NWS2009/Buffett_Company_NWS2006.pdf>.

E. Buffett, quoted in S. Overman, "Measuring the Success of EAPs", *Employee Benefit News Canada*, 2006, available online at: <http://www. accessmylibrary.com/coms2/summary_0286-13897917_ITM>.

Canadian Institute of Actuaries (CIA), *Long-term Disability Causes* (Ottawa: CIA Group Experience Committee, 1997).

Canadian Mental Health Association, *Fast Facts: Mental Health/Mental Illness*, available online at: <http://www.cmha.ca/bins/content_page.asp?cid=6-20-23-43>.

Canadian Mental Health Association, "Canadian Mental Health Association (CMHA): Depression in the Workplace" (Presented at the Psychological Disabilities in the Workplace: Prevention, Rehabilitation and Cost Control Conference, Toronto, June 10-11, 1996) [unpublished].

CCH, "Unscheduled Absenteeism Rises to a Five-year High" *Human Resources Management: Ideas & Trends* (October 2005, Issue No. 616).

CCH, *CCH 2007 Unscheduled Absence Survey* (October 2007), available online at: <http://www.cch.com/press/news/2007/20071010h.asp>.

Concern: EAP, *Cost Effectiveness* (2005), available online at: <http://www. concern-eap.com/html/bc-cost-effective.htm>.

Conference Board of Canada, *Compensation Planning Outlook* (Ottawa: Conference Board of Canada, 1997).

Conference Board of Canada, *Caring about Caregiving: The Eldercare Responsibilities of Canadian Workers and the Impact on Employers* (Ottawa, Ontario: Conference Board of Canada, 1999).

Conference Board of Canada, "Survey of Canadian Workers on Work-Life Balance" (Ottawa: Conference Board of Canada, 1999).

Conference Board of Canada, *News Release*, "Workplace Solutions for Stressed Out Workers" (September 7, 1999).

D.J. Conti, "The Management of Psychiatric Short-term Disability" (Presented at the American Psychiatric Association Annual Meeting, Miami, FL, May 21, 1996) [unpublished].

B.A. Cryer, "Neutralizing Workplace Stress: The Physiology of Human Performance and Organizational Effectiveness" (Presented at the Psychological Disabilities in the Workplace: Prevention, Rehabilitation and Cost Control Conference, Toronto, June 10-11, 1996) [unpublished].

R. Csiernik, "From Employee Assistance Program to Wellness: Program Evolution and Service Provider Selection" (Presented at the Psychological Disabilities in the Workplace: Prevention, Rehabilitation and Cost Control Conference, Toronto, June 10-11, 1996) [unpublished].

L. Duxbury, C. Higgins & K. Johnson, *An Examination of the Implications and Costs of Work-life Conflict in Canada* (Ottawa: Health Canada, 1999).

D. Dyck, "Directions in Disability Management" (1997) 44:2 EAP Digest 16

J. Eakin, "Psychological Aspects of Workplace Health" (April 1992) Canadian Centre for Occupational Health and Safety 8.

EAP, "Why Your Company Needs an EAP" (2005), available online at: <http://www.eap4u.com/cms/need>.

Essi Systems, *Stress Map: A Personal Exploration* (Collingwood: Essi Systems, 1987).

FGI, "One Workplace, Four Generations: Managing their Conflicting Needs" (September 2004) 7 *Working Well for Managers*, available online at: <http://www.mta.ca/hr/managers/workingwell_sept2004.pdf>.

R.W. Francis, "Medcan Health Management" (Presentation at The Disability Management Conference, Toronto, May 27-28, 1996) [unpublished].

D. Goleman, *Emotional Intelligence: Why it Can Matter More Than IQ* (New York: Bantam Books, 1995).

Institut de sante publique du Quebec, reported in "Taboos and Prejudices" (2008), available online at: <http://www.fondationdesmaladiesmentales.org/en/p/help-a-person/our-assistance-programs/managers-and-employees/mental-illness/taboos-and-prejudice>.

Ipsos Reid, "Mental Health in the Workplace Study" (November 2007), available online at: <http://www.ipsos.ca>.

R. Karasek & T. Theorell, *Healthy Work: Stress, Productivity and Reconstruction of Working Life* (New York: Basic Books, 1990).

S. Klitzman, J. House, B. Israel & R. Mero, "Work Stress, Nonwork Stress and Health" (1990) 13:3 Journal of Behavioural Medicine 221.

J. Kranc, "Fact Check", *Benefits Canada* (March 2004) 70.

L. Lewis, "Employers Place More Emphasis on Managing Employee Stress" (1993) 11:2 Business & Health 46.

J. MacBride-King, "Caring about Caregiving: The Eldercare Responsibilities of Canadian Workers and the Impact on Employers" (Ottawa: The Conference Board of Canada, 1999).

J. MacBride-King, "Wrestling with Workload: Organizational Strategies for Success", *Conference Board of Canada Report* (Ottawa: Conference Board of Canada, 2005).

S.T. Maier, L.R. Watkins & M. Fleshner, "Psychoneuroimmunology: The Interface Between Behaviour, Brain and Immunity" (1994) 40 American Psychologist 771.

P. Stuart, "How McDonnell Douglas Cost-justified Its EAP, *Personnel Journal* (February 1993) 72:2 at 48, available online at: <http://www.workforce.com/archive/feature/22/21/86/223227.php>.

Mental Health Roundtable, *Employers Getting Started: On the Road to Mental Health and Productivity* (March 28, 2006), available online at: <http://www.mentalhealthroundtable.ca/20060328/part4module3.pdf>.

Mercer & The Canadian Alliance on Mental Illness and Mental Health (CAMIMH), *2008 Mental Health in the Workplace Survey* (2008), available online at: <http://www.mercer.ca/referencecontent.htm?idContent=1313070>.

H. Minuk, "The Mercantile and General Disability Claims Survey, 1994" (Presented at the Psychological Disabilities in the Workplace: Prevention, Rehabilitation and Cost Control Conference, Toronto, June 10-11, 1996) [unpublished].

National Institute of Mental Health, *News Release* (May 7, 2008) "Mental Disorders Cost Society Billions in Unearned Income", available online at: <http://www.nimh.nih.gov/science-news/2008/mental-disorders-cost-society-billions-in-unearned-income.shtml>.

A. Nicoll, "Time for Action: Managing Mental Health in the Workplace" (September 29, 2008), available online at: <http://www.mercer.ca/referencecontent.htm?idContent=1322990>.

Ontario Ministry of Labour, "Counting the Cost of Absenteeism" (1993) 1:1 Group Healthcare Management 9.

Out of the Shadows at Last, Final Report of The Standing Senate Committee on Social Affairs, Science and Technology, Senator Kirby, May 2006, available online at: <http://www.parl.gc.ca/39/1/parlbus/commbus/senate/Com-e/SOCI-E/rep-e/pdf/rep02may06part1-e.pdf>.

J. Prohofsky, "Speaking to Your CEO About EAPs: Three Strategies that Can Make EAP Believers Out of CEO Skeptics", *EAP Digest* (May 2005).

R.J. Price, "Absenteeism and Disability" (1995) The ACPM Reporter, at 34-37.

M. Ross, "Psychiatric Disability Management" (Presentation at The Disability Management Conference, Toronto, May 27-28, 1996) [unpublished].

K. Seward, "Employee Benefits — The State of EAPs in Canada, Benefits and Pensions Monitor" (June 2005) 21, available online at: <http://www.bpmagazine.com>.

C. Sherman, "Who is the Problem Employee", *Human Resources Management in Canada* (February 1989) at 70, 507-70.

Statistics Canada, *Work Absence Rates, 2007*, Cat. No. 71-211-X (Ottawa: Statistics Canada, 2008), available online at: <http://www.statcan.gc.ca/pub/71-211-x/71-211-x2008000-eng.htm>.

D.G. Tate, R.V. Habeck & D.E. Galvin, "Disability Management: Origins, Concepts and Principles for Practice" (1986) 17:3 Journal of Applied Rehabilitation Counselling 5.

Watson Wyatt Worldwide, "Addressing Mental Health in the Workplace" (June 2003), available online at: <http://www.watsonwyatt.com>.

Watson Wyatt Worldwide, *Staying@Work 2005* (Canada 2005), available online at: <http://www.watsonwyatt.com>.

W. Weeks, "Stressing Prevention", *Benefits Canada* (May 2004) 54, available online at: <http://www.benefitscanada.com/content/legacy/Content/2004/05-04/ benefits.pdf>.

B. Wilkerson, "Perspective on Mental Health in the Workplace", reported in Watson Wyatt Worldwide, *Staying@Work Report, 2005* (Canada 2005), available online at: <http://www.watsonwyatt.com>.

World Health Organization (WHO) reported in Watson Wyatt Worldwide, "Addressing Mental Health in the Workplace" (June 2003), available online at: <http://www.watsonwyatt.com>.

Chapter 8

Management of Chronic Fatigue Syndrome: Case Study[1]

INTRODUCTION

Some of the most difficult disability management cases to deal with are the ones that are poorly understood, and have primarily subjective symptomatology. This includes illnesses such as chronic fatigue syndrome, fibromyalgia and multiple chemical sensitivities. This chapter has been included to demonstrate an industry practice in dealing with employees absent due to chronic fatigue syndrome.

CHRONIC FATIGUE SYNDROME

Chronic fatigue syndrome is a complex disorder marked by incapacitating fatigue of uncertain etiology which results in at least a 50 per cent reduction in activity and is of at least six months in duration.[2] Although women aged 20 to 50 years are the most susceptible to chronic fatigue syndrome, anyone at any age can be affected.

Chronic fatigue syndrome has been called many things; for example, "Yuppie Flu", 20th Century Disease, chronic Epstein-Barr virus, M.E. (myalgic encephalomyelitis) yet it is not a new disorder. In fact, the same syndrome, or similar ones, can be found in various pieces of medical literature under such names as yeast syndrome, epidemic vegetative neuritis, chronic brucellosis, nervous exhaustion, ads neurasthenia, or Iceland disease.[3]

Several different agents have been proposed as the potential causes of chronic fatigue syndrome, ranging from fatigue due to a chronic overachieving or "type A" personality, to viral infections such as Epstein-Barr virus or an unknown retrovirus; to sleep disorders; to psychosomatic disorders; to psychiatric illness; or to deconditioning. Whatever the cause, the person with chronic fatigue syndrome experiences debilitating fatigue that is extremely frustrating and distressing to live with.

---

[1] D. Dyck, "Management of Chronic Fatigue Syndrome: Case Study" (1996) 44:2 AAOHN Journal 85. Reprinted with permission.
[2] G.P. Holmes, J.E. Kaplan *et al.*, "Chronic Fatigue Syndrome: A Working Case Definition" (1988) 108 Annals of Internal Medicine 387.
[3] S.E. Abbey & S.D. Shafran, "Chronic Fatigue Syndrome: It's Real, It's Treatable" (March 1993) Patient Care 35.

DIAGNOSING CHRONIC FATIGUE SYNDROME

When a person develops chronic fatigue syndrome, getting a definitive diagnosis can be very challenging.[4] There are no markers to objectively identify the presence of chronic fatigue syndrome. Diagnosing depends heavily on the presence of subjective complaints. Unfortunately, many physicians are unfamiliar with chronic fatigue syndrome and have difficulty diagnosing it.[5] Typically, the person with chronic fatigue syndrome travels from physician to physician looking for a cause for the fatigue, only to be subjected to more tests and investigative procedures. This process can reinforce the **sick role**, or the expression of illness behaviours, and can increase health care costs through repetitive tests and procedures.

This phenomenon partly stems from the U.S. Center for Disease Control's definition of chronic fatigue syndrome (Figure 8.1).

Figure 8.1: Diagnosing Chronic Fatigue Syndrome: Case Definition 2005[6]

Major Criteria

- Incapacitating exhaustion or fatigue of at least six or more consecutive months in duration with over 50% reduction in activity level
- Exclusion of medical and psychiatric causes
- Concurrently have four or more of the following symptoms:

  - Substantial impairment in short-term memory or concentration
  - Sore throat
  - Tender lymph nodes
  - Multi-joint pain without swelling or redness
  - Headaches of a new type, pattern or severity
  - Unrefreshing sleep
  - Post-exertional malaise lasting more than 24 hours

To be diagnosed with chronic fatigue syndrome, the person must experience incapacitating fatigue of longer than six consecutive months in duration and 50 per cent reduction in activity level *to the exclusion* of all other medical and psychiatric conditions. This means ruling out the presence of malignancies, infectious diseases, endocrine disease, autoimmune disease, sleep disorders, neuromuscular or neurological disease, exposure to toxic agents, and psychiatric disorders. As well, the definition relies on the presence of four or more other signs and symptoms, which must also not have predated the fatigue.

---

[4]	K. Fukuda, S. Straus, I. Hickie, *et al.*, "The Chronic Fatigue Syndrome: A Comprehensive Approach to Its Definition and Study" (1994) 121:12 American College of Physicians 953.

[5]	S.E. Abbey & S.D. Shafran, "Chronic Fatigue Syndrome: It's Real, It's Treatable" (March 1993) Patient Care 35.

[6]	Centers for Disease Control and Prevention, *Chronic Fatigue Syndrome* (2005), available online at: <http://www.cdc.gov/ncidod/diseases/cfs/index.htm>.

PREVALENCE OF CHRONIC FATIGUE SYNDROME

Between 1 and 4 million Americans suffer from Chronic Fatigue Syndrome (CFS),[7] which impairs them and prevents about 25 per cent of them from working.[8] Chronic Fatigue Syndrome is a serious illness and poses a dilemma for patients, their families, and health care providers.

According to Dr. Buchwald, the belief that chronic fatigue syndrome occurs mainly with Caucasians and women, is a myth. Research indicates that there is a one to one ratio for men and women and that all races can contract chronic fatigue syndrome. She believes this myth developed because women and men express the condition differently. Her research demonstrates that women tend to present primarily with painful lymph nodes and fibromyalgia, whereas men complain of painful lymph nodes and exhibit more alcohol abuse.[9] The result is a difference in diagnosing.

PROGNOSIS

People with chronic fatigue syndrome can present with a wide range of physical symptoms ranging from obvious invalidism to looking perfectly well. They can experience any of the physical symptoms outlined in Figure 8.1, with overwhelming fatigue being the major complaint. Since weight gain is common, family and friends often question the legitimacy of the illness.

The earlier a person with Chronic Fatigue Syndrome receives medical treatment, the greater the likelihood of a successful recovery. Yet, only about half will consult a physician for their illness. Equally important, about 40 per cent of the general population who report symptoms of Chronic Fatigue Syndrome have a serious, treatable, previously unrecognized medical or psychiatric condition (such as diabetes, thyroid disease, systemic lupus, or substance abuse).[10]

Recovery can be a very slow process. Symptoms may last six years or more.[11] The best prognosis for recovery occurs if the person experiences a high fever at the onset, and if he or she has a job or occupation to return to after recovery.[12]

---

[7]   Centers for Disease Control and Prevention, *Chronic Fatigue Syndrome*, available online at: <http://www.cdc.gov/cfs/cfsbasicfacts.htm>.

[8]   *Ibid.*

[9]   D. Buchwald, "Current Concepts in Assessment and Treatment of Chronic Fatigue" (Understanding Chronic Fatigue Conference. Symposium conducted at Health Science Theatre, Medical Sciences, University of Calgary, October, 1994) [unpublished]

[10]   Centers for Disease Control and Prevention, *Chronic Fatigue Syndrome*, available online at: <http://www.cdc.gov/cfs/cfsbasicfacts.htm>.

[11]   S.E. Abbey & S.D. Shafran, "Chronic Fatigue Syndrome: It's Real, It's Treatable" (March 1993) Patient Care 35.

[12]   D. Buchwald, "Current Concepts in Assessment and Treatment of Chronic Fatigue" (Understanding Chronic Fatigue Conference. Symposium conducted at Health Science Theatre, Medical Sciences, University of Calgary, October, 1994) [unpublished].

MANAGEMENT OF CHRONIC FATIGUE SYNDROME

There are numerous management approaches for helping chronic fatigue syndrome patients cope with their illness. One of the most popular models is based on Butler's Vicious Circle model (Figure 8.2).

According to this model, the patient develops the chronic fatigue syndrome symptoms and avoids activity, which results in deconditioning and a reduced tolerance for activity. This leads to resentment because the person is unable to do the activities of normal daily living. The patient tries to resume his or her familiar activities and is thwarted and left feeling helpless. This produces more symptoms and the circle continues.

Figure 8.2: Vicious Circle Model of Chronic Fatigue Syndrome[13]

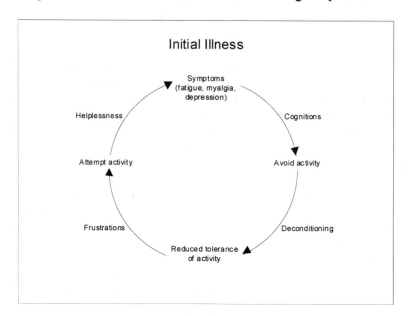

The current trend in chronic fatigue syndrome management is to use a multi-disciplinary approach incorporating the following rehabilitation goals:

- restore a sense of self-efficacy and control;
- gradually increase physical activity; and
- decrease the restrictions imposed by chronic fatigue syndrome.[14]

---

[13]   S. Butler *et al.*, "Cognitive Behavior Therapy in Chronic Fatigue Syndrome" (1991) 54 Journal of Neurological and Neurosurgical Psychiatry 153.

[14]   S.E. Abbey & S.D. Shafran, "Chronic Fatigue Syndrome: It's Real, It's Treatable" (March 1993) Patient Care 35.

The techniques involved to achieve these goals vary. However, the following are some common suggestions for chronic fatigue syndrome rehabilitation:

- validate the condition: acknowledge that chronic fatigue syndrome is a recognizable illness that many people suffer from;
- educate the person regarding chronic fatigue syndrome, the effects of physical deconditioning and the cognitive effects of inactivity;
- encourage the person to consider a wide range of explanations other than "virus" for an increase in, or return of, symptoms;
- identify dysfunctional thought patterns and demonstrate ways to think more functionally;
- focus on the person's capabilities not disabilities;
- gradually increase activities and monitor tolerance for activities;
- record all activity; and
- help the person recognize the progress that is occurring.

A WORKPLACE APPLICATION

Background

In 1994, a major Canadian oil and gas company faced the challenge of rehabilitating two employees diagnosed with chronic fatigue syndrome. Both employees developed severe flu-like symptoms in the fall of 1993. They experienced an acute onset of fever, sore throat, coughing and swollen glands. Later, they developed unexplained muscle weakness and discomfort, all-encompassing fatigue, arthralgia, forgetfulness, confusion, inability to concentrate, depression and sleep disturbances (*i.e.*, restless legs, snoring, insomnia, and fitful sleep). Both exhibited thyroid dysfunction and hoarse voices to the point of laryngitis.

During the short-term disability phase, these employees attempted to return to work in a modified work capacity, but had to withdraw due to increased fatigue and a return of symptoms. After six months of short-term disability, both were transferred to long-term disability with the company's third party insurance carrier.

Rehabilitation Program Plan

Active rehabilitation of employees on short-term disability and long-term disability was within the mandate of the company's Managed Rehabilitation Care Program. As a result, a number of health and fitness care practitioners were invited to work on a plan to actively rehabilitate these two employees. They developed the chronic fatigue syndrome rehabilitation program's goals, strategies and plan, which is outlined in Figure 8.3.

Figure 8.3: Chronic Fatigue Syndrome Rehabilitation Program

Goals
- To provide a multi-disciplinary rehabilitation program for people suffering from chronic fatigue syndrome.
- To support the participants in reaching an optimal level of functioning and an improved quality of life.
- To decrease the restrictions associated with the disability and to focus on wellness and moving on with life.
- To restore a sense of self-efficacy and control.
- To promote an early return to work.

Strategies
- To provide a holistic approach towards dealing with disability through the use of the available fitness facilities, Employee Assistance Program services, occupational health services and vocational rehabilitation services.
- To increase activity tolerance through a graduated physical fitness program, relaxation and stretching guidance, nutritional counselling, physiotherapy instruction and massage therapy.
- To increase psychological tolerance through developing strategies for coping with disability and achieving a sense of wellness.
- To increase vocational tolerance through developing strategies for work re-entry.

Plan
- To educate the patient about chronic fatigue syndrome by providing information about:
  1. the nature of chronic fatigue syndrome;
  2. the effects of physical deconditioning on muscle; and
  3. the phenomenon of increased anxiety when a failed activity is re-attempted.
- To identify the dysfunctional thought patterns and to try to change cognition about health status.
- To encourage the participant to consider a range of explanations other than a "virus" for an increase in, or return of symptoms.
- To focus on what the participant can do, rather than what he or she cannot do.
- To gradually increase activity levels.
- To record activity so that progress can be monitored.
- To institute fitness twice a week under the guidance of a personal trainer.
- To provide instruction on relaxation and stretching techniques.
- To provide massage therapy for each participant.
- To provide dietary counselling.
- To provide physiotherapy counselling.
- To provide a forum for exploring strategies for living with a disability.
- To explore vocational issues related to the disability.
- To use peer support to help deal with the effects of chronic disease.

A multi-disciplinary program was designed to operate out of the company's fitness facility for two 90-minute sessions per week conducted over a three-month period. Each session was designed to include an educational component lasting 30 minutes, fitness activities with a personal trainer lasting 30 minutes and stretching and relaxation techniques also lasting 30 minutes. The educational component encompassed information about chronic fatigue syndrome, sleep problems, psychological support for living with a disability, dietary counselling, vocational counselling, and physiotherapy guidance. The psychological support was provided weekly, while the other topics rotated through the remaining session.

Educational sessions were also offered to the family members, co-workers and the involved work groups. In addition, the participants were provided with weekly massage sessions arranged outside of the set rehabilitation program time. To evaluate the value of the rehabilitation program, individual pre-intervention and post-intervention assessments were made. These will now be described, as a part of the post-intervention results.

Results

PSYCHOLOGICAL TESTS

The participants were asked to complete scales and questionnaires that measure:

- *Attribution* — the individual's perception of disease, in particular physical versus psychological etiologies.
- *Coping* — the ability to deal with illness and life issues.
- *Fatigue Rating* — the characteristics of fatigue.
- *Functional Status* — the ability to function in daily life.
- *General Health History* — the experienced somatic and psychological distress.
- *Locus of Control* — the belief that health is determined by behaviour.
- *Quality of Life* — the perceived satisfaction with daily activities and relationships.
- *Social Supports: Family and Friends* — the emotional, instrumental and problem-solving support obtained from family and friends.
- *Stress* — the stress factors identified in the areas of environmental pressures and satisfactions, coping responses, cognition and signals of distress.

The scores from psychological tests were used for pre-intervention and post-intervention comparison purposes.

In general, the participants showed either gradual improvements or no change between the pre-intervention and post-intervention results (Figure 8.4).

Figure 8.4: Psychological Test Results

Scale/Questionnaire	Case 1	Case 2
Attribution Scale	Shift in belief that the problem was purely physical to believing that psychological factors were impacting the condition	Shift in belief that the problem was purely physical to believing that psychological factors were impacting the condition
Coping Scale: Problem-based	Increased ability to manage the source of difficulties	Increased ability to manage the source of difficulties
Coping Scale: Emotion-based	Reduced ability to minimize distress	No change in ability to cope
Fatigue Rating	Less interference in daily activities due to fatigue	Less interference in daily activities due to fatigue
Functional Status Questionnaire (Medical Measures)		
Physical function	Improvement	Improvement
Role function	Improvement	Improvement
Social function	Improvement	Improvement
Mental health	Improvement	No change
General health	Improvement	No change
Body pain	Improvement	Improvement
Vitality	Improvement	Improvement
General Health History Questionnaire **(Distress Measure)**	No distress	Change from being "in distress" to "not being in distress"
Locus of Control Scale	Slight shift to externality	Slight shift to externality
Quality of Life Scale	General improvement	General improvement
Social Support Scale (Family)	High score originally: Unchanged	Increased support

Scale/Questionnaire	Case 1	Case 2
Social Support Scale (Friends)	Moderately high score originally: Unchanged	Moderately high score originally: Unchanged
Stress Map		
Work world	Improvement	Not applicable*
Personal world	Improvement	Improvement
Coping responses	Improvement in self-care, direct action, support seeking, situation mastery and adaptability: negative change in time management	Improvement in self-care, direct action, situation mastery and adaptability: no change in support seeking and time management
Thinking patterns	Improvement in self-esteem and positive outlook: no change in personal power — at the burnout stage	Improvement in self-esteem, support seeking and positive outlook
Feeling patterns	Improvement in connection and compassion: negative change in expression	Improvement in connection: no change in expression and compassion
Symptoms	Improvement in physical symptoms, behavioural symptoms and emotional symptoms: all were at the level of burnout originally	Improvement in physical symptoms, behavioural symptoms and emotional symptoms: at the level of burnout originally

* At the time of pre-and post-testing, this participant was not working.

FITNESS TESTS

A treadmill test was used to assess cardiovascular fitness. Subjects were asked to maintain heart rates within their Target Heart Rate Zones[15] as the speed and grade of the treadmill was gradually increased. Their tolerance for this activity over three minutes was then measured and recorded.

The fitness consultants were unable to implement other standardized fitness tests as the participants did not possess the necessary grip or upper body strength for even the most elementary level of testing. Consequently, the participants were asked to give maximum effort to the use of the rowing machine and free weights, and measurements of those activities were made and documented.

Improvements were seen in tolerance for activity, level of fitness and strength training as summarized in Figure 8.5.

Figure 8.5: Fitness Results

Assessment	Case 1	Case 2
Treadmill	Increased speed 1.3 miles per hour Increased endurance by 9 minutes Increased grade by 2%	Increased speed 1.5 miles per hour Increased endurance by 14 minutes Increased grade by 5%
Rowing Machine	Rowing 10 minutes at 26 strokes per min.	Rowing 12 minutes at 26 strokes per min.
Weight Training	2 x 10 reps at 3 kg biceps curls 2 x 10 reps at 3 kg bent over row 2 x 10 reps at 2 kg lateral raise 2 x 10 reps at 35 lb. leg curls 2 x 10 reps at 40 lb. leg extensions	2 x 15 reps at 3 kg biceps curls 2 x 15 reps at 3 kg bent over row 2 x 15 reps at 2 kg lateral raise 2 x 15 reps at 35 lb. leg curls 2 x 15 reps at 35 lb. leg extensions 2 x 15 reps at 20 lb. triceps press downs

---

[15] Canadian Society for Exercise Physiology (CSEP), *Physical Fitness Testing: Certified Fitness Appraiser, Resource Manual* (Gloucester, ON: CSEP, 1993).

PAIN TESTING

At the first massage session, the participants were administered the following series of massage tests:

- *Resisted Active Test*
  Therapist immobilizes the joint and provides resistance against client's muscular contraction (about 20 per cent to 39 per cent of maximum strength). This test determines muscular strains and trigger points.

- *Relaxed Passive Test*
  The therapist manually moves the client's limb through a full range of motion while the client relaxes the surrounding joint muscles. This test helps to determine joint pathologies.

- *Free Active Test*
  The client moves the limb through a full range of motion. This allows for assessment of the presence or absence of pain and abnormalities in the movement mechanics.

- *Trigger Point Test*
  A trigger point is pain in a muscle that, when pressed, allocates pain locally and/or refers pain to other areas of the body. They can be latent (pain present only upon application of stimulus), or active (pain present without the application of pressure).

During the baseline massage assessment, both participants indicated pain when simple techniques were administered. Their pain and sensitivity were more intense on the left side of the body. Both reported having muscle cramps associated with movement, and, at times, these cramps were present without movement.

Trigger point testing was done on the shoulder, cervical and lumbar joints. Initially, pain was indicated on resisted active and passive tests. There was an absence of pain with free active testing indicating the lack of joint pathology. Trigger points were active and referring pain in the following muscles:

1. *levator scapula* (left) causing pain into the cervical, suboccipital and shoulder area;
2. *quadratus lumborum* (left) causing pain in the lumbar, hip and gluteals; and
3. tricep, lateral head (left) being localized and extremely sensitive to the touch.

The initial massage treatment was extremely painful and the body was hypersensitive to touch. Using a pain scale of 1 to 10, 1 being ticklish and 10 being intolerable, the weight of the hand on their bodies registered 9-10. It took two to three sessions before the pain and discomfort was reduced enough (to a 5-6 level) to allow the implementation of therapeutic techniques. By the sixth session, massage was reportedly enjoyable and beneficial.

Likewise, relaxation was initially difficult for both participants to achieve. This was probably associated with the pain experienced during massage treatments. By the sixth treatment, both were able to relax enough to allow the masseur to incorporate joint mobilizations.

Figure 8.6: Massage Results

Assessment	Case 1	Case 2
Trigger Points	Referred trigger point pain was lessened. Local trigger point pain was reduced in intensity.	Referred trigger point pain reduced in all initial trigger points. Therapeutic pressure was reached by the third session.
Relaxation	Remarkable improvement in relaxation state. Developed ability to trust and relax enough to allow joint mobilizations after fifth session.	Relaxation easily achieved by third session.

DIETARY ASSESSMENT

The participants were asked to complete a dietary history, which includes a physical symptom history, weight history, brief family history, lifestyle history, height, weight, age and a three-day food record. The three-day food record was then computer-analyzed using the Nuts 3.7 nutrient assessment program for nutritional adequacy.[16]

The Nomogram[17] (Mayo Clinic, 1994) was used to calculate the caloric recommendations. The only subjective information used in this equation was the activity factor, which was estimated at a low level for both participants. Weights were monitored throughout the study using a Gold Brand beam scale. Gastrointestinal symptoms were obtained by self-report.

Prior to the program, both participants were consuming calories well below their basal caloric requirements. This finding was consistent with nutritional

---

[16]   Quichena Consulting Limited, *Nuts Version 3.7* (Victoria: Quichena Consulting, 1992).

[17]   J. K. Nelson *et al., Mayo Clinic Diet Manual: A Handbook of Nutritional Practices*, 7th ed. (St. Louis: C.V. Mosby, 1994).

literature on chronic fatigue syndrome.[18] The basal metabolic rate decreases primarily due to muscle tissue breakdown common to starvation states, and, combined with decreased activity due to fatigue, the person gains weight even on a low caloric intake.

Post-intervention, both participants reported a greater awareness of the gap between their dietary deficits and the recommended daily nutritional requirements.[19] One participant was able to attain the recommended daily caloric intake, while the other came close to doing likewise. Food sensitivities were identified and addressed by one participant. This resulted in a reduction of gastrointestinal symptoms. The other participant reported an increase in the number of "positive feeling" days, improved appetite, less insomnia and fewer episodes of laryngitis and swollen glands. However, both participants gained significant weight from the onset of the illness, and, even now, remain unable to lose the extra weight.

FUNCTIONAL ASSESSMENT

Daily activity logs (Figure 8.7) were kept by the two participants for the duration of the program. The intent was to track sleep patterns, activity levels and tolerance, fatigue levels and mood. As well, health status was regularly monitored through the company's occupational health centre.

The daily activity logs that each participant completed showed a gradual increase in activities and an increased tolerance for those activities. Not only did the participants look and feel better, but also they were able to begin a gradual re-entry process back into the workplace.

VOCATIONAL ASSESSMENT

Standardized vocational tests were not conducted; however, a number of observations were made. Prior to the program, one participant was attempting modified work for one to two hours, the other was unable to work. Both participants expressed fears that their jobs would be abolished and that they would be unable to secure employment when they were well enough to return to work. Lack of confidence in their ability to market themselves to potential employers was a noted source of anxiety.

---

[18] I.J. Russell, "Neurohormonal Dysfunction in Chronic Fatigue and Fibromyalgia" (7th International Symposium of Physical Medicine Research Foundation on Repetitive Strain Injuries, Fibromyalgia, and Chronic Fatigue Syndrome, June 1994) [unpublished]; and M. Winther, "Essential Fatty Acid Therapy for Myalgic Encephalomyelitis" in *The Clinical and Scientific Basis of Myalgic Encephalomyelitis — Chronic Fatigue Syndrome*, B. Hyde, ed. (Ottawa: Nightingale Research Foundation, 1992) 628.

[19] Canadian Diabetic Association (CDA), *Good Healthy Eating Guide, Resource Manual* (Edmonton: CDA, 1994).

Figure 8.7: Daily Activity Log

Date: _____

Hour of Awakening: _____ Sedation Used: Yes _____ No _____

No. of Sleep Disturbances: _____ Dream Activity: Low ___ Medium ___

High ___

	Exhausted							Totally Refreshed		
Refreshed:	1	2	3	4	5	6	7	8	9	10

Comments: _____

_____

_____

Calendar of Activities

6:00 a.m.	
7:00 a.m.	
8:00 a.m.	
9:00 a.m.	
10:00 a.m.	
11:00 a.m.	
12:00 noon	
1:00 p.m.	
2:00 p.m.	
3:00 p.m.	
4:00 p.m.	
5:00 p.m.	
6:00 p.m.	
7:00 p.m.	
8:00 p.m.	
9:00 p.m.	
10:00 p.m.	
11:00 p.m.	

Appraisal of the Day

	Low									High
Activity Level	1	2	3	4	5	6	7	8	9	10
Fatigue Level	1	2	3	4	5	6	7	8	9	10
Mood Level	1	2	3	4	5	6	7	8	9	10

Comments: _____

Both participants demonstrated an increased awareness of their marketable skills, particularly in the areas of personal and transferable skills. The initial reluctance to take ownership of their strengths and skills was gradually reduced.

There was an increased willingness to accept that a broad range of vocational options exists in the labour market, and that these options are obtainable through a strategic job search.

Discussion

Chronic fatigue syndrome is a multifaceted condition and requires a team approach to produce positive recovery results. The following is a discussion of how the Chronic Fatigue Syndrome Rehabilitation Program strategies were met and the findings that emerged:

Strategy 1: Provide a holistic approach towards dealing with disability through the use of available company resources: the fitness centre, Employee Assistance Program, occupational health services and vocational rehabilitation services.

The program operated as planned, however the original design of the program failed to include a transitional period from dependency on the program providers, to self-sufficiency by the participant. During the course of the program, the designers recognized that this aspect was important if the demonstrated recovery behaviours were to be sustained. Thus, the program was extended by a month.

Strategy 2: Support the participant in attaining an optimal level of functioning and an improved quality of life.

The functional status questionnaire (medical measures), Figure 8.4, indicated improvements in physical function, role function, social function, mental health, general health and vitality. As well, there was an improvement in quality of life and a reduction in chronic fatigue syndrome symptomatology (stress map).

In the pre-intervention test, both participants scored high on the social support scale (friends) (Figure 8.4). As a result, change was not expected or seen. As for family support, one participant indicated an increase in family support at the post-intervention test. This was probably associated with the psychological counselling, which encouraged the participants to control perfectionist tendencies, lower expectations and accept help from family members.

As for the cognitive and behavioural coping strategies for dealing with internal and external demands in stressful situations, both participants increased their ability to manage problems, but neither demonstrated an improvement in coping with the associated emotional issues. In fact, one participant demonstrated a reduced ability to cope with emotional problems on the stress map and emotion-based coping scale (Figure 8.4). When this was examined further, it was noted that at the time of the post-intervention test, this person was reacting to the deaths of a number of family members. Interestingly, the grieving process lasted a normal period of time without a setback in the recovery process.

Some credit for this degree of coping may be attributable to the psychological support provided by the Chronic Fatigue Syndrome Rehabilitation Program.

Although there were some improvements in the participants' feeling patterns, Figure 8.4, more help may have been warranted in some areas. For example, the test results indicated negative, or no change, in expression and compassion. Expression is sharing what one thinks and how one feels with others through direct and indirect communication.[20] Compassion is the capacity to empathize with another person, understanding another point of view and recognizing other peoples' strengths and limits.[21] In discussion with the program designers, it was believed to be unrealistic to expect change in these areas as a result of a three-month program. Healthy people can function adequately at lower levels of both these values.

One area where no change was noted was time management. Given the fact that both participants had been absent for many months and were returned to a scheduled program and into a modified work program, the designers of the program should have anticipated that time management would be a challenge. If a similar program were repeated, inclusion of a time management session, as well as help with balancing home and work life pressures, would be recommended.

Strategy 3: Decrease the restrictions associated with the disability and focus on wellness and "moving on with life".

An increase in activity tolerance was illustrated by the fitness test results, massage results, activity logs and gradual return-to-work initiatives. Now, three months after the end of the program, both participants have sustained their activity levels, and, in fact, they are increasing their hours of work.

The fatigue rating results indicated less interference in daily activities due to fatigue. Part of this finding appears to be due to the physical reconditioning: part may be due to the psychological counselling which encouraged a gradual increase in activity and also encouraged the participants not to be frustrated by trying to "do it all at once". In this way, the vicious circle of chronic fatigue syndrome was interrupted.

The results of the related psychological tests appear to indicate that the counselling around living with a chronic disability helped both participants. Prior to the program, they believed that chronic fatigue syndrome was strictly physical in nature. Attempts to explore any associated emotional factors in the earlier stages of the recovery process proved unsuccessful. By the end of the Chronic Fatigue Syndrome Rehabilitation Program, there was a shift in belief

---

[20]   Essi Systems, *StressMap: A Personal Exploration* (Collingwood, ON: The Centre for High Performance, 1987).

[21]   *Ibid.*

that some psychological factors were impacting the conditions. In short, psychological tolerance was increased.

A reduction in some of the physical symptoms of chronic fatigue syndrome may also have been due to dietary changes. For example, an improved nutrient intake can increase blood sugar and glycogen stores and aid in greater tissue anabolism instead of tissue catabolism. Tissue catabolism from inadequate caloric and nutrient intake can result in ketosis and the resulting elevated uric acid levels. These can promote a "gouty condition" creating joint pain, weakness, fatigue, poor exercise tolerance, *etc.*, paralleling the symptoms seen with chronic fatigue syndrome.

One month into the program, it became apparent that sleep disturbances remained a barrier to the participants' successful recovery. Dr. Adam Moscovitz, of the University of Calgary Sleep Disorder Clinic, was consulted. He recommended that sleep logs be kept by each participant for screening purposes. He also agreed to conduct an educational session on the abnormalities of sleep in persons with chronic fatigue syndrome. Both participants tested positively for the presence of sleep disturbances and were referred for extensive investigations. Sleep disturbances often co-exist with chronic fatigue syndrome and are potentially treatable.[22] For this reason, the participants attended a sleep clinic.

Strategy 4: Restore a sense of self-efficacy and control.

Both participants reported a heightened sense of control over their recovery process and their lives. When the Chronic Fatigue Syndrome Rehabilitation Program ended, both employees chose to continue their rehabilitation efforts by continuing their fitness programs, psychological counselling, dietary counselling and massage therapy. Their goal was to sustain and build on the gains that they had already made.

Strategy 5: Promote an early return to work.

In association with the program, both participants worked modified work duties. However, due to a changing work environment, guarantees of a return to a permanent job are uncertain. For this reason, a referral for focused job search assistance was made to a private career-coaching program that has a philosophy consistent with the goals of the Chronic Fatigue Syndrome Rehabilitation Program. The outcome was that one participant chose to do a thorough career

---

[22] D. Buchwald *et al.*, "Sleep Disorders in Patients with Chronic Fatigue" (1994) 18 (Supp. 1) Clinical Infectious Diseases 68; L. Krupp *et al.*, "Sleep Disturbance in Chronic Fatigue Syndrome" (1993) 37:4 Journal of Psychosomatic Research 325; and R. Morriss *et al.*, "Abnormalities of Sleep in Patients with the Chronic Fatigue Syndrome" (1993) 306 British Medical Journal 1161.

evaluation, while the other decided to do on-the-job training with the department in which modified work was available.

In summary, this multi-disciplinary approach to chronic fatigue syndrome rehabilitation did make a difference, and the gains in recovery appear to be sustainable. Some recommendations for future Chronic Fatigue Syndrome Rehabilitation Programs are:

- document baseline states so that progress can be measured;
- include a transitional period prior to discharge from the program so that participants can move towards self-sufficiency;
- build "Time Management" and "Achieving Balance Between Work and Family Life" sessions into the program;
- anticipate and investigate the possible presence of sleep disturbances so they can be treated;
- incorporate dietary counselling into the program, as it can help to reduce the underlying physical symptoms; and
- offer vocational counselling to promote employability once a return to full-time work has been achieved.

SUMMARY

Case management and rehabilitation of "hot illnesses", like chronic fatigue syndrome, are challenging processes. To result in a successful return to a productive lifestyle for the employee, a goal-oriented plan of action is required that encompasses a team effort, a multi-disciplinary approach and collaboration by all stakeholders.

CHAPTER REFERENCES

S.E. Abbey & S.D. Shafran, "Chronic Fatigue Syndrome: It's Real, It's Treatable" (March 1993) Patient Care 35.

D. Buchwald, "Current Concepts in Assessment and Treatment of Chronic Fatigue" (Understanding Chronic Fatigue Conference. Symposium conducted at Health Science Theatre, Medical Sciences, University of Calgary, October, 1994) [unpublished].

D. Buchwald *et al.*, "Sleep Disorders in Patients with Chronic Fatigue" (1994) 18 (Supp. 1) Clinical Infectious Diseases 68.

S. Butler *et al.*, "Cognitive Behavior Therapy in Chronic Fatigue Syndrome" (1991) 54 Journal of Neurological and Neurosurgical Psychiatry 153.

Canadian Diabetic Association (CDA), *Good Healthy Eating Guide, Resource Manual* (Edmonton: CDA, 1994).

Canadian Society for Exercise Physiology (CSEP), *Physical Fitness Testing: Certified Fitness Appraiser, Resource Manual* (Gloucester, ON: CSEP, 1993).

Centers for Disease Control and Prevention, *Chronic Fatigue Syndrome* (2005), available online at: <http://www.cdc.gov/ncidod/diseases/cfs/index.htm>.

D. Dyck, "Management of Chronic Fatigue Syndrome: Case Study" (1996) 44:2 AAOHN Journal 85.

Essi Systems, *StressMap: A Personal Exploration* (Collingwood, ON: The Centre for High Performance, 1987).

K. Fukuda, S. Straus, I. Hickie, *et al.*, "The Chronic Fatigue Syndrome: A Comprehensive Approach to Its Definition and Study" (1994) 121:12 American College of Physicians 953.

G.P. Holmes, J.E. Kaplan, *et al.*, "Chronic Fatigue Syndrome: A Working Case Definition" (1988) 108 Annals of Internal Medicine 387.

L. Krupp *et al.*, "Sleep Disturbance in Chronic Fatigue Syndrome" (1993) 37:4 Journal of Psychosomatic Research 325.

R. Morriss *et al.*, "Abnormalities of Sleep in Patients with the Chronic Fatigue Syndrome" (1993), 306 British Medical Journal 1161.

J.K. Nelson *et al.*, *Mayo Clinic Diet Manual: A Handbook of Nutritional Practices*, 7th ed. (St. Louis: C.V. Mosby, 1994).

Quichena Consulting Ltd., *Nuts Version 3.7* (Victoria: Quichena Consulting, 1992).

I.J. Russell, "Neurohormonal Dysfunction in Chronic Fatigue and Fibromyalgia (7th International Symposium of Physical Medicine Research Foundation on Repetitive Strain Injuries, Fibromyalgia, and Chronic Fatigue Syndrome, June, 1994) [unpublished].

M. Winther, "Essential Fatty Acid Therapy for Myalgic Encephalomyelitis" in *The Clinical and Scientific Basis of Myalgic Encephalomyelitis — Chronic Fatigue Syndrome*, B. Hyde, ed. (Ottawa: Nightingale Research Foundation, 1992) 628.

Chapter 9

Workplace Attendance Support and Assistance

INTRODUCTION

Companies are increasingly being challenged to meet the needs of customers, expectations of shareholders, and obligations to the community at large in their daily operations. Meeting these challenges requires the commitment and support of every employee. For this reason, management attention is being paid to supporting employee attendance.

Disability management involves assisting ill or injured employees in managing their medical absence and return to work, having policies and procedures in place, providing education to stakeholders, clarifying stakeholder roles and responsibilities in the process, having graduated return-to-work opportunities available, and addressing workplace wellness (Chapter 1, "Disability Management: Overview", Figure 1.1). Encouraging employees to attend work on a regular basis should be part of any organization's disability management efforts.

> Unscheduled absenteeism is a problem that no organization can afford to ignore — either from a cost or productivity standpoint. With the appropriate programs in place, businesses can significantly reduce the number of last minute no-shows, improve the work environment for all employees and realize substantial savings.[1]

To this end, many companies have chosen to assist their employees through the use of a formalized workplace attendance support program.

EMPLOYEE ABSENTEEISM

Employee absenteeism is defined as unplanned work absence due to illness, injury or personal reasons, or just failing to come to work. Often there are discernible absence patterns such as Monday and Friday absences.[2] Some reasons for unscheduled work absences, which can lead to chronic absenteeism, are:

*   chronic medical conditions;

---

[1]   P. Wolf, "CCH Survey Finds Most Employees Call in 'Sick' for Reasons Other Than Illness", CCH Inc., *2007 CCH Unscheduled Absence Survey* (Riverwoods, IL: CCH Inc., 2007), available online at: <http://www.cch.com/press/news/2007/20071010h.asp>.

[2]   *Ibid.*

- personal problems;
- problems balancing work-family life demands;
- medical, dental or personal appointments;
- increased caregiving responsibilities;
- more women in the workforce, especially mothers with young children;
- high stress among workers, especially women over 40 years of age;
- frequent illness/injuries;
- job dissatisfaction or disinterest in work;
- low employee morale;[3]
- lack of awareness of attendance expectations;
- irresponsible work attitudes;
- poor quality of supervision;
- decaying employee-employer relations; and/or
- increased prevalence of generous sick and family-related leave (design of benefit plans).

WHY MANAGE EMPLOYEE ABSENTEEISM?

Employee absenteeism is a costly and complex problem for employers in all segments of Canada's economy. In the 1970s, when productivity was high, many employers chose to ignore employee attendance problems. Through the "leaner years" of the 1980s, 1990s and into the 2000s, the challenge for companies has been to ensure a consistent level of productivity and service in a climate of downsizing.

Employee Absenteeism Costs:

- In 2007, 8.8% of all full-time employees were absent from work for all or part of any given week. This is a significant increase from 1997 when about 5.5% of all full-time employees were absent.[4]
- In 1994 unplanned absences cost Canadian employers about $15 billion per year;[5] by 2001 this increased to $17 billion.[6] Today, this number is $24.4 billion.[7]

---

[3]   CCH Inc., *CCH 2007 Unscheduled Absence Survey* (Riverwoods, IL: CCH, 2007).

[4]   Statistics Canada, *Work Absence Rates, 2007*, Cat. No. 71-211-XWE (Ottawa: Statistics Canada, May 2008); and E. Akyeampong, *Work Absence Rates, 1987 to 1998*, Cat. No. 71-535-MPB, No. 10 (Ottawa: Statistics Canada, 1999).

[5]   D. Thompson, "The Dollars and Sense of Managing Absenteeism" (1995) 3:8 Group Healthcare Management 17.

[6]   J. Kranc, "Fact Check" *Benefits Canada* (March 2004) 70, 86.

[7]   Calculated by multiplying the number of lost-time workdays in 2007 (147,918,000 lost workdays) by the average daily wage for full-time Canadian employees as of November 2007 ($167.44 per day). Data obtained from Statistics Canada, *Work Absence Rates, 2007*, Cat. No. 71-211-XWE (Ottawa: Statistics Canada, May 2008) and Statistics Canada, *Average Hourly*

- In Canada, direct costs of employee absenteeism in 1991 averaged $1,112 per employee per year.[8] Now, it equals $1,708 per full-time employee per year.[9] This translates to $2.4 million per year (1.2% of payroll) for many Canadian employers.[10]
- Over the last 10 years, American companies experienced absenteeism rates ranging from a high of 2.9% in 1998 to a low of 1.9% in 2003. Likewise, the per employee costs ranged between $572 in 1997 to the all time high of $789 in 2002 (Figure 9.1).[11] In 2007, job absences cost American employers $660 per employee per year.[12]
- Absenteeism costs approximately 1.2 – 6% of payroll.[13]
- Restated, American employers paid 0.2% of their **total health care dollars** on employee absenteeism.[14]
- By managing absenteeism, a reduction of 30-50% or more can be realized.[15]

Wages of Employees by Selected Characteristics and Profession, available online at: <http://www40.statcan.ca/l01/cst01/labr69a-eng.htm>.

[8] Peat, Marwick & Kellogg, *Data Produced on 1991 Employee Benefit Costs in Canada* (1993) [unpublished].

[9] Calculated by determining the daily wage from the average daily wage for full-time Canadian employees as of November 2007 ($167.44 per day), and multiplying that value by the average number of lost time days per Canadian worker (10.2 days). Data obtained from: Statistics Canada, *Work Absence Rates, 2007*, Cat. No. 71-211-XWE (Ottawa: Statistics Canada, May 2008), and Statistics Canada, *Average Hourly Wages of Employees by Selected Characteristics and Profession*, available online at: <http://www40.statcan.ca/l01/ cst01/labr69a.htm>.

[10] Watson Wyatt Worldwide, *Staying@Work: Effective Presence at Work — 2007 Survey Report — Canada* (2007), available online at: <https://www.watsonwyatt.com>.

[11] CCH Inc., News Release, "2004 CCH Unscheduled Absence Survey: Unscheduled Employee Absenteeism Rises to Five-Year High" (October 7, 2004), available online at: <http://www. cch.com/Press/News/2004/20041007h.asp>.

[12] CCH Inc., *CCH 2007 Unscheduled Absence Survey* (Riverwoods, IL: CCH, 2007).

[13] D. Thompson, "The Dollars and Sense of Managing Absenteeism" (1993) 3:8 Group Healthcare Management 17; Peat, Marwick & Kellogg, *Data Produced on 1991 Employee Benefit Costs in Canada* (1993) [unpublished]; Watson Wyatt Worldwide, *Staying@Work: Effective Presence at Work — 2007 Survey Report — Canada* (2007), available online at: <https://www.watsonwyatt.com>; and Mercer Inc., "The Total Financial Impact of Employee Absences — Survey Highlights" (2008) at 4, available online at: <http://www.kronos.com/ absenceanonymous/media/Mercer-Survey-Highlights.pdf>.

[14] S. Aldana, *Top Five Strategies to Enhance the ROI of Worksite Wellness Programs*, Wellness Council of America (January 2009), available online at: <http://www.welcoa.org/freeresources/ pdf/top_5_strategies.pdf>.

[15] D. Thompson, "The Dollars and Sense of Managing Absenteeism" (1993) 3:8 Group Healthcare Management 17; and Aon Consulting, "The Case for Absence Management" (2005) *Aon Workforce Strategies*, available online at: <http://www.aon.com/default.jsp>.

Figure 9.1: Rate and Cost of Absenteeism: United States of America[16]

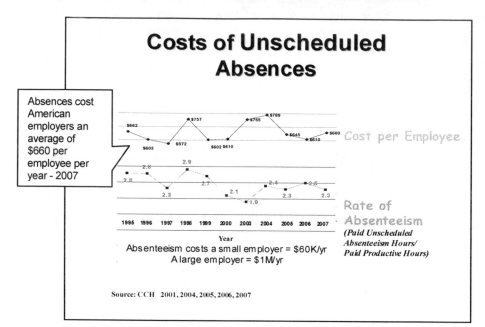

TRACKING EMPLOYEE ABSENTEEISM

Employee absenteeism, although costly in terms of lost productivity and employee benefit costs, is not well tracked, or quantified, by employers.[17] Employers tend to recognize the cost of lost wages (direct cost of absenteeism), but not the indirect costs such as:

- worker replacement costs;
- overtime costs;
- supervisory time to rearrange work schedules;
- negative employee morale;
- reduction in productivity;
- "catch-up time" for the returning employee;
- administration time and costs to deal with the absence claims and costs; and
- increased benefit and insurance premiums.

---

[16] CCH Inc., *CCH 2007 Unscheduled Absence Survey* (Riverwoods, IL: CCH, 2007). Permission for Use Granted, © CCH, Wolters Kluwer Law & Business, 2007, available online at: <http://www.cch.com/Absenteeism2007/Images/Rate.asp>.

[17] Watson Wyatt Worldwide, *Staying@Work: Effective Presence at Work — 2007 Survey Report — Canada* (2007), available online at: <https://www.watsonwyatt.com>.

According to Lori Rosen, J.D., a CCH workplace analyst, and author of *HR Networking: Work-Life Benefits*,[18] the tight economy seems to have:

> ... helped companies in holding the per-employee cost of absenteeism steady, but with the rate of unscheduled absences increasing, the overall out-of-pocket cost to employers rises accordingly. This trend makes it all the more important to closely examine why employees aren't showing up for work and what work-life and absence control programs can be used to help stem the tide.[19]

WHAT DOES AN ATTENDANCE SUPPORT AND ASSISTANCE PROGRAM INVOLVE?

There is no one "best", or "standard", way to manage employee absenteeism. Some aspects of absenteeism are within managerial control and some are not, depending on the type of absenteeism and its severity, frequency, concentration, and causes. The Annual CCH Unscheduled Absences Surveys (1995 to 2007) determined that "sick time" is not the single leading reason for employee absence from work. The five main reasons for unscheduled absences are as follows:[20]

Figure 9.2: Reasons for Unscheduled Absences: 1995-2007

Reasons	1995	1996	1997	1998	1999	2000	2001	2002	2003	2004	2005	2006	2007	Average
Personal Illness	45	28	26	22	21	40	32	33	36	38	35	35	34	32%
Personal Needs	13	20	22	20	20	20	19	21	18	18	18	18	18	19%
Family Issues	27	26	26	26	21	21	21	24	22	23	21	24	22	23%
Entitlement Mentality	9	15	14	16	19	14	9	10	13	10	14	13	11	13%
Stress	6	11	12	16	19	5	19	11	18	11	13	12	13	12%

---

[18] Chicago, IL: CCH, 2004.

[19] L. Rosen, CCH Inc., News Release, "2004 CCH Unscheduled Absence Survey: Unscheduled Employee Absenteeism Rises to Five-Year High" (October 7, 2004), available online at: <http://www.cch.com/Press/News/2004/20041007h.asp>.

[20] CCH Inc., "The 7th Annual CCH Unscheduled Absences Survey" (1997) 412 Human Resources Management: Ideas and Trends 121; Peat, Marwick & Kellogg, *Data Produced on 1991 Employee Benefit Costs in Canada* (1993) [unpublished]; CCH Inc., News Release, "2004 CCH Unscheduled Absence Survey: Unscheduled Employee Absenteeism Rises to Five-Year High" (October 7, 2004), available online at: <http://www.cch.com/Press/News/2004/20041007h.asp>; CCH Inc., *2006 CCH Unscheduled Absence Survey* (Riverwoods, IL: CCH, 2006); and CCH Inc., *CCH 2007 Unscheduled Absence Survey* (Riverwoods, IL: CCH, 2007).

Using this data, personal illness seems to account for only 32 per cent of unscheduled work absence while 68 per cent of the absences are related to factors such as personal needs, family issues, entitlement mentality, and stress.

Cultural absenteeism, which can be a self-fulfilling prophecy, is defined as employee absenteeism that is supported and nurtured by the beliefs of the work culture. If people perceive that attendance is of little concern to management and co-workers and that their attendance does not matter, cultural absenteeism will prevail.[21]

Coming to work is an important part of a person's normal activities. People gain intrinsic and extrinsic benefits from working. The intrinsic benefits include self-actualization, job satisfaction, pride in a strong work ethic and loyalty to co-workers and company. The extrinsic benefits are compensation, rewards and recognition for good performance.

A few suggestions to encourage and promote greater job satisfaction among employees are:

- strive to make jobs interesting and challenging;
- provide opportunities for personal achievement (*i.e.*, opportunities to make suggestions for improvement, special projects, *etc.*);
- ensure that employees are recognized appropriately for their achievements;
- encourage employee participation in setting organizational goals and solving problems;
- maintain regular communication with all employees;
- address presenteeism, that is, the phenomenon of employees coming to work sick and passing their illness onto other employees;[22] and
- promote a positive level of employee morale.[23]

A number of companies have introduced attendance management programs only to learn that what has been implemented is negatively perceived by employees and unions. Programs with an "enforcement approach" have met with unanticipated resistance.

An Attendance Support & Assistance Program, on the other hand, is a pro-active approach to promoting and supporting employee attendance at work. Although an attendance program can be called many different things, like attendance management, attendance support, employee wellness, workplace wellness, *etc.*, the term Attendance Support & Assistance Program will be used in this text.

Over the years, human resources personnel have come to realize that successful attendance program implementation requires:

- internal partnerships to address employee attendance;

---

[21] L. Kelly, *Absenteeism: Manual* (Kingston: International Research, 1991).
[22] CCH Inc., *CCH 2007 Unscheduled Absence Survey* (Riverwoods, IL: CCH, 2007).
[23] *Ibid.*

- increased employee understanding of the impact lost work time has on the organization and its employees;
- standards involving regular work attendance;
- reliable tracking of employee work attendance;[24]
- employee accountability for work attendance;
- fair and consistent treatment of employees;
- a focus on supporting and helping the employee attend work;
- the capacity to work with individual employees who are having difficulty maintaining regular work attendance; and
- workplace solutions to maintain regular employee attendance and reduce absenteeism.

To be successful, an Attendance Support & Assistance Program must be custom-made to fit the organization and the attendance problems identified. Although there is no such thing as a "standard" program, there are many common features of a successful attendance support program. The key functions of a successful Attendance Support & Assistance Program include:

- identifying the importance to the organization of employee dependability and responsibility, as demonstrated through good attendance;
- indicating the concern of the organization regarding excessive absenteeism for any reason;
- identifying the relationship between absence and performance management;
- defining culpable or "blameworthy" absences and non-culpable or "innocent" absences, and the measure for dealing with these separately, that is, progressive discipline for culpable absence and counselling or resource assistance for non-culpable absence;
- clearly outlining the rules of the organization on reporting absences, for example:

  (a) the frequency and direction of reporting;
  (b) when and if a medical certificate is required; and
  (c) the nature and frequency of any additional information required by the employer during a period of absence from work.

- being consistently enforced, while at the same time flexible enough to allow for some discretion on the part of the employer in the case of emergencies or unusual circumstances;
- providing guidance to managers on what information is required from the absent employee, and what type of information is necessary for tracking purposes; and
- ensuring that there is a method for documentation and follow-up in the management of absenteeism.

---

[24] Hewitt Associates, *Disability Absence Index Survey 2007* (2007) at 5, available online at: <http://www. hewittassociates.com/Intl/NA/en-CA/KnowledgeCenter/ArticlesReports/DAIS_highlights. aspx>.

HOW CAN THIS BE DONE?

Commitment

By working together to build an attendance support policy, an organization can assist employees to understand the importance of regular work attendance, while clearly outlining the consequences of chronic absenteeism. Of particular note, the name of the program can either make or break the program intent. For this reason, I suggest the title "Attendance Support & Assistance Program". It denotes support, and, as the acronym ASAP indicates, responsiveness.

Policy Development

As with any program, a policy statement is required. A sample policy on attendance could be:

POLICY

The Company and its Unions recognize that a standard of excellence in service delivery can be achieved and maintained through the regular attendance of all employees.

   Employees have a duty to attend work as part of the job requirements for which they were hired. Employees encountering difficulties in maintaining their regular work attendance are encouraged to take advantage of the employee supports available. The Company and its Unions are committed to assisting employees who experience difficulty in attending work.

Definitions

Operative definitions are needed to ensure clarity. One of the key terms to define is "excessive absenteeism". In Canada, "excessive absenteeism" is "employee absence from work that exceeds two to three times the average absenteeism rate for the employee population within an organization". Another measure is employee absence that is in excess of the national standard for employee absenteeism.

Stakeholder Responsibilities

Of paramount importance is the task of defining the roles and responsibilities of each stakeholder in the proposed attendance program. Some examples will be provided later in this chapter.

Reporting an Absence

Clear instructions regarding the reporting practices must be provided. For example:

The employee is to contact his or her direct supervisor as soon as possible, either via a designated contact person, or through the use of a voice recorded message. The information provided should cover the name, reason for the absence, the anticipated return-to-work date, and what provisions, if applicable, have been made to cover his or her duties.

For an absence of greater than five consecutive workdays in duration, the employee will be required to produce a medical certificate and to submit it to the occupational health service.

In a case of excessive absenteeism, the Company may request a medical certificate or a signed statement from the employee identifying the cause of absences of five or less days.

Measuring and Monitoring Attendance

One of the basic tools that supervisors require when implementing an effective Attendance Support & Assistance Program is a set of reliable statistics on sick leave usage. Supervisors must be aware of the overall absence records for their work group and for each individual employee. This need not be a complex process. Some companies put the onus on the employee to record absences in a logbook, on individual time sheets or in a computerized database. Other companies have administrative or clerical personnel collect this data and enter it into an absence tracking system.

Regardless of the practice, minimally, a company should record and summarize the following:

- absences of ten days or less;
- absences of more than ten days;
- absences due to illness at work, or for medical/dental appointments;
- absences due to an injury on duty (Workers' Compensation);
- absences due to long-term disability;
- absences due to tardiness; and
- unauthorized absences.

Reports

Plans should be made so that regular monthly reports are generated to assist employees, managers or supervisors, and human resources personnel in the administration of the Attendance Support & Assistance Program. Annual reports are also required to determine the overall effectiveness of the program.

Attendance should be monitored by the manager or supervisor. Employees with excessive absenteeism would be identified by the manager or supervisor. In these cases, it would be the manager or supervisor's responsibility to initiate the Attendance Support & Assistance Program Action Steps.

Action Steps

The action steps are designed for the:

(a) early detection of employees experiencing work attendance problems;
(b) provision of assistance;
(c) encouragement of employees to address attendance problems; and
(d) addressing of problem attendance issues in a fair and consistent manner.

   The Attendance Support & Assistance Program Flow Chart (Figure 9.3) outlines the steps and actions that can be taken. It is the employee's responsibility to take charge of his or her attendance problems. However, support and assistance is consistently offered and available through the Employee Assistance Program, Disability Management Program, or through human resources programs and services.

ATTENDANCE SUPPORT AND ASSISTANCE PROGRAM: AN INDUSTRY EXAMPLE

Concepts for an Attendance Support and Assistance Program

In very basic terms, the Attendance Support & Assistance Program should be based on the following concepts:

AWARENESS

- The supervisor should be aware of the exact level of attendance for the work unit and for each individual employee in the work unit. As discussed earlier, this necessitates comprehensive and effective absenteeism recording and analysis.
- The supervisor should pay regular attention to reviewing attendance information and examining all situations where absence is a concern.
- The supervisor should pay careful attention to pattern absences or increases in absenteeism.

EXPECTATIONS

- Employees must be aware that full attendance is expected. This expectation is to be communicated to all employees on a regular basis.
- The importance of regular attendance should be officially communicated to employees, discussed at regular meetings and performance reviews and reiterated to those whose attendance is of concern.
- The importance of regular attendance should be emphasized during a new employee's induction and during the probationary period.

- Misconceptions regarding attendance should be cleared up on an ongoing basis (*e.g.*, some employees feel that they are "entitled" to a certain number of sick days a year).

ROLE MODELLING

- Each supervisor sets the standard for attendance by his or her personal attendance. Role modelling good attendance is critical to promoting regular attendance by employees.

RECOGNITION

- Good attendance warrants as much attention as poor attendance. Recognize employees with consistent good attendance, as well as those who improve poor attendance. This may be done either orally or in writing, *e.g.*, with a copy to the employee's official file.

ATTENTION

- Some employees need more supervisory support than others, whether regarding job performance or regular work attendance record. It is important to meet with employees informally after periods of absence. More specific discussions are required with employees who are not meeting attendance expectations.

ACTION

- Some situations, particularly those involving chronic absenteeism, require other direct action by the supervisor.

Provisions for Authorizing or Not Authorizing Absences

COLLECTIVE AGREEMENT

- Usually, the applicable collective agreement clearly stipulates the work leaves available to employees.

TERMS OF EMPLOYMENT

- The terms of employment clearly stipulate the work leaves available to non-unionized employees.

DEPARTMENT RULES

- In line with providing quality service, rules are established to assist the organization in meeting the operational needs of the department, for example, service or operational hours are from 8:00 a.m. to 4:00 p.m. on weekdays, lunch hour is at 12 noon.

- Other rules may be required for the operational requirements of the organization or a department. Supervisors should ensure that employees are aware of these rules by direct communication, by posting the rules on bulletin boards and through reinforcement at employee meetings or when confronting an employee about a work absence.

Stakeholder Responsibilities

SENIOR MANAGEMENT RESPONSIBILITIES

Senior Management is responsible for ensuring that employees and customers have a safe and healthy environment in which to work. They are also charged with the responsibility of providing this service in an effective and cost-efficient manner using good business practices.

HUMAN RESOURCES DEPARTMENT RESPONSIBILITIES

Senior Management usually authorizes the implementation of an Attendance Support & Assistance Program, which helps employees understand the costs of uncontrollable absenteeism and enlists employee support for attendance management. In collaboration with the employees and administration, human resources is responsible for setting the Attendance Support and Assistance Policy and Program, and the associated performance targets.

EMPLOYEE RESPONSIBILITIES

Every employee is responsible for maintaining an acceptable attendance record at work. Employees should also be aware of the provisions of the governing collective agreement, available sick leave or short-term disability benefits, and the Attendance Support & Assistance Policy and Program procedures around reporting absences, proof of illness, and other workplace requirements relating to work attendance.

It is the employee's responsibility to:

- understand the intent of the various disability plan benefits;
- understand the obligation to perform, with regularity, the prescribed duties;
- be at work regularly and on time;
- be interested in their own health and well-being;
- make every effort to live and work safely;
- attend to personal affairs and obligations outside of working hours;
- make every effort to schedule medical appointments outside of working hours;
- follow the procedures set out for reporting illness or injuries;

- personally keep the supervisor informed on their recovery when absent due to illness or injury;
- report to the supervisor upon their return to work;
- provide any required documentation verifying the absence; and
- recognize the benefit of a formal rehabilitation program for recovering employees.

Expectations regarding work attendance need to be communicated on a regular basis. Efforts should not be focused only on problem or crisis situations. The following are examples of some opportunities to discuss attendance with employees:

- *During the orientation and training of a probationary employee* — This is an appropriate time to ensure the employee's awareness of the Attendance Support & Assistance Program, the supervisory expectations regarding attendance and the requirements for reporting work absences.
- *During the performance appraisal cycle* — This is the ideal time to discuss and document expectations and to recognize good or improved attendance. For example, set specific attendance goals and document effects of the absence on the employee's performance.
- *When an employee reports an illness or injury* — This is an opportunity to discuss the reasons for the absence, the expected length of the absence, the value that the employee provides to the company and customers and any concern for the employee's well-being.
- *When an employee returns to work after an absence* — This is an ideal time to convey genuine concern for the person's health and well-being. Inquire in a positive and caring manner about how the employee is feeling. Let it be known that he or she was missed and that the workplace is glad to have him or her back.

THE ROLE OF THE UNION

In this model, the union is responsible for:

- supporting the Attendance Support & Assistance Policy and Program;
- assisting with the implementation of the Attendance Support & Assistance Policy and Program;
- promoting communication with employees as to the related attendance standards and expectations;
- identifying situations where an employee needs help;
- participating in attendance reviews, if required; and
- participating in the review of attendance targets and recommending changes at a department level.

SUPERVISOR RESPONSIBILITIES

It is the supervisor's responsibility to ensure the proper and efficient management of the employees in his or her department and to be accountable for managing acceptable attendance rates of all employees.

The supervisor's responsibilities include:

- provision of leadership and a positive attendance role model;
- application and administration of the Attendance Support & Assistance Policy and Program for employees;
- communication about the Attendance Support & Assistance Policy and Program;
- promotion of communication with employees as to the related attendance standards and expectations;
- tracking employee attendance;
- identification of situations where an employee needs help;
- implementation of regular attendance reviews with employees;
- reinforcement of good attendance with employees with exemplary attendance and encouragement for attendance improvement with employees who have poorer attendance records;
- investigation of barriers to regular work attendance;
- provision of a safe and healthy workplace;
- adherence to the set procedures for managing excessive employee absenteeism; and
- data management for reporting purposes.

REPORTING AN ABSENCE

The employee is to contact the department, or his or her direct supervisor, as soon as possible either via a designated contact person or through the use of a voice recorded message. The employee should provide his or her name, reason for the absence, the anticipated return-to-work date and what provisions, if any, have been made to cover his or her duties.

A medical certificate is usually not required for an absence of three days or less. However, the absence is recorded on a monthly basis and submitted to the human resources payroll system.

For an absence between three and ten days in length, the process is the same as above. However, the employee may be required to produce a medical certificate (Chapter 10, "Disability Management Practice Standards", Appendix 3, Forms 2a and 2b).

For absences longer than ten days, the process is the same; however, the employee remits a medical certificate to the Disability Management Program for processing.

Reports and Monitoring Absenteeism

REPORTS

As already mentioned, various attendance reports are needed to assist employees, supervisors and human resources in the administration of the Attendance Support & Assistance Program. These reports should be prepared weekly/monthly for the department so that timely action can be taken by the supervisor. An annual report that reports attendance performance to the company along with any related recommendations is critical. It allows the organization the opportunity to assess employee attendance and the related costs.

MONITORING

Annual interviews regarding attendance are to be conducted by the supervisor with each and every employee. This is one way to reinforce good attendance and to address attendance concerns.

Employees with "**excessive absenteeism**"[25] are to be identified by the supervisors. It is the supervisors' responsibility to initiate the Attendance Support & Assistance Action Steps.

Attendance Support and Assistance Plan Action Steps: Preparation

When an employee's work attendance begins to cause concern, a supervisor must be prepared to discuss the matter with the person. During these discussions, the goal is for the supervisor to encourage and support the employee to achieve an acceptable level of work attendance.

Before entering into an employee interview, the supervisor should take the time to do the following:

1. Review the employee's attendance record. Have both the specific information about the employee's work absence and a summary of the past absences available. Identify any patterns of absences, such as Friday and Monday absences, extended vacation or holiday periods or seasonal absences. Consider any available information on the causes of the employee's absence and fitness to work.
2. Consider the employee's performance. Is it declining due, in part, to poor attendance? Are there other factors at play?
3. Determine if it is necessary or appropriate to meet privately with the employee. For example, if an employee with a good attendance record suffers a heart attack and is absent for a lengthy recovery period, a private discussion about absenteeism is inappropriate. However, if the employee

---

[25] **Excessive absenteeism** is defined as absenteeism that exceeds either the corporate average for employee absence, or the Canadian national average of ten days (2007).

has been inexplicably absent from work on many occasions and his or her work performance has deteriorated, meeting in private with the employee is appropriate.

4. Inform the employee when the discussion will be held and the reason for the discussion, preferably giving one to two days' notice. The discussion should not be disciplinary in nature; rather it is an exploration of how the supervisor/company can assist the employee in regaining an acceptable level of work attendance.

When interviewing the employee, it is advisable to meet in a comfortable, private environment. Privacy is strongly recommended as the employee may choose to reveal information about him- or herself, the workplace or other work relationships that should be kept confidential between the employee and supervisor.

Always remember that the purpose of the meeting is to avoid intimidating the employee.

Attendance Support and Assistance Plan Action Steps: Implementation

STEP 1

An employee is absent for three days or less, but does not exceed the company's absenteeism standard:

*   The supervisor briefly meets with the employee to acknowledge the absence.
*   If the employee is off for more than four days, the supervisor contacts the employee to inquire as to his or her return-to-work status.

STEP 2

The absence exceeds the company's standard and is unrelated to a documented medical condition:

*   The supervisor arranges for an interview with the employee on the day of his or her return to work, or as soon as possible thereafter.
*   The supervisor advises the employee as to the reason for the interview.
*   The supervisor and employee set realistic objectives for improvement in attendance, taking individual circumstances into account.
*   The supervisor asks the employee if any assistance is required in order to meet the expected attendance standard. This will include a discussion as to the services available, which include the occupational health services or corporate programs such as the Employee Assistance Program.
*   The supervisor reinforces the impact of absenteeism on the department, students and co-workers.

- The supervisor completes an Attendance Support & Assistance Program Action/Status Initial Concern Letter (Appendix 1), and provides the employee with a copy. This letter forms part of the employee's personnel record.
- If required, a process of workplace accommodation may be initiated and supported by proper medical documentation.
- A follow-up meeting with the employee is arranged. The meeting is held three to six months after the Step 2 interview, depending on the situation. The supervisor continues to monitor the employee's attendance during this period. If required, the follow-up interview may be held earlier based on individual circumstances, or if the objectives are exceeded.

STEP 3

At the follow-up meeting with the supervisor, one of the following conditions will exist:

CASE A. THE EMPLOYEE'S ATTENDANCE IMPROVES

- The supervisor gives a Letter of Congratulations (Appendix 2) to the employee with a copy sent to the human resources department. The letter forms part of the employee's personnel record.
- Attendance continues to be monitored by the supervisor.

CASE B. THE EMPLOYEE'S ATTENDANCE MEETS THE OBJECTIVE BUT IS STILL ABOVE THE COMPANY'S ABSENTEEISM STANDARD

- The supervisor gives a Letter of Recognition of Attendance Improvement (Appendix 3) to the employee.
- The supervisor clearly indicates that continued improvement is expected and new attendance objectives are set.
- The supervisor and employee agree to a follow-up meeting and repeat Step 3 (please note that some employees may be at Step 3 for several months as they continue to show improvement).

CASE C. THE EMPLOYEE'S ATTENDANCE SHOWS NO IMPROVEMENT

- The supervisor holds a meeting with the employee (and a union representative if requested by the employee).
- The supervisor reviews the employee's attendance statistics.
- The supervisor asks the employee if any assistance is required in order to meet the attendance expectations. This includes a discussion as to services available, including referral to the occupational health services or to corporate programs such as the Employee Assistance Program.
- The supervisor establishes short-term objectives. While efforts are made to help the employee achieve the attendance expectations, attendance continues to be monitored.

- Employees are to be reminded that regular attendance is a condition of employment.
- The company may require additional information through medical documentation that may be utilized if workplace accommodation is required. Appendix 4 illustrates two sample letters that can be used to request medical documentation — one designed for the unionized workplace and one for the non-unionized environment.
- The supervisor completes the Attendance Support & Assistance Program: Action/Status Advanced Concern Letter (Appendix 5), and provides the employee with a copy. This letter will form part of the employee's personnel record.
- A follow-up meeting occurs within three months of the Step 3 interview.
- If required, the process of accommodation may be initiated and supported by proper documentation.

STEP 4

At the follow-up meeting to Step 3, one of the following conditions will exist:

CASE A. THE EMPLOYEE'S ATTENDANCE IMPROVES

- The supervisor gives a Letter of Congratulations to the employee with a copy to the human resources department. The letter forms part of the employee's personnel record.
- Attendance continues to be monitored by the supervisor.

CASE B. THE EMPLOYEE'S ATTENDANCE MEETS THE OBJECTIVE BUT IS STILL ABOVE COMPANY'S STANDARD

- The supervisor gives a Letter of Recognition of Attendance Improvement (Appendix 3) to employee.
- The supervisor clearly indicates that continued improvement is expected and new attendance objectives are set.
- The supervisor arranges a follow-up meeting and repeats Step 3 (please note that some employees may be at Step 3 for several months as they continue to show improvement).

CASE C. THE EMPLOYEE'S ATTENDANCE SHOWS NO IMPROVEMENT

- The Director of Human Resources and the supervisor meet with the employee. In a unionized workplace, the employee may have union representation if requested.
- The Director of Human Resources reviews the attendance statistics and asks the employee if he or she requires any assistance to achieve the expected level of attendance.
- The Director of Human Resources sets short-term targets and a follow-up meeting is held within three months.

- The Director of Human Resources may require the employee to bring in a medical certificate to substantiate every absence, and may use other mechanisms deemed appropriate to guide the employee towards achieving the expected standard of attendance.
- Employees should be alerted to the fact that regular attendance is a condition of employment.
- The process of accommodation may be initiated if required and supported by proper documentation.
- A follow-up meeting is set for three months.

STEP 5

- The Director of Human Resources continues to follow up with the employee until he or she is satisfied that there is sustainable improvement. If the employee does not achieve the objectives within the allotted time period, and every effort has been made to assist the employee including accommodation (if necessary), the need to terminate the employment may arise. The Director of Human Resources and the supervisor should be very clear as to the expectations and objectives that are to be met in the given time period.

Figure 9.3 is a graphic depiction of how an Attendance Support & Assistance Program could function. As well, Appendices 1 to 5 contain sample letters that could be used at various stages of the Attendance Support & Assistance Program Action Steps.

SUMMARY

Assisting employees in attending work on a regular basis is critical to the success of any Disability Management Program. The process begins by clearly setting corporate expectations, and continues through an established action plan to address excessive employee absenteeism. Having a functional process in place allows for a supportive but fair manner in which to deal with absenteeism. As well, it promotes early assistance for "troubled" employees. In essence, it is part of the preventative aspects of disability management.

Employee attendance is crucial to the effective functioning of a company. Employee absenteeism is costly. By being proactive and addressing employee attendance in a supportive manner, employees are shown that the company cares about them. However, the corollary is also true:

> If people perceive that attendance is of no concern to a company, that it doesn't matter if they are at work or not, cultural absenteeism will prevail.[26]

---

[26] CCH Inc., "The 7th Annual CCH Unscheduled Absences Survey" (1997) 412 Human Resources Management: Ideas and Trends 121.

Figure 9.3: Company XYZ: Attendance Support & Assistance Program (ASAP)

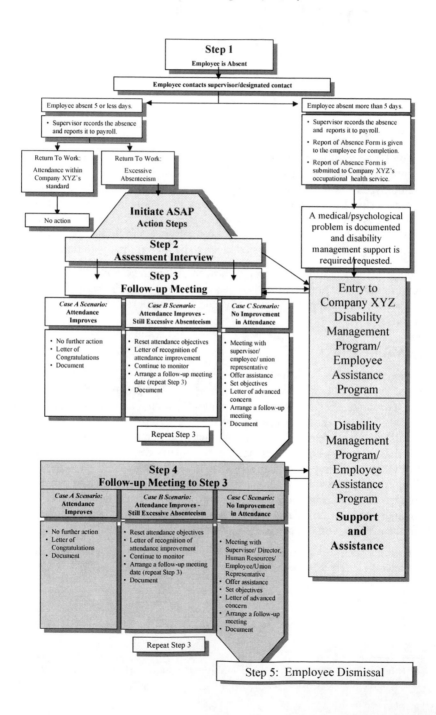

Appendix 1

Sample — ASAP Action/Status Initial Concern Letter

Date: _____   _____

To: [EMPLOYEE] _____   _____

From: Manager/Supervisor

Dear [EMPLOYEE]:

The purpose of this letter is to confirm our discussion of [DATE] regarding your attendance at work.

At that time, it was brought to your attention that the number of your absent days has reached a level of concern to the [DEPARTMENT].

The expectations of Company XYZ with respect to attendance were reviewed as well as the problems caused by your absenteeism.

The Company is willing to provide you with whatever assistance it is able to maintain your attendance at an acceptable level. It was noted that, should your absenteeism increase further, the Company will have to take further action.

Please note that neither our meeting nor this letter of communication is disciplinary.

Sincerely,

_____

Manager/Supervisor

cc: Union Representative (if applicable)
     Employee File

Appendix 2

Sample — Letter of Congratulations

Date: _____

To: [EMPLOYEE] _____

From: Manager/Supervisor

Dear [EMPLOYEE]:

Congratulations! You have made a significant improvement on your attendance record over the past [NUMBER] months.

As work absences cost us all in the long run, I thank you for your cooperation in this matter.

Please accept my best wishes for your good health as you strive for good work attendance.

Sincerely,

_____
Manager/Supervisor

cc: (Human Resources)
     Union Representative (if applicable)
     Employee File

Appendix 3

Sample — Letter of Recognition of Attendance Improvement

Date: _____

To: [EMPLOYEE] _____

From: Manager/Supervisor

Dear [EMPLOYEE]:

Congratulations! You have made improvements on your work attendance over the past [NUMBER] months.

Your goal is to increase your attendance target of [NUMBER] days this year. Company XYZ and I are willing to provide you with support and assistance in your endeavour. Our plan is to continue to monitor your work attendance and to review your progress in [NUMBER] months.

As absences cost us all in the long run, I thank you for your cooperation in this matter. Please accept my best wishes for your good health as you strive for good work attendance.

Sincerely,

_____
Manager/Supervisor

cc: (Human Resources)
     Union Representative (if applicable)
     Employee File

Appendix 4

Sample — Letter Requesting Medical Documentation

TWO EXAMPLES OF A LETTER REQUESTING REQUIRED MEDICAL DOCUMENTATION

Option 1 — For Unionized Employees

To: Dr. _____

Re: [EMPLOYEE]

The above named person is an employee of Company XYZ employed as a _____ in the _____ [DEPARTMENT].

It is our primary objective that [EMPLOYEE NAME] is healthy and able to attend work regularly. However, our concern is that the employee's absences over the past year have been significantly higher than the Company XYZ average for worker absenteeism.

During the past 12 months, [EMPLOYEE NAME] has been absent from work, for reasons of illness or injury, on _____ occasions for a total of _____ days.

The Collective Agreement between Company XYZ and the Union states that:

Before payment is made under the foregoing provisions, the Employee may be required to provide:

for illness of three (3) consecutive days or less, statement in a form provided by the Employer, signed by the Employee substantiating the illness;

for illness of more than three (3) consecutive days, a medical certificate in a form approved by the Employer, from a qualified medical or dental practitioner.

[Editorial Note: This will differ with each Collective Agreement.]

[EMPLOYEE NAME] has requested that you conduct this examination and release your findings to us. We are requesting that your examination and report address the following issues:

1. The nature of the employee's illnesses or injuries and whether or not these are likely to continue to affect his or her ability to work now and in the future. This may require that you consult with other physicians who have treated [EMPLOYEE NAME].

2. Your assessment of the employee's present abilities to perform the full duties of a [JOB TITLE].

In order to assist you, the following is a list of duties that [EMPLOYEE NAME] may be asked to perform.

[LIST DUTIES]

Company XYZ agrees to pay a maximum of $50 in medical fees for this examination. Please submit your report and invoice to the Company, Occupational Health Nurse, Company XYZ Occupational Health Centre.

Should you wish to discuss these duties more fully, please contact me at your convenience. If a visit to the workplace would aid you in reaching your prognosis or completing your report, I will arrange that at your convenience.

Sincerely,

_____

Manager/Supervisor

cc: Human Resources
     Union Representative
     Occupational Health Nurse
     Employee File

Option 2 — For Non-Unionized Employees

To: Dr. _____

Re: [EMPLOYEE]

The above named person is an employee of Company XYZ employed as a _____ in the [DEPARTMENT].

It is our primary objective that [EMPLOYEE NAME] be healthy and able to attend work regularly. However, our concern is that the employee's absences over the past year have been significantly higher than Company XYZ average for worker absenteeism.

During the past 12 months, [EMPLOYEE NAME] has been absent from work, for reasons of illness or injury, on _____ occasions for a total of _____ days.

Company XYZ has an Attendance Support & Assistance Policy which states that for an absence greater than five (5) consecutive workdays in duration, the employee will be required to produce a medical certificate and to submit it to the Occupational Health Service. It also states that, in a case of excessive absenteeism, a medical certificate may be requested for absences of five (5) days or less.

[EMPLOYEE NAME] has requested that you conduct this examination and release your findings to us. We are requesting that your examination and report address the following issues:

The nature of the employee's illnesses or injuries and whether or not these are likely to continue to affect his or her ability to work now and in the future. This may require that you consult with other physicians who have treated [EMPLOYEE NAME].

Your assessment of the employee's present abilities to perform the full duties of a [JOB TITLE].

In order to assist you, the following is a list of duties that [EMPLOYEE NAME] may be asked to perform.

[LIST DUTIES]

Company XYZ agrees to pay a maximum of $50 in medical fees for this examination. Please submit your report and invoice to the Company, Occupational Health Nurse, Company XYZ Occupational Health Centre.

Should you wish to discuss these duties more fully, please contact me at your convenience. If a visit to the workplace would aid you in reaching your prognosis or completing your report, I will arrange that at your convenience.

Yours sincerely,

_____

Manager/Supervisor

cc: Human Resources
     Occupational Health Nurse
     Employee File

Appendix 5

Sample — Attendance Support & Assistance Program: Action/ Status Advanced Concern Letter

Date: _____

To: [EMPLOYEE] _____

From: Manager/Supervisor

Dear [EMPLOYEE]:

The purpose of this letter is to confirm our discussion of [DATE] regarding your attendance at work.

At that time, I referred to our earlier meeting of [DATE], at which time you were alerted to our concern with the number of your work absence days at that point.

You were notified that, since that discussion, the number of absent days has increased to the point where further action is now necessary and you are requested to attend a meeting with the Company, Occupational Health Advisor, on [DATE and TIME] for the purpose of discussing, in confidence, detailed reasons for your absenteeism and determining what you and Company XYZ can do to improve this situation.

You were reminded that should your absence record not improve, Company XYZ will have to take further action.

As well, please note that neither our discussion nor this letter of communication is disciplinary.

Sincerely,

_____
Manager/Supervisor

cc: Human Resources
     Union Representative (if applicable)
     Employee File

CHAPTER REFERENCES

S. Aldana, *Top Five Strategies to Enhance the ROI of Worksite Wellness Programs*, Wellness Council of America (January 2009), available online at: <http://www.welcoa.org/freeresources/pdf/top_5_strategies.pdf>.

Aon Consulting, "The Case for Absence Management" (2005), *Aon Workforce Strategies*, available online at: <www.aon.com/default.jsp>.

E. Akyeampong, *Work Absence Rates, 1987 to 1998*, Cat. No. 71-535-MPB, No. 10 (Ottawa: Statistics Canada, 1999).

CCH Inc., "The 7th Annual CCH Unscheduled Absences Survey" (1997) 412 Human Resources Management: Ideas and Trends 121.

CCH Inc., News Release, "2004 CCH Unscheduled Absence Survey: Unscheduled Employee Absenteeism Rises to Five-Year High" (October 7, 2004), available online at: <http://www.cch.com/Press/News/2004/20041007h.asp>.

CCH Inc., *2005 Unscheduled Absence Survey* (CCH 2005).

CCH Inc., *2006 CCH Unscheduled Absence Survey* (Riverwoods, IL: CCH 2006).

CCH Inc., *CCH 2007 Unscheduled Absence Survey* (Riverwoods, IL: CCH 2007).

Hewitt Associates, *Disability Absence Index Survey 2007* (2007) at 5, available online at: <http://www.hewittassociates.com/Intl/NA/en-CA/KnowledgeCenter/ArticlesReports/DAIS_highlights.aspx>.

L. Kelly, *Absenteeism: Manual* (Kingston: International Research, 1991).

J. Kranc, "Fact Check", *Benefits Canada* (March 2004) at 70, 86

Mercer Inc., "The Total Financial Impact of Employee Absences — Survey Highlights" (2008) at 4, available online at: <http://www.kronos.com/absenceanonymous/media/Mercer-Survey-Highlights.pdf>.

Peat, Marwick & Kellogg, *Data Produced on 1991 Employee Benefit Costs in Canada* (1993) [unpublished].

L. Rosen, CCH Inc., News Release, "2004 CCH Unscheduled Absence Survey: Unscheduled Employee Absenteeism Rises to Five-Year High" (October 7, 2004), available online at: <http://www.cch.com/Press/News/2004/20041007h.asp>.

Statistics Canada, *Work Absence Rates, 2007*, Cat. No. 71-211-XWE (Ottawa: Statistics Canada, May 2008).

Statistics Canada, *Average Hourly Wages of Employees by Selected Characteristics and Profession*, available online at: <http://www40.statcan.ca/l01/cst01/labr69a.htm>.

D. Thompson, "The Dollars and Sense of Managing Absenteeism" (1993) 3:8 Group Healthcare Management 17.

Watson Wyatt Worldwide, *Staying@Work: Effective Presence at Work* (2007), available online at: <https://www.watsonwyatt.com>.

P. Wolf, "CCH Survey Finds Most Employees Call in 'Sick' for Reasons Other Than Illness", CCH Inc., *CCH 2007 Unscheduled Absence Survey* (Riverwoods, IL: CCH Inc., 2007), available online at: <http://www.cch.com/press/news/2007/20071010h.asp>.

Chapter 10

Disability Management Practice Standards

INTRODUCTION

To assist Disability Case Managers, many organizations and insurers have developed practice standards, or codes of practice, for disability management. Unlike disability guidelines, which advise on expected length of absences for various illnesses or injuries, these standards or practice codes outline the best practice rehabilitation strategies and steps the organization expects health professionals to follow.

Practice standards are stated approaches to care and practice based on recognized and accepted principles of clinical practice for planned processes, such as disability management. They form the guidelines and rules for the practice, provide the boundaries for the practice activity, clarify stakeholder roles and responsibilities, and can act as a benchmark.

Practice standards can be beneficial because they:

* promote a consistent approach to case management;
* provide meaningful direction to the practice in question; and
* promote effectiveness and efficiency of practice through a reduction of errors, complications, and costs.

To remain current and credible, practice standards must be regularly reviewed and updated.

RECOMMENDED DISABILITY MANAGEMENT PRACTICE STANDARDS

The key practice standards required for a Disability Management Program address issues such as claim management, case management, confidentiality, and documentation. The following sections describe in detail each of these practice standards.

Some of the materials contained in these practice standard examples have been covered elsewhere in this book. However, the intent is to present each of the relevant Disability Management Practice Standards in a format that can be adapted for the reader's use.

DISABILITY CLAIM MANAGEMENT STANDARD OF PRACTICE

Introduction

Disability Claim Management is the service provided in administering income loss claims through employee benefit plans such as short-term disability, Workers' Compensation, or long-term disability. This activity includes the determination of eligibility contained in the plan contract, collective agreement or contract of insurance; the facilitation of income loss replacement; and the processing of the claim towards a resolution or termination.

Disability Claim Management Steps

DETERMINING ELIGIBILITY FOR INCOME REPLACEMENT BENEFITS

WORKERS COMPENSATION BENEFITS (OCCUPATIONAL)

The Workers' Compensation system is designed to compensate ill or injured workers for work-related diseases and injuries. It is a no-fault insurance system funded entirely by the employers. The provincial Workers' Compensation Acts govern the functioning of the Workers' Compensation Board. It is important to remember that Workers' Compensation benefits are a worker's statutory right. An effective claim management system never attempts to prevent workers from receiving benefits to which they are legitimately entitled.

Workers

Workers employed in industries to which provincial Workers' Compensation Acts apply are protected from loss of earnings due to a work-related injury or disease. The provincial Workers' Compensation Acts generally define "worker" as a person who enters into, or works under, a contract of service or apprenticeship.[1] This contract can be written or verbal, express or implied, for manual labour or otherwise. This includes trainees, apprentices, clerks, sales staff, office staff, and supervisors. It includes individuals employed on a part-time, full-time, casual or commission basis. It also includes any other individuals the Workers' Compensation Board deems to be a worker.

---

[1]   Alberta: *Workers' Compensation Act*, R.S.A. 2000, c. W-15, s. 1(1)(z); British Columbia: *Workers' Compensation Act*, R.S.B.C. 1996, c. 492, s. 1; Ontario: *Workplace Safety and Insurance Act, 1997*, S.O. 1997, c. 16, Sch. A, s. 2(1).

Contractors and Subcontractors

Individuals hired on a contract or subcontract basis are workers of the principal,[2] unless these individuals have a Workers' Compensation Board account or are incorporated as a limited company. The Workers' Compensation Board will determine if an individual is considered a worker of the principal, or required to establish his or her own account with the Workers' Compensation Board.

A contractor or subcontractor is not considered a worker when performing the work as:

- an employer;
- a worker of another employer;
- a director of a corporation;
- a proprietor with personal coverage; or
- a partner in a partnership with personal coverage.

The Workers' Compensation Board may, at its discretion, deem any or all persons (or classes of persons) performing work for the principal to be the principal's workers.

Before engaging a contractor, a company should check with the applicable provincial Workers' Compensation Board to determine if the contractor has an account in good standing.

Other Groups Considered by the Workers' Compensation Board to be Workers

Some other individuals or groups may be covered under provincial Workers' Compensation Acts, such as:

- proprietors;
- partners;
- individuals sharing labour;
- students on a work experience; and
- workers engaged in volunteer activities.

As provincial Workers' Compensation Acts vary, care must be taken to determine the applicable conditions for the organization.

COMPENSABLE ILLNESS OR INJURY

If an illness or injury occurs in the course of employment, the illness or injury is compensable unless there is evidence that the illness or injury was caused by factors extrinsic to employment.

---

[2] "Principal" refers to a contractor or subcontractor hired to perform work or services by a person or entity.

A worker may be compensated when an illness or injury is progressive and occurs over a period of time rather than resulting from a specific incident. However, for an illness or injury to be compensable there must be evidence that the employment was a significant factor in producing the injury or illness. Speculation is insufficient to prove that the illness or injury is compensable.

Pre-existing Conditions

There are instances where a medical condition has reached a critical point, and that some immediate workplace activity triggers an injury. If it were not for a specific work-related activity or accident, a worker may not have experienced an injury. The Workers' Compensation Board may accept the initial acute stage of the disability, but may not accept the ongoing disability as it relates to the underlying, pre-existing condition. Claims of this type should be followed closely for cost-relief purposes.[3]

SICK LEAVE BENEFITS (NON-OCCUPATIONAL)

There are a number of short-term, non-occupational disability benefits in existence that tend to be uniquely defined by organizations in which they operate. Some typical plans are:

- *Casual Sick Leave* — coverage for a non-occupational absence that extends for less than five consecutive workdays.
- *Sick Leave/Short-term Disability* — income replacement for the employee while recuperating from a non-occupational illness or injury.
- *Long-term Disability* — an insurance program through which eligible employees may derive income replacement for long-term illness or injury.

INFORMATION REQUIRED TO SUPPORT A CLAIM FOR INCOME REPLACEMENT

The type of information required to support the employee's claim for income replacement varies with the benefit desired. The following are some common examples of required information:

WORKERS' COMPENSATION BENEFITS

- An employee is legally bound to report a work-related injury to the employer as soon as it is practical, and to submit a Worker's Report of Injury to the provincial Workers' Compensation Board. In most provinces, a copy of the Worker's Report of Injury form should then accompany the

---

[3]   Alberta: *Workers' Compensation Act*, R.S.A. 2000, c. W-15, s. 65; British Columbia: *Workers' Compensation Act*, R.S.B.C. 1996, c. 492, s. 39(1)(e); Ontario: *Workplace Safety and Insurance Act, 1997*, S.O. 1997, c. 16, Sch. A, s. 21(3).

Employer's Report of Injury to the WCB. Refusal by the worker to complete the form can result in denial of the WCB claim.

- The employer is obliged to submit an Employer's Report of Injury to the provincial Workers' Compensation Board within a set time frame of becoming aware of the accident.
- The employee must consult his or her physician regarding the illness or injury. The physician is legally required to submit a medical report to the Workers' Compensation Board. Subsequent physician's progress reports are also sent to the Workers' Compensation Board as a means of monitoring the ill or injured employee's recovery.

SICK LEAVE BENEFITS

- The employee is to contact his or her direct supervisor as soon as possible, either via a designated contact person or through the use of a voice recorded message. The information provided should cover his or her name, reason for the absence, the anticipated return-to-work date and what provisions, if applicable, have been made to cover his or her duties.
- The supervisor should notify the appropriate department, either by a time-recording system or telephone call, once the employee returns to work.

SHORT-TERM DISABILITY

- For an absence of greater than five consecutive workdays in duration, the employee is required to produce a medical certificate and to submit it directly to occupational health services (if available), or human resources.
- The Report of Absence Form (Appendix 3: Form 2a and 2b) is to be completed by the attending physician and signed and dated by the employee. Additional information may be required by occupational health services.

LONG-TERM DISABILITY

- Typically, the long-term disability claim application must be initiated once the employee has been on short-term disability for half of the short-term elimination period,[4] or earlier if it is apparent that a long-term disability claim is inevitable.
- The insurance company's long-term disability claim forms should be completed as indicated.
- The insurance company's application for waiver of premium under life insurance should also be initiated.

---

[4] The **short-term elimination period** is the time of illness/injury prior to applying for long-term disability benefits. This period of time varies in length depending on the long-term disability plan design. It may be 17 weeks, six months, 12 months, or 24 months.

- Additional information for the insurer may be requested from the employee or employer as required.

PROCESSING CLAIM FORMS

As with the type of information collected to support a claim, claim processing also varies. The following are the usual steps required for processing a claim for each type of disability benefit plan:

WORKERS' COMPENSATION BENEFITS

Submit the Employer's Report of Injury and the Worker's Report of Injury on the required provincial Workers' Compensation Board forms to ensure that the Worker's Compensation Board Claim Adjudicator has the necessary information to appropriately adjudicate the claim.

An injury report must be sent to the Workers' Compensation Board if the injury results in medical treatment and/or subsequent time loss. Generally, if there is no time loss, there is no need to submit a report of accident to the Workers' Compensation Board. However, there are exceptions that do require reporting. These might include injuries requiring the modification of work duties beyond the day of accident, the need to purchase drugs and dressings, eyeglasses replacement, dental damage, chiropractic treatment and physiotherapy and motor vehicle accidents. If uncertain about whether or not to file a claim, the employer is advised to err on the side of caution and send one. There are provisions in the provincial Workers' Compensation Acts for a penalty assessment for late injury reporting.[5]

SICK LEAVE BENEFITS

- The employee phones his or her supervisor on the first day of absence.
- The absence is documented on the company payroll time accounting system.

SHORT-TERM DISABILITY

- The Report of Absence Form is generated by the employee and attending physician.
- The Report of Absence Form is reviewed by the occupational health nurse.
- The occupational health nurse then advises the company Claim Administrator regarding the employee's fitness to work.
- If unfit for work, then the employee is eligible for short-term disability in accordance with the employee's earned sick leave.

---

[5]   **Cost Relief** is defined as a reduction in a company's Workers' Compensation (WCB) claims costs as the result of a reassignment of those costs to the other industry members. This is done to spread out the costs so that an individual company is not overburdened by its WCB claims costs.

- If the employee is fit to work modified duties, the occupational health nurse advises the Claim Administrator of the employee's work capabilities.
- If the employee is fit to work, the occupational health nurse advises the Claim Administrator and short-term disability is denied.

LONG-TERM DISABILITY

- The company Claim Administrator initiates the long-term disability claim by contacting the long-term carrier.
- Complete the required insurance carrier's claim forms. These usually include:
  - an employee form;
  - a physician form; and
  - an employer form.

Claim Adjudication

Claim adjudication is the process of determining whether a claim is eligible under the terms of the benefit contract or plan for benefit coverage.

Claim Adjudication Steps

The claim adjudication process includes:

- Receipt and review of the claim.
- Establishment of the claimant's status and eligibility for benefit coverage. Is this a work-related claim? Is the employee applying for the proper coverage given the nature of the situation?
- Review of the eligibility requirements according to the contract/plan, and/or the collective agreement.
- Consideration of the issue of any limitations or exclusions. Limitations occur when the employee is eligible for benefits, but cannot receive payments for a specific cause. Exclusions occur when the employee cannot receive payment because the illness or injury resulted from a situation not covered by the plan. For example, for short-term disability coverage, exclusions would be appropriate for injury due to work-related accident, riot, war, *etc.*
- Consideration of pre-existing conditions. Pre-existing conditions are typically defined in the contract or plan as conditions of illness or injury that occurred prior to the employee being covered by the plan. Coverage for subsequent illness or injury, or a recurrence within a specific time frame, is not allowed.
- Consideration of the existence of specialized clauses that would preclude the claimant from benefit coverage. Policyholders can place additional exclusions in benefit plans or contracts, such as participation in risky events or sports.

- Determination for eligibility.
- Acceptance or rejection of the claim.

Figure 10.1 is a checklist which the claim adjudicator can use to assist with this process. This is not meant to be all-inclusive, rather a quick reference guide.

Figure 10.1: Checklist for Claim Adjudication

- Appropriate physician completes the form/letter, *i.e.*, information is sent to the appropriate source.
- Work-related issues have been addressed. (This is not a Workers' Compensation Claim.)
- The evidence is objective.
- The employee is under treatment.
- Rehabilitation/resource initiatives have been implemented.
- File documentation supports a well-managed case, based on a well-thought-out process approach, *i.e.*, the problems are identified, actions implemented, results evaluated, costs and consequences considered.
- This is a work-related illness or injury.
- If information is insufficient to support disability, suspension or termination of benefits has been considered.
- If long-term disability is pending, medical information has been requested to support the long-term disability claim.

The Role of the Physician in Determining Disability

In determining an employee's eligibility to receive income replacement benefits, physicians are frequently put in the position of verifying a disability. The Canadian Medical Association and many provincial medical associations have produced position statements clarifying that the role of the physician is "to diagnose and treat the illness or injury, to advise and support the patient, to provide and communicate appropriate information to the patient and the employer, and to work closely with other involved health care professionals to facilitate the patient's safe and timely return to [work]".[6] They support the shift towards using a variety of means to determine if an employee is fit to work or not. Ultimately, it is the employer who determines the type of work available and whether or not the physician's recommendations can be accommodated.

The following position papers regarding the role of the physician in determining disability have been released:

---

[6]   Canadian Medical Association, *The Physician's Role in Helping Patients Return to Work After an Illness or Injury* (update 2000) at 1, available online at: <http://policybase.cma.ca/dbtw-wpd/POLICYPDF/PD01-09.pdf>

- Ontario Medical Association — Ontario Medical Association (OMA), *Position Paper: OMA Position in Support of Timely Return to Work Programs and the Role of the Primary Care Physician* (Toronto: OMA, 1994).[7]
- Alberta Medical Association — Alberta Medical Association (AMA), *An Information Sheet for Patients: Early Return to Work After Illness or Injury* (Edmonton: AMA, February 1994) still current, this information is available online.[8]
- Canadian Medical Association — Canadian Medical Association (CMA), *The Physician's Role in Helping Patients Return to Work After an Illness or Injury* (update 2000). This position was reviewed by the CMA in February 2005 and found to still be relevant.[9]

These position papers imply that physicians can determine employee eligibility for benefits or level of work accommodation. Eligibility for a disability benefit (including short-term disability, long-term disability, and Workers' Compensation Board) is a contractual decision determined by comparing the job requirements with the contract provisions and the impairment of the employee. It is the Claim Administrator who must determine whether the definition of disability is met.

Claim Referral Triggers

As a claim is processed, certain triggers for referral may occur. These are listed as:

- the short-term disability or Workers' Compensation Board claim is beyond the duration of disability suggested in medical guidelines;
- the nature of injury is severe enough to warrant referral (*i.e.*, prognosis for return to work greater than six weeks);
- a history of frequent absences from work, multiple previous sick leaves or Workers' Compensation Board claims;
- no contact from employee for past three weeks;
- a claim goes beyond six weeks in length;
- a claimant is referred to a Workers' Compensation Board Vocational Rehabilitation Caseworker;
- notification that treatment does not appear to be appropriate;
- notification of non-compliance with treatment;

---

[7]   Ontario Medical Association, *Position Paper: OMA Position in Support of Timely Return to Work Programs and the Role of the Primary Care Physician* (1994), available online at: <http://www.oma.org/phealth/position.htm>.

[8]   Alberta Medical Association (AMA, 1994), *An Information Sheet for Patients: Early Return to Work After Illness or Injury* (Edmonton: AMA, 1994) in the "Advocacy and Positions" section of the AMA's website, available online at: <http://www.albertadoctors.org/bcm/ama/ama-website.nsf/frmHome?OpenForm>.

[9]   Canadian Medical Association, *The Physician's Role in Helping Patients Return to Work After an Illness or Injury* (Update 2000), available online at: <http://policybase.cma.ca/dbtw-wpd/POLICYPDF/PD01-09.pdf>.

- notification of no known diagnosis;
- notification of a vague diagnosis; and/or
- notification that case is failing to progress.

Development of Claim Management Action Plans

Claim Management plans are tools designed to facilitate the disability management claim process by helping key players to focus their actions towards a claim resolution.

IDENTIFYING HIGH-RISK CLAIMS

Some claims are of a more lengthy duration than others are and hence, are termed "high-risk claims". The characteristics associated with lengthy disability claims are:

- an expected duration of disability exceeding one month;
- hospitalization greater than one week;
- a Workers' Compensation claim that lasts longer than one week;
- an employee, aged 50 years or older;
- "stress" as the medical diagnosis;
- diagnoses of cardiovascular, cancer, digestive, skeletal (repetitive strain injury), neurological, or psychological conditions;
- multiple diagnoses;
- cases which fail just before the expected return-to-work date;
- frequent changes in health caregivers;
- employees with limited social acceptance and support;
- job dissatisfaction;
- presence of labour relations problems;
- presence of performance problems;
- presence of pending litigation associated with the illness or injury;
- an injured or ill employee with a high rate of absenteeism; and
- any multiple of the above.

These claims should be referred to the Occupational Health Nurse or Disability Case Manager for case management and warrant careful claim management.

IDENTIFYING WORK LIMITATIONS

FITNESS-TO-WORK

To determine employee fitness-to-work, two pieces of information are required:

- the physical and psychological job demands for the position; and
- the employee's work capabilities and limitations.

These two pieces of information are then compared to determine the gap between the employee's current level of functioning and the level of functioning required to safely and effectively do the job.

HOW IS THIS INFORMATION OBTAINED?

The best way to gather information about an employee's work restrictions and abilities is to provide the attending practitioner (whether that is the physician, physiotherapist, or chiropractor) with a job demands analysis that outlines the demands of the employee's job. If that is not available, ask the employer if a checklist outlining the job requirements could be completed by an occupational health professional, the health and safety representative, or the supervisor. More detailed information can be obtained by referring the employee for a functional capacity evaluation.

While disability benefits are approved based on an employee's restrictions, the employee and employer should be focusing on work abilities. Gathering information about the employee's work abilities by interviewing the employee, and confirming that information with the practitioner, can be invaluable in paving the way for a modified return-to-work opportunity.

PHYSICAL JOB REQUIREMENTS

Physical job demands are the physical activities that the employee is required to do in the course of doing his or her job. These may include the ability to:

- sit, stand, walk, bend, squat, climb;
- drive;
- lift, push, pull, twist, reach, crawl;
- write, handle small objects, pinch;
- see, hear, taste, smell;
- read;
- speak;
- travel;
- tolerate heat, cold, altitude; and/or
- other specific work-related physical activities or conditions.

PSYCHOLOGICAL JOB REQUIREMENTS

The psychological job requirements are the cognitive and emotional demands of the job. They may include the ability to:

- comprehend and follow instructions;
- perform simple and repetitive tasks;
- maintain a work pace appropriate to a given workload;
- perform complex or varied tasks;
- relate to other people beyond giving and receiving instructions;
- influence people;

- make generalizations, evaluations and decisions without immediate supervision;
- accept and carry out responsibility for direction, control and planning of work; and/or
- deal with multiple tasks or activities.

USING DISABILITY GUIDELINES

Comprehensive disability guidelines incorporate the background information about the medical condition, treatment regimes, and the estimated duration of the condition with established timelines for a return to work. Some sources of information for disability guidelines include:

- the ICD-9 or 10 Codes - the World Health Organization (WHO) developed an international system for the classification of diseases and signs, symptoms, abnormal findings, complaints, social circumstances and external causes of injury or diseases. The International Statistical Classification of Diseases and Related Health Problems 10th Revision (ICD-10) allows more than 155,000 different codes and permits tracking of many new diagnoses and procedures, a significant expansion on the 17,000 codes available in ICD-9. A complete listing of the ICD-10 Codes is available online at <http://www.who.int/classifications/apps/icd/icd10 online>;
- publications including *The Medical Disability Advisor*, *The Comprehensive Textbook of Modern Synopsis of Psychiatry II*, and the *Presley Reed Disability Advisor*;
- the AMA and the various provincial Workers' Compensation Guidelines;
- Millimand and Robertson, *Healthcare Management Guidelines*;
- the guidelines provided by the Work-loss Data Institute;
- actuarial analysis and past claim experience; and
- consultation with occupational health professionals.

Disability guidelines help the Claim Administrator to:

- develop the expected absence duration for the average employee;
- determine when an independent medical examination or referral to a specialist may be warranted; and
- promote the use of consistent practices between Claim Adjudicators (important for client satisfaction with services provided).

These guidelines are valuable, but should not be used as the only basis for a decision on benefit eligibility. Other tools that can be used are a second medical opinion, referrals, claim management action plans, and case conferences.

SECOND OPINION REFERRALS

A second opinion regarding the employee's health status and functional capabilities is often required. This can be obtained through a number of avenues:

1. Independent Medical Examinations

The decision to request a second opinion, or independent medical examination, is based on several factors including:

- concerns about the duration of the claim;
- availability of adequate information to determine function;
- direction needed regarding prognosis or treatment;
- concerns about the validity of the claim;
- difficulty in obtaining information from the treating practitioner;
- inconsistent information submitted from different sources; and
- differences of opinion in the interpretation of medical information.

2. Functional Capacity Assessments

A functional capacity assessment may be chosen instead of, or in addition to, an independent medical examination for the following reasons:

- it provides more detailed information needed for the development of a rehabilitation plan;
- it clarifies prognosis for return to own job duties;
- it assists in identifying work abilities which may be needed to assess employability for other occupations; and
- it assists in outlining appropriate treatment.

Some of the terms used in this process are provided in Figure 10.2.

Figure 10.2: Definition of Terms

The following is a list of terms that may appear on the reports obtained:

Physical Capacity Evaluation —	An assessment of the functional abilities of an individual.
Work Hardening/Conditioning —	Improving tolerance to perform a job.
Work Sample Evaluations —	Simulate real jobs or tasks for the purpose of evaluation.
Ergonomics —	A study of human interface with work.

Claim Management Action Plan

DEVELOPING CLAIM MANAGEMENT ACTION PLANS

A claim management action plan is the planned approach for managing a specific claim. It includes:

- employee information;
- employee's current health status;
- an estimate of the likelihood of the employee returning to work;
- the proposed claim management action plans; and
- the claim and case management activity tracking.

A sample claim management action plan is provided in Appendix 1.

DOCUMENTATION

A claim management action plan should be documented and regularly updated. Documentation is crucial for effective claim management. It serves to provide:

- a profile of the claim status and the claim management services provided;
- a means of communication among members of the disability management team contributing to claim management;
- a basis for planning and for continuity of claim management for each case;
- a basis for review, study and evaluation of the claim;
- some protection for the medical and legal interests of both the employee and the company; and
- an audit trail of activities completed which can serve as a "due diligence" tool if required.

REVIEW/UPDATE ACTION PLANS

Claim management action plans should be regularly reviewed and updated. Actions and plans should be noted, assigned, and completion dates established. Progress against these plans needs to be monitored and recorded.

COMMUNICATING ACTION PLANS TO KEY STAKEHOLDERS

All players in a disability management claim need to be kept current on the progress of the claim and the employee's fitness to work. How often this is done and to whom, depends on the complexity and chronicity of the case. Typically, weekly to bimonthly reports need to be made.

Confidentiality

All persons who collect, maintain, handle and use employee health information are required to protect the confidentiality of the information. To ensure compliance, human resource personnel involved in claim administration are bound by an oath of confidentiality (Figure 10.6). The oath is to be reviewed annually and the form dated, signed, and witnessed.

Administration Responsibility

Primary responsibility for the administration and update of this standard of practice rests with senior management. Revision dates should be noted.

DISABILITY CASE MANAGEMENT STANDARD OF PRACTICE

Companies and professionals involved in disability management should provide a planned approach to remove barriers so that employees can return to work as quickly as possible without risk to their health or the health of others. The purpose of this standard is to provide guidelines for disability case management.

Disability Case Management

DEFINITION

A collaborative process for assessing, planning, implementing, coordinating, monitoring, and evaluating the options and services available to meet an individual's health needs through communication and accessible resources to promote quality, cost-effective outcomes [10] Case management promotes:

- safe and timely return-to-work efforts;
- early identification of disability claims for services and coordination of services, such as early intervention;
- maintaining contact with disabled employees;
- developing and monitoring modified/alternate work opportunities; and
- coordinating issues with the insurer and arranging for vocational rehabilitation when required.

GOAL

Case management is intended to assist ill and injured employees in reaching the highest level of medical improvement possible and to facilitate a return to work in the most cost-effective manner.

DISABILITY CASE MANAGERS

Disability Case Managers ensure that appropriate rehabilitative care is underway with the employee, and that the goal from the onset of injury or illness is to return the employee to productive work as soon as possible.

---

[10] Case Management Society of America (CMSA), *Standards of Practice for Case Management* (Little Rock, AR: CMSA, 1995).

QUALIFICATIONS

The qualifications necessary for a Disability Case Manager are:

- Maintenance of current professional licensure or national certification in a health and human services profession, or both.
- Completion of a baccalaureate or higher-level educational program in a health care related field of study, such as occupational health nursing, rehabilitation therapy, occupational therapy, *etc.*
- Completion of specific training and a minimum of 24 months of experience with the health needs of the population to be served.
- Demonstration of knowledge of occupational health, organizational behaviour, employee group benefits plans, and community health care services.
- Maintenance of continuing education appropriate to disability case management and professional licensure.
- Maintenance of case management certification. Certifications that are equivalent to case management certification (CCM) include the certified occupational health nurse (COHN), and certified insurance rehabilitation specialist (CIRS).

ROLE OF DISABILITY CASE MANAGER

The Disability Case Manager:

- initiates and maintains contact with injured or ill employees, health professionals, the insurance carrier, the employer and other involved parties;
- reviews medical care of injured or ill employees and their response to treatment;
- facilitates and coordinates sharing of information among all involved parties;
- communicates and educates stakeholders regarding graduated return-to-work guidelines;
- facilitates graduated return-to-work strategies, including modified/alternate work opportunities;
- monitors modified/alternate work efforts;
- establishes vocational rehabilitation when required; and
- collects data to show cost-effectiveness of the Disability Management Program and any identified trends for illness or injury prevention.

Disability Case Management Process

The Disability Case Manager functions as the catalyst and liaison to facilitate the recovery of employees with non-occupational and work-related illness or injury in the most expedient and cost-effective manner. To accomplish this, the Disability Case Manager utilizes the foundation of good business management coupled with good medical, nursing, and disability management knowledge.

Specifically, the Disability Case Manager performs the following functions in an orderly manner:

1. ASSESSMENT

Disability management requires a comprehensive approach. The following are some of the factors that need to be assessed when determining the need for case management:

Physical factors, such as:

- physical capabilities;
- job demands;
- potential for job modification;
- potential for use of adaptive devices; and
- potential for worksite/environmental modifications.

Personal factors, such as:

- changes in the family since the onset of the illness or injury;
- the presence of a personal crisis compounding the disability (*i.e.*, legal, domestic problems, job insecurity, *etc.*);
- the employee's cultural orientation to illness/injury and disability management;
- the health status of other family members; and
- how the family dynamics impact the current disability situation.

Vocational factors, such as:

- degree of job satisfaction;
- the occurrence of recent changes at work (*i.e.*, hours, assignment, performance, availability of work, *etc.*);
- any previous work activities and other marketable skills;
- the employee's vocational interests and aptitudes; and
- the supervisor's and human resource professional's promotion of a graduated return to work.

Medical factors, such as:

- diagnosis;
- prognosis;
- treatment plan;
- expected return-to-work date;
- employee confidence and satisfaction with medical treatment;
- potential residual limitations;
- presence of pain and coping skills;
- presence of other health problems; and

- independent practitioner, nutritional guidance, adaptive devices, aids to daily living, home help, and/or home care services, *etc.*

Psychological factors, such as:

- the employee's reaction to illness/injury;
- the employee's thoughts and feelings, level of self-esteem, outlook, locus of control, and degree of personal power;
- cultural factors;
- the employee's interests and attitude about work and the illness or injury;
- reliance on alcohol and/or drugs;
- stress management needs; and
- the employee's willingness to try modified work/alternate work duties.

Performance issues, such as:

- quality of the relationship between the employee and his or her supervisor;
- quality of relationships with co-workers;
- level of social acceptance and credibility;
- employee's past and recent work performance; and
- past history of absenteeism.

Educational factors, such as:

- formal education; and
- specialized training.

Financial factors, such as:

- available employee benefits;
- income;
- financial assets/liabilities; and
- treatment/rehabilitation expenses.

Organizational factors, such as:

- willingness to host case management conferences to expedite a successful graduated return-to-work plan; and
- resources to meet the employee's rehabilitation needs.

Effective case management requires the appropriate assessment and evaluation of the employee's needs; of the availability and utilization of appropriate medical treatment; and of the factors that may impede the employee's successful recovery and reintegration into the workforce (Chapter 5, "An Integrated Disability Management Program: The Managed Rehabilitative Care Program", Figure 5.2). By providing parallel assistance with work and medical issues, return-to-work barriers can be eliminated.

2. PROBLEM IDENTIFICATION

BACKGROUND

An overwhelming majority of injured, ill, or disabled employees return to work without difficulty. For approximately 15 per cent to 20 per cent of employees on short-term and long-term disability and Workers' Compensation, disability provokes a constellation of personal, emotional, and work-related issues that delay return to work. The existence of person-job mismatch, workplace discord, and a performance problem usually indicates a prolonged absence from work.

Some factors associated with a delayed return to work are:

- the absence of graduated return-to-work opportunities;
- time lags in obtaining medical care or other forms of therapy;
- lack of knowledge on the part of the community practitioner about the workplace and what accommodations can be made for the disabled employee;
- disability insurance plans that promote a "reward" for being disabled;
- unreliable methods for tracking the ill or injured worker;
- employee fear of losing disability income if he or she attempts an unsuccessful return to work;
- physical/psychological pain;
- employee fear of relapse or re-injury;
- employee anxiety concerning poor job performance due to disability;
- decreased self-confidence;
- a physical illness with strong psychological overtones;
- a work situation perceived as intolerable by the employee;
- a negative industrial relations climate,
- layoffs due to "downsizing";
- cultural differences in illness/injury response;
- limited social acceptance and supports;
- a breakdown in communication between the employee and employer; and
- lack of understanding by all stakeholders of the real costs associated with disability.

The factors associated with a timely and safe return to work are:

- job satisfaction;
- respect for the worker;
- open communication between the employer and worker;
- existence of a modified/alternate work program; and
- use of a team approach (*i.e.*, employee, supervisor, union, insurance company, human resource professionals, physician, Employee Assistance Program counsellors, occupational health professionals, *etc.*) towards a graduated return to work with the employee being the key player.

Recent changes in the workers' compensation and human rights regulations in Canada demand workplace accommodation for the disabled worker. For larger companies, this can mean workplace and/or work duty modifications, or necessitate the development of alternate job positions.

3. DISABILITY CASE MANAGEMENT

Disability Case Managers identify cases, non-occupational or occupational in origin that will benefit the most from case management intervention. Criteria for early identification include:

*   the absence of graduated return-to-work opportunities;
*   time lags in obtaining medical care or other forms of therapy;
*   lack of knowledge on the part of the community practitioner about the workplace and what accommodations can be made for the disabled employee;
*   disability insurance plans that promote a "reward" for being disabled;[11]
*   unreliable methods for tracking the ill or injured worker;
*   employee fear of losing disability income if he or she attempts an unsuccessful return to work;[12]
*   physical/psychological pain;
*   employee fear of relapse or re-injury;[13]
*   employee anxiety concerning poor job performance due to disability;
*   decreased self-confidence;[14]
*   a work situation perceived as intolerable by the employee;
*   a negative industrial relations climate;
*   layoffs due to "downsizing";
*   cultural differences in illness/injury response;
*   few or limited social credits and supports (refer to Chapter 15, "Disability Management: The Social Capital Theory-Perspective for Managing Disability Claims", for details on social credits);
*   a breakdown in communication between the employee and employer; and
*   lack of understanding by all stakeholders of the real costs associated with disability.

4. OUTCOME IDENTIFICATION

Disability case management is a goal-directed process. Information is gathered and evaluated to form an assessment of an injured or ill employee's needs. When

---

[11]   P. Booth, *Employee Absenteeism: Strategies for Promoting an Attendance-Oriented Corporate Culture* (Ottawa: The Conference Board of Canada, 1993) at 3.

[12]   L. Gross, "Managing Your Escalating Health and Safety Costs" (Presented to the Petroleum Industry's Annual Safety Seminar, Alberta, May 1993) [unpublished].

[13]   *Ibid.*

[14]   *Ibid.*

these needs have been identified, the Disability Case Manager, in collaboration with the medical care provider, employee, employer, and other involved parties, identifies cost-effective and appropriate resources that can be utilized to facilitate the worker's recovery. For each identified resource, or intervention, the Disability Case Manager must be able to report, in quantifiable terms, its impact on quality of care or quality of life in order to appropriately evaluate outcomes.

5. PLANNING PROCESS

The Disability Case Manager facilitates the planning of care and the selection of resources. This facilitation is not conducted in a vacuum but rather in partnership with the employee, management, union, physician, Employee Assistance Program counsellor, and often, family members. All of the factors identified in the assessment process are considered in deciding on appropriate care, the delivery of that care, and necessary resources, such as equipment, supplemental assistance, available Employee Assistance Programs (own and spousal), and extended health care plans.

A rehabilitation action plan is developed for each employee who can benefit from proactive intervention. This is accomplished by gathering data using the following techniques:

- *Job Analysis* — The job description and physical demand requirements of the employee's job are reviewed to identify capabilities, as well as any limitations.
- *Attending Physician Support* — The purpose of the case management process is to work as a team to benefit the employee. This includes involvement of the attending physician. The Disability Case Manager needs to explain the benefits and corporate support available for the employee to the physician, if appropriate.
- *Job or Work Site Modification* — The opportunity for job changes, or the reassignment of parts of a job, are considered so that the employee can return to work in a safe and timely manner. Once the employee's capabilities have been identified by an occupational health professional, the supervisor, union representative, Return-to-Work Coordinator, and human resource personnel are usually the leaders of a modified/alternate work opportunity.
- *Employee Assistance Program Support* — The Disability Case Manager should offer Employee Assistance Program support to the employee and family as appropriate. Many disabled employees need help to cope with a disability, work stress, personal issues, and any mental health component of the existent medical conditions.
- *Coordination with a Specialist* — When warranted, a Disability Case Manager may arrange to obtain an earlier appointment for the employee. Under certain circumstances, it may be advantageous to fund a medical assessment, especially if it facilitates getting an earlier appointment.

- *Third Party Functional Capacity Assessment/Evaluation (FCA/FCE)* — A third party FCA/FCE may be sought to determine the employee's fitness to work.
- *Adaptive Devices* — Special clothing, devices, or equipment that allow adaptation of the work to the employee's limitations are considered where possible. From the beginning, the disabled employee and supervisor are involved in selecting and learning how to use any device that assists in the workplace accommodation of the returning employee. The occupational hygiene professionals can be an excellent team resource in this area.
- *Job Finding* — Human resources personnel should be advised as early as possible of the likelihood that the employee will not be able to return to his or her own job. In that way, an internal job search can be instituted.
- *Employee Education* — Company resources may be used to help the employee understand and cope with his or her disability. This is important when trying to encourage a positive attitude towards illness or injury management. The employee must feel a sense of control over life if he or she is to successfully cope with the situation.
- *Case Conferences* — It is critical to invite all the relevant stakeholders to attend any required case management meetings. Specific goals and time frames are developed and communicated to the team, of which the employee is the key player. A decision tree, like the one provided in Chapter 3, "The Supportive Infrastructure for an Integrated Disability Management Program", Figure 3.3, can help the team remain focused. Another useful tool is the Rehabilitation Action Plan, (Chapter 5, "An Integrated Disability Management Program: The Managed Rehabilitative Care Program", Figure 5.5). In this way, all the stakeholders can review and address any identified rehabilitation or return-to-work barriers. This is particularly important if the employee will not be able to return to his or her own job.

Rehabilitation action plans should be regularly reviewed and updated to reflect the progress being made. The Disability Case Manager documents the effectiveness of each step of the plan, identifies any unforeseen obstacles, and prepares all participants in the plan for the subsequent steps. By involving the employee in case management decisions, the employee retains a sense of control over his or her life.

6. MONITORING AND COORDINATION

The Disability Case Manager:

- provides for the assessment and documentation of quality of care and of services and products delivered to the employee;
- determines if rehabilitation goals are being met;
- determines whether the case management goals and the expected outcomes are realistic and appropriate;

- continuously monitors the rehabilitation process through good oral and written communication;
- ensures effective coordination of care and services for the injured or ill employee;
- documents the rehabilitation process;
- ensures a timely response to rehabilitation issues; and
- ensures prompt reporting to the management of any relevant workplace issues.

A Disability Case Management Flow Chart like the one presented in Chapter 3, "The Supportive Infrastructure for an Integrated Disability Management Program", Figure 3.2, can be used by Disability Case Managers to assess the employee's progress throughout the case management process.

7. EVALUATION

Evaluation of the case's progress and outcomes is necessary to determine the effectiveness of the case management plan and the quality of medical care, services, and products from providers. Evaluation is most effective if metrics, or medical case measurements, are used. Comparing the results of a particular case management scenario against the case plan metrics can be a valuable exercise when it comes to appropriately evaluating outcomes. Figure 10.3 is a listing of some of the possible Disability Case Management Metrics.

Individual case management process and results are reviewed continually and process improvements sought. The Disability Case Management Assessment and Evaluation Checklist (Figure 10.4) can be a useful evaluation tool for Disability Case Managers.

Program results, costs, system concerns, and recommendations are tabulated and reported annually to management and the Disability Management Program Steering Committee. Confidentiality of individual information is maintained as per the company's Disability Management Standard of Practice for Confidentiality of Personal Health Information.

Annual auditing of the Disability Case Management, peer review, and self-auditing are recommended evaluation techniques.

Figure 10.3: Disability Case Management Metrics[15]

Metric	Best Practice
Diagnosis verified.	Diagnosis verified by appropriate test or observations. If diagnosis is not verified, Disability Case Manager will challenge diagnosis until it is verified.
Evidence-based practice protocols.	Ten most common diagnoses will have practice protocols.
Existence of "red flag" alerts Disability Case Manager to institute or increase case management.	Disability Case Manager has established criteria or indicators for increased case acuity.
Disability Case Manager has specific diagnosis-based disability-duration guidelines to follow.	Low variances from disability-duration guidelines.
Resources used for hospital and ambulatory care.	Most appropriate resources are identified and used.
Average number of disability days per diagnosis.	Documented decrease in disability days.
Case cost with case management.	Decreased case cost with case management.
Case notes/documentation.	Well-documented treatment plan, decision making.
Hospitalization.	Low hospitalization rates (below 5%) coupled with good outcomes.
Re-admissions.	Low re-admission rate (below 1%).
Medical management.	Treatment process changes based on case management information.
Individual (worker/patient) satisfaction.	Improved patient satisfaction with case management (using a survey tool).

---

[15] Printed with permission: D. DiBenedetto *et al.*, *OEM Occupational Health and Safety Manual* (Boston: OEM Press, 1996).

Figure 10.4: Disability Case Management Assessment and Evaluation Checklist[16]

Information to be Obtained	Rationale
Age	Age affects recovery time and rate of rehabilitation.
Gender	Gender plays a role in the recovery time.
Years of service with the company	Raises the issue of motivation to return to work, interest in medical retirement, *etc.*
Length of time in the current job position	In-depth knowledge of position will aid in developing opportunities for modified work.
Previous workers' compensation injury	If yes, what is the employee's views towards return to modified work, litigation, *etc.*
Current injury, diagnosis and treatment	In addition to gathering the particulars, it is important to note any areas in which the employee, provider, or adjuster lacks all the needed information.
Diagnostic testing	Determine what tests have been done and the results but also review what tests, which might be expected for a particular diagnosis, have not been done.
Medications: (a) Appropriateness of use (b) Use of other personal medications (c) Outcomes of (a) and/or (b)	Some personal medications may have an addictive or negative combination effect. Patients may not be taking medication in the appropriate time frame or manner, thus delaying recovery. Medications that seem ineffective, or have side-effects, should be brought to the attention of the physician.
Physical medicine modalities and results	Modalities should be scientifically based, and if a patient is not showing progress after 4 to 6 weeks, a re-evaluation by the physician should be initiated.
Expectations of the disability duration	Expectations of disability duration by the physician, patient and family may subtly influence the recovery.
Psychosocial variables	Family and social issues may be incentives or disincentives in the recovery process. This is an area in which Disability Case Managers may frequently uncover hidden agendas or issues that would have delayed recovery if not addressed.

---

[16]   *Ibid.*

Information to be Obtained	Rationale
Communication	Employee's failing to receive a timely Workers' Compensation payment, or his or her uncertainty as to how the Workers' Compensation system works, has one of the highest correlations with the employee's initiation of litigation. The Disability Case Manager fills a vital role as liaison with the employee, insurance providers, employer, and third-party administrator.

8. DOCUMENTATION

Refer to the "Disability Management Standard of Practice — Documentation in Personal Health Records" section below.

CONSENT FOR HANDLING

Disability case management requires information on the employee's physical and emotional capabilities and restrictions. Input from the employee's attending physician is essential.

According to Canadian legislation, an employer must obtain the consent of the employee before approaching the employee's physician for personal medical information. Thus the company, or its representative, must make efforts to obtain the employee's written consent before seeking such input from the employee's physician.[17]

Appendix 3 contains sample forms for this practice standard:

1.   Letter to Absent Employee
2.   Report of Absence Form
3.   Modified/Alternate Work Plan Form
4.   Restricted Work Form
5.   Physician's Statement of Medical Status
6.   Return-to-Work Report
7.   Consent Form

Confidentiality

Refer to the "Disability Management Standard of Practice — Confidentiality of Personal Health Information" section below for information on maintaining the confidentiality of personal health information.

---

[17]   A. Legault *et al.*, "How to Cope with Absenteeism, Part IV: Requesting a Medical Opinion" (1996) Focus on Canadian Employment and Equality Rights 126.

Administration Responsibility

Primary responsibility for the administration and update of this standard of practice rests with senior management. Revision dates should be noted.

DISABILITY MANAGEMENT STANDARD OF PRACTICE — CONFIDENTIALITY OF PERSONAL HEALTH INFORMATION

Introduction

All persons who collect, maintain, handle, and use personal health information are required to protect the confidentiality of the information.

This standard is based on the *Model Code for the Protection of Personal Information*[18] and the various pieces of provincial and federal privacy legislation. It details the procedures for collection, retention, storage, security access, disclosure, transmittal, reproduction, and destruction of identifiable personal health information held by the company or organization.

All staff must comply with the Disability Management Standard of Practice document on confidentiality of personal health information when interpreting personal health information to the employer-client without divulging any privileged information.

General

The company or organization recognizes the individual's right to privacy in relation to personal health information collected.

The principles governing confidentiality are:

- personal health information is only used on a "need-to-know" basis;
- personal health information should be relevant to the purposes for which it is to be used;
- personal health information is restricted to the company or organization staff who sign a pledge of confidentiality and who are subject to a recognized professional code of ethics;
- upon request, an employee has the right to access all information regarding his or her health;
- personal health information is protected by reasonable security safeguards;
- documented personal and health information is the property of the company or organization entrusted to occupational health staff for safeguarding and protection; and
- compliance with this standard is the responsibility of the Disability Case Manager.

---

[18] CAN/CSA, *The Model Code for the Protection of Personal Information*, CAN/CSA - Q830-96, (Ottawa: CSA, 1996).

Definitions

Collection — The act of gathering, acquiring, or obtaining personal information from any source, including third parties, by any means.

Confidentiality — The maintenance of trust and the avoidance of invasion of privacy through accurate reporting and authorized communication.

Consent — The voluntary agreement with what is being done or proposed. Consent can be either expressed or implied. Expressed consent is given explicitly, either orally, or in writing. It is unequivocal and does not require any inference on the part of the organization seeking consent. Implied consent arises where consent may reasonably be inferred from the action or inaction of the individual.

Designated Representative — Any individual or organization to whom an employee gives written authorization to exercise a right to access.

Disclosure — The act of making employee personal information available to others outside the organization.

Personal Health Information — An accumulation of data relevant to the past, present and future health status of an individual which includes all that the company or organization staff learn in the exercise of their responsibilities. It is the information about an identifiable individual that is recorded in any form.

Privacy — The claim of individuals, groups, or institutions to determine for themselves when, how and to what extent information about them is communicated to others.

Application

These guidelines apply to all occupational health and disability management staff, and include contract employees and all other support staff whether permanent, temporary, or volunteers.

Collection of Personal Health Information

The primary purpose for collecting and retaining personal health information is disability management. All information collected is subject to confidentiality and must be treated with respect.

Knowledge and consent of the employee are required for the collection and disclosure of personal health data relevant to disability management. Figure 10.5 shows how personal information should be collected. In essence, personal health information is not to be collected indiscriminately. Only the personal health information relevant to disability management should be collected.

Figure 10.5: Collection of Information

- Request for information will be in writing and contain the following:
  - Name and address of recipient of information.
  - Purpose or need for information.
  - Full name, address, and date of birth of person whose information is being requested.
  - Specific definition of the type and extent of information required.
- All requests will be accompanied by the appropriate "Release for Medical Information" form signed by the employee whose personal health record is being requested.
- A record of all requests will be maintained on the employee's personal health record.

Personal health information is collected using various methods, including interviewing, written documentation (*i.e.*, insurance claims, Workers' Compensation Board forms, *etc.*) and electronic data processing, all of which are subject to confidentiality. Appendix 2 provides standards for computerized employee health information management.

The personal health information collected relates to medical assessments, Employee Assistance Program treatment reports, illness and injury reports, personal and family history, and consultant reports.

Personal health information is only collected by designated staff subject to a pledge of confidentiality (Figure 10.6). Personal health information should be as accurate, complete, and current as possible.

Figure 10.6: Pledge of Confidentiality

- All personal health information related to an identified employee will be treated as confidential. This information may be in writing, oral, electronic or in any other format.
- Confidentiality extends to everything Company XYZ staff learns in the exercise of their responsibilities. It extends to both obviously important and apparently trivial information and includes the nature of the employee's contact with the staff, all information an employee discloses and all information learned from external caregivers.
- Personal health information related to the disability claim can be shared with occupational health professionals employed by Company XYZ in privacy to enhance continuity of care and a coordinated disability management approach.
- The dissemination of personal health information will be considered a breach of confidentiality and will be reported to Director, Human Resources and the CEO, Company XYZ. Disciplinary action will be taken up to and include immediate termination of employment with cause.

- Senior Management is responsible for ensuring that the Company XYZ staff involved in the disability management function are aware of the Pledge of Confidentiality and that they sign the pledge acknowledging this awareness.
- To acknowledge and emphasize the serious responsibility in safeguarding employee health information, all Company XYZ staff (permanent or temporary), or contract staff involved with disability management will be required to sign a pledge of confidentiality on the first day of work and annually thereafter, which will be worded as follows:

Pledge of Confidentiality

I have read and reviewed Company XYZ's Standard of Practice on Confidentiality of Personal Health Information. I understand that all employee personal health information, to which I may have access, is confidential and will not be communicated except as outlined in the Disability Management Standard of Practice.

Signed	Witness	Date
Signed	Witness	Date
Signed	Witness	Date

Note: This pledge is to be signed annually. The original form is to be sent to the staff member's file, Company XYZ HR Department. Copies are to be retained by the area Manager and the Company XYZ staff person.

Retention, Storage and Security

All personal health information must be stored separately from other employee information. The storage location is checked regularly and safeguarded from fire, water, and other potential disasters.

All computerized health information must be secured using passwords and access codes.

All activities of employees and visitors to the company or organization offices must be supervised in order to protect the confidentiality of personal health information.

During active use, records and other personal health information must be kept in private offices, always ensuring that identifiable information is protected from the observation and the hearing of other individuals.

All personal health information must be retained for a period of seven years from the last date of contact.

Personal health records of employees who have left the company are retained as outlined in Figure 10.7.

Figure 10.7: Retention, Storage and Security

- The medical records of terminated employees are to be pulled from the active files, placed in a designated envelope marked *"Confidential Personal Health Document: To Be Opened By Authorized Personnel Only"*, labelled and placed in a storage box. The box is to be numbered.
- A list of the medical files in the storage box is to be created. Three sets of this list are to be made: one copy to go with the storage box, another is to be sent to the employee, and a third is to be retained by Company XYZ.
- A system of archiving that links the file with the storage box is required.
- Files are to be stored in a location that is safeguarded from water, fire and access by unauthorized persons.

Accessibllity

Upon request, an employee is to be informed of the existence, use and disclosure of personal health information and is given access to that information.

Employees, former employees and other properly designated representatives have the right to inspect and copy, all or in part, personal health records. All such written requests are to be honoured within a reasonable time that should not exceed 15 days.

> **Note:** *The actual health record is the property of the company; however, the information contained in the record belongs to the employee.*

To the extent practicable, inspection of a personal health record is to be made in the presence of a representative of the company or organization, who endeavours to explain the meaning of the contents of the record to the employee. Rebuttal of information contained in the personal health record by the employee will be included in the record, signed, and dated by the employee. The representative will add a note to the file concerning explanation and agreement, or disagreement.

The company or organization personnel may delete the identity of a family member, personal friend, or fellow employee who has provided confidential information concerning an employee's health status from the requested health records.

It is recommended that employees:

- accept a summary of material facts and opinions in lieu of copies of the records requested; or
- accept a release of the requested information only to the family physician or other qualified health care professional.

Access to health information that may have an adverse impact upon the health of the employee will only be provided to a designated physician of the employee.

No other personnel, except designated staff, have the right to access health information unless disclosure obligations have been met.

Internal Disclosure to the Employer-Client

Personal health information released to management (managers and/or supervisors) is limited to the following:

- report of fitness to work following a mandated or statutory health assessment;
- determination that a medical condition exists and that the employee is under medical care. This could include the dates or follow-up appointments or referrals to specialists or treatment programs;
- time that the employee has been or is expected to be off work;
- medical limitations, if any, to carry out work in a safe and timely manner;
- medical restrictions, if any, regarding specific tasks; and/or
- estimated date for a realistic return to work, or a return to modified/alternate work.

However, if, in the opinion of a health professional, disclosure is necessary because of a *clear danger* to the employee, other employees, the workplace or the public at large, and:

- the employee consistently refuses to give consent; and
- a second opinion is obtained from the employee's personal physician when the concern is for the health of the employee or fellow employees-clients, or from the medical officer of health when the risk is to the public;

the appropriate staff member may make the disclosure to the appropriate manager after giving notice in writing to the employee, indicating that confidential information will be disclosed.

External Disclosure

Subject to the exceptions specified below, the company or organization should not disclose personal health information regarding employees, or former employees, to external sources unless the individual has authorized such release by providing a signed and dated consent form for release of medical information or its equivalent. Disclosure will follow the checklist provided in Figure 10.8, and the Requirements for Informed Consent in Figure 10.9.

Figure 10.8: Disclosure of Information Checklist

- All requests for disclosure of information will be directed to the Company XYZ Disability Case Manager.
- Any authorization for release of information will be an original form and will specify the source, content, recipient, purpose and time limitations. The form will identify the:

    - Name of the individual or institution who is to disclose the information.
    - Name of the individual or institution who is to receive the information.
    - Full name, address, and date of birth of the person whose information is being requested.
    - Purpose or need of information, unless included in accompanying request.
    - Extent or nature of information to be released, including date(s) of treatment or contact (blanket authorizations requesting "any" or "all" information will not be honoured).
    - Date that consent/authorization is signed which must be subsequent to the date of treatment or contact in question and within sixty (60) days of signature of person whose information is to be released, or that of his or her legally authorized representative.
    - Information released to legally authorized persons is not to be made available to any other party without further authorization. The recipient will be so informed by including a copy of the following letter with the information:

Sample Letter

To Whom It May Concern:

The enclosed information is being forwarded to you from our records, which are the property of Company XYZ and managed by Company XYZ. Such copies are released only to persons authorized according to law and the policy of Company XYZ. In this way, we seek to uphold the trust vested in us by the individual and ensure that his or her wishes and best interests are served at all times. Accordingly, this information is released on the following conditions:

- that it not be further copied, transmitted, or disseminated without further specific authorization of the person concerned;
- that it be used only for the purpose as outlined in your request; and
- that it be destroyed by shredding or incineration when the original purpose has been served.

Your cooperation and compliance with the above is appreciated.

Figure 10.9: Requirements for Informed Consent

- There is an obligation on the employer to ensure that sufficient information is provided to employees about the nature and consequence of the intended action to allow the employee to come to a reasoned decision.
- The employee is mentally competent, and has the ability to understand and appreciate the nature and consequences of the procedure.
- Consent is freely given.
- Consent is not obtained through misrepresentation or fraud.
- Consent is in relation to the specific act contemplated unless the employee's life is immediately endangered and it is impractical to obtain consent.
- Consent cannot be given to the performance of an illegal procedure.

Routine Request for Release of Medical Information — A written request by a physician, medical institution, another health agency, or insurance company, for abstracts or copies of part or all of the individual's health record is honoured when the consent form (Appendix 3, Form 7) or its equivalent is signed by the employee.

Release of Pertinent Medical Data to Appropriate Public Health Authorities — When it is determined that a public health issue or risk has been uncovered, as in the case of a reportable communicable disease, appropriate notification to provincial or municipal health authorities will be made in accordance with the statutory requirement.

Disclosure to Government Agencies — To preserve the confidentiality of employee health records, the company or organization usually requests government agencies for consent for release of medical information signed by the employee. However, government legislation may have the authority to require immediate access to employee and former employee medical information. Whenever access is necessary without the prior written consent of the employee, a government agency must present a written access order to the company or organization.

Disclosure to Designated Representative — The company or organization, upon presentation of a written consent by an employee or former employee, will release copies of the individual's medical record to the designated representative. With respect to medical information that may be deemed to have a detrimental impact upon the health of the employee, medical information will be provided only to the employee's family physician. Information received in confidence from external sources that is part of the health record will not be divulged to the employee's designated representative.

Disclosure of Subpoenaed Information — A company or organization should respond to a subpoena as follows:

- with the server present, the employee's name and the validity of the subpoena are verified;
- the Chief Executive Officer is notified;
- only the specific material requested in the subpoena is collected and photocopied;
- authorization to release information is given by the Chief Executive Officer and the Senior Counsel, Corporate; and
- without written authorization of the employee, subpoenaed records are not available for review by outside counsel prior to being established as evidence.

Reproduction and Transmittal

Reproduction of any individualized health information is to be done by designated staff in privacy.

Transmittal of individualized health records can be faxed to a recipient with a confidentiality notice. Information can also be mailed or couriered in envelopes clearly marked "Confidential: To Be Opened by Addressee Only".

Transmittal of individualized health records will be in sealed envelopes or boxes. The envelopes or boxes must be clearly marked "Confidential: To Be Opened by Addressee Only".

Destruction

When it becomes appropriate to dispose of health information, including formal health records, notes and messages pertaining to an individual employee, they will be rendered completely and permanently unidentifiable through destruction by burning, shredding, or automated erasure.

When burning, shredding, or automated erasure is not feasible, health information will be transmitted to the closest office with the ability to destroy such information.

Company or organization staff will personally transmit the information to be destroyed and remain with the information until it is destroyed.

Misuse of Personal Health Information

Any individual who becomes aware of an abuse of confidentiality of health information will document and report the incident to the Chief Executive Officer.

Administration Responsibility

Primary responsibility for the administration and update of this standard of practice rests with senior management.

DISABILITY MANAGEMENT STANDARD OF PRACTICE — DOCUMENTATION IN PERSONAL HEALTH RECORDS

Introduction

This standard of practice is intended to provide guidance and direction to Disability Case Managers in the initiation, maintenance, and disposal of employee health records.

When completed properly, the personal health record can:

- provide a profile of the health status and the health care provided to each employee;
- provide a means of communication among members of the Disability Management Team contributing to the disability case management process;
- provide a basis for planning and for continuity of rehabilitation care for employees;
- provide a basis for review, study and evaluation of the case; and
- assist in the provision of protection for the medical and legal interests of both the employee and the company.

General

Disability Case Managers are required to discharge their legal responsibilities by providing accurate and timely records of events and information affecting the health of the employee.

Information recorded in the employee health record is confidential. The Disability Management Standard of Practice — Confidentiality of Personal Health Information applies to all Disability Case Managers documenting and handling employee personal health records.

Personal health records are to be cumulative and sequential. Filing in the chart is done in such a way that the most current information in each selection is on top when the file is opened.

Application

These guidelines apply to all professionals and contract employees who gather information for the purpose of disability case management.

PERSONAL HEALTH RECORD FORMAT

The employee's health record is kept in an appropriately labelled data file folder in a secure manner. The employee's name must appear on every page of the record.

Each record will contain the following information:

- reports of sickness and injury absences;
- reports of all medical examinations and consultations;
- a record of all inquiries related to health problems, whether presented in person or by phone;
- copies of disability claim forms;
- correspondence with other health care professionals or agencies;
- copies of Workers' Compensation claims;
- memos or notes regarding discussions relevant to the case (*e.g.*, discussions between professionals, medical experts, Employee Assistance Program counsellors);
- a record of communication with other health and safety related bodies (*e.g.*, Workers' Compensation Board, insurance companies and government agencies); and/or
- a record of all communication with management, unions and employees. These signed notes should include time and date of call.

RECORDING

The general guidelines for recording are:

- all entries are to be recorded on the Disability Case Management Status Report (Figure 10.10);
- all entries should be dated and entered sequentially;
- every entry must be signed. The accepted format for a signature is the initial, surname and professional designation (if applicable);
- entries are to be made in ink or typed;
- entries should be made at the earliest opportunity following contact;
- writing in the record must be legible;
- entries should be continuous, do not skip lines between entries or leave space within an entry;
- entries in the record are permanent. Do not obliterate material on the record by scratching out, using correction fluid, felt tip pen or typewritten XXXs; and
- when content corrections are required, the following procedure is to be observed:
  - draw a single line through each line of inaccurate recording making certain it is still legible;
  - date and initial the line;
  - enter corrections in chronological order;

- time the entry and sign;
- make certain to indicate which entry the correction is replacing; and
- in questionable situations, it is wise to have the corrected material witnessed by an occupational health colleague. Countersigning of the record is completed with the signature of the responsible party and the witness or counter-signatory (signature should be in the standard format).

ACCESS TO THE HEALTH RECORD

Refer to the "Disability Management Standard of Practice — Confidentiality of Personal Health Information" section regarding the topics of:

- accessibility; and
- internal and external disclosure.

RETENTION OF HEALTH RECORD

Refer to the "Disability Management Standard of Practice — Confidentiality of Personal Health Information" section regarding:

- retention, storage, security; and
- Retention of Inactive Health Records — Appendix B.

TRANSMITTAL OF HEALTH RECORD

Refer to the "Disability Management Standard of Practice — Confidentiality of Personal Health Information" section regarding:

- Reproduction and Transmittal.

DESTRUCTION OF HEALTH RECORD

Refer to the "Disability Management Standard of Practice — Confidentiality of Personal Health Information" section.

Figure 10.10: Disability Case Management Status Record

COMPANY XYZ
LOGO/ADDRESS

Employee Name
Company/Organization
Employee Number/Identifier

Date	Status	Signature

Review of Health Record

Regular and periodic review of personal health records is conducted to ensure that policies and practices are implemented, and that forms and records continue to capture appropriate information without duplication.

Administration Responsibility

Primary responsibility for the administration and update of this standard of practice rests with senior management. Revision dates should be noted.

SUMMARY

These four disability management practice standards comprise the key elements of a responsible Disability Management Program. Companies that offer disability management services of any sort should have these safeguards in place. This is one way to protect themselves against costly litigation, and to demonstrate their "due diligence".

Appendix 1

Claim Management Action Plan Form

```
COMPANY XYZ
LOGO/ADDRESS
```

Claim Management Action Plan

Employee Information

Name: _____   Employee #: _____

Phone: (H)_____

       (W)_____

Job Title: _____   Manager: _____

Occupation: _____   Phone: _____

Return-to-Work Probability

Expected date of return to work: _____

      Likely to return to own job   ☐

      Unlikely to return to own job   ☐

      Job modifications necessary   ☐

Current Status

Last Day Worked: _____

Previous Work Absence in the Last Six (6) Months: _____ (Dates)

Functional Limitations:

Lifting   _____   Bending   _____

Sitting   _____   Reaching   _____

Standing   _____   Psychological _____

Other   _____

Comments:

_____

_____

_____

COMPANY XYZ
LOGO/ADDRESS

Employee Name: _____   Employee #: _____

Treatment Program:

_____

_____

_____

Able to Return to Work   ☐

Date: _____   Full-time ☐   Part-time ☐
Restrictions: _____

Unable to Return to Work ☐

Expected Date of Return to Work: _____

Next Case Management Assessment Date: _____

Action Plan
Claim Management Plan:

		Comments	Date Requested
☐	Standard Physician Form	_____	_____
☐	Diagnosis Specific Form	_____	_____
☐	Attending Physician's Narrative	_____	_____
☐	Functional Evaluation	_____	_____
☐	Specialist Consult Report	_____	_____
☐	Investigative Studies	_____	_____
☐	IME (Independent Medical Evaluation)	_____	_____
☐	Other	_____	_____

| COMPANY XYZ |
| LOGO/ADDRESS |

Employee Name: _____   Employee #: ____ _____

Claim and Case Management Tracking

#	Date	Claim Action Plan	Rehabilitation Action Plan
1.			
2.			
3.			
4.			
5.			
6.			
7.			
8.			
9.			
10.			
11.			
12.			

Additional Comments:

_____
_____
_____
_____
_____

Appendix 2

Computerized Employee Health Information Management[19]

COMPUTERIZED EMPLOYEE HEALTH INFORMATION MANAGEMENT

Security of Computerized Health Information

1. Company XYZ recognizes the individual's right to privacy in relation to health information. Computerized health information is subject to the same security as written information:

    *   Company XYZ has the property right to the computerized health information that is compiled.
    *   All Company XYZ offices shall safeguard computerized health information against loss or unwarranted access.
    *   All Company XYZ offices shall establish policies and procedures concerning the confidentiality and security of computerized health information.
    *   The office policies and procedures for access to written information must serve as a minimum standard for computerized information.

2. It is recognized that a computerized health information system can be as secure as a paper system and should allow relative ease of use for authorized personnel while eliminating unauthorized access:

    *   The issue of confidentiality shall not be used as a barrier to the implementation of computerized information systems.

3. An individual's access to his or her own computerized health information shall follow the guidelines on Accessibility of this Standard of Practice:

    *   Management and employees shall be informed as to existence, purpose and type of information contained in the computerized health information system.

---

[19] Adapted from: Petro-Canada, "Confidentiality Code of Practice, Reference Number 130" in *Occupational Health Manual* (Calgary: Petro-Canada, 1994) at 12-14.

4. Information from computerized health information used or maintained to facilitate information exchange in support of employee care shall be accessible only to authorized persons.
5. Data security shall include data integrity. Steps must be taken to ensure the reliability of data input.

   - Data shall be protected so that it cannot be altered or purged without the proper authorization.
   - Principles of documentation and context of health information shall be adhered to in order that computer charting will meet legal and professional standards.

Note: *Records should not be computerized without obtaining the advice of legal counsel to determine whether the "hard copy" will be acceptable as evidence, and whether the act of computerization conflicts with any provincial enactment regarding written or other traditional forms of records. Special care must be taken regarding confidentiality and errors. Since there is very little law on this matter, the computerization of records must be kept under constant review with respect to possible legal changes.*

Policies and Procedures Regarding Security of Computerized Health Information

1. Physical Protection — The facility must ensure:

   - The physical protection of the system by guarding against threats from electrical failure/fluctuations, fire, flood and temperature variations.
   - Terminals located in such a way that the screen cannot be viewed by unauthorized persons.
   - Back-up copies of vital files are stored in a physically separated and secure area.
   - Documented manual systems to enable ongoing operation during a down period of the computerized systems.
   - Written agreements from computer vendors involved with health care data that specify methods by which information is handled and transported.

2. Access of Information in System — There shall be:

   - Controlled access to terminals. Categories of personnel shall be identified to indicate authorized access to these terminals.
   - Defined access, specifying information to which users may be granted access.

- A personal security passcode for each authorized individual.
- Immediate removal of passcode upon an individual's denial to access.
- A provision for change of passcode where access has been restricted or redefined.
- A policy for access to the system. It shall be available at every point of access.

3. General Administrative — Policies and procedures shall include:

- Development of, or change to any computerized health record and/or health information system governed by a committee of multi-disciplinary health professionals.
- Administrative responsibility for ensuring the security of the system which shall be designated to an individual and that responsibility shall be defined and documented.
- Appropriate security which must be inherent in the software when computer facilities are shared.

4. User Responsibility:

- The users are expected to guard their identification and passwords to prevent a breach of security.

Appendix 3

Disability Case Management Sample Forms

1. Letter to Absent Employee
2. Report of Absence Forms

    - Sample (a)
    - Sample (b)

3. Modified/Alternate Work Plan Forms

    - Sample (a)
    - Sample (b)

4. Restricted Work Form
5. Physician's Statement of Medical Status
6. Return-to-Work Report
7. Consent Form

Form 1: Letter to the Employee

```
COMPANY XYZ
LOGO/ADDRESS
```

Date _____

Dear _____ _____
          (Employee)

RE: Disability

We have been advised by your supervisor that you are unable to work due to illness/injury. We sincerely hope that you will experience an early recovery and we wish to assist you wherever possible.

As part of our corporate Disability Management Program, we require the following:

- a completed attending physician's report (as attached); and
- a signed consent form for release of medical information to our Disability Case Manager(s), and our insurers/adjudicators (_____).

The attending physician report must be completed and returned to Company XYZ's Occupational Health Department within three (3) working days. Your signed consent form must accompany this physician report.

Your supervisor will be in contact on a weekly basis to determine if there are any opportunities for modified/alternate work. We would encourage you to utilize the Employee Assistance Program should you require such services during your disability.

If there is any additional assistance the company can provide, please contact _____.

We look forward to having you return to your job in the very near future.

Yours truly,

_____
Supervisor

Form 2a: Report of Absence Form[20]

Sample (a):   For Organizations with Occupational Health Services:

REPORT OF ABSENCE FORM

EMPLOYEE AUTHORIZATION: *(To be completed by the employee)*

Name:			Employee Number:	
Address:			Home Phone Number:	
Work Injury ☐	Work Illness ☐		Work Phone Number:	
Non-work Injury ☐	Non-work Illness ☐		Start Date of Injury/Illness:	

Is your injury or illness related to your work?   ☐ Yes   ☐ No   If yes, please explain below:

I hereby authorize my insurer and attending physician to release any information related to this injury/illness, or copies thereof acquired in the course of examination or my treatment, Company XYZ's Occupational Health Service. I further authorize the Occupational Health Service to release to my insurer/employer any information required to determine my eligibility for short term disability benefits and any information related to the employment relationship. I understand that this information will be used to determine my eligibility for disability benefits, and to assist with the management of my claim, and to remedy any work-related factors contributing to my illness or injury or my return to work. This consent is valid for 180 days.

Signature:		Date:	

COMPANY PHILOSOPHY

Company XYZ has a Disability Management Program designed to assist the safe and timely return of employees who are recovering from injury/ illness, or who have ongoing health problems. We would appreciate your assistance and co-operation. If you have any questions or suggestions about the Disability Management Program, and/or the placement of this employee, please contact at____.

Submit form to: The Occupational Health Service at above address, or in the confidential envelope provided, or by confidential fax **(XXX-XXXX).** Thank you for the time and consideration you have provided to Company XYZ and this employee.

PHYSICAL WORK RESTRICTIONS: *(To be completed by the attending physician)*

Please check and complete either Section A or Section B:

Section A:	The employee will be able to return to **Regular Work** on:	Date:	
Section B:	The employee may return to **Modified Work** on:	Date:	
	And may return to Regular Work on:	Date:	

If Modified Work is required, please complete the following **Work Restrictions:**

☐ Lifting - from waist	(weight/frequency)		☐ Typing	(how long)	
☐ Lifting - from shoulder	(weight/frequency)		☐ Sitting	(how long)	
☐ Prolonged standing	(how long/frequency)		☐ Walking	(how long)	
☐ Working in the cold	(how long/frequency)		☐ Bending	(how long)	
☐ Working in the heat	(how long/frequency)		☐ Kneeling	(how long)	
☐ Working outdoors	(how long/frequency)		☐ Twisting	(frequency)	
☐ Repetition (hand/arm)	(how long/frequency)		☐ Crawling	(frequency)	
☐ Operating heavy machinery	(frequency)		☐ Working shift work		
☐ Climbing ladders	(frequency)		☐ Driving		
☐ Working at heights			☐ Climbing stairs		

Other Comments:

Temporarily reduced or gradually increasing hours are available. Please indicate any restriction of this type:

DIAGNOSIS: *(To be completed by the attending physician)*

Diagnosis of the *Present Health Condition*:

1. Primary Diagnosis:

2. Pre-existing condition or complications that may affect the work absence:

3. Date of next follow-up visit	Day	Month	Year

4. Is the present condition the result of, or complicated by, a pre-existing condition?	Yes ☐	No ☐

If Yes, please explain:

Date of Hospitalization (if applicable):		Date of Injury/Illness Onset:	
Nature of Treatment (e.g., surgery, physiotherapy)		Name of Specialist (if applicable):	
Duration/ Frequency of Treatment:			
Date of First Treatment:		Date of Last Treatment:	
Name of Physician:		Physician Phone Number:	
Address:		Physician Fax Number:	
Physician's Signature:		Date:	

Thank you for your assistance in supporting this employee through this injury or illness, and a timely return to work.

---

[20]   Adapted from: L. Ydreos, "Medical Status Report Forms" (Presented at the Absenteeism and Disability Management Seminar, Toronto, May 9-10, 1995) [unpublished].

Form 2b: Report of Absence Form

Sample (b):   For Organizations without Occupational Health Professional Support

---

Return-to-Work Certificate

This must be completed and signed by an employee returning to work after an absence of 3 (three) or more days

Non-Work Related: ☐ *i.e.*, the flu, sports injury	Work Related: ☐ *i.e.*, a possible Workers' Compensation claim

1.(a)   ☐   I have seen a physician and he advised me that I would be medically fit to work on this date: _____

(b)   ☐   To the best of my knowledge I am fit for work.
(check one)

2.   Specify any work restrictions recommended by your physician:

_____

_____

_____

Physician's Name and Address:

_____

_____

Employee Name: (please print) _____	Employee Signature: _____
Employee Number: _____	Date: _____

Return-to-work date:

_____

Form 3a: Modified/Alternate Work Plan Form — Sample (a)

```
COMPANY XYZ
LOGO/ADDRESS
```

Date: _____

To: _____

Department: _____

The following employee is to be placed in a Modified/Alternate Work Plan due to a medical condition:

Name: _____

Employee Number: _____

Title: _____

Company: _____ Department: _____

Work Restriction:
Length of
restriction: _____ days: _____ weeks: _____ months:

MWP begins (date): _____ (time): _____

THE EMPLOYEE WILL BE
RE-EVALUATED ON (DATE): _____ (TIME): _____

Please contact our office if you
have any questions at (telephone): _____

Completed by: _____ MD/OHN

Title: _____

Address (of contract provider): _____

_____

Form 3b: Modified/Alternate Work Plan Form — Sample (b)

| COMPANY XYZ |
| LOGO/ADDRESS |

Modified/Alternate Work Plan:
[To be completed by the Disability Case Manager]

Employee Name:	
Last Day Worked:	Supervisor:
Regular Work Location:	Regular Occupation:
Information Provided by Employee:	

Modified/Alternate Work Requirements:

Permanent: ☐   Starting Date: _____

Temporary: ☐   Starting Date: _____   Expected Ending Date: _____

Modified/Alternate Work Plan Details:

Location:	Supervisor:
Modified/Alternate Work Description:	
Comments/Special Considerations:	
Next Medical Reassessment:	Next Review:

Signed: _____   Date: _____
        (Supervisor)

Signed: _____   Date: _____
        (Modified/Alternate Work
        Supervisor, if applicable)

Signed: _____   Date: _____
        (Employee)

cc: For WCB — Manager, Occupational Health
       All others — Manager, Employee Benefits

Form 4: Restricted Work Form[21]

| COMPANY XYZ |
| LOGO/ADDRESS |

Date: _____

Employee Name: _____

Employee Number: _____

Department: _____ Title: _____

Work Location: _____

Work Restrictions are: ☐ job-related (WC)   ☐ non-occupational
Explain physical limitations: (and reasons for them on the medical copy only)

_____

_____

_____

_____

_____

_____

_____

_____

_____

_____

Expected length of restriction/limitation: _____ days _____ weeks

Restriction is (check one):   ☐ Temporary   ☐ Permanent
Employee will be re-evaluated on: (date) _____

Signature: _____

Examiner: (print name) _____

Telephone No.: _____

Date: _____

---

[21]   Adapted from: OEM Health Information Inc., "Restricted Work Form IB-21" in *OEM Occupational Health and Safety Manual* (Beverly, MA: The OEM Press, 1996).

Form 5: Physician's Statement of Medical Status Form[22]

```
COMPANY XYZ
LOGO/ADDRESS
```

Company   XYZ
Representative: _____   Department: _____
Title: _____   Telephone No.: _____
Address: _____

Instructions to the Attending Physician/Health Care Provider:
Please complete all information requested regarding your patient and return this form within 3 days to the Company Representative (address provided above). Thank you.

Date: _____

Employee Name: _____   Employee Number: _____
Job Title: _____   Department: _____
Date of Injury/Illness: _____   First Day out of Work: _____

Is this absence an occupational/workers' compensation ☐ or non-occupational/
disability ☐ related diagnosis/condition
  (Please explain/list chief complaints, signs, symptoms): _____

_____
Date of first treatment for this condition: _____
Date of most recent treatment/diagnostic examination: _____
What were the findings of the above treatment/examination: _____

_____
What treatment/therapy and medication regimen are you prescribing? Please indicate frequency and expected duration of treatment, *etc.*:

_____
Physician's signature: _____   Date: _____
Physician's name (please print): _____   Telephone No.: _____
Address: _____   Fax No.: _____
Thank you for this information. It is essential to our efforts of safely returning employees back to work.

Company XYZ Disability Case Manager

---
[22] Adapted from: OEM Health Information Inc., in "Physician's Statement of Medical Status, IB-16" *OEM Occupational Health and Safety Manual* (Beverly, MA: The OEM Press, 1996).

Form 6: Return-to-Work Report[23]
(For use by Occupational Health Professional)

COMPANY XYZ
LOGO/ADDRESS

Employee Name: (print last, first, middle)   _____

Employee Number: _____

I hereby authorize my attending physician to release any information or copies thereof acquired in the course of examination or treatment for the injury/illness identified below to my employer or their representative.

Employee Signature: _____   Date: _____

To be completed by personal physician:
Employee diagnosis: _____

_____

Date of first injury/illness: _____

Date of latest visit/treatment: _____

Date last worked: _____

Current medical status:

☐ Recovered (may return to work with no limitations on _____ date).

☐ May return to work with the following limitations:* _____

_____

_____

*These limitations   or until employee is
are in effect until: _____   reevaluated on: _____
                    (date)   (date)

☐ Employee remains totally incapacitated at the
    present time and will be reevaluated on: _____
                                            (date)

Physician's comments: _____

_____

Physician's signature: _____   Date: _____
Physician's name: Telephone
(please print)   _____   No.:   _____
Address: _____   Fax No.:   _____

Note: Both employee and physician must complete form.

_____

[23]   Adapted from: OEM Health Information Inc., "Return-to-Work Notification: Report to Employer, IB-19" in *OEM Occupational Health and Safety Manual* (Beverly, MA: The OEM Press, 1996).

Form 7: Consent Form

COMPANY XYZ
LOGO/ADDRESS

I hereby authorize all physicians, practitioners, hospitals and other institutions by this form or photographic copy thereof to give Company XYZ's representatives, The Occupational Health Services, for inclusion in medical files, any information they may have regarding the status of my health when I was under observation for my disability.

_____   _____
        Employee Signature   Date

Please note that all information received will be kept in STRICT CONFIDENCE and will be used for adjudication, rehabilitation, and return to work purposes.

CHAPTER REFERENCES

Alberta Medical Association (AMA), *An Information Sheet for Patients: Early Return to Work After Illness or Injury* (Edmonton: AMA, 1994), available online at: <http://www.albertadoctors.org/bcm/ama/ama-website.nsf/frmHome? Openfrm>.

Alberta: *Workers' Compensation Act*, R.S.A. 2000, c. W-15, s. 65.

P. Booth, *Employee Absenteeism: Strategies for Promoting an Attendance-Oriented Corporate Culture* (Ottawa: The Conference Board of Canada, 1993).

British Columbia: *Workers' Compensation Act*, R.S.B.C. 1996, c. 492, s. 39(1)(e).

CAN/CSA, *The Model Code for the Protection of Personal Information*, (CAN/CSA - Q830-96) (Ottawa: CSA, 1996).

Canadian Medical Association (CMA), *The Physician's Role in Helping Patients Return to Work After an Illness or Injury* (update 2000), available online at: <http://policybase.cma.ca/dbtw-wpd/POLICYPDF/PD01-09.pdf>.

Case Management Society of America (CMSA), *Standards of Practice for Case Management* (Little Rock, AR: CMSA, 1995).

D. DiBenedetto *et al.*, *OEM Occupational Health and Safety Manual* (Boston: OEM Press, 1996).

L. Gross, "Managing Your Escalating Health and Safety Costs" (Presented to the Petroleum Industry's Annual Safety Seminar, Alberta, May 1993) [unpublished].

A. Legault *et al.*, "How to Cope with Absenteeism, Part IV: Requesting a Medical Opinion" (1996), Focus on Canadian Employment and Equality Rights 126.

OEM Health Information Inc., "Physician's Statement of Medical Status, IB-16" in *OEM Occupational Health and Safety Manual* (Beverly, MA: The OEM Press, 1996).

OEM Health Information Inc., "Restricted Work Form IB-21" in *OEM Occupational Health and Safety Manual* (Beverly, MA: The OEM Press, 1996).

OEM Health Information Inc., "Return-to-Work Notification: Report to Employer, IB-19" in *OEM Occupational Health and Safety Manual* (Beverly, MA: The OEM Press, 1996).

Ontario Medical Association (OMA), *Position Paper: OMA Position in Support of Timely Return to Work Programs and the Role of the Primary Care Physician* (Toronto: OMA, 1994), available online at: <http://www.oma.org/ health/position.htm>.

Ontario: *Workplace Safety and Insurance Act, 1997*, S.O. 1997, c. 16, Sch. A, s. 21(3).

Petro-Canada, "Confidentiality Code of Practice, Reference Number 130" in *Occupational Health Manual* (Calgary: Petro-Canada, 1994).

L. Ydreos, "Medical Status Report Forms" (Presented at the Absenteeism and Disability Management Seminar, Toronto, May 9-10, 1995) [unpublished].

Chapter 11

Prevention of Workplace Illness and Injury

INTRODUCTION

Organizations vary in the degree of coordination that exists between the Disability Management Program and other company programs such as the Employee Assistance Program, Occupational Health & Safety Program, Attendance Management Program, Workplace Wellness Program, Human Resources Programs, and management human resource theories and practices. Some of these programs/services function independently as "silos", while others are integrated to form a comprehensive workplace support system. This chapter supports the latter approach.

ROLE OF EMPLOYEE ASSISTANCE PROGRAMS IN THE PREVENTION OF WORKPLACE ILLNESS AND INJURY

Employee Assistance Program professionals can assist the employees and the organizations they serve, by focusing on attendance and disability management. Occupational, non-occupational, and casual absences and disabilities drain millions of dollars from the Canadian economy, not to mention the toll exacted on the individual organizations, and on employees and their families.

In Chapter 7, the role of the Employee Assistance Programs in disability management is discussed in detail. Chapter 9, "Workplace Attendance Support and Assistance" describes an effective approach to attendance support and required links to the company's Employee Assistance Program. However, an Employee Assistance Program can provide other valuable illness and injury prevention services such as:

- Critical incident stress debriefing following a tragedy within the workplace or community. This reactive approach can mitigate the traumatic effect for employees of experiencing a workplace/community disaster hence avoiding conditions like post-traumatic stress disorder.

- Assistance in identifying and addressing the contributing causes of workplace accidents/injuries. Some contributing accident/injury causes that the Employee Assistance Program may help the organization to identify are employee fatigue, grief, preoccupation with personal problems or workplace discord, dysfunctional workgroups, substance abuse, *etc.* By proactively addressing these recognized accident/injury causes, prevention of workplace accidents/injuries can occur.

- Providing anticipatory guidance on the identification and management of "new" addictions such as gambling addiction, various computer addictions, sexual preoccupations, *etc.* By assisting the workplace to understand these conditions, individuals are better prepared, if need be, to identify and respond appropriately.

- Development and presentation of both workplace and personal change management seminars. Assisting managers and employees with a change process can enable them to successfully cope with the challenges of a future state in their lives.

- Coaching clinics for supervisory staff on how to deal with the troubled employee, on developing people skills, or on gaining an appreciation of the impact that troubled home situations can have on employees and workgroups.

- Counselling management on the effect that various human resource management practices can have on the workplace and employees. This is a preventative measure that can combat employee stress, presenteeism, burnout, and other mental health illness. Management theories and practices have a strong association with the health and well-being of employees as will be discussed later in this chapter, and in Chapter 15, "Disability Management: The Social Capital Theory — Perspective for Managing Disability Claims" and Chapter 16, "Effective Management of Disability Claims with Strong Psychosocial Aspects".

With incidents of workplace violence on the rise, Employee Assistance Programs can play a significant role in assisting workers to constructively address life stressors. As well, they can assist victims of workplace violence to come to grips with what has happened and how to move forward with their recovery process.

ROLE OF OCCUPATIONAL HEALTH & SAFETY IN THE PREVENTION OF WORKPLACE ILLNESS AND INJURY

Workers' compensation costs are significant. As well, substantial other costs are incurred when injury/illness occurs. These costs directly impact an organization's/company's operational costs and hence profits.[1] For example, in 2007 the average workers' compensation cost for a work-related injury in

---

[1]   Workplace Safety & Insurance Board (WSIB), *Business Results Through Health & Safety* (Toronto, ON: WSIB, 2002) at 3, available online at: <http://www.wsib.on.ca/wsib/ wsibsite.nsf/Public/ BusinessResultsHealthSafety>.

Canada was $9,891 per claim.[2] If a company has a 10 per cent profit margin, it requires $98,910 in product sales/services to cover these injury costs.

The message presented in *Business Results Through Health & Safety* is that Occupational Health & Safety Programs have an important role to play in the prevention of workplace illness or injuries. Typically, prevention strategies are achieved through:

- developing Occupational Health & Safety standards;
- identifying and controlling work hazards;
- providing Occupational Health & Safety training for everyone in the workplace, particularly supervisors, managers and employers;
- providing and maintaining personal protective equipment and fit-testing;
- enabling ergonomic accommodations to be made;
- conducting work site walk-through assessments;
- auditing workplace practices;
- responding, reporting and investigating occupational illness/injuries;
- tracking workplace illness/injuries; and
- enabling Occupational Health & Safety to become part of the fabric of the work, as opposed to being seen as an "add-on" program.

An effective Occupational Health & Safety Program can result in "zero tolerance" for occupational injuries or illness. In addition, many elements of an Occupational Health & Safety Program are legislated, either federally or provincially. Hence, they are the minimum performance standard that the organization must meet.

When an Occupational Health & Safety Program operates in conjunction with a Disability Management Program, synergies can be realized. For example, by having a people-oriented work culture, strong Occupational Health & Safety leadership, and by being duly diligent about worker safety, organizations can positively impact their disability claims numbers and costs.[3] From an operational perspective, an existing Joint Health & Safety Committee can address some disability management issues, such as return-to-work practices, modified work opportunities, and workplace hazard risk reduction.

Recently, Occupational Health & Safety Programs have focused on off-the-job safety. This has been in response to the fact that for every workplace illness or injury, 8 to 14 non-occupational illnesses or injuries occur. Some of the off-the-job safety initiatives have included home safety, sport safety, water safety, cycling safety, fire prevention, sun safety, domestic violence, and street safety.

[2]   Association of Workers' Compensation Boards of Canada, *Key Statistical Measures for 2007, Key Statistical Measures (KSMs)* — Data Tables (December 2008), available online at: <http://www.awcbc.org/common/assets/ksms/2007ksms.pdf>.

[3]   R. Williams, *A Survey of Disability Management Approaches in Ontario Workplaces (2005)*, available online at: <http://www.wsib.on.ca/wsib/wsibsite.nsf/Public/ResearchResultsSurveyDisabilityMgnt>.

ROLE OF ATTENDANCE MANAGEMENT PROGRAMS IN THE PREVENTION OF WORKPLACE ILLNESS AND INJURY

Attendance Management Programs have traditionally adopted a "reactive approach" aimed at dealing with employee absenteeism. Although a "tried and true" approach as noted in Chapter 9, "Workplace Attendance Support and Assistance", organizations can more effectively position this program to enhance employee wellness and prevent workplace illness and injury. By providing workplace support and assistance as earlier recommended, organizations empower employees to address their work/life problems. This prevents ruminating on and being distracted by life-issues, hence, employees are better able to remain focused on their job tasks and the hazards of the work environment in which they are operating.

Attendance Support & Assistance Programs can also be expanded to address employee "**presenteeism**" — the phenomenon of employees being at work, but because of wasted time, failure to concentrate, sleep deprivation, distractions, poor health, and/or lack of training, they may not be working at all. Presenteeism is associated with low employee morale and poor management practices.

Recently, presenteeism is gaining management attention — 56 per cent of organizations indicate that they were concerned about presenteeism and its negative effects.[4] As well, presenteeism is costly. It is estimated that the price of presenteeism equates to:

Presenteeism = 1.8 × Organization's Annual Health Care Costs[5]

In comparison, absenteeism costs would be:

Absenteeism = 0.2 × Organization's Annual Health Care Costs[6]

For a company of 1,000 employees that spends $8 million on health care per year, this equates to presenteeism costs of 1.8 × $8 million = $14,400,00; and absenteeism costs of 0.2 × $8 million = $1,600,000.

> Presenteeism can take a very real hit on the bottom line, although it is often unrecognized. After all, the employee is at work. But if he doesn't feel well, he is not going to be as productive and the quality of work will suffer. Meanwhile, he may be spreading illnesses to other employees further adding to the problem. So the indirect costs are high while often not captured.
>
> Brett Gorovsky, CCH Employment Law Analyst[7]

---

[4]   CCH, Survey, *2006 CCH Unscheduled Absence Survey*, "CCH Survey Finds Unscheduled Absenteeism Up in U.S. Workplaces" (2006), available online at: <http://www.cch.com/press/news/2006/20061026h.asp>.

[5]   S. Aldana, *Top Five Strategies to Enhance the ROI of Worksite Wellness Programs*, Wellness Council of America (February 2009), available online at: <http://www.welcoa.org/freeresources/pdf/top_5_strategies.pdf>.

[6]   *Ibid.*

[7]   CCH Inc., *2006 CCH Unscheduled Absence Survey*, "CCH Survey Finds Unscheduled Absenteeism Up in U.S. Workplaces" (2006), available online at: <http://www.cch.com/press/ news/2006/20061026h.asp>.

By using an Attendance Support & Assistance Program in consort with the Disability Management Program as presented in Chapter 9, "Workplace Attendance Support and Assistance", organizations can mitigate these preventable employee health care and lost productivity costs.

ROLE OF WORKPLACE WELLNESS PROGRAMS IN THE PREVENTION OF WORKPLACE ILLNESS AND INJURY[8]

Workplace wellness can be viewed as having two key elements — organizational wellness and personal wellness. **Organizational wellness** involves managing both business functions and employee well-being in a manner that allows the organization to be more resistant to environmental pressures. **Personal wellness** involves managing both psychological and physical issues in response to environmental stress, including the work environment. These two forms of wellness are interdependent. For example, in companies where employee morale is low, the rates of unscheduled absence are 50 per cent higher than in companies with strong employee morale.[9]

INTEGRATION OF WORKPLACE WELLNESS

Some human resources leaders shy away from workplace wellness because of the vagueness of the topic and the anticipated extra costs. However, Canadian organizations tend to have most of the workplace wellness components already in place. For example, as early as 1997, approximately 80 per cent of Canadian companies (500 or more employees) had EAPs available for their employees and families.[10] The current market penetration of EAP services is estimated to be 71 per cent of the mid- to large-sized companies that offer EAP services.[11]

In the United States, as early as 1996, 85 per cent of medium- to large-sized companies surveyed had smoke-free workplaces; 78 per cent put out wellness newsletters; 76 per cent had Health Risk Assessments (HRA) with blood pressure tests and cholesterol testing; 50 per cent hosted health fairs; 48 per cent had employer-sponsored sports; 41 per cent had employer-owned fitness facilities; 39 per cent had financial incentive programs for smoking cessation and weight

---

[8]   Adapted with permission from the Human Resources Association of Calgary. D. Dyck, "Workplace Wellness: What is Your Potential Return on Investment?", *Human Resources Association of Calgary: A Newsletter on Human Resources Management* (November 1998). Adapted with permission from D. Dyck, "Wrapping Up the Wellness Package" (January 1999) Benefits Canada 16.

[9]   CCH Inc., "Unscheduled Absenteeism Rises to Five-Year High" (2004) 592 Human Resources Management Ideas & Trends 145.

[10]   Conference Board of Canada, *Compensation Planning Outlook* (Ottawa: Conference Board of Canada, 1997).

[11]   Buffett & Company Worksite Wellness Ltd., *National Wellness Survey Report 2006* (Whitby, ON: Buffett and Company 2006), available online at: <http://www.buffettandcompany.com/NWS2009/Buffett_Company_NWS2006.pdf>.

control programs; 33 per cent had discounted fitness facilities; and 25 per cent offered Health Risk Assessments surveys to their employees.[12]

As of 2006, 79 per cent of Canadian organizations/companies had one or more wellness initiatives in place,[13] namely:

- Employee Assistance Programs — 71 per cent of organizations/companies;
- flu immunization — 70 per cent;
- employee recognition initiatives — 62 per cent;
- wellness education and newsletters — 54 per cent;
- flexible work program — 45 per cent;
- health awareness/education programs — 41 per cent;
- smoking cessation — 40 per cent;
- nutrition education — 38 per cent;
- stress management programs — 33 per cent;
- blood pressure screening — 31 per cent;
- work/family balance programs — 25 per cent;
- time management education — 24 per cent;
- on-site fitness program — 24 per cent;
- back care program — 21 per cent;
- cholesterol screening — 20 per cent;
- employee health risk assessments — 19 per cent;
- childcare — 11 per cent; and
- eldercare — 9 per cent.[14]

It is ironic that, although 79 per cent of Canadian organizations/companies have many workplace wellness components in place,[15] the various programs such as the Disability Management Program, Employee Assistance Program, Occupational Health & Safety Program, Attendance Support & Assistance Program, and Human Resources Programs and supports tend to be disjointed operating in isolation and focusing solely on their individual program goals. There is no overall scheme in place for a comprehensive support system. The opportunity for collective synergies and for demonstrating both individual and composite return on investment results are missed.

The challenge for organizations/companies is not to find the resources to implement programs, but rather, to integrate the existing components, and to channel those efforts and outcomes to meet business needs.

---

[12]   Hewitt, "Health Promotion Programs on the Increase", Aon Comments (September 2, 1996).
[13]   Buffett & Company Worksite Wellness Ltd., *National Wellness Survey Report 2006* (Whitby, ON: Buffett and Company 2006), available online at: <http://www.buffettandcompany.com/NWS2009/Buffett_Company_NWS2006.pdf>.
[14]   *Ibid.*
[15]   *Ibid.*

An *integrated approach* to tracking, measuring, and addressing the *key determinants* of workforce and organizational health is necessary to achieve and maintain a *healthy organization.*[16]

WORKPLACE WELLNESS PROGRAM: DEVELOPMENT

Prior to the introduction of a Workplace Wellness Program, baseline data should be obtained for the outcome measures that are to be used. Jumping on the "bandwagon" without knowing the current state of the organization's/company's level of performance can lead to inappropriate expenditure of resources and failed desired outcomes. The first step is to conduct a needs assessment (or gap analysis), followed by the development of a strategic plan for the Workplace Wellness Program.[17]

Targets based on health promotion/workplace wellness research[18] can then be set for each program performance measure. Achievements should be assessed regularly to determine whether the process is meeting its established objectives. The Workplace Wellness Program should be aligned with and be part of the existing corporate business strategy. As well, the Workplace Wellness Program should have long-term, mid-range, and short-term goals to justify and sustain its existence. Program evaluation and continuous improvement activities will help the organization to sustain the Workplace Wellness Program.

AN INDUSTRY APPLICATION

The following workplace wellness model (Figure 11.1) was designed by Aon Consulting Inc. and the City of Calgary to graphically display workplace wellness, what it involves, and how it functions.

---

[16] Watson Wyatt Worldwide, *Staying@Work: Effective Presence at Work — 2007 Survey Report — Canada* (2007) at 2, available online at: <http://www.watsonwyatt.com>.

[17] Hewitt, Disability *Absence Index Survey, 2007* (2007) at 2, available online at: <www.hewittassociates.com/lib/assets/na/en-ca/pdf/dais_2007_highlights.pdf>.

[18] The American Institute for Preventative Medicine is a valuable resource for information on the health and economic implications for Workplace Wellness programs. Refer to <http://www.healthylife.com/template.asp?pageID=75>.

Figure 11.1: Workplace Wellness Model

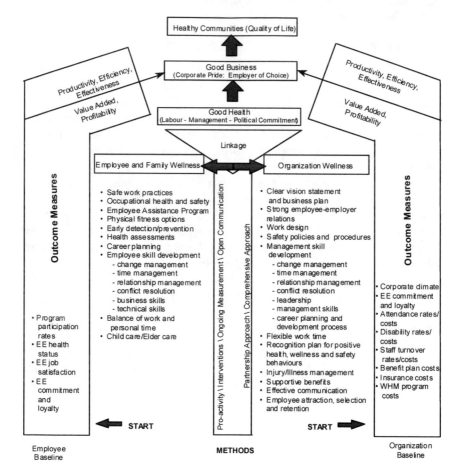

In this model, employee and family wellness and organizational wellness operate side by side and are linked through a partnership approach. Open communication, proactivity, timely interventions and ongoing measurement focus the Workplace Wellness Program on employee and organizational well-being. Outcome measures for both employee and organizational wellness are geared towards productivity, effectiveness, efficiency, "value addedness", and profitability and resource optimization.

WHY CONSIDER IMPLEMENTING A WORKPLACE WELLNESS STRATEGY?

Companies that focus on reactive business health culture approaches (*i.e.*, dealing with attendance and disability rates and costs; accident rates and costs;

Employee Assistance Program utilization rates and costs; and/or staff turnover rates and costs), tend to focus their resources and energies on "failure costs".

However, detective and preventive business health culture approaches can positively impact an organization's business outcomes. By definition, **detection activities** focus on identifying workplace concerns and issues before they become problematic. Organizational climate evaluation, health, and safety audits, employee health risk appraisals, pre-placement screenings, and incident or "near-miss" investigations are some examples of detection activities.

On the other hand, **prevention activities** focus on addressing and eliminating the identified concerns and issues so that they do not lead to health problems. Traditionally, fitness programs, nutrition counselling, smoking cessation, stress management, on and off the job safety training, immunization, and financial planning have been examples of workplace prevention initiatives. A study conducted by Aon Consulting in 1999 has shown that high performance leadership, communication, support of work-personal life balance, meaningful participation in and control over one's work, and development of effective interpersonal skills can also help avoid workplace "failures" (*i.e.*, the failure of an employer to respond to the needs of its employees resulting in an accident).

In essence, organizations should approach health as an investment rather than a cost. Judicious investment in detection and prevention can significantly reduce "failure" costs. Research has shown that companies that focus on detection and prevention activities realize lower "failure" costs.[19]

BUSINESS CASE FOR WORKPLACE WELLNESS

A business case for a Workplace Wellness Program should focus on demonstrating the positive impact that a Workplace Wellness Program can have on the "bottom-line". This means examining a number of outcome measures when establishing what return on investment a Workplace Wellness Program can offer.

These outcome measures include:

- the status of the corporate climate/culture;
- level of employee commitment and loyalty;
- level of employee job satisfaction;
- participation rate in various health promotion/workplace wellness programs;
- employee self-reported stress levels;
- employee productivity levels;
- employee attendance rates and costs;
- disability rates and costs;

---

[19] D. Pratt, "Competitiveness and Corporate Health Promotion: The Role of Management Control" (Graduate paper in Management Accounting, University of Western Ontario Business School, 1992) [unpublished]; Watson Wyatt, *Staying@Work: Effective Presence at Work — 2007 Survey Report — Canada* (2007), available online at: <http://www.watsonwyatt.com>.

- staff turnover and costs;
- benefit costs;
- insurance premiums and costs; and
- costs required to implement a Workplace Wellness Program.

According to Danielle Pratt, President, Healthy Business Inc., Calgary, Alberta, the required themes in a business case for workplace wellness are:

- the impact of health, safety and wellness problems on the company's effectiveness;
- the projected impact of doing nothing to address problems and how doing nothing will affect future costs, organizational resilience, employee morale, and corporate culture;
- the magnitude of the potential improvement, which can be achieved by implementing workplace wellness best practices; and
- the opportunity to achieve a level of excellence in employee health, safety, and wellness. High organizational performance can be achieved.[20]

In his work on workplace health and well-being, Dr. Martin Shain, University of Toronto, reinforces the need to link workplace wellness with corporate business strategy.[21] He has developed a Business Health Culture Index (BHCI) which is based on the relationship between job stressors (demand and pressure versus effort and fatigue) and job satisfiers (recognition and reward versus control).

The BHCI is a summary indicator of the extent to which the *health culture* of an organization supports its *business objectives*. It provides a simple basis for conceptualizing workplace health cultures as "business-positive", "business-neutral", or "business-negative". Business-negative health cultures actively obstruct the achievement of business objectives. Business-positive cultures facilitate the achievement of business objectives, and business-neutral cultures have no impact on business objectives.

The BHCI has the potential to yield benchmarks. Internally it provides a baseline for action plans aimed at abating job stressors and enhancing job satisfiers. For example, a Workplace Wellness Program objective may be to move the organization from a BHCI of 0.96 to one of 1.5, signalling an important shift in the ratio between workplace stress and job satisfaction. Externally, the index can provide a basis for comparisons within industry sectors, such as municipalities, hospitals, school settings, manufacturers, *etc.*

Measurement tools, such as corporate climate surveys, employee commitment (loyalty) surveys, rates of program utilization/participation, job satisfaction surveys, benefit rates, and costs can be used to demonstrate the Workplace Wellness Program's influence on an organization's business objectives.

---

[20] *Ibid.*
[21] M. Shain, "Managing Stress at its Source in the Workplace" (Presented at the Health Work and Wellness Conference '98, Whistler, BC, September 27-30, 1998) [unpublished].

The Workplace Wellness Program business case and plan should undergo the same rigour and requirements of any other business function. To be sustainable, the Workplace Wellness Program must speak in business terms and demonstrate targeted returns on investment.

INDUSTRY FINDINGS

Many companies in Canada and the United States are now reporting their Workplace Wellness Program outcomes. The cost of workplace wellness per employee per year varies depending on whether a comprehensive approach or a single program is presented. As well, costs vary according to the formulae used and variables perceived to be program costs. Based on 13 research studies, the savings realized from Workplace Wellness Programs are much greater than their programming costs, with health cost savings averaging $3.48 per dollar, and absenteeism savings averaging $5.82 per dollar invested in the Workplace Wellness Programs.[22]

For every dollar spent on Workplace Health Promotion Programs, the returns have been cost savings of between $2.30 and $10.10[23] in the areas of decreased absenteeism, fewer sick days, decreased Workers' Compensation Board claim costs, lowered health and insurance costs, and improvements to employee performance and productivity.[24]

As for the benefits noted from Workplace Wellness Programs, the following are the outcomes reported by a variety of organizations/companies:

- Canada Life developed a health promotion program in 1978 and had it independently evaluated over a ten-year period. The program showed a return of $6.85 on each corporate dollar invested. "Reduced employee turnover, greater productivity, and decreased medical claims by participating employees were primarily cited as the benefits contributing to this economic and health success."[25]

---

[22] D. Anderson, *The Health Promotion First Act, Stay Well Health Management* (January 13, 2009), available online at: <http://wellnessintheworkplace.net/workplace-wellness-programs-supporting-scientific-research-and-wellness-statistics/>.

[23] The average return on investment (ROI) is $3.50 in Canada. Source: S. Pridham, "Different Strokes for Different Folks: Three Companies Take Unique Paths to Wellness", Employee Benefit News Canada 16, available online at: <http://ebn.benefitnews.com/news/different-strokes-different-folks-three-companies-560461-1.html>.

[24] Administration, *Workplace Wellness Plan: ROI* (December 21, 2008), available online at: <http://costofcorporatewellness.com/workplace-wellness-plan-roi/>.

[25] R. Kirby, "The ROI of Health Workplaces" (October 20, 1997) Canadian HR Reporter 31.

- DuPont (2002) reported an 8 per cent differential in the reduction of the incidence rates of off-the-job illness between industrial worksites that offered health promotion programs and those that did not.[26]

- Providence Everett Medical Center, Everett, Washington, saved an estimated three million, or a cost-benefit ratio of 1 to 3.8, over nine years through its employee health benefit program called the Wellness Challenge®.[27]

- Xerox Corp (2001) reported a 3.3 per cent differential in the decrease in frequency of WCB claims and a $2,976 differential in the average cost per claim between participants and non-participants in their workplace wellness program.[28]

- One of the longest and best-known case studies is the Johnson & Johnson Health and Wellness Program, which has been operating since the early 1980s. Reporting on data from 1990 to 1999, with more than 18,000 members, the program reported annual savings of more than $8 million, translating to savings of $225 per employee per year since 1995.[29]

- DundeeWealth, Toronto, Ontario launched in 2006 its formal Workplace Wellness Program that embraced the slogan of "Health is Wealth". Focusing on three priorities — nutrition and weight management, physical activity, and life balance — the company was already able to report positive employee participation rates. Going forward, the company is tracking program participation rates, sick leave, absenteeism, and employee engagement rates.[30]

- Enbridge Inc., North York, Ontario, has operated their "Health Wise" program — an integrated Disability Management Program — for the past 20 years. In 2000, a Workplace Wellness Program was introduced. It offered onsite physiotherapy, massage therapy, wellness seminars, nutrition counselling, and a work site fitness facility. In 2006, Enbridge was

---

[26]   Wellness Councils of America (WELCOA), "Corporate Wellness Makes a Bottom-Line Difference, The Cost Benefit of Worksite Wellness", (2009), available online at: <http://www. welcoa.org/worksite_cost_benefit.html>.

[27]   *Ibid.*

[28]   S. Musich, D. Napier, D. Edington, "The Association of Health Risks with Workers' Compensation Costs" (2001) 43(6) *Journal of Occupational and Environmental Medicine* 534-541, available online at: <http:www.hmrc.umich.edu/research/pdf/associationofhealthrisks.pdf>.

[29]   R. Goetzel, R. Ozminkowski, J. Bruno, K. Rutter, F. Isaac, S. Wang, "The Long-Term Impact of Johnson & Johnson's Health & Wellness Program on Employee Health Risks" (2002) 44 Journal of Occupational and Environmental Medicine 417.

[30]   S. Pridham, "Different Strokes for Different Folks: Three Companies Take Unique Paths to Wellness" (March-April 2008) Employee Benefit News Canada 16, available online at: <http://ebn.benefitnews.com/news/different-strokes-different-folks-three-companies-560461-1.html>.

recognized as a Top 100 Employer in Canada. Then in 2007, Enbridge reported long-term disability savings of $466,000 (23 per cent reduction).[31]

- Campbell Company of Canada, Listowel, Ontario, launched a "Winning Within" program in 2003. A highly interactive Workplace Wellness Program approach, the Campbell Company offered its employees an individual health assessment, followed by one-on-one professional counselling aimed at lifestyle changes. Using an integrative approach, Campbell's Workplace Wellness Program is linked with its Disability Management Program and Employee Assistance Program to integrate the wellness themes. The high rate of employee involvement (>50 per cent) and below industry health claims speaks volumes about the program's success.[32]

Some other notable research and industry workplace wellness findings include:

- British employees who feel little or no control at work have a greater risk of heart disease – 50 per cent more than those with executive positions. This study was conducted with 7,372 male and female British civil servants from 1985 to 1993.[33]

- Employees who smoke cost Canadian companies, on average, $3,396 more per year than non-smoking employees. This is due to increased absenteeism, lost productivity and increased health and life insurance premiums.[34]

- In 1996, Dr. Roy Shephard studied the effectiveness of workplace fitness programs. He found that regular participation resulted in reduced body mass by 1-2 per cent with a reduction of body fat of 10-15 per cent. Muscle strength and aerobic capacity increased by up to 20 per cent.[35] Shepherd also reported on the effects of wellness on productivity as follows: "Up to half of the burden of medical costs could be prevented by changes in personal lifestyle. Physical activity in particular has the potential to reduce both acute and chronic demands on the medical care system, with a

---

[31] S. Pridham, "Different Strokes for Different Folks: Three Companies Take Unique Paths to Wellness" (March-April 2008) Employee Benefit News Canada 16, available online at: <http:// ebn.benefitnews.com/news/different-strokes-different-folks-three-companies-560461-1.html>.

[32] *Ibid.*

[33] D. Pratt, "Competitiveness and Corporate Health Promotion: The Role of Management Control" (Graduate Paper in Management Accounting, University of Western Ontario Business School, 1992) [unpublished].

[34] Health Canada, *Smoking Cessation in the Workplace — A Guide to Helping Your Employees Quit Smoking*, "Section V: Tools for Employers and Others Who Promote Health in the Workplace — Estimating the Cost of Smoking in Your Workplace" (2008) at 7, available online at: <http://www.hc-sc.gc.ca/hc-ps/pubs/tobac-tabac/cessation-renoncement/section-5-eng.php>.

[35] R. Shephard, "Worksite Fitness and Exercise Programs: A Review of Methodology and Health Impact" (1996) 10 Am. J. Health Promotion 436.

reduction in employee turnover, an increase in productivity, a reduction in absenteeism, and a decreased risk in industrial injury."

• In 2002, the CDC estimated that U.S. employers could save up to $12 billion annually by providing flu shots to employees. These savings were projected to come from reduced lost-time days and lower health care costs.[36]

• The 1996 Wellness Survey by Buffett Taylor,[37] cited the top ten success markers of a wellness program as depicted in the following graph (Figure 11.2).

Figure 11.2: Effectiveness of a Wellness Program: Top 10 Success Markers by Industry Sector[38]

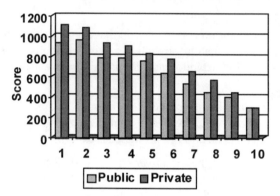

Key: Success Markers

1. Improved employee health
2. Reduced absenteeism
3. Cost to benefit ratio
4. Fewer WCB claims
5. Increased workplace morale
6. Lower employee extended health care costs
7. Fewer employees in higher risk categories
8. Length of time before return on investment
9. Initial start-up costs
10. Lower provincial health care premiums

Ten years later, participant companies in the Buffett & Company 2006 National Wellness Survey reported positive participant feedback, improved employee morale, increased worker participation, and reduced absenteeism as the top four results from their organization's wellness efforts (Figure 11.3). Interestingly, reduced employee absenteeism and improved employee morale remain high in terms of the observed results.

---

[36] D. McReynolds, ed., *Worksite Wellness Programs: A Better Health Plan In Which Everyone Benefits* (Personal Best Publications, Scott Publishing, 2003), available online at: <http://www. trale.com> at 7 (date accessed: August 3, 2007).

[37] Buffett Taylor & Associates Ltd., *The First Comprehensive Canadian Wellness Survey* (Whitby, ON: Buffett Taylor, 1996).

[38] Reprinted with permission from Buffett Taylor & Associates, "Wellness Survey" (1997), available online at: <http://www.buffetttaylor.com>.

Figure 11.3: Buffett & Company, 2006 National Wellness Survey: Respondents' Experiences from Company Wellness Efforts[39]

FIGURE 12 (NATIONAL): Respondents' Experiences from Wellness

- Positive feedback from participants — 84.7%
- Improved employee morale — 52.0%
- Increased participation — 48.0%
- Reduced absenteeism — 29.1%
- Fewer disability claims — 20.2%
- Decreased health risks — 19.4%
- Reduced group and extended health care costs — 11.7%
- Positive return-on-investment — 8.2%
- Reduction in the rate of prescription drug cost escalation — 4.8%

Percentage of Total Respondents

• The Alberta Centre for Active Living (2004) conducted an environmental scan of workplace wellness programs and initiatives. The results were that:

- larger companies are more likely to provide bicycle racks, exercise facilities and showers (all of which may support employees' efforts to be physically active);
- fitness testing and counselling are typically more available in larger companies;
- in most companies, the physical activity program is most likely to fall under the jurisdiction of a combination of departments (*i.e.*, human resources, occupational health, occupational safety, *etc.*);
- availability of group exercise programs did not depend on the size of the company (*i.e.*, a higher percentage of small and medium-size companies in our sample offered group exercise programs); and

---

[39] Reprinted with permission from Buffett & Company Worksite Wellness Ltd. (2006). *National Wellness Survey Report 2006* (Whitby, ON: Buffett & Company, 2006), available online at: <http://www.buffettandcompany.com/NWS2009/Buffett_Company_NWS2006.pdf>.

- up to 60 per cent of the participating organizations conduct some form of evaluation of their wellness programs.[40]

The bottom line is that workplace wellness programs and initiatives positively impact company productivity and profitability. According to the Wellness Councils of America (WELCOA), well companies:

- understand that employees do not get or stay healthy by chance;
- recognize that a healthy workforce means investing hard dollars;
- appreciate the diverse needs of employees; and
- understand that not everything that counts is visible on a balance sheet.[41]

ROLE OF THE HUMAN RESOURCES PROFESSIONAL

The Workplace Wellness Program model presented in this chapter is a futuristic model (refer back to Figure 11.1). It was designed to encourage a partnership approach to employee well-being. Unlike past workplace health promotion models, it is meant to encourage employee responsibility for wellness. The organization's role is to provide a receptive environment and support for positive health and well-being. However, the organizational goal is to achieve good business results through good health. In essence, workplace wellness is more than a service or a benefit it is a management strategy.

Human resources personnel are well positioned to assist management with this business strategy. Human resources personnel can contribute to the Workplace Wellness Program by:

- determining the current status of workplace wellness efforts within a company;
- collecting objective outcome data (*i.e.*, attendance, staff retention, disability, benefit program, and corporate culture data);
- influencing policies and procedures to improve employee and organizational health;
- developing a business case for workplace wellness; and
- evaluating the program outcomes.

Human resources personnel can also actively reinforce the idea that workplace wellness is a management issue — one that has cost drivers and expected outcomes.

---

[40] Alberta Centre for Active Living (2004). *2004 Environmental Scan of Workplace Wellness Programs in Alberta*, available online at: <http://www.centre4activeliving.ca/publications/ reports.html>.

[41] D. McReynolds, ed., *Worksite Wellness Programs: A Better Health Plan In Which Everyone Benefits* (Personal Best Publications, Scott Publishing Inc., 2003), at 15 available online at: <http://www.trale.com>.

CONCLUSION

For a Workplace Wellness Program to be effective it must:

*   have "buy-in" by all stakeholders;
*   be proactive in its approach;
*   meet stakeholder needs;
*   be aligned with the business strategy; and
*   add value to the organization and employees in terms of effectiveness, efficiency, productivity, and profitability (or resource optimization).

Organizations are willing to commit time and resources to workplace wellness, but need assurance that there is a reasonable return on their investment for doing so; that is, there is a reduction in health care costs, increased employee health satisfaction, and increased worker productivity. [42]

How companies implement a Workplace Wellness Program will vary depending on individual culture, business, and needs. Regardless of implementation, workplace wellness has been demonstrated to be cost-effective and to be valued by employees and organizations alike. In short, "good health is good business".

ROLE OF HUMAN RESOURCES PROGRAMS IN THE PREVENTION OF WORKPLACE ILLNESS AND INJURY

Human Resources Programs have a major role to play in the prevention of employee illness/injury. As a staff-support service, human resources professionals/ practitioners provide guidance and counselling services to management and employees. They oversee the selection and management of employee group benefits. They undertake the selection and recruitment of employees. They assist management with employee management and growth and development. Compensation and pension functions, along with succession and business continuity planning are part of the Human Resources Program.

In terms of disability management outcomes, the following human resources practices that have a profound impact on disability rates:

*   the degree of employee involvement and participation in work decisions;
*   the robustness of the organization's/company's conflict resolution and grievance instruments;
*   the degree of workforce stability; and
*   disability management policies that emphasize early supportive assistance measures.

Although in many organizations/companies, Human Resources Programs can look and function in a unique manner, they all can prevent workplace illness and injuries through:

---

[42] Watson Wyatt Worldwide, *Staying@Work: Effective Presence at Work — 2007 Survey Report — Canada* (2007), at 9, available online at: <http://www.watsonwyatt.com>.

- counselling and coaching management on the effects that various human resource management practices can have on the workplace and employees. Preventative measures that can combat employee stress, presenteeism, burnout, and other mental health illness include:

  - encourage management to "walk the talk" — that is, to lead by example;[43]
  - provide clarity on the organization's vision, philosophy and business strategies, and on the associated expectations of managers/employees;
  - promote human resource management theories and practices that align and support the organization's vision, philosophy and business strategies;
  - encourage management to develop and use fair and comprehensive workplace policies and practices;
  - implement employee support systems, such as a Disability Management Program, Employee Assistance Program, Attendance Support & Assistance Program, Occupational Health & Safety Program, Workplace Wellness Program, and Human Resources Programs, that are comprehensive and robust in nature and servicing;
  - offer employee group benefit plans that support employees experiencing mental health illness and disorders;
  - create a work environment that maximizes human performance by:

    - enabling employees to know how to do their jobs;
    - ensuring employees are able to do their jobs;
    - equipping employees to do their jobs;
    - motivating employees to do their jobs; and
    - encouraging constructive workplace interactions.[44]

  - when hiring, ensure that there is a "good person-job fit";
  - encourage management to adopt work practices that counter high-demand/low-control and high-effort/low reward situations for employees;[45]
  - provide appropriate education and training empowering managers/employees to be competent and confident in exercising their specific roles;[46] and

---

[43] I. Taylor, "Managers Play an Important Supporting Role in Workplace Mental Health" (November-December 2008), Employee Benefit News Canada 16, available online at: <http://ebnc.benefitnews.com/ebnc_issues/archives.html>.

[44] T. Roithmayr, The Performance Maximizer®, presented in Chapter 5: "OH&S Leadership and Commitment", in D. Dyck, *Occupational Health & Safety: Theory, Strategy and Industry Practice* (Markham, ON: LexisNexis Canada, 2007) at 274-75.

[45] M. Shain, "Managing Stress at its Source in the Workplace" (Presented at the Health Work and Wellness Conference '98, Whistler, BC, September 27-30, 1998) [unpublished].

[46] I. Taylor, "Managers Play an Important Supporting Role in Workplace Mental Health" (November-December 2008), Employee Benefit News Canada 1, available online at: <http://ebnc.benefitnews.com/ebnc_issues/archives.html>.

- educate the workplace about mental health and illness, and the negative impacts of stigma.[47]

- counselling and coaching supervisors/managers on their roles, responsibilities, and limitations, namely:

  - creating and contributing to a healthy work environment;
  - respecting work-life balance and emotional needs;
  - extending care and concern and a guiding hand to troubled employees;
  - recognizing the signs of mental illness;
  - documenting the employee's observed performance declines;
  - addressing relevant performance issues using a constructive action plan;
  - fairly and consistently applying workplace policies;
  - accommodating employees' special needs and circumstances; and
  - mitigating the negative effects on disability on the workgroup.[48]

Supervisory support and understanding has been associated with positive work attendance and strong employee performance.

In addition to the above tasks, human resources professionals/practitioners have a role to play in the following areas:

Employee Engagement

In 2000, Aon conducted the *Canada@Work*[49] study to investigate the organizational factors and conditions that build strong workforce commitment. This survey provided a unique source of information on employees and the effectiveness of various human resources and organizational practices. A similar study was produced a year earlier in the United States — *America@Work.*[50]

Employees who give their best to an organization and help to meet the business goals are characterized as *committed*. How are they recognized? The survey found that these employees:

---

[47] I. Taylor, *ibid.*; A. Nicoll, "Time for Action: Managing Mental Health in the Workplace", *Fall 2008 Bulletin, Mercer Bulletin* (September 29, 2008), available online at: <http://www.mercer.ca/referencecontent.htm?idContent=1322990>; Global Business and Economic Roundtable on Addictions and Mental Health, *News Release*, "Ground-breaking Survey on Mental Health in the Workforce" (November 19, 2007), available online at: <http://www.gwlcentreformentalhealth.com/english/userfiles/news/pdf/s7_004756.pdf>.

[48] I. Taylor, "Managers Play an Important Supporting Role in Workplace Mental Health" (November-December 2008), Employee Benefit News Canada 16, available online at: <http://ebnc.benefitnews.com/ebnc_issues/archives.html>.

[49] Aon Consulting Inc., *Canada@Work* (Chicago, IL: Aon Group, 2000).

[50] Aon Consulting Inc., America@Work: An Overview of Employee Commitment in America (Chicago, IL: Aon Group, 1999).

- work hard to improve themselves, thereby increasing their value to the employer, and make personal sacrifices to ensure the organization's success;
- recommend their company as being "a good place to work", and their employer's products and services as "valuable"; and
- believe that their workplace is one of the best around, and intend to stay.

What are the drivers of employee commitment? The study found the following:

- employees who believe that management recognizes the importance of their personal and family lives are committed employees;
- most committed employees believe they have benefits that meet their needs and are fairly paid;
- employers of committed employees communicate more effectively about a variety of topics: employee benefits, compensation and change initiatives; and
- employers of committed employees provide training to help employees remain current with the increased technical demands of today's jobs.

- ***Recognition of the Importance of Personal and Family Life***

The Aon Study also noted that stress plays a major role in reduced employee commitment. Stress can be attributed to the difficulty in balancing the conflicting demands of work and personal and family life. An appreciation of the importance of employee personal and family life can result in increased employee productivity and the resulting increased organizational/company profitability.

(a) Family-friendly Policies

Attracting, retaining, and motivating the "best people" is a challenge for most organizations. For this reason programs need to be created that recognize the needs of individuals and diverse family situations. Employers note that flexible work scheduling is one of the most important recruiting tools. Studies indicate that flexible work programs lower employee stress levels.[51] As well, providing support for employees and families can translate into decreased employee absenteeism and tardiness.

Women, who are a significant part of today's workforce, have traditionally been the caregivers in their family. Although men are assuming more childcare responsibilities today, women remain the major caregivers. The pressure of juggling work and family tasks is strongly associated with the

---

[51] Conference Board of Canada, News Release, "Eldercare Taking its Toll on Canadian Workers", (November 10, 1999); HRM Guide, "Flexible Working Reduces Absenteeism" (July 12, 2001), available online at: <http://www.hrmguide.co.uk/flexibility/flexibility_absenteeism.htm>.

stress employees perceive in their lives. In general, work-family stress stems from two sources:

- *role interference* — the roles played by individuals overlap and conflict; and
- *role overload* — the daily work-family tasks are simply too much for one individual to handle.

Role interference and role overload can make life very difficult for the employee and, indirectly, for the employer.

A study done in the early 1990s by the Conference Board of Canada indicated that nearly one third of employees reported experiencing stress or anxiety as a result of balancing work and family life responsibilities. At that time, Statistics Canada estimated that stress-related disorders due to overwork cost Canadian businesses $15 billion per year.[52]

In 1999, a Health Canada study reported that 40 per cent of working Canadians experienced high levels of work-family conflict. For women, this conflict was especially acute.[53] However, work-life programs, flexible work hours, and paid time-off programs had positive effects on reducing "last minute" employee absences.[54]

The annual CCH Unscheduled Absences Survey shows a significant increase in the percentage of employee absenteeism due to worker stress between 1995 (6 per cent) and 2007 (12 per cent). Personal illness and family issues were the most cited reasons for "last minute" employee absences in American organizations/companies.[55] The ten most effective mitigation strategies (Figure 11.3), in order of their effectiveness are:

1. alternative work arrangements (most effective);
2. telecommuting;
3. compressed work week;
4. flu immunization program;
5. leave for school function;
6. emergency child care program;
7. job sharing;
8. Employee Assistance Program support;
9. Wellness Program; and
10. satellite workplaces (least effective).[56]

---

[52] Conference Board of Canada, *Compensation Planning Outlook* (Ottawa: Conference Board of Canada, 1997).

[53] Human Resources Development Canada, Labour Program, "Business Case for Work-Life Balance" (Benefits & Costs) (2002).

[54] *Ibid.*

[55] CCH Inc., "Special Report: 1999 CCH Unscheduled Absences Survey" (1999) 467 Human Resource Management: Ideas and Trends 149.

[56] CCH Inc., *CCH 2007 Unscheduled Absence Survey* (Riverwoods, IL: CCH, 2007), available online at: <http://www.cch.com/absenteeism2007/>.

Figure 11.3: Effectiveness and Use of Work-life Programs, 2007[57]

WORK-LIFE PROGRAM	EFFECTIVENESS RATING*	PERCENTAGE USE
Alternative Work Arrangements	3.6	54%
Telecommuting	3.5	53%
Compressed Work Week	3.3	45%
Flu Shot Programs	3.2	66%
Leave for School Functions	3.2	54%
Emergency Child Care	3.1	32%
Job Sharing	3.0	38%
Employee Assistance Plans	2.9	72%
Wellness Programs	2.9	60%
Satellite Workplaces	2.9	36%
On-site Child Care	2.9	32%
Fitness Facility	2.8	52%
On-site Health Services	2.8	33%
Work-life Seminars	2.6	43%
Career Counseling	2.6	41%
Child Care Referrals	2.6	38%
Holidays/Summer Camp	2.6	29%
Sabbaticals	2.5	35%
Concierge Services	2.4	30%
Elder Care Services	2.4	33%

*1: Not Very Effective to 5: Very Effective

Unfortunately, the effectiveness rating of the mitigation strategy does not determine its frequency of use in the workplace. For example, the following is a comparison of the effectiveness and use of work-life programs, 2007 (Figure 11.3). The most effective programs, like the use of alternative work arrangements, telecommuting, and the compressed workweek, are used less than 55 per cent of the time, while the less effective programs like Employee Assistance Programs, flu immunization programs, and workplace wellness programs are used the most. Obviously, a workplace that affords employees the flexibility to balance their work and personal commitments can significantly reduce employee stress levels, while enhancing business objectives.

---

[57]   *Ibid.*

(b) Options for the Family-responsive Workplace

Making the workplace family-friendly involves much more than implementing a set of programs designed to address one or two issues. Helping workers cope with work and family demands involves a strategic commitment to engage in a comprehensive transformation of the workplace culture.

This reconfiguration of the workplace involves changes in attitude as well as clearly articulated program goals, preferably linked to the organization's strategic plan. Achieving this *is no easy task and the process takes time.* Although research shows that there are positive relationships between work and family programming and the bottom line, such evidence fails to convince leaders who do not believe in this new role for business. This can require a quantum leap in management attitudes and belief systems.

In order to create a family-responsive workplace, management must:

(a) determine employee needs; and
(b) tailor incentives to meet those needs.

Although this sounds elementary, many Canadian employers (over 60 per cent) have not created family-responsive workplaces.

What can an employer do to help employees balance work and family life? In general, offer or promote:

*   flexible work arrangements;
*   flexible work time — job sharing, compressed work week, shorter workweek, shorter workday;
*   greater employee control/autonomy over the workload;
*   childcare assistance — information and referral assistance, onsite daycare, family home care, emergency/sick-child care, daycare subsidy;
*   eldercare assistance;
*   Employee Assistance Program support; and
*   a change in the corporate culture — the attitudes, practices, values and relationships within the organization that impact family-friendly practices. This includes belief in the legitimacy of work-family policies and practices as part of the workplace, available policies and procedures, supervisory understanding of the issues, and flexibility in dealing with situations, to name a few.

There is an incontestable relationship between work and family-related stresses, and workplace productivity, absenteeism and staff turnover. For example, absence rates fell from 8 to 6.5 days per employee when companies introduced flexible annual leave, flexible work hours, and the ability to work from home occasionally.[58] Organizations can realize improvements by making decisions on specific options and methods of implementation that will help employees alleviate some of these pressures.

The onus is on the human resources professionals/practitioners to assist in the selection of suitable employee group benefit plans and approaches that best fit the organization's/company's corporate culture and business strategies.

- ### *Supportive Versus Punitive Attendance Management Programs*

Attendance management programs that are more punitive than supportive in their focus of regular employee attendance tend to fail at meeting the anticipated program outcomes.

Dr. Lawrence Kelly[59] recommends attendance management programs that focus on employee well-being and support their regular work attendance. This means having employee assistance, ergonomic, return-to-work, eldercare, childcare, and flex-time programs in place to assist the employee in balancing work and home life issues and responsibilities.

Human resources professionals/practitioners can play an important role in developing an attendance management approach that best fits the organization's/company's corporate culture and business strategies (refer to Chapter 9, "Workplace Attendance Support & Assistance" for more details).

- ### *Reinforce/Enhance Employee Morale*

Employee morale is defined as the employee group's general level of confidence or optimism about the workplace and management theories and practices, especially as it affects discipline and willingness. Employee morale is subject to environment, work, economic factors, and corporate culture.

There are many business situations where employee morale warrants a "boost" such as:

- unsafe work environment;
- numerous employee-supervision issues such as conflict, poor relationships, *etc.*;
- promotion of unpopular personnel;
- demanding, rigid supervision that is too controlling;
- unsupportive, weak supervision that offers insufficient input or guidance;
- overwork;
- feeling unappreciated or underappreciated for the work done;
- problems within a department or businesses challenges;
- layoffs;

---

[58] HRM Guide, "Flexible Working Reduces Absenteeism" (July 12, 2001), available online at: <http://www.hrmguide.co.uk/flexibility/flexibility_absenteeism.htm>.

[59] L. Kelly, "Attendance Management" (Presented at the Alberta Occupational Health Nurses 21st Annual Conference, Calgary, May 24-26, 1998) [unpublished].

- merger or acquisition situations;
- if a company is going through an outside government investigation or a lawsuit; and
- anything that can draw attention to the organization/company.

When employee morale is high, the management of employees is rewarding. Employees perform better when they are satisfied with their work and their work environment. They miss less work time and perform more effectively when they are at work.[60]

Human resources professionals/practitioners can prevent workplace presenteeism, casual sickness, and short- and long-term disabilities by encouraging workplace interventions that enhance employee morale. Some examples are:

- improve the workplace environment — occupational health & safety enhancements, ergonomic changes, housekeeping, *etc.*;
- provide clarity about business strategy and stakeholder roles and responsibilities;
- use management practices that recognize and praise desired employee's work performance;
- encourage the right mix of job benefits and job satisfactions, such as offering employees:

  - educational programs;
  - time to do charitable, volunteer work for outside organizations;
  - an opportunity to do/learn something different within the company — cross-transferrable learning and skills experience; and
  - expand their job definition or scope; and

- be honest about the organization's/company's business/financial standing.

- *Address Employee Presenteeism*

Employee presenteeism is a concern for many organizations/companies. As already noted, it is characterized by employees being at work, but because of wasted time, failure to concentrate, sleep deprivation, distractions, poor health, and/or lack of training, they may not be working at all. Employee presenteeism costs American employers dearly — approximately 1.8 times their health care costs per year. That is nine times more than their employee absence costs.

How can human resources professionals/practitioners address and prevent workplace employee presenteeism? Some interventions are:

---

[60] Watson Wyatt Worldwide, *Staying@Work: Effective Presence at Work — 2007 Survey Report — Canada* (2007), available online at: <http://www.watsonwyatt.com>.

- educate the workforce on the detrimental effects of employee presenteeism for employees and the organization/company;
- promote open communication between employees and management;
- seek employee perception feedback on "what will work well and what is not working";
- address any identified occupational health & safety issues;
- confront employee education and training issues;
- promote **transformational leadership** — inspired leadership that influences the beliefs, values, and goals of followers so that they can perform in an extraordinary manner;
- assist management to confront employee substandard performance, providing support and remediation. This intervention could emulate the response to the Chapter 3, "The Supportive Infrastructure for an Integrated Disability Management Program", Figure 3.5 "Employee and Family Assistance Program" flow chart; and
- refer identified health issues.

By addressing employee presenteeism, human resources professionals/ practitioners can prevent the related human, business, and financial costs.

MANAGEMENT HUMAN RESOURCE THEORIES AND PRACTICES: IMPACT ON WORKPLACE ILLNESS/INJURY

Until recently, organizations have focused on program issues when trying to understand attendance and disability management program outcomes. However, research indicates that management practices and human resource management theories can have a significant impact on Disability Management Program outcomes. This section will deal with the relevance of management practices and human resource management theories in attendance and disability management.

STRESS RISK MANAGEMENT IN THE WORKPLACE: RESEARCH BY DR. MARTIN SHAIN, UNIVERSITY OF TORONTO[61]

Job-related stress results from human interactions in the workplace. It needs to be managed like production and operational activity. It is up to management to address job stress at the source instead of dealing solely with the symptoms of job stress through the Employee Assistance Program, Disability Management Program, and Occupational Health & Safety Program. This can best be achieved by balancing the organizational and programmatic approaches to stress risk management.

The key ingredients for good employee mental health in the workplace are:

- mutual respect and appreciation;
- employees feeling heard and appreciated;

---

[61] M. Shain, "Managing Stress at its Source in the Workplace" (Presented at the Health Work and Wellness Conference '98, Whistler, September 27-30, 1998) [unpublished].

- open communication;
- freedom from feelings of hostility and anger; and
- a sense of self-worth and confidence.[62]

The work factors that threaten employee mental health and physical safety and contribute to workplace stress are:

- work overload and time pressures;
- lack of influence over daily work;
- too many changes within the job;
- lack of training and/or job preparation;
- too little or too much responsibility;
- discrimination;
- harassment;
- poor communication;
- lack of quality supervision/management; and
- neglect of legal and safety obligations.[63]

Excess workplace stress can erode employee self-efficacy and social supports — both key elements to employee well-being. In their book *Healthy Work: Stress, Productivity and the Reconstruction of Working Life,*[64] Robert Karasek and Töres Theorell identified the combination of high pressure (too much work in too short a period of time) and lack of influence over day-to-day work as a key contributor to cardiovascular disease. This "deadly duo" also threatens people's health by making it harder for them to take care of themselves. Getting too little exercise, smoking and drinking too much, poor nutrition, insomnia or hypersomnia and sleeping poorly, and feeling generally out of control and miserable are a few of the signs that stress is becoming disruptive.

A 24-year study of workers found that workers in low-control jobs are 43 per cent more prone to premature death; likewise those in jobs lacking meaningful content tend to take greater risks. This study is consistent with the Whitehall studies of British civil servants. Workers with less decision-making latitude died sooner from heart disease and other similar ailments.[65]

Overwhelming pressure and lack of influence do not occur by chance. They result directly from how work is organized (*i.e.*, the allocation of work and relationship between employees) and how it is designed (the structure and content of work). The organization and design of work are dictated by both the job's technological requirements and human decisions. These two factors determine how employees relate to one another and to their jobs; they also contribute to the increase or decrease of stress levels and have an important impact on mental and physical health (Figure 11.5). When stress from other sources — especially the home — is thrown into the equation, health is even more likely to be adversely affected.

---

[62] *Ibid.*

[63] *Ibid.*

[64] R. Karasek & T. Theorell, Healthy Work: Stress, Productivity, and the Reconstruction of Working Life (Toronto: Harper Collins, 1992).

[65] Editor, "Low-Control Jobs are Hazardous to Health" (July/August 2002) O.H.S. Canada 23.

Figure 11.5: Organization and Design of Work[66]

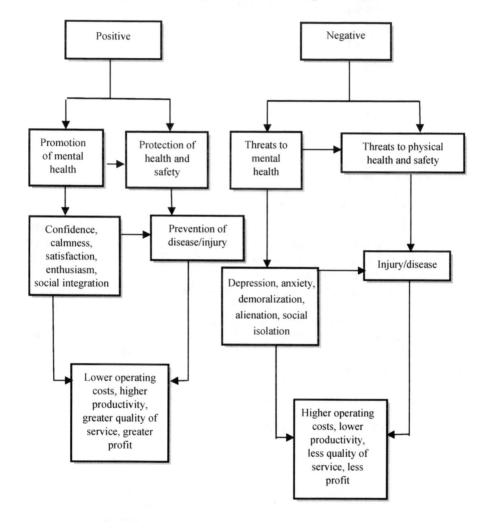

It is not simply a matter of benefiting the "weak" by increasing their resiliency to stress. It is an issue of work conditions that can be modified to manage the risks of job-related stress.

In April 1998, the Families and Work Institute released a study that supports Dr. Shain's work.[67] It found that productivity is far more likely to be hurt by job-

---

[66] Adapted from M. Shain, "A New Take on Stress: Strategies that Work" (November 1997) Health Policy Forum 12.

[67] M. Jackson, "Worker Squeeze: Employee Stress Cuts Productivity, Study Declares", *Calgary Herald* (April 15, 1998) A5.

related stress than by family problems. Until recently, organizations tended to focus on helping employees to address family problems to improve productivity. The Families and Work Institute study revealed that pay and benefits are far less important to workers than the quality of work and supportiveness of the organization.

A study by MacMillian-Bloedel, British Columbia[68] showed that job stress due to high employee effort and low reward, coupled with home stress can lead to anger and a sense of unfairness. This anger can manifest in two ways: overtly in the form of conflict (*e.g.*, workplace/home violence, road rage, sabotage); or covertly in the form of substance abuse. Anger caused by the discrepancy between effort and compensation can cause workplace injuries. Workplace injuries will occur if the employee perceives that he or she is unable to control or avoid hazards. Overt and covert anger due to work conditions end up increasing employee absenteeism and disability.

An organization can have a positive influence on the workforce and workplace outcomes by promoting good mental health and protecting employees from injury and illness. This is described as an "upstream" approach — dealing with the root causes instead of the symptoms of the problem.

Dr. Shain notes that management can have a positive influence on the health and well-being of employees as well as the Occupational Health and Safety Program outcomes.[69] Dr. Shain calls the influence of management on well-being the Zone of Management Discretion, which is not paternalistic towards employees, but rather focuses on prevention (Figure 11.6).

Dr. Shain also supports management recognition and control of threats to employee well-being such as high energy and effort output, high job demands, low recognition for work done, and little control over the job. The last two conditions are easily changed. Employees should actively help the organization lower risks and increase mental health benefits. Being part of the problem helps people to determine workable solutions and to own the remediation when introduced.

---

[68] M. Shain, "Stress, Satisfaction and Health at Work: Tuning for Performance (Presented at the Health & Wellness Conference '99, Vancouver, October 24-27, 1999) [unpublished].

[69] *Ibid.*

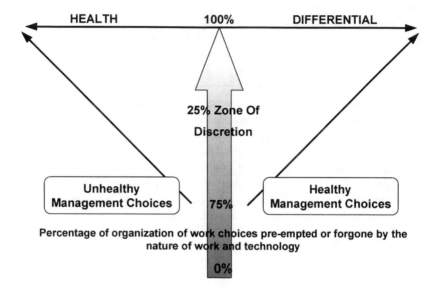

Figure 11.6: The Health Differential[70]
Technological Determinants Versus Management
as Influences on Employee Health

Dr. Shain promotes management prevention of the harmful consequences of stress. He presented a Best Practice model at the 1998 Work, Health and Wellness Conference (Figure 11.7).

---

[70] Adapted from M. Shain, "A New Take on Stress: Strategies that Work" (November 1997) Health Policy Forum 12.

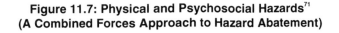

**Figure 11.7: Physical and Psychosocial Hazards[71]
(A Combined Forces Approach to Hazard Abatement)**

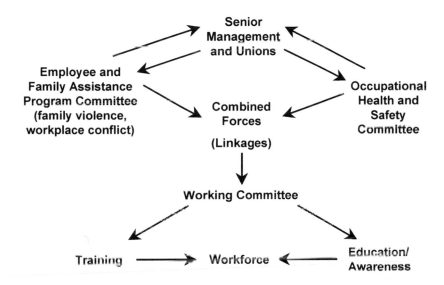

Dr. Martin Shain's early work has culminated into a recent endeavour produced by the Consortium for Organizational Mental Healthcare (COMH).[72] Guarding Minds @ Work — an approach that provides an evidence-based process that employers can easily and quickly implement to protect psychological safety and promote psychological health in their workplace.

According to the Consortium for Organizational Mental Healthcare (COMH):

> Guarding Minds @ Work is a response to current and emerging legal requirements in Canada for the protection of employee mental health and the promotion of civility and respect at work. Legal standards increasingly require employers to develop comprehensive strategies for ensuring a psychologically safe workplace. Prudent employers need to develop policies and programs that meet these new legal standards.[73]

---

[71] *Ibid.*

[72] The **Consortium for Organizational Mental Healthcare (COMH)** is a collective of mental health researchers, consultants, and practitioners who are experienced in working with a range of public and private sector organizations. Its goal is to further the creation and translation of mental health knowledge and practice into real-world settings. To achieve this objective, the Consortium forms collaborative relationships with committed organizations, leaders, and experts to achieve specific outcomes. For more information refer to the Consortium's website at: <http://www.comh.ca>.

[73] Guarding Minds @ Work, available online at: <http://www.guardingmindsatwork.ca/Gmaw What.aspx>.

Most human resources managers are unaware of the magnitude of stress risks and hazards in the workplace. By identifying stress risks, they can then have a positive impact on reducing employee absenteeism and disability. To improve employee health, managers must:

- encourage two-way communication with employees;
- articulate and communicate a clear vision for the future;
- train employees in new competencies and capabilities for success;
- articulate the desired organizational culture;
- re-engineer work processes to meet current demands;
- encourage employees to challenge the status quo;
- develop change management competencies of leaders; and
- educate managers/supervisors to be more sensitive to employee concerns.

POSITIONING OF THE DISABILITY MANAGEMENT PROGRAM

Integration of the Disability Management Program with the Employee Assistance, Occupational Health & Safety, Attendance Support & Assistance, Workplace Wellness, Human Resources, and management human resource theories and practices is vital to achieving a comprehensive approach to individual wellness and organizational wellness. To begin with, organizations/ companies need to establish their Disability Management Program. The steps required for developing a Disability Management Program include:

1. *Determine the current state* — define the need for a disability management program by collecting information on the current disability rates and costs, illness/injury management practices, outcome data, stakeholders involved, *etc.*

2. *Determine the desired state* — What does the organization/company want its Disability Management Program to look like and to achieve?

3. *Define the gaps between the two states* — How great and how many gaps exist between the two states? What is it going to take to eliminate or reduce those gaps? This approach is often termed a **gap analysis** or a **needs assessment**.

4. *Develop a strategic plan* — Working from the identified gaps, determine which ones are feasible to address, and how. From there, create an action plan, as well as the desired deliverables. The Disability Management Program should have set goals, objectives, and outcome targets. Policies and procedures along with practice standards have to be adopted. A supportive infrastructure is required.[74] Stakeholder roles and responsibilities

---

[74] Refer to Chapter 3, "The Supportive Infrastructure for an Integrated Disability Management Program".

must be established[75] and communicated. A communication strategy and program marketing[76] is needed. Plans for program evaluation are required.

5. *Implement the Disability Management Program* — Implementation includes the "doing parts",[77] but also the monitoring of the Disability Management Program processes and approaches. The aim is to address the identified process issues as early as possible.

6. *Program evaluation* — At set points in time, the Disability Management Program must be evaluated against the stated Disability Management Program goals, objectives, and targets.[78] Successes and failures need to be recognized and serve as a "learning". Successes should be celebrated and built upon; failures should be corrected.

7. *Continuous Improvement* — Disability Management Programs are developed to address an identified need. Once that need is no longer paramount, other needs surface. The Disability Management Program must continuously evolve to be viable and sustained.

When developing a Disability Management Program, all the relevant stakeholders should be involved. Having everyone participating enhances the chance that the Disability Management Program will be designed to meet the needs of each stakeholder group. Being "part of the problem-solving" helps the solution to be acceptable.

Once the Disability Management Program is functional, the next step is to seek opportunities for integration. There are two levels of integration:

1. **Level I Integration:** This involves the integration of the disability management of all types of medical disabilities — occupational, non-occupational disability management, as well as the short- and long-term disabilities. There are many proponents for this approach because it:

    • minimizes the administration staffing needs, overhead, and costs;
    • results in the collection of disability claim and case management data on all types of disabilities;
    • provides data with which to identify employee injury/illness/absence patterns, major causes for lost time, durations of medical absences, and the overall costs of medical absences;
    • leads to seamless links between the various disability benefit plans;
    • provides the ability to track and quantify the true costs of employee medical absences and disabilities; and

---

[75] Refer to Chapter 4, "The Disability Management Program: Stakeholder Roles".
[76] Refer to Chapter 11, "Marketing Disability Management Programs".
[77] Refer to Chapter 5, "An Integrated Disability Management Program: The Managed Rehabilitative Care Program".
[78] Refer to Chapter 6, "Integrated Disability Management Program: Outcome Measurements".

- serves as evidence of corporate due diligence in the management of employee disabilities of all types and the legal requirement for workplace accommodation.

Excitingly, more companies are integrating certain elements of their disability management programs. For example, in 2002, 62 per cent of American employers reported using a consistent approach to managing occupational and non-occupational return-to-work programs. This was a 32 per cent increase over 2001. Fifty-one per cent had integrated their short-term disability and long-term disability coverage, an increase of 39 per cent from 2001.[79]

In Canada, many organizations like Red Deer College,[80] have instituted a Disability Management Program that uses a coordinated approach to managing employee disabilities regardless of cause — casual illness, short-term disability, Workers' Compensation, or long-term disability.

As companies recognize the financial and administrative benefits of integrated services, the expectation is that they will opt for this approach.

2. **Level II Integration:** This involves the integration of the Disability Management Program with the organization's Employee Assistance Program, Occupational Health & Safety Program, Attendance Support & Assistance Program, Workplace Wellness Program, and Human Resources Programs.

   In most companies, these programs/services tend to function independently, and can be a mix of internally- and externally-resourced and operated programs/services. The result is a "silo" effect, with each program/service functioning in isolation. The opportunities to provide integrated services that can offer comprehensive programming and services, and to benefit from the activities and learning of each discipline and service, are lost. As well, consolidation and analysis of the data is not possible. That means the organization/company is unable to truly understand what is going on with its employees, or with the organization's overall health.

   A few Canadian organizations have implemented integrated services. For example, The University of Calgary (1998) has combined the Staff Assistance Program (Employee Assistance Program), Managed Rehabilitation Program (Occupational Health Centre [OHC]) dealing with attendance and disability

---

[79] Marsh Risk Consulting, *Workforce Risk: Fourth Annual Marsh Mercer Survey on Employers' Time-Off & Disability Programs* (2003), available online at: <http://www.hr.com/SITEFORUM?&t=/Default/gateway&i=1116423256281&application=story&active=no&ParentID=1119278006229&StoryID=1119656728609&xref=http%3A//search.yahoo.com/search%3Fp%3DWorkforce+Risk%253A+Fourth+Annual+Marsh+Mercer+Survey+on+Employers%25E2%2580%2599+Time-Off+%2526+Disability+Programs%26ei%3DUTF-8%26fr%3Dmoz2>.

[80] Red Deer College, *Disability Management Process for Red Deer College* (2009), available online at: <http://www.rdc.ab.ca/current_students/getting_started/health_safety_wellness/disability_management.html>.

management), and human resources support in its approach to workplace wellness.[81] This service is integrated at a number of levels:

- *Organizational Commitment* — support of key players (senior executive, leaders, unions, staff) and integration with policies and procedures.
- *Team Approach* — appropriate sharing of information and cross referral of cases between OHC, Staff Assistance Program, human resources, and the health care community.
- *Case Management* — management of all cases associated with potential lost productivity (incidental absence, long-term disability, Workers' Compensation Board, and short-term disability).

The result has been in considerable savings for the University. In 1997, 3,785 days were saved with a $400,000 productivity recovery (cost avoidance). In 1998, 4,563 days were saved with a productivity recovery of $477,362. The return on investment (ROI) in the first year was roughly 1:1. However, for years two and three of this program, the ROI has been 2:1 — that is, for every dollar spent on the program $2 have been saved.[82]

Staff responded positively to this approach, rating their level of satisfaction with the service as good-excellent (96.9 per cent). As well, 100 per cent indicated they would use the service again and would make referrals to peers, and 93.4 per cent said that the presenting problem was improved.[83]

A second example is Petro-Canada. They have used an Occupational Health Services model that integrates occupational health, disability management, occupational safety, industrial hygiene, Employee Assistance Program, Workers' Compensation claims management, and human resources practices for a number of years. The outcome is a comprehensive, integrated Disability Management Program that has low absenteeism and disability management costs.

Level II Integration offers organizations a number of advantages, namely:

- better coordination of existing program, policies, and benefits;
- the ability to understand the issues associated with employee health, safety, and well-being;
- the ability to understand the issues associated with organizational health, productivity, and profitability;
- the ability to balance employee health needs with business operational needs;

---

[81] B. Daigle & G. Schick, "Early Intervention, Integration and Successful Resolution of Employee Health Issues" (Presented at the Health Work and Wellness Conference '98, Whistler, September 27-30, 1998) [unpublished].

[82] *Ibid.*

[83] *Ibid.*

- a comprehensive approach to employee health and productivity;
- programs designed to promote workplace wellness by focusing on the detection and prevention of situations/conditions that can lead to system failures;
- ability to consolidate data from all the various programs;
- benchmark results against other data sources;
- the ability to streamline and amalgamate various program supports such as the data management system, communication strategy, program marketing, stakeholder education, performance measurement, program evaluation, and continuous improvement action;
- a better return on investment for the various programs; and
- a healthy workforce and organization.

There is an appetite for Level II Integration given that respondents to the 2007 Staying@Work survey indicated that organizational health and productivity effectiveness was greatly increased through program integration.[84] Employers who have Integrated Disability Management Programs experience an average reduction of 19-25 per cent in their total disability costs.[85] The Hewitt 2006 Absence Data Survey supports the concept of program integration,[86] as does Liberty Mutual which purports that an integrated disability management program could cut company employee group benefit costs by 15 per cent to 35 per cent depending on which employee group benefits are offered.[87] It is important to note that these reports define integration less broadly than the total integration being proposed by this author. Their focus is more on the integration of the Disability Management Program with employee group benefit plans. However, it is a "start" in the right direction.

INTEGRATED DISABILITY MANAGEMENT PROGRAMS: ADMINISTRATION

Typically, the Integrated Disability Management Program is operated independently from other company-funded programs. This phenomenon tends not to vary by industry sector, but rather by the philosophies and

[84] Watson Wyatt Worldwide, *Staying@Work: Effective Presence at Work — 2007 Survey Report — Canada* (2007), at 9, available online at: <http://www.watsonwyatt.com>.

[85] Watson Wyatt Worldwide, News Release, "Employers that Measure Results from Integrated Disability Programs Report Big Savings" (October 15, 1998), available online at: <http://www.watsonwyatt.com/news/press.asp?ID=6900>.

[86] Hewitt, *Disability Absence Index Survey, 2007* (2007), available online at: <http://www.hewitt associates.com/lib/assets/na/en-ca/pdf/dais_2007_highlights.pdf>.

[87] N. Vimadalal & J. Wozniak, "Best Practices to Help Employers Capture the Benefits of Integrated Disability Management", Employee Benefits News (March 1, 2008), available online at: <http://ebn.benefitnews.com/asset/article/548491/best-practices-help-employers-capture-benefits.html?pg=>.

preferred practices of the organization/company and involved service providers.

More progressive organizations/companies integrate their Human Resources Programs, Attendance Support & Assistance Program, Employee Assistance Program, Workplace Wellness Program, and Disability Management Program. Using an employee absenteeism problem as an example, the Human Resources professional/practitioner refers the employee to the Employee Assistance Program. The Employee Assistance Program assesses the attendance problem and either counsels the employee, or refers the employee for appropriate assistance. If a health issue exists, then the Employee Assistance Program counsellor refers the employee to the organization's/company's Disability Management Program for additional help. This arrangement also works if the initial point of contact comes through either the Disability Management Program or Employee Assistance Program.

However, the following issues tend to exist that can negatively impact an integrated approach:

1. Not all Disability Case Managers are familiar or comfortable with attendance management practices, nor with their potential role in the corrective counselling process. However, Disability Case Managers are well positioned to support the employee and supervisors with health-related issues if they are part of the reason for the employee's absence.

2. Not all Employee Assistance Program, disability management, and human resources personnel understand how to address an employee's attendance problem. Many service providers need coaching on this practice.

3. Many organizations fail to have systems that facilitate the Human Resources-Disability Management Program-Employee Assistance Program linkage. To function properly, a workable structure, process and method of outcome measurement is needed. This translates to a system in which there is clarity of roles and processes; availability of consents for information exchange; identified performance measures and targeted outcomes; and follow-up mechanisms.

There is less of a difference in program structure by nature of the industry sector than there is by level of awareness of an organization's attendance, employee presenteeism, and disability rates and costs. Organizations that know the cost of employee absence, presenteeism, and disability tend to be far more interested in using an integrated approach to managing employee productivity in terms of work behaviour, absenteeism, and disability rates.

INTEGRATED DISABILITY MANAGEMENT PROGRAM: SUPPORTIVE INFRASTRUCTURE

A supportive infrastructure is the system and environment within which an Integrated Disability Management Program operates. It encompasses the corporate culture, attendance and disability-related policies and procedures, employee group benefit plans, and linkages between the Integrated Disability Management Program and other organizational resources.

CORPORATE CULTURE

The corporate culture consists of learned values, assumptions, and behaviours that convey a sense of identity for employees and management. It acts to encourage employee commitment, organizational stability, and desired behaviours.

Depending on the nature of the corporate culture, employees and management may be receptive to:

- helping each other;
- looking for innovative ways to accommodate recovering employees back into the workplace;
- taking risks on certain workplace rehabilitation approaches; and/or
- implementing benefit plans that encourage a return to employability for the ill/injured employee.

As well, the corporate culture dictates what type of Disability Management Program model can be successfully adopted. For instance, a paternalistic culture tends to adopt a model that is more organizational-operated and directed. Here, the onus for the person's successful return-to-work is assumed by the organization. This is typical of the more traditional models of attendance and disability management. On the other hand, a democratic corporate culture tends to encourage employee responsibility for absence and successful return to work. In this model, the organization works with the employee to affect a successful rehabilitation plan leaving the employee ultimately in control of his or her situation. This is exemplified by the direct case management model for attendance and disability management.

In a more subtle fashion, the corporate culture affects **occupational bonding**. When an organization has a corporate culture that promotes pride in belonging to the organization and that adheres to a strong work ethic, employees are more likely to see personal value in belonging to the social group and in working for the organization. They are less likely to be absent, except for valid reasons, and more likely to return to work as soon as possible. In this instance, the occupational bond is difficult to break.

However, the reverse can also be true. When employees do not experience corporate pride, a sense of belonging, or a feeling of adding value to the organization, the occupational bond is easy to break and remaining off work on disability is more likely.

To attain a successful Attendance Support & Assistance Program and Disability Management Program, the corporate culture should value the employee and convey the message that all employees are valuable and that absence from the workplace is of great concern. That is, the culture should be people-oriented in which trust between the employer and employees exists. It should also value having a safe workplace and strong safety performance (Occupational Health & Safety leadership), as well as adherence to the applicable Occupational Health & Safety legislation (Safety due diligence). All these conditions are associated with fewer disability claims.[88]

WORKPLACE ILLNESS/INJURY PREVENTION STRATEGY

In 2007, Watson Wyatt undertook the *Staying@Work Survey* in Canada and the United States. The results speak to how organizations can attain a healthy status. The secret to a healthly organization is attaining a balance between the organization's health practices and the workforce's health practices (Figure 11.8).

Figure 11.8: Healthy Organization[89]

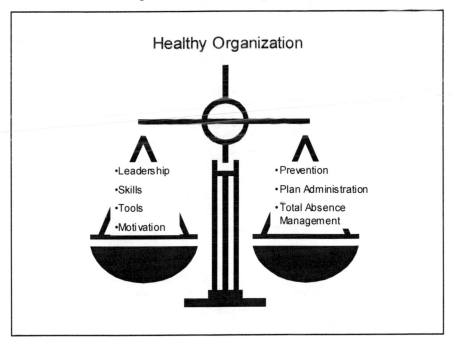

---

[88]   R. Williams *et al.*, *A Survey of Disability Management Approaches in Ontario Workplaces*, (2005), McMaster University and WSIB Ontario, at 2, available online at: <http://www.wsib.on.ca/wsib/wsibsite.nsf/Public/ResearchResultsSurveyDisabilityMgnt>.

[89]   A **healthy organization** achieves a balance between the organization's health practices and the workforce's health practices.

The organizational health practices include:[90]

- *Leadership* — Providing strategic communication on the organization's/ company's business goals and plans, as well as role clarity to the various stakeholders. Succinctly said, what is to be done, how, and by whom?

- *Skills* — Addressing the requisite employee capabilities, learning needs, and application of knowledge to maximize employee performance and productivity.

- *Tools* — Providing the needed tools, data systems, information, workload, and work facilitation.

- *Employee motivation* — Inspiring employees through monetary/non-monetary rewards, performance management, job opportunities, corporate culture, and management to maximize employee performance and productivity.

These recommended elements of work health and productivity mirror the human performance elements of the Roithmayr Performance Maximizer® described in Chapter 12, "Toxic Work Environments: Impact on Employee Illness/Injury". It advocates that the work environment should:

- enable employees to know how to do their jobs;
- ensure employees are able to do their jobs;
- equip employees to do their jobs;
- motivate employees to do their jobs;[91] and
- include workplace interactions — the "glue that brings it all together", namely the trust, honesty, respect, openness, and involvement of all stakeholders.[92]

The workforce's health practices proposed by Watson-Wyatt, 2008, include:[93]

- *Prevention* — Through the use of Occupational Health & Safety Programs, Health Risk Appraisals, health management, disease management, control of employee presenteeism, conflict management, and workplace harassment and violence prevention the workforce can prevent workplace illness and injury;

---

[90] Watson Wyatt Worldwide, *Staying@Work: Effective Presence at Work*, available online at: <http://www.watsonwyatt.com>.

[91] T. Roithmayr, "The Performance Maximizer®", presented in Chapter 5: "OH&S Leadership and Commitment", in D. Dyck, *Occupational Health & Safety: Theory, Strategy and Industry Practice* (Markham, ON: LexisNexis Canada, 2007) at 274-75.

[92] *Ibid.*

[93] Watson Wyatt Worldwide, *Staying@Work: Effective Presence at Work*, available online at: <http://www.watsonwyatt.com>.

- *Plan Administration* — To effectively operate, business practices such as vendor management, plan design, and financial management are required to be in place; and

- *Total Absence Management* — To address the human aspects of work, attendance management, integrated disability management, program administration, claim management, case management, and return-to-work measures and management are great assets to an organization/company.

From their 2007 Survey, Watson-Wyatt determined that organizations with effective health and productivity programs experience:[94]

- greater financial returns and productivity improvements. The results observed include 20 per cent more revenue per employee, 16.1 per cent higher market value, and 57 per cent higher shareholder returns;
- 5 per cent lower casual absence rates and costs;
- 4 per cent lower short-term disability rates and costs;
- 4.5 per cent lower long-term disability rates and costs;
- 3.5 per cent lower health care costs (American organizations);
- lower payroll costs for Workers' Compensation Board claims;
- lower presenteeism rates and costs;
- integrated health management programs;
- healthier workforce; and
- a healthier organization and bottom line.

Extrapolating all the above information, as well as the materials presented in this chapter, a model of a Workplace Health & Productivity is provided (Figure 11.9).

---

[94] *Ibid.*

Figure 11.9: Value of Workplace Health and Productivity Approaches[95]

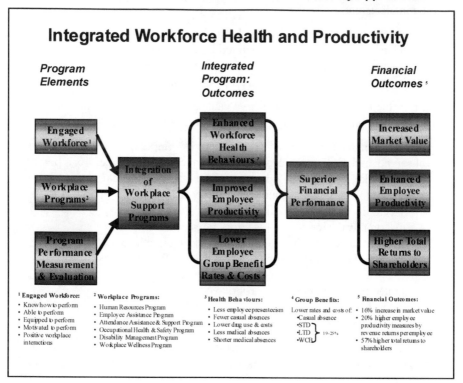

In this model, the mix of an engaged workforce, effective workplace programs, and program performance measurements and evaluation, can lead to an integrated approach to workplace health, and to improved workplace health behaviours, productivity, and health outcomes and costs. These health and productivity outcomes in turn, lead to superior financial performance.

[95] Adapted from T. Roithmayr, "The Performance Maximizer®" (Calgary, AB: Performance by Design) available online at: <http://www.performance–bydesign.com>; Watson Wyatt Worldwide, "Health and Productivity — Drives Organizational Effectiveness" (October 25, 2007), *2007/2008 Staying@Work™ Report* (2008), available online at: <http://www. businessgrouphealth.org/meetings/forum2007/presentations/thursdaywatsonwyatt_survey.pdf>; Watson Wyatt Worldwide, *Staying@Work: Effective Presence at Work*, available online at: <www.watsonwyatt.com>; and Watson Wyatt Worldwide, News Release, "Employers that Measure Results from Integrated Disability Management Programs Report Big Savings" (October 15, 1998), available online at: <http://www.watsonwyatt.com/news/press.asp?ID=6900>.

SUMMARY

By linking an organization's disability management efforts with its Employee Assistance Program, Occupational Health & Safety Program, Attendance Support & Assistance Program, Workplace Wellness Program, and Human Resources Program; and by recognizing the impact that management and human resource management theories can have on a workforce and workplace wellness; the opportunity to significantly reduce illness or injury incidence and impact exists. The challenge for management is to act on that knowledge in a proactive manner.

CHAPTER REFERENCES

Administration, *Workplace Wellness Plan: ROI* (December 21, 2008), available online at: <http://costofcorporatewellness.com/workplace-wellness-plan-roi/>.

Alberta Centre for Active Living (2004), *2004 Environmental Scan of Workplace Wellness Programs in Alberta*, available online at: <http://www.centre4 activeliving.ca/ publications/reports.html>.

S. Aldana, *Top Five Strategies to Enhance the ROI of Worksite Wellness Programs*, Wellness Council of America (February 2009), available online at: <http://www.welcoa.org/freeresources/pdf/top_5_strategies.pdf>.

D. Anderson, The Health Promotion First Act, *StayWell Health Management* (January 13, 2009), available online at: <http://wellnessintheworkplace.net>.

Aon Consulting Inc., *America @Work: An Overview of Employee Commitment in America* (Chicago, IL: Aon Group, 1999).

Aon Consulting Inc., *Canada@Work* (Chicago, IL: Aon Group, 2000).

Association of Workers' Compensation Boards of Canada, *Key Statistical Measures for 2007, Key Statistical Measures (KSMs) — Data Tables* (December 2008), available online at: <http://www.awcbc.org/common/assets/ksms/2007ksms.pdf>.

Buffett Taylor & Associates Ltd., *The First Comprehensive Canadian Wellness Survey* (Whitby, ON: Buffett Taylor, 1996).

Buffett Taylor & Associates, "Wellness Survey" (1997), available online at: <http://www.buffetttaylor.com>.

Buffett & Company Worksite Wellness Ltd. (2006). *National Wellness Survey Report 2006* (Whitby, ON: Buffett & Company, 2006), available online at: <http://www.buffettandcompany.com/NWS2009/Buffett_Company_NWS2 006.pdf>.

CCH Inc., "Special Report: 1999 CCH Unscheduled Absences Survey" (1999) 467 Human Resource Management: Ideas and Trends 149.

CCH Inc., "Unscheduled Absenteeism Rises to Five-Year High" (2004) 592 Human Resources Management Ideas & Trends 145.

CCH Inc., *Survey, 2006 CCH Unscheduled Absence Survey*, "CCH Survey Finds Unscheduled Absenteeism Up in U.S. Workplaces" (2006), available online at: <http://www.cch.com/press/news/2006/20061026h.asp>.

CCH Inc., *CCH 2007 Unscheduled Absence Survey* (2007), (Riverwoods, IL: CCH, 2007), available online at: <http://www.cch.com/absenteeism2007/>.

Conference Board of Canada, *Compensation Planning Outlook* (Ottawa: Conference Board of Canada, 1997).

Conference Board of Canada, *News Release,* "Eldercare Taking its Toll on Canadian Workers" (November 10, 1999).

Consortium for Organizational Mental Healthcare (COMH), available online at: <http://www.comh.ca>.

B. Daigle & G. Schick, "Early Intervention, Integration and Successful Resolution of Employee Health Issues" (Presented at the Health Work and Wellness Conference '98, Whistler, September 27-30, 1998).

D. Dyck, "Workplace Wellness: What is Your Potential Return on Investment?" *Human Resources Association of Calgary: A Newsletter on Human Resources Management* (November 1998).

D. Dyck, "Wrapping Up The Wellness Package" (January 1999) Benefits Canada 16.

Editor, "Low-Control Jobs are Hazardous to Health" (July/August 2002) O.H.S. Canada 23.

Global Business and Economic Roundtable on Addictions and Mental Health, *News Release*, "Ground-breaking Survey on Mental Health in the Workforce" (November 19, 2007), available online at: <http://www. gwlcentreformentalhealth.com/english/userfiles/news/pdf/s7_004756.pdf>.

R. Goetzel, R. Ozminkowski, J. Bruno, K. Rutter, F. Isaac, S. Wang, "The Long-Term Impact of Johnson & Johnson's Health & Wellness Program on Employee Health Risks" (2002) 44 Journal of Occupational and Environmental Medicine 417.

Guarding Minds@Work available online at: <http.//www.guardingmindsatwork.ca/GmawWhat.aspx>.

Health Canada, *Smoking Cessation in the Workplace — A Guide to Helping Your Employees Quit Smoking*, "Section V: Tools for Employers and Others Who Promote Health in the Workplace — Estimating the Cost of Smoking in Your Workplace" (2008) at 7, available online at: <http://www.hc-sc.gc.ca/hc-ps/pubs/tobac-tabac/cessation-renoncement/section-5-eng.php>.

Hewitt, "Health Promotion Programs on the Increase", *Aon Comments* (September 2, 1996).

Hewitt, *Disability Absence Index Survey, 2007* (2007), available online at: <http:// www. hewittassociates.com/lib/assets/na/en-ca/pdf/dais_2007_highlights.pdf>.

HRM Guide, "Flexible Working Reduces Absenteeism" (July 12, 2001), available online at: <http://www.hrmguide.co.uk/flexibility/flexibility_absenteeism.htm>.

Human Resources Development Canada, Labour Program, "Business Case for Work-Life Balance" (Benefits & Costs) (2002).

M. Jackson, "Worker Squeeze: Employee Stress Cuts Productivity, Study Declares" *Calgary Herald* (April 15, 1998) A5.

R. Karasek & T. Theorell, *Healthy Work: Stress, Productivity, and the Reconstruction of Working Life* (Toronto: Harper Collins, 1992).

L. Kelly, "Attendance Management" (Presented at the Alberta Occupational Health Nurses 21st Annual Conference, Calgary, May 24-26, 1998) [unpublished].

R. Kirby, "The ROI of Healthy Workplaces" (October 20, 1997) Canadian HR Reporter 31.

D. McReynolds, ed., *Worksite Wellness Programs: A Better Health Plan in Which Everyone Benefits* (Personal Best Publications, Scott Publishing, 2003), available online at: <http://www.trale.com>.

A. Nicoll, "Time for Action: Managing Mental Health in the Workplace", *Fall 2008 Bulletin, Mercer Bulletin* (September 29, 2008), available online at: <http://www.mercer.ca/referencecontent.htm?idContent=1322990>.

Marsh Risk Consulting, *Workforce Risk: Fourth Annual Marsh Mercer Survey on Employers' Time-Off & Disability Programs* (2003), available online at: <http://www.hr.com/SITEFORUM?&t=/Default/gateway&i=1116423256281 &application=story&active=no&ParentID=1119278006229&StoryID=11196 56728609&xref=http%3A//search.yahoo.com/search%3Fp%3DWorkforce+ Risk%253A+Fourth+Annual+Marsh+Mercer+Survey+on+Employers%25E2 %2580%2599+Time-Off+%2526+Disability+Programs%26ei%3 DUTF-8% 26fr%3Dmoz2>.

S. Musich, D. Napier & D. Edington, "The Association of Health Risks with Workers' Compensation Costs" (2001) 43(6) *Journal of Occupational and Environmental Medicine* 534-541, available online at: <http://www.hmrc. umich.edu/research/pdf/associationofhealthrisks.pdf>.

D. Pratt, "Competitiveness and Corporate Health Promotion: The Role of Management Control" (Graduate paper in Management Accounting, University of Western Ontario Business School, 1992) [unpublished].

S. Pridham, "Different Strokes for Different Folks: Three Companies Take Unique Paths to Wellness" (March-April 2008) Employee Benefit News Canada 16, available online at: <http://ebn.benefitnews.com/news/different-strokes-different-folks-three-companies-560461-1.html>.

Red Deer College. *Disability Management Process for Red Deer College* (2009), available online at: <http://www.rdc.ab.ca/current_students/getting_started/ health_safety_wellness/disability_management.html>.

T. Roithmayr, "The Performance Maximizer®" (Calgary, AB: Performance by Design), available online at: <http://www.performance-bydesign.com/>.

T. Roithmayr, "The Performance Maximizer®", presented in Chapter 5: "OH&S Leadership and Commitment", in D. Dyck, *Occupational Health &Safety: Theory, Strategy and Industry Practice* (Markham, ON: LexisNexis Canada, 2007) at 274-75.

M. Shain, "A New Take on Stress: Strategies that Work" (November 1997) Health Policy Forum 12.

M. Shain, "Managing Stress at its Source in the Workplace" (Presented at the Health Work and Wellness Conference '98, Whistler, BC, September 27-30, 1998) [unpublished].

M. Shain, "Stress, Satisfaction and Health at Work: Tuning for Performance" (Presented at the Health and Wellness Conference '99, Vancouver, October 24-27, 1999) [unpublished].

R. Shephard, "Worksite Fitness and Exercise Programs: A Review of Methodology and Health Impact" (1996), 10 Am. J. Health Promotion 436.

I. Taylor, "Managers Play an Important Supporting Role in Workplace Mental Health" (December 1, 2008), Employee Benefit News Canada 16, available online at: <http://ebnc.benefitnews.com/ebnc_issues/archives.html>.

N. Vimadalal & J. Wozniak, "Best Practices to Help Employers Capture the Benefits of Integrated Disability Management", Employee Benefits News (March 1, 2008), available online at: <http://ebn.benefitnews.com/asset/ article/548491/best-practices-help-employers-capture-benefits.html?pg=>.

Watson Wyatt Worldwide, News Release, "Employers That Measure Results from Integrated Disability Programs Report Big Savings" (October 15, 1998), available online at: <http://www.watsonwyatt.com/news/press.asp?ID=6900>.

Watson Wyatt Worldwide, *Staying@Work: Effective Presence at Work*, available online at: <http://www.watsonwyatt.com>.

Watson Wyatt Worldwide, "Health and Productivity — Drives Organizational Effectiveness" (October 25, 2007), *2007/2008 Staying@Work™ Report* (2008), available online at: <http://www.businessgrouphealth.org/meetings/ forum2007/presentations/thursdaywatsonwyatt_survey.pdf>.

Wellness Councils of America (WELCOA), *"Corporate Wellness Makes a Bottom-Line Difference, The Cost Benefit of Worksite Wellness"* (2009), available online at: <http://www.welcoa.org/worksite_cost_benefit.html>.

R. Williams, *A Survey of Disability Management Approaches in Ontario Workplaces* (2005), available online at: <http://www.wsib.on.ca/wsib/ wsibsite.nsf/Public/ResearchResultsSurveyDisabilityMgnt>.

Workplace, Safety & Insurance Board (WSIB), *Business Results Through Health & Safety* (Toronto, ON: WSIB, 2002) at 3, available online at: <http:// www.wsib.on.ca/wsib/wsibsite.nsf/Public/BusinessResultsHealthSafety>.

Chapter 12

Toxic Work Environments: Impact on Employee Illness/Injury[1]

By Tony Roithmayr[2]

INTRODUCTION

Over the years, occupational health and human resources personnel have witnessed the effects of organizational stressors on employee and manager health. Workers who perceive themselves as being "stressed":

- report making more mistakes;
- feel angry with their employers for creating the stressful situation; and
- resent their coworkers who they feel are not working as hard as they are, which can lead to a desire to leave the job.[3]

Overstressed workers also cost their employers 50 per cent more in terms of health care expenditures, lost workdays, staff turnover costs,[4] and accident costs.

Typically, the response is "What can we do? Things have been this way for years". The purpose of this chapter is to encourage understanding of the impact that a stressful, toxic work environment can have on both the employee and organization, and to present a plausible argument for initiating realistic workplace changes to help "break the cycle" of workplace stress and contain disability costs.

The bottom line is that workers vary in their tolerance of workloads. What is desirable for one worker is an intolerable level for another.[5] It is important for managers to understand the drivers of stress and to respect the individual differences of each employee in the workplace.

---

[1]   Excerpts taken from: D. Dyck & T. Roithmayr, "Organizational Stressors and Health: How Occupational Health Nurses Can Help Break the Cycle" (2002) 50:5 AAOHN Journal 213. Reprinted with permission from the AAOHN Journal.

[2]   Tony Roithmayr, BA, MEd, is the president of Performance by Design (<http://www.performance–bydesign.com>).

[3]   J. MacBride-King, "Wrestling with Workload: Organizational Strategies for Success" (Ottawa: Conference Board of Canada, 2005).

[4]   *Ibid.*

[5]   *Ibid.*, at 1.

HAVE ORGANIZATIONS BECOME TOXIC TO HUMAN LIFE?

In too many workplaces, the following things have happened, or are happening:

Too many and conflicting priorities	Employees experiencing frequent headaches, workplace accidents, anxiety attacks, ulcers, or high blood pressure	Poor employee morale
Lack of understanding about how performance is measured		Workplace tension
		High absenteeism
Poor communications	Employees reporting insomnia	Staff turnover
Little or no feedback and recognition for work done	Employees experiencing irritability, anger, or depression	Rising employee benefit plan costs
	Increased drug or alcohol abuse	Disappointing financial results

These three lists are causally-related and this relationship tends to have a destructive cycle. The cumulative effect of a multitude of organizational stressors manifests in deteriorating employee health, lost productivity, and escalating disability and employee group benefit plan costs.[6]

For example, Dr. Martin Shain reports that employees who experience high stress due to high work effort and low reward (recognition), and high strain due to high work demands and limited control over their job, suffer a threefold increase in the incidence of heart problems, back pain, work/family conflicts, substance abuse, infections, mental health problems, and injuries; and a fivefold increase in the incidence of certain cancers like colorectal cancer.[7] Other studies have shown that employees who experience chronic low job control are more prone to premature death. The primary cause was cardiovascular in nature.[8]

The Conference Board of Canada's *Survey of Canadian Workers on Work-Life Balance* reports that high stress levels due to the difficulty of balancing the demands of work and personal commitments are associated with health problems and work absence. Respondents experiencing high stress miss twice as much work time as those who report being in low stress situations (7.2 versus 3.6 days absence).[9]

---

[6]   R. Karasek & T. Theorell, *Healthy Work: Stress, Productivity, and the Reconstruction of Working Life* (New York, NY: Basic Books Inc., 1992).

[7]   M. Shain, "Managing Stress at its Source in the Workplace" (Presented at the Health Work and Wellness Conference 1998, Whistler, BC, September 27-30, 1998) [unpublished].

[8]   J. Siegrist, "Adverse Health Effects of High-Effort/Low-Reward Conditions" (1996) 1:1 Journal of Occupational Health Psychology 27; B.B. Marmot *et al.*, "Contribution of Job Control and Other Risk Factors to Social Variations in Cardiovascular Heart Disease Incidence" (1997) 350 (9073) Lancet 235; J. Johnson, "Long-term Psychological Work Environment and Cardiovascular Mortality among Swedish Men" (1996) 86:3 American Journal of Public Health 324; A. LaCroix, *Occupational Exposure to High Demand/Low Control Work and Coronary Heart Disease Incidence in the Framingham Cohort* (Ann Arbor, MI: University of North Carolina, UMI Dissertation Services, 1984).

[9]   Conference Board of Canada, *Survey of Canadian Workers on Work-Life Balance* (Ottawa: Conference Board of Canada, 1999).

According to a Health Canada survey (2003), employees who perceive that they have "too much to do in too little time" are:

- 5.6 times more likely to report high levels of job stress;
- 3.5 times more likely to experience high absenteeism rates due to emotional, physical or mental fatigue;
- 2.3 times more likely to report the intent to leave their current job; and
- 1.6 times more likely to have high absenteeism rates and to miss six or more days per year.[10]

Stress situations result in the release of the hormones epinephrine (or adrenaline) and norepinephrine into the bloodstream. At the same time, the adrenal glands also release cortisol, a hormone that sends the body the message to release fatty acids for a burst of energy. Chronically high stress levels can negatively impact body metabolism, elevate blood pressure, damage white blood cells, worsen autoimmune disorders and inflammatory conditions (eczema and colitis), and contribute to gastrointestinal problems. Conditions like heart disease, strokes, diabetes, and kidney failure have all been linked to chronic stress situations.[11]

Stress-related absences cost Canadian employers approximately $3.5 billion annually.[12] Workplace stress contributes to:

- 19 per cent of absenteeism costs;
- 40 per cent of staff turnover costs;
- 55 per cent of Employee Assistance Program costs;
- 30 per cent of short-term disability and long-term disability costs;
- 60 per cent of occupational incidents; and
- 10 per cent of prescription drug plan costs.[13]

So what can be done? How can organizations eliminate or mitigate the impact of organizational stressors? Experts in the field recommend eliminating stress at its source:[14] "to achieve high levels of employee productivity, efficiency and morale, leading executives have learned that they need to address workplace

---

[10] L. Duxbury & C. Higgins, *Work-Life Conflict in Canada in the New millennium: A Status Report* (prepared for Health Canada, Healthy Communities Division) (Ottawa: Health Canada, 2003), available online at: <http://www.phac-aspc.gc.ca/publicat/work-travail/pdf/rprt_2_e.pdf>.

[11] M. Haiken & E. Herscher, "Stress & Chronic Illness" (2008), available online at: <http://www.ahealthyme.com/topic/stressill>.

[12] Canadian Policy Research, reported in *IAPA: Creating Healthy Workplaces Everywhere – Healthy Workplace Week* (2006), available online at: <http://www.iapa.ca/main/articles/2006_oct_healthy_workplace_week.aspx>.

[13] Chrysalis Performance Inc., reported in *IAPA: Creating Healthy Workplaces Everywhere – Healthy Workplace Week* (October 19, 2005), available online at: <http://www.iapa.ca/main/articles/2006_oct_healthy_workplace_week.aspx>.

[14] M. Shain, "Managing Stress at its Source in the Workplace" (Presented at the Health Work & Wellness Conference 1998, Whistler, B.C., September 27-30, 1998) [unpublished].

health and wellness in an integrated fashion".[15] This can be done effectively by focusing on the environment in which the work is being done.

The following model provides insight into how to create a healthy and productive workforce through an integrated approach that enables employees to do their job and gain enjoyment and growth from the experience.

THE PERFORMANCE MAXIMIZER™ MODEL

We will start with some of the fundamental aspects about human performance in the workplace. To sustain success, organizations must provide a supportive environment that enables and supports employee performance in a variety of ways. Using The Performance Maximizer™ (Figure 12.1), we will examine the nature of a supportive work environment. This tool focuses on the factors that shape optimal human performance in the workplace. It describes, in a simple and memorable way, the conditions that exist when successful human performance occurs in the workplace.

Figure 12.1: The Performance Maximizer Model[16]

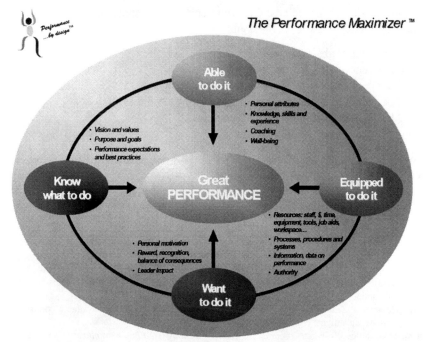

---

[15]   K. Bachmann, *More Than Just Hard Hats and Safety Boots: Creating Healthier Work Environments* (Ottawa: Conference Board of Canada, 2000) at 1.

[16]   T. Roithmayr, "The Performance Maximizer™" (Calgary, AB: Performance by Design) available online at: <http://www.performance–bydesign.com>.

Simply stated, employees and work leaders need to jointly create a work environment in which everyone will:

☐ *Know* what to do   ☐ be *Equipped* to do it
☐ be *Able* to do it   ☐ *Want* to do it

In the absence of these conditions, "organizational stressors" develop which cause problems with employee health and on-the-job performance, and ultimately, impact the organization's bottom line. The premise is that by focusing on the leading indicators for creating great human performance, lagging indicators such as employee absence, disability-related costs, reduced productivity, and poor profits will gradually decrease.

ORGANIZATIONAL STRESSORS AND HEALTH

The essential elements of Organizational Stressors and Health are presented in Figure 12.2.[17] It describes a situation that requires human performance improvement techniques to solve formidable and serious business problems. Intuitively, we recognize that a causal relationship exists among the elements presented below. But, how does this model actually work?

The cycle begins and ends with organizational stressors, defined as the absence of the conditions that enable performance. (For a comprehensive list of stressors, see items 1 through 26 in the Organizational Stressors Survey, Figure 12.4). Following the arrows, the model illustrates how organizational stressors impact individuals and then, ultimately, organization performance.

Explanation of the Model

The cycle begins and ends with organizational stressors. Organizational stressors are defined as the absence of conditions that enable maximum performance. Starting with the individual (the employee), the elements include:

DEGREE OF THREAT

Sustained exposure to organizational stressors can impact even the most resilient of individuals.[18] The more stressors there are and the longer the duration of the exposure, the more likely that detrimental effects will occur.

In general, personal impact depends on individual strengths and social supports — personality, the degree of self-confidence, level of self-esteem, emotional well-being and personal support system all play a role in mitigating the effects of workplace stressors.

---

[17] T. Roithmayr, *Performance by Design* (2000).
[18] R. Karasek & T. Theorell, *Healthy Work: Stress, Productivity, and the Reconstruction of Working Life* (New York, NY: Basic Books Inc., 1992).

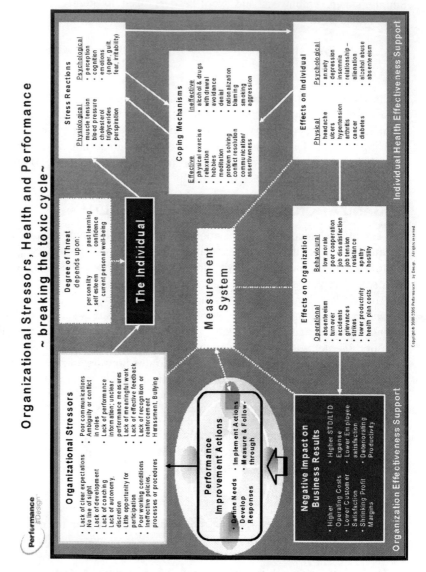

Figure 12.2:   Organizational Stressors and Health: Breaking the Toxic Cycle

STRESS REACTIONS

Workplace stress produces stress reactions. Physiologically, there may be changes in blood pressure or cholesterol levels, heightened awareness of the environment, or increases in muscle tension. Psychologically, judgement may be impaired. The person may experience irritability, anxiety, anger, an inability to concentrate, or short-term memory loss.

Today, the estimate is that employees process 190 messages per day (voice mail, e-mail, faxes, *etc.*). This constant information processing and overloading can lead to increased stress.[19] As well, life in general is deemed to be more stressful that it was 30 years ago.[20]

A recent study indicates that 62 per cent of workers report experiencing "a great deal of stress" at work. For 34 per cent of workers, "stress has been so overwhelming that it has made me physically ill at times".[21] This is consistent with previous studies.[22]

COPING MECHANISMS

Everyone has individual ways of dealing with everyday stressors. Good communication and problem solving skills, regular exercise, relaxation and social supports, as well as a variety of personal interests can serve to lessen the effects of stress. However, when stress is prolonged, many people respond in ineffective ways: avoidance, withdrawal, panic, or aggressive behaviour — even an increased use of drugs and alcohol. These ineffective coping mechanisms can temporarily help an individual deal with the stress of the moment, but can seriously impair physical and emotional health in the long run.

EFFECTS ON INDIVIDUALS

For years, health professionals have recognized the symptoms of workplace stress: headaches, ulcers, infections, hypertension, cardiovascular disease, substance abuse, anxiety, hostility and clinical depression.[23] However, society is just now beginning to appreciate the tremendous costs associated with workplace stress: productivity losses; human suffering; increased disability management and employee group benefit plan costs; and the enormous burden on our health care system.

Organizations are not solely responsible for the negative effects of organizational stress. However, when the average worker spends as much as two-thirds of his or her waking hours at work, or with concerns of work, it begs the question: What is the appropriate level of organizational responsibility?

---

[19]   Conference Board of Canada, *News Release*, "Workplace Solutions for Stressed Out Workers" (September 7, 1999).

[20]   B.A. Cryer, "Neutralizing Workplace Stress: The Physiology of Human Performance and Organizational Effectiveness" (Presented at the Psychological Disabilities in the Workplace: Prevention, Rehabilitation and Cost Control Conference, Toronto, June 10-11, 1996) [unpublished].

[21]   Aventis Pharma-Canada, *The Aventis Healthcare Survey* (2001).

[22]   T. Roithmayr, "The Performance Maximizer™" (Calgary, AB: Performance by Design), available online at: <http://www.performance-bydesign.com/>.

[23]   Health Canada, *Best Advice on Stress Risk Management in the Workplace* (Ottawa: Minister of Public Works and Government Services Canada, 2000); J. Siegrist, "Adverse Health Effects of High-Effort/Low-Reward Conditions" (1996) 1:1 Journal of Occupational Health Psychology 27.

- Three million Canadians suffer depressive episodes in any 12-month period.[24]
- One in four cases are detected and diagnosed.[25]
- Less than 8 per cent are being properly treated.[26]
- North American price tag for direct costs and productivity losses is $60 billion annually.[27]
- 26 per cent of Canadian workers have been diagnosed with depression.[28]
- Only 36 per cent of individuals get treatment.[29]
- Of the 62 per cent of individuals who related themselves as being "highly stressed", only 2 per cent reported that their work environment was detrimental or that their co-workers/supervisors were abusive.[30]
- In the past 12 months, 19 per cent of Canadian employees missed three or more workdays due to depression, stress, and anxiety.[31]

INDIVIDUAL HEALTH EFFECTIVENESS SUPPORT (HEALTH AND WELLNESS PROGRAMS)

Our organizations and institutions are not typically uncaring, nor do they choose to deliberately ignore stress-related problems. Many of the workplace leaders are themselves affected. In response, organizations have put supportive services in place to help employees develop effective coping mechanisms, for example:

- Employee Assistance Programs (EAPs);
- flexible benefit plans;
- flexible work hours;
- Disability Management Programs;
- fitness centres or subsidies;
- exercise and relaxation programs;
- child care services;
- elder care services; and
- education programs.

---

[24] Centre for Addiction and Mental Health (CAMH) (2001), Research, CAMH homepage, available online at: <http://www.camh.net>.

[25] *Ibid.*

[26] *Ibid.*

[27] *Ibid.*

[28] IPSOS-Reid, *Mental Health in the Workplace: Largest Study Ever Conducted of Canadian Workplace Mental Health and Depression* (Toronto: IPSOS-Reid, 2007), at 10, available online at: <http://www.ipsos.ca>.

[29] *Ibid.*

[30] *Ibid.*, at 11.

[31] *Ibid.*, at 13.

ARE WE TREATING SYMPTOMS INSTEAD OF ROOT CAUSES?

No doubt, these good and very necessary employee support services do help the individual. However, should organizations address the "root causes" of workplace stress instead? We maintain that a significant causal factor is the organizational environment in which the employee works. In essence, many workplace environments are "toxic to human life".

In support of this premise, we will examine below the second part of this model, the organizational elements.

Effects on Organizations

The cost of workplace stress is not borne by employees alone. Organizations pay a huge price for the emotional mismanagement of their human capital (employees) in the form of increased operational and benefit expenses, and productivity losses.[32] Low morale, lack of cooperation, workplace conflict, apathy and hostility are some of the behavioural outcomes. The operational outcomes of this stressors cycle include high rates of employee absenteeism, staff turnover, productivity losses and increased employee benefit plan costs. In the final analysis, the overall result impacts the organization's "bottom line".

Measurement

Dealing with the causes can break this unfortunate "cycle of harm". To achieve this, an organization must truly understand what is going on. Measurement is the key.

Measurement enables an organization to make evidence-based decisions about which remedies will produce the desired improvements. This is not only about tracking Employee Assistant Program usage, or monitoring drug plan usage, or counting union grievances, or determining the number of absent employees. Measurement must track all the components of the cycle illustrated in Figure 12.2 and bring the data together to form a holistic picture of the relationships active within the cycle.

"If you don't measure it, you can't manage it!

If you can't manage it, you can't control it."

Measurement provides information about:

- The degree to which stressors are being experienced by employees.
- The physical and psychological effects on individuals.

---

[32] M. Shain, "Stress, Satisfaction and Health at Work: Tuning for Performance" (Presented at the Health & Wellness Conference '99, Vancouver, BC, October 24-27, 1999) [unpublished].

- The effects on the organization:

  - behavioural outcomes; and
  - operational results.

- The financial or "balanced scorecard" results of the organization.

Performance Improvement Actions

Performance and Organizational Effectiveness consultants have the "soft technology" for improving human performance in the workplace — by dealing with the "organizational stressors" as the root causes they are. Occupational Health Nurses and Disability Managers can assist Performance and Organizational Effectiveness consultants in:

1. conducting needs assessments;
2. analyzing the "root causes" of the problems;
3. selecting and implementing interventions; and
4. tracking results and evaluating the outcomes.

Through an effective organization analysis, remedies such as the following can be utilized:

- *Education*: provide comprehensive briefings to top executives and senior management using both external and internal data to illustrate the business case associated with workplace stress and enhancing employee health and well-being.

- *Measurement system*: develop and implement measurement that includes indicators for "stress toxicity" as well as individual health and financial results.

- Promote *access* to and the use of a Wellness program (Individual Effectiveness Support).

- Improve the capacity of management to *recognize* and respond to causes of workplace stress and employee distress.

- *Performance Support Practices*: become better at managing people. The most effective and enduring remedy is to implement and sustain performance support practices that focus on the "four Es" of people management:

  - Establish purpose
  - Enable performance
  - Expect results and
  - Encourage success.

The importance of effective people management is not a new proposal. We realize it is not just "nice to do", but essential to creating an environment that fosters employee loyalty and in the long-term, sustainable success.

USE OF GOOD PERFORMANCE SUPPORT PRACTICES IS GOOD BUSINESS

Dennis Kravetz studied the correlation between people management practices and financial success. He developed an index for rating an organization's performance in people management practices (PMP score). In 1996, he published a study that looked at the correlation of PMP scores to financial performance over a 10-year period. The following chart (Figure 12.3) compares companies having low PMP scores with companies having high PMP scores:

Figure 12.3: Comparison of Companies with High and Low PMP Scores[33]

Financial Factors	Companies with High PMP Scores	Companies with Low PMP Scores
Sales growth	16.1%	7.4%
Profit growth	18.2%	4.4%
Profit margin	6.4%	3.3%
Growth (earnings/share)	10.7%	4.7%
Total return (stock appreciation + dividends)	19.0%	8.8%

ESTABLISH PURPOSE

- help employees understand the organization's vision, values, goals and business strategies; and
- guide the development of individual performance and learning plans that will achieve organizational goals.

ENABLE PERFORMANCE

- align resource allocations with performance expectations;
- coach employees to overcome difficulties and to build skill and knowledge;
- foster and maintain effective work groups; and
- resolve performance issues and remove barriers that are beyond the control of individuals and teams.

EXPECT RESULTS

- facilitate the measurement of progress, contribution and development; and
- hold people accountable for delivering agreed upon results.

---

[33] D. Kravetz, *People Management Practices and Financial Success: A Ten-Year Study* (Bartlet, IL: Kravetz Associates, 1996).

ENCOURAGE SUCCESS

- sustain communication that maintains focus, fosters commitment, and facilitates implementation; and
- recognize and celebrate progress, development, and the achievement of desired results.

ORIGINAL RESEARCH

An informal survey (Figure 12.4) was conducted to measure the degree of organizational stress in one Canadian city. The survey looked at specific factors within the conditions we know are needed to foster and sustain successful performance.[34] The results suggest that significant organizational stressors exist in some workplaces.

In general, the number of people who responded "disagree" or "strongly disagree" is low on most items. It is a concern that few people can say "this is not a stressor" for most items.

Highlights from the survey are organized below into the "four conditions for great performance".[35] In choosing the highlights, focus was placed on the percentage of combined "agree" and "strongly agree" responses and the percentage of combined "disagree" or "strongly disagree" responses. The numbers in brackets that appear below refer to the item numbers in Figure 12.4.

KNOW WHAT TO DO

- 72 per cent of the respondents said employees are faced with conflicting priorities and demands (item 2).
- 42 per cent of the respondents reported that employees are unclear about how their performance is measured (item 5).
- Less than 25 per cent of the respondents reported goal alignment (items 1 and 4).

ABLE TO DO IT

- Half the respondents reported that employees do not get the coaching and learning support they need (items 6 and 7).

EQUIPPED TO DO IT

- Few (10 per cent) of the respondents believed that employees get measurement data about their progress (item 12).
- Few (7 per cent) of the respondents believed that employees have clear and effective work processes and procedures (item 19).

---

[34] T. Roithmayr & D. Dyck, "The Toxic Workplace" (2001) 25:3 Benefits Canada 52.
[35] *Ibid.*

- 63 per cent of the respondents reported that employees do not have the time to do the work required of them (item 21).

WANT TO DO IT

- Half the respondents said that employees lack the recognition they need to stay motivated while only 5 per cent indicate that they do receive recognition (item 22).
- 15 per cent reported that employees get positive feedback while only 10 per cent say they get helpful corrective feedback (items 23 and 24).

The 44 respondents who completed this survey acknowledged the proposed "cycle of harm".[36] Their work experience supports a causal relationship among organizational stressors, health and operational results (items 27, 28 and 29).

This finding is consistent with research reported in 1998 by Dr. Martin Shain, University of Toronto.[37] He advocates dealing with workplace stress at the source in terms of "work design, work control, work demand and work effort" as opposed to trying to address the negative outcomes – *i.e.*, workplace injuries, increased operational costs, human suffering, and increased employee group benefit plan costs.

On a positive note, 83 per cent of the survey respondents believed that organizations can reduce or eliminate organizational stressors while maintaining or growing their business results (item 30).

These survey results can be compared with the *Top Ten Sources of Workplace Stress* reported by the Global Business and Economic Roundtable on Addiction and Mental Health (2001):

1. Treadmill Syndrome: too much to do at once requiring a 24-hour workday.
2. Random work interruptions.
3. Doubt: employees unsure what is happening, or where things are headed.
4. Mistrust: vicious office politics that disrupt positive behaviour.
5. Unclear company direction and policies.
6. Career/job ambiguity: things happen without employees knowing why.
7. Inconsistent performance management: employees get raises without a performance review and positive feedback and then get laid off.
8. Feeling unappreciated.
9. Lack of two-way communication between employees and management.
10. Experiencing a feeling of not contributing and having lack of control over the work and workplace.[38]

---

[36]   *Ibid.*

[37]   M. Shain, "Managing Stress at its Source in the Workplace" (Presented at the Health Work & Wellness Conference 1999, Vancouver BC, October 24-27, 1999) [unpublished].

[38]   Global Business and Economic Roundtable on Addiction and Mental Health, Top 10 Sources of Workplace Stress (2001), available online at: <http://www.mentalhealthroundtable.ca/ avg_round_pdfs/ Top%20Ten%20Sources%20of%20Stress.pdf>.

Figure 12.4: Organizational Stressors Survey

An informal survey of organizations in a Canadian city shows the degree to which Human Resource, Organizational Effectiveness and Occupational Health professionals perceive stressors within the organizations they serve. Forty-two people from about 30 organizations responded.

The percentage of people who replied 0 or 1, percentage who replied 2 or 3, and percentage who replied 4 or 5 to each item are shown below.

0 = Strongly Disagree	3 = Somewhat Agree
1 = Disagree	4 = Agree
2 = Somewhat Disagree	5 = Strongly Agree

Strongly Disagree						Strongly Agree
0	**1**	**2**	**3**	**4**	**5**	

1. are NOT clear about the specific performance expectations (<u>results</u>) for which they are accountable

25%	45%	30%

2. are faced with CONFLICTING priorities and demands

03%	25%	72%

3. are NOT clear about the behavioural expectations (personal <u>conduct</u>) that is consistent with the organization's values

30%	52%	18%

4. are NOT clear about how their individual work will contribute to the goals of the organization

22%	55%	23%

5. do NOT understand the standards for their success and how their progress and contributions will be measured

13%	45%	42%

6. do NOT get the coaching they need to succeed in their current roles

08%	40%	52%

7. do NOT get the learning support they need to further develop their capabilities

20%	32%	48%

8. are in jobs that do NOT match their own personal interests and attributes; do NOT find their work meaningful

28%	65%	07%

	Strongly Disagree					Strongly Agree
	0	1	2	3	4	5

9. are <u>often</u> involved in POOR working relationships

33%	50%	17%

10. encounter workplace situations in which they feel emotionally or psychologically VULNERABLE

22%	48%	30%

11. encounter workplace situations in which they feel physically UNSAFE

68%	32%	00%

12. do NOT get measurement data about their progress

10%	63%	27%

13. do NOT get sufficient communications about developments in the organization or information that affects their job

33%	47%	20%

14. have little or NO involvement in decisions that affect their work

20%	45%	35%

15. do NOT have the necessary autonomy and discretion to successfully deliver on their accountabilities

27%	53%	20%

16. feel they have NO influence over things that happen to them at work

26%	52%	22%

17. feel their roles are UNCLEAR or are <u>in conflict</u> with the roles of other employees

27%	43%	30%

18. do NOT have access to the tools, equipment, job aids or other resources they need to succeed in their jobs

35%	52%	13%

19. feel encumbered with unclear or ineffective work practices or procedures

07%	63%	30%

20. feel their physical work environment is NOT conducive to working efficiently or effectively

22%	48%	30%

21. feel they <u>lack sufficient time</u> to do the work required of them

05%	32%	63%

22. do NOT get the recognition they need to stay energized and motivated in their work

05%	47%	48%

Strongly Disagree							Strongly Agree
	0	1	2	3	4	5	

23. get little or NO positive feedback on how they do their work

15%	45%	40%

24. get little or NO <u>helpful</u> corrective feedback on how they do their work

10%	55%	35%

25. believe they are not treated with fairness, trust and respect

40%	43%	17%

26. believe that how well they perform DOES NOT really matter — that there are NEITHER positive consequences for good performance NOR negative consequences for poor performance

37%	40%	23%

No Effect At All	SOMEWHAT DETRIMENTAL				Highly Detrimental
	0	1	2	3	4
5					

27. In your experience, to what degree do "organizational stressors" have detrimental physical and psychological effects on individuals?

00%	18%	82%

28. In your experience, to what degree do "organizational stressors" have detrimental operational and behavioural effects on organizations?

03%	30%	67%

29. In your professional opinion, are stressors <u>in the organization(s) you are rating</u> detrimental to...
   a) employee health and wellness

04%	30%	65%

   (b) the "bottom line" of the organization

04%	48%	48%

Not at all		Somewhat		Greatly	
	0	1	2	3	4	5

30. In your professional opinion, can organizations reduce or eliminate stressors while maintaining or growing required results

00%	17%	83%

SUMMARY

Based on the experience of Occupational Health, Human Resources, and Workplace Wellness practitioners/professionals, unmanaged organizational stress leads to increased employee stress, failing employee health, decreased productivity, increased absence and disability costs, and lowered financial results. However, the task is to prove this statement. To our knowledge, not enough data is available to tie all the elements described in this article into a holistic framework of cause and effect.

Organizations want to make evidence-based decisions regarding the allocation of their limited resources. To do this, a commitment is needed to:

- implement a measurement system to track the entire "cycle of harm";
- implement evidence-based actions to reduce or eliminate stressors;
- track progress for three to five years and share the results publicly in order to motivate others to follow suit.

Through the use of a multi-disciplinary approach, occupational health, human resources, and organizational effective professionals can take action and find workable solutions to mitigate organizational stressors and the resultant employee illness/injury.

CHAPTER REFERENCES

Aventis Pharma-Canada, *The Aventis Healthcare Survey* (2001).

K. Bachmann, *More Than Just Hard Hats and Safety Boots: Creating Healthier Work Environments* (Ottawa: Conference Board of Canada, 2000) at 1.

Canadian Policy Research, reported in *IAPA: Creating Healthy Workplaces Everywhere — Healthy Workplace Week* (2006), available online at: <http://www.iapa.ca/main/articles/2006_oct_healthy_workplace_week.aspx>.

Centre for Addiction and Mental Health (CAMH), "Research", CAMH Homepage, available online at: <http://www.camh.net/>.

Conference Board of Canada, *Survey of Canadian Workers on Work-Life Balance* (Ottawa: Conference Board of Canada, 1999).

Conference Board of Canada, News Release, "Workplace Solutions for Stressed Out Workers" (September 7, 1999).

B.A. Cryer, "Neutralizing Workplace Stress: The Physiology of Human Performance and Organizational Effectiveness" (Presented at the Psychological Disabilities in the Workplace: Prevention, Rehabilitation and Cost Control Conference, Toronto, June 10-11, 1996) [unpublished].

Chrysalis Performance Inc., reported in *IAPA: Creating Healthy Workplaces Everywhere — Healthy Workplace Week* (October 19, 2005), available online at: <http://www.iapa.ca/main/articles/2006_oct_healthy_workplace_week.aspx>.

L. Duxbury & C. Higgins, *Work-Life Conflict in Canada in the New millennium: A Status Report* (prepared for Health Canada, Healthy Communities Division) (Ottawa: Health Canada, 2003), available online at: <http://www.phac-aspc.gc.ca/publicat/work-travail/pdf/rprt_2_e.pdf>.

J. MacBride King, "Wrestling with Workload: Organizational Strategies for Success" (Ottawa: Conference Board of Canada, 2005).

D. Dyck & T. Roithmayr, "Organizational Stressors and Health: How Occupational Health Nurses Can Help Break the Cycle" (2002) 50:5 AAOHN Journal 213.

Global Business and Economic Roundtable on Addiction and Mental Health, Top 10 Sources of Workplace Stress (2001), available online at <http://www.mentalhealthroundtable.ca/aug_round_pdfs/Top%20Ten%20 Sources%20of%20Stress.pdf>.

Health Canada, *Best Advice on Stress Risk Management in the Workplace* (Ottawa: Minister of Public Works and Government Services Canada, 2000).

M. Haiken & E. Herscher, "Stress & Chronic Illness" (2008), available online at: <http://www.ahealthyme.com/topic/stressill>.

IPSOS-Reid, *Mental Health in the Workplace: Largest Study Ever Conducted of Canadian Workplace Mental Health and Depression* (Toronto: IPSOS-Reid, 2007), available online at: <http://www.ipsos.ca>.

J. Johnson, "Long-term Psychosocial Work Environment and Cardiovascular Mortality among Swedish Men" (1996) 86:3 American Journal of Public Health 324.

R. Karasek & T. Theorell, *Healthy Work: Stress, Productivity, and the Reconstruction of Working Life* (New York, NY: Basic Books Inc., 1992).

D. Kravetz, *People Management Practices and Financial Success: A Ten-Year Study* (Bartlet, IL: Kravetz Associates, 1996), available online at: <www.kravetz.com>.

A. LaCroix, *Occupational Exposure to High Demand/Low Control Work and Coronary Heart Disease Incidence in the Framingham Cohort* (Ann Arbor, MI: University of North Carolina, UMI Dissertation Services, 1984).

B.B. Marmot *et al.*, "Contribution of Job Control and Other Risk Factors to Social Variations in Cardiovascular Heart Disease Incidence" (1997) 350 (9073) *Lancet* 235.

T. Roithmayr, *Performance by Design* (2000).

T. Roithmayr, "The Performance Maximizer[TM]" (Calgary, AB: Performance by Design), available online at: <http://www.performance–bydesign.com>.

T. Roithmayr & D. Dyck, "The Toxic Workplace" (2001) 25:3 Benefits Canada 52.

M. Shain, "Managing Stress at its Source in the Workplace" (Presented at the Health Work & Wellness Conference 1998, Whistler, BC, September 27-30, 1998) [unpublished].

M. Shain, "Stress, Satisfaction and Health at Work: Tuning for Performance" (Presented at the Health & Wellness Conference 1999, Vancouver, BC, October 24-27, 1999) [unpublished].

J. Siegrist, "Adverse Health Effects of High-Effort/Low-Reward Conditions" (1996) 1:1 Journal of Occupational Health Psychology 27.

Chapter 13

Marketing Disability Management Programs and Communicating the Results[1]

INTRODUCTION

The shortfall of most Disability Management Programs is that although they exist and function, few people know about them until they need to use them. In essence, attention to program marketing is missing. This chapter addresses the concepts of program marketing and communication, and how they can be applied to promoting a Disability Management Program.

PROGRAM MARKETING

Marketing is defined as a social and managerial process through which individuals and groups obtain what they need and want by creating and exchanging products or services and value with others.

Marketing Components

The components of marketing include:

* *Customer Needs, Wants and Demands*

Customer needs, wants, and demands must be taken into account when producing products or developing services to be delivered. This means that program developers need to know what each stakeholder needs, wants and expects from the program. In terms of marketing a Disability Management Program, the program leaders must demonstrate how the program and its services meet those specific needs, wants, and expectations.

[1]   D. Dyck, "Disability Management Program: Communication Plan & Marketing Strategy" (Presented as a class offering in the Fundamentals of Disability Management Course, University of Alberta, Calgary, Alberta, 2002) [unpublished].

- ### *Products or Services*

Products and services involve anything that can be offered to a market to satisfy a customer need or want. This includes both tangible (products) and intangible items (services). Disability Management Services provided to employees and workplace operations are shown in (Figure 13.1).

Figure 13.1: An Example of Some Disability Management Program Products and Services[2]

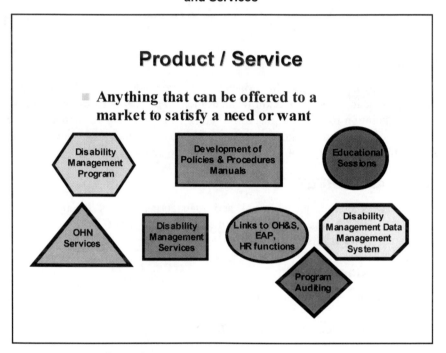

- ### *Product Value, Consumer Satisfaction and Product Quality*

Consumers buy based on their *needs* and the perception of the value the product or service offers — its *features*. Satisfaction depends on the product or service's perceived performance relative to buyer expectations and needs. When the product or service quality meets or exceeds customer expectations, the customer is satisfied. This means that for employees and managers to view the Disability Management Services as valuable, they must perceive that they have received more value than what they initially expected. For Disability Management professionals/practitioners, the message is "not to over-promise and under-deliver", but rather to keep your promises realistic regarding what you can do.

---

2   *Ibid.*

- ### *Exchange*

The exchange is the actual delivery of the product or service. How the product or service is made available to the customer is important. It can be either a negative, or a positive experience. This is where customer service principles come into play. The strategy is to provide the right product or service to the right person at the right time and for the right price.

- ### *Market*

The market is the potential customers for whom the product or service has been designed. In a Disability Management Program, this would include the employees, management, unions and various external stakeholders like health care providers, insurers, and family members.

Marketing Management

Effective marketing can be equated to effective marketing management. Marketing management involves managing customer demand which, in turn, involves managing customer relationships. Marketers need to build long-term relationships with valued customers, distributors, dealers, and suppliers.

Disability Management professionals/practitioners can promote their programs by nurturing strong relationships with program champions and those employees who have benefited from the services offered. Union leaders, line managers, and human resources personnel can be valuable allies. They are well positioned to help market the program and its services.

Key Marketing Concepts

Marketing management involves a thorough understanding of a key marketing concept. Successful marketing depends on determining customer **needs and wants**, and delivering the desired services (**features**) more effectively and efficiently than one's competitors can/do. The sales equation is:

$$\textit{Features } + \textit{ Needs } = \textit{ Benefits}^{3}$$

What does this mean to the promoters of a Disability Management Program? Simply stated, "*acknowledge stakeholder needs and demonstrate* **what** *and* **how** *the program and its services can meet those needs*".

For example, employees care about what the Disability Management Program can do for them and their families, that is, what is in it for them? They care less about how the Disability Management Program is going to improve the company bottom line. Thus, the marketing message for the Disability

---

[3] R. Buttenshaw, *Ready, Set, Sell: How to Succeed in Selling*, (Wellington, NZ: Generator, 2008) at 27, available online at: <http://www.acxionaddix.co.nz>.

Management Program needs to focus on how the Disability Management Program can assist them when they are ill/injured — a vulnerable time in their lives. The employee-directed message needs have a personal touch. It should indicate concern and caring for the employee and family members; a message indicating that the employee is wanted and valued even when ill/injured.

Employers, on the other hand, are interested in the company bottom-line and to want to know how effective the Disability Management Program is at mitigating disability rates and costs. This message should be delivered in financial terms.

Figure 13.2: Core Marketing Concepts

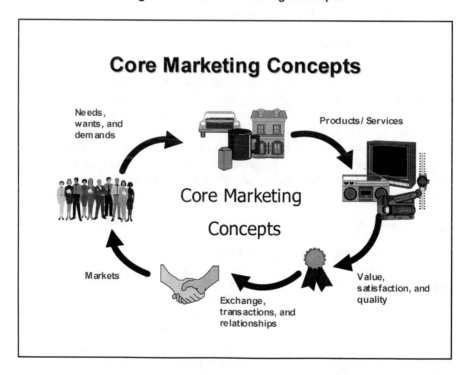

General Marketing Principles

The following are some general principles that can be followed so that this key marketing concept can be operationalized:

PROMOTE THE BENEFITS OF THE DISABILITY MANAGEMENT PROGRAM

Articulate to stakeholders the benefits that the Disability Management Program can offer to each of them. For example:

1. Employee regains income and a chance to remain in the workplace.
2. Union able to protect the employability of members while retaining rights and principles.
3. Employer retains a valuable employee and realizes decreased disability costs.

These benefits can be broadly stated, or specifically defined. Some general statements that can be made are:

CORPORATE BENEFITS

For the organization, the Disability Management Program allows for:

- Risk management:
  - at any time, 8-12 per cent of the workforce are off due to a disability;
  - employee absenteeism costs the employer about 250 per cent of the employee's salary;
  - the total direct and indirect disability absence costs for 1,000 employees would range from $3,500,000 to $3,675,000;[4] and
  - reduces casual absence, short-term disability, Workers' Compensation and long-term disability rates and costs.

- Fewer lost days and lower Workers' Compensation insurance premium rates and costs.
- Cost-containment of approximately 19-25 per cent can be realized through:
  - lower disability costs;
  - lower insurance premiums and rates; and
  - higher Workers' Compensation Board rebates.

- Lower employee group benefit costs by 15-35 per cent.
- Reduced costs associated with hiring replacement workers.
- Enhancing accident prevention.
- Higher level of employee productivity.
- Supporting a healthy workforce.
- Enhancing financial returns by:
  - increasing the revenue per employee by 20 per cent;
  - attaining a 16.1 per cent higher market value; and
  - 57 per cent higher shareholder returns.

- Meeting the organization's legislative obligations.

---

[4]   Hewitt Associates, *Disability Absence Index Survey 2007* (2007), available online at: <http://www. hewittassociates.com/Intl/NA/en-CA/KnowledgeCenter/ArticlesReports/DAIS_highlights.aspx>.

UNION BENEFITS

For the Union, the Disability Management Program affords the union members an opportunity to:

- contribute to company profitability and competitiveness;
- problem-solve addressing areas of mutual interest and concern;
- interact and build relationships;
- protect employability of its members;
- maintain labour rights and principles; and
- promote employee well-being.

EMPLOYEE BENEFITS

The employee (and his or her family) benefits from the Disability Management Program because the personnel and services:

- encourage a speedy rehabilitation;
- allow the employee to maintain contact and support from co-workers;
- reduce the time for optimal recovery;
- enable the employee to maintain self-identity and respect;
- enable the employee to remain current in his or her field; and
- result in the illness/injury experience being less disruptive in normal family/workplace relationships.

As one employee who went through a lengthy illness and received considerable Disability Management Program support stated:

"This program was great and it allowed me to:

- concentrate on getting better and to not worry about my financial and vocational future;
- keep a regular routine despite medical appointment interruptions;
- maintain a sense of self-worth;
- make a contribution to the company;
- work at regular duties for as many hours as I could tolerate;
- keep my work contacts;
- remain current with the changing work duties and responsibilities within my department;
- remain current with changing technology;
- gradually re-adjust to full-time work; and
- return to work without upgrading."

FIT THE MESSAGE TO THE TARGET AUDIENCE

The message must fit the "corporate culture". This means the message sender must know the target audience and the culture(s) within which that audience operates. Doing a "mini" culture assessment is advisable. For example, what are the group's beliefs and values? What are the symbols, rituals and rites that they observe? Who do they recognize as the group's heroes? Who are their leaders — informal or formal? Once this information is obtained, design the appropriate marketing message.

USE SOUND SELLING TECHNIQUES

Selling is the act of promoting a product or concept in such a way as to get another individual to adopt the product or concept. Selling is much like leadership in that both are aimed at influencing another person to achieve and objective.[5]

Selling success means using effective marketing techniques. In the world of Disability Management, that might look like:

- marketing Disability Management services, internally and externally, through the use of:

  - Disability Management Program educational sessions;
  - Disability Management Program brochures/posters;
  - Disability Management Program educational presentations;
  - media boards (*e.g.,* bulletin boards, electronic information boards, computer message boards, *etc.*); and/or
  - articles in the company newsletter.

- use of Disability Management Program web pages;
- provision of one-on-one coaching on sound disability management practices for employees and management;
- use of recognition/rewards for a performance of the desired disability management practices by line management;
- provision of regular Disability Management Program reporting to all levels; and
- use of disability trend analysis data to identify issues and reinforce the message(s) presented.

BE PREPARED TO ANSWER TOUGH QUESTIONS

Promoters of the Disability Management Program must know how to answer the following questions:

1. Why is a Disability Management Program needed in our company?
2. What are the benefits to the company and the various stakeholders?
3. What data are required to build a business case that promotes the existence of this program?
4. What are the real costs related to employee disability?

---

[5] R. Buttenshaw, *Ready, Set, Sell: How to Succeed in Selling* (Wellington, NZ: Generator, 2008) at 27, available online at: <http://www.acxionaddix.co.nz>.

5.   What savings can be realized due to having a Disability Management Program?

6.   What return on investment (ROI) can be realized?

Program evaluation is usually ignored or done badly and feeding back the great results — benefits — to stakeholders enables ongoing marketing. These are also the questions that need answering in the program evaluation report which is discussed later in this chapter.

To effectively answer these questions, the Disability Management Program promoters have to do some internal and external research and legwork. To assist with this process, the following facts may prove helpful (Table 13.1):

Table 13.1 Relevant Facts

- The total cost of time off and disability programs averages 14.9% of company payrolls.[6]

- National Institute of Disability Management & Research worker disability costs eight cents for every dollar earned in British Columbia, Canada. The breakdown of costs is as follows:
  - 35% of the cost borne by employers
  - 27% borne by employees
  - 38% borne by government agencies[7]

- In the first six months of a disability:
  - 1 in 3 employees experience an additional disability
  - 1 in 3 employees experience marital problems
  - 1 in 4 employees experience financial problems
  - 1 in 5 employees experience a clinical depression
  - 1 in 6 employees become involved in substance abuse.

  Each of these outcomes results in an additional cost for those paying for the disability.

- The cumulative weight of evidence supports a strong link between health and productivity.[8]

- Increasingly, employers are recognizing that the manner in which they integrate their employee benefit systems (*e.g.,* linking medical care, disability management, and return to work) is important to their future productivity and ongoing competitiveness.

---

[6]   Marsh Risk Consulting, *2003 Marsh/Mercer Survey of Employers' Time-Off and Disability Programs*, cited in "Employee Absence: Absence Management Means Ensuring that Your Employees are Both Present and Productive at Work", available online at: <http://www.marshriskconsulting.com/st/PSEV_C_228064_SC_229050_NR_303.htm>; and Hewitt Associates,

Build a Business Case for an Integrated Disability Management Program

The business case for an Integrated Disability Management Program must demonstrate the benefits and return on investment that could be realized by having the program in place. This is important when initiating the program and should be repeated regularly thereafter. Stakeholders need to know the rationale for initially supporting the program and then why they should continue to offer that support.

Some suggestions that can be made to garner support from the various stakeholders are:

For the Organization:

An Integrated Disability Management Program is a management tool for:

- managing employee medical absenteeism and the related costs;
- identifying the reasons for medical absences through data collection and trend analysis;
- preventing employee illness/injuries;
- containing disability related costs; and
- improving financial outcomes.

Selling an Integrated Disability Management Program as such can help management to see the value it can provide to the company.

Add to this "personal-hook message", the financial reasons for having an Integrated Disability Management Program. For example, Watson-Wyatt (2007-2008) measured the financial returns for having health and productivity programs, like the Disability Management Program, as being:

- 16.1% increase in the organization's/company's market value;
- 20% greater employee productivity; and
- 57% higher total return on investment to shareholders.[9]

Disability Absence Index Survey, 2007 (2007), available online at: <http://www.hewittassociates.com/Intl/NA/en-CA/KnowledgeCenter/ArticlesReports/DAIS_highlights.aspx>.

[7] National Institute of Disability Management and Research (NIDMAR), *The Effects of Disability on the BC Economy* (1997), available online at: <http://www.nidmar.ca/products/products_details.asp?id=15>.

[8] Refer to Chapter 11, "Prevention of Workplace Illness and Injury", Figure 11.9.

[9] Watson Wyatt Worldwide, *2007/2008 Staying@Work Report: Building an Effective Health & Productivity Framework — Executive Summary* (2008), available online at: <http://www.heissmann.at/research/resrender.asp?id=2007-US-0216&page=1>.

To put this into perspective for the company, state this information into well-recognized terms for the company. For example, how many telephone installations would a telephone company have to do to cover these costs?

Lastly, determine what the organization's total losses/costs for employee presenteeism, absenteeism, and disabilities would be with and without an Integrated Disability Management Program (Figure 13.3). Then calculate the savings realized by having an Integrated Disability Management Program. The return on investment (ROI) for having an Integrated Disability Management Program is the savings realized divided by the program costs of the Integrated Disability Management Program.

Figure 13.3: Model for a Cost/benefit Analysis of an Integrated Disability Management Program (IDMP)[10]

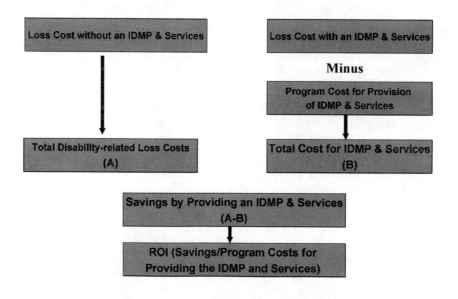

IDMP: Outcome Evaluation

In addition to the financial benefits, an Integrated Disability Management Program can add value to an organization and its business operations by supporting efforts that:

---

[10] D. Dyck, "Fundamentals of Disability Management" (Presented as a pre-conference offering at the Industrial Accident Prevention Association conference in Toronto, April 18-19, 2008).

- improve employee morale, and in turn, reduce employee presenteeism, and absenteeism;
- maintain a healthy workforce;
- lessen business interruptions;
- lower business costs;
- lessen government sanctions against the organization;
- reduce WCB claim and insurance premiums and costs; and
- maintain the organization's/company's image and reputation as a good corporate citizen and healthy and safe place to work.

Although the financial and business reasons for having an Integrated Disability Management Program are of interest to Boards of Directors and Senior Management, Union Leaders and employees are more interested in what is relevant to them as exemplified by the following:

For the Union:

An opportunity to:

- promote employee well-being;
- maintain labour rights and principles;
- protect the employability of members;
- demonstrate the union's "due diligence" in terms of helping injured workers to return to work;
- interact and build relationships;
- problem-solve mutual concerns and issues; and
- contribute to the company's profitability and competitiveness.

For Employees:

The Integrated Disability Management Program enables the employee to:

- have a speedy rehabilitation;
- maintain self-identity and respect;
- maintain social supports;
- remain technically competent;
- sustain financial and vocational stability;
- minimize family disruption; and
- maintain a sense of self-control.

INTEGRATED DISABILITY MANAGEMENT PROGRAM: A COMMUNICATION STRATEGY AND PLAN

The Integrated Disability Management Communication Strategy defines the corporate disability management message, how it will be delivered, to whom, through what means, and when.

The Integrated Disability Management Program: Communication Goal and Objectives

To begin with, determine the communication goal for the Integrated Disability Management Program. This goal will vary as the program evolves. Initially, it may be as follows:

INTEGRATED DISABILITY MANAGEMENT PROGRAM: SAMPLE COMMUNICATION GOAL

All stakeholders are to be knowledgeable about the Integrated Disability Management Program and of their roles and responsibilities in regards to the program.

From that point, strategies to enable the realization of this goal can be developed. These are the steps that the program promoters would take to move towards the completion of the goal. Some examples may be:

INTEGRATED DISABILITY MANAGEMENT PROGRAM: SAMPLE COMMUNICATION OBJECTIVES

By January 2011, 100 per cent of the stakeholders will know about the Integrated Disability Management Program and their specific roles and responsibilities as evidenced by their level of program awareness and/or their level of participation in the program.

By June 2011, all the key stakeholders will have an in-depth knowledge about the Integrated Disability Management Program and be able to enact their specific roles and responsibilities, as evidenced by their level of program awareness and their participation in the program.

These objectives can be operationalized by:

1. Achieving the overall endorsement of the Integrated Disability Management Program.
2. Providing general education about the program to all.
3. Providing specific education for key players in the program (Supervisors/Managers, Union Representatives, Occupational Health Nurse, and Disability Management Coordinator).
4. Provision of introductory and regular communication about the program.
5. Providing ongoing education about the Integrated Disability Management Program to all.
6. Provision of introductory and regular communication with external stakeholders (physician, insurers, and Employee Assistance Program).
7. Development of regular reports on the Integrated Disability Management Program outcomes (quarterly/annual).
8. Implementation of a mechanism for communicating employee fitness to work between relevant stakeholders.

Integrated Disability Management Program: Communication Plan

The next step is to create a communication plan and the accompanying tools to tell the key stakeholders about the Integrated Disability Management Program. As in the development of an Integrated Disability Management Program, a plan of action is required. This means determining what message(s) will be provided to each stakeholder group. Using the Integrated Disability Management Program Manual and the stakeholder roles and responsibilities as guidelines, determine the message(s) for each stakeholder group. The following is a graphic representation of a sample communication plan for an Integrated Disability Management Program (Figure 13.4).

Figure 13.4: Integrated Disability Management Program: Sample Communication Plan

Stakeholder	What?	How?	When?	Accountability?

For each stakeholder, determine the desired message to be delivered, the appropriate approach and timing, the best medium, and who will be accountable for delivering the message.

Different stakeholders have different informational needs. For example, senior management will be interested in how the introduction of the Integrated Disability Management Program will allow for the fair and consistent management of employee illness/injury, save money and demonstrate compliance to the applicable legislation. The financial officer for the company will want to hear about the objective measures about the program and the expected return on investment from the Integrated Disability Management Program. Line managers will be interested in outcomes such as increased employee attendance, lowered sickness and accident costs, and increased productivity. Employees will want to know how the Integrated Disability Management Program will provide them greater access to medical and vocational support, timely income continuance payments, and a speedy return to a productive lifestyle. Occupational health and safety personnel will value information on how the program will enable them to enhance employee health and wellness and how workplace injuries can be reduced. Lastly, union personnel will want to know what the Integrated Disability Management Program will offer to their members in terms of fair and equitable treatment for ill/injured members and job security.

The following are some sample communication plans that were industry-created (Figures 13.5 and 13.6).

Figure 13.5: Communication Plan For Employees

Stakeholder	What?	How?	When?	Accountability?
Employees	— History of the sick leave, STD, LTD, and the WCB experiences; the effects of doing nothing — Overview of the IDMP — Benefits (direct and indirect) of the IDMP — Future plans re: · Sick Leave · STD · LTD · WCB	— Overview of the IDMP; presentations using real examples; explain the business case — Training re: disability management and IDMP: · Introductory · Ongoing — Scheduled union meetings (shift employees) — Handouts	— Scheduled meetings (introductory, follow-up, new-hire orientation)	— Union Reps — Management — Advisory Council — HR — Home department

Figure 13.6: Communication Plan For Senior Management and Corporate Directors

Stakeholder	What?	How?	When?	Accountability?
Senior Management	Knowledge of IDMP; understanding of the purpose; understanding of the benefits; gain support for IDMP; seek endorsement of IDMP and its goals	· Presentation: overview outlining issues, implications, business plan · Entire program document	After ratification by union	Person's Name
Corporate Services & Human Resources	Knowledge of IDMP; understanding of IDMP	Status Reports	Monthly	Person's Name
Board of Directors	Knowledge of IDMP to level of application; understanding	· Review entire document · Overview presentation	Specific timeframe	Person's Name
Senior Management &Board of Directors	Program outcome data (ongoing reports)	Slides (graphs) on outcome trends	Annually Quarterly	Person's Name

Through the use of similar communication plans, a plan of action for promoting the Integrated Disability Management Program to each stakeholder is developed. Typically, these stakeholders are:

- Senior Management /Board of Directors,
- Employees,
- Managers/Supervisors,
- Union Executive Officers/Shop Stewards,
- Human Resources personnel,
- External insurers, and
- Health care Providers.

An industry example of a Disability Management Program: Communication Plan is provided in Appendix 1.

Integrated Disability Management Program: Communication Tools

As part of the Integrated Disability Management Communication Plan, the Integrated Disability Management Program promoters have to develop communication tools. These tools can be presentations, educational sessions, company newsletter announcements or articles, a web page, posters, and brochures marketing the Integrated Disability Management Program. The following is a discussion of the various communication tools designed to promote the Integrated Disability Management Program and to explain the related services.

INTEGRATED DISABILITY MANAGEMENT PROGRAM: BROCHURE

A sample brochure marketing the Integrated Disability Management Program is contained in Appendix 2. Critical to producing such a brochure is to ensure that:

- the message contained is accurate;
- contact personnel are included to enhance user access to the service;
- the tool is attractively presented and aligned with company branding and other marketing techniques;
- the graphics are appropriate to the audience and the purpose of the brochure;
- the reading level is at a grade 6-8 level so all employees can understand the message contained;
- in workplaces with multilingual workers, the brochure is translated; and
- where worker literacy is an issue, the use of pictograms where possible is considered.

INTEGRATED DISABILITY MANAGEMENT PROGRAM: WEB PAGE

In today's workplaces, one of the best methods for marketing the Integrated Disability Management Program is the creation of an Integrated Disability Management Program web page. The use of an existing and accepted company communication vehicle can be a powerful approach for getting the word out about the Integrated Disability Management Program.

INTEGRATED DISABILITY MANAGEMENT PROGRAM: OUTCOME REPORT

Disability Management professionals are expected to prepare program outcome reports. These reports can serve dual purposes: to describe the company's Integrated Disability Management Program results as well as to educate stakeholders on the value and benefits of the Integrated Disability Management Program. To do this successfully, there are a number of report preparation and writing principles that need to be understood.

As the business environment increases in complexity, the importance of skillful communication becomes increasingly important. In addition to possessing sound disability management technical skills, the Disability Management professional must develop effective communication skills. It is of little use to formulate solutions to business problems without being skilled at transmitting this information to others involved in the problem-solving process. In this section, the preparation of an Integrated Disability Management Program business report is discussed.

TARGET AUDIENCE AND MESSAGE

When developing an Integrated Disability Management Program business report, it is critical to first identify two key factors, *"who is the target audience?"* and *"what is your message?".*

REPORT FORMAT

Written reports enable the efficient presentation of factual data. Many Disability Management Program reports require a formal report, allowing the Disability Management professional/practitioner the opportunity to carefully verbalize the findings, to provide a historical record of the information being shared, and to share the same message with a wide audience in an expedient manner.

The Disability Management professional/practitioner must prepare the formal report so that it has a professional appearance and tone. The standard report elements include:

- *Title Page* — It contains the title of the report, the name of the organization/company, the name and contact details of the Disability Management professional/practitioner, and the preparation date.

- *Executive Summary* — The intent of the Executive Summary is to provide the time-constrained reader with the important facts and findings contained in the report. It summarizes these findings and conclusions, along with any recommendations, and places them at the beginning of the study. This placement provides easy access to the more important information relevant to any decision that an organization/company must make. If interested in more details, the reader is able to read the main body of the report.

  The Executive Summary should be written in a non-technical manner. It is intended for senior managers whose expertise often lies in business management and not in technical fields such as Disability Management. They usually have little concern for the technical aspect of the report. They primarily want to be assured that all the relevant business factors have been considered, and that appropriate procedures have been followed. If the reader decides that a more complete technical explanation is needed, that portion of the report can be reviewed.

Although the Executive Summary precedes the main body of the report when it is submitted in its final form, it is written after the completion of the rest of the report. The Executive Summary should not include new information or offer conclusions based on data or information not contained in the report.

- ***Table of Contents*** — Presents all the relevant sections and subsections so that the reader can readily access the desired information.

- ***Program Evaluation Description*** — This is the body of the report that houses:

  - a brief introduction describing the nature and scope of the evaluation question;
  - any relevant history or background material essential to gaining a thorough understanding of the evaluation question and to providing clarification of the program evaluation project;
  - a statement made that explains why the answer to this evaluation question is important;
  - the program evaluation goals and objectives;
  - the program evaluation workplan;
  - the method of program evaluation implementation (***Methodology***) and the techniques used to answer the program evaluation question; and
  - the program evaluation findings/outcomes (the relevant raw data) with any associated comments that add clarity to the data or draw attention to relevant factors that will be discussed in the next section.

- ***Discussion of the Disability Management Program Results*** — Based on the findings from the previous section, a discussion, and interpretation of the major implications of the Integrated Disability Management Program results are provided in a meaningful and non-technical manner. This section has considerable impact on the formulation of the action to be taken.

- ***Recommendations*** — They should be presented as advice for improvement as opposed to an edict. This section tends to repeat some of the information that is found in the Executive Summary, yet allows for greater explanation as to how and why these conclusions were reached. It is important that this section be based on the Integrated Disability Management Program results and not other conclusions or recommendations unsupported by the analysis presented.

- ***Conclusion*** — It summarizes the main objectives and results from the perspective of the reader who has read the body of the report and is reminded of what it was all about.

- ***Appendix*** — This part of the report can house supporting documentation on findings, recommendations, support documentation, and such.

If Integrated Disability Management Program business reports are prepared in an organized format, they are more useful and credible. As well, the report will command respect from those who sponsored/supported the program evaluation and who are relying on its content to make program decisions.

REPORT CONTENTS

When preparing an Integrated Disability Management Program business report, it is important to write so the contents are presented in a concise and factual manner. The report should, in most cases, satisfy the needs of two somewhat different types of audiences. One type of reader could be someone with a reasonable knowledge of the Integrated Disability Management Program and services, wishing to use the findings of the report as a reference for further action. This person requires relevant theory and specific results written in a precise business style. The other type of reader is someone with a business interest in the Integrated Disability Management Program, but with no specific knowledge of the area. This type of person would be looking to gain, not a trivial explanation, but more of an understanding of the issues, and if necessary, be able to skip the theoretical sections without losing flow or context. The best type of project report achieves a balance between these requirements.

Consider the attitude of the target audience(s). How will they react towards the report? If they may be somewhat hostile toward the report, offer more supporting evidence and documentation than if their anticipated reception to the report content is expected to be favourable.

The educational background and work experience of the audience(s) is a key consideration factor. In terms of style, word usage, and complexity, a report written for top executives differs considerably from the report prepared for line management. Even age, gender and other demographic characteristics might serve to shape the report writing.[11]

The text of the report should be written in a professional format, using short precise sentences and avoiding the use of unnecessary and redundant information. If there has been some salient issue or problem with program evaluation project, note it, but do not keep repeating it throughout the main body of the text. It is quite possible that an important aspect of the Integrated Disability Management Program outcome findings may need to be referred to in various sections of the report. If so, then describe the aspect fully in one section and reference this section where required. In short, avoid repetition.

Write the report so it does justice to the work contained within. The primary aim is clarity.[12] Minimize the use of technical jargon.[13] Be sure to remain

---

[11] W. Allen, "Business Report Writing" (2006) Applied Statistics for Business and Economics 957, available online at: <http://business.clayton.edu/arjomand/business/writing.html>.

[12] D. Inman, "Project Report Writing" (London South Bank University, 2004), available online in *Project Web Guide* at: <http://www.scism.lsbu.ac.uk/inmandw/projects/writing.htm>.

[13] S. Portny, *Project Management for Dummies*, 2nd ed. (Hoboken, NJ: Wiley Publishing, 2007).

focused on the program evaluation project, the outcomes, and the results. Use the report as an opportunity to fully explain what the results mean and what is perceived as useful recommendations for the customer. Be sure to clearly describe the recommended actions and the rationale for those actions.

Another consideration is the tone of the report. To the reader, is the tone of the report positive? Is it respectful of the customer and the customer's commitment to the project? Does the content read so that the reader feels like an "equal" in the discussion process? Take time to assess the tone of the report as it can be more influential than the content contained in the report.

In terms of a writing approach, start with a general overview and then move into coverage of the more detailed information. Consider how a person normally reads. Close attention is paid to the first page or two, and then if the gist of the content is missed, the person loses interest and skims idly through the remainder of the report trying to find significant ideas and relevant points. To avoid this, engage the reader early and hold his or her attention by presenting the information in a logical and sequential manner. By the end, the reader should be well-enough informed to responsibly action the related business decisions.

Some additional tips for report writing include:

- Keep it interesting — tell people what they want/need to know.
- Ensure the writing style, grammar, punctuation and spelling are acceptable.
- Write in the "third-person", avoiding the use of personal pronouns.
- Know and use the customer's accepted report writing style where possible.
- Use subheadings to help focus the reader's attention.
- Compare the actual project performance with the planned project performance.
- Proofread the report — one suggestion is to proof the report yourself and then to have someone who is unfamiliar with the project read and comment on it. If they can understand it and accurately explain what it contains, then the report is ready.

LIMITATIONS OF WRITTEN REPORTS

Report writing is a science and an art. Learning how to write well is a critical skill for Disability Management professionals/practitioners. However, as important as learning to write effectively is, it is just as vital to recognize the limitations associated with report writing, namely:

- Reports do not allow for verbal exchange, feedback, or other forms of interaction between the author and audience.
- The author cannot verify that the audience interpreted the intended message.
- The author never really knows if the report was read.

It is also important to realize that Disability Management Program reports rarely stand alone. Oral presentations are often required because the reader/ audience will seek further clarification of the Integrated Disability Management

Program issues as part of their problem-solving and decision-making process. This aspect is part of the report writing — the Disability Management professional/practitioner should be prepared to develop and present an oral presentation.

INTEGRATED DISABILITY MANAGEMENT PROGRAM: PRESENTATIONS

Disability Management professionals are expected prepare and deliver presentations on the company's Integrated Disability Management Program. The purpose of such presentations is usually informational and educational.

Oral presentations differ from written communication in that the presenter is talking rather than writing. Although a seemingly silly statement, the point being made is that by virtue of the communication delivery, there are two critical points that influence how one prepares and delivers an oral project report presentation:

- ***There is no written record.***

   Usually there is no complete written record for the audience to consult — the presenter talks, and hopefully, they listen. This means that simple, direct presentations are best: otherwise there is a risk of losing the audience's attention. Periodically, remind them of the overall structure of the presentation, and how the information fits together. In other words, do not just present the Integrated Disability Management Program data/findings to them; guide the audience through the presentation and the Integrated Disability Management Program Results report.

- ***Understand and use non-verbal communication techniques (body language) carefully.***

   When personally delivering a message to other people, the message sent is not just ***what*** is being said, it also includes ***how*** it is said. Attention to voice, posture, hand gestures, use of eye contact, and overall appearance is critical because they are all sending their own messages and must align with what is being said. In fact, lots of studies show that people pay more attention to the "***hows***" of a presentation than to the "***whats***".

PREPARING THE PRESENTATION

In preparing an oral presentation, there are six key steps:

Step 1: Planning

As with all communication tasks, before actually preparing a presentation, determine the intended audience and their anticipated reaction to the program evaluation project report. Design your main idea or topic. That is your intended message. Decide on the information and evidence needed to support this message and how to structure its presentation. This forms the presentation outline or plan. Remember, you are leading the audience through the Integrated Disability Management Program results and guiding them to the conclusions and recommended actions. Finally, decide the presentation length.

Tip: The higher up the company hierarchy, the shorter the presentation length and allotted time for questions.

Step 2: Preparing the introduction

The presentation introduction is critical; it lays the foundation for the entire presentation. Always connect and develop a rapport with the audience at the onset. Get their attention and show how the Integrated Disability Management Program results relate and are important to them. Preview the main idea/topic (message) and explain the structure for the presentation. To remember these four aspects, think of the acronym RAMP — **R**apport, **A**ttention, **M**ain message, and **P**lan.

Step 3: Preparing the body of the presentation

The body of the oral presentation is where the actual information, details, and evidence to support the main idea are provided. This part consumes the majority of the time allotted for the presentation.

There should be a number of slides in the body of the presentation, each corresponding to one of the main points in the presentation outline. Here the argument for the main message is developed. It involves providing clear data/evidence, relevant examples, pertinent anecdotes, and supporting disability management practice/research findings.

Since there is no written record of the oral presentation for the audience to consult, make sure that they are periodically re-oriented to the structure of the presentation. Do this verbally (*"now we'll move on to the second of my three main points ..."*), and by using overheads. Always ensure they know where they are within the presentation, and why a given section is relevant to the overall topic or idea. Otherwise the audience will lose interest, and the presentation will fall short of its intended impact.

Step 4: Preparing the conclusion

The presentation conclusion reinforces the main message. Briefly summarize the key elements and points of the Integrated Disability Management Program Results report, and, if appropriate, motivate the audience to act. Take advantage of the fact that an audience's attention level increases dramatically towards the end of a presentation.

Step 5: Preparing for questions

Questions are an essential part of most presentations. They allow for audience reaction and interaction; the opportunity to clarify ideas; or simply to get more information. In general, it is advisable to hold questions until the end of the presentation. This prevents repeated interruptions and provides an opportunity for the presenter to thoroughly explain the program evaluation project report before having to defend it. As well, the presentation tends to answer many potential questions.

If possible, prepare and practice answers to likely questions before the presentation. Anticipate and prepare for the tough questions. In particular, be able to explain and support any assumptions made during the program evaluation project.

When appropriate, set and adhere to a time limit for the question period. Before finishing the question period, remind people that it is almost over by saying something like, *"We're almost out-of-time. I can take one more quick question"*. If someone persistently asks questions, offer to provide more information at the end of the presentation.

Step 6: Preparing the visual aids

Visual aids must be simple, clear, and pertinent. Their purpose is to reinforce key presentation points and sections, not detract from the presentation by confusing people. Accordingly, they must be carefully planned and properly used.

Computerized overheads are preferable because they are effective, inexpensive, reliable, and easy to produce and use. Overheads should be text, or a mixture of text and graphics. They include:

1. A visual *title page* which provides introductory information like the title of the presentation and the presenter's company and name.

2. An *overview page* which previews your presentation's structure and main sections. It can be used several times during the course of a longer presentation to re-orient the audience.

3. *Charts, graphs, tables, photos* or other image-based material.

Importantly, avoid crowding material onto overheads; keep them free of visual clutter. It should go without saying that your overheads must be free of any grammatical, typographic, or spelling errors.

Plan which points in the overhead materials warrant emphasizing, determine which type of overhead is the best for doing this and create clear, dynamic, and colourful visual support materials that enhance the presentation message. A sample presentation made to management on an Integrated Disability Management Program and its performance results is provided in Appendix 3.

PRESENTING

Nervousness is part of delivering a good presentation. It enables the presenter to "get energized and up" for the experience. However, for some people that nervousness is more detrimental than useful. As Jerry Seinfeld put it: "People are afraid of public speaking … . In fact, most say that it's their number one fear. Death, apparently, only comes second."

The sweaty palms, the stomach butterflies, and dry throat are all signs that the person's body is in distress.

Yet, the ability to verbally persuade or inform a group of people — to make effective oral presentations, in other words — is arguably the single-most valuable skill in business. Its importance, very simply, cannot be overstated.

How can presenters overcome their fears so that they can perform to the best of their abilities? The following tips have been found to be useful:

- Prepare the presentation materials yourself.
- Have key notes on each slide.
- Plan out the time required for each presentation and adhere to it.
- Know the contents of the related OH&S report.
- Know and rehearse your presentation.
- Write down the opening statements so that you can get started without any verbal hesitation.
- Make sure you know what the anticipated audience reaction to the report will be.
- Rehearse the presentation. Try walking around, speaking each segment, and then speaking aloud the entire presentation. Rephrase ideas that are difficult to say — these will likely be hard for the audience to follow.
- Be sure to time the presentation so that it does not exceed the time limit.
- Keep the presentation as short as possible — avoid distractions.
- If possible, become familiar with the room where the presentation will be delivered to know how loudly to talk and how people will be seated.
- Practise and be comfortable with an effective delivery style (Table 13.2).

Table 13.2: An Effective Presentation Delivery Style

- Clearly demarcate the beginning and end of each point and segment in the presentation.
- Announce each main topic. That way, the audience knows when one topic has been completed and a new one is beginning.
- Allow a slight pause to occur after the completion of the presentation introduction then, announce the first topic.
- After finishing the final topic in the main body of the presentation, allow a slight pause before beginning the conclusion.
- Speak slowly, vigorously, and enthusiastically. Be sure you enunciate the words carefully, particularly if addressing a large group.
- Use gestures to accentuate points. Use body movements to aid in announcing major transition points. In short, avoid standing still.
- Maintain eye contact with the audience.

> - Avoid memorizing the presentation: one forgotten part will end up with confusion and panic. Use brief notes on a hardcopy of the slides. Highlighted key points help to refresh one's memory.
> - If possible, record the rehearsed presentation. Listen objectively to what was said. Consider the main issues of audience, purpose, organization, context, content, and style. Listen for tone, attitude, and clarity. Is the tone appropriate to the audience and purpose? Is each sentence easy to understand? Is the speaking pace appropriate? Are the major divisions in the presentation easy to hear? Are any sentences difficult to understand? Make any necessary adjustments to the presentation materials or delivery.

No matter what type of presentation, ultimate success as a speaker and the success of the presentation depend on the presenter's ability to establish credibility with the audience. Guidelines on planning, structuring, and delivering the presentation are important because they are designed to build your credibility with your audience. However, no amount of planning and organization will substitute for practice, which builds confidence. Practice also enhances and displays planning and the value of the presenter's ideas.

INTEGRATED DISABILITY MANAGEMENT PROGRAM: SUPERVISOR AND EMPLOYEE EDUCATION

Disability Management Program education is an effective way to promote the Integrated Disability Management Program and its features to supervisors and employees. Chapter 14, "Disability Management Education" addresses how to increase the Disability Management Program awareness, knowledge, and application levels.

SUMMARY

For Integrated Disability Management Programs and services to remain visible and viable, they must be promoted within the organization. In return, the program promoters must demonstrate that the program is adding value to the organization and stakeholders. This information must be reported back to all the stakeholders in order for them to understand that the program is providing them with what they value the most. This is the only way that they will support the implementation and sustainability of the Integrated Disability Management Program.

APPENDIX 1

Sample Integrated Disability Management Program (IDMP) Communication Plan

IDMP Message	Media	Senior Management Team	Managers	Front Line Supervisors	Staff	Employees	Unions	External Stakeholders
IDMP Policy	IDMP Web site	✓	✓	✓	✓	✓	✓	
	Bulletin Board Postings	✓	✓	✓	✓	✓	✓	
	IDMP Program Manual	✓	✓	✓	✓	✓	✓	
	Employee Benefits Handbook	✓	✓	✓	✓	✓	✓	
IDMP Program	IDMP: Web site version	✓	✓	✓	✓	✓	✓	
Employee Benefits Handbook	IDMP Web site	✓	✓	✓	✓	✓	✓	
	Hardcopy version	✓	✓	✓	✓	✓	✓	✓
IDMP Action Plan	IDMP Web site	✓	✓	✓	✓	✓	✓	
IDMP	IDMP Web site	✓	✓	✓	✓	✓	✓	
	IDMP Brochure	✓	✓	✓	✓	✓	✓	✓
Department Personnel	IDMP Training Materials		✓	✓	✓	✓		

IDMP Message	Media	Senior Management Team	Managers	Front Line Supervisors	Staff	Employees	Unions	External Stakeholders
General IDMP Information	IDMP Web site	✓	✓	✓	✓	✓	✓	
	Bulletin Board	✓	✓	✓	✓	✓	✓	
	Safety Meetings		✓	✓	✓	✓		
	Safety Training		✓	✓	✓	✓	✓	✓
	Posters			✓	✓	✓	✓	✓
	IDMP Brochures	✓	✓	✓	✓	✓	✓	✓
IDMP Education	Brochures	✓	✓	✓	✓	✓	✓	✓
	Employee Newsletter	✓	✓	✓	✓	✓		
General Worker IDMP Education and Training	New Employee Orientation	✓	✓	✓	✓	✓		
	Worker IDMP Training		✓	✓	✓	✓		
	IDMP Refresher Training		✓	✓	✓	✓		
IDMP Program Outcomes/Results	IDMP Web site	✓	✓	✓	✓	✓	✓	✓
	Reports	✓	✓			✓	✓	
	Trend analyses	✓	✓			✓	✓	
	Annual Report	✓	✓			✓	✓	

APPENDIX 2

Integrated Disability Management Program Brochure

At COMPANY XYZ, employees are our most important assets. COMPANY XYZ is committed to providing programs and services to support employee wellness and regular work attendance. We support initiatives to assist employees experiencing a diminished work capacity and to help ill/injured employees to return to work.

THE INTEGRATED DISABILITY MANAGEMENT PROGRAM

COMPANY XYZ's Integrated Disability Management Program is designed to:

*   Support employees and business operations during an employee illness/injury period
*   Promote employee health and recovery
*   Assist employees to return to work in a safe and timely manner
*   Lower the associated absence cost
*   Promote a healthy work environment

HOW DOES IT WORK?

The ill/injured employee notifies the immediate supervisor/line manager of the medical absence, who in turn, notifies the Disability Management Coordinator, hence initiating the claim submission process.

The Disability Management Coordinator contacts the employee to assess the situation, to identify the need for employee supports, and to determine the anticipated length of absence.

The Disability Management Coordinator may request the employee's written consent to have medical information released by his or her family physician, specialist, or other health service provider. Information released to the Disability Management Coordinator is used to aid in the evaluation of the employee's fitness-to-work status.

Confidential medical information about the employee is not shared. What is disclosed is the source of the injury/illness — work-related or not — as well as the employee's fitness-to-work status, the identified work limitations and capabilities, and a realistic return-to-work date.

Case management meetings involving the Return-to-Work Team may occur at any time throughout the Disability Management process. The aim is to address any barriers to a safe and timely return to work that the employee may be experiencing.

THE INTEGRATED DISABILITY MANAGEMENT TEAM

COMPANY XYZ's Integrated Disability Management Program uses a coordinated team approach for facilitating the employee's safe and timely return to work following an illness/injury. The team may include any or all of the following:

- Employee
- Supervisor/Line Manager
- Union Representative (if applicable)
- Attending Health Care Providers
- COMPANY Disability Management Services
- Employee and Family Assistance Service provider
- COMPANY Employee Services
- Rehabilitation specialists
- Insurance company representatives

BENEFITS OF THE INTEGRATED DISABILITY MANAGEMENT PROGRAM

FOR THE EMPLOYEE:

- Encourages a timely recovery
- Maintains contact and support from co-workers
- Decreases the risk of relapse
- Offers the ability to maintain self-identity and respect
- Lessens the disruption in normal family and work life
- Supports a return to work in a safe and timely manner
- Reduces the associated financial hardships

FOR THE EMPLOYER:

- Supports and promotes a healthy workforce
- Maintains valuable employees within the workplace
- Meets legislative obligations
- Manages illness/injury costs effectively

NEED MORE INFORMATION?

If you require more information, please contact one of the following:

- ☐ COMPANY XYZ Intranet
- ☐ Your Line Manager
- ☐ Your Union Representative
- ☐ COMPANY XYZ Disability Management Coordinator
- ☐ COMPANY XYZ Employee Services

CONTACTS:

Disability Management Coordinator
Address: [insert address]

Phone: [insert number]
Cell: [insert number]
Fax: [insert number]

Union Office
UNION — [insert number]

APPENDIX 3

Disability Management Program Presentation

Company XYZ
Disability Management
Program

Presented:
October 2009

Disability Management

Definition

An active process of minimizing the impact of an impairment on the employee's ability to function within the workplace

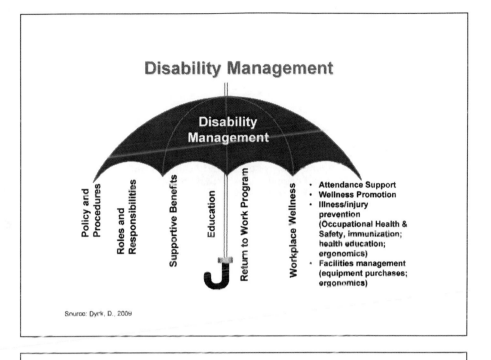

Disability Management

Key Elements

- Joint Labour-Management endorsement and support
- Management-Labour commitment and supportive policies
- Supportive benefit plans
- Stakeholder education and involvement
- Coordinated approach to injury/illness management
- Early Intervention
- Graduated return-to-work opportunities
- Program performance measurement and evaluation
- Integration with other company programs
- Workplace Wellness

Source: Dyck, D., 2009

Disability Management Program

Purpose

- To attain the best performance in managing all workplace disabilities – casual sickness, STD, LTD and WCB

- To promote employee recovery and health through active claim and case management, in addition to a safe and timely return to work

Disability Management Program

Principles

- To reinforce the factors promoting return to work, and to mitigate those factors acting as barriers to a safe and timely return to work

- To provide a planned approach to minimize the barriers so employees can return to work in a timely manner without risk to their health, or to the health of others

- Integration with other company programs, Human Resources, Attendance Support & Assistance Program, Employee Assistance Program, Occupational Health & Safety Program, and Workplace Wellness Program

Disability Management Program

Benefits

- Manage absences due to illness or injury

- Intervene at the very onset of an illness/injury

- Facilitate the rehabilitation of employees while expediting a safe return to work through a return-to-work plan

- Follow confidentiality guidelines

- Respond to the corporate/union vision of providing employees with a safe and healthy workplace

Disability Management Program

Benefits

- Convey the message that employees are valued

- Focus on illness/injury prevention

- Promote the image of a caring and responsible employer

- Contain human and financial costs

- Demonstrate compliance with legislation and regulations *(e.g., Workers' Compensation Act, Duty to Accommodate and Human Rights Legislation, OH&S Act, Privacy legislation, and applicable Collective Agreements)*

Disability Management Program

Stakeholders

- Employees
- Managers and supervisors
- Co-workers
- Employer
- Unions
- Healthcare Providers
- Insurance carriers

Disability Management Program

Stakeholder Roles and Responsibilities

- Understand your rights, role and responsibilities
- Report employee absence
- Ensure completion of claim reports and forms
- Submit all applicable medical information
- Participate in and/or support return-to-work initiatives
- Provide feedback on the DMP process and outcomes
- Respect the collective agreements
- Refer employees to the EAP when appropriate
- Identify positions suitable for return-to-work opportunities

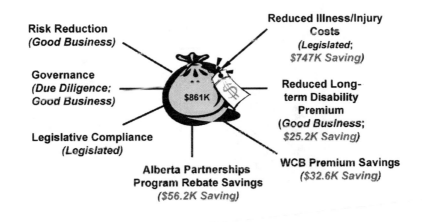

Value of Disability Management Program: 2008

Risk Reduction
(Good Business)

Governance
(Due Diligence;
Good Business)

Legislative Compliance
(Legislated)

Alberta Partnerships
Program Rebate Savings
($56.2K Saving)

$861K

Reduced Illness/Injury
Costs
(Legislated;
$747K Saving)

Reduced Long-
term Disability
Premium
(Good Business;
$25.2K Saving)

WCB Premium Savings
($32.6K Saving)

Value of Disability Management Program: 2008

To operate the Disability Management Program
(DMP), Company XYZ spent $251K

DMP
Budget
Costs
$251K

Direct
Dollar
Returns
$861K

Return on Investment = $3.43 per $1 spent

Disability Management Program

Discussion / Questions

CHAPTER REFERENCES

W. Allen, "Business Report Writing" (2006) Applied Statistics for Business and Economics 957, available online at: <http://business.clayton.edu/arjomand/business/writing.html>.

R. Buttenshaw, *Ready, Set, Sell: How to Succeed in Selling* (Wellington, NZ: Generator, 2008) at 27, available online at: <http://www.acxionaddix.co.nz>.

D. Dyck, "Disability Management Program: Communication Plan & Marketing Strategy" (Presented as a class offering in the Fundamentals of Disability Management Course, University of Alberta, Calgary, Alberta, 2002) [unpublished].

D. Dyck, "Fundamentals of Disability Management" (Presented as a pre-conference offering at the Industrial Accident Prevention Association conference in Toronto, April 18-19, 2008).

Hewitt Associates, *Disability Absence Index Survey 2007* (2007), available online at <http://www.hewittassociates.com/Intl/NA/en-CA/KnowledgeCenter/ArticlesReports/DAIS_highlights.aspx>.

D. Inman, "Project Report Writing" (London South Bank University, 2004), available online in *Project Web Guide* at: <http://www.scism.lsbu.ac.uk/inmandw/projects/writing.htm>.

Marsh Risk Consulting, *2003 Marsh/Mercer Survey of Employers' Time-Off and Disability Programs*, cited in "Employee Absence: Absence Management Means Ensuring that Your Employees are Both Present and Productive at Work", available online at: <http://www.marshriskconsulting.com/st/PSEV_C_228064_SC_229050_NR_303.htm>.

National Institute of Disability Management and Research (NIDMAR), *The Effects of Disability on the BC Economy* (1997), available online at: <http://www.nidmar.ca/products/products_details.asp?id=15>.

S. Portny, *Project Management for Dummies*, 2d ed. (Hoboken, NJ: Wiley Publishing, 2007.

Watson Wyatt Worldwide, *2007/2008 Staying@Work Report: Building an Effective Health & Productivity Framework — Executive Summary* (2008), available online at: <http://www.heissmann.at/research/resrender.asp?id=2007-US-0216&page=1>.

Chapter 14

Disability Management Education

INTRODUCTION

People learn new things everyday and tend to apply what they learn to new and different situations. This is often done in an effortless manner. Based on this premise, most government and community agencies that promote public health interventions use an educational component to elicit the desired human behavioural change. Their belief is that once people know what to do, they will do what is recommended. However, from experience, "knowing" does not lead to "doing".

This chapter is dedicated to disability management education and how disability management professionals/practitioners can enable employers to design and deliver effective Disability Management Education Programs or educational sessions.

DISABILITY MANAGEMENT PROGRAM EDUCATION

To be effective, an Integrated Disability Management Program requires a strong educational component. The education of management, union leaders, and employees is a critical element in promoting stakeholder understanding, passion, and endorsement for an Integrated Disability Management Program. From that foundation, comes stakeholder support for the program as well as for its individual components — the disability case management, disability claim management, gradual return-to-work initiatives, along with the necessary program resources.

Disability management education can be defined as providing management and workers with the information, concepts, and models to undertake and deliver an effective Integrated Disability Management Program. It includes helping stakeholders develop the requisite skills and judgment to assist ill/injured employees to return to work in a safe and timely manner. It also addresses the assessment of the disabled employee and the work situation.

The objectives of disability management education are to facilitate the implementation of an Integrated Disability Management Program, and to raise stakeholder awareness and skill levels to an acceptable performance standard. While all employees can benefit from disability management education, special attention should be given to the education offered to management, union leaders, supervisors, human resources personnel, and occupational health & safety practitioners/professionals. These players have a greater duty of responsibility and accountability for assisting disabled employees, and hence, require a broader scope and deeper breadth of knowledge to be able to effect their assigned duties.

DISABILITY MANAGEMENT EDUCATION: IMPORTANCE

According to Canadian Human Rights, specifically the Duty to Accommodate legislation, employers, unions and ill/injured employees have a tripartite obligation to ensure that reasonable work accommodation for employees with a physical or mental disability are made. The primary obligation rests with the employer to accommodate employees with disabilities (both physical and mental) to the point of "undue hardship". To meet this obligation, employers are advised to ensure that all the relevant stakeholders involved in the process of accommodating disabled employees are knowledgeable about the company's Integrated Disability Management Program and their respective roles.

The provision of disability management education offers additional benefits. An informed workplace and union lends themselves to the effective functioning of the Integrated Disability Management Program: one in which the stakeholders know "why" and "how" to participate effectively, and in which the stakeholders are "owners of the program" and are hence invested in the continued success of the program. It also promotes worker motivation to participate in the Integrated Disability Management Program and gradual return-to-work initiatives.

DISABILITY MANAGEMENT EDUCATION: IMPORTANT ELEMENTS

Disability management education can be formal, informal, classroom instruction, or on-the-job instruction. It should be instructive, clear, relevant, accurate, and tailored to the intended audience's needs and learning styles.

Adult Learning Principles

The use of adult learning principles as originally identified by Malcolm Knowles,[1] is important when providing disability management education. In most cases, the target audiences are responsible adults who bring with them extensive work histories and experiences.

Adult learning principles include:

- recognizing that adult learners have unique learning needs;
- respecting the adult learner's previous experiences and seeking ways to incorporate those experiences into the current learning experience;[2]

[1]   National-Louis University, "Malcolm Knowles: Apostle of Andragogy", available online at: <http://www.nl.edu/academics/cas/ace/resources/malcolmknowles.cfm>.
[2]   S. Lieb, "Principles of Adult Learning", available online at: <http://honolulu.hawaii.edu/intranet/committees/FacDevCom/guidebk/teachtip/adults-2.htm>.

- understanding that teaching/learning procedures are determined by the adult learner's needs;
- appreciating that adult learners are goal- and relevancy-oriented and relating how the current education/training applies to the learner's work situation;[3]
- recognizing that adults are autonomous and self-directed, and need the freedom to direct themselves and to be actively involved in the learning process;[4]
- using thoughtful, relevant learning situations that include the adult learner's perspectives;
- recognizing that adult learners learn from each other through class interaction;
- recognizing that adult learning is informational, and involves skill development and attitudinal change;
- understanding that adult learners are practical and need to be instructed on how the lesson will be of value to them;
- understanding that teaching should be focused on the adult learner, not the subject being taught;
- making teaching and learning a shared responsibility for the instructor and adult learner;
- continually evaluating the learning process so that both the instructor and adult learner can assess the learning achieved; and
- being willing, both the instructor and adult learner, to progress from an area of comfort to a learning environment that challenges their knowledge levels.[5]

Factors Impacting Workplace Learning

Workplace learning often occurs in relation to an employee's need to make decisions regarding workplace situations. Factors that can impact workplace learning are:

- *The contingent* — The unplanned and informal nature of work that often requires impromptu decisions.
- *The practical* — The need to solve problems efficiently and effectively.
- *The process* — The need for the worker to think about past actions to learn and value professional growth.
- *The particular* — The need to address current situations, compromising wisely as required.
- *The affective and social domains* — The ability to make decisions that align with the learner's professional and personal emotional and social values.[6]

---

[3] *Ibid.*
[4] *Ibid.*
[5] Hatscan, "WHMIS Training" (Presented in Edmonton, AB, February 26-27, 2007).

Motivation for Behavioural Change

Although worker disability management education can enhance awareness on work-related topics and impart knowledge, education may not be enough to elicit the desired work behaviours. The age-old belief that by just "merely telling people what they should do" will lead to the adoption of desired behaviours has proven time and again to be faulty. Rather, behavioural change is complex and requires motivation.

Motivators for behavioural change by workers are:

- understanding, valuing, and embracing the importance of the behavioural change;
- management rewarding the adoption and display of the desired behavioural change;
- cultural support for the desired behavioural change; and
- management passion for and demonstration of the desired behaviours.[7]

Additional motivators for adult learners include:

- *Social relationships*: to make new friends, to meet a need for associations and friendships.
- *External expectations*: to comply with instructions from someone else; to fulfil the expectations or recommendations of someone with formal authority.
- *Social welfare*: to improve ones ability to serve mankind, prepare for service to the community and improve the ability to participate in community work.
- *Personal advancement*: to achieve higher status in a job, secure professional advancement, and stay abreast of competitors.
- *Escape/Stimulation*: to relieve boredom, provide a break in the routine of home or work and provide a contrast to other exacting details of life.
- *Cognitive interest*: to learn for the sake of learning, seek knowledge for its own sake and to satisfy an inquiring mind.[8]

---

[6] Beckett and Hager (2000) as reported in K. Sitzman, "Learners Reframed" (2006) 54 American Association of Occupational Health Nurses Journal 292.

[7] T. Roithmayr, "The Great Safety Performance Model", in D. Dyck, *Occupational Health & Safety: Theory, Strategy & Industry Practice* (Markham, ON: LexisNexis Canada, 2007), c. 5, "Occupational Health And Safety Leadership and Commitment".

[8] S. Lieb, "Principles of Adult Learning", available online at: <http://honolulu.hawaii.edu/intranet/committees/FacDevCom/guidebk/teachtip/adults-2.htm>.

Factors Impacting Effective Disability Management Education

Some factors that impact the delivery and effectiveness of disability management education are:

- *Group size*:

   Groups of fewer than 25 attendees tend to result in effective learning.[9]

- *Session length and frequency*:

   Attendance at multiple training courses along with the use of frequent, short educational sessions works the best.

- *Mode of training*:

   Demonstrations and interactive learning techniques are more effective than the use of written instructions, lectures, or training videos.

- *Transfer of training*:

   Transfer of learning occurs best with the use of contrasting illustrations of the "desired" versus the "undesirable" behavioural practices.

- *Promotional activities*:

   Learning is best supported by the use of rewards to reinforce the learning, as well as incorporating the desired practices into the manager or employee's performance appraisal.

- *Management role*:

   Management support and endorsement of the Disability Management Program and the related practices. There is an old saying, "*What interests the boss, fascinates employees.*"

- *Learner retention*:

   Learner retention is impacted by the teaching modes used. Research has shown that 72 hours post-instruction, learner retention is as follows:

---

[9] K. Saarela, "An Intervention Program Utilizing Small Groups: A Comparative Study" (1990) 21 J. of Safety Research 149; T. Robins *et al.*, "Implementation of the Federal Hazard Communication Standard: Does Training work?" (1990) 32 Occupational Medicine 1133.

Figure 14.1: The Relationship between Instructional Modes and Learner Retention[10]

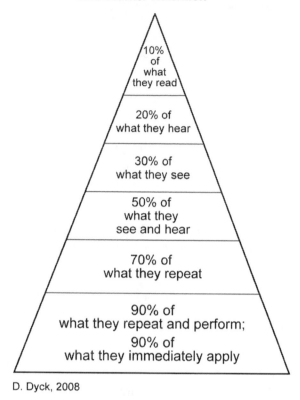

10% of what they read

20% of what they hear

30% of what they see

50% of what they see and hear

70% of what they repeat

90% of what they repeat and perform; 90% of what they immediately apply

D. Dyck, 2008

The message is to reinforce learning and to design courses so learners can apply the provided content.

Other Considerations

- To enhance the use of desired behaviours or practices, management should make doing those behaviours or practices the "path of least resistance"[11] — that is, make the disability management-related processes as logical and as easy to follow as possible.

---

[10] D. Dyck, *Occupational Health & Safety: Theory, Strategy & Industry Practice* (Markham, ON: LexisNexis Canada, 2007) at 358.

[11] Linneman, Cannon & DeRonde & Lamphear (1991), Lynch *et al.* (1990), Seto, Ching, Chu & Fielding (1990) and Wong *et al.*, (1991), cited in M. Colligan & A. Cohen, "The Role of Training in Promoting Workplace Safety and Health", in J. Barling & M. Frone, eds., *The Psychology of Workplace Safety* (Washington, DC: American Psychological Association, 2004) at 223.

- For education/training on disability management practices to be effective, supervisors/line management/foremen need to model the desired behaviours and practices.

- Disability management education is not a general panacea, or a "quick fix", for relationship problems within an organization. Its effectiveness is a function of the organization's overall commitment to providing a caring, responsible, and safe work environment, and the employees' perception and recognition of that commitment.[12]

DISABILITY MANAGEMENT EDUCATION: DEVELOPING A DISABILITY MANAGEMENT EDUCATIONAL SESSION

The following are the recommended steps for developing a disability management educational session:

1. Identify the Disability Management Education Needs

When planning a disability management educational program or individual instructional session, the first step is to determine the disability management educational needs of the target work group. Experienced educators recommend that a needs assessment be conducted so that the disability management educational session is relevant, timely, and related to a desired behavioural change or performance improvement.

A **needs assessment** is a form of gap analysis — it is the systematic exploration of the way things are (the current state) and the way they should be (the desired state). The desired outcome is to define the need — that is the gap(s) between the current and desired states with a view to reducing or eliminating those gaps.

Some recommended needs assessment techniques are:

- ***Review of Relevant Literature*** — Enables the educator to establish the "best practices" in disability management; that is, the "desired state".

- ***Consultation with Persons in Key Positions*** — Allows the educator to identify key problem areas that warrant improvement.

- ***Performance Analysis*** — Allows the educator to separate manager/employee disability management educational needs from other organizational issues by using a systematic approach to ensure that the instructional solutions address the identified problem.[13]

---

[12] M. Colligan & A. Cohen, "The Role of Training in Promoting Workplace Safety and Health", in J. Barling & M. Frone, eds., *The Psychology of Workplace Safety* (Washington, DC: American Psychological Association, 2004) 223 at 226.

[13] F. Bird & G. Germain, *Loss Control Management: Practical Loss Control Leadership*, rev. ed. (Loganville, GA: Det Norske Veritas, 1996).

- *Workgroup Analysis* — Enables the educator to identify the dynamics of the workgroup(s) of interest.[14]

- *Direct Observation* — Provides an evaluation of the manager/employee performance against industry disability management best practices. It helps to identify specific educational needs for individual workers.

- *Interviews* — Interviews would be held with employees and managers/supervisors who have been involved with the organization's Integrated Disability Management Program. The intent is to identify the associated knowledge/performance gaps and weaknesses.

- *Perception Surveys* — Bird identifies two survey methods — interviews and questionnaires. Interviews allow managers/employees to express their disability management learning needs to the interviewer. Questionnaires can be used to enable managers/employees to identify disability-related problems in which they feel they need further knowledge and skills.[15]

- *Incident and Injury Data* — By reviewing the company's short-term disability, Workers' Compensation, and long-term disability plan process and outcome experience, trends may indicate educational needs.

- *Focus Groups* — Once all the data have been collected and hypotheses for educational topics have been established, it is advisable to seek validation of those conclusions through the use of focus groups. A **focus group** is a representative sample of the target workplace population assembled to obtain their feedback on a particular issue or concern. Typically they are asked their opinion on a product, service, concept or idea. Open-ended questions are asked in an interactive-group setting, thereby encouraging the participants to freely express their thoughts and observations with other group members. In this instance, the intended outcome is to validate that the selected educational topics are indeed appropriate.

These tools can be used by the Disability Management professional/ practitioner to define the learner's disability management educational needs, the work conditions/relationships that could impact the educational sessions, and the specific educational topics to be covered.

The results can then be compared against the "best practices" in the field of disability management, with the noted differences identified as the "practice gaps". Those gaps deemed as "substandard", most likely would be the subjects or topics for the upcoming disability management education.

---

[14] *Ibid.*
[15] *Ibid.*

2. Decide the Disability Management Education Priorities

Once the disability management education needs and options have been identified, the next step is to decide which of the identified disability management educational topics to pursue. To do this, determine which disability management educational topics:

- are legally required;
- if not addressed, have the potential for causing the greatest harm;
- are necessary for new or inexperienced employees;
- would benefit the largest number of employees; and
- are of top priority to employees and/or the employer.

Based on these considerations, choose a suitable disability management topic or series of topics.

3. Establish the Disability Management Education Objectives

Objectives are the specific aims for the disability management education program. They are statements of intentions, prepared in such a way that they guide problem-solving (or instructional) behaviours, and form the basis for measuring the results. They address two questions:

1. What must be taught?
2. What will success look like?

Objectives state the desired outcomes in a manner that is meaningful, relevant, realistic, actionable, sustainable, useful, measurable, and result-oriented. Each content,[16] learning[17] and teaching[18] objective should be written so that it is:

- specific, that is it measures only one thing;
- measurable;
- attainable, but challenging;
- realistic; and
- time-specific.

---

[16] **Content objective** is a specific statement that speaks to the content to be covered in a training session/course. For example: *"At the end of this educational session, the manager will be aware of the legislative requirement for accommodating ill/injured employees back into the workplace."*

[17] **Learning objective** is a specific statement that speaks to the worker learning. For example: *"At the end of this educational session, the manager will know how to report an employee medical absence."*

[18] **Teaching objective** is a specific statement that speaks to what the worker must do to demonstrate what he or she knows or how to apply a learned skill. For example: *"At the end of this educational session, the manager will be able to demonstrate the organization's absence recording practice."*

In terms of what must be taught and what success would look like, it is important to first determine the level of learning required. There are four levels of learning:

1. *Awareness* — the aim of the instruction is to create a level of basic understanding and knowledge about the topic. When applied to the field of disability management, this would involve providing employees, management, and other stakeholders with information on a specific Integrated Disability Management Program.

2. *Knowledge* — the desired outcome is that the participants will understand and be able to recall the information provided. For example, this level of instruction would be more detailed with an expected outcome of the learners being able to recite the information provided should they be asked.

3. *Application* — in many workplace situations, the level of learning required is the participant's ability to learn and be able to apply a defined skill. In terms of disability management, this would entail a worker knowing what to do should he or she experience an illness/injury. Likewise, it would involve the supervisor being able to apply the company's Integrated Disability Management principles and practices.

4. *Synthesis* — the intent of the instruction is to prepare the learner to be able to take the disability management concepts, principles and practices and apply them to a number of scenarios. As the word synthesis suggests, it is the ability to "build on" to known information. An example would be the Disability Management Steering Committee being able to enhance a company's Integrated Disability Management Program based on knowledge about disability management concepts, principles, and industry best practices.

Once the desired level of learning is established, the next step is to decide what can be done to achieve the desired level of learning and what success would then look like.

There are a number of disability management education measures that can be used to promote general understanding of the value and benefits of an Integrated Disability Management Program:

• *General Disability Management Program education provided to all stakeholders*. This measure is informational and aimed at awareness-raising.

• *Specialized education on the various stakeholder roles and responsibilities in the Integrated Disability Management Program.* This measure is aimed at achieving a functional level of knowledge and application.

• *Specialist education and training for Disability Management practitioners on the "best practices" in Disability Management*. This measure is designed to enable the learner to apply the knowledge gained and to be able to "build on" that information.

- *A new employee Occupational Health & Safety Orientation*, designed to provide an overview of the company's Occupational Health & Safety standards, is an excellent opportunity to explain the company's Integrated Disability Management Program and how it works. It should include an explanation of the:
  - company's commitment to Disability Management;
  - company's Integrated Disability Management Program and policy;
  - how the Integrated Disability Management Program works;
  - the employee's Integrated Disability Management Program responsibilities;
  - reporting work injuries/illnesses; and
  - return-to-work procedures after injury or illness.

This approach promotes a level of awareness about the Integrated Disability Management Program and the new employee's role in that program.

- Employee education can be reinforced through the use of ongoing disability management presentations held at Safety Meetings or other employee group meetings.

- **Coaching** and **mentoring** are two other means of reinforcing disability management education.

- Online training courses are an additional instructional measure. They can include videos, interactive modules, task-based exercises, *etc.*, designed for reinforcing other disability management education measures.

4. Develop a Plan for Achieving the Disability Management Education Objectives

Select content, teaching methods, media, and materials that will best meet the target audience's needs and enable the achievement of the stated disability management education objectives. To begin with, research the topic, find relevant information, and select the content to be presented.

Decide on the appropriate instructional method(s). Will it be educator-led instruction, self-directed learning guided by instructional materials; or a combination of both methods? Will it be delivered in a traditional teaching setting; in a work site setting; or through the use of online learning techniques?

There are many different instructional media and materials from which to choose. The crucial thing is to pick an instructional approach that best suits the audience and yields the best outcome(s). This means attention to details like:

- How will the disability management educational session(s) be delivered?

- Who is best suited to provide the disability management education, to assist with the educational session, and to attend the educational session?
- When to schedule the disability management educational session?
- What materials are best used to enhance the learning experience?
- Where to best host the disability management educational session?

5.   Prepare the Teaching/Lesson Plan and Related Materials

Preparing the teaching/lesson plan means operationalizing the stated objectives. In addition to being the agenda for the disability management educational session, it describes the how, who, when, what and where's stated above. A typical disability management teaching plan is provided in Table 14.1.

6.   Deliver the Disability Management Educational Session

(i) **Preparation**: The key to a successful disability management educational session is the preparation. Be well-versed on the educational topic and then create a presentation that effectively delivers the desired message(s). Appendix 1 provides a sample disability management educational presentation — *"Supervisor's Role: WCB Claims and Disability Management"*.

Next, be fully familiar with the instructional materials and the related media equipment. Test the audio/video aids to ensure that they work properly and can be seen and heard throughout the room. Have the handouts ready and arranged for timely and easy distribution during the session.

Finally, make sure the facilities are set up to support a positive learning experience. The teaching method, media and materials dictate how the room should be arranged. Lectures are best delivered in a classroom setting, whereas the use of "application exercises", such as case studies or role playing, requires tables for group work. An instructional session that uses computer online training requires the preparation of specialized equipment.

(ii) **Rehearse the presentation**: Rehearsal allows the presenter to test the timing of the instructional events and to make adjustments as necessary. Take the time to run through the actual presentation, noting any needed content or time changes that need to be made. It also is an opportunity to get a feel for the room and how best to position oneself to best get the educational messages across.

Presenting evokes many strong emotions, some of which are not that pleasant for the presenter. The important thing is to recognize nervousness and to prepare for it. One suggestion is to have the opening statements for the presentation written out. Once underway, most presenters are comfortably able to proceed.

When presenting, there are a number of "golden rules" to uphold, namely:

- speak clearly and loudly enough for people to comfortably hear;
- use plain, simple language: avoid the use of metaphors and awkward examples;
- use conversational hand gestures;
- move around comfortably;
- stick with the jargon and technical terms that are familiar to the audience;
- use concrete examples;
- look at the audience when speaking;
- avoid playing with a pen, pocket items, keys, coins, laser pointer, *etc.*;
- only use diagrams and teaching aids that enhance the learners' understanding of the spoken materials;
- create a friendly atmosphere;
- encourage and reward audience participation;
- stay on topic;
- seek audience feedback on the pace of the teaching, the relevancy of the materials and the participants' satisfaction levels; and above all,
- **start and end the session on time** — it shows respect for the participants.

7. Evaluate the Disability Management Educational Session

Evaluation is the only way to ensure that the disability management education is effective and that it meets the stated objectives. It is also an important way to improve Disability Management Education Programs and sessions. This topic is covered in detail in the following section.

Table 14.1 Worker Disability Management Education: Teaching Plan[19]

DISABILITY MANAGEMENT TEACHING PLAN

Title: **Disability Management: Overview**

Educator: **Joe Black**

Type: ✓ **One-hour Session**   •Half-day Workshop (3 hours)   •Full-day Workshop (6 hours)

Objectives *By the end of the session, the participants will.....*	Content (Topics)	Time Frame	Presenter	Teaching Strategy
1. Understand the term, Disability Management	Provide an operational definition of Disability Management	5 minutes	Joe Black	Presentation
2. Learn why Disability Management is important	• Explain the costs of disabilities • Demonstrate that these costs are increasing • Discuss the factors that impact employee absenteeism	10 minutes	Joe Black	Presentation

---

[19] D. Dyck, "Worker Disability Management Training Plan" (Calgary, AB: Progressive Health & Safety Consulting, 2009).

Objectives *By the end of the session, the participants will.....*	Content (Topics)	Time Frame	Presenter	Teaching Strategy
3. Understand what companies can do to manage the human losses and the associated financial and business costs	Explain how companies can: • effectively address employee absenteeism • manage disabilities	15 minutes	Joe Black	Presentation
4. Appreciate the need for joint labour-management involvement in Disability Management Programs	Discuss the importance of joint labour-management involvement and commitment	5 minutes	Joe Black	Presentation
5. Learn the benefits of an Integrated Disability Management Program	Explain the benefits that an Integrated Disability Management Program affords to all stakeholders.	10 minutes	Joe Black	Presentation
6. Discover how an Integrated Disability Management Program can benefit this company and its stakeholders	Explain how an Integrated Disability Management Program can benefit this company and its stakeholders	15 minutes	Joe Black	Presentation and participant discussion

DISABILITY MANAGEMENT EDUCATION: MEASUREMENT OF EFFECTIVENESS

There are two levels of measurement available for evaluating Disability Management Education Programs. One is a high-level evaluation of the entire Disability Management Education Program; the other is the measurement of the effectiveness of an individual Disability Management Education Program session.

Evaluation of the Entire Disability Management Education Program

Program success can be measured in a number of ways. By **auditing** a Disability Management Education Program, one can measure the program structure, procedures, and outcomes against the established program objectives and/or standards. This measurement technique allows for the identification of the gaps between the current and ideal state of the program. Typically, the evaluation process includes recommendations for reaching the ideal state.

A second approach to measuring program success is to undertake a **cost-benefit analysis** projection. This involves determining the losses a company would incur without a Disability Management Education Program and compare that against the losses the company experiences when disability management education is provided. The financial differences are deemed the "*benefits realized*".

A third approach is to establish the **return on investment (ROI)** as a result of the Disability Management Education Program. The ROI is a performance measure used to evaluate the efficiency of an investment or program, or to compare the efficiency of a number of different investments or programs. In this particular circumstance, the ROI is calculated by dividing the benefits realized through the Disability Management Education Program by the cost of the education program. A positive ROI indicates that a benefit exists because of the Disability Management Education Program. The ROI is a popular metric because of its versatility and simplicity. That is, if an investment/program does not yield a positive ROI, or if there are other opportunities with a higher ROI, then the investment/program should be not be undertaken.

Benchmarking program data against that of external parties is a fourth approach. **Benchmarking** is a continual and collaborative discipline that involves measuring and comparing the results of the key process with "best performers" or with one's own previous achievements. Internally, benchmarking can be used to compare against previous program outcomes, processes, practices, and performance. Externally, benchmarking involves comparing a company's Disability Management Education Program, processes, and/or results against those of another organization/company, or group of organizations/companies.

Typically, benchmarking is undertaken to improve the quality of the service or product, address an identified problem, learn "best practices", or in response to increased pressures to improve performance. It is not an exact science, but rather a methodology designed to determine the best way to do things.

When benchmarking a Disability Management Education Program, the process should be to:

1. plan what, and who, to benchmark;
2. collect and analyze the relevant data;
3. integrate the findings into a familiar frame of reference; and
4. develop an action plan that would implement, monitor and evaluate the changes made.

The benefit of benchmarking is that the methodology provides a rational and objective framework for observing what other companies are doing in terms of providing disability management education, how they are doing it, and what can be done to improve the process even more. In essence, it is a quality improvement tool because the decision-making is based on facts, and on learning from the actions of others.

A fifth approach is a **client satisfaction survey** regarding the disability management education offered. The typical approach is to ask those employees who participated in the Disability Management Education Program for their impressions of the session(s), presenter(s), and outcomes. Typically, the questions asked are designed to measure specific elements of the program such as timeliness, accessibility, appropriateness, and universality of the program.

Evaluation of a Specific Disability Management Educational Program/Session

Educational programs/sessions should be designed so that evaluation is one of the elements of the delivery of the session/program. Evaluation can be done before the program/session begins (pre-assessments), during the program/session (process evaluations), or at the end (outcome evaluations).

The **pre-learning assessments** are a baseline measure of level of awareness/knowledge/skills/abilities that the participant possesses prior to the educational session. This can be done using checklists, surveys, interviews, or demonstrations.

Process evaluations or **formative evaluations** are measures of how the learning experience is progressing. Some educators call this "a temperature-taking" exercise. The intent is to determine if the teaching approach is aligning with the audience's expectations and needs. It is a test of relevancy. The results enable the educator to make the appropriate adjustments to the teaching plan. This can be done formally using a checklist or multiple-choice questionnaire, or informally, using a show of hands to questions posed by the educator. It is also a teaching tool that enables the learners to test and evaluate their own levels of comprehension, and to reinforce the teaching. Thus, it increases the potential for retention of the materials learned.

Outcome evaluations are more complex. In essence, they are designed to determine if the disability management education program/session met the participants' expectations in terms of the pre-stated disability management education objectives. They are summative evaluations and include a measurement of:

- *Participant reaction to the instruction*: Participant satisfaction questionnaires are the "tool of choice" to determine the degree to which the session/ program met participant expectations and needs; and whether the participant believes that the instruction will make a difference in future job performance/work behaviours.

- *Change in participant awareness/knowledge levels*: "Before and after" tests are used to establish if the session/program objectives have or have not been met.

- *Change in skills/behaviours/attitudes*: Through proficiency tests, direct observation of disability management practices/behaviours and/or self-reports on skill improvement or application of the learning concepts, educators can measure the difference(s) made as a result of the disability management educational session.

- *Change in Disability Management Program performance measures*: These are objective markers that occur as a result of the disability management education, such as improved reporting of disability claims or an increase in the rate of work accommodations.

- *Organizational impact*: Changes to outcome measures related to the Integrated Disability Management Program are often used, for example, a reduction in disability claim costs. One common example is a reduction in the Short Term Disability plan claim costs as a result of the disability management education.

When evaluating an educational session/program, controlling for confounding variables poses a huge challenge for the program designers. A **confounding variable** is a variable that confuses the relationship between the dependent and independent variables and that needs to be controlled through the design of the evaluation plan or via statistical procedures. The **dependent variable** is the outcome variable of interest; the variable that is hypothesized to depend on or be caused by another variable. The **independent variable** is the variable that is believed to cause or influence the dependent variable. In a research scenario, it is the variable that is manipulated.

Disability Management Education: Measurement Model

A measurement model for evaluating a Disability Management Education Program/session (Figure 14.2) can be used to evaluate an entire education program or a specific educational session. It illustrates the measurement the cycle for educational session/program objectives, beginning with the educator setting the instructional objectives.

Figure 14.2: Disability Management Education Session/Program Measurement Model[20]

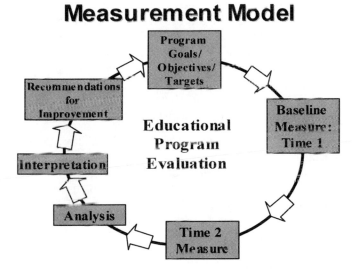

The model suggests measurement of each of the educational session program objectives prior to and following the delivery of the education. The difference in the results between Time 1 and Time 2 is then determined, analyzed, and interpreted. From the outcome of that exercise, the evaluator can reach a conclusion as to whether or not the educational session/program was successful, and the degree to which it did or did not make a difference.

WORKER DISABILITY MANAGEMENT EDUCATION: MAKING IT FUN

Adult learning principles tell us that teaching should be self-paced, meaningful, relevant, and interesting for the target audience. With these

---

[20] D. Dyck, *Occupational Health & Safety: Theory, Strategy & Industry Practice* (Markham, ON: LexisNexis Canada, 2007).

principles in mind, making learning fun requires innovative approaches. The following section provides some industry examples of creative educational approaches, techniques, and tools.

Disability Management: Role-playing

Role-playing is an instructional technique used when participants are expected to be able to apply a specific skill. For example, the participants can be placed in groups of three players — the disabled employee, the supervisor, and an observer. The disabled employee and the supervisor are assigned a defined role to play. The purpose of the exercise is for the supervisor to be able to interact with the employee in such a way as to be able to successfully craft a gradual return-to-work plan. The duty of the observer is to provide feedback to the supervisor in regards to the approach taken. The observer also elicits feedback from the employee as to how he or she felt about the interaction.

Role-playing is a very effective teaching-learning tool. Participants tend to really enjoy the experience.

Disability Management: Situation Critique

Another effective way to instruct supervisors, Disability Case Managers, Disability Claim Managers, *etc.* is to have them watch and then critique the Disability Management-related actions of actors depicted a videoed scenario. The intent is for the participants to identify "what worked well", "what could have been done differently", and "how they might have handled the situation". This is another popular approach with participants, and one that tends to promote sustainable learning.

Disability Management Crossword Puzzle

On the theme of being innovative in getting Disability Management Program and practice messages across, the use of crossword puzzles can be implemented. They can be used as part of an educational session, or online as a "learning challenge". Figure 14.3 is an example of a disability management crossword puzzle.

One Canadian company developed a series of crossword puzzles, each with different messages, and posted them on their company intranet for employees to complete and submit to the Occupational Health & Safety Department. All the correctly answered puzzle submissions received a reward that supported injury/ illness prevention, and positive Disability Management Program practices.

Figure 14.3: Disability Management Crossword Puzzle[21]

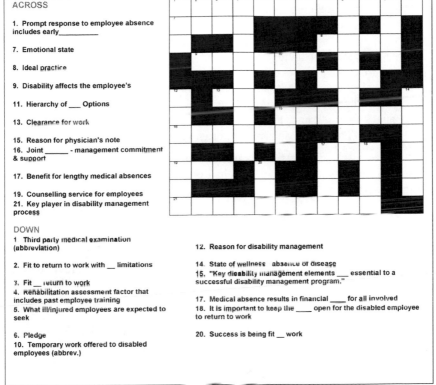

ACROSS

1. Prompt response to employee absence includes early_____

7. Emotional state

8. Ideal practice

9. Disability affects the employee's

11. Hierarchy of ___ Options

13. Clearance for work

15. Reason for physician's note
16. Joint _____ - management commitment & support

17. Benefit for lengthy medical absences

19. Counselling service for employees
21. Key player in disability management process

DOWN

1 Third party medical examination (abbreviation)

2. Fit to return to work with __ limitations

3. Fit __ return to work
4. Rehabilitation assessment factor that includes past employee training
5. What ill/injured employees are expected to seek

6. Pledge
10. Temporary work offered to disabled employees (abbrev.)

12. Reason for disability management

14. State of wellness absence or disease
15. "Key disability management elements ___ essential to a successful disability management program."

17. Medical absence results in financial ____ for all involved
18. It is important to keep the ____ open for the disabled employee to return to work

20. Success is being fit __ work

THE VALUE OF DISABILITY MANAGEMENT EDUCATION PROGRAMS

Like any other business endeavour, Integrated Disability Management Programs and the education offered must demonstrate value to the organization. Education is expensive, and the effectiveness and sustainability of the learning is often questioned. So how can disability management professionals/practitioners demonstrate a positive return on the company's investment in disability management education?

Research has shown that what employers value, is whether or not the educational or training programs demonstrate significant changes in worker behaviours, the way workers do their jobs, and the manner in which workers think and talk about their jobs.[22] With that in mind, disability management professionals/practitioners can use

---

21   See page 507 for Crossword answers.
22   Bongarde Holdings Inc., "How to Demonstrate the Value of Training Programs", 4:2 Safety Compliance Insider 14, available only through subscription: <http://www.safetysmart.com>.

the measurements discussed earlier in this chapter, to demonstrate the value of disability management education. For example:

- participant reaction to the disability management education;
- change in participant awareness/knowledge levels about the Integrated Disability Management Program and their responsibilities/accountabilities;
- change in skills/behaviours/attitudes towards mitigating the disability losses and costs;
- change in Disability Management Program practices and performance as a result of the knowledge attained; and
- changes to outcome measures related to employee disability and the Integrated Disability Management Program .

Research also indicates that company leaders are influenced by case studies illustrating the impact that education had on the behaviour of workers at other companies/organizations.[23]

SUMMARY

Providing disability management information and education helps employers to:

- ensure that union leaders and employees are prepared to address and learn from the human losses and costs associated with illness/injury;
- develop a positive workplace culture, where assistance to disabled employees and mitigation of disability losses are the norm;
- identify ways to continually improve the Integrated Disability Management Program and ultimately the overall health and safety of the workplace; and
- be compliant with the related Canadian Human Rights (Duty to Accommodate) and Workers' Compensation legislation.

Disability management education can lead to effective learning with the deliverables being:

- stakeholders competent in their Integrated Disability Management Program roles and responsibilities;
- reduced disability-related losses and costs;
- accurate collection of disability data and outcomes;
- identified illness/injury prevention measures; and
- avoidance of unnecessary human and financial costs.

Additionally, the provision of effective disability management education exceeds the minimum level of worker education and training mandated by Occupational Health & Safety legislation and serves to demonstrate to employees/ union leaders that the employer cares and is committed to assisting employees when they are ill or injured. That message holds true for the community at large. Hence, Disability Management Education Programs can contribute to enhancing employee morale and the organization's corporate image.

---

[23]   *Ibid.*

APPENDIX 1

Sample Disability Management Educational Presentation

Supervisor's Role

WCB Claims
&
Disability
Management

Injured Worker's WCB Package

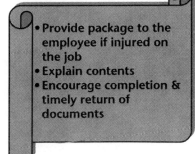

- Provide package to the employee if injured on the job
- Explain contents
- Encourage completion & timely return of documents

WCB Worker's Report

- Encourage provision of complete details on the incident & injury
- Employee to submit form to WCB directly

WCB Employer's Report

- Complete company incident report & WCB Employer's Report
- Answer all questions
- Submit to Disability Management Coordinator
- Employer's Report must be sent to WCB within 72 hours
- WCB must be notified of MW arrangements within 24 hours of employee's return-to-work

WCB Physician's First Report

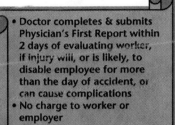

- Doctor completes & submits Physician's First Report within 2 days of evaluating worker, if injury will, or is likely, to disable employee for more than the day of accident, or can cause complications
- No charge to worker or employer

WCB Physician's Progress Report

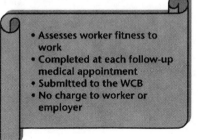

- Assesses worker fitness to work
- Completed at each follow-up medical appointment
- Submitted to the WCB
- No charge to worker or employer

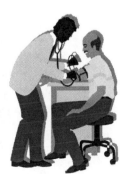

Disability Management Program

Definition:

An active process of minimizing the impact of an impairment on the individual's ability to compete in the workplace

Disability Management Program

Company DMP is based on:

- ❏ Early intervention
- ❏ Access appropriate medical care
- ❏ Modified/alternate work
- ❏ Ergonomic accommodations
- ❏ Helping employees to get back to work in a safe & timely manner

Disability Management Program

Management Role:

- Be responsible & accountable for assisting ill/injured employees
- Make every attempt to accommodate the employee
- Ensure modified work (MW) is meaningful, safe & provided in a timely manner for a successful return-to-work (RTW)

Disability Management Program

Supervisor's Role:

- Give injured employee the WCB package
- Complete & submit WCB & company forms within 24 hours
- Determine if MW is available
- Work with Disability Management Coordinator to arrange MW details
- Support employee
- Assist co-workers to understand the MW arrangement
- Monitor the MW arrangement
- Provide feedback on the MW & DMP, & how it can be enhanced

Disability Management Program

Discussion / Questions

APPENDIX 2

Disability Management — Crossword Answer

CHAPTER REFERENCES

Beckett and Hager (2000) as reported in K. Sitzman "Adult Learners Reframed" (2006), 54 American Association of Occupational Health Nurses Journal 292.

F. Bird & G. Germain, *Loss Control Management: Practical Loss Control Leadership*, rev. ed. (Loganville, GA: Det Norske Veritas, 1996).

Bongarde Holdings Inc., "How to Demonstrate the Value of Training Programs", *Safety Compliance Insider*, Vol. 2 (4), at 14. Available through <www.safetysmart.com>.

M. Colligan & A. Cohen, "The Role of Training in Promoting Workplace Safety and Health", in J. Barling & M. Frone, eds., *The Psychology of Workplace Safety* (Washington, DC: American Psychological Association, 2004).

D. Dyck, *Occupational Health & Safety: Theory, Strategy & Industry Practice* (Markham, ON: LexisNexis Canada, 2004) at 358.

D. Dyck, "Worker Disability Management Training: Teaching Plan" (Calgary, AB: Progressive Health Consulting, 2009).

Hatscan, "WHMIS Training" (Presented in Edmonton, AB, February 26-27, 2007).

S. Lieb, "Principles of Adult Learning", available online at: <http://honolulu.hawaii.edu/intranet/committees/FacDevCom/guidebk/teachtip/adults-2.htm>.

Linneman, Cannon & DeRonde & Lamphear (1991), Lynch *et al.* (1990), Seto, Ching, Chu & Fielding (1990) and Wong *et al.*, (1991), cited in M. Colligan & A. Cohen, "The Role of Training in Promoting Workplace Safety and Health", in J. Barling & M. Frone, eds., *The Psychology of Workplace Safety* (Washington, DC: American Psychological Association, 2004).

National-Louis University, "Malcolm Knowles: Apostle of Andragogy", available online at: <http://www.nl.edu/academics/cas/ace/resources/malcolmknowles.cfm>.

T. Robins *et al.*, "Implementation of the Federal Hazard Communication Standard: Does Training work?" (1990) 32 Occupational Medicine 1133.

T. Roithmayr, "The Great Safety Performance Model", in D. Dyck, *Occupational Health & Safety: Theory, Strategy & Industry Practice* (Markham, ON: LexisNexis Canada, 2007), c. 5, "Occupational Health And Safety Leadership and Commitment".

K. Saarela "An Intervention Program Utilizing Small Groups: A Comparative Study" (1990) 21 J. of Safety Research, 149.

Saarela et al. (1989), Borland *et al.* (1991) and Karmy & Martin (1980), cited in M. Colligan & A. Cohen, "The Role of Training in Promoting Workplace Safety and Health", in J. Barling & M. Frone, eds., *The Psychology of Workplace Safety* (Washington, DC: American Psychological Association, 2004).

Chapter 15

Disability Management: The Social Capital Theory Perspective for Managing Disability Claims

By Kelly Williams-Whitt[1]

INTRODUCTION

The role of business in contemporary society has changed in recent years. A narrow customer and market focus has been forced to expand as corporations interact in an increasingly complex social context. In addition to making a profit, organizations are also expected to behave in ways that are socially responsible.

The underlying idea is that organizational action has an influence beyond traditional "business" boundaries. Therefore, they should not only generate profit, but should also take into account the social and ecological environment. This challenges the belief that social issues, like disability in the workplace, are not the concern of corporate management. Organizations are connected to, and dependent on, society; so what was once "outside" the organization is now "inside" and vice versa. Organizations are forced to be **open systems**[2] operating as flexible networks in an unpredictable and complex environment.[3]

Since businesses are open systems, change inside or outside of the system alters how the individual parts function and how well the parts work together. When employee disability occurs, whether it originates from an occupational (internal) or non-occupational (external) event, the organization is expected to respond in a socially responsible manner. This means minimizing the negative

[1] Dr. K. Williams-Whitt, RN, has an MBA and a PhD in labour relations and teaches labour arbitration, collective bargaining, corporate social responsibility, and workplace diversity at the University of Lethbridge. She has conducted research in disability accommodation, speaks frequently at conferences, and has authored a number of peer reviewed journal articles on this subject. Dr. Williams-Whitt co-authored, *Employment Law for Business and Human Resource Managers in British Columbia and Alberta* (Toronto: Emond Montgomery, 2008), and co-edits, *Perspectives on Disability and Accommodation* (Victoria, BC: NIDMAR, 2009 forthcoming), a National Institute of Disability Management and Research publication.

[2] An **open system** is a system that is permeable to external influences.

[3] M. Schoemaker, A. Nijhof, & J. Jonker, Human Value Management: "The Influence of the Contemporary Developments of Corporate Social Responsibility and Social Capital on HRM" (2006) 17:4 Management Review 448.

and maximizing the positive impacts for the affected stakeholders (*e.g.*, the disabled employee, colleagues, shareholders, *etc.*). Furthermore, the way that organizations manage these impacts internally, will have an effect on society as a whole. For example, the success that a business has with its Disability Management Program and practices influences:

- employment rates for disabled persons;
- the number and nature of social programs necessary to support those who are unable to work; and
- productivity effects both internally (affecting shareholders) and externally (affecting tax rates, gross domestic product, *etc.*).

To maximize the positives and minimize the negatives, it helps if organizations think in *system terms* when they are managing disability in the workplace. In other words, creative problem-solving can be enhanced by using a *social-network lens* to view the world of work.

Social networks are how work gets done. Goods are produced with raw materials that are accessed through supply *networks*. Transformation of the raw materials occurs through *collaboration* with employees whose roles are interdependent. Businesses sell their products and services by utilizing the knowledge, skills, and *relationships* of their marketing and sales teams. Social networks are the people we know, and how well we know them. Some networks (*e.g.,* family or work teams) involve daily interaction and require a great deal of trust and goodwill to function well. Others may require less maintenance because they involve infrequent interactions, or the nature of the interactions is restricted to information exchange.

By understanding how disabilities in the workplace affect these social networks, Disability Management professionals/practitioners may be better able to understand and address complex issues and situations. Social Capital Theory offers one way to analyze the impact of workplace disability on social relationships. This chapter uses Social Capital Theory to discuss internal workplace networks, but it should be recognized that the effect of disability in the workplace is far-reaching. Social networks extend beyond the walls of the corporation and can positively, or negatively, influence the system. Disability Management professionals/practitioners can use the example of internal relations discussed below and apply a similar analysis to respond creatively to disability challenges originating from external network relations (*e.g.,* Workers' Compensation Boards, the employee's medical team, *etc.*).[4]

---

[4]   For further discussion of external network relations see K. Williams, "Accommodating Disability in the Workplace" (PhD dissertation, University of Calgary, Alberta, 2004) [unpublished].

SOCIAL CAPITAL THEORY

Social Capital Theory suggests that our willingness to help others is based on the quality of our social relationships. We are willing to help (exchange favours) only when we feel a sense of goodwill, trust, and empathy towards other members of our social group. We are also more likely to grant favours if we know that at some point in the future, the same courtesy will be returned, either directly by the recipient, or by someone else within our social group.[5] So social capital actually belongs to "the social group as a whole" (it is one element of organizational culture), but access to it, depends on one's degree of individual social credit.[6]

Membership in a group ensures that individuals understand how others expect him or her to behave. Just belonging to a work group allows some access to social capital, but employees increase or decrease their individual "goodwill credits" by the effort they put toward building and maintaining ties with their colleagues. Employees can build up their social capital credits by:

- following group norms (*e.g.,* being courteous, being respectful of others, taking responsibility for mistakes, *etc.*),
- behaving in a trustworthy manner (*e.g.,* keeping confidences, being honest, being reliable, *etc.*);
- meeting role-identity expectations (*e.g.,* arriving at work on time, performing in an expected manner, being productive, *etc.*); and
- participating in the repayment of obligations (*e.g.,* working in groups/teams, assisting others, *etc.*).[7]

Disability can influence an employee's ability to participate effectively in the activities that build and maintain access to social capital. Employees, who begin a return-to-work opportunity with few social capital credits, and those who deplete their social credits as a result of multiple health episodes, often face distinct social sanctions. For example, the assistance necessary for accomplishing work tasks may be intentionally delayed or denied. They may be given the least desirable jobs/shifts as a form of punishment by managers. They may be subjected to incivility, or negative hyper-vigilance, where peers and managers look for indications of exaggeration or falsification of the health condition. The effect of these social sanctions is to decrease successful re-integrations because the psychological environment at work becomes intolerable.[8]

---

[5]   R. Putnam, "Bowling Alone: America's Declining Social Capital" (1995) 6:1 Journal of Democracy 65.

[6]   J. Coleman, "Social Capital in the Creation of Human Capital" (1988) 94 (Supp.), American Journal of Sociology S95.

[7]   J.M. Podolny & J.N. Baron, Resources and Relationships: Social Networks and Mobility in the Workplace" (1997) 62 American Sociological Review 673.

[8]   K. Williams-Whitt, "Impediments to Disability Accommodation" (2007) 62 *Relations Industrielles* 405.

RELEVANT TERMS

Social capital — The goodwill available to individuals through their social networks.

Social capital credits — Employees gain access to the goodwill of others when they have worked to establish personal credits. Credits are built by following group norms, being trustworthy, meeting group expectations, and returning favours.

Norms — Rules of behaviour agreed upon by a particular social group.

Social group/network — Any group of people with whom we have social relations. This can be a workplace team, a family, or any other group of individuals who engage in social exchange on a regular basis.

Organizational culture — A pattern of thinking, feeling, and acting that members of an organization pass along to new members as the "correct" way to perceive and behave.

Social sanctions — Any penalty imposed by a social group on a member who violates accepted standards of behaviour.

Social capital deficit — Occurs when a member of a social group is unable to build enough social capital credits to access the goodwill of the group.

Post-return absences — Employee absenteeism that continues after a disabled employee has returned to work in a temporarily or permanently modified position.

Expectancy violation — Occurs when an individual's behaviour does not conform to the expectations of others.

High-status employee — Any employee who is well regarded within the organization. High status may derive from an employee's formal position in the hierarchy, from a special level of expertise, or from the employee's social networking skills (*e.g.,* social capital credits).

DISABILITY MANAGEMENT AND SOCIAL CAPITAL THEORY

The Social Capital Theory is a concept that helps to illustrate the importance of relationships in terms of disability management and return-to-work situations. The following sections discuss how the employee's pre-diagnosis work history, the nature of a disability, and return-to-work behaviour patterns interact with the employee's and workgroup's social capital to affect return-to-work outcomes. Social capital will then be used as a tool to develop recommendations that help supervisors/ line management and Disability Management professionals/practitioners increase the likelihood of successful reintegration of the recovering employee back into the workplace.

Pre-diagnosis Work History

There are four problems that arise in an employee's work history that contribute to decreased social capital for those with disabling health conditions:[9]

1. Pre-diagnosis absenteeism;
2. A history of discipline-attracting conduct;
3. Difficult peer/manager relationships; and
4. Prior task performance.

1. PRE-DIAGNOSIS ABSENTEEISM

It is well understood that absenteeism after return-to-work is a significant challenge that needs to be well managed in order to successfully reintegrate an employee.[10] It makes scheduling difficult and can mean managers fail to meet their production targets. Absenteeism complicates relationships because peers become frustrated when they are too frequently required to cover the absent employee's missed shifts. It can also negatively affect the employee's skill maintenance if the occupation is one that requires technical proficiency. However, absenteeism *prior* to diagnosis, or time off for recovery, is also problematic, and has a detrimental effect that hangs on through the post-return-to-work phase.

Employees who are frequently absent before their disabilities are diagnosed may be attempting to re-enter the workplace with a social capital deficit. They are already seen as "attendance norm violators" when they begin their modified work program. There is also likely to be a period of time where absence levels continue to be quite high as the employee juggles ongoing treatment and the gradual return-to-work obligations. It is during this time that the employee must continue to rely on the goodwill of others and there is little opportunity to reciprocate favours that were granted earlier.

The absence-effect can be particularly poisonous when the cause of the pre-disability absenteeism is unclear or unknown. If early absences are believed to be within the employee's control (*e.g.,* not health-related, or preventable), then the employee's credibility is damaged, which further reduces access to any social capital.

---

[9] K. Williams-Whitt & D. Taras, "Disability and the Performance Paradox: Can Social Capital Bridge the Divide?" British Journal of Industrial Relations (2009, forthcoming).

[10] M. Baldwin & R. Butler, "Upper Extremity Disorders in the Workplace: Costs and Outcomes Beyond the First Return to Work" (2006) 16:3 Journal of Occupational Rehabilitation 296.

2.   A History of Discipline-Attracting Conduct

Engaging in discipline-attracting behaviours before the identification of a health condition can also result in a social capital deficit. Examples of discipline-attracting behaviours may include frequently arriving late for work, falling asleep on the job, or viewing inappropriate material on the Internet, among other activities. These behaviours may be characteristic of an unrecognized/untreated psychosocial problem, such as alcoholism or depression. But they can also be activities the employee would engage in whether ill or not. Engaging in discipline-attracting behaviour is considered a breach of workplace trust. As noted earlier, trust is critical in order to gain access to social capital. Confusion about whether the discipline-attracting behaviour is culpable (choice-based) or non-culpable (disability-driven) complicates the affected employee's ability to build goodwill at work.

3.   Difficult Peer/Supervisor Relationships

Conflict between ill or injured employees and their peers or managers also affects social support and acceptance. Furthermore, when conflict exists before the disability diagnosis, it often escalates after the employee's return-to work. The social capital of conflict for a disabled employee is more complicated to analyze than absence or discipline-worthy behaviour, because it involves the active engagement of more than one party. In other words, "*it takes two to tango*"; so it may affect the social capital credits of more than one person (and therefore the work team as a whole). Research has shown that people who differ significantly from their peers on the personality characteristic of "agreeableness" are more likely to engage in conflict.[11] So if a health condition affects the employee's "agreeableness", the disabled employee is less likely to be integrated into the social network and less likely to be categorized by others as a friend.[12] Since integration, liking, and friendship affect access to social capital, employees with a history of difficult peer/co-worker interactions, may find themselves without support should they become disabled.

4.   Prior Task Performance

The final work history factor that impacts social capital is task function. This refers to an employee's performance reputation, and illustrates an interesting paradox. Employees who were historically considered to be very high performers can have as much difficulty returning to work from an illness/injury as do employees who were considered to be poor performers.

The relationship between poor performance and social capital is self-evident. An individual who violated productivity or performance norms prior to illness or

---

[11]   M. Barrick, G. Stewart, M. Neubert, & M. Mount, "Relating Member Ability and Personality to Work-Team Processes and Team Effectiveness" (1998) 83:3 Journal of Applied Psychology 377.

[12]   *Ibid.*

injury is expected to continue to do so upon returning to the workplace. In essence, if the employee was not a "shining star" before getting ill or injured, the employee will not be a "shining star" upon his or her return. In this instance, access to social capital begins low and remains low.

Employees who have been high performers, however, run into two problems. Firstly, they may be more likely to suffer from mental health problems related to high levels of stress. Secondly, this group may have a difficult time accepting new life and work limitations. They believe they can quickly resume previous levels of task function. Peers and managers may contribute to this situation by applying pressure on the returning employee to conform to prior work performance standards. Consequently the high performer exceeds his or her medical restrictions. The result is often the onset of secondary stress-related health problems. So while this person may initially benefit from strong social support because he or she has built a "nest egg of social capital credits", repeated illness begins to deplete the stores quickly. Multiple illness and absence episodes eventually make it difficult for the high achiever to meet role expectations, comply with performance norms, and reciprocate favours. Eventually, access to social capital may be denied (Figure 15.1).

Figure 15.1: Relationship of Task Performance to Social Capital Credits

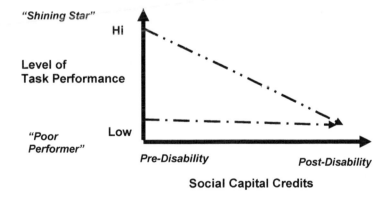

Nature of the Disability

Factors associated with the nature of a disability also can significantly affect how well the employee is reintegrated when returning to work. Return-to-work success is affected by the:

- acuity level of the health condition at the time of return;
- chronic, recurring nature of some health conditions;
- invisibility of the condition; and
- perceived degree of control the employee has over the onset or continuing manifestations of the condition.

The disability management literature generally advocates an early return to modified duties in order to prevent the development of social complications associated with health problems. An early return-to-work can decrease the financial impact on the employee, ease the process of adjustment, reduce costs for the employer, and increase the likelihood of successful rehabilitation.

Unfortunately, the empirical work evaluating the effects of "early returns" is very limited,[13] so it is difficult to establish what "early" is or should be. In some cases, employees have been aggressively pushed back to work during the acute stage of an illness. While it is true that sometimes the only way to find out if employees can perform tasks is to have them try, returning employees to work before they are well enough to meaningfully contribute means they are being forced to draw more heavily upon their social capital credits. Precipitous returns may exacerbate the original illness, or initiate another illness. If this occurs, the cycle of repetitive absence and capital depletion described for super-achievers begins.

The chronic, recurring nature of health conditions such as back pain, fibromyalgia, or depression also creates some very unique challenges. It can be more difficult to arrange long-term rather than temporary accommodations, and the unpredictable nature of these conditions may mean a larger number of work restrictions, or the need for sudden changes to planned work schedules. Post-return absences are also likely to be higher. The health and welfare of co-workers can be negatively affected, particularly if responsibility for the most physically or emotionally demanding tasks is permanently placed on peers who are already performing a full roster of duties.

There also are negative ramifications when expectations of a "full recovery" are not met. For example, an employee with a condition like multiple sclerosis, or amyotrophic lateral sclerosis (ALS), is faced with permanent changes to self-image, family relationships, and financial stability. Employers and co-workers struggle with a long-term increase in workload, and may mistakenly believe employees who have been recuperating and in receipt of disability benefits should be fully functional within a short period of their return to work. Work-expectancy violations[14] that occur when full recovery is not achieved, damage the reputation of even the most conscientious employee with a disability, and hence, their social capital.

A third disability feature that contributes to difficult accommodations for some employees is "visibility". It has traditionally been thought that the more visible the disability, the greater the discomfort experienced by observers;

---

[13]   R. Baril, D. Berthelette, & P. Massicotte, "Early Return to Work of Injured Workers: Multidimensional Patterns of Individual and Organizational Factors" (2003) 41:4 Safety Science 277.

[14]   B. Bettencourt, K. Dill, S. Greathouse, K. Charlton, & A. Mulholland, "Evaluations of Ingroup and Outgroup Members: The Role of Category-Based Expectancy Violation" (1997) 33 Journal of Experimental Social Psychology 244.

therefore, the greater the negative responses to the individual.[15] Newer research, however, suggests that being disabled "appearing healthy" may actually be more treacherous[16] for the ailing employee.

Disability visibility affects perceptions of illness legitimacy. Many health conditions do not change an individual's physical appearance. There is often no wheelchair, and no blood test, or X-ray that can confirm the existence of what is not visible to the naked eye. If an illness or health condition relies heavily on self-report for diagnosis and treatment, observers may believe that the employee is exaggerating the illness/injury to gain some "benefit". They may believe that the disability claim is being used to excuse bad behaviour, or to "cherry pick" the most favourable work shifts and duties. Therefore invisible conditions such as chronic pain or psychological illness are more likely to trigger suspicion and reduce the trust of the social group.

Furthermore, when colleagues feel intentionally betrayed, they want greater punishment for the perpetrator than if the breach of trust was accidental.[17] This means that in addition to the withdrawal of physical and psychological support that normally accompanies low levels of trust, employees with invisible health conditions may also become targets of social harassment campaigns. They face increased pressure to perform, along with the pressure of persistent and invasive medical investigation required by the employer seeking a definitive diagnosis.[18] When a disabled employee does not feel believed by others regarding the authenticity of his or her condition, there is a statistically significant likelihood that disability duration will actually increase.[19]

A fourth factor associated with the nature of the employee's disability is the onset and symptom control. Research suggests that the origin of a disability impacts acceptance in the workplace.[20] Employers and colleagues will respond negatively to individuals with disabilities if they perceive that those individuals are personally responsible for their own illness/injury. For example, an employee suffering from alcoholism will receive different co-worker response than an individual with a congenital heart defect. Since many illnesses have ongoing symptoms (*e.g.*, diabetes, colitis, alcoholism, migraine headaches, *etc.*) that are episodic and sometimes difficult to control, relapse is common.

---

[15] D. Stone & A. Colella, "A Model of Factors Affecting the Treatment of Disabled Individuals in Organizations" (1996) 21:2 The Academy of Management Review 352.

[16] K. Williams-Whitt & D. Taras, "Disability and the Performance Paradox: Can Social Capital Bridge the Divide?" British Journal of Industrial Relations (2009, forthcoming).

[17] K. Hong, & I. Bohnet, "Status and Distrust: The Relevance of Inequality and Betrayal Aversion" (2007) 28:2 Journal of Economic Psychology 197.

[18] K. Williams-Whitt, "Impediments to Disability Accommodation" (2007) 62:3 *Relations Industrielles* 405.

[19] J. Smith, V. Tarasuk, S. Ferrier, & H. Shannon, "Prognosis of Musculoskeletal Disorders: Effects of Legitimacy and Job Vulnerability" (Toronto: Institute for Work and Health, Working paper # 67, 1998).

[20] D. Stone & A. Colella, "A Model of Factors Affecting the Treatment of Disabled Individuals in Organizations" (1996) 21:2 The Academy of Management Review 352.

Managers and peers who think the employee is "cured" when they return-to-work, may also believe any reoccurrence of symptoms is because of a deliberate "failure to follow medical advice". So even if the employee is not blamed for the onset of the condition, co-workers and managers may still assign guilt.

When employees are thought to be responsible for the onset or ongoing control of symptoms, stereotyping occurs. Colleagues attribute other personality traits to the ill/injured employee such as being irresponsible, threatening, or lacking in integrity and impulse control.[21] Social capital requires that individuals feel connected to, and identify with, others in their network. When the social group members assign stereotypes, they do not want to believe that they share these negative characteristics, so they distance themselves from the individual. The social group decreases communications (avoidance) and when the members do interact, individuals become less friendly and more uncomfortable (*e.g.,* decreased eye contact, abrupt conversations, unfriendly demeanor, physical avoidance, *etc.*).

Human beings also tend to seek others who agree with their assessments of a situation or person. They endorse the shared negative beliefs and support policies and practices that are consistent with their beliefs and values, resulting in disadvantages to the disabled employee.[22]

Return-To-Work Cooperation

A final dynamic that influences the social capital accumulation for disabled employees is return-to-work cooperation. Two opposing behaviour patterns affect how observers characterize the returning employee, and therefore, how much social capital is made available. Co-workers and managers view cooperation as a continuum where the most successful accommodations are associated with employees who fall in the midrange. The least successful return-to-work outcomes occur for those employees at the extreme ends of the continuum, that is, those employees who are characterized as "too gung ho" and those who are characterized as "woe is me" (Figure 15.2).

---

[21]   *Ibid.*

[22]   D. Amodio & P. Devine "Stereotyping and Evaluation in Implicit Race Bias: Evidence for Independent Constructs and Unique Effects on Behaviour" (2006) 91:4 Journal of Personality and Social Psychology 652.

Figure 15.2: Continuum of Employee Level of Cooperation

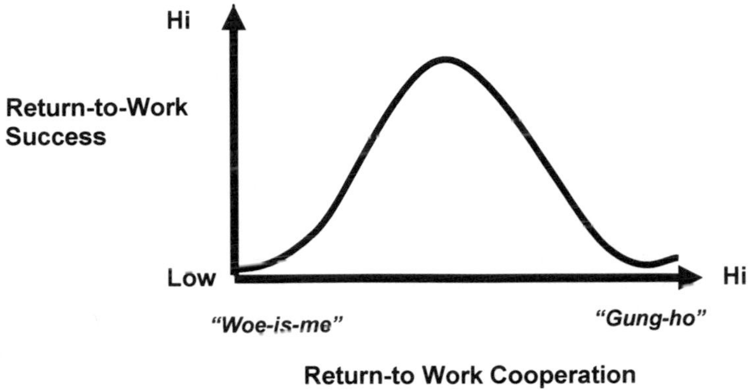

Return-to Work Cooperation

In general, enthusiastic employees earn social credits because they appear willing to follow group norms, and others believe they will eventually be able to reciprocate any favours granted. However, those employees who are unrealistically "gung ho" engage in less productive rehabilitation behaviours such as declining medical or psychological assistance, or refusing to follow treatment regimens. They may also push for a very early return-to-work or demand tasks that exceed the medical recommendations for their chance of a successful rehabilitation.

Alternatively employees who appear unenthusiastic about returning to work engage in behaviours that are viewed as evasive — switching physicians, refusing to release medical information, alternately accepting and then rejecting proposed work accommodations, and being inconsistent in communications with the employer (*e.g.,* not returning phone calls, providing different information to different individuals, being non-committal about a potential return-to-work date, *etc.*).

There are many reasons why employees may engage in the counterproductive return-to-work behaviours. The conduct may be a manifestation of the illness itself (*e.g.,* anxiety or paranoia). It may be that the employee is simply not psychologically ready or able to return to work.[23] The employee may be in denial about the existence of the disability or very fearful about disclosing a stigmatized illness. If an employee is new to the workgroup, he or she may not realize that their behaviours are inappropriate, or are being negatively viewed.

---

[23]   J. Prochaska & C. Diclemente, "Stages and Processes of Self-Change of Smoking: Toward an Integrative Model of Change" (1983) 51:3 Journal of Consulting Clinical Psychology 390.

The behaviours may also be part of the grieving process,[24] or a method of coping with the illness.[25]

Regardless of the cause, the impact on the employee's social capital is consistent. Employees who engage in behaviours associated with the "woe is me" end of the continuum are often believed to be lying or lazy. Their behaviours violate norms of trust, reciprocity, productivity, and responsibility, which decrease access to goodwill. Social capital for employees who engage in behaviours associated with an extremely "gung ho" attitude, may take longer to decline because they are initially perceived as exceeding the social group's norm-based expectations. However, over time, illness episodes are likely to increase because these employees tend to refuse treatment and to believe that they can manage both their jobs and their health conditions without help. Repeated illness and absence episodes tax the patience of peers/managers, and their initially high access to social capital dwindles.

Social Capital Theory: Recommendations for Action

Disability Management Coordinators face unique challenges when the social capital of employees has been damaged. It is important to understand that the challenge is not only to re-integrate the employee, but also to help him or her mend some of the "bridges burned" prior to the disability absence. Disability Managers can also enable them to develop the skills needed to earn social credits that would help them better fit back into the workplace.

The following are twelve recommendations for organizations and Disability Management professionals/practitioners that utilize the social capital concepts:

1. ***Educate the Workforce***: Changing attitudes is difficult, but organizations that systematically educate their leaders, and validate disability accommodation as a social responsibility of the organization are more likely to have success. Crossovers between unrecognized symptoms and emerging performance and relationship problems often occur. Symptoms of illness are frequently mistaken for the employee being insubordinate or possessing a poor work attitude. Educating managers/supervisors so they are familiar with the "tell-tale" signs and symptoms that indicate there may be an emerging health condition (*e.g.,* significant changes in behaviour or personality, altered visual appearance, *etc.*) may improve the likelihood that appropriate health intervention can occur before social capital loss is significant.

---

[24] J. Rothaupt & K. Becker, "A Literature Review of Western Bereavement Theory: From Decathecting to Continuing Bonds" (2007) 15:1 The Family Journal: Counseling and Therapy for Couples and Families 6.

[25] R. Moss-Morris, "Symptom Perception, Illness Beliefs, and Coping in Chronic Fatigue Syndrome" (2005) 14:3 Journal of Mental Health 223.

Teaching employees about the concept of social capital and its influence on return-to-work outcomes may also be beneficial. Most employees require assistance with a health condition at some point in their work experience, which means it benefits everyone to build access to social capital in workplace and other social networks. Assisting others during a return-to-work is one of many ways to accumulate individual credits. It is like *"money in the bank"*. Hence, managers should discuss ways that employees can build social capital specific to their workplaces.

2. ***Redesign Work Processes***: To decrease the likelihood of relapse and secondary health conditions that are so detrimental to social capital, employers may wish to consider redesigning work processes to decrease physical and psychological stress. This may mean integrating job-task rotation so that employees get regular relief, or hiring more part-time employees to even-out the distribution of strenuous or demanding work.

Increasing job flexibility and choices are also beneficial practices. Jobs with high task demands and little control over how the tasks are completed are the most likely to result in employee disability.[26] So even if the demand-side of the equation cannot be addressed, it may be possible for employers to increase individual autonomy by allowing employees to control the pace and organization of their work.

Develop a plan for intermittent employee absences. This can be done by adding a contingent workforce — individuals who prefer to work "on-call", casual, or part-time shifts, so that the core workgroup is not always required to cover for disability-related employee absenteeism. This can also be accomplished by building some "slack into the system" so that productivity can be maintained comfortably even if the workgroup is short-staffed.

If there is no way to redesign work processes that better incorporate long- and short-term accommodations, employers should reward or increase vacation time for those employees who take on the heavier workload while covering for an employee absence. Rewarding activities that accrue social capital encourages more employees to participate and increases the total pool of social capital as well as individual credit slips.

3. ***Collaborate***: Perhaps one of the simplest steps that employers can take to reduce conflict is to involve the affected employee and the union early in the return-to-work planning. The employer must initiate contact with the ill/injured employee and can also issue an invitation to the union. The union is a contractual resource for the employee and will often be necessary (from both practical and legal perspectives) to be part of the implementation of complex work accommodations. So it makes sense to involve union

---

[26] R. Karasek, "Job Demands, Job Decision Latitude and Mental Strain: Implications for Job Redesign" (1979) 24:2 Administrative Science Quarterly 285.

representatives early in the return-to-work planning to prevent, rather than promulgate, any misunderstandings.

Employees who are involved from the onset of the disability claim and return-to-work planning have a clearer understanding of the lengths that the employer went to, to find an appropriate work accommodation. If employees feel their concerns have been heard and addressed, the resulting sense of procedural justice may help to decrease fear, counterproductive behaviours, and grievance filing.[27]

Furthermore, combative relations between employers and unions may spill over, affecting organizational trust and social capital, thus decreasing the likelihood of future successful return-to-work options.[28]

4. ***Communicate and Document***: In order to increase cooperation for psychologically ill employees, Disability Management Program and return-to-work processes must be transparent and easily understood. Giving regular "in-service" education regarding the Disability Management Program and return-to-work processes increases the workforce's exposure to the return-to-work concepts. This tactic enables all employees/managers/ union representatives to identify appropriate actions at the time of employee illness/injury, and decreases the likelihood of preventable stress.

   Employers should also regularly communicate with employees who are on sick leave, following up their conversations with documentation that is copied to the employee and perhaps the union. This approach is helpful for confirming mutual understandings, and may be invaluable for employees who are on medication or recovering from conditions that may affect their ability to recall details.

5. ***Investigate Accommodation Options***: In order to decrease the occurrence of social capital problems associated with precipitous returns to work, employers should investigate the "fit" between the employee's work capabilities and the duties of the target work position. A physical and psychological job demands analysis of the target work position should be conducted. The capabilities of the returning employee should then be matched to tasks that provide observable value to the organization (*i.e.,* meaningful work), and to others in the work group; and therefore, provide the employee and workforce as a whole, with an opportunity to replenish social capital accounts.

6. ***Reintegrate Slowly***: For employees who are fearful of failure or illness/injury relapse, Disability Management professionals/practitioners (in conjunction with medical practitioners) should develop a return-to-work

---

[27]   Y. Cohen-Charash & P. Spector, "The Role of Justice in Organizations: A Meta-Analysis" (2001) 86:2 Organizational Behavior and Human Decision Processes 278.

[28]   K. Williams-Whitt, "Impediments to Disability Accommodation" (2007) 62 *Relations Industrielles* 405.

plan that builds confidence. Motivation is positively influenced by setting goals that are somewhat difficult — that is, a stretch, but attainable in nature. Achieving the goal promotes self-efficacy so the next goal can be set slightly higher.[29]

Employees benefit from **work hardening**[30] that occurs in small increments and allows some flexibility for managing illness symptoms. Giving employees time/opportunity to manage symptoms helps prevent the blaming (loss of capital) that occurs when others believe the disabled employee is not following prescribed treatment regimens.

7. *Manage Expectations*: This applies to the expectations of the returning employee as well as the expectations of colleagues/managers/union representatives. Firstly, it is important to regularly confirm the importance of cooperating with the return-to-work plan and following the recommended medical restrictions. Explain to the returning employee that success is more likely for returning employees in the middle of the performance continuum than those at either extreme.

Secondly, when task limitations mean psychologically ill employees are not able to meet productivity norms or fulfill all role expectations, managers may be able to work with them to find ways that work favours can be reciprocated without creating undue stress.

Thirdly, employers can also manage peer expectations by verifying which tasks the affected employee can fulfill, and which tasks are prohibited, being careful to maintain the confidentiality of protected employee personal health information. Peers should be encouraged to avoid pressuring the affected employee and should be acknowledged for their assistance.

8. *Legitimize the Work Accommodation*: In order to decrease the negative evaluations associated with invisible conditions, onset control, and symptom control, employers need to legitimize the work accommodation of the returning employee. Some of this can be done by Disability Management professionals/practitioners. They can tackle misinformation "head on" and debunk myths about work safety and disability authenticity. They can teach the workplace how to assist the disabled employee rather than blaming the employee when he or she experiences symptoms or a relapse at work.

Employers can also utilize social capital principles to more specifically legitimize accommodated employees. An individual's position in a network

---

[29] A. Tolli & A. Schmidt, "The Role of Feedback, Causal Attributions and Self-Efficacy on Goal Revision" (2008) 93:3 Journal of Applied Psychology 692.

[30] **Work hardening** is the post-injury/illness work experience aimed at gradually increasing the recovering employee's ability to tolerate a particular level of physical and psychological work tasks.

(the individual's power and the power of those with whom he or she is affiliated) can significantly influence the way the individual is treated by peers.[31] It may therefore be beneficial to accommodate, or retrain, disabled employees in positions that build or require special expertise. Employers can also create opportunities for increased engagement between "high status employees" and accommodated employees, which may be mimicked by others.[32]

9. ***Resolve Conflict***: Conflict resolution is critical for re-integrations to be successful. Conflict decreases trust,[33] liking, and therefore, social capital. Although conflict may be inevitable when individuals work closely together, and particularly when tasks and rewards are interdependent, employers can prevent the escalation of burgeoning differences. Employees can be taught the requisite skills to resolve conflict themselves, or selected workers can be trained as mediators who can be called upon to "step in" when others require neutral third-party assistance.

If work conflict contributed to stress-related illness in the first place, or was a significant problem prior to the affected employee's disability leave, it may be necessary to bring in a mediator from outside of the organization. Finally, if relationships have been damaged beyond repair or conflict continues despite intervention, it may be advisable to return the recovering employee to a different work unit within the organization.

10. ***Correct the Situation***: In order to prevent the escalation of workplace conflict and perceptions of favoritism, employers must also develop a fair and transparent process for investigating discipline-worthy conduct. However, it is important to consider the possibility that the observed behaviours may be linked to employee's illness or injury.

Managers and employees should be taught to recognize signs of illness, elevated physical and psychological stress, or sudden behavioural shifts. The moment the investigator becomes aware that the "discipline-worthy behaviour" may be linked to a health problem, the employee should be referred to an Employee Assistance Program and the employer's approach must transform from discipline to work accommodation. For further elaboration regarding performance management and distinguishing between

---

[31] K. Aquino & K. Lamertz, "A Relational Model of Workplace Victimization: Social Roles and Patterns of Victimization in Dyadic Relationships" (2004) 89:6 Journal of Applied Psychology 1023.

[32] H. Weiss "Subordinate Imitation of Supervisor Behaviour: The Role of Modeling in Organizational Socialization" (1977) 19 Journal of Organizational Behaviour and Human Performance 89.

[33] C. Langfred, "The Downside of Self-Management: A Longitudinal Study of the Effects of Conflict on Trust, Autonomy, and Task Interdependence in Self-Managing Teams" (2007) 50:4 Academy of Management Journal 885.

performance and mental health issues, see the "Rule-Out-Rule" approach presented later in this chapter.

11. ***Reward***: Classic business literature encourages and rewards super-productivity.[34] Bonuses are often tied to early completion of projects, above average production levels, and cost-cutting measures. These reward systems can, however, be counterproductive if they decrease the trust and amount of social capital that builds within the organization as a whole (*e.g.,* frequent layoffs, creating competition between employees for pay and bonuses, *etc.*). In order to decrease the likelihood of stress-related illnesses, and to improve accommodation of valued employees when they return from sick leave, employers should also reward balance. Managers should receive incentives for maintaining healthy work teams and for successfully accommodating employees from other business units. Likewise, employees should be rewarded for following medically sanctioned work restrictions and for assisting in the accommodation of co-workers.

12. ***Avoid Assumptions***: A final recommendation and the one that is perhaps the most difficult to implement, is to avoid making assumptions about an employee's performance credibility while they are ill. There are many reasons why employees may engage in counterproductive behaviour during an illness and in the gradual return-to-work phase. While some employees may be consciously attempting to scam the system, true malingering and fraud are actually quite rare.[35] Employers should be wary of embarking on campaigns that attempt to reveal employee malingering. They can easily slide toward harassment of the employee resulting in costly grievances, investigations, and human rights challenges.

Research on the "secondary gains" associated with disability, indicates that to successfully manage counterproductive behaviours, employers must first have a trusting relationship with employees.[36] Social capital flows in both directions. If the employment relationship is trusting, it enables those involved in the work accommodation process to identify underlying problems such as financial instability, conflict, or anxiety, without triggering conflict. Once underlying issues are resolved, rehabilitation and return-to-work plans can be prepared with the affected employee that include goal setting and rewards for achieving realistic productivity targets.[37]

---

[34] T.J. Rodgers, "No Excuses Management" (1990) 68:4 Harvard Business Review 84.

[35] J. Dersh, P. Polatin, G. Leeman & R. Gatchel, "The Management of Secondary Gain and Loss in Medicolegal Settings: Strengths and Weaknesses" (2004) 14:4 Journal of Occupational Rehabilitation 267.

[36] *Ibid.*

[37] *Ibid.*

These 12 recommendations are applicable to the case management of all types of disabilities, physical or psychological in nature. In most instances, the employer will not be privy to the nature of the employee's disability. Hence, it is recommended that all disability situations be approached in the same manner, with a focus on employee performance and, if required, suitable work accommodation.

In terms of the occupational health professionals and physicians who will have access to the employee's medical information, the case management and successful return to work by the employee experiencing a psychological disability poses a number of challenges. The remainder of this chapter is dedicated to addressing the effective management of psychological disabilities.

PSYCHOLOGICAL DISABILITIES

By Dianne Dyck

The incidence of mental health disorders and claims is on the rise.[38] The World Health Organization estimates that 25% of the population will be affected by a mental health disorder at some time in their lives,[39] and by 2020, depression is predicted to be the second leading cause of disability worldwide.[40]

Despite all the advances made in medicine, mental health disabilities remain poorly understood and stigmatized.[41] We all, from time to time, experience sadness, anxiety, forgetfulness, poor concentration, or mood swings. But when our mental state becomes such that we cannot function as we normally would, a mental health problem or condition exists.

Workers suffering from mental health conditions tend to try to work through their condition, which often goes unrecognized and untreated. Most physicians find it a challenge to help these workers return to gainful employment.[42]

---

[38] Watson Wyatt Worldwide, *Staying@Work 2005 — Canada* (2005), available online at: <http://www.watsonwyatt.com/research/resrender.asp?id=w-860&page=1>; and
Marsh Risk Consulting, *Workforce Risk: Fourth Annual Marsh Mercer Survey of Employers' Time-off and Disability Programs*, (2003), available online at: <http://www.marshriskconsulting.com>.

[39] World Health Organization (2005), reported in National Quality Institute (NQI), "So What Are Canadian Organizations Doing to Improve Mental Health? With Some Exceptions, Not Enough" (September 9, 2005), available online at: <http://www.nqi.ca/articles/article_details.aspx?ID=532>.

[40] OMA Committee on Work and Health "Return to Work for Patients with Mental Disorders" (January 2005), available online at: <http://www.oma.org/home.asp>.

[41] Global Business and Economic Roundtable on Addiction and Mental Health, "*News Release*: Ground-breaking Survey on Mental Health in the Workforce" (November 19, 2007), available online at: <http://www.gwlcentreformentalhealth.com/english/userfiles/news/pdf/s7_004756.pdf>; and IPSOS-Reid, *Mental Health in the Workplace: Largest Study Ever Conducted of Canadian Workplace Mental Health and Depression* (November 19, 2007), available online at: <http://www.ipsos.ca>.

[42] S. Calhoun & P. Strasser, "Generations at Work" (2005) 53:11 American Association of Occupational Health Nurses Journal 469.

Likewise, it is frustrating for employers/co-workers to understand why a worker, who looks fine, needs to be off work for extended periods of time.

To gain a better understanding of this situation, consider some of the following facts. Depressive disorders rank as the second most common reason for visiting a Canadian physician.[43] People dealing with depression experience difficulty in maintaining their level of productivity both at home and at work. Fewer than 20 per cent of the people who need mental health treatment actually get it. Serious depression can result in a work absence of 40 or more days.[44] As well, returning to work after weeks of disability leave can be a "punishing experience" for the employee.

Depression

Depression is a physical condition that is centred in the brain, but affects the whole body. It can strike early in the person's life creating life-long problems and costs. The manifestations of depression are:

- slumping home and work performance;
- poor timekeeping;
- increased substance abuse;
- frequent headaches and backaches;
- withdrawal from social contact;
- demonstrations of poor judgment;
- indecisiveness;
- constant fatigue or lack of energy; and
- unusual displays of emotion.[45]

Depression is also associated with other conditions like diabetes, hypertension, asthma, heart disease, and stroke (cerebral vascular accident).

So who is at "*high risk*"? According to the Global Business and Economic Roundtable on Addictions and Mental Health, the workers most vulnerable to developing a clinical depression are those who are in their prime working years; employees with 10 to 15 years with the same company; and workers new to the

---

[43] OMA Committee on Work and Health, *Mental Illness and Workplace Absenteeism: Exploring Risk Factors and Effective Return to Work Strategies* (April 2002), available online at: <http://www.oma.org/home.asp>.

[44] Global Business and Economic Roundtable on Addiction and Mental Health, *Roundtable Roadmap to Mental Health Disability Management in 2004-05* (Working document prepared June 25, 2004), available online at: <http://www.mentalhealthroundtable.ca/june_2004/monitor_june2004.pdf>.

[45] Global Business and Economic Roundtable on Addiction and Mental Health, *Roadmap to Mental Health and Excellence At Work in Canada, Summer Draft.* Presented to The Ontario Chamber of Commerce, Economic Summit on Mental Health and Productivity in Ontario, A Pilot for Canada, Sutton Place Hotel, Toronto, Ontario, Canada, June 8, 2005 (2005) at 24, available online at: <http://www.bcmentalhealthworks.ca/files/roadmap-mentalhealth-at-work.htm>.

workforce.[46] As well, women over 40 years of age experience more stress than any other worker age group due to combined work and home stressors, and the inability to effectively balance the two.[47]

Middle managers are especially vulnerable.[48] Caught between senior management demands and subordinate expectations, middle managers tend to experience the negative effects of workplace pressures. Some "tell-tale" signs and symptoms of work distress are:

- increased irritability and impatience;
- lack of concentration and an inability to stay focused;
- avoidance and distancing from work situations and social interactions;
- open frustration;
- demonstration of "back stabbing" and/or passive aggressive actions;
- ever-lengthening work days;
- persistently late for meetings;
- "working at home" to avoid the negative energy at work;
- avoidance behaviours;
- missing deadlines and commitments;
- physical symptoms; and
- periodic work absences.[49]

The following table (Table 15.1) provides a number of relevant statistics on depression and mental health.

---

[46] Global Business and Economic Roundtable on Addiction and Mental Health, *Roundtable Roadmap to Mental Health Disability Management in 2004-05* (Working document prepared June 25, 2004), available online at: <http://www.mentalhealthroundtable.ca/june_2004/monitor_ june2004.pdf>.

[47] CCOHS, "Stress Higher Among Working Women Over Forty, Study Finds" (September 5, 2005) CCOHS 5.

[48] Global Business and Economic Roundtable on Addiction and Mental Health, *Roadmap to Mental Health and Excellence At Work in Canada, Summer Draft*. Presented to The Ontario Chamber of Commerce, Economic Summit on Mental Health and Productivity in Ontario, A Pilot for Canada, Sutton Place Hotel, Toronto, Ontario, Canada, June 8, 2005 (2005) at 43, available online at: <http://www.bcmentalhealthworks.ca/files/roadmap-mentalhealth-at-work.htm>.

[49] *Ibid.* at 24.

Table 15.1: Depression — Facts and Figures

Depression — Facts and Figures

Based on numerous research and surveys, the following data has been complied:

- 18% of Canadians will be diagnosed with depression at some point in their lives.[50]
- 8% of Canadians will experience depression, but go undiagnosed, at some point in their lives.[51]
- 43% of Canadians felt that acknowledging depression would prove detrimental to their careers.[52]
- 66% of Canadians who experienced depression linked its onset to a non-work triggering event, such as a relationship breakdown, death, *etc.*[53]
- Managers estimate the average cost of employee depression to Canadian organizations to be $7K in terms of "presenteeism" — at work, but not fully functional, and $10K in terms of absenteeism.[54]
- Although willing to help depressed employees, the direct supervisors are unsure how to go about that task. 43% of Canadians felt that acknowledging depression would prove detrimental to their careers.[55]
- A majority (82%) of employees think that senior leaders should make helping employees experiencing depression a Human Resources priority.[56]
- The rates of depression and suicide are higher among high-stress occupations such as physicians, nurses, soldiers, police officers and farmers. There are also gender differences with men being four times more likely to commit suicide than women.[57]
- Employees who are diagnosed with depression and take appropriate medication will save their employer an average of 11 days a year in prevented absenteeism.[58]

---

[50] IPSOS-Reid, *Mental Health in the Workplace: Largest Study Ever Conducted of Canadian Workplace Mental Health and Depression* (November 19, 2007), available online at: <http://www.ipsos.ca>.

[51] *Ibid.*

[52] *Ibid.*

[53] *Ibid.*

[54] *Ibid.*

[55] *Ibid.*

[56] *Ibid.*

[57] W. Glenn, "Depression, Suicide Rate Linked to Occupations" (July/August 2008) 24:5 O.H.S. Canada 20.

[58] M. Wilson, R. Joffe & B. Wilkerson, *The Unheralded Business Crisis in Canada: Depression at Work*, An Information Paper for Business, incorporating "12 Steps to A Business Plan to Defeat Depression" (Toronto: Global Business and Economic Roundtable on Addiction and Mental Health, 2002) at 22, available online at: <http://www.mentalhealthroundtable.ca/aug_round_pdfs/Roundtable%20report_Jul20.pdf>.

Management Intervention

Management can "make a difference" by promoting an awareness of the relationship between workplace practices and the promotion of positive mental health among employees. Intervention can exist at a "systems level", "management-practices level", and "individual-employee level". Some constructive approaches are to:

- Clearly state the organization's/company's commitment to mental health and excellence at work.
- Make mental health practices part of the organization's/company's vision of a healthy workplace as per the Wilson Principle to Mental Health Excellence at Work[59] (Figure 15.3).
- Evaluate the status of the organization's/company's mental health level of awareness, practices, and status.
- Incorporate mental health into organizational/company workplace systems, such as management accountability, Human Resources practices, and Occupational Health & Safety Programs.
- Develop policy objectives that support employee mental health well-being, namely:

  - education and training;
  - primary prevention;
  - secondary prevention; and
  - graduated return-to-work.

- Target and eliminate common management stress-producing practices.
- Guide managers/supervisors to help them evaluate work stress levels — theirs and that of the employees.
- Educate supervisors/managers on how to distinguish between developing medical conditions and work performance problems, *e.g.*:

  - educate supervisors and managers to ask questions of an employee which both respect the employee's privacy and help him or her to consider whether a health consultation is worth doing before the performance issues are reviewed in more conventional terms;
  - encourage the employee to consult a family physician, other health professional, or EAP service provider; and
  - defer a discussion on work performance until the completion of a health review.[60]

---

[59] The Wilson Principle to Mental Health Excellence is advocated by the Honourable Michael Wilson, Chairman of UBS Canada and Senior Chairman of the Global Business and Economic Roundtable on Addiction and Mental Health.

[60] *Ibid.* at 28.

Figure 15.3: The Wilson Principle to Mental Health Excellence at Work[61]

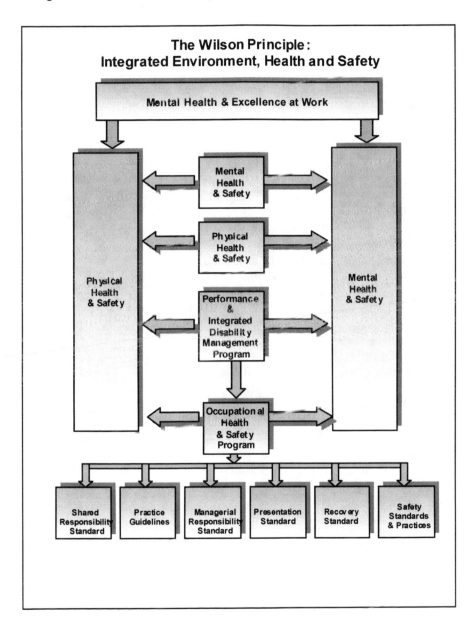

---

[61]   Global Business and Economic Roundtable on Addiction and Mental Health, *Roadmap to Mental Health and Excellence At Work in Canada, Summer Draft.* Presented to The Ontario Chamber of Commerce, Economic Summit on Mental Health and Productivity in Ontario, A Pilot for Canada, Sutton Place Hotel, Toronto, Ontario, Canada, June 8, 2005 (2005) at 18, available online at: <http://www.bcmentalhealthworks.ca/files/roadmap-mentalhealth-at-work.htm>.

- Promote a shared responsibility by all stakeholders for the management of employee mental health conditions.
- Address mental illness using a shared responsibility approach towards the road for recovery for the employee and the workgroup(s) (Figure 15.4).

EFFECTIVE MANAGEMENT OF EMPLOYEE PSYCHOLOGICAL DISABILITIES

By Dianne Dyck

To better understand the issues that employees with mental health disability face, consider psychological disability in terms of the Social Capital Theory. Recapitulating, Social Capital Theory suggests that an individual's willingness to help others is based on the quality of social relationships. People are willing to help (exchange favours) only when they feel a sense of goodwill, trust, and empathy towards other members of a social group.

In terms of a psychological disability, social relationships become disturbed; and when Disability Management professionals/practitioners work to facilitate and implement a gradual return-to-work plan, they are asking members of a particular social group to renegotiate their social relationships with the returning employee. Hence, the return-to-work period becomes a "testing ground" for workplace social relationships.

As previously noted, many psychological illnesses go unrecognized for a period of time — time in which the ill employee may act inappropriately and damage many social relationships. Hence, the return-to-work period is also a time for "damage control" and for "rebuilding social relationships". This is a serious challenge if the employee and social group are ill-prepared for the task, or if they lack the guidance and supports to achieve a successful resolution of the situation.

The 12 social capital recommendations for action proposed by Dr. Kelly Williams-Whitt nicely compliment the key principles for managing mental health disabilities provided by the Global Business and Economic Roundtable on Addiction and Mental Health, 2004-05.[62] The two approaches together can enable Disability Management professionals/ practitioners to broker a successful return-to-work opportunity for the recovering employee.

---

[62] Global Business and Economic Roundtable on Addictions and Mental Health, *Module 3, Guidelines for Mental Disability Management, Managing Employers Getting Started: On the Road to Mental Health and Productivity* (2006), available online at: <http://www.mentalhealthroundtable.ca>.

**Figure 15.4: The Road to Recovery: Return to Work —
A Shared Responsibility**[63]

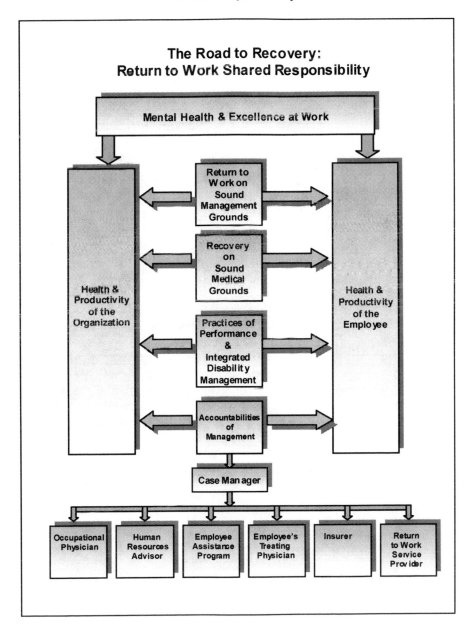

Roadmap to Recovery[64]

The suggested approach for organizations/companies and Disability Management professionals/practitioners is to embrace the **Roadmap to Recovery** as a means to effectively manage mental health issues in the workplace. The Roadmap to Recovery is designed to promote a **shared responsibility for mental health in the workplace by a variety of stakeholders** — investors, corporate directors, senior management, supervisory staff, insurers, physicians, Disability Management professionals/practitioners, clinical psychologists, and employees.[65]

A SYSTEMS APPROACH TO PROMOTING GOOD MENTAL HEALTH

Investors, when undertaking business investments, are encouraged to assess the quality of the management of the workforce mental health and well-being of the targeted companies. Boards of Directors are challenged to ensure that they uphold their duty towards promoting good employee mental health. Chief Operating Officers and presidents must provide responsible leadership and care for employee mental health and well-being. Frontline managers/supervisors should embrace and be held accountable for creating a workplace environment that enables human performance maximization and well-being. Insurers, in consort with client companies, are expected to develop insurance standards and best practices that counter the increased incidence and costs of mental health disability in the workplace. Health care providers — physicians, psychologists, occupational health nurses — are to enhance the identification, diagnosis, and treatment of mental health disorders, as well as to seek ways to effectively manage a return to optimal functioning for mentally ill employees. Lastly, employees, the stakeholder group most affected by mental illness, need to be responsible for their own mental health and well-being, as well as for that of co-workers.

AN ORGANIZATIONAL APPROACH TO PROMOTING GOOD MENTAL HEALTH

Organizations/companies can make a substantial difference in the mental health of their employees and the workplace environment. As well, should a mental health disability occur organizations/companies can mitigate the outcomes by:

- ensuring through education and training, that the workforce is aware of mental health disorders;

---

[64] Global Business and Economic Roundtable on Addiction and Mental Health, *Roadmap to Mental Health and Excellence At Work in Canada, Summer Draft.* Presented to The Ontario Chamber of Commerce, Economic Summit on Mental Health and Productivity in Ontario, A Pilot for Canada, Sutton Place Hotel, Toronto, Ontario, Canada, June 8, 2005 (2005) at 24, available online at: <http://www.bcmentalhealthworks.ca/files/roadmap-mentalhealth-at-work.htm>.

[65] *Ibid.* at 28.

- promoting the acceptance of mental health disorders;
- integrating good mental health practices into existing workplace systems and programs, such as management theories and practices, workplace policies and procedures, Human Resources Programs, Occupational Health & Safety Programs, Disability Management Programs, Workplace Wellness Programs, *etc.*;
- identifying and addressing the barriers to effective management of mental health disorders;
- establishing an acceptable approach to promoting early diagnosis and treatment of mental health disorders;
- implementing effective workplace programs and supports for employees experiencing mental illness; and
- actively promoting good mental health as an integral part of the work culture.

AN OPERATIONAL APPROACH TO PROMOTING GOOD MENTAL HEALTH

Operationally, the Roadmap to Recovery promotes the use of The Rule-Out-Rule — a management tool. The Rule-Out-Rule Approach is a means of effective management of employee performance. It is a management tool designed to enable a discussion about an employee's ability to perform in the workplace. It enables management to "tease apart" the presence of a developing medical condition from non-medically-related work performance issues as illustrated in Figure 15.5. In essence, it is a management tool for addressing and identifying mental health issues in the workplace.

Through regular performance management combined with empathetic communication between the employee and supervisor, the symptoms of mental and physical health problems can be identified in a timely manner. This performance management approach aligns well with the "Management of Personal Health Problems" (Figure 3.4) discussed in Chapter 3, "The Supportive Infrastructure for an Integrated Disability Management Program", as well as with the "Workplace Attendance Support and Assistance Program" described in Chapter 9.

Figure 15.5: Rule-Out-Rule — Performance Management[66]

Rule-Out-Rule

Step 1: As a result of observed changes in the employee's work performance, relationships, affect, energy levels, and other behavioural signs, the manager/supervisor plans to privately meet with the employee to identify concern for the employee's well-being and to express concern as well as to offer support and assistance.

Note: *To effectively verify if health problems are impacting the employee's work performance, management requires the knowledge and skills to address work performance problems.*

Step 2: The manager/supervisor privately meets with the employee to express care and concern about the employee's substandard work performance. The focus centers on work performance. However, the employee is encouraged to consult with his or her family physician or another health professional to rule out any related health issues. This step typically occurs when the employee is still functioning within the workplace.

Step 3: If the employee agrees to seek a medical assessment, the manager/supervisor defers from further discussion regarding work performance until the medical review has been completed and a fitness-to-work clearance has been received.

If the employee refuses, then the focus returns to work performance and what the employee plans to do about addressing the identified issues.

There may be some workplace issues that must be addressed as part of the conditions for remaining at work. For example, employees who have threatened, bullied, or physically assaulted other employees need to be informed that to remain in the workplace, this type of behaviour will not be tolerated. Under the various provincial and federal Occupational Health & Safety Acts, employers have a "duty of care" to protect all workers. However, this can be done in a constructive manner by setting the parameters around acceptable work behaviours.

---

[66] Global Business and Economic Roundtable on Addiction and Mental Health, *Roundtable Roadmap to Mental Health Disability Management in 2004-05* (Working document prepared June 25, 2004), available online at: <http://www.mentalhealthroundtable.ca/june_2004/monitor_june2004.pdf>.

THE CASE MANAGEMENT APPROACH TO RECOVERY TO GOOD MENTAL HEALTH

Early intervention is critical to a timely and successful return to work post illness. In terms of mental illness, the crucial time to arrest the potential disabling effects are within the first two weeks post-development of symptoms. Given the tendency for employees to try to "work through" a mental illness, early intervention may well involve action prior to a work absence.

To promote a safe, timely, and supportive return to work, it is very important to maintain contact and open communication between the workplace and the employee throughout the absence and return-to-work period of time. As previously mentioned, isolation worsens the employee's situation. Hence, organizations/companies are encouraged to adopt a system of clear communication among the major stakeholders, especially between the Occupational Health professionals and the healthcare providers. The aim is to ensure that employer and employee needs are identified and addressed. One option is the use of the Green Chart (Figure 15.6), and the associated communication tools:

(1) *The Case Manager's Roadmap to Recovery* (Figure 15.7).

(2) *The Physician's Roadmap to Recovery* (Figure 15.8).[67]

The Green Chart, which is designed specifically for use by Occupational Health professionals and treating physicians, promotes a dialogue on the relevant workplace concerns and employee performance issues. The intent is to identify the current state of affairs so that appropriate treatment and return-to-work plans can be developed and implemented. It also enables the workplace to put forth their concerns so that the health care providers can appreciate the magnitude of the challenges faced by the employee and employer.

The Green Chart: Case Manager's and Physician's Roadmap to Recovery

To successfully carry out their responsibilities, Occupational Health professionals are encouraged to use The Green Chart — Case Manager's Roadmap to Recovery (Figure 15.7). This tool is designed to track the case management details of the employee's illness in terms of the employee's mental health capabilities, as well as the steps for his or her re-entry into the workplace. It includes the physician's rating of the employee's capabilities, the physician's recommendations, a plan of action, and the desired outcomes.

The Green Chart — Physician's Roadmap to Recovery (Figure 15.8) is an assessment tool, as well as a communication tool. It enables the physician to rate the employee's mental/emotional functioning in terms of work performance, *e.g.*, the ability to understand and follow instructions, the ability to perform simple and repetitive tasks, *etc.* The collection of workplace information, historical employee performance information, and other details is also enabled.

---

[67] *Ibid.* at 17.

Within the disability period, it is paramount for the internal/external Occupational Health professional to:

- promote appropriate medical treatment for the employee;
- support the workgroup throughout the absence and return-to-work periods; and
- facilitate a successful resolution of the absence and return-to-work for the employee and workgroup.

Figure 15.6: The Green Chart[68]

(Specifically designed for use by Occupational Health Professionals
and attending physicians)

The Green Chart

Goal:
Facilitate a safe, timely, and supported return to work for the employee
suffering from a mental health problem.

Approach:
Implement the use of charts like the ones provided in Figure 15.7 and 15.8 to
house:

1. Information that the attending physician needs in order to clearly
   understand the implications of the mental health disorder on the
   individual's ability to function in the workplace. It would include:

   - the employee's job and functions;
   - the required skills such as technical skills, planning skills, attention
     to critical details, interpersonal skills, organizational skills, ability to
     concentrate, retention of information, time management, *etc.*; and
   - the work demands: pace, dynamics, need for interpersonal exchange
     and features of the work environment.

2. Information the employer needs to support the employee's recovery and
   return to work, such as:

   - the nature of communication recommended between work to home
     and home to work; and
   - the information the employee needs in order to understand,
     participate, and "own" the return-to-work plan.

---

[68] *Ibid.* at 17. Developed by Diane Rogalski for the Global Business and Economic Roundtable on
Addictions and Mental Health, and endorsed by Dr. Bruce Rowat, Medical Director, Sun Life of
Canada and the Bank of Montreal; and Dr. Sol Sax, Global Medical Director, Dupont Inc.

Figure 15.7: The Green Chart: Case Manager's Roadmap to Recovery[69]

Case Manager's Roadmap to Recovery — Green Chart

Employee: _____

Case Manager: _____

Date: _____　　　　Date of Next Case Meeting: _____

	Physician's Rating (1 to 5)	Physician Recommendations	Plan of Action	Desired Outcome
General work skills				
Understanding and following instructions				
Performing simple and repetitive tasks				
Maintaining a work pace appropriate to the work load				
Relating to other people beyond giving and receiving instructions				
Influencing others, accepting instructions, planning				
Specific job functions or requirements (not covered above as outlined by the case manager)				

Additional tasks for Case Manager	Date	Comments
Re-entry interview scheduled		
People invited to bring friend, family member, or physician to re-entry interview		
Employee assured his/her job is waiting for him/her		
Employee formally welcomed back by employer		
Re-entry plan established and reviewed; a realistic timeline implemented		

---

[69] Reprinted with permission from the Global Business and Economic Roundtable on Addiction and Mental Health. Global Business and Economic Roundtable on Addiction and Mental Health, *Roadmap to Mental Health and Excellence At Work in Canada, Summer Draft*. Presented to The Ontario Chamber of Commerce, Economic Summit on Mental Health and Productivity in Ontario, A Pilot for Canada, Sutton Place Hotel, Toronto, Ontario, Canada, June 8, 2005 (2005) at 20, available online at: <http://www.bcmentalhealthworks.ca/files/roadmap-mentalhealth-at-work.htm>.

Figure 15.8: The Green Chart: Physician's Roadmap to Recovery[70]

Physician's Roadmap to Recovery — Green Chart

(In the space provided explain and/or list specific accommodations that can be made by the employer to ease the Return to Work Process)

	1	2	3	4	5
	At this time, this task is impossible for the employee to perform	The employee can perform some aspects of this task with accommodations	The employee can perform this task with accommodations	The employee performs this task well although some accommodations are still necessary	The employee can easily perform this task with little or no special assistance
General work skills					
Understanding and following instructions					
Performing simple and repetitive tasks					
Maintaining a work pace appropriate to the work load					
Relating to other people beyond giving and receiving instructions					
Influencing others, accepting instructions, planning					
Specific job functions or Requirements (not covered above as outlined by the case manager)					
Information Required by the Physician					
Characteristics of the workplace — pace, dynamics and history					
Patterns of absence or downtime in the last 30 days					
Any other relevant information					

---

[70] *Ibid.*

Privacy Considerations

Although a desirable approach, the collection of personal health information poses some interesting challenges, especially in terms of mental illness situations. Personal health information received by employers must be used for a specific and stated purpose, and obtained with the employee's **informed consent**.[71] However, during a mental health illness, many employees are medically unfit to provide an informed consent. As well, *a priori* "blanket consents" for the collection of personal health information tend to not withstand court review.

Secondly, Canadian Human Rights legislation prohibits employers from accessing employee diagnosis. Hence, being able to identify whether or not a disability claim is due to mental or physical health reasons is not feasible. Although assumptions can be made as the reason for the employee's substandard performance, employers are left to treat all disabilities equally and to focus on work performance.

Lastly, when employers collect employee personal health information, they become subject to the provincial or federal privacy legislation. This means security and protection of confidential medical information. For more details refer to Chapter 20, "Disability Management: Legal Aspects".

SUMMARY

The field of Disability Management continues to be fraught with interesting challenges. To practice effectively, Disability Management professionals/ practitioners need to be equipped with:

- current knowledge;
- unique ways of viewing workplace relationships and practices;
- sound disability claim and case management principles and standards;
- honest and open communication skills;
- good relationship-building and nurturing skills; and
- regular practice evaluation techniques.

They also need to gain an appreciation that a "systems approach" to managing workplace disability is more effective and sustainable than a case-by-case approach.

---

[71] **Informed consent:** There is an obligation on the employer to ensure that sufficient information is provided to employees about the nature and consequence of the intended action to allow the employee to reach a reasoned decision. The employee must be mentally competent, and possess the ability to understand and appreciate the nature and consequences of the procedure. The consent must be freely given; not obtained through misrepresentation or fraud. Consent cannot be given to the performance of an illegal procedure. The consent given must be in relation to the specific act contemplated unless the employee's life is immediately endangered and it is impractical to obtain consent.

A systems approach impacts every stakeholder in the system, is aimed at prevention, and is proactive in nature. The case-by-case approach, on the other hand, helps one employee and employee workgroup. Being reactive in nature, it is aimed at damage control and remediation. Ideally, organizations/companies use both approaches as a means of promoting good mental health and supporting the road to recovery when employees experience mental health conditions.

CHAPTER REFERENCES

D. Amodio & P. Devine, "Stereotyping and Evaluation in Implicit Race Bias: Evidence for Independent Constructs and Unique Effects on Behaviour" (2006) 91:4 Journal of Personality and Social Psychology 652.

K. Aquino & K. Lamertz, "A Relational Model of Workplace Victimization: Social Roles and Patterns of Victimization in Dyadic Relationships" (2004) 89:6 Journal of Applied Psychology 1023.

BCTel, *BCTel Evaluation of Occupational Health 1998 Program Costs* (British Columbia: BCTel, 1999) [unpublished].

M. Baldwin & R. Butler, "Upper Extremity Disorders in the Workplace: Costs and Outcomes Beyond the First Return to Work" (2006) 16:3 Journal of Occupational Rehabilitation 296.

R. Baril, D. Berthelette & P. Massicotte, "Early Return to Work of Injured Workers: Multidimensional Patterns of Individual and Organizational Factors" (2003) 41:4 Safety Science 277.

M. Barrick, G. Stewart, M. Neubert & M. Mount, "Relating Member Ability and Personality to Work-team Processes and Team Effectiveness" (1998) 83:3 Journal of Applied Psychology 377.

D. Bettencourt, K. Dill, S. Greathouse, K. Charlton & A. Mulholland, "Evaluations of Ingroup and Outgroup Members: The Role of Category-Based Expectancy Violation" (1996) 33 Journal of Experimental Social Psychology 244.

T. Buller, "A Flexible Combination", *Benefits Canada* (November 2004) at 99, Available on line at: <http://www.benefitscanada.ca>.

S. Calhoun & P. Strasser, "Generations at Work" (2005) 53:11 American Association of Occupational Health Nurses Journal 469.

CCOHS, "Stress Higher Among Working Women Over Forty, Study Finds" (September 5, 2005) CCOHS 5.

Y. Cohen-Charash & P. Spector, "The Role of Justice in Organizations: A Meta-Analysis" (2001) 86:2 Organizational Behavior and Human Decision Processes 278.

J. Coleman, "Social Capital in the Creation of Human Capital" (1988) 94 (Supp.), American Journal of Sociology S95.

Conference Board of Canada, *From Payer to Payer: The Employer's Role in the Canadian Health Care System Report #246-98* (Ottawa: Conference Board of Canada, 1998) at 3.

J. Cowell, "Fitness to Work" (Presented at the Conference on Workers' Compensation, Calgary, 1996) [unpublished].

J. Dersh, P. Polatin, G. Leeman & R. Gatchel, "The Management of Secondary Gain and Loss in Medicolegal Settings: Strengths and Weaknesses" (2004) 14:4 Journal of Occupational Rehabilitation 267.

W. Glenn, "Depression, Suicide Rate Linked to Occupations" (July/August 2008) 24:5 O.H.S. Canada 20.

Global Business and Economic Roundtable on Addiction and Mental Health, *Roundtable Roadmap to Mental Health Disability Management in 2004-05* (Working document prepared June 25, 2004), available online at: <http://www.mentalhealthroundtable.ca/june_2004/monitor_june2004.pdf>.

Global Business and Economic Roundtable on Addiction and Mental Health, *Roadmap to Mental Health and Excellence At Work in Canada, Summer Draft*. Presented to The Ontario Chamber of Commerce, Economic Summit on Mental Health and Productivity in Ontario, A Pilot for Canada, Sutton Place Hotel, Toronto, Ontario, Canada, June 8, 2005 (2005), available online at: <http://www.bcmentalhealthworks.ca/files/roadmap-mental health-at-work.htm>.

Global Business and Economic Roundtable on Addictions and Mental Health, *Module 3, Guidelines for Mental Disability Management, Managing Employers Getting Started: On the Road to Mental Health and Productivity* (2006), available online at: <http://www.mentalhealthroundtable.ca>.

Global Business and Economic Roundtable on Addiction and Mental Health, *CFO Framework for Mental Health and Productivity* (November 2007). Available on line at: <http://www.mentalhealthroundtable.ca/nov_07/CFO_Report_FINAL%20Nov%202007.pdf?blank>.

Global Business and Economic Roundtable on Addiction and Mental Health, "News Release: Ground-breaking Survey on Mental Health in the Workforce" (November 19, 2007), available online at: <http://www.gwlcentreformentalhealth.com/english/userfiles/news/pdf/s7_004756.pdf>.

K. Hong & I. Bohnet, "Status and Distrust: The Relevance of Inequality and Betrayal Aversion" (2007) 28:2 Journal of Economic Psychology 197.

IPSOS-Reid, *Mental Health in the Workplace: Largest Study Ever Conducted of Canadian Workplace Mental Health and Depression* (November 19, 2007), available online at: <http://www.ipsos.ca>.

R. Karasek, "Job Demands, Job Decision Latitude, and Mental Strain: Implications for Job Redesign" (1979) 24:2 Administrative Science Quarterly 285.

C. Langfred, "The Downside of Self-Management: A Longitudinal Study of the Effects of Conflict on Trust, Autonomy, and Task Interdependence in Self-Managing Teams" (2007) 50:4 Academy of Management Journal 885.

Marsh Risk Consulting, *Workforce Risk: Fourth Annual Marsh Mercer Survey of Employers' Time-Off and Disability Programs* (2003), available online at: <http://www.marshriskconsulting.com>.

R. Moss-Morris, "Symptom Perception, Illness Beliefs, and Coping in Chronic Fatigue Syndrome" (2005) 14:3 Journal of Mental Health 223.

OMA Committee on Work and Health, "Return to Work for Patients with Mental Disorders" (January 2005), available online at: <http://www.oma.org/home.asp>.

OMA Committee on Work and Health, "Mental Illness and Workplace Absenteeism: Exploring Risk Factors and Effective Return to Work Strategies" (April 2002), available online at: <http://www.oma.org/home.asp>.

J.M. Podolny & J.N. Baron, "Resources and Relationships: Social Networks and Mobility in the Workplace" (1997) 62 American Sociological Review 673.

J. Prochaska & C. Diclemente, "Stages and Processes of Self-Change of Smoking: Toward an Integrative Model of Change" (1983) 51:3 Journal of Consulting Clinical Psychology 390.

R. Putnam, "Bowling Alone: America's Declining Social Capital" (1995) 6:1 Journal of Democracy 65.

T.J. Rodgers, "No Excuses Management" (1990) 68:4 Harvard Business Review 84.

D. Rogalski, B. Rowat, & S. Sax, *Green Chart for the Global Business and Economic Roundtable on Addictions and Mental Health,* available online at: <http://www.mentalhealthroundtable.ca/june_2004/monitor_june2004.pdf>

J. Rothaupt & K. Becker, "A Literature Review of Western Bereavement Theory: From Decathecting to Continuing Bonds" (2007) 15:1 The Family Journal: Counseling and Therapy for Couples and Families 6.

M. Schoemaker, A. Nijhof, & J. Jonker, "Human Value Management: The Influence of the Contemporary Developments of Corporate Social Responsibility and Social Capital on HRM" (2006) 17:4 Management Review 448.

J. Smith, V. Tarasuk, S. Ferrier, & H. Shannon, "Prognosis of Musculoskeletal Disorders: Effects of Legitimacy and Job Vulnerability" (Toronto: Institute for Work and Health, Working paper # 67, 1998).

D. Stone & A. Colella, "A Model of Factors Affecting the Treatment of Disabled Individuals in Organizations" (1996) 21:2 The Academy of Management Review 352.

A. Tolli & A. Schmidt, "The Role of Feedback, Causal Attributions and Self-Efficacy on Goal Revision" (2008) 93:3 Journal of Applied Psychology 692.

Watson Wyatt Worldwide, *Staying@Work 2005 — Canada* (2005), available online at: <http://www.watsonwyatt.com/research/resrender.asp?id=w-860&page=1>.

H. Weiss, "Subordinate Imitation of Supervisor Behaviour: The Role of Modeling in Organizational Socialization" (1977) 19 Journal of Organizational Behaviour and Human Performance 89.

K. Williams, "Accommodating Disability in the Workplace" Ph.D. dissertation, University of Calgary, Alberta 2004) [unpublished].

K. Williams-Whitt, "Impediments to Disability Accommodation" (2007) 62 *Relations Industrielles* 405.

K. Williams-Whitt & D. Taras, "Disability and the Performance Paradox: Can Social Capital Bridge the Divide?", British Journal of Industrial Relations (2009, forthcoming).

M. Wilson, R. Joffe & B. Wilkerson, *The Unheralded Business Crisis in Canada: Depression at Work*, An Information Paper for Business, incorporating "12 Steps to A Business Plan to Defeat Depression" (Toronto: Global Business and Economic Roundtable on Addiction and Mental Health, 2002) at 22, available online at: <http://www.mentalhealthround table.ca/aug_round_pdfs/Roundtable%20report_Jul20.pdf>.

World Health Organization (2005), reported in National quality Institute (NQI), "So What Are Canadian Organizations Doing to Improve Mental Health? With Some Exceptions, Not Enough" (September 9, 2005), available online at: <http://www.nqi.ca/articles/article_details.aspx?ID=532>.

Chapter 16

Effective Management of Disability Claims with Strong Psychosocial Overtones

INTRODUCTION

Work is central to a person's identity and social roles. When individuals are unable to work or lose their jobs, it is a life crisis. In terms of a medical absence from work, recovering and getting back to work requires prompt attention — attention from competent disability management professionals/practitioners who are focused on assisting the employee to return to work in a safe and timely manner. Garnering support from and receptivity by the employer and the workplace for the employee's return is a vital component of this endeavour.

The reason for timely (prompt) attention is that after 12 weeks (three months) of absence from work, the chance of the employee returning to work is 50 per cent. This percentage decreases significantly as the months pass; by 24 weeks (six months), the percentage of employees that return to work post-physical/psychological illness/injury was found to be 20 per cent. At the 48-week point (12 months), only 2 per cent of the disabled employees returned to work (Figure 16.1).

Figure 16.1: Relationship Between Time Away and Return to Work[1]

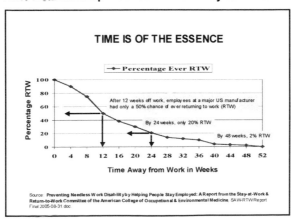

---

[1] Partnership for Workplace Mental Health, *Assessing and Treating Psychiatric Occupational Disability*, Report released by the American Psychiatric Foundation (2005) at 21, available online at: <http://www.workplacementalhealth.org/pdf/disabilityreportpart1.pdf>.

When the inability to work is due to a mental illness, the need for timely, focused, and considerable professional attention is greater. As well, a multidisciplinary approach is recommended.

TREATMENT PRINCIPLES

Disability claims are best managed by using sound case and claim management approaches as discussed in Chapter 5, "An Integrated Disability Management Program: The Managed Rehabilitative Care Program" and Chapter 10, "Disability Management Practice Standards". To reiterate, the best practices for disability management are:

- *Early assessment* — early intervention is a key component of preventing and minimizing dysfunction.

- *Intensive treatment* — the development and implementation of medically-appropriate treatment.

- *Treatment focus* — the goal of the treatment is the safe and timely return to work by the employee. Setting up this expectation early in the treatment process, has been found to positively impact the employee's recovery.[2] Employees' expectations about a return to normal recovery are strongly associated with their understanding of their condition and their beliefs about the problem. Employees' beliefs about their ability to achieve their return-to-work goals is termed, "self-efficacy". In short, what employees expect to/believe will occur, influences what actually occurs.

- *Active collaboration and communication* — open, honest, and continual collaboration and communication of stakeholders in the disability situation are vital to a successful return to work by the employee. This factor is graphically displayed in Figure 16.2.

- *Graduated Return to Work* — Based on the recognition that illness and impairment can coexist with adequate work performance, treatment providers are advised to recommend and employers are advised to offer and support graduated return-to-work opportunities for recovering employees. Graduated return-to-work practices have been shown to reduce the duration and outcomes of employee medical absences (Chapter 5, "An Integrated Disability Management Program: The Managed Rehabilitative Care Program").

---

[2]   D. Gross & M. Battié, "Work-related Recovery Expectations and the Prognosis of Chronic Low Back Pain Within a Workers' Compensation Setting" (2005) 47:4 Journal of Occupational and Environmental Medicine 428.

Figure 16.2: Everyone Has a Role to Play[3]

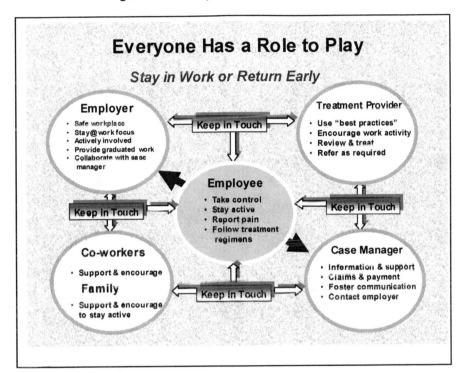

DISABILITY CASE MANAGEMENT CHALLENGES

As noted, work is central to a person's identity — his or her income, self-esteem, and purpose in life. When an employee is on medical absence from work, a number of case management challenges occur which must be addressed if a successful return-to-work outcome is to be achieved. They include:

- In terms of employee illness/injury, physicians address the employee's mental status, but not his/her functional status.[4] Due to human rights and privacy legislation, the workplace is limited to managing the employee's work performance (the demonstration of functional abilities). Hence, a "disconnect" exists.

---

[3] Accident Compensation Corporation (ACC) and the National Health Committee, *Active and Working! Managing Acute Low Back Pain in the Workplace — An Employer's Guide* (Wellington, NZ: ACC and National Health Committee, 2000). Available for public use.

[4] Partnership for Workplace Mental Health, *Assessing and Treating Psychiatric Occupational Disability*, report released by the American Psychiatric Foundation (2005), available online at: <http://www.workplacementalhealth.org/pdf/disabilityreportpart1.pdf>.

- The attending physician may view the employer as "part of their patient's problem": that is, the employer's interests are in opposition to the patient's (employee) health and recovery interests.[5] This may or may not be a true assessment, but that perception can negatively impact the employee's expectations for recovery and a successful return-to-work.

- Physical conditions can lead to mental health problems. For example, following a serious and sudden heart attack, the individual may develop a reactive depression, or bouts of anxiety. Likewise, post-injury, instances of drug dependence and addiction have occurred.

- The side-effects of medication use have been found to lead to psychiatric symptoms.[6]

- A disability may be attributed to a physical condition, when actually the functional impairment is due to an undiagnosed and untreated psychiatric condition. Psychiatric conditions often present as physical conditions, *e.g.,* chronic fatigue, chronic pain, depression, *etc.* Diagnosing the primary problem can be difficult.[7]

- Chronic disability situations can lead to the development of "secondary gains". The employee's focus becomes centred on the disability as opposed to his/her capabilities. The outcome is that the employee becomes "stuck in a realm of disability", unable to see life beyond that point — unable to move forward.

These are some of the case management challenges with which many disability management professionals/practitioners can identify.

In response, WorkSafeBC organized a staff in-service for their Occupational Health Nurses.[8] The goal of this interactive workshop was: "*To develop an approach and tool(s) to manage disability claims with strong psychosocial overtones.*"

The focus of this chapter is to examine the known "facts" about the management of disability cases that exhibit strong psychosocial overtones; to review the available research data; to discuss the related treatment concepts and principles; to discuss recognized models of disability management and intervention; and to provide a "workable" assessment approach and tool(s) adaptable to a number of industry/workplace settings.

---

[5]   *Ibid.*

[6]   *Ibid.*

[7]   *Ibid.*

[8]   WorkSafeBC ("Staff In-service — Interactive Workshop on Disability Management: Management of Disability Claims with Strong Psychosocial Overtones", facilitated by D. Dyck, May 14, 2009).

WHAT DOES "PSYCHOSOCIAL" MEAN?

The term, "**psychosocial**", means the interaction between the person and his or her social environment, and the influences on the person's behaviour. In regards to "pain", the psychosocial factors that affect the individual's response to pain are graphically demonstrated in Figure 16.3.

Figure 16.3: Psychosocial Factors Associated with Pain[9]

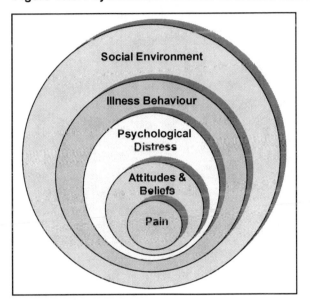

The employee's response to pain is associated with individual attitudes and beliefs about pain and what pain signifies. For example, the employee's response to pain differs if the personal view is that pain is a body signal that can be tolerated and "worked through", as opposed to being harmful and signalling the need for inactivity.

Likewise, the psychological distress that arises from the pain experience differs. For some individuals pain is a sensation to be managed; for others it is catastrophic and they respond accordingly.

The illness behaviour that ensues differs as does the social response to the individual's pain response. Some individuals accept the challenge to manage their pain and to work though it; others assume a "sick role" — that is, a societal-sanctioned role that ill or injured individuals assume once they become

---

9   Accident Compensation Corporation (ACC) and the National Health Committee, *New Zealand Acute Low Back Pain Guide, January 1997 edition* (Wellington, NZ: ACC and National Health Committee, 1999) at 46.

ill or injured. The societal response (social environment) can be supportive of either response, depending on the prevailing cultural beliefs.

PSYCHOSOCIAL FACTORS

"How come two employees with the same injury/illness respond so differently when it comes to returning to work?"

Psychologists tell us that there are two types of disability markers, individual markers and workplace markers. The individual markers include:

- demographic variables — age, gender, generation, culture, geographic location, *etc.*;
- pain and pain beliefs;
- perception of function and expected recovery;
- individual resiliency as per:

    - coping skills;
    - self-esteem, self-efficacy;
    - locus of control;
    - the value placed on health and well-being;
    - level of optimism;
    - social supports (friends and family);
    - perceived employer support;
    - having a job to return to;
    - receptive work environment; and
    - lifestyle.

The workplace markers include the physical and psychological workplace environment, a receptive workplace (*e.g.,* employer support, supervisory support and peer support), and the nature of the work.

Social Capital Theory

To better understand the issues surrounding employee disabilities in which a number of psychosocial factors are "at play", consider disability in terms of the Social Capital Theory. To reiterate, the Social Capital Theory holds that a person's willingness to do something to help another person is dependent on his or her belief that "good" will come back to him or her. Applying this theory to the workplace, the concept is that employees have a "bank" of individual social credits (goodwill) that they accumulate based on their degree of involvement and commitment to the workplace and to other employees. Throughout their employment, employees collect these "banked credits" and draw on them as required.

Employees who are active team players; who invest in the interests of the company and other workers; who work with and assist other employees; and who shoulder their share of the work and responsibilities tend to earn lots of social credits. In times of hardship, like illness/injury, they are the ones that other people rally around and are willing to help them to successfully recover and return to work.

Employees, who are less engaged in the company, its activities and its people; who are withdrawn or lack social skills; who are viewed as insubordinate and difficult to manage; and/or who are frequently absent, tend to have few, if any, social credits. In fact, they may be in a deficit position for social credits. These employees are the ones who, when ill/injured, go unsupported by the workplace. The validity of their absence is questioned. Questions about whether or not they really belong in this workplace emerge. Return-to-work issues occur, making the return-to-work experience feel more like a "punishment" than a rehabilitation effort.

Employees with mental health conditions often fit into this latter category. It is important for Disability Management Coordinators to recognize this and understand that the challenge is not only to re-integrate the employee, but also to help him or her mend some of the "bridges burned" prior to the disability absence. It is also important to enable them to develop the skills needed to earn social credits that would help them to better fit into the workplace.

Likewise, the supervisor and workgroup can benefit from understanding the importance of their support for the employee. As noted in Chapter 15, "Disability Management: The Social Capital Theory Perspective for Managing Disability Claims", garnering an understanding of social capital and the positive impact it can have on the successful return of the disabled employee, can prove extremely valuable to the various stakeholders and the organization/company.

RECOMMENDED WORKPLACE INTERVENTIONS

Similar to the treatment principles recommended earlier, employers should respond to an employee medical absence by:

- intervening early;
- maintaining regular, caring contact as noted in Figure 16.2;
- developing a standard method of accurately assessing and reporting on the mental/cognitive demands of any job. Typically, this is achieved by creating a bank of Job Demands Analysis (refer to Figure 5.4, Chapter 5);
- using a team-based approach to managing a disability and the return-to-work process. A multidisciplinary team consists of the employee, attending physician, employer, Employee Assistance Program, occupational health, and disability plan representatives;
- maintaining regular and open communication with all stakeholders;
- focusing on a safe and timely return to work right from the onset of the illness/injury;
- offering graduated return-to-work opportunities that support a successful return to full duties; and
- providing feedback to all stakeholders on the success of the disability management processes and their valuable contributions.

ADDRESSING PSYCHOLOGICAL BARRIERS TO RETURN TO WORK: INTERVENTION MODELS

Although there are a number of disability management models used in industry (Chapter 1, "Disability Management: Overview"), few models address the management of psychosocial factors and barriers to recovery and a successful return-to-work. The following are three disability management models designed to identify and address psychosocial factors and barriers, and effective interventions:

1.   The ECM Model[10]

The disability management model developed and successfully used by The Effective Case Management Group (ECM),[11] Calgary, Alberta has the motto of *"Taking control of disability"*. The message is that the employee is the one that must be "in the driver's seat" — in control. The issue is that disability situations often leave the employee feeling "out of control" and at the mercy of the illness/injury situation, health care providers, insurance companies, employer representatives, circumstances, *etc.*

Equally important, the ECM Model and approach offers the employer a sense of control. Through good communication and a strong focus on fitness-to-work efforts, the ECM Model enables the employer to overcome the typical feelings of minimal control and powerlessness that accompany employee medical absence. The model promotes a collaborative approach to disability management.

The Intake Assessment Form (questionnaire) used by The ECM Group Nurse Consultants (Appendix 1), is designed to gather the relevant information about the employee, the workplace, and the disability situation. The approach used is deemed to be as critical as the information collected. Nurse Consultants are instructed to use open-ended questions, and to begin by asking non-threatening questions, such as the employee's occupational history, and then work towards asking the more sensitive questions about medical information, the current disability, and the perceived barriers to recovery and return-to-work.

The ECM Model emphasizes the importance of listening with the intent of understanding the employee/employer's situation. Through open-ended questioning, the Nurse Consultant, encourages the employee to "control the conversation" and explain the disability situation from his or her perspective.

---

[10]   Information approved for publication by Fay Benard, RN, MN, OHNC, President of The ECM Group, a Canadian company specializing in the provision of disability management services to large and small public and private employers. Fay has experience in the development, implementation, evaluation, and supervision of disability management and occupational health programs.

[11]   The Effective Case Management Group is owned by three Occupational Health Nurses. For more information, refer to the ECM Group website available online at: <http://www.ecmgroup.ca>.

This approach allows for the telephonic collection of the needed information, while building a caring relationship with a view to engagement of the employee.

By way of comparison with the Traditional Rehabilitation and Managed Care Models, the ECM Model fosters employee/employer "ownership" and "control" of the disability situation through:

- *Early involvement* — Early intervention and disability case management practices aimed at understanding the disability situation and the factors at play. In addition to undertaking a thorough case management review and assessment, they determine the drivers and barriers for the employee to successfully return to work.

- *Collaborative approach* — ECM works closely with the employee, health care provider(s), Employee Assistance Program, employer, union, insurers, family, *etc*. The aim is to facilitate a timely recovery to an optimal level of functioning.

- *Enhances existing resources* — Using the internal and external resources available to the various stakeholders, ECM assists the employee, family, and employer move forward in the recovery process.

- *Focuses on "capabilities"* – Putting the employee in the driver's seat is vitally important to prevent the employee from adopting a passive attitude to recovery and return to work. Injury/illness tends to leave one feeling very vulnerable and "disabled"; neither of which are conducive to bolstering ones self-esteem, self-identity, self-efficacy, or locus of control. By focusing on the employee's capabilities, it channels the "energy" towards those capabilities and away from the disability factors.

- *Workplace involvement* — With the movement of employee rehabilitation out of the hospital and community rehabilitation settings, and into the workplace, the need for workplace involvement in the rehabilitation process emerged. This translates into the employer and union having disability roles and responsibilities. In the ECM Model open communication on the employee's fitness to work and capabilities is a critical element. Collaboration with the supervisor has proven invaluable in brokering a safe and timely return to work for the recovering employee.

- *Combines medical and vocational rehabilitation* — Through the timely use of a combination of medical (physical and psychological) and vocational rehabilitation practices, the ECM Model supports the concept of active rehabilitation of the employee within the work setting to which he or she will be returning. This approach leverages recovery on the employee's work knowledge and skills, while maximizing the social supports available to the employee.

- *Communication with all parties* — Information is power. By keeping all stakeholders in the disability management process informed, a "level-playing field" is established. It also enables the employee and workplace to anticipate and be prepared for the appropriate actions during the recovery and return-to-work phases. Open and honest communication also prevents assumptions, "misconceptions", and distrust — extremely dysfunctional elements that can prevent progress.

*   ***Employee assisted to maintain control*** — Although previously mentioned, it is worth emphasizing how critical it is to enable the employee to be "in control" of the disability management process. To some caregivers, this concept is extremely threatening. In fact the term, "caregiver" seems to imply that the giving of care equates to "ownership", in some instances, rendering the care receiver dependent on the caregiver. The end product tends to be a "passive response" to treatment and recovery — a condition that is counterproductive to a successful return to work.

The ECM Model promotes the opposite approach. As depicted in the series of cartoons in Figure 16.4, the ideal approach is to have the employee "in the driver's seat" with the Nurse Consultant facilitating, coordinating, guiding, coaching, and mentoring the recovery and return-to-work process.

In the first cartoon — the Traditional Rehabilitation Model — control of the disability rests with the vocational rehabilitation professional. As depicted by the "dated biplane", intervention occurs late in the disability situation. There are many barriers to getting the employee back to work — the plane needs to be "kick started", the plane is off the runway, and the flying conditions are cloudy and ominous. The employee is in the "passenger seat", a passive and fearful "observer" in the recovery and return-to-work process. Given the late start, the intervention focuses on vocational rehabilitation, work hardening, and alternate work.

The second cartoon, the Managed Care Model, is driven by the Case Manager using disability guidelines and preferred providers to guide the flight towards recovery and return to work. The process begins earlier and the techniques used are more in line with current disability management practices. However in this model, the employee's situation must "fit within a distinct set of parameters"; there is no room for individual differences. Again, the employee is the passenger, dependent on the case manager and the service provider(s) to get him or her to the desired destination. Confusion, uncertainly, and fear are the felt emotions as the employee proceeds along this "unsettling flight".

The ECM Model is depicted in the last two cartoons. Initially, the Nurse Consultant helps to "navigate" the recovery and return-to-work processes with the employee "piloting the flight". Through timely facilitation and coordination of these processes, the Nurse Coordinator guides, coaches, and mentors the employee. Working with the workplace and the Nurse Consultant, the employee is able to pilot the flight to recovery and to a successful return to work.

Part of the ECM Model includes preparing the workplace for the employee's return, and working with the supervisor and co-workers to support the employee's graduated return to work. The goal, as depicted in cartoon #4, is for the employee to succeed and to "fly solo" once it is mutually agreed that the time is right. The ECM Model is robust enough to accommodate individual rehabilitation needs and to support the employee beyond the "solo flight", especially in situations where the disability involved a psychological disability.

- ***Measured Outcomes*** — Outcome focused, the ECM Model includes a comprehensive system of measurement that measures not only the absence and modified workdays, but also the barriers and contributing factors for a successful return-to-work. By identifying these barriers/contributing factors, remedial action(s) can be developed to eliminate or reduce them. Additionally, outcome measurement allows for meaningful information on the cost-effectiveness of the workplace disability management interventions, and for continuous improvement.

Figure 16.4: Comparison of the ECM Model with the Traditional Rehabilitation and Managed Care Models[12]

Traditional Rehabilitation Model

Managed Care Model

ECM's Model

ECM's Model

---

[12] Reprinted with permission from The ECM Group, Calgary, AB.

2.   New Zealand Model

The recommended approach for dealing with workplace disabilities, especially those with strong psychosocial overtones, is to treat the disability, not the pain. This involves ruling out the physical or organic factors related to the disability, and then addressing the psychological factors and other workplace barriers.

To distinguish between the various contributing factors/barriers to recovery and return to work from low back pain, the New Zealand Model uses a system of "flags".

THE FLAG SYSTEM FOR LOW BACK PAIN

The **Red Flags** are the factors that are indicative of the presence of medical problems. In terms of low back pain, they:

- constitute organic medical issues;
- are identifiable by symptoms/signs of severe worsening of pain, especially at night, groin numbness, weight loss, fever, evidence of abnormal test results, *etc.*;
- are associated with significant trauma and injury;
- are related to a history of cancer or other degenerative conditions;
- are related to the use of intravenous drugs or prescribed steroids; and
- are associated with aging — older than aged 50 years.

If detected, these factors need to be medically investigated and addressed.

Yellow Flags are the psychosocial barriers — factors that increase the risk of chronicity, disability, and work loss. They include factors such as:

- the belief that pain and the related activity are harmful (cultural);
- evidence of "sick role and behaviours";
- the presence of fear;
- the use of inappropriate diagnostic and treatment modalities — not "best practices";
- the presence of disability claim and compensation issues;
- evidence of negative moods, social withdrawal, anger, and depression;
- evidence of poor or declining work performance;
- a job in which heavy work (manual labour) is required;
- unsociable hours leading to social isolation for the employee;
- family issues such as an overprotective/unsupportive family; and
- cultural impacts counter to the focus of the disability management and return-to-work practices.
- inadequate control of pain increases the likelihood of the development of chronic pain syndrome.
- inactivity due to disability is detrimental to the quality of life and the individual's general well-being.
- successful return to work, and hence, the mitigation of work loss, depends on the quality of case management practices.

It is important to recognize that Red Flags and Yellow Flags can exist simultaneously and hence, to be properly addressed, they must be teased apart. The Red Flags have to be medically investigated and treated; while the Yellow Flags are addressed through the use of clinical assessment and intervention. There are two other types of flags — Blue Flags and Black Flags. Blue Flags are the *"employee's perceived"* features of work that are associated with work loss and delayed recovery from injury/illness. They include:

- a "perceived" high work demand and low control work situation;
- time pressures;
- monotonous work or non-challenging work;
- lack of job satisfaction;
- unsupportive management style;
- low social support from colleagues/supervisor;
- unrealistic performance expectations;
- peer pressure; and
- poor/substandard work performance.

The **Black Flags** signify the *"actual"* features of work that can be "real" barriers to a successful return to work such as the:

- nature of the work;
- job context;
- actual work conditions;
- rates of pay, negotiated sick leave, and salary continuance rates;
- lack of modified/alternate work opportunities;
- management style;
- level of union support/involvement; and
- the size and structure of the organization/company.

The treatment approaches for the Red, Yellow, Blue and Black Flags are provided in Figure 16.5. In each case, the aim is timely action and resolution of the contributing factor or barrier to recovery and a successful return to work.

Figure 16.5: New Zealand Model: System of "Flags"

 Red Flags (Barriers/ Contributing Factors)	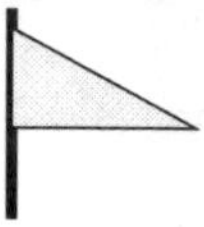 Yellow Flags (Barriers/ Contributing Factors)	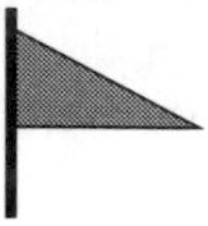 Blue Flags (Barriers/ Contributing Factors)	 Black Flags (Barriers/ Contributing Factors)
• Medical investigation, assessment and management • Scans/X-rays/MRIs • Neurological assessment • Blood work Look for other pathologies	• Clinical assessment • Identification of psychosocial factors Identify appropriate cognitive and behavioural management strategies	• Clinical assessment • Identification of perceived barriers & fears Identify appropriate cognitive & behavioural management strategies	• Workplace assessment (Figure 16.6) • Identification of actual workplace barriers Identify appropriate risk management strategies (Figure 16.7)
↓ **Immediate Action** ↓	↓ **Immediate Action** ↓	↓ **Immediate Action** ↓	↓ **Immediate Action** ↓
Aimed at: An appropriate recovery response	**Aimed at:** 1. *Decision:* Is a more detailed assessment needed? 2. *Identification:* Salient conditions/factors for intervention	**Aimed at:** 1. *Decision:* Are these fears and barriers valid (*Black Flags*)? 2. *Identification:* Salient conditions/factors for intervention	**Aimed at:** Workplace change and receptivity

RED, YELLOW, BLUE, AND BLACK FLAGS: CLINICAL ASSESSMENT

According to the New Zealand Model, the prescribed case management steps when addressing low back pain are to:

1. assess for the Red Flags and refer the disabled employee as appropriate; and then
2. assess for the Yellow Flags, Blue Flags and Black Flags and address them.

By way of an industry example, the Accident Compensation Corporation (ACC) in New Zealand, developed a model for the clinical assessment and management of acute low back pain (Figure 16.6). Triggered by the initial presentation of acute low back pain, the occupational health professional undertakes an Initial Assessment which consists of a history of the condition, an examination of the employee, and an assessment for Red Flags and for Yellow Flags. If Red Flags are detected, the employee is referred to a medical specialist for further investigation of underlying organic health problems.

If there are no Red Flags detected, the employee is provided an explanation of the etiology, prognosis, and recommended treatment for acute low back pain (analgesics, and manipulation for 4-6 weeks only). Assurance that there is nothing seriously wrong is provided and the employee is encouraged to continue activities as tolerated and to avoid bed rest. This model includes a review of the employee's condition in one week.

For most cases, the acute low back pain will resolve and the employee will be deemed recovered. However, if the pain continues, consideration of a specialist referral may be entertained.

If by the fourth week, the employee is still experiencing acute low back pain, a full assessment is recommended. It includes a history of the condition, a physical and neurological examination of the employee, screening for Red and Yellow Flags, investigations as clinically required, and consideration of the available treatment options. This is a more in-depth assessment. If Red Flags are detected, a referral to the specialist is made. In terms of the Yellow Flags, the following factors are examined:

- Why has the employee not resumed normal activities? What are the barriers and contributing factors?
- Why has the employee not returned to work? What are the barriers and contributing factors?
- Why has the response to the recommended treatment been poor? What are the barriers and contributing factors?

Figure 16.6: Clinical Assessment and Management of Acute Low Back Pain[13]

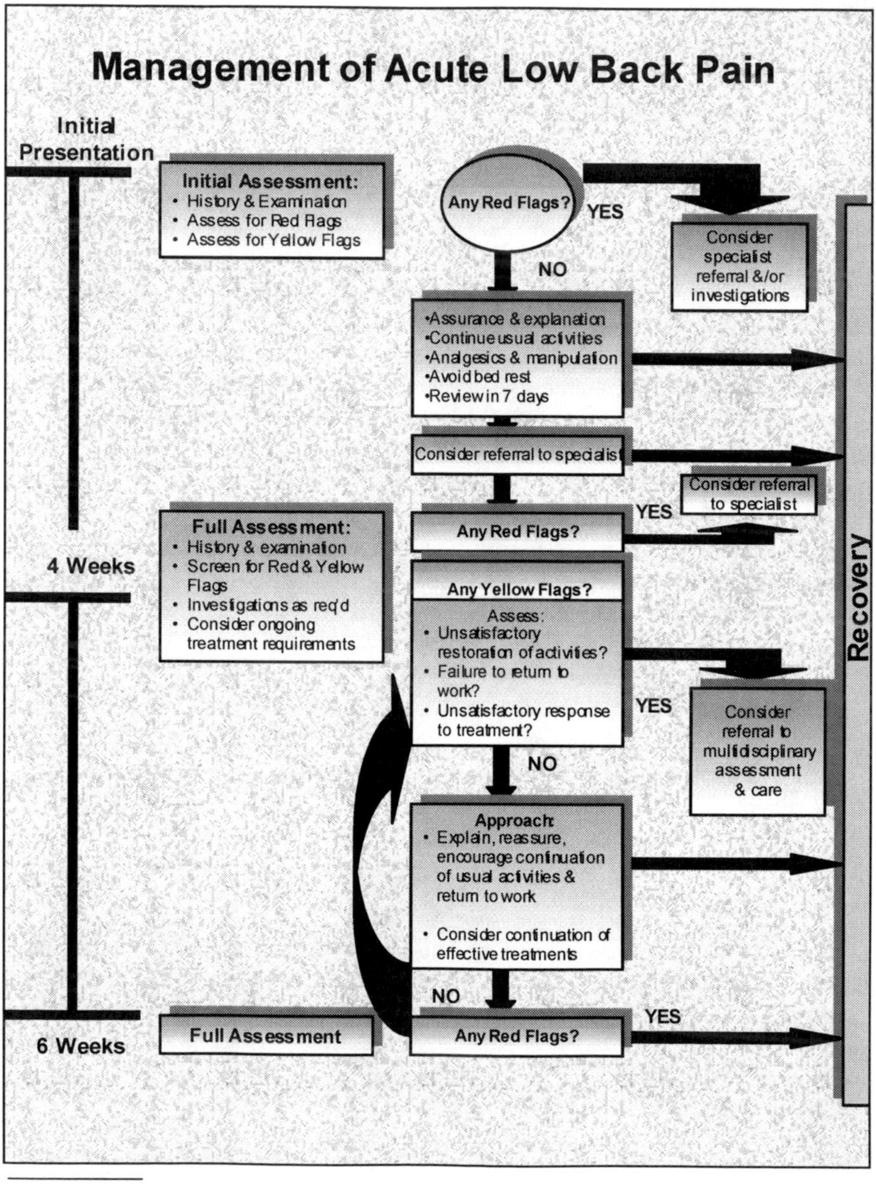

Management of Acute Low Back Pain

Initial Presentation

Initial Assessment:
- History & Examination
- Assess for Red Flags
- Assess for Yellow Flags

Any Red Flags? **YES** → Consider specialist referral &/or investigations

NO

- Assurance & explanation
- Continue usual activities
- Analgesics & manipulation
- Avoid bed rest
- Review in 7 days

Consider referral to specialist

4 Weeks

Full Assessment:
- History & examination
- Screen for Red & Yellow Flags
- Investigations as req'd
- Consider ongoing treatment requirements

Any Red Flags? **YES** → Consider referral to specialist

Any Yellow Flags?
Assess:
- Unsatisfactory restoration of activities?
- Failure to return to work?
- Unsatisfactory response to treatment? **YES** → Consider referral to multidisciplinary assessment & care

NO

Approach:
- Explain, reassure, encourage continuation of usual activities & return to work
- Consider continuation of effective treatments

NO

6 Weeks   Full Assessment   Any Red Flags? **YES**

Recovery

---

[13]   N. Kendall, S. Linton, & C. Main, *Guide to Assessing Psychological Yellow Flags in Acute Low Back Pain: Risk Factors for Long-Term Disability and Work Loss* (Wellington, NZ: Accident Compensation Corporation and the New Zealand Guidelines Group, 1997) at 11-13. Available for public use.

The identification of numerous barriers and contributing factors resulting in failure to resume normal activities, work and recovery, is indicative of a need for referral of the employee to a multi-disciplinary team for assessment and care. If barriers (flags) are not detected, then the suggested approach is to explain, reassure, and encourage the employee to continue the usual activities and to return to work. As well, continued use of the effective treatments and a review in two week are recommended.

At the six-week point, if the employee has not recovered, the full assessment is repeated. The efforts to unearth the underlying reasons for failure to recover are increased, with particular focus on the detection of Red and Yellow Flags.

The goals and rationale for assessing the Yellow Flags (psychological factors) are to address:

- *Pain* — Inadequate pain control increases the employee's risk of developing chronic pain syndrome.
- *Disability* — Inactivity is detrimental to the employee's quality of life and general well-being.
- *Work Loss* — Successful return to work by the employee is dependent on the quality of the case management.

These undesired outcomes are prevented by:

- initiating effective interventions early;
- enabling the employee to stay active, and to retain work skills and work relationships;
- identifying psychological risk factors; and
- reducing the psychological risk factors which lead to inactivity, disability and work loss.

The focus of the clinical assessment is to determine what can be done to help the employee experience less distress and disability. It covers:

- *Emotional Factors*:

  - fear of increased pain with activity or work;
  - depression, loss of sense of enjoyment in life;
  - more irritable than usual;
  - anxiety about, and heightened awareness of, body sensations;
  - feeling under stress and unable to maintain sense of control;
  - presence of social anxiety or disinterest in social activity;
  - feeling useless and not needed; *etc.*

- *Family Factors*:

  - over-protective partner/spouse who emphasizes fear of harm or encourages catastrophizing of the disability;
  - solicitous behaviour from spouse, *e.g.*, taking over the employee's usual tasks;

- socially-punitive responses from spouse, *e.g.,* ignoring, expressing frustration;
- extent to which family members support any attempt to return to work;
- lack of a support person to talk to about problems; *etc.*

- ***Attitudes and Beliefs about Back Pain*:**
    - belief that pain is harmful or disabling, and resulting in fear-avoidance behaviour, *e.g.,* the development of guarding and fear of movement;
    - belief that all pain must be abolished before attempting to return to work or to doing normal activities;
    - expectation of increased pain with activity or work;
    - lack of ability to predict capability;
    - catastrophizing, thinking the worst, misinterpreting bodily systems and body cues;
    - belief that pain is uncontrollable;
    - passive attitude to rehabilitation; *etc.*

- ***Behaviours*:**
    - use of extended rest; disproportionate "downtime";
    - reduced activity level with a significant withdrawal from activities of daily living;
    - irregular participation or poor compliance with physical exercise; the tendency for activities to be in a "boom-bust" cycle;
    - avoidance of normal activity and progressive substitution of lifestyle away from productive activity;
    - report extremely high level of pain intensity;
    - excessive reliance on use of medication, aids, or appliances;
    - sleep quality reduced since onset of back pain;
    - excessive intake of alcohol or other substances with an increase since the onset of back pain;
    - smoking; *etc.*

- ***Claim and Compensation Issues*:**
    - lack of a financial incentive to return to work;
    - delay in accessing income support and treatment cost; disputes over claim eligibility;
    - history of claim(s) due to other injuries or pain problems; knowledge of the claim system;
    - history of extended time off work due to injury or other pain problem;
    - history of previous back pain, with previous claim(s) and time off work;
    - previous experience of ineffective case management; *etc.*

- *Diagnosis and Treatment Factors*:

  - the health professional sanctioning the disability and/or not providing interventions that will improve the employee's ability to function;
  - experience of conflicting diagnoses or explanations for back pain, resulting in confusion;
  - diagnostic language leading to catastrophizing and fear;
  - dramatization of back pain by health professional producing a dependency on treatments by the employee and the continuation of passive treatment(s);
  - the number of times the employee visited health professional(s) in the last year (excluding the present back pain episode);
  - expectation of a "techno-fix", *e.g.,* requests to treat as if body were a machine;
  - lack of satisfaction with previous treatment for back pain;
  - advice from a health care provider to the employee to withdraw from job; *etc.*

- *Work Factors*:

  - history of manual work, notably from:

    - fishing, forestry, and farming,
    - construction,
    - nursing,
    - truck driving, and
    - labour-intensive occupations;

  - work history, including patterns of frequent job changes, experiencing stress at work, job dissatisfaction, poor work relationships, lack of vocational direction;
  - belief that work is harmful; that it will do damage or be dangerous to the employee's health;
  - an unsupportive or unhappy current work environment;
  - low-educational background, low-socioeconomic status;
  - job involves significant bio-mechanical demands, such as lifting, manual handling heavy items, extended standing, driving, vibration, maintenance of constrained or sustained postures, inflexible work schedule preventing appropriate breaks;
  - job involves shift work or working "unsociable hours", low social contact;
  - minimal availability of selected duties and graduated return-to-work opportunities with unsatisfactory implementation of these;
  - negative experience of workplace management of back pain, *e.g.,* absence of a reporting system, discouragement to report, punitive response from supervisors and managers;

- absence of interest in the employee's recovery and return to work by the employer; *etc.*

HOW TO DETERMINE IF THE EMPLOYEE IS AT "HIGH RISK"?

As part of the clinical assessment, the Disability Management Coordinator needs to decide the level of risk that the claimant is displaying (Figure 16.7). Claimants at "high risk" are identified if there is:

- A cluster of a few very salient factors, *e.g.,*

  - the presence of the belief that pain is harmful, or disabling.
  - the exhibition of fear-avoidance behaviour(s).
  - evidence of low mood or anxiety.
  - social withdrawal. The expectation that "passive treatment" versus "active treatment" will help the claimant to recover.

- A group of several less important factors that combine cumulatively.

SCREENING QUESTIONNAIRE

The New Zealand Model includes a screening questionnaire (Appendix 2) which is aimed at identifying and assessing the psychosocial risk factors for chronic low back pain. This industry example was developed for the management of acute low back pain. However, it does have a strong potential for a more generalized application.

Figure 16.7: How to Assess Psychosocial Factors of Acute Low Back Pain[14]

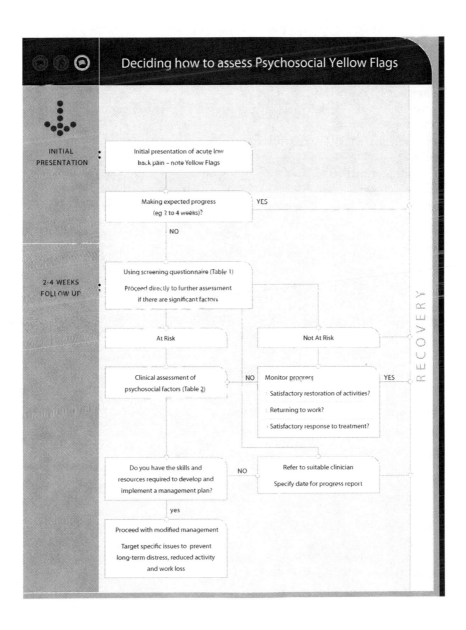

---
[14] *Ibid.*

WHAT CAN BE DONE FOR EMPLOYEES AT "HIGH RISK"?

The New Zealand Model advocates that physicians and Disability Management Coordinators:

- provide the employee with positive return-to-work expectations;
- be directive in scheduling regular progress reviews;
- keep the employee active and at work in some capacity;
- acknowledge that the employee may experience some difficulties with daily living; but that he or she should avoid inactivity;
- promote the collaboration and cooperation of worker, employer, insurer, and health care providers;
- communicate that time from work can negatively impact the employee's chances of successfully returning to work;
- be alert for evidence that the employee holds the belief that time off work should continue until "one is cured";
- promote self-management and self-responsibility for recovery and return to work;
- seek a second opinion when required;
- avoid confusing the employee's symptomology reports with the presence of emotional distress;
- avoid suggesting to the employee that he or she should "work at home" — that leads to isolation at a time when social support is required;
- encourage pain control and the management and continuation of the employee's normal daily and work activities; and
- use a multidisciplinary approach for complex claims.[15]

3. The Risk-Factor Intervention Model

The Risk-Factor Intervention Model is based on the premise that early and effective intervention prevents an acute condition from becoming chronic. Simple in its conception, but what constitutes "effective intervention"?

- interventions that alleviate causal risk factors should lead to effective chronic disability prevention; and
- risk factor screening should provide a basis for determining "who" is likely to benefit from a specific intervention.

The intent is to match the claimant to various early intervention techniques which have proven outcomes (effective interventions), and hence, to reduce the cost of early intervention. However, there are a number of issues related to the implementation of this endeavour. For example:

---

[15]   *Ibid.*

- not all "risk factors" have been clinically proven to have a "cause-effect" relationship;
- many risk variables overlap, thus confounding the ability to predict outcomes; and
- some clinical studies in this area suffer from measurement and confounding biases.

So, the question remains: *"How do you 'identify claimants' needing certain interventions?"*

- demographic variables — age, gender, race, income, educational attainment, employment status, *etc.*;
- pain and pain beliefs;
- perceptions of function and expected return to activities and recovery; and
- workplace physical and psychosocial environment.

The known effective interventions are:

- early contact and return-to-work facilitation;
- reduced ergonomic hazards;
- improved supervisor supports;
- improved coworker supports;
- managing and coordinating medical care, or modifying health care provider behaviour; and
- improving claimant readiness for work through physical training, education, or counselling.

The components of the risk factor-based intervention model are depicted in Figure 16.8.[16] The challenge of the screening process is to match prognostic factors with suitable interventions strategies to identify the effective interventions. There are a number of screening approaches; for example some practitioners chose to intervene with the "high risk" cases only, while others opt to target a "single risk factor" for intervention, and then, screen claimants on that risk factor.

---

[16]   W. Shaw, S. Linton & G. Pransky, "Reducing Sickness Absence from Work due to Low Back Pain: How Well do Intervention Strategies Match Modifiable Risk Factors?" (2006) 16:4 J. Occup Rehabil 591 at 600. Reprinted with permission.

Figure 16.8: Components of Risk Factor-based Interventions

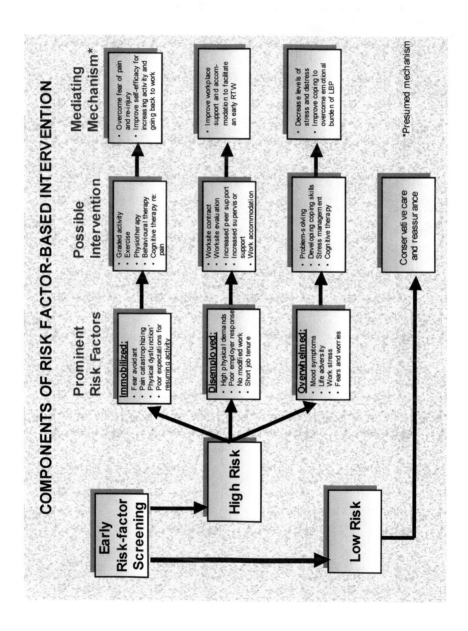

COMPARISON OF THE MODELS

There are a number of similarities between the three models. For example, they have a common goal — *a safe and timely return to work*. They are designed to promote early and effective intervention(s). All three models identify the psychological social factors and barriers for recovery and a successful return to work. All are aimed at employee rehabilitation within the workplace. Open communication and collaboration between the stakeholders is paramount.

Some of the noted differences are:

- The ECM Model addresses the employee's perceptions of the contributing factors and barriers to recovery and return to work in terms of the workplace, the home, and his or her own medical situation.

- The New Zealand Model is designed to identify the employees at "high risk" for psychosocial flags (barriers) by "scoring" the questionnaire responses provided by the employee. The interventions recommended are based on the score attained and the nature of the psychosocial flags.

- The Risk-factor Intervention Model focuses on identifying effective interventions.

Importantly, the contributions made by these models can be used to design an approach and tools to effectively employee disability management in the workplace.

MANAGEMENT OF DIFFICULT HEALTH CONDITIONS

There are a number of well-recognized and challenging health conditions — conditions that are commonly associated with difficult reintegration of the disabled employee back into the workplace. The rationale is that these conditions tend to have a higher potential for complexity. For example:

1. Acute Low Back Pain

Acute low back pain (LBP) is defined as back pain lasting less than three months. It is characterized by non-specific pain making a precise diagnosis impossible. The employee experiences acute episodes of persistent or fluctuating back pain for a period of a few weeks or months. Then improvement occurs, resulting in no loss of function.

Acute LBP is best managed by simple measures (Figure 16.9), namely:

- reassurance that there is nothing seriously wrong;
- support;
- explanations of the condition and its prognosis;
- supportive treatment of the acute low back pain;
- promoting activity as usual;
- encouraging the employee to remain at work; and

- providing ongoing management of the acute low back pain and regularly reviewing.

In terms of treatment modalities for acute low back pain, a summary of the effective treatment modalities for acute low back pain are provided in Figure 16.10. The key treatment approaches are to reinforce that:

- Pain does not equate to damage: the low back pain will settle and there is no sign of anything seriously wrong.
- Staying "active as tolerated" promotes recovery.
- Movement and activity will not cause harm.
- Staying at work is beneficial. It:

  - reduces the risk of job loss;
  - encourages self-confidence;
  - promotes a gradual recovery;
  - eases the adjustment to full-time work; and
  - results in less disruption to the employee, workgroup, and family.

Summarized, there are a number of useful work accommodation tips that can be offered, namely:

  - reduce the work duration;
  - offer and undertake work duties as tolerated;
  - use pain relief as needed; and
  - gradually increase work activities when tolerated.

Figure 16.9: Management of Acute Low Back Pain[17]

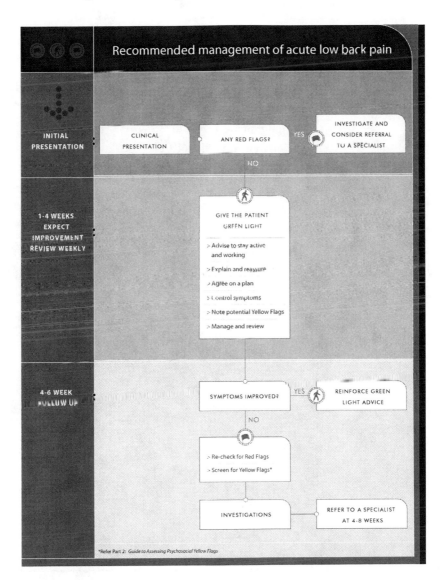

---

[17] Accident Compensation Corporation (ACC), *Active and Working! Managing Acute Low Back Pain in the Workplace — An Employer's Guide* (Wellington, NZ: ACC and National Health Committee, 2000). Available for public use.

Figure 16.10: Treatment Options for Acute Low Back Pain[18]

Treatment Options for Acute LBP

EVIDENCE	TREATMENT OPTIONS	EVIDENCE STRENGTH
IMPROVEMENT	• Advise to stay active	A
	• Analgesics as required	A
	• Manipulation – first 4-6 weeks	A
	• Multidisciplinary approach	B
NO IMPROVEMENT	• TENS	A
	• Traction	A
	• Specific back exercises	A
	• Education pamphlets on LBP	A
	• Massage	A
	• Acupuncture	A
	• Surgery	A
HARMFUL	• Use of narcotics or diazepam	A
	• Bed rest for more than 2 days	A
	• Bed rest, with/without traction	A
	• Manipulation under anesthesia	A
	• Immobility splint	A
INSUFFICIENT EVIDENCE	• Core conditioning	
	• Aerobic conditioning	
	• Epidural steroidal injections	
	• Shoe lifts/corsets	
	• Biofeedback	
	• Physical agents & passive modalities (ice, heat, ultrasound, short wave diathermy)	

---

[18]   W. Shaw, S. Linton & G. Pransky, "Reducing Sickness Absence from Work due to Low Back Pain: How Well do Intervention Strategies Match Modifiable Risk Factors?" (2006) 16:4 J. Occup Rehabil 591 at 600.

2. Depression and Other Mental Health Conditions

As noted in Chapter 9, "Workplace Attendance Support and Assistance" and Chapter 15, "Disability Management: The Social Capital Theory Perspective for Managing Disability Claims", mental health conditions are on the increase. With employees tending to try to *"work through their condition"*, mental health conditions are commonly encountered in the workplace. Yet, less than 20 per cent of these employees get treatment. Added to this situation, mental health conditions are poorly understood and heavily stigmatized. The employee looks fine, but is having difficulty maintaining productivity, or is off work.

Some of the challenges for the employee and the workgroup are that mental health conditions tend to result in disturbed social relationships. Likewise, the return-to-work is a "a fragile period"; it is a time for "damage control" and the "rebuilding social relationships". It ends up being a "testing ground" for *new* workplace social relationships. The re-entry can be challenging if the employee and the workgroup are ill-prepared, or lack anticipatory guidance and support from the Disability Management Coordinator.

3. Post-Traumatic Stress Disorder

As a result of workplace incidents such as robberies, assaults, a life-threatening incident/experience, a disaster, *etc.*, employees can develop an anxiety disorder that occurs following involvement in, or observation of, a traumatic event. Following a critical incident, most employees experience "short-term effects" with "no" or "very little time loss".

Post Traumatic Stress Disorder (PTSD) tends to develop when there is a lack of support from others post-incident. Prevention can be achieved through the delivery of Critical Incident Stress Debriefing (CISD)

Another risk factor is when the employee who is experiencing signs and symptoms of PTSD, waits too long to seek help.

Exposure to a similar incident can trigger PTSD. Likewise an accumulation of trauma over the employee's lifespan can render him or her more vulnerable to PTSD.

PTSD SIGNS AND SYMPTOMS

Employees, who experience PTSD, demonstrate signs and symptoms such as:

- *Increased Arousal* (insomnia, irritability, hyper-vigilant, heightened startle response, poor concentration).

- *Avoidance* (avoidance of conversation, thoughts, feelings; avoidance of activities, places, people that arouse recollections; recall problems; loss of interest and enjoyment; emotional restriction; tunnelled vision).

- *Intrusive Experiences* (nightmares, scary thoughts, reliving the experience, flashbacks, anxiety attacks).

PREVENTION AND MANAGEMENT OF PTSD

Key to the prevention and management of PTSD is the need for Disability Management Coordinators to recognize the potential or occurrence of PTSD. Providing Critical Incident Stress Debriefing has been shown effective in increasing worker awareness of the signs and symptoms of PTSD, and when and how to get help.

In terms of the management of PTSD, the three recognized treatments are:

- *psychosocial first aid*;
- *psychotherapy* — personalized cognitive therapy — changing emotions, thoughts, and behaviours in regards to the traumatic event; and
- *pharmacology*.

Employees returning to work from PTSD require unique work accommodation. The work environment should be modified so as not to "trigger" a recurrence of PTSD. The incidence of conflict, or emotional provocativeness, in the workplace should be reduced because it arouses the central nervous system. Activities requiring a high degree of concentration and alertness, especially if the employee is taking a tranquilizing medication, should be temporarily restricted. As the recovery process progresses, the introduction of events that could be PTSD "triggers" should be done gradually.

THE MANAGEMENT OF PSYCHOSOCIAL FACTORS: WHAT IS KNOWN SO FAR?

The purpose of this chapter is to examine the research and established clinical data about the psychosocial factors involved in a disability. The recognized treatment concepts and principles, as well as some of the models for disability management and intervention have been discussed.

So far, it has been determined that there is a need to identify the "high risk" versus "low risk" claims. The right screening approach and tool(s) can make possible this task. The New Zealand Model and tools could be adapted to include all types of disabilities, not just acute low back pain. The knowledge from the other disability models and disability management research can be incorporated into a "new model". One important factor is the use of clinical assessment and sound clinical assessment techniques. One approach for the management of disabilities with strong psychosocial overtones is depicted in Figure 16.11.

Figure 16.11: An Approach to the Management of Psychosocial Factors

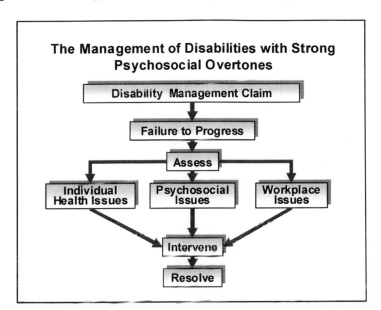

CONTRIBUTION MADE BY THE WORKSAFEBC OCCUPATIONAL HEALTH NURSES – MAY 14, 2009

The task of the WorkSafeBC Occupational Health Nurses was to develop a "workable" assessment model and tool(s) for use in the insurance setting. Through the use of an interactive workshop approach, a model for the management of an occupational disability claim by the WorkSafeBC was created (Figure 16.12).

Management of a Disability Claim: The Approach

At the onset of the occupational claim, a *Level 1 — Early/Initial Assessment* is conducted. It consists of an evaluation of the presenting injury/illness, clinical data, and claim data. Claims identified as "serious injury claims" are automatically referred to a multidisciplinary team within WorkSafeBC. The remaining claims are assessed and managed as follows:

1. Are there any noted Red Flags? If "yes", refer the claim for medical assessment and management. If "no", proceed with the next step.

2. Assurance and education, rehabilitation planning and return-to-work planning. A majority of the occupational claimants will return to work and recover without additional intervention.

3. At the 1-2 week post-injury point, assess if the worker is recovering as expected? If "yes", allow the claim to resolve as anticipated. If "no", monitor and reassess at the 2-4 week point.

4. At the 2-4 week point, conduct a **Level 2 — Full Assessment** of the claim. At this point, undertake:

    - a clinical history;
    - screen for Flags — the Red, Yellow, Blue and Black Flags;
    - identify and investigate the return-to-work barriers; and
    - consider the ongoing treatment requirements.

    The planned approach is to address the identified flags through referral to a multidisciplinary team. In instances when no flags are evident, continue to monitor the claim and to:

    - explain, reassure, and encourage continuation of usual activities and return to work; and
    - consider the continuation of the effective treatments.

5. At 6 weeks post the date of injury, a reassessment of the claim is to be undertaken. The question to be addressed is whether or not this claim is progressing as anticipated. If "yes", then assist the worker to move towards recovery and return to work. If "no", then repeat the *Level 2 — Full Assessment* and step 5.

6. At the 8-12 week point, the claim is reassessed once more. Again, the question to be addressed is whether or not this claim is progressing as anticipated.

Figure 16.12: Management of a Disability Claim (WorkSafeBC Model)

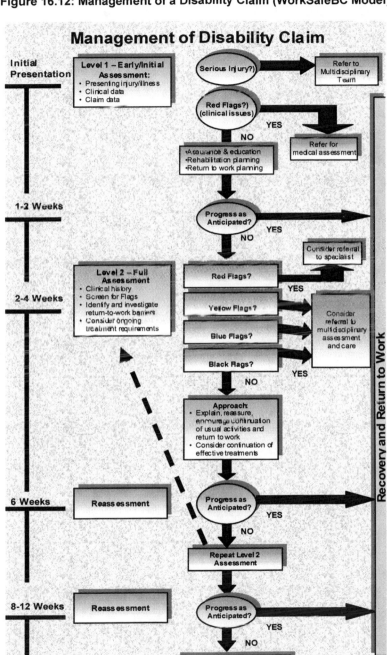

Management of a Disability Claim: The Tools

The tools prepared for use with this model include:

- *A System of Flags* — a system designed for the identification of the medical, psychosocial, cognitive and workplace barriers to a successful recovery and return to work (Figure 16.13).

- *A Model for the Clinical Assessment of Psychosocial Yellow Flags* — a model that directs the assessment of the worker's level of risk for the negative psychosocial factors (Figure 16.14). Part of this process is the screening questionnaire to identify the level of risk for work absence associated with the presence of negative psychosocial factors (Appendix 3 — Nurse Advisor administered, and Appendix 4 — Self-administered by the injured/ill worker). A clinical assessment tool of the in-depth evaluation of the negative psychosocial factors that can serve as barriers to a successful recovery and return to work (Figure 16.14 and Figure 16.15).

- *A Workplace Assessment* — a tool designed for use by the WorkSafeBC Nurse Advisor to assess the relevant parameters of the workplace (Figure 16.16). The intent is to be able to identify and address workplace barriers to worker return to work.

- *Employer Aids* — three educational tools are provided to enhance the level of employer workplace practices in the field of disability management. The aim is to reduce or eliminate organizational barriers for a worker's successful return to work. They are:

    1. *Workplace Checklist* — an educational tool designed to enhance employer awareness about and appreciation for worker illness/injury management and early return to work (Figure 16.17).
    2. *Keeping Employees@Work* — an educational tool designed to identify the roles of the employee, employer and the health care provider in keeping employees at work (Figure 16.18).
    3. *Everyone Has Role to Play* — a companion document to *Keeping Employees@Work*. This diagram explains the stakeholder roles as well as the need for open communication. The employee plays a pivotal and active role in this process (Figure 16.19).

Figure 16.13: System of Flags

Flag	Indicators	Treatment
Red Flags	• Organic medical issues • Pain • Significant trauma/injury • Weight loss • Fever • Evidence of abnormal tests • History of neurological, respiratory, cardiac, inflammatory, or other degenerative conditions Use of I/V or prescribed drugs	• •Medical investigation, assessment & management • Scans/X-rays/MRIs • Blood work Assess for other pathologies
Yellow Flags	**Worker Issues** • Belief that pain and activity are harmful (cultural) • Evidence of "sick role and behaviours" • Fear, frustration, stressed • Mistrust in the claim/case management processes. • Negative moods, social withdrawal, anger, depression • Passive approach to recovery • Sleep disturbances • Hypervigilent of body sensations • Substance abuse/smoking • Inactivity • Low self-esteem, locus of control, self-efficacy **Medical Management Issues** • Frustration with the medical system • Conflicting diagnoses /unknown diagnosis • Inappropriate diagnostic and treatment(s) — not "best practices" • "Enabling" health care providers • Lack of timely intervention • Using medical jargon to catastrophize their situation	• Clinical assessment • Identification of psychosocial factors • Verification of the presence of psychosocial factors • Involve the worker • Identify appropriate cognitive and behavioural management strategies • Act quickly and remain involved Use a multi-disciplinary approach as required

Flag	Indicators	Treatment
Yellow Flags	**Family/Society Issues** • Family issues — overprotective/unsupportive • Cultural impacts **Compensation/Financial Issues** • Entitlement of claim and benefits • Past disability claim experience • Financial incentives to remain off • Claim management issues • Perceived need to prove validity of the disability Litigation drivers	
Blue Flags	• "Perceived" features of work associated with work loss and delayed recovery from injury/illness such as: High work demand and low control situation • Shiftwork • Time pressures • Monotonous/non-challenging work • Lack of job satisfaction • Unsupportive management style • Low social support from colleagues • High "perceived" workloads Unrealistic expectations	• Clinical assessment • Identification of perceived barriers and fears Identify appropriate cognitive and behavioural management strategies
Black Flags	• "Actual" features of work that can be "real" barriers to return-to-work such as: • Job context and work conditions • Nature of work • Rates of pay, negotiated sick leave, salary continuance rates • Lack of modified/alternate work • Management style • Union support/involvement Organizational size and structure	• Workplace assessment • Identification of actual workplace barriers Identify appropriate risk management strategies

Figure 16.14: Clinical Assessment of Psychosocial Factors

Clinical Assessment of Psychosocial Factors (Yellow Flags)

Key Question:

What can be done to help this worker experience less distress and disability?

Assess the Following Factors

Worker's Emotions:
- Fear of increased pain with activity or work
- Fear of re-injury associated with return to work
- Depression, loss of sense of enjoyment
- More irritable than usual
- Anxiety about and heightened awareness of body sensations
- Feeling under stress and unable to maintain sense of control
- Presence of social anxiety or disinterested in social activity
- Feeling useless and not needed
- Anger due to loss of job position, role, occupational licence, *etc.*

Family's Reactions:
- Over-protective partner/spouse/child/parent, emphasizing fear of harm or encouraging catastrophizing
- Solicitous behaviour from spouse, *e.g.*, taking over tasks
- Socially punitive responses from spouse, *e.g.*, ignoring, expressing frustration
- Extent to which family members support any attempt to return to work
- Lack of support person to talk to about problems
- Assuming family chores, daily errands and child care
- Financial savings due to child care savings, fewer work and travel costs, *etc.*

Worker's Attitudes and Beliefs:
- Belief that pain is harmful or disabling resulting in fear-avoidance behaviour, *e.g.*, the development of "guarding" and fear of movement
- Belief that all pain must be abolished before attempting to return to work or normal activity
- Expectation of increased pain with activity or work, lack of ability to predict capability
- Catastrophizing, thinking the worst, misinterpreting bodily systems
- Belief that pain is uncontrollable
- Passive attitude to rehabilitation
- Enjoyment of the increased attention due to injury

- Sense of entitlement due to injury
- Reliance on analgesics, self-medication
- Fear that injury and impairment will be life-long
- Adherence to total disability beliefs
- Learned helplessness

Worker's Behaviours:
- Use of extended rest, disproportionate "downtime"
- Reduced activity level with significant withdrawal from activities of daily living
- Irregular participation or poor compliance with physical exercise, tendency for activities to be in a "boom-bust" cycle
- Avoidance of normal activity and progressive substitution of lifestyle away from productive activity
- Report extremely high intensity of pain
- Excessive reliance on use of aids or appliances
- Sleep quality reduced since onset of back pain
- High intake of alcohol or other substances with an increase since the onset of back pain
- Smoking

Compensation Issues:
- Lack of financial incentive to return to work
- Insurance benefits viewed as "a free ride"
- Delay in accessing income support and treatment cost, disputes over eligibility
- History of claim(s) due to other injuries or pain problems
- History of extended time off work due to injury or other pain problem
- History of previous back pain, with previous claim(s) and time off work
- Previous experience of ineffective case management
- Insurance pays less than regular pay
- Feels pressured to return to work when unfit to do so

Diagnosis and Treatment:
- Physician "shopping": multiple health care providers
- Health professional sanctioning disability, not providing interventions that will improve function
- Experience of conflicting diagnoses or explanations resulting in confusion
- Diagnostic language leading to catastrophizing and fear
- Dramatization of back pain by health professional producing dependency on treatments and continuation of passive treatment instead of active treatment
- Number of times visited health professional in the last year (excluding the present back pain episode)

- Expectation of a "techno-fix", *e.g.*, requests to treat as if body were a machine
- Lack of satisfaction with previous treatment for back pain
- Advice to withdraw from his or her own job or seek retraining
- Surfing the Internet for a diagnosis and suitable treatment options
- Refusing to attempt MW while awaiting a definitive diagnosis

Work:
- Unsafe working conditions according to the worker's perceptions
- Nature of work
- Work history, including length of service, frequent job change, stress levels at work, job dissatisfaction, poor work relationships, lack of vocational direction, no job to return to, *etc.*
- Belief that work is harmful; that it will do damage or be dangerous
- Unsupportive or unhappy current work environment
- Low educational background, low socioeconomic status
- Job involves shift work or working "unsociable hours"
- Minimal availability of selected duties and graduated return-to-work pathways, with unsatisfactory implementation of these
- Lack of interest by the employer in bringing the worker back to work
- Presence of labour relations issues
- Lack of job autonomy
- Level of support from co-workers
- Return to work support by a central figure in the workplace
- Poor employee-supervisor relationship
- Position-specific job demands — physical and psychological
- Limited modified work opportunities
- Employee's perceptions of their responsibilities while on claim:
  - Maintaining regular contact
  - Active participation in the recovery process
  - Compliance with treatment and rehabilitation

Figure 16.15: Clinical Assessment of Psychosocial Factors

Nature of Psychosocial Factors to Be Assessed

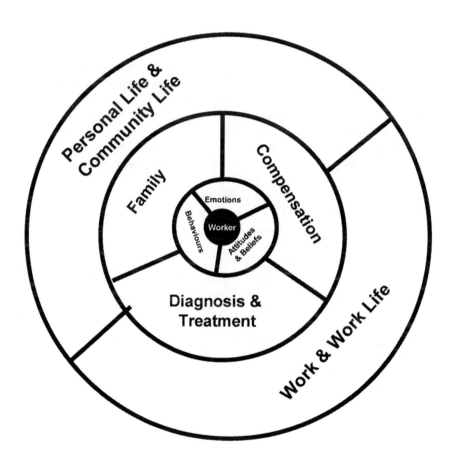

Figure 16.16: A Workplace Assessment — A Nurse Advisor Assessment Tool

Nurse Advisor
Workplace Checklist

✓

- ❏ Does your company have a Health & Safety Program? If yes, please describe.
- ❏ Is there an OHS practitioner dedicated solely to the Health & Safety Program?
- ❏ Does the company have clear reporting and recording procedures for all accidents, injuries and illnesses?
- ❏ Does the company support injured workers "to stay at work" or "to return to work early"? Please describe.
- ❏ Does the company have an internal person to develop workplace assessment and return-to-work plans?
- ❏ Are you aware that WorkSafeBC Nurse Advisors assist employers with the development of workplace assessment and return-to-work plans?
- ❏ How successful are your return to work efforts?
- ❏ Do you have a process for reviewing difficult return-to-work situations? Please describe.

WHEN AN EMPLOYEE REPORTS AN INJURY......

- ❏ Does the company review the circumstances of the injury?
- ❏ Does the company implement recommended changes to job tasks, content, or to the worksite? *(prevention of injury recurrence)*
- ❏ Could the employee stay at work doing normal tasks, or do modified tasks or hours as necessary? *(mitigation of injury consequences)*
- ❏ Does the company let the health care provider/WorkSafeBC know about the available modified work opportunities?
- ❏ Is someone assigned to assist the injured worker?
- ❏ Is an Action Plan developed?

IF YOUR EMPLOYEE IS OFF WORK.....

- ❏ Does the company implement a graduated return-to-work plan?
- ❏ Does the company maintain regular contact with the absent worker?
- ❏ Does the company require a physician's note verifying the absence and then, regular follow-up?
- ❏ Does the company need help to set up return-to-work plans?
- ❏ When return to work is proving difficult, does the company hold a meeting with everyone involved to resolve the situation?

Adapted from the ACC. *Active and Working! Managing Acute Low Back Pain in the Workplace - An Employer's Guide* (2000). NZ.

Figure 16.17: A Workplace Checklist — Employer Educational Tool

Workplace
Checklist

✓

☐ Does your company have a Health & Safety Program?
☐ Does the company continuously improve health and safety of the work environment?
☐ Are there clear reporting and recording procedures for incidents, injury & illness?
☐ Are ill/injured employees encouraged to stay at work or to return to work in a timely manner?
☐ Does the company have a Disability Management Program? Is it working as designed

WHEN AN EMPLOYEE REPORTS AN INJURY......

☐ Are the circumstances leading up to the injury examined?
☐ As a result of the incident, are recommended changes to job tasks, content, or worksite implemented?
☐ Are modified work and alternate work opportunities available for ill/injured employees?
☐ Does the company advise the health care providers about the available modified work and alternate work opportunities?
☐ Is someone assigned to assist ill/injured employees?
☐ Are modified work plans in place and used?

IF YOUR EMPLOYEE IS OFF WORK.....

☐ Does the company stay in regular contact with the injured employee?
☐ Is the employee required to submit a physician's verification of the injury and fitness to work?
☐ Does the company use disability management claim and case management practices when employees are off work?
☐ Does the company offer graduated return-to-work opportunities to injured employees?
☐ Are return-to-work plans developed and used?
☐ If return to work is proving difficult, are case conferences used to identify and resolve the barriers to a successful return to work?
☐ Is the company aware that WorkSafeBC can assist with this process?

Adapted from ACC. *Active and Working! Managing Acute Low Back Pain in the Workplace - An Employer's Guide* (2000). NZ.

Figure 16.18: Keeping Employees@Work — Employer Educational Tool[19]

Keeping Employees@Work

	The employee can...	The employer can...	The health care provider can...
Before problem occurs	• Recognize and address workplace issues and opportunities for improvement	• Set up your systems • Identify advisors you can use • Prepare functional job descriptions	
Onset of Pain (up to 1 wk)	• Use self-help approach • Take simple pain relief Stay active; modify activities as needed	• Encourage early reporting of pain	• Encourage employee to remain at work
Report Pain (up to 1 wk)	• Report pain if task/safety affected Tell work about difficult tasks	• Activate your systems • Respond quickly with modified work • Review work site factors • Make recommended changes • Be aware of "flags" & serious symptoms Keep records	• Encourage employee to remain at work
Seek Treatment (if no improvement)	• Stay active • Stay @ work • Follow treatment regimen (pain relief) Follow treatment advice about work, hours and activities	• Foster "stay @ work" • Identify suitable MW tasks and hours Assign someone to stay in touch	• Encourage "stay @ work" • Reassure and explain • Advise on work tasks, hours, activities & pain relief Monitor for additional

---

[19] Accident Compensation Corporation (ACC), *Active and Working! Managing Acute Low Back Pain in the Workplace — An Employer's Guide* (Wellington, NZ: ACC and National Health Committee, 2000).

	The employee can...	The employer can...	The health care provider can...
			medical issues
If Off Work	• Keep in touch with work • Attend work meetings & social events Stay active	• Set RTW plan • Get OH&S advice as needed • Keep in touch weekly Liaise with treatment providers — advise of available MW	• Set RTW plan • Encourage activity • Refer for expert treatment Identify & address Yellow Flags
Return to Work (RTW)	• Gradually increase hours and tasks Continue as many usual activities as possible	• Start graded RTW plan Get OH&S advice if needed	• Review regularly • Encourage activity Address ongoing Yellow Flags
Ongoing Symptoms (4-12 wks)	• Tell about tasks that remain difficult • Stop unhelpful treatment Consider job options	• Suggest all parties meet to discuss employment options	• Intensify RTW efforts • Stop unhelpful treatments • Use rehab expertise Liaise with Case Manager

Figure 16.19: Everyone Has Role to Play — Employer Educational Tool[20]

The key messages that emerged from this WorkSafeBC Conference are that:

• "You do not get people better to get them back to work; you get them back to work, to get better."

• "Workplace conditioning is the best form of conditioning."

Employers, employees, health care providers, and disability management professionals/practitioners are advised to use the aforementioned approach and tools to encourage employees to stay at work or to return to work in a safe and timely manner.

SUMMARY

This chapter addresses the system and applications that enable the effective management of worker disability claims where psychological overtones are negatively impacting the worker's chance for a successful return to work. The suggestions put forth have been tailored to a specific insurer's needs. However, the approach used demonstrates how to test and refine the presented approaches and tools to effectively manage difficult disability claims that exhibit strong psychosocial overtones.

---

[20] Adapted from ACC, *ibid.*

APPENDIX 1

THE ECM GROUP: INITIAL ASSESSMENT FORM[21]

Initial Assessment Form

Case Number	Employee Number	Employee Name
_____	_____	_____

EMPLOYEE INFORMATION
Date Off Work _____   Referral Date _____
Assessment Date _____   Nurse Consultant _____
Gender □ Male □ Female   DOB _____ Age Group   □ <20   □ 30-39   □ 50-59
                                                      □ 20-29   □ 40-49   □ 60 +

Address _____
City _____   Prov _____   Home Phone _____
Postal Code _____   Work Phone _____

WORK INFORMATION
Job Classification _____   Employer:
Supervisor Name_____   Department _____
                                             Job Location _____
                                             City Work _____
Key Job Demands (Duties, shift, hours, breaks, hazards)
_____
_____
_____

Occupational History (Job history, education, transferable skills, relationship with supervisor &
                      coworkers, current contact, possible work modifications or alternatives for
                      transitional work)

MEDICAL INFORMATION   DIAGNOSIS: _____
History of Illness/Injury (Onset, contributing factors, signs & symptoms, systems review)
_____
_____
_____
_____

Page #1

---

[21]   Printed with permission from The ECM Group, Calgary, AB. See company website at:
<http://www.ecmgroup.ca>.

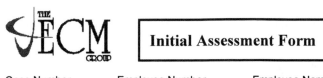

Initial Assessment Form

Case Number   Employee Number   Employee Name

_____   _____   _____

Current Health Status

_____
_____
_____

Current Treatment and Medications

_____
_____
_____

Previous Treatment

_____
_____
_____

Primary Practitioner Name _____   TYPE _____

Address _____   Phone _____   **Signed Consent**
                                                □ On File
City _____   Fax _____   □ At Practitioner's Office
Postal _____   □ With Employee

Additional Practitioner(s) Name   Phone   Fax   Type
1. _____   _____   _____   _____
2. _____   _____   _____   _____
3. _____   _____   _____   _____

PSYCHOSOCIAL INFORMATION
FAMILY & SOCIAL SUPPORT

_____
_____
_____

PERCEIVED CONTROL

_____
_____

ACTIVITIES (Daily living, recreation, hobbies, capabilities with examples - sitting, standing, walking, kneeling, bending, lifting, reaching, climbing, twisting, stooping, reaching pushing, pulling, gripping, writing, typing, level of perceived function at 1 month, 6 months, 1 year)

_____
_____
_____

BARRIERS TO REHABILITATION (Include barrier client sees as largest barrier to return to work)

_____
_____
_____

Page #2

APPENDIX 2

QUESTIONNAIRE FOR ASSESSMENT OF PSYCHOSOCIAL FACTORS[22]

ACUTE LOW BACK PAIN SCREENING QUESTIONNAIRE	(LINTON & HALLDÉN, 1996)

Today's Date >

Name >   ACC Claim Number :-

Address :-

Telephone :-HOME (   )   > WORK (   )

Job Title > OCCUPATION   Date stopped work for this episode >   /   /

These questions and statements apply if you have aches or pains, such as back, shoulder or neck pain. Please read and answer each question carefully. Do not take too long to answer the questions. However, it is important that you answer every question. There is always a response for your particular situation.

1. What year were you born?   19

2. Are you   ◯ male   ◯ female

3. Were you born in New Zealand?   ◯ yes   ◯ no   2x COUNT

4. Where do you have pain? Place a ✓ for all the appropriate sites.

   ◯ neck   ◯ shoulders   ◯ upper back   ◯ lower back   ◯ leg

5. How many days of work have you missed because of pain during the past 18 months? Tick (✓) one.

   ◯ 0 days [1]   ◯ 1-2 days [2]   ◯ 3-7 days [3]   ◯ 8-14 days [4]   ◯ 15-30 days [5]

   ◯ 1 month [6]   ◯ 2 months [7]   ◯ 3-6 months [8]   ◯ 6-12 months [9]   ◯ over 1 year [10]

6. How long have you had your current pain problem? Tick (✓) one.

   ◯ 0-1 weeks [1]   ◯ 1-2 weeks [2]   ◯ 3-4 weeks [3]   ◯ 4-5 weeks [4]   ◯ 6-8 weeks [5]

   ◯ 9-11 weeks [6] ◯ 3-6 months [7]   ◯ 6-9 months [8]   ◯ 9-12 months [9]   ◯ over 1 year [10]

7. Is your work heavy or monotonous? **Circle** the best alternative.

   0   1   2   3   4   5   6   7   8   9   10
   < *Not at all*   *Extremely* >

8. How would you rate the pain that you have had during the past week? **Circle** one.

   0   1   2   3   4   5   6   7   8   9   10
   < *No pain*   *Pain as bad as it could be* >

9. In the past 3 months, on average, how bad was your pain? **Circle** one.

   0   1   2   3   4   5   6   7   8   9   10
   < *No pain*   *Pain as bad as it could be* >

10. How often would you say that you have experienced pain episodes, on average, during the past 3 months? **Circle** one.

   0   1   2   3   4   5   6   7   8   9   10
   < *Never*   *Always* >

11. Based on all the things you do to cope, or deal with your pain, on an average day, how much are you able to decrease it? **Circle** one.   10x

   0   1   2   3   4   5   6   7   8   9   10
   < *Can't decrease it at all*   *Can decrease it completely* >

12. How tense or anxious have you felt in the past week? **Circle** one.

   0   1   2   3   4   5   6   7   8   9   10
   < *Absolutely calm and relaxed*   *As tense and anxious as I've ever felt* >

---

[22] N. Kendall, S. Linton & C. Main, *Guide to Assessing Psychological Yellow Flags in Acute Low Back Pain: Risk Factors for Long-Term Disability and Work Loss* (Wellington, NZ: Accident Compensation Corporation and the New Zealand Guidelines Group, 1997) at 11-13. Available for public use.

13. How much have you been bothered by feeling depressed in the past week? **Circle** one.

0	1	2	3	4	5	6	7	8	9	10
< Not at all										Extremely >

14. In your view, how large is the risk that your current pain may become persistent? **Circle** one.

0	1	2	3	4	5	6	7	8	9	10
< No risk										Very large risk >

15. In your estimation, what are the chances that you will be working in 6 months? **Circle** one.   `10x`

0	1	2	3	4	5	6	7	8	9	10
< No chance										Very large chance >

16. If you take into consideration your work routines, management, salary, promotion possibilities and work mates, how satisfied are you with your job? **Circle** one.   `10x`

0	1	2	3	4	5	6	7	8	9	10
< Not at all satisfied										Completely satisfied >

Here are some of the things which other people have told us about their back pain. For each statement please circle one number from 0-10 to say how much physical activity, such as bending, lifting, walking or driving would affect your back.

17. Physical activity makes my pain worse. **Circle** one.

0	1	2	3	4	5	6	7	8	9	10
< Completely disagree										Completely agree >

18. An increase in pain is an indication that I should stop what I am doing until the pain decreases. **Circle** one.

0	1	2	3	4	5	6	7	8	9	10
< Completely disagree										Completely agree >

19. I should not do my normal work with my present pain. **Circle** one.

0	1	2	3	4	5	6	7	8	9	10
< Completely disagree										Completely agree >

Here is a list of five activities. Please circle the one number which best describes your current ability to participate in each of these activities.

20. I can do light work for an hour. **Circle** one.   `10x`

0	1	2	3	4	5	6	7	8	9	10
< Can't do it because of pain problem								Can do it without pain being a problem >		

21. I can walk for an hour. **Circle** one.   `10x`

0	1	2	3	4	5	6	7	8	9	10
< Can't do it because of pain problem								Can do it without pain being a problem >		

22. I can do ordinary household chores. **Circle** one.   `10x`

0	1	2	3	4	5	6	7	8	9	10
< Can't do it because of pain problem								Can do it without pain being a problem >		

23. I can go shopping. **Circle** one.   `10x`

0	1	2	3	4	5	6	7	8	9	10
< Can't do it because of pain problem								Can do it without pain being a problem >		

24. I can sleep at night. **Circle** one.   `10x`

0	1	2	3	4	5	6	7	8	9	10
< Can't do it because of pain problem								Can do it without pain being a problem >		

SUM >

TABLE 1: ACUTE LOW BACK PAIN SCREENING QUESTIONNAIRE – TO PREDICT RISK OF LONG-TERM WORK LOSS (LINTON & HALLDÉN,1996)

a sample questionnaire is included in the back of this guide.

You may photocopy this.

SCORING INSTRUCTIONS – ACUTE PAIN SCREENING QUESTIONNAIRE

> For question 4, count the number of pain sites and multiply by 2

> For questions 6, 7, 8, 9, 10, 12, 13, 14, 17, 18 and 19 the score is the number that has been ticked or circled

> For questions 11, 15, 16, 20, 21, 22, 23 and 24 the score is 10 minus the number that has been ticked or circled

> Write the score in the shaded box beside each item – questions 4 to 24

> Add them up, and write the sum in the box provided – this is the total score

Note: the scoring method is built into the questionnaire

INTERPRETATION OF SCORES – ACUTE PAIN SCREENING QUESTIONNAIRE

QUESTIONNAIRE SCORES GREATER THAN 105 INDICATE THAT THE PATIENT IS AT RISK.

This score produces:

> 75% correct identification of those not needing modification to ongoing management

> 86% correct identification of those who will have between 1 and 30 days off work

> 83% correct identification of those who will have more than 30 days off work

THE USE OF THIS QUESTIONNAIRE IN NEW ZEALAND

A prospective study is under way to determine the validity of the cut-off score of 105 in New Zealand using a local sample. Information regarding any amendment to this scoring system will be provided as soon as it becomes available.

APPENDIX 3

Two versions of this questionnaire were prepared — one for a clinical assessment conducted by the Nurse Advisor (Appendix 3), and a self-assessment version for use by an injured/ill worker (Appendix 4).

QUESTIONNAIRE FOR ASSESSMENT OF PSYCHOSOCIAL FACTORS — NURSE-ADVISOR ADMINISTERED[23]

Screening Questionnaire – Assessment of Disability Psychosocial Factors

Name:		Claim Number:	
Address:			
Telephone: Home ( )-		Work ( )-	
Occupation:		Date of Injury:	
Height:	BMI: *(calculated)*	Hand Dominance: R □: L □	
Weight:			
Year of Birth:		Gender: Male □ : Female □	
Preferred Language:			

General Questions:

These questions apply if the worker reports aches or pain associated with the injury. Please complete each question.

1. Where do you have pain? Place a (✓) for all the appropriate sites.

Neck	□	Shoulders	□	Upper back	□	Lower back	□	Leg	□	Other	□

2. How many days of work have you missed due to pain in the last 18 months? Tick (✓) one.

0 days	□	1-2 days	□	3-7 days	□	8-14 days	□	15-30 days	□
1 month	□	2 months	□	3-6 months	□	6-12 months	□	More than 1 year	□

3. How long have you experienced your pain? Tick (✓) one.

0 days	□	1-2 days	□	3-7 days	□	8-14 days	□	15-30 days	□
1 month	□	2 months	□	3-6 months	□	6-12 months	□	More than 1 year	□

4. Is your work heavy? Circle the best rating.

0	1	2	3	4	5	6	7	8	9	10
Not at all										*Extreme*

5. Is your work repetitive/monotonous? Circle the best rating.

0	1	2	3	4	5	6	7	8	9	10
Not at all										*Extreme*

6. How would you rate the pain that you experienced during this past week? Circle one.

0	1	2	3	4	5	6	7	8	9	10
No pain										*Extreme*

7. Since the day of your injury, how bad was your pain? Circle one.

0	1	2	3	4	5	6	7	8	9	10
No pain										*Extreme*

8. Prior to this injury, did you ever experience pain in this area?

Never	□		Once	□		Frequently	□

9. On average and since your injury, how often would you say that you have experienced bouts of pain? Circle one.

0	1	2	3	4	5	6	7	8	9	10
Never										*Always*

10. Based on the things you do to manage your pain, on an average day, how much are you able to decrease the pain? Circle one.

0	1	2	3	4	5	6	7	8	9	10
Can't decrease it										*Can completely decrease its*

11. How tense or anxious have you felt in the past week? Circle one.

0	1	2	3	4	5	6	7	8	9	10
Calm and relaxed										*As tense and anxious as ever felt*

12. How would you rate your mood in the past week? Circle one.

0	1	2	3	4	5	6	7	8	9	10
Low										*Upbeat*

13. Are you concerned that your pain may not resolve? Circle one.

0	1	2	3	4	5	6	7	8	9	10
No concern										*Very concerned*

14. In your estimation, what are the chances that you will be working in 2 months? Circle one.

0	1	2	3	4	5	6	7	8	9	10
No chance										*Will be back*

15. If you take into consideration your work routines, management, salary, co-workers, how satisfied are you with your job? Circle one.

0	1	2	3	4	5	6	7	8	9	10
No satisfied										*Extremely satisfied*

---

23 Developed at the WorkSafeBC Conference, May 14, 2009, and adapted from N. Kendall, S. Linton & C. Main, *ibid.*

Screening Questionnaire – Assessment of Disability Psychosocial Factors

Your Current Level of Physical Activity:

Here are some things which people tell us about their pain. For each statement, please circle a number from 1-10 to describe how much physical activity affects your pain.

16. Physical activity makes my pain worse. Circle one.

0 Strongly disagree	1	2	3	4	5	6	7	8	9	10 Strongly agree

17. An increase in pain is an indication that I should stop doing what I am doing until the pain subsides. Circle one.

0 Strongly disagree	1	2	3	4	5	6	7	8	9	10 Strongly agree

18. I should not do my normal work with my present pain Circle one.

0 Strongly disagree	1	2	3	4	5	6	7	8	9	10 Strongly agree

Your Current Level of General Activity:

Here is a list of activities. Please circle the one number which best describes your current ability to participate in each of these activities.

19. I can do light work for an hour. Circle one.

0 Can't due to pain	1	2	3	4	5	6	7	8	9	10 Can without any problem

20. I can walk for an hour. Circle one.

0 Can't due to pain	1	2	3	4	5	6	7	8	9	10 Can without any problem

21. I can do my regular household chores Circle one.

0 Can't due to pain	1	2	3	4	5	6	7	8	9	10 Can without any problem

22. I can go shopping. Circle one.

0 Can't due to pain	1	2	3	4	5	6	7	8	9	10 Can without any problem

23. I can sleep at night. Circle one.

0 Can't due to pain	1	2	3	4	5	6	7	8	9	10 Can without any problem

Additional Comments noted by the Worker:

_____

_____

_____

Additional Comments from the Nurse Advisor:

_____

_____

_____

APPENDIX 4

QUESTIONNAIRE FOR ASSESSMENT OF PSYCHOSOCIAL FACTORS — SELF-ASSESSMENT[24]

Screening Questionnaire – Assessment of Disability Psychosocial Factors

Name:		Claim Number:	
Address:			
Telephone: Home ( )-		Work ( )-	
Occupation:		Date of Injury:	
Height:	BMI: *(calculated)*	Hand Dominance: R ☐ or L ☐	
Weight:			
Year of Birth:		Gender: Male ☐ ; Female ☐	
Preferred Language:			

General Questions:

Please read and answer the following questions if you have aches or pain.

1. Where do you have pain? Place a (✓) for all the appropriate sites.

Neck	☐	Shoulders	☐	Upper back	☐	Lower back	☐	Leg	☐	Other	☐

2. How many days of work have you missed due to pain in the last 18 months? Tick (✓) one.

0 days	☐	1-2 days	☐	3-7 days	☐	8-14 days	☐	15-30 days	☐
1 month	☐	2 months	☐	3-6 months	☐	6-12 months	☐	More than 1 year	☐

3. How long have you experienced your pain? Tick (✓) one.

0 days	☐	1-2 days	☐	3-7 days	☐	8-14 days	☐	15-30 days	☐
1 month	☐	2 months	☐	3-6 months	☐	6-12 months	☐	More than 1 year	☐

4. Is your work heavy? Circle the best rating.

0	1	2	3	4	5	6	7	8	9	10
Not at all										*Extreme*

5. Is your work repetitive/monotonous? Circle the best rating.

0	1	2	3	4	5	6	7	8	9	10
Not at all										*Extreme*

6. How would you rate the pain that you experienced during this past week? Circle one.

0	1	2	3	4	5	6	7	8	9	10
No pain										*Extreme*

7. Since the day of your injury, how bad was your pain? Circle one.

0	1	2	3	4	5	6	7	8	9	10
No pain										*Extreme*

8. Prior to this injury, did you ever experience pain in this area?

Never	☐	Once	☐	Frequently	☐

9. On average and since your injury, how often would you say that you have experienced bouts of pain? Circle one.

0	1	2	3	4	5	6	7	8	9	10
Never										*Always*

10. Based on the things you do to manage your pain, on an average day, how much are you able to decrease the pain? Circle one.

0	1	2	3	4	5	6	7	8	9	10
Can't decrease it										*Can completely decrease its*

11. How tense or anxious have you felt in the past week? Circle one.

0	1	2	3	4	5	6	7	8	9	10
Calm and relaxed										*As tense and anxious as ever felt*

12. How would you rate your mood in the past week? Circle one.

0	1	2	3	4	5	6	7	8	9	10
Low										*Upbeat*

13. Are you concerned that your pain may not resolve? Circle one.

0	1	2	3	4	5	6	7	8	9	10
No concern										*Very concerned*

14. In your estimation, what are the chances that you will be working in 2 months? Circle one.

0	1	2	3	4	5	6	7	8	9	10
No chance										*Will be back*

15. If you take into consideration your work routines, management, salary, co-workers, how satisfied are you with your job? Circle one.

0	1	2	3	4	5	6	7	8	9	10
No satisfied										*Extremely satisfied*

---

[24] Developed at the WorkSafeBC Conference, May 14, 2009, and adapted from N. Kendall, S. Linton & C. Main, *ibid.*

Screening Questionnaire – Assessment of Disability Psychosocial Factors

Your Current Level of Physical Activity:

Here are some things which people tell us about their pain. For each statement, please circle a number from 1-10 to describe how much physical activity affects your pain.

16. Physical activity makes my pain worse. Circle one.

0 Strongly disagree	1	2	3	4	5	6	7	8	9	10 Strongly agree

17. An increase in pain is an indication that I should stop doing what I am doing until the pain subsides. Circle one.

0 Strongly disagree	1	2	3	4	5	6	7	8	9	10 Strongly agree

18. I should not do my normal work with my present pain Circle one.

0 Strongly disagree	1	2	3	4	5	6	7	8	9	10 Strongly agree

Your Current Level of General Activity:

Here is a list of activities. Please circle the one number which best describes your current ability to participate in each of these activities.

19. I can do light work for an hour. Circle one.

0 Can't due to pain	1	2	3	4	5	6	7	8	9	10 Can without any problem

20. I can walk for an hour. Circle one.

0 Can't due to pain	1	2	3	4	5	6	7	8	9	10 Can without any problem

21. I can do my regular household chores Circle one.

0 Can't due to pain	1	2	3	4	5	6	7	8	9	10 Can without any problem

22. I can go shopping. Circle one.

0 Can't due to pain	1	2	3	4	5	6	7	8	9	10 Can without any problem

23. I can sleep at night. Circle one.

0 Can't due to pain	1	2	3	4	5	6	7	8	9	10 Can without any problem

Do you have any additional comments that you would like to add?

_____

_____

_____

_____

Thank you for your time and honesty in completing this questionnaire.

APPENDIX 5

LIST OF CONTRIBUTORS

Thanks are extended to all the Occupational Health Nurses who participated in the development of an effective approach to the management of disability claims with strong psychosocial overtones at the WorkSafeBC OHN Conference, May 14, 2009. Special mention is offered to Jan Beesley, Margaret Smithson, Jocelyne Fidyk, WorkSafeBC, and Barbara Roberts who without their expertise and support, this work would not have been possible.

Occupational Health Nurse	Occupational Health Nurse
Rupel Amershi	Suzanne Ledet
Lydia Arnold-Smith	Patrick Madden
Paulette Baker	Anu Manhas
Shelley Barnard	Julie Matear
Marla Barnes	Abha McDonell
Susan Bates	Sandra McGuire
Mary Beeksma	Joan Meidl
Jan Beesley	Candice Moore
Kyra Bell	April Negrin
Juliana Boratto	Sundeep Nijjar
Mary-Anne Brittain	Patricia O'Brien
Elizabeth Brydon	Dee Ogden
Arvin Cajigas	Nan Ouimet
Jim Cariaso	Pearl Pacheco
Barbara Carter	Heather Palmer
Cordia Chung	David Poelzer
Eva Clegg	Stacy Purewal
Barb Curtis	Usha Reddy
Patricia Doiron	Nicole Richards
Arlene Dyer	Barb Roberts
Kathy Fast	Karin Rolfes-Kubik
Jo-Anne Finley	Kathy Romano
Barbara Flesh	Penny Ross
Steve Fur	Bernadette Rudolphi
Simone Gardezy	Helen Ryan
Patricia Garnham	Eva Sadowski
Lynda Goodman-Bell	Lucy Samuel
Rachelle Grace	Tammy Scott

Occupational Health Nurse	Occupational Health Nurse
Donna Graham	Margaret Smithson
Diana Grant	Melanie Solari
Catherine Guy	Susan Stryck
Alison Hannah	Sheila Thiessen
Helene Heppner	Cheryl Walilko
Stephanie Higgins	Susan Wood
Nicole Hough	Juanita Woodrow
Tess Juliano	Benita Yan
Elise Kobylanski	Doreen Yanick
Jennifer Kullman	

CHAPTER REFERENCES

Accident Compensation Corporation (ACC) and the National Health Committee, *Active and Working! Managing Acute Low Back Pain in the Workplace — An Employer's Guide* (Wellington, NZ: ACC and National Health Committee, 2000).

Accident Compensation Corporation (ACC) and the National Health Committee (1999), *New Zealand Acute Low Back Pain Guide, January 1997 edition* (Wellington, NZ: ACC and National Health Committee, 1999).

F. Benard, The ECM Group (2009), Calgary, AB, available online at <http://www.ecmgroup.ca>.

D. Gross & M. Battié, "Work-related Recovery Expectations and the Prognosis of Chronic Low Back Pain Within a Workers' Compensation Setting" (2005) 47:4 Journal of Occupational and Environmental Medicine 428.

N. Kendall, S. Linton, & C. Main, *Guide to Assessing Psychological Yellow Flags in Acute Low Back Pain: Risk Factors for Long-Term Disability and Work Loss* (Wellington, NZ: Accident Compensation Corporation and the New Zealand Guidelines Group, 1997).

Partnership for Workplace Mental Health, *Assessing and Treating Psychiatric Occupational Disability,* report released by the American Psychiatric Foundation (2005), available online at: <http://www.workplacemental health.org/pdf/disabilityreportpart1.pdf>.

W. Shaw, S. Linton & G. Pransky, "Reducing Sickness Absence from Work due to Low Back Pain: How Well do Intervention Strategies Match Modifiable Risk Factors?" (2006) 16:4 *J. Occup Rehabil* 591.

WorkSafeBC ("Staff In-service — Interactive Workshop on Disability Management: Management of Disability Claims with Strong Psychosocial Overtones", facilitated by D. Dyck, May 14, 2009).

Chapter 17

Disability Management
Best Practices

DISABILITY MANAGEMENT BEST PRACTICES DEFINED

Disability management, in its entirety, can be defined as the process of preventing and managing absence from work. Operationally, it is an active process directed towards promoting and supporting regular workplace attendance and minimizing the impact of impairment on the ill or injured employee's ability to compete in the workplace.

As noted in Chapter 1, "Disability Management: Overview", the *key elements* of any Integrated Disability Management Program are:

- management-employee commitment and supportive policies;
- stakeholder education and involvement;
- supportive benefit plans;
- a coordinated approach to injury/illness management with a focus on early intervention;
- a communication strategy;
- graduated return-to-work opportunities;
- performance measurement of outcomes;
- workplace wellness; and
- disability prevention, including Workplace Wellness, Attendance Support & Assistance, and Occupational Health & Safety Program initiatives.

Best practices are a form of benchmarking that result from direct observation of clinical practices.[1] They are based on real examples and can be used to gradually promote system improvement. Best practices can serve as guidelines for practice and measurement of outcomes. However, changes in technology, knowledge and practice advancements can alter any best practice. This means that benchmarks and guidelines must undergo frequent reviews and updates to remain current and credible.

---

[1] R. Bruckman & J. Harris, "Occupational Medicine Practice Guidelines" (1998) 13:4 Occupational Medicine: State of the Art Reviews 679.

DISABILITY MANAGEMENT: BEST PRACTICES

The intent of this chapter is to present current best practices in the field of Disability Management. A discussion of each topic will be followed by a list of the relevant best practices.

(1)   Joint Labour-Management Commitment to a Disability Management Program

The most successful workplace models of Disability Management Program involve joint labour-management support and participation. In terms of legalities, management is obliged to work with union leaders to offer effective disability services, Employee Assistance Programs, and rehabilitation services. The rationale is that the union is the certified bargaining agent for the employee. As noted in Chapter 2, "Joint Labour-Management Support and Involvement", the employee relinquishes his or her individual bargaining position on behalf of a stronger collective voice with the union. In return, the union has a duty to review any employment decisions made between the employer and employee. If the union fails to do so, the employee can sue the union.[2]

The union has a duty to fairly represent a union member when a complaint comes forward about the employee's work capacity, or likelihood of risk due to health conditions. The employer and the union have the duty to accommodate the ill or injured worker; and the worker has the right to be accommodated unless there is a Bona Fide Occupational Requirement preventing the accommodation, or if the accommodation is to the point of undue hardship on the employer's part.

BEST PRACTICES

1.   Encourage joint labour-management participation in the Disability Management Program Steering Committee.
2.   Encourage joint labour-management involvement in all the disability management initiatives and activities.
3.   Invite and strongly encourage union/employee promotion and participation in graduated return-to-work activities.
4.   Seek ways to collaboratively lower the high absenteeism rate of unionized employees.

---

[2]   D.B. Mercer, "Roles and Responsibilities in Job Modification and Accommodation" (Seminars in Occupational Health and Medicine, Faculty of Medicine, Continuing Education, University of Calgary, February 3, 1999) [unpublished].

(2) Integrate Disability Management Program Efforts

For effective disability management, a design or model for an Integrated Disability Management Program should exist. An **Integrated Disability Management Program** is a planned and coordinated approach to facilitate and manage employee health and productivity. It is a human resource risk management and risk communication approach designed to integrate all organizational/company programs and resources to minimize or reduce the losses and costs associated with employee medical absence regardless of the nature of those disabilities.

An Integrated Disability Management Program model (Chapter 1, "Disability Management: Overview", Figure 1.2) contains the following elements:

- joint union-labour-management endorsement, commitment and involvement;
- supportive policies, procedures and systems;
- a system that ensures accountability by all parties;
- employee absenteeism and disability data collection for analysis and evaluation;
- claim management and adjudication;
- case management and coordination;
- multi-disciplinary interventions — occupational safety, human resources, Employee Assistance Program, medical, vocational, and/ or occupational rehabilitation;
- early intervention;
- graduated return-to-work opportunities;
- data collection, management and consolidation with other organizational/ company employee support programs;
- attendance support and disability prevention strategies;
- workplace wellness; and
- leveraging of the available company-program offerings to enhance employee health and productivity.

According to Watson Wyatt Worldwide, employers who have integrated Disability Management Programs experience an average reduction of 19-25 per cent in their total disability costs.[3] Additionally, employers can anticipate a 15-35 per cent reduction in company group benefit costs depending on the nature of the suite of benefits offered by the organization.[4]

---

[3] Watson Wyatt Worldwide, *News Release*, "Employers That Measure Results from Integrated Disability Management Programs Report Big Savings" (October 15, 1998), available online at: <http://www.watsonwyatt.com/news/press.asp?ID=6900>.

[4] N. Vimadalal & J. Wozniak, Best Practices to Help Employers Capture the Benefits of Integrated Disability Management, *Employee Benefits News* (March 1, 2008), available online at: <http://ebn.benefitnews.com/news/best-practices-help-employers-capture-benefits-548491-1.html>.

BEST PRACTICES

1. Have a joint labour-management committee act as a steering committee for the Integrated Disability Management Program.[5] This committee would be the foundation of the Integrated Disability Management Program. Roles assigned to members of the committee have been defined in Chapter 4, "Integrated Disability Management: Stakeholder Roles".

    The steering committee advises and consults with management and union leaders, evaluates concerns, and receives advice and suggestions for the Integrated Disability Management Program from various stakeholders in the company or organization. The committee also receives reports regarding the usage of the Integrated Disability Management Program, which assess the program's overall effectiveness. The information provided to the committee and to management is population, or aggregate data to prevent the identification of individual employees.

    Typically, the steering committee membership has representatives from management and labour, and the chairperson is elected by the members for a set term.

2. Ensure effective functioning by having one central figure oversee the daily operations of an Integrated Disability Management Program. This is typically a Disability Management Coordinator — an occupational health nurse or a Disability Management professional/practitioner with advanced education in the field of Disability Management.

3. Ensure that resources, such as the Disability Management Coordinator, the claim administrator, and internal/external consultants, are available as internal consultants to the steering committee.

4. Conduct a comprehensive needs-analysis to identify specific organizational needs, and to establish baseline data before implementing an Integrated Disability Management Program. This should include an assessment of labour/management attitudes towards disability management practices, the identification of the company or organization's disability profile, an acknowledgment of the types of assistance available to the ill or injured employee and an estimate of the level of disability support required.

5. Examine all related disability policies and procedures in terms of their impact on the Integrated Disability Management Program.

6. Review and revise, where necessary, the current disability-related policies and procedures.

7. Identify and communicate the roles and responsibilities of all major stakeholders involved in the Integrated Disability Management Program.

8. Define the available return-to-work options to all the stakeholders.

---

[5] National Institute for Disability Management and Research (NIDMAR), *Disability Management in the Workplace: A Guide to Establishing a Joint Workplace Program* (Port Alberni, BC: NIDMAR, 1995).

9. Identify the milestones or specific steps to be taken in the return-to-work process.
10. Review and revise, as appropriate, the current return-to-work strategies.
11. Assess, where necessary, the disability claim forms with a view to their functionality and contribution to the effectiveness of the Integrated Disability Management Program. Forms should focus on the claimant's capabilities versus disabilities.
12. Develop an absence and disability database for all types of absences — casual absence, short-term disability, occupational absence (Workers' Compensation), and long-term disability. Link this system with the company or organization's Occupational Health, Employee Assistance Program, Occupational Health & Safety Program, employee benefit plans, and Workplace Wellness Program outcomes.
13. Use the above outcome data along with other Human Resources and employee group benefit plan outcomes to assist in the interpretation of disability management issues.
14. Seek ways to maximize the integration of all the organizational/company programs so as to maximize the individual program efforts and outcomes.

(3) Disability Management Program Policies and Procedures

Policies and procedures for maintaining contact with absent staff members, accessing treatment or rehabilitation, and ensuring an expedient return to work can be applied to the entire continuum of absence regardless of cause, including casual absence, short-term disability, Workers' Compensation Board, and long-term disability illness/injuries. The intent of policies and procedures is to ensure that processes are in place and are applied fairly, equally and consistently[6]

BEST PRACTICES

1. Develop and implement policies and procedures that deal with:

    - disability leaves (*i.e.*, casual absence, sick leave, short-term disability, Workers' Compensation Board, long-term disability, *etc.*);
    - rehabilitation measures (*i.e.*, case/claim management, vocational rehabilitation, *etc.*);
    - claim management standards of practice;
    - case management standards of practice;
    - confidentiality standard of practice;
    - documentation standard of practice;
    - return-to-work practices;

---

[6]   Canadian Centre on Disability Studies, *Best Practices in Contemporary Disability Management: Executive Summary* (1998) at 8, available online at: <http://www.disabilitystudies.ca>.

- alcohol and drug policy; and
- harassment and respectful workplace policies.

More detail on relevant policies and procedures is provided in Chapter 3, "The Supportive Infrastructure for an Integrated Disability Management Program".

2. Regularly review and update these policies to evaluate their continued applicability.

(4) Graduated Return-to-Work

Graduated return-to-work initiatives can be an effective method of systematically returning employees to health and work, and can contribute to cost-containment.[7]

The recommended components of a graduated return-to-work initiatives are:

- employee and supervisor submission of all the necessary claim forms;
- active involvement by the supervisor;
- early intervention;
- communication with the employee and attending physician regarding the availability of modified/alternate work;
- regular follow-up with the employee and physician regarding the employee's fitness-to-work status;
- availability of modified/alternate work for the recovering employee;
- documented return-to-work plans;[8]
- placement of the employee into suitable modified/alternate work;
- monitoring of the employee's progress and fitness to work;
- a gradual return to full-time duties;
- evaluation of the claim management practices and outcomes;
- evaluation of the case management practices and outcomes; and
- data collection and management.

Companies who have implemented graduated return-to-work initiatives have noted significant success at returning employees to work, and at containing their disability rates and costs. As well, they are able to demonstrate compliance with the Canadian Human Rights duty to accommodate legislation.

The Canadian duty to accommodate legislation varies by province. In general, this legislation indicates that the employer, employee, and unions have a

---

[7]   D. Lyons, "Integrated Disability Management: Assessing Its Fit for Your Company", *Ideas at Work* (Winter 2004), available online at: <http://online.wsj.com/ad/LibertyMutual/>; and Watson Wyatt Worldwide, *Staying@Work: Effective Presence at Work. 2007 Survey Report — Canada: Executive Summary* (2007) at 10, available online at: <http://www.easna.org/documents/WatsonWyattStayingatWorkSurvey.pdf>.

[8]   Watson-Wyatt, *ibid.*

tripartite responsibility to accommodate the injured or ill employee back into the workplace, up to the point of "**undue hardship**".[9]

The key practices of successful graduated return-to-work plans are:

*   arranging acceptable practices with unions for modified/alternate work opportunities within the collective agreements;
*   ensuring that the modified/alternate work offered is meaningful and gainful employment;
*   having set time lines for the modified/alternate work opportunity; and
*   clearly defining the differences between modified and alternate work.

This topic of graduated return-to-work plans is covered in more in Chapter 5, "An Integrated Disability Management Program: The Managed Rehabilitative Care Program".

BEST PRACTICES

1. Develop and implement corporate-wide use of graduated return-to-work plans that involve labour and management support and participation.
2. Communicate the roles, responsibilities, and accountabilities of the key stakeholders.
3. Elicit employee, union and line identification of modified/alternate work options.
4. Manage safe and timely return-to-work activities.
5. Develop flexible and creative return-to-work options.
6. Collect and manage modified/alternate work data, and the graduated return-to-work outcomes.
7. Evaluate the graduated return-to-work initiatives, plans, and outcomes regularly.
8   Communicate the benefits, challenges, and outcomes to all key stakeholders.

(5) Centralize the Responsibility for an Integrated Disability Management Program

To ensure effective functioning, one central figure should coordinate the daily operations of an Integrated Disability Management Program.[10] This is typically a Disability Management Coordinator. The functions for this position are discussed in detail in Chapter 4, "Disability Management Program: Stakeholder Roles and Responsibilities", and in Chapter 5, "An Integrated Disability Management Program: The Managed Rehabilitative Care Program".

---

[9]   L. Steeves & R. Smithies, "Foresight is Your Best Defence" (1996) 4:2 Group Healthcare Management 29.

[10] L. Steeves & R. Smithies, *ibid.*; and D. Lyons, "Integrated Disability Management: Assessing Its Fit for Your Company", *Ideas at Work* (Winter 2004), available online at: <http://online.wsj.com/ad/LibertyMutual>.

BEST PRACTICES

1. Delegate the coordination of the Disability Management Program to one central person. The Disability Management Coordinator is responsible for the overall management (including data organization and analysis) of all employee disabilities; acts as a point of contact for all stakeholders; is an active supporter of the ill or injured employee and family members; and functions as a catalyst for facilitating the reintegration of the disabled worker into the workplace.
2. Coordinate disability management initiatives with the Employee Assistance Program, Occupational Health & Safety Program, Workplace Wellness Program, and Human Resources Program.
3. Advise the company's Occupational Health & Safety department of the cause and nature of all Workers' Compensation Board claims as part of the overall Disability Management Program. The intent is to seek workable illness and injury prevention strategies.

(6) Disability Management Program Communication Strategy

An essential component of any successful Integrated Disability Management Program is the widespread understanding and support of stakeholders both within the workplace and in the broader community. This is a dynamic process. Education and open, honest communication about program objectives, successes, failures and future plans are powerful tools that can alter entrenched attitudes and build trust between individuals. The reality is that attendance support and disability management is built on relationships, and these relationships need to be constantly nurtured.

BEST PRACTICES

1. Develop a communication strategy and plan to promote awareness and overcome organizational barriers to implementing an Integrated Disability Management Program (Chapter 13, "Marketing Disability Management Programs and Communicating the Results", provides more details).
2. Keep all key stakeholders in the information loop and part of the decision-making process.
3. Provide stakeholders with relevant outcome data and benefits realized by the Integrated Disability Management Program. This garners continued support for the Integrated Disability Management Program.
4. Use the available communication vehicles to spread the word about the Integrated Disability Management Program, both internally and externally, to supervisors and managers, union leaders and employees. In this manner, the stakeholders can be part of an ongoing solution for employee attendance support and disability management.

(7)   Disability Management Program Education and Training

The purpose of Disability Management Program education and training is to create awareness around the need for and value afforded by workplace-based attendance and Disability Management Programs. Recent studies indicate that the response of the supervisor to the worker's medical absence is one of the most important factors in the worker's timely return to work. For example, workers who felt blamed, penalized, mistrusted, or belittled by their supervisor when they first reported a work-related injury had a significantly longer work absence.[11]

Supervisors, union leaders, and management benefit from specific information on:

*   assisting employees to attain regular workplace attendance;
*   the values and objectives of attendance support and disability management practices;
*   communicating effectively with the ill/injured employee and family;
*   identifying markers that indicate a potential problem situation;
*   overcoming barriers to graduated return-to-work efforts;
*   tracking of absences and modified/alternate work initiatives;
*   the related cost/benefit issues; and
*   success and failure indicators for an Integrated Disability Management Program.

Ongoing training is required for a Disability Management Coordinator to develop and maintain the specific skills and knowledge necessary to facilitate a safe and timely return to work for ill or injured employees. A Disability Management Coordinator must have a practical knowledge of:

*   the various roles and responsibilities of health professionals who affect the return-to-work process (*i.e.*, physicians, occupational health nurses, physiotherapists, occupational therapists, rehabilitation specialists, *etc.*);
*   the field of Ergonomics;
*   the principles of Occupational Health & Safety;
*   "best practice" claim management methods;
*   "best practice" case management methods;
*   barriers to graduated return-to-work efforts within the organization and how to overcome them;
*   the accepted dispute resolution procedures for the organization/company;
*   Disability Management Program performance measurement methods;
*   "best practice" data collection and management practices;
*   "best practice" Disability Management Program evaluation techniques;
*   program reporting and presentation of results;

---

[11]   G. Pransky & W. Shaw, "Injury Response: Optimizing the Role of Supervisors", *Ideas at Work* (Spring 2002) at 11-12, available online at: <http://www.libertymutual.com>.

- "best practice" integration techniques to maximize the programming resources; and
- the principles of Workplace Wellness Programs.

BEST PRACTICES

1. Specialized education and training in disability management is required for the Disability Management Coordinator.
2. Generalized training for all supervisors and human resource staff in dealing with ill or injured employees and family members.
3. Disability management education for union and other staff leaders facilitates Disability Management Program implementation.[12] This may be possible through a government or private agency specializing in the delivery of disability management education.
4. Continuing education in the field of disability management and other related fields (e.g., in Employee Assistance Programs, Human Resources principles, Occupational Health & Safety, risk management and risk communication, Workplace Wellness Programs, management human resource theories and practices, etc.) is required for the Disability Management Coordinator.

(8)   Link the Disability Management Program with the Employee Assistance Program

External services can play an important role in effective employee attendance support and disability management. Companies that integrate the Employee Assistance Program services with attendance support and Disability Management Programs experience the need for a comprehensive Employee Assistance Program service when dealing with the psychological and physiological aspects of absence. Workplace-focused programs can be designed to assist with the identification and resolution of personal concerns that can impair employee attendance and productivity and lead to increased disability costs. The rationale for such an approach is detailed in Chapter 7, "The Role of Employee Assistance Programs in Disability Management".

The most effective formal linkages are the ones in which there is a predetermined working relationship between Disability Case Managers and the Employee Assistance Program service providers. Appropriate consents are put in place so that the relevant issues surrounding the employee's fitness to work, treatment plans and workplace accommodations can be discussed. Issues are discussed on a need-to-know basis and pertain to a successful re-entry to the workplace.

---

[12]   Canadian Centre on Disability Studies, *Best Practices in Contemporary Disability Management: Executive Summary* (1998), available online at: <http://www.disabilitystudies.ca>.

BEST PRACTICES

1. Ensure that the proposed Integrated Disability Management Program model includes a formal linkage with company or organization's Employee Assistance Program. Effective linkage can be achieved before, during or after the disability occurs.
2. Ensure that all the service providers attain a mutual understanding of and respect for the individual program goals and objectives, as well as for the overall Integrated Disability Management Program goals and objectives.
3. Promote a partnership approach that allows for multi-disciplinary interventions.
4. Examine the outcome measures on the cases served jointly by the Employee Assistance Program and Integrated Disability Management Program personnel. Knowledge of utilization rates, types of cases served, trend analyses and success or failure rates, and anticipatory guidance for illness and injury prevention can be provided using aggregate data.

The intent is to be able to assess the value of the linkage and its contribution to the overall process. This outcome data can also be compared to those cases that were not co-managed to determine the value of the Disability Management Program-Employee Assistance Program linkage.

(9) Medical Consents and Certificates

In regards to the medical consents and certificates obtained for disability management purposes, this area is governed by the following:

*   the various provincial Freedom of Information and Protection of Privacy Acts;
*   Canadian Life and Health Insurance Association Guidelines; and
*   *Model Code for the Protection of Personal Information.*[13]

The *Model Code for the Protection of Personal Information* defines "consent" as "the voluntary agreement with what is being done or proposed". While consent may be expressed or implied, organizations should seek express consent where information is sensitive. The person must provide consent in an informed manner. Consent of the individual must be obtained unless legal, medical, security or other reasons make it impossible or impractical.

The following are the requirements for **informed consent**:

*   There is an obligation to ensure that sufficient information is provided to employees concerning the true nature and consequences of the intended use of information in order to allow the employee to come to a reasoned decision.

---

[13] Canadian Standards Association (CSA), *Model Code for the Protection of Personal Information,* (CAN/CSA – Q830-96) (Ottawa: CAN/CSA, 1996).

- The employee is mentally competent and has the ability to understand and appreciate the nature and consequences of the procedure.
- Consent is freely given; not coerced in any way.
- Consent is not obtained through misrepresentation or fraud.
- Consent cannot be given to the performance of an illegal procedure.
- Consent is in relation to a specific act contemplated and provided in a timely manner in relation to the information sought.

Personal health information should not be collected indiscriminately. Rather, it must be relevant to the purposes for which it is to be used and restricted to staff that sign a pledge of confidentiality (see Chapter 10, "Disability Management Practice Standards", Figure 10.6).

The process of obtaining consent to collect personal health information creates a reasonable expectation of privacy by the employee. This requires the employer to take all reasonable steps to ensure the level of confidentiality promised in the consent form is not compromised. Some reasonable steps include:

- maintaining confidentiality;
- retaining information;
- secure storage of information;
- appropriate disclosure of information internally and externally;
- proper transmittal of information;
- appropriate methods of destruction; and
- identification of the consequences for staff violations, if any should occur.

BEST PRACTICES

1. Ensure the existence of a consent form that is to be signed by the ill or injured worker before any contact is made with the physician.
2. Review disability claim forms, and revise forms that fail to gather the necessary information in a manner that is in compliance with applicable legislation.
3. Establish measures to protect the confidentiality of personal health information.
4. Assess the degree of compliance of the Integrated Disability Management Program practices and medical forms with the human rights and protection of personal information legislation and relevant guidelines.

(10) Policies and Procedures to Protect the Confidentiality of Medical Data

Medical diagnoses and health-related data are obtained during the course of claims and case management. Policies and procedures are required to deal with confidentiality and access to medical files, as well as with the retention, storage, transfer, or disposal of medical data.

BEST PRACTICES

1. Develop a policy that deals with the confidential management of employee medical data. This should comply with applicable legislation (see Chapter 3, "The Supportive Infrastructure for an Integrated Disability Management Program", and Chapter 10, "Disability Management Practice Standards", for more details).
2. Develop a protocol for the retention, maintenance, release, and disposal of medical documentation (see Chapter 10 for more details).
3. Retain all medical data in a secure and confidential manner with access by authorized personnel and only on a need-to-know basis.
4. Retain all medical documentation for a minimum period of seven years from the last point of activity.
5. Limit the dissemination of medical diagnoses to broad categories or neutral descriptors, such as occupational injury, occupational illness, non-occupational injury, or non-occupational illness. When diagnoses are used, limit them to disease classifications or aggregate the data so individual diagnoses cannot be determined.

(11) Disability Case Management Practices

As already noted, case management is a collaborative process for assessing, planning, implementing, coordinating, monitoring and evaluating the options and services available to meet individual health needs through communication and accessible resources. Effective case management promotes quality, cost-effective outcomes in terms of human and financial savings.[14]

The Case Manager:

- maintains contact with the injured/ill employee, health care professionals, the long-term disability insurance carrier, the Workers' Compensation Board, supervisor, Employee Assistance Program service providers, and others;
- assesses the biological, psychological and social factors involved in the disability;
- reviews the medical or psychological care and the response to treatment;
- facilitates and coordinates information sharing;
- communicates and educates return-to-work guidelines to all involved;
- facilitates return-to-work strategies;
- monitors return-to-work (modified/alternate work and alternate work) activities;
- establishes vocational rehabilitation and monitors the outcomes; and

---

[14] Watson Wyatt Worldwide, *Staying@Work: Effective Presence at Work. 2007 Survey Report — Canada: Executive Summary* (2007) at 10, available online at: <http://www.easna.org/documents/WatsonWyattStayingatWorkSurvey.pdf>.

- collects data to show cost-effectiveness of the intervention and the need for proactive measures.

To assist Case Managers, many organizations and insurers have developed practice standards or codes of practice for illness and injury management. Unlike disability guidelines, which merely advise on expected length of absences for various illnesses or injuries, these standards or codes outline rehabilitation strategies and steps.

Case management standards are a guide to professional practices. They define the practice, goal, role, and qualifications of the Case Manager, the case management process, the problem and outcome identification process, the planning process, monitoring and coordination, evaluation techniques, documentation, document handling, confidentiality and administrative responsibilities for the program. An example of a generic version of a case management practice standard is provided in Chapter 10, "Disability Management Practice Standards".

The case management approaches that have proven most effective:

- use an established planned and systematic approach;
- use early intervention;
- use direct, face-to-face contact with the employee to promote engagement in the process;
- provide support to the absent employee, workplace and union representative;
- develop written rehabilitation plans with goals, time frames and lines of accountability for action for all cases;[15]
- use a multi-disciplinary approach when indicated (*i.e.*, medical, nursing, psychological, vocational and rehabilitation interventions, *etc.*);
- maintain a regular progress review of all open cases;
- follow up on the employee throughout the absence, modified/alternate work period and return to work for at least until two weeks following the return to full-time duties;
- promote a mechanism for the early identification of cases;
- encourage self-reporting by employees of illness/injury before the absence occurs; and
- maintain ongoing process evaluation to ensure quality delivery of services.

There is no conclusive research indicating which specific case management practices result in the best rates of return to work for employees.

---

[15] Watson Wyatt Worldwide, *Staying@Work Report, 2005 — Canada* (2005) at 5, available online at: <http://www.watsonwyatt. com/research/resrender.asp?id=w-860&page=1>.

BEST PRACTICES

1. Establish case management standards and educate Case Managers on their use.
2. Institute documented rehabilitation plans for all ill or injured employees who are offered case management.
3. Continue to track long-term disability data, plus hours of modified/alternate work, dollars saved with modified/alternate work and types of cases that were the most successful with early return-to-work initiatives.
4. Evaluate the case management process through the use of peer or internal, reviews, or external quality assurance measures (audits).
5. Track occupational health and vocational rehabilitation activities, such as the amount of time required to case manage each claim, administer the service, train supervisors, undertake process development, conduct follow-up activities and pursue professional development. A data management software program can facilitate this process.
6. Evaluate, case-by-case, the return on investment of the case management interventions.
7. Continue to review long-term disability insurance claim outcomes, paying special attention to claims that are closed. Use the closed claims as indicators of case management outcomes.
8. Support regular evaluation of the Disability Management Program as part of the improvement process.

(12) Early Intervention

Research and industry experience has supported the importance of early intervention in any absence.[16] Informally, many organizations report more success with returning the recovering employee to the workplace if intervention begins at, or soon after, the time of injury. By maintaining the person in the workplace, the occupational bond, the identity of the employee with the workplace, is not broken.

Early intervention is discussed in detail in Chapter 1, "Disability Management: Overview" and Chapter 5, "An Integrated Disability Management Program: The Managed Rehabilitative Care Program".

BEST PRACTICES

1. Institute early contact with the ill or injured employee. Ideally, the supervisor should do this on the first day of absence.

---

[16] Canadian Centre on Disability Studies, *Best Practices in Contemporary Disability Management: Executive Summary* (1998) at 6-7, available online at: <http:www.disabilitystudies.ca/cdmes.htm>; and M. Creen, "Best Practices for Disability Management" (Winter 2002) Journal of the Ontario Occupational Health Nurses Association 5.

2. If required, implement early case management (within the first three to five days).
3. Involve the Employee Assistance Program in situations as appropriate.

(13) The Claim Adjudication Process

Typically, the claim adjudication process involves deciding if an individual is eligible to receive an income replacement benefit and the associated services. It involves:

- determining eligibility to receive a benefit;
- determining eligibility based on the nature of the medical condition; and
- the critical match between the person's abilities and the employee's job demands.

Third party insurers adjudicate the Workers' Compensation and long-term disability claims. However, for self-insured short-term disability plans, employers require a documented process for claim adjudication. This helps to ensure that a standardized approach is used. The exact criteria used to determine eligibility depend on the terms of the benefit plan in place. The typical steps for claim adjudication include:

Step 1:   Receipt and coding of claim.

Step 2:   Determination of eligibility:
   (a)   eligibility requirements are reviewed according to the benefit plan or insurance contract; and
   (b)   determination of acceptance or rejection is made on the basis of eligibility.

Step 3:   Determination of any limitations or exclusions:
   (a)   pre-existing conditions (if applicable);
   (b)   pregnancy, maternity or parental leave; or
   (c)   specialized clauses by plan design or contract.

Step 4:   Assessment of medical profile:
   (a)   existing medical information is reviewed (fit or unfit to work);
   (b)   resources for review of the claim are used, such as:
      (i)   medical consultant;
      (ii)   independent medical examiner;
      (iii) functional capacity examination; or
      (iv)   rehabilitation.

Step 5:   Determination of acceptance, rejection or need for more detailed information.

Step 6:   Approval for a specific time.

Step 7:   Creation of a management strategy.

Step 8:   Closing the file:
   (a)   appeal;

(b)   close; and
(c)   return to work.[17]

Using these steps, the employee's eligibility for disability plan coverage is determined. However, claim adjudication is not a one-time event — rather it is an ongoing process. In general, adjudication should occur at a number of points in the disability management process:

*   at the onset of illness/injury;
*   during the short-term absence period;
*   at the transition point to long-term disability insurance coverage;
*   during the long-term disability period; and
*   at the transition of the "own occupation" period to the "any occupation" period.

Best Practices

1.   Incorporate critical points for claims adjudication along with the definitive eligibility criteria in the design of the Disability Management Program. In general, special attention should be paid to the onset of illness or injury, the short-term disability period and to the transition from the "own occupation" period to the "any occupation" in the long-term disability period.
2.   If human resources policies and procedures are not in place to accommodate the establishment of satisfactory benefit plan eligibility requirements, ensure that they are created and adopted.

(14) Effective Management of Disabilities

The workplace is a social system in which people come together to work towards common business goals. In the course of "doing business", people interact and build relationships. According to the Social Capital Theory (Chapter 15, "Disability Management: The Social Capital Theory Perspective for Managing Disability Claims"), individuals amass social credits that enable them to effectively interact and work together. Employee's willingness to help others is based on the quality of their social relationships.

People are willing to help (exchange favours) only when they feel a sense of goodwill, trust, and empathy towards other members of their social group. They are also more likely to grant favours to individuals if they know that, at some point in the future, the same courtesy will be returned, either directly by the recipient, or by someone else within the social group. So social capital actually belongs to "the social group as a whole" (it is one element of organizational culture), but access to it depends on the individual's level of social credit.

When a disability occurs, the status of the employee's social credits impacts the workgroup's willingness to support the employee through the illness/injury

---

[17]   A. Leckie, *Disability Claims Management*, 2nd ed. (Markham, ON: Butterworths, 2001).

period, as well as in the return-to-work process. Employees, who begin a return-to-work opportunity with few social capital credits, and those who deplete their social credits as a result of multiple health episodes, often face distinct social sanctions. Employees with strong social credits fare well and gain the support of the workgroup. This concept helps to explain why some employees successfully return to work without "a hitch"; while others struggle, facing many hurdles.

BEST PRACTICES

1. Educate the workplace about the impact of workplace disabilities and how to recognize when an employee is experiencing health problems. Add to that, an explanation of the concept of social capital and its influence on the return-to-work process.
2. Redesign work processes to decrease physical and psychological stress and hence, to decrease the likelihood of relapse and secondary health conditions that are so detrimental to employee/workgroup's social capital.
3. When designing a rehabilitation and return-to-work plan, involve the employee, supervisor, and union. Working collaboratively enhances relationships and provides clarity as to the plans and processes.
4. Regularly communicate with employees who are on sick leave, using documented conversations to reinforce the agreed-upon decisions and action plans. Be sure to provide copies to line management and the union representative.
5. Ensure a good person/job fit when offering work accommodation opportunities.
6. Seek to develop a return-to-work plan that builds the employee's confidence, particularly when employee fear of relapse or pain is evident. Motivation is positively influenced by setting goals that are somewhat difficult — a stretch, but attainable. Achieving the goal promotes self-efficacy so the next goal can be set slightly higher.
7. Manage the expectations of the returning employee as well as the expectations of colleagues/managers/union representatives. Ensure they remain realistic as to what "a successful rehabilitation and return-to-work" looks like.
8. Legitimize the work accommodation of the returning employee. Some of this can be done by tackling misinformation "head on" — debunking myths about work safety and authenticity; then teaching how to assist rather than blame, when an employee experiences symptoms or a relapse at work.
9. Resolve conflict. Conflict decreases trust, liking, and therefore, social capital — all detrimental to a successful return to work for the recovering employee.
10. Develop a fair and transparent process for investigating discipline-worthy conduct. This will go a long way to prevent the escalation of workplace conflict and perceptions of favouritism.
11. Reward managers for maintaining healthy work teams and for successfully accommodating employees from other business units. Likewise, employees

should be rewarded for following medically-sanctioned work restrictions and for assisting in the accommodation of co-workers.

12. Avoid making assumptions about the validity of an employee's illness/ injury. There are many reasons why employees may engage in counterproductive behaviour during an illness and in the gradual return-to-work phase.

(15) Management of Mental Health Disabilities

A. MITIGATION

The incidence of mental health claims is on the rise. These claims tend to be lengthy, with many non-medical issues, and are the most challenging disability claims to successfully resolve. For example, serious depression can result in workplace absences of 40 or more days and include many workplace and performance issues. Partly due to denial and partly due to trying to work through their depression, the person not only has to recover from the illness but also deal with the "burned bridges" and damaged relationships that occurred before they left the workplace.

Recent research indicates that return-to-work plans specific to the management of mental illness should be used in the workplace.[18] This is consistent with the work undertaken by the Global Business and Economic Roundtable on Addictions and Mental Health.[19]

B. PREVENTION

The Consortium for Organizational Mental Healthcare (COMH) has developed an industry-focused approach that enables employers to easily and quickly implement effective strategies to protect the psychological safety of employees and to promote psychological health in their workplace. "[Guarding Minds @ Work] is a response to current and emerging legal requirements in Canada for the protection of employee mental health and the promotion of civility and respect at work. Legal standards increasingly require employers to develop comprehensive strategies for ensuring a psychologically safe workplace. Prudent employers need to develop policies and programs that meet these new legal standards."[20]

---

[18] Watson Wyatt Worldwide, *Staying@Work: Effective Presence at Work. 2007 Survey Report — Canada: Executive Summary* (2007) at 10, available online at: <http://www.easna.org/documents/WatsonWyattStayingatWorkSurvey.pdf>.

[19] Global Business and Economic Roundtable on Addictions and Mental Health, Module 3, Guidelines for Mental Disability Management, *Managing Employers Getting Started: On the Road to Mental Health and Productivity* (2006), available online at: <http://www.mentalhealthroundtable.ca>.

[20] Guarding Minds @ Work, homepage, available online at: <http://www.guardingmindsatwork.ca/GmawWhat.aspx>.

BEST PRACTICES: MITIGATION

1. Institute early contact with the ill or injured employee. Ideally, the supervisor should do this on the first day of the medical absence.
2. Implement early case management (within the first three to five days).
3. Involve the Employee Assistance Program or some other form of counselling as part of the treatment plan.
4. Use a technique such as The Green Chart (Chapter 15, "Disability Management: The Social Capital Theory Perspective for Managing Disability Claims"), to open the lines of communication between the health care providers and the occupational health professionals or Disability Management professionals/practitioners who represent the workplace interests.
5. Work with a significant person in the individual's life to ensure that workplace issues/concerns are properly addressed.
6. Ensure that support is available to the employee upon a return to work.
7. Maintain that support for a number of months post-return to work.

BEST PRACTICES: PREVENTION

1. Develop effective strategies for protecting the psychological safety of employees and promoting psychological health in the workplace.
2. Implement those strategies.
3. Monitor and evaluate the effectiveness of the implemented strategies.
4. Enhance the prevention approaches as required.

(16) Cultural Diversity and Disability Management

Cultural diversity in Canadian and American workplaces is here to stay. By becoming culturally competent, employers can appreciate and maximize the strengths of each of the various cultures present in their workplaces. Cultural diversity brings challenges to managing employee disabilities. Reaction to illness/injury and recovery is culturally-based (Chapter 21, "Disability Management: Impact of Cultural Diversity" and Chapter 22 "Disability Management: Impact of Four Generations in the Workplace").

BEST PRACTICES

1. Promote cultural competence within the organization.
2. Communicate effectively with the various cultures.
3. Identify areas of potential cultural conflict and seek ways to address them.
4. Provide clarity on the Integrated Disability Management Program while being culturally respectful.
5. Compromise by showing respect for different beliefs and by being willing to work with those beliefs to reach a "win-win" solution for the stakeholders.
6. Help workers understand their options so that they can make informed consents to treatment and return-to-work options.
7. Ensure that support is available to the employee upon a return to work.

(17) Disability Data Management

Data collection and analysis is the foundation on which the successful development and maintenance of an Integrated Disability Management Program is based. Companies that choose not to measure disability-related costs miss information that could help them identify their health and productivity issues. As well, disability data can play a major role in justifying the need for an Integrated Disability Management Program, for demonstrating the value added to the company by the program and the other related programs, and for making informed decisions on continuous improvement efforts.

Information regarding workplace absence can be obtained from both internal and external areas and is often accumulated without thought to integration or management. Some examples of information pockets are discussed below:

SHORT-TERM ABSENCES

In general, employee absence from work is affected by a number of variables:

- *Industry Sector* — workers in the public sector tend to miss, on average, 12.8 workdays per year, while private sector workers miss 9.5 workdays per year. [21] This was an increase in both sectors since 2004 when the public sector workers missed 12 workdays and the private sector missed 8.4 days. [22]

- *Industry* — health care and social assistance workers (14.3 days), public administration employees (12.2 days), and transportation and warehousing workers (12.2 days) posted the most absence time in 2007. Those in professional, scientific, and technical industries missed the least time (6.6 workdays per year). [23]

- *Size of Organization* — larger organizations (*i.e.*, more than 500 employees) experience higher absenteeism (11.8 workdays per year) than smaller ones, with less than 20 employees (8.8 workdays per year). [24]

- *Work Status* — permanent full-time employment is associated with more sick time than part-time employment status. Those with permanent job status miss 10.4 workdays per year versus 8.3 workdays per year for those with non-permanent job status. [25]

---

[21] Statistics Canada, *Work Absence Rates 2007*, Catalogue No. 71-211-XIE (Ottawa: Statistics Canada, May 2008), available online at: <http://www.statcan.gc.ca/pub/71-211-x/2008000/5204138-eng.htm>.

[22] *Ibid.*

[23] *Ibid.*

[24] *Ibid.*

[25] *Ibid.*

- *Union Status* — union coverage is associated with almost twice the absence rate (14.0 workdays per year) of non-union coverage (8.4 workdays per year).[26]

- *Occupation* — employees in more physically demanding, hazardous, or stressful occupations lose the most time. For example, labourers lost 14.4 days per year, health care occupations lost 15.6 workdays; while those in managerial occupations experienced the least absence days (6.4 workdays per year). Two occupations topped the list — nursing at 16.2 lost workdays per year and health support staff at 19.5 workdays.[27]

- *Job Tenure* — in 2004, workers with the most tenure missed the most time from work. New workers (12 months or less on the job) missed only 7.8 days. Workers who had been on the job for over 14 years missed an average of 12.2 days per year.[28]

- *Educational Attainment* — the more education attained, the less likely the employee was off work. In 2007, employees with a university degree missed 7.9 days/year, while those with less than grade 9 education missed 13.9 days;[29]

- *Gender* — as a rule, women miss more days from work per year than do men (Figure 17.1).

Figure 17.1: Work Absence by Gender[30]

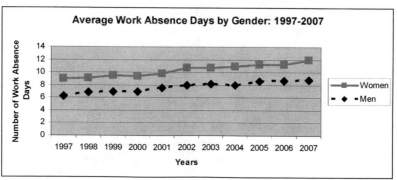

In 2007, women were away on average, 20 days, while men missed on average 8.8 workdays. For the actual lost workdays data, refer to Appendix 1, Table 17.1.

- *Geographic Location* — in 2007, Nova Scotia and Québec had the highest work absence rates (12.0 each); while Alberta and Ontario (9.0 and 9.3 workdays per year) had the lowest. This is a variable factor as can be seen in the following table:

Table 17.2: Days Lost per Canadian Worker due to Illness or Disability (I/D) & Personal or Family Responsibility (P/F) [31]

Province	Year																					
	1997		1998		1999		2000		2001		2002		2003		2004		2005		2006		2007	
	I/D	P/F	I/D	P/F	I/D	P/F	I/D	P/F	I/D	P/F	I/D	P/F	I/D	P/F	I/D	P/F	I/D	P/F	I/D	P/F	I/D	P/F
Canada	6.2	1.2	6.6	1.2	6.7	1.3	6.7	1.3	7.0	1.5	7.4	1.7	7.5	1.7	7.5	1.7	7.8	1.8	7.6	2.1	8.1	2.1
Newfoundland & Labrador	6.1	1.5	8.1	1.3	7.6	0.7	7.7	1.4	7.4	1.3	6.9	1.7	9.1	1.4	8.8	1.5	8.1	1.4	8.2	1.5	8.2	1.6
Prince Edward Island	6.4	1.3	5.1	1.4	6.7	1.8	5.8	1.1	6.5	1.2	6.9	1.6	6.4	1.3	6.0	1.6	6.9	1.6	6.9	1.6	6.8	1.6
Nova Scotia	6.0	1.0	6.6	1.2	6.9	1.1	8.2	1.3	8.3	1.4	8.8	1.6	8.1	1.7	0.1	1.9	9	1.8	8.9	1.8	9.9	2.1
New Brunswick	6.5	0.8	7.0	0.9	6.7	1.1	7.6	1.0	0.8	1.4	8.4	1.3	8.7	1.4	8.0	1.7	8.5	1.8	9.7	1.7	8.8	1.8
Quebec	7.4	1.0	7.4	1.0	7.7	1.0	7.8	1.0	7.9	1.2	8.4	1.4	9.3	1.5	9.4	1.4	0.0	1.6	9.3	2.2	9.8	2.2
Ontario	5.4	1.2	6.0	1.3	5.8	1.3	5.7	1.3	6.0	1.6	0.6	1.9	6.5	1.8	6.7	1.9	6.7	1.9	6.6	2.2	7.2	2.2
Manitoba	6.7	1.3	6.9	1.0	7.0	1.4	7.1	1.6	7.7	1.7	8.4	1.7	7.8	1.6	8.0	1.8	7.9	2	8.1	1.9	8.7	2.2
Saskatchewan	5.8	1.6	6.7	1.5	7.0	1.7	7.7	1.6	8.1	1.8	8.4	2.0	8.6	1.8	8.0	2.2	8.9	2.2	8.7	2.3	8.3	2.2
Alberta	5.2	1.3	5.5	1.4	6.2	1.7	6.1	1.5	6.5	1.7	6.7	1.8	6.2	1.8	5.6	1.9	6.5	2.1	6.6	2.1	0.9	2.1
British Columbia	7.2	1.5	7.4	1.2	8.2	1.5	7.4	1.3	8.3	1.4	7.8	1.7	8.1	1.7	7.3	1.5	8.5	1.9	7.6	1.8	8.2	1.9

- *Age* — older workers are absent more often than younger workers (55 to 64 years = 12.5 missed workdays per year; and 45 to 54 years = 9.9 workdays per year, versus 20-to-24-year-olds = 6.4 workdays per year).[32]

- *Childcare* — workers with children miss more workdays, 10.8 workdays (women = 12.9; men = 9.2) than do workers without any children. Those without children are absent 9.8 workdays per year (women = 11.3; men = 8.6). Workers with preschoolers (under 5 years of age) miss, on average, 12.7 workdays per year (women = 14.7; men = 11.7);[33]

---

[31] *Ibid.*
[32] *Ibid.*
[33] *Ibid.*

- *Eldercare* — workers who care for aging relatives report spending 60 hours per month with those needing care.[34] The impact of providing eldercare can be great. These workers are more likely to report sleep loss, lack of time for personal care and health problems. The result is an increase in employer costs due to more work absenteeism, increased employee benefit costs, lower productivity while at work, and a reluctance to taking on expanded job opportunities or duties.

- *Other Factors* — Shift work and access to a sick leave plan are two other factors noted as factors that impact work absence. Although not measured in 2007, those workers entitled to a sick leave plan in 1997 are absent more (4.2 workdays per year) than those who are without (3.0 workdays per year).[35] As well, shift workers experienced higher absence days (4.3 workdays per year) than non-shift workers (3.6 workdays per year).[36]

Thus, there are many factors that impact workplace absence. Astute employers are beginning to recognize this and look for ways to address these issues. On average, the absenteeism and disability costs for Canadian and American employers are approximately 14.9% of payroll.[37]

The bottom line is that work absence has increased over the past 10 years. In 1997, the average time lost to medical absenteeism in Canada was 7.4 workdays, with 6.2 workdays due to medical reasons and 1.2 workdays due to personal or family reasons. In 2000, this number increased to 9.0 workdays (6.7 lost due to illness/disability and 1.3 days lost due to personal/family reasons). By 2004, workers lost 9.2 workdays with 7.5 days away due to illness or disability and 1.7 days due to personal or family reasons. Now in 2007, the average number of lost workdays equals 10.2 workdays per full-time worker with 8.1 workdays away due to personal health reasons and 2.1 workdays away for family reasons (non-health reasons). In 10 years, Canadian employers have witnessed a 38% increase in absenteeism, and increased costs.

ABSENCE REASONS — SHORT-TERM DISABILITY

Typically, the main reasons for short-term, non-occupational disabilities are musculoskeletal and psychological disorders. However, this can vary by industry and with the length of the short-term disability absence. For example, the reasons for going on short-term disability and those for remaining on claim are demonstrated in Table 17.3.

---

[34] Conference Board of Canada, *News Release*, "Eldercare Taking Its Toll on Canadian Workers" (November 10, 1999).

[35] E. Akyeampong, *Work Absences: New Data, New Insights, Spring 1998 Perspective*, Cat. No. 75-001-XPE (Ottawa: Statistics Canada, 1998) at 16-22.

[36] *Ibid.*

[37] Marsh Risk Consulting, *Workforce Risk: Fourth Annual Marsh Mercer Survey of Employers' Time-Off and Disability Programs* (2003), available online at: <http://www.marshriskconsulting.com/st/PSEV_C_228064_SC_229050_NR_303.htm>.

Table 17.3: Reasons for Remaining on Short-Term Disability - 1998[38]

Reason	Percentage of Short-Term Disability Claims	Remaining on Short-Term Disability
Accident	36%	19%
Mental/Nervous Disorder	11%	22%
Musculoskeletal Disorder	11%	15%
Circulatory Disorder	5%	12%

Eleven years ago, "non-occupational accidents" were the main reason for employees going on short-term disability; while "mental/nervous disorders" were the top reason for an employee remaining on short-term disability. Today, the Watson Wyatt 2007 Staying@Work Survey indicates that mental health disorders remain the number one reason for employees remaining on short-term disability, followed by musculoskeletal disorders, accidents and cancers.[39]

WORKPLACE ILLNESS OR INJURY

The trends in work-related illness and injuries are:

- most injuries tend to occur to workers between the ages of 19 and 26 years;[40]
- young workers, males and inexperienced workers account for a majority of the lost-time claims;
- the accident types are primarily the result of overexertion, falls, and being struck by an object;[41]

---

[38] The Mutual Group, *Block of Business: January 01, 1998 to December 31, 1998, STD Claims Management Report — Statistics* (Waterloo, ON: The Mutual Group, 1998).

[39] Watson Wyatt Worldwide, *Staying@Work: Effective Presence at Work. 2007 Survey Report — Canada: Executive Summary* (2007) at 5, available online at: <http://www.easna.org/documents/WatsonWyattStayingatWorkSurvey.pdf>.

[40] WorkSafeBC, *Key Statistics, 2007 Annual Report* (2008), available online at: <http://www.worksafebc.com/publications/reports/annual_reports/2007/key_statistics.asp>; and Alberta Workers Compensation Board, "Number of LTCs Table, Provincial Synopsis", 2008, available online at: <https://lcr.wcb.ab.ca/public/RetrieveReports.aspx>.

[41] Alberta Workers Compensation Board, *ibid.*; and Alberta Labour, *Occupational Injury and Disease in Alberta, 2007 Summary: Lost-time Claims and Claim Rates* (Edmonton: Alberta Labour, 2008), available online at: <http://employment.alberta.ca/documents/WHS/WHS-PUB_oid_2007.pdf>.

- the primary causes for work-related lost-time claims are strains and sprains (54%), contusions or concussions (11%), cuts (11%), and fractures or dislocations (7%);[42]
- the parts of the body most frequently injured are the back, foot, torso and hands;[43]
- the primary sources of lost-time claims were 1) persons, plants, animals and minerals (24.5%); and 2) structures and walking surfaces (17.4%). These sources of injury accounted for 23.6% and 15.1% of the disabling injury claims respectively;[44] and
- the duration of lost time claims is usually less than 10 days (55.6% of the claims) — however, about 21% of these claims last longer than 31 days in length.[45] The median number of lost time claim days was 7 in 2007.[46]

LONG-TERM ABSENCES

In 2005-2006, there were 291,226 Canada Pension Plan (CPP) claimants. This count does not represent all employees on long-term disability because some claimants qualify for private long-term disability insurance coverage without being eligible for Canada Pension Plan coverage. This was an increase over the number of Canada Pension Plan claimants for the past two years (Table 17.4).

Table 17.4: Canada Pension Plan Claimants: 2003 – 2006[47]

Timeframe	Number of Claimants	Benefit Dollars Paid
2003-2004	281,345	$2,815M
2004-2005	284,213	$2,919M
2005-2006	291,226	$3,074M

Based on 1997 long-term disability insurance data, the incidence rates for long-term disability vary depending on the type of work done by the claimant (Table 17.5).

---

[42]   WorkSafe BC, *Key Statistics, 2007 Annual Report* (2008), available online at: <http://www.worksafebc.com/publications/reports/annual_reports/2007/key_statistics.asp>.

[43]   Alberta Workers Compensation Board, "Number of LTCs Table, Provincial Synopsis, 2008", available online at: <https://lcr.wcb.ab.ca/public/RetrieveReports.aspx>.

[44]   Alberta Labour, *Occupational Injury and Disease in Alberta, 2007 Summary: Lost-time Claims and Claim Rates* (Edmonton: Alberta Labour, 2008), available online at: <http://employment.alberta.ca/documents/WHS/WHS-PUB_oid_2007.pdf>.

[45]   *Ibid.*

[46]   *Ibid.*

[47]   Institute of Health Economics, *Mental Health in Your Pocket* (2006) at 19, available online at: <http://www.ihe.ca/publications/library/2006/mental-health-in-your-pocket>.

Table 17.5: Long Term Disability Incidence by Occupation[48]

Occupation	Long-Term Disability Incidence
Professionals[49]	4.5/1000
White Collar Workers[50]	5.5/1000
Blue Collar Workers[51]	10.0/1000
Service Providers[52]	8.0/1000

Using the same 1997 data set, the top six reasons, by cause, for long-term disability insurance coverage are as follows (Table 17.6):

Table 17.6: Long Term Disability Claims by Cause[53]

Cause of Disability	New Long-Term Disability Claims	Ongoing Long-Term Disability Claims
Mental Disorder	25%	22%
Musculoskeletal System and Connective Tissue Disorder	24%	30%
Cancer	14%	6%
Circulatory System Disease	11%	14%
Non-work Accident	9%	7%

These earlier findings are supported by the Watson Wyatt 2007 Staying@Work Survey which noted that the primary reason for employees remaining on long-term disability was mental health disorders, followed by cancer, by musculoskeletal disorders, cardiovascular disorders, and accidents.[54]

---

[48]   The Mutual Group, *LTD Claims Trends: 1996* (Waterloo, ON: The Mutual Group, 1996).

[49]   *Professionals* include accountants, computer operators, dentists, engineers, physiotherapists, doctors, lawyers, registered nurses.

[50]   *White Collar Workers* include technicians, managers, letter carriers, cashiers, administrators, contractors, clerks, and tellers.

[51]   *Blue Collar Workers* include craftsmen, foremen, inspectors, labourers, electricians, mechanics, machine operators, and miners.

[52]   *Service Workers* include hotel staff, police, firefighters, nurses' aides, orderlies, registered nursing assistants, janitors, and restaurant staff.

[53]   WorkSafe BC, *Key Statistics, 2007 Annual Report* (2008), available online at: <http://www.worksafebc.com/publications/reports/annual_reports/2007/key_statistics.asp>; and Alberta Workers Compensation Board, "Number of LTCs Table, Provincial Synopsis, 2008", available online at: <https://lcr.wcb.ab.ca/public/displayreport.aspx?id=1042109>.

[54]   Watson Wyatt Worldwide, *Staying@Work: Effective Presence at Work. 2007 Survey Report — Canada: Executive Summary* (2007) at 5, available online at: <http://www.easna.org/documents/WatsonWyattStayingatWorkSurvey.pdf>.

Thus, the reasons for going on long-term disability differ from the reasons for continuing on claim.

Likewise, the causes for long-term disability claim coverage differ by occupation (Table 17.7).

Table 17.7: Musculoskeletal and Mental Disorders by Occupation[55]

Occupation	Musculoskeletal Disorders	Mental Disorders
Professionals	27%	28%
White Collar Workers	23%	26%
Blue Collar Workers	34%	15%
Service Providers	38%	18%

Note:

Getting an accurate picture of the incidence and nature of long-term disability in Canada is difficult. There is no central repository for the collection of statistical long-term disability data. Rather, individual private insurers guard their long-term disability insurance data claiming it to be proprietary in nature.

The associated costs for short-term and long-term disability insurance coverage are difficult to ascertain. However, an indication of these insurance costs is provided by the Institute of Health Economics. In 2004, the total direct private insurance claims were $461M for short-term disability insurance coverage, and $2.2 B for long-term disability insurance coverage.[56]

DATA SYSTEMS — COLLECTION AND MEASUREMENT

The types of data that organizations tend to collect include the:

- number and duration of casual illness, short-term disability, Workers' Compensation and long-term disability;
- nature of disability reason (either as illness/injury or actual diagnosis);
- total number of lost time days and costs (in salary);
- number and types of modified/alternate work opportunities;
- duration of modified/alternate work;
- savings (cost-avoidance) realized through modified/alternate work;
- assessment, treatment and rehabilitation costs; and

---

55   *Ibid.*
56   Institute of Health Economics, *Mental Health in Your Pocket* (2006) at 17, available online at: <http://www.ihe.ca/publications/library/2006/mental-health-in-your-pocket>.

- outcome measures, such as the number of short-term disability days or the amount of Workers' Compensation that proceed long-term disability cases in which the employee returns to work, dies, terminates or moves to another form of leave.

Unfortunately, standardization of data collection and measurement techniques is rare, making data comparisons difficult, if not impossible.

Data can be tabulated to calculate the total cost of an organization's/company's workplace disability claims for a given period of time (Table 17.8).

Table 17.8: Company Disability Management Program Costs

Disability Cost Components per Claim	Average Cost
Average Workers' Compensation claim cost	$
Average medical costs (non-occupational claims)	$
Average salary continuation costs	$
Average long-term disability costs	$
Average rehabilitation costs	$
Average labour replacement wages	$
Average cost of supervisory hours to manage a claim	$
Average overtime payments to other worker(s) to maintain department daily productivity in the absence of the disabled worker	$
Average unit cost of lost productivity	$
Average lost opportunity costs	$
Average staff turnover cost	$
Average human resources costs in time to recruit and arrange temporary help, orient new workers to workplace, worker training, *etc.*	$
Average cost of disability claim management activities	$
Average cost of disability case management activities	$
Average fitness to work assessment costs	$
Average cost of return-to-work planning and monitoring activities	$
Average costs of work accommodations	$
Average permanent disability settlements	$

Disability Cost Components per Claim	Average Cost
Average miscellaneous costs (*e.g.,* transportation costs, accommodation costs, *etc.*)	
Average legal/grievance costs	$
Subtotal	$
Multiplied by Number of Employees Ill/Injured	
Total Disability Costs	$

As well, the cost of disability to an employee can be calculated using the worksheet provided in Table 17.9.

Table 17.9: Employee Disability Costs

Disability Component Costs	Average Cost/ Employee
Lost wages not covered by Workers' Compensation or other wage replacement plan	$
Lost wages from inability to do a second job	$
Lost wages from inability to receive overtime wages	$
Decreased accrual of paid time off	$
Non-reimbursed medical/drug costs	
Non-reimbursed rehabilitation costs	$
Miscellaneous disability costs (*e.g.,* transportation costs, assistive devices, *etc.*)	
Litigation and grievance costs	$
Total	$

These two spreadsheets can be used to demonstrate the costs of disability to the organization and the employee.

Many companies or organizations have realized the need for a computerized system to facilitate the collection of disability management, Workers' Compensation Board claims and occupational health and safety data; to follow up on case management of claims; to analyze employee benefit programs, Workers' Compensation Board, occupational health and safety programs and Employee Assistance Program data; and to examine linkages between these three areas.

In fact, more proactive organizations are combining the above data with Employee Assistance Program utilization, case mix, and costs; Group Benefit

Plan experience and costs; and management practices. The intent is to identify all the **prevention**,[57] **detection**,[58] and **failure**[59] costs related to employee and organizational well-being.

BEST PRACTICES

1. Capture all absence and disability data in a format that can be compared with other Canadian industry disability databases.
2. Ensure that the claims and case management data collected includes incidental, short-term and long-term disability absence rates and costs.
3. Monitor the Workers' Compensation Board data, investigate opportunities for cost avoidance and cost savings and seek guidance regarding Workers' Compensation Board claims management techniques. Canadian Workers' Compensation Board legislation and practices are in a state of constant flux. Best practice organizations remain current by seeking guidance from the Workers' Compensation Board (*i.e.*, employer services, seminars, *etc.*) and industry safety associations; by verifying the quality of Workers' Compensation Board claims submissions; by monitoring claims cost summaries; by training Workers' Compensation Board claims personnel and supervisors; and by ensuring timely reporting and follow-up.
4. Investigate the potential implementation of an integrated occupational health and safety data management system that can link Disability Management Program outcomes (*i.e.*, short-term disability, Workers' Compensation Board claims, long-term disability, *etc.*) with Occupational Health and Safety Programs, Employee Assistance Programs, employee benefits and Workplace Wellness Programs.
5. Seek opportunities to link employee absence data with human resource information on employees. Some companies do this through a linkage with a Human Resources Information System (HRIS). This allows for a comprehensive picture of employee characteristics, workplace situation and absence nature and outcome.
6. Use the company's available communication systems (*e.g.*, email, internal mail, cheque inserts, newsletters, reports, *etc.*) to encourage the transmission of absence, disability and modified/alternate work data. This allows for the timely receipt of data and dissemination of information about absenteeism and Disability Management Program efforts from various work locations.
7. Ensure that all stakeholders are aware of the reasons for, and costs of, medical absenteeism. This is an essential step towards encouraging ownership of the problem, and disability management solutions.

---

[57] **Prevention Activities** are described as the focus on addressing and/or eliminating the identified concerns or issues so they do not worsen.

[58] **Detection Activities** are described as the focus on identifying concerns or issues before they become problematic.

[59] **Failure Activities** are described as the losses an organization incurs due to breakdowns in the system.

8. Use standardized data collection and data measurement techniques, thereby enabling comparisons with other databases.
9. Support industry disability benchmarking such as the Institute for Work and Health's Workplace Disability Benchmarking Project[60] — an initiative aimed at identifying disability management trends and best practices. By tracking disability performance, organizations can determine what is working and not working for them.

(18) Measurement, Monitoring and Continuous Improvement of the Integrated Disability Management Program

Workplace-based Attendance and Disability Management Programs must evolve to meet the changing needs of businesses and employees. Changes in operating or management styles open new avenues for the reintegration of injured or ill employees. As well, technological advancements and changing attitudes create modified/alternate work opportunities not before available.

To establish program goals, objectives and targets that relate to workplace productivity, programs like the Integrated Disability Management Program demonstrate evidence-based and outcome-based practices. To meet this requirement, the Integrated Disability Management Program must demonstrate continuous evaluation and modifications to:

- justify the program;
- improve workplace health and safety practices;
- ensure that the program objectives are met; and
- ensure that employer and employee needs are met.

BEST PRACTICES

1. Develop short-term disability performance measures that include absentee rates, lost time hours, lost time costs, average absentee length, percentage of hours saved on modified/alternate work, dollars saved due to modified/alternate work activities, percentage of employees who returned to work, number and types of interventions used and number of short-term disability claims that were successfully resolved.
2. Review the Workers' Compensation Board data, investigate opportunities for cost avoidance and cost savings, and seek guidance regarding Workers' Compensation Board claim management techniques.
3. Institute program outcome measures in the long-term disability period which include the following: reduced disabled lives liability, reduced long-term disability claims and costs, increased cost avoidance due to early intervention and modified/alternate work initiatives, case-by-case return on investment due to intervention, and return on investment using a formula customized to suit

---

[60] Institute for Work and Health, "Workplace Disability Benchmarking Project", available online at: <http://www.iwh.on.ca/wdb>.

the company or organization's needs (see Chapter 6, "Integrated Disability Management Program: Outcome Measurements", Figure 6.5 for a model to calculate the return-on-investment for an Integrated Disability Management Program).

4. Establish the contributing factors for absenteeism and disability such as employee age, lifestyle, drug or alcohol use, work environment, employee-employer relationships, seasonal issues, legal issues, financial issues and existence of pre existing health conditions.

5. Measure the effectiveness of the Integrated Disability Management Program through interviews, surveys, data analyses, return on investment for the services provided and associated benefit costs.

6. Set program management targets for each year and measure success.

7. Use the disability management data to provide insight into opportunities for corporate occupational health and safety initiatives and prevention strategies.

8. Regularly disseminate this information to all the departments along with the related costs.

9. Justify the Integrated Disability Management Program in terms of the return on investment attained through lower disability costs, reduced use of employee group benefits, improved employee well-being and health, and increased employee productivity.

SUMMARY

The listing of best practices for disability management in this chapter is not meant to be exhaustive in nature. Rather, this chapter merely presents some examples of currently held beliefs in disability management practices. As noted in the opening of this chapter, these beliefs will change as technology, knowledge and practice advancements occur. The key is to be sensitive to the changes in disability management practices, and to adapt them to your program and practices.

Appendix 1

Table 17.10: Work Absence by Gender[61]

Work Absence by Gender (workdays/year)		
Year	Women	Men
1997	9.0	6.2
1998	9.1	6.8
1999	9.5	7.0
2000	9.4	7.0
2001	9.8	7.6
2002	10.7	8.0
2003	10.7	8.2
2004	10.9	8.0
2005	11.2	8.6
2006	11.2	8.7
2007	12.0	8.8

---

[61] Statistics Canada, *Work Absence Rates 2007*, Catalogue No. 71-211-XWE (Ottawa: Statistics Canada, May 2008), available online at: <http://www.statcan.gc.ca/pub/71-211-x/2008000/5204138-eng.htm>.

CHAPTER REFERENCES

E. Akyeampong, *Work Absences: New Data, New Insights*, Spring 1998 *Perspective*, Cat. No. 75-001-XPE (Ottawa: Statistics Canada, 1998) at 16-22.

Alberta Labour, *Occupational Injury and Disease in Alberta, 2007 Summary: Lost time Claims and Claim Rates* (Edmonton: Alberta Labour, 2008), available online at: <http://employment.alberta.ca/documents/WHS/WHS-PUB_oid_2007.pdf>.

Alberta Workers Compensation Board, "Number of LTCs Table, Provincial Synopsis, 2008", available online at: <https://lcr.wcb.ab.ca/public/ Retrieve Reports.aspx>.

R. Bruckman & J. Harris, "Occupational Medicine Practice Guidelines" (1998) 13:4 Occupational Medicine: State of the Art Reviews 679.

Canadian Centre on Disability Studies, *Best Practices in Contemporary Disability Management: Executive Summary* (1998), available online at: <http://www. disabilitystudies.ca>.

Canadian Standards Association (CSA), *Model Code for the Protection of Personal Information* (CAN/CSA - Q830-96) (Ottawa: CAN/CSA, 1996).

Conference Board of Canada, *Compensation Planning Outlook 2000* (Ottawa: Conference Board of Canada, 1999).

Conference Board of Canada, *News Release*, "Eldercare Taking its Toll on Canadian Workers" (November 10, 1999).

M. Creen, "Best Practices for Disability Management" (Winter 2002) Journal of the Ontario Occupational Health Nurses Association 5.

Global Business and Economic Roundtable on Addictions and Mental Health, Module 3, Guidelines for Mental Disability Management, *Managing Employers Getting Started: On the Road to Mental Health and Productivity* (2006), available online at: <http://www.mentalhealthroundtable.ca>.

Guarding Minds @ Work available online at: <http://www.guardingmindsat work.ca/GmawWhat.aspx>.

Institute for Work and Health, "Workplace Disability Benchmarking Project", available online at: <http://www.iwh.on.ca/wdb>.

Institute of Health Economics, *Mental Health in Your Pocket* (2006), available online at: <http://www.ihe.ca/publications/library/2006/mental-health-in-your-pocket>.

A. Leckie, *Disability Claims Management*, 2nd ed. (Markham, ON: Butterworths, 2001).

D. Lyons, "Integrated Disability Management: Assessing Its Fit for Your Company", *Ideas at Work* (Winter 2004), available online at: available online at: <http://online.wsj.com/ad/LibertyMutual/>.

Marsh Risk Consulting, *Workforce Risk: Fourth Annual Marsh Mercer Survey of Employers' Time-Off and Disability Programs* (2003), available online at: <http://www.marshriskconsulting.com/st/PSEV_C_228064_SC_229050_N R_303.htm>.

D.B. Mercer, "Roles and Responsibilities in Job Modification and Accommodation" (Seminars in Occupational Health and Medicine, Faculty of Medicine, Continuing Education, University of Calgary, February 3, 1999) [unpublished].

The Mutual Group, *LTD Claims Trends: 1996* (Waterloo, ON: The Mutual Group, 1996).

The Mutual Group, *Block of Business: January 01, 1998 to December 31, 1998, STD Claims Management Report — Statistics* (Waterloo, ON: The Mutual Group, 1998).

National Institute for Disability Management and Research (NIDMAR), *Disability Management in the Workplace: A Guide to Establishing a Joint Workplace Program* (Port Alberni, BC: NIDMAR, 1995).

G. Pransky & W. Shaw, "Injury Response: Optimizing the Role of Supervisors", *Ideas at Work* (Spring 2002), at 11-12, available online at: <http://www.libertymutual.com>.

Statistics Canada, *Work Absence Rates 2007*, Catalogue No. 71-211-XWE (Ottawa: Statistics Canada, May 2008), available online at: <http://www.statcan.gc.ca/ pub/71-211-x/2008000/5204138-eng.htm>.

L. Steeves & R. Smithies, "Foresight is Your Best Defence" (1996) 4:2 Group Healthcare Management 29.

N. Vimadalal & J. Wozniak, "Best Practices to Help Employers Capture the Benefits of Integrated Disability Management", *Employee Benefits News* (March 1, 2008), available online at: <http://ebn.benefitnews.com/news/best-practices-help-employers-capture-benefits-548491-1.html>.

Watson Wyatt Worldwide, *News Release*, "Employers That Measure Results from Integrated Disability Management Programs Report Big Savings" (October 15, 1998), Available online at: <http://www.watsonwyatt.com/news/press. asp?id=6900>.

Watson Wyatt Worldwide, *Staying@Work Report, 2005 — Canada* (2005), available online at: <http://www.watsonwyatt.com/research/resrender.asp? id=w-860&page=1>.

Watson Wyatt Worldwide, *Staying@Work: Effective Presence at Work. 2007 Survey Report — Canada: Executive Summary* (2007), available online at: <http://www.easna.org/documents/WatsonWyattStayingatWorkSurvey.pdf>

WorkSafe BC, *Key Statistics, 2007 Annual Report* (2008), available online at: <http://www.worksafebc.com/publications/reports/annual_reports/2007/key_statistics.asp>.

Chapter 18

Disability Management: Nursing Best Practices

INTRODUCTION

Disability management best practices, as noted in the previous chapter, are aimed at organizational/company disability management practices. Operationalizing these identified best practices will now be undertaken by focusing on the disability management nursing best practices.

THE NURSING PROCESS

The **nursing process** is a systematic, rational method of planning and providing individualized nursing care. It is the process by which registered nurses deliver nursing care to patients, clients, companies, or workers. The process is supported by nursing philosophies and concepts. A deductive theory, the nursing process was originally an adapted form of the problem-solving process.

A patient-centred, goal-oriented method of "caring", the **nursing process** provides a framework to nursing care. It involves five major steps:

- assessment (of company/worker's needs);
- diagnosis (of human response needs that nursing can assist with);
- planning (of company/worker's care);
- implementation/intervention (of care); and
- evaluation (of the success of the implemented care).

The characteristics of the nursing process are that it is:

- *Cyclic and dynamic* — The nursing process, which exists for every problem that the patient/client/company/worker has, is a cyclical and ongoing process that can end at any stage if the problem is solved (Figure 18.1).

Figure 18.1: The Nursing Process[1]

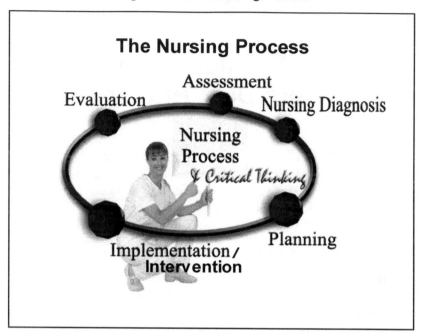

- *Goal-directed and client-centred* — The nursing process focuses on the patient/client/ company/worker and the individual's specific needs.

- *Interpersonal and collaborative* — The nursing process is not only centred on ways to improve the patient/client/company/worker's physical needs, but also on the social and emotional needs. Working in consort with the patient/client/company/worker, the nurse is able to facilitate/deliver nursing care that addresses the identified bio-psychosocial needs.

- *Universally applicable* — The nursing process applies to all peoples, regardless of race, religion, and geographic location.

- *Systematic* — The nursing process is a planned and coordinated approach to providing nursing care.

---

[1]   Adapted from F. Ferozali, *The Nursing Process*, available online at: <http://www.porterville college.edu/ferozali/folder3/Nursing_Process_online.ppt>.

DISABILITY MANAGEMENT: NURSING BEST PRACTICES — DEFINED

Disability management nursing best practices are defined as solutions which work best when linked to existing problems, or even to specific disability management crises within a workplace. These nursing solutions stem from "real-life" examples and direct observation of clinical disability management nursing practices. In essence, nursing best practices are a form of benchmarking which can serve as guidelines for nursing practice and measurement of outcomes. They are used to promote system and practice improvements.

DISABILITY MANAGEMENT: NURSING BEST PRACTICES

At the May 13, 2009 National Conference, Vancouver, British Columbia, the following disability management nursing best practices were identified by the 103 Canadian Occupational Health Nurses that were in attendance (Appendix 1):

(1) Joint Labour-Management Commitment to a Disability Management Program

The most successful workplace models of an Integrated Disability Management Program involve joint labour-management support and participation.

NURSING BEST PRACTICES

1. Educate the labour and management on the value of a Disability Management Program for the organization/company.
2. Explain the potential benefits for the union and management of having an Integrated Disability Management Program in the workplace.
3. Correct misconceptions regarding employee disability and the related disability management practices.
4. Invite and strongly encourage union/employee promotion and participation in the graduated return-to-work activities.
5. Facilitate the development of a good Disability Management Program and the related structure, processes, and outcomes.
6. Seek ways to collaboratively address employee absenteeism and lower the organization's/company's absenteeism rate.

(2) Integrate Disability Management Efforts

For effective disability management, a design or model for an Integrated Disability Management Program should exist. An **Integrated Disability Management Program** is a planned and coordinated approach to facilitate and manage employee health and productivity. It is a human resources risk management and risk communication approach designed to integrate all organizational/company programs and resources to minimize or reduce the losses and costs associated with employee medical absence regardless of the nature of those disabilities.

NURSING BEST PRACTICES

1. Promote the establishment of a joint labour-management steering committee to oversee the Integrated Disability Management Program.
2. Actively participate as the disability management subject matter expert.
3. Assist in conducting a comprehensive needs-analysis to identify specific organizational needs, and to establish baseline data before implementing the Integrated Disability Management Program.
4. Participate in assessing the related disability policies and procedures in terms of their impact on the Integrated Disability Management Program, and recommend changes if warranted.
5. Assist with the development of the roles and responsibilities of all major stakeholders involved in the Integrated Disability Management Program.
6. Promote the development of an inventory of modified work/alternate work positions.
7. Assist with the development of the organization's return-to-work program and processes.
8. Develop suitable disability claim and case management forms. These forms should focus on the claimant's functional abilities versus disabilities (*i.e.*, diagnosis).
9. Develop an absence and disability database for all types of absences — casual absence, short-term disability, occupational absence (Workers' Compensation), and long-term disability. Link this system with the company or organization's/company's Occupational Health Program, Employee Assistance Program, Occupational Health & Safety Program, employee benefit plans, and Workplace Wellness Program outcomes.
10. Use the above outcome data along with other human resources and group benefit plan outcomes to assist in the interpretation of the disability management issues.
11. Seek ways to maximize the integration of all the organizational/company programs so as to maximize the individual program efforts and outcomes.

(3) Disability Program Policies and Procedures

Policies and procedures for maintaining contact with absent staff members, accessing treatment or rehabilitation, and ensuring an expedient return to work can be applied to the entire continuum of employee medical absence regardless of cause, including casual absence, short-term disability, Workers' Compensation Board, and long-term disability illness/injuries. The intent of the Integrated Disability Management Program policies and procedures is to ensure that the appropriate processes are in place and that they are applied fairly, equally, and consistently.

NURSING BEST PRACTICES

1. Serve as a subject matter expert in the development and implementation of policies and procedures that deal with:

   - disability leaves (*i.e.*, casual absence, sick leave, short-term disability, Workers' Compensation Board, long-term disability, *etc.*);
   - rehabilitation measures (*i.e.*, case/claim management, vocational rehabilitation, *etc.*);
   - claim management standards of practice;
   - case management standards of practice;
   - confidentiality standards of practice;
   - documentation standards of practice;
   - return-to-work practices;
   - alcohol and drug policy; and
   - harassment and respectful workplace policies.

   More detail on the policies and procedures relevant to the Integrated Disability Management Program is provided in Chapter 3, "The Supportive Infrastructure for an Integrated Disability Management Program".

2. Provide governance and stewardship regarding the content of these policies.
3. Identify deficits in these policies and advise management.

(4)   Graduated Return-to-Work Initiatives

Graduated return-to-work initiatives can be an effective method of systematically returning employees to health and work, and can contribute to cost-containment.

NURSING BEST PRACTICES

1. Serve as a subject matter expert in the development and implementation of graduated return-to-work initiatives that involve labour and management support and participation.
2. Communicate the roles, responsibilities, and accountabilities of the key stakeholders.
3. Elicit employee, union, and line identification of modified/alternate work options.
4. Manage safe and timely return-to-work activities.
5. Endorse the development of flexible and creative return-to-work options.
6. Act as a neutral participant in the return-to-work process.
7. Promote a collaborative approach to the return-to-work process — employee, supervisor, union, human resources, health care provider(s), and insurer involvement.
8. Develop individualized return-to-work plans for employees that enable them to return to work in a safe and timely manner.
9. Promote respectful and healthy employment relationships.
10. Identify the need for conflict resolution and assist with this process.

11. Monitor the accommodation process, making adjustments as required.
11. Collect and manage modified/alternate work data, and the graduated return-to-work outcomes.
12. Evaluate the graduated return-to-work initiatives, plans, and outcomes regularly.
13. Communicate the benefits, challenges, and outcomes of the Integrated Disability Management Program to all the key stakeholders.

(5) Centralize the Responsibility for an Integrated Disability Management Program

To ensure effective functioning, one central figure should coordinate the daily operations of an Integrated Disability Management Program. Because of their nursing education and work experience as a generalist, Occupational Health Nurses tend to be ideal candidates for this role.

NURSING BEST PRACTICES

1. Assist the Integrated Disability Management Program steering committee to identify the duties of the Disability Management Coordinator, as well as the requisite skills for the position.
2. If deemed appropriate, manage the Integrated Disability Management Program — this includes the planning, organizing, directing, evaluating, and continuous improvement activities.
3. Coordinate the Disability Management Program with other organizational/company programs such as the Employee Assistance Program, Occupational Health & Safety Program, Workplace Wellness Program, and Human Resources Program/services.
4. Advise the company's Occupational Health & Safety department of the cause and nature of all occupational claims. The intent is to seek workable illness and injury prevention strategies.
5. Advise Human Resources of the cause and nature of the non-occupational claims. The intent is to seek workable illness and injury prevention strategies.

(6) Disability Management Program Communication Strategy

An essential component of any successful Integrated Disability Management Program is the widespread understanding and support of stakeholders both within the workplace and in the broader community.

NURSING BEST PRACTICES

1. Assist in the development of the Integrated Disability Management Program's communication strategy and plan. The aim is to promote awareness and overcome organizational barriers to implementing an Integrated Disability Management Program (refer to Chapter 13, "Marketing Disability

Management Programs and Communicating the Results", for more details on this subject).

2. Assist with the identification of the key stakeholders along with their respective needs and wants from the Integrated Disability Management Program.

3. Assist with the development of the key messages that are to be delivered to each stakeholder group as well as with the appropriate communication media and vehicles.

4. Play a major role in informing the key stakeholders about the Integrated Disability Management Program, and its successes and problems. That is, keep them in the "decision-making loop".

5. Provide stakeholders with the relevant outcome data and benefits realized by the Integrated Disability Management Program. This approach garners continued support for the Integrated Disability Management Program.

(7)   Disability Management Program Education and Training

The purpose of Disability Management Program education and training is to create awareness around the need for and value afforded by workplace-based attendance and disability management programs.

Nursing Best Practices

1. Assist with the development and delivery of generalized training for all supervisors and Human Resources staff in dealing with ill or injured employees and family members.

2. Provide specialized disability management education for supervisors, union, and other staff leaders involved in the implementation of the Integrated Disability Management Program.

3. Develop and deliver "train-the-trainer" sessions for employee/union peer counsellors if appropriate.

4. Provide coaching and mentoring to supervisors/managers involved in disability management situations. Timely feedback on the performance of the Integrated Disability Management Program enhances the overall management of claims.

5. Develop and deliver quality educational sessions (refer to Chapter 14, "Disability Management Education", for more details on this subject).

6. Avail oneself of specialized education and training in disability management. This should include continuing education in the field of disability management and other related fields (*e.g.,* in Employee Assistance Programs, Human Resources principles, Occupational Health & Safety, risk management and risk communication, Workplace Wellness Programs, management human resource theories and practices, *etc.*).

(8)   Link the Disability Management Program with the Employee Assistance Program

External services can play an important role in effective employee attendance support and disability management. Companies that integrate the Employee Assistance Program services with attendance support and Disability Management Programs tend to encounter the need for a comprehensive Employee Assistance Program service when dealing with the psychological and physiological aspects of absence.

NURSING BEST PRACTICES

1. Partner with the organization's Employee Assistance Program to develop an effective manner in which to link the Integrated Disability Management Program with the Employee Assistance Program. The focus is on the employee's functional ability, the characteristics of workplace environment, and the job demands. Hence, both parties can reach a common ground on which to jointly assist the ill/injured employee.
2. Ensure that all the service providers attain a mutual understanding of and respect for the individual program goals and objectives, as well as for the overall Integrated Disability Management Program goals and objectives.
3. Promote a partnership approach that allows for multi-disciplinary interventions.
4. Develop the appropriate channels of information and consent forms through which information on the employee's functional ability, the characteristics of workplace environment, and the job demands can be shared.
5. Evaluate the outcome measures on the cases served jointly by the Employee Assistance Program and Integrated Disability Management Program personnel. Knowledge of utilization rates, types of cases served, trend analyses and success or failure rates, and anticipatory guidance for illness and injury prevention can be attained using aggregate data.

(9)   Medical Consents and Certificates

The process of obtaining consent to collect personal health information creates a reasonable expectation of privacy by the employee. This requires the employer to take all reasonable steps to ensure the level of confidentiality promised in the consent form is not compromised. Some reasonable steps include:

- maintenance of confidentiality;
- retention of information;
- secure storage of information;
- appropriate disclosure of information internally and externally;
- proper transmittal of information;
- appropriate methods of destruction; and
- identification of the consequences for staff violations, if any should occur.

NURSING BEST PRACTICES

1. Review the disability claim forms and medical certificates; revise any forms/certificates that fail to gather the necessary information in a manner that is in compliance with the applicable legislation.
2. Ensure the form/certificate is clear, concise and designed to gather only the information relevant to the current disability.
3. Develop and communicate the procedures for the submission and retention of consent forms and medical certificates (refer to Chapter 3, "The Supportive Infrastructure for an Integrated Disability Management Program", for more details on this subject).
4. Educate unions, management, and employees on the elements of **informed consent**.[2]
5. Serve as the custodian of informed consent.
6. Ensure the existence of a consent form signed by the ill or injured worker before any contact with the physician is initiated.

(10) Policies and Procedures to Protect the Confidentiality of Medical Data

Medical diagnoses and health-related data are obtained during the course of claim and case management. Policies and procedures are required to deal with confidentiality and access to medical files, as well as with the responsible retention, storage, transfer, or disposal of medical data.

NURSING BEST PRACTICES

1. Assist with the development of a confidentiality policy and code of practice. This should comply with the applicable legislation (refer to Chapter 3, "The Supportive Infrastructure for an Integrated Disability Management Program" and Chapter 10, "Disability Management Practice Standards", for more details).
2. Develop a protocol for the retention, maintenance, release, and disposal of medical documentation (refer to Chapter 10 "Disability Management Practice Standards", for more details).
3. Retain all medical data in a secure and confidential manner with access by authorized personnel, and only on a "need-to-know" basis.

---

[2] **Informed consent** — There is an obligation on the employer to ensure that sufficient information is provided to employees about the nature and consequence of the intended action to allow the employee to reach a reasoned decision. The employee must be mentally competent, and possess the ability to understand and appreciate the nature and consequences of the procedure. The consent must be freely given; not obtained through misrepresentation or fraud. The consent given must be in relation to the specific act contemplated unless the employee's life is immediately endangered and it is impractical to obtain consent. Consent cannot be given to the performance of an illegal procedure.

4. Retain all medical documentation for a minimum period of seven years from the last point of activity.
5. Limit the dissemination of medical diagnoses to broad categories or neutral descriptors, such as occupational injury, occupational illness, non-occupational injury, or non-occupational illness. When diagnoses are used, limit them to disease classifications or aggregate the data so that individual diagnoses cannot be determined.
6. Provide governance and stewardship in terms of current case law and legislative changes that impact the disability management practices.

(11) Disability Case Management Practices

Effective case management promotes quality, cost-effective outcomes in terms of human and financial saving.

NURSING BEST PRACTICES

1. Serve as a subject matter expert in the development of the organization's/company's case management practice standards.
2. Educate stakeholders on what case management is and what it is not, thereby managing the expectations of the key stakeholders.
3. Uphold the established case management standards (refer to Chapter 5, "An Integrated Disability Management Program: The Managed Rehabilitative Care Program", for more details on this subject).
4. Develop disability management nursing plans that are based on the nursing process, and which include the use of evidence-based data, as well as knowledge of the workplace and its culture.
5. Track the disability data, plus the hours of modified/alternate work, dollars saved with modified/alternate work, and types of cases that were the most successful with early return-to-work initiatives.
6. Evaluate the case management process employed through the use of peer or internal reviews, or external quality assurance measures (audits).
7. Track occupational health and case management activities, such as the amount of time required to case manage each claim, administer the service, train supervisors, undertake process development, conduct follow-up activities, and pursue professional development.
8. Evaluate, on a case-by-case basis, the return on investment of the case management interventions.
9. Continue to review disability claim outcomes, paying special attention to claims that are closed. Use the closed claims as indicators of the case management outcomes.

(12) Early Intervention

Research and industry experience strongly endorses the importance of early intervention in any employee absence situation.

NURSING BEST PRACTICES

1. Educate the workplace on the value of early intervention and what early intervention looks like.
2. Promote the development of a work culture that actively supports early intervention.
3. Manage the case management expectations of the key stakeholders.
4. Promote early contact between the supervisor and the ill/injured employee ideally on the first day of absence; by the third day at the latest.
5. If required, implement early case management (within the first three to five days of the absence).
6. Function as an advocate,[3] not an enabler,[4] to the disabled employee and family.
7. Involve the Employee Assistance Program in employee absence and disability situations as appropriate.
8. Encourage open communication and positive relationships within organization.

(13) The Claim Adjudication Process

Employers require a documented process for claim adjudication. This helps to ensure the use of a standardized approach. The exact criteria used to determine claim eligibility depend on the terms of the benefit plan in place. Most of this task is undertaken by non-nursing personnel. The claim management skills are discussed in Chapter 4, "Integrated Disability Management Program: Stakeholder Roles". They vary greatly from nursing skills in that they involve adherence to claim management criteria, as opposed to being based on concepts, principles and practices. However, the occupational health nurse does have a significant role to play in the claim management processes.

NURSING BEST PRACTICES

1. Determine employee fitness-to-work.
2. Communicate that information to management/human resources services in a timely manner.
3. Assist with the ongoing monitoring of the employee's fitness-to-work status.
4. Communicate the degree of employee compliance with the recommended treatment and rehabilitation.
5. Communicate the expected return-to-work date along with any identified work limitations.

---

[3] **Advocate** — the role of pleading or representing an employee's cause to management, or to external individuals or agencies.

[4] **Enabler** — the role of enabling another to persist in self-destructive behaviour (such as substance abuse) by providing excuses or by making it possible to avoid the consequences of such behaviour.

6. Consider the use of flow charts and visual aids to depict the claim management process, and how and when the occupational health nurse can assist.

(14) Effective Management of Disabilities

Disability management is highly dependent on workplace relationships. Employee willingness to help each other is based on the quality of their social relationships. The stronger the social relationships, the more tolerant the workplace culture is of employee disabilities; and the greater the likelihood that the workplace will support the recovering employee through the return-to-work process.

NURSING BEST PRACTICES

1. Educate the workplace about the impact of workplace disabilities and how to recognize an employee who is experiencing health problems. Add to that, an explanation of the concept of social capital and its influence on the return-to-work process (refer to Chapter 15, "Disability Management: The Social Capital Theory Perspective for Managing Disability Claims", for more details on this subject).
2. Encourage the workplace to redesign work processes to decrease certain physical and psychological stressors, and hence, to decrease the likelihood of relapse and secondary health conditions when the employee does return to work.
3. When designing a rehabilitation and return-to-work plan, involve the employee, supervisor, and union. Working collaboratively enhances relationships and provides clarity as to the plans and processes.
4. Regularly communicate with employees who are on sick leave. Document conversations to reinforce the agreed-upon decisions and action plans. Include line management and the union representative on this correspondence.
5. Reinforce that the occupational health nurse is qualified to receive and interpret medical information. In most workplaces, the occupational health nurse will be the only professional qualified to do so.
6. Promote a good person/job fit when offering work accommodation.
7. Seek to develop return-to-work plans that build the employee's confidence, particularly when employee fear of relapse or pain is evident.
8. Manage the expectations of the returning employee as well as the expectations of co-workers, managers, and union representatives. Ensure they remain realistic as to what "a successful rehabilitation and return-to-work" looks like, and how long it might take to complete.
9. Seek to legitimize the work accommodation of the returning employee. Some of this can be done by tackling misinformation "head on" — debunking myths about workplace safety and authenticity, and teaching line management how to "assist" rather than to "blame", when an employee experiences symptoms or a relapse at work.

10. Encourage the resolution of conflict. Conflict decreases trust, liking, and therefore, social capital — all detrimental to a successful return to work.
11. Promote the development of a fair and transparent process for investigating discipline-worthy conduct. This will go a long way to prevent the escalation of workplace conflict and perceptions of favouritism.
12. Seek ways to recognize and reward managers for maintaining healthy work teams and for successfully accommodating employees from other business units. Likewise, employees should be positively recognized for following medically-sanctioned work restrictions and for assisting in the accommodation of co-workers.

(15) Management of Mental Health Disabilities

A. MITIGATION

With a rising incidence rate of mental health claims in Canada and the United States, the recommended approach is the use of return-to-work plans specific to the management of mental illness in the workplace. This is consistent with the work undertaken by the Global Business and Economic Roundtable on Addictions and Mental Health.

BEST PRACTICES: MITIGATION

1. Promote early contact with the ill or injured employee by the supervisor.
2. Implement early case management (within the first three to five days).
3. Involve the Employee Assistance Program or some other form of counselling as part of the treatment plan.
4. Use a technique such as The Green Chart (refer to Chapter 15, "Disability Management: The Social Capital Theory Perspective for Managing Disability Claims", for more details) to open the lines of communication between the health care providers and the occupational health professionals, or disability management professionals/practitioners, who represent the workplace interests.
5. Work with a significant person in the individual's life to ensure that workplace issues or concerns are properly addressed.
6. Ensure that support is available to the employee upon his or her return to work.
7. Maintain that support for a number of months post-return to work.

B. PREVENTION

Prevention of mental health problems in the workplace is a "best practice" — an approach that is cost-effective in terms of the human and financial aspects.

BEST PRACTICES: PREVENTION

1. Promote the development of effective strategies for protecting the psychological health and safety of employees (refer to Chapter 15, "Disability

Management: The Social Capital Theory Perspective for Managing Disability Claims", for more details.
2. Participate in the implementation of those strategies.
3. Assist with the monitoring and evaluation of the effectiveness of the implemented strategies.
4. Assist with the enhancement of the identified prevention approaches.

(16) Cultural Diversity and Disability Management

By becoming culturally competent, Canadian and American employers can appreciate and maximize the strengths of each of the various cultures present in their workplaces. Cultural diversity brings challenges to managing employee disabilities. Reaction to illness/injury and recovery is culturally-based. Nurses recognized this fact many years ago. Hence, the early focus on cross-cultural nursing (refer to Chapter 21, "Disability Management: Impact of Cultural Diversity", for more details on this subject).

NURSING BEST PRACTICES

1. Assist with the identification of the cultural mix within the organization.
2. Promote cultural competence within the organization (refer to Chapter 21, "Disability Management: Impact of Cultural Diversity", and Chapter 22, "Disability Management: Impact of Four Generations in the Workplace").
3. Seek to communicate effectively with the various cultures — use of translators or multi-lingual communication tools.
4. Identify areas of potential cultural conflict and seek ways to address them.
5. Provide clarity on the Integrated Disability Management Program while being culturally respectful.
6. Compromise by showing respect for different beliefs and by being willing to work with those beliefs to reach a "win-win" solution for the stakeholders.
7. Help workers understand their options so that they can make informed consents to treatment and return-to-work options.
8. Ensure that support is available to the employee upon a return to work.
9. Remain current on cross-cultural nursing and the related best practices.
10. Seek ways to continuously improve the organization's approach to cultural diversity, especially in the area of disability management.

(17) Disability Data Management

Data collection and analysis is the foundation on which the success of an Integrated Disability Management Program is based

NURSING BEST PRACTICES

1. Use evidence-based research when designing the data management processes for the Disability Management Program.

2. Capture all absence and disability data in a format that can be compared with other Canadian disability databases.
3. Ensure that the claim and case management data collected includes casual sick time, short-term disability, Workers' Compensation, and long-term disability absence rates and costs.
4. Monitor the Workers' Compensation Board data, investigate opportunities for cost avoidance and cost savings, and seek guidance regarding Workers' Compensation Board claim management techniques.
5. Investigate the potential implementation of an integrated occupational health and safety data management system that can link Disability Management Program outcomes (*i.e.*, short-term disability, Workers' Compensation Board claims, long-term disability, *etc.*) with Occupational Health and Safety Programs, Employee Assistance Programs, employee benefits, and Workplace Wellness Programs.
6. Seek opportunities to link employee absence data with other pieces of human resources information.
7. Use the company's available communication systems (*e.g.*, email, internal mail, cheque inserts, newsletters, reports, *etc.*) to encourage the transmission of absence, disability, and modified/alternate work data.
8. Ensure that all stakeholders are aware of the reasons for, and costs of, medical absenteeism and disability.
9. Encourage industry disability management benchmarking such as the Institute for Work and Health's Workplace Disability Benchmarking project to determine what is working and not working in the organization's Disability Management Program.
10. Monitor and evaluate the effectiveness of the data management processes, making improvements as required.

(18) Measurement, Monitoring, and Continuous Improvement of the Disability Management Program

Integrated Disability Management Programs must demonstrate continuous evaluation and modifications to:

*   justify the program;
*   improve workplace health and safety practices;
*   ensure that the program objectives are met; and
*   ensure that employer and employee needs are met.

NURSING BEST PRACTICES

1. Develop short-term disability performance measures that include absentee rates, lost time hours, lost time costs, average absentee length, percentage of hours saved on modified/alternate work, dollars saved due to modified/alternate work activities, percentage of employees who returned to work, number and types of interventions used and number of short-term disability claims that were successfully resolved.

2. Review the Workers' Compensation Board data, investigate opportunities for cost avoidance and cost savings, and seek guidance regarding Workers' Compensation Board claim management techniques.
3. Institute program outcome measures in the long-term disability period which include the following: reduced disabled lives liability, reduced long-term disability claims and costs, increased cost avoidance due to early intervention and modified/alternate work initiatives, case-by-case return on investment due to intervention, and return on investment using a formula customized to suit the company or organization's needs (see Chapter 6, "Integrated Disability Management Program: Outcome Measurements", Figure 6.5 for a model to calculate the return-on-investment for an Integrated Disability Management Program).
4. Establish the contributing factors for employee absenteeism and disability such as employee age, lifestyle, drug or alcohol use, work environment, employee-employer relationships, seasonal issues, legal issues, financial issues, and the existence of pre-existing health conditions.
5. Measure the effectiveness of the Integrated Disability Management Program through interviews, surveys, data analyses, and return on investment for the services provided and associated benefit costs.
6. Set program management targets for each year and measure success/failures.
7. Use the disability management data to provide insight into opportunities for corporate occupational health and safety initiatives and prevention strategies.
8. Regularly disseminate disability management data to all the departments along with the related costs.
9. Justify the Integrated Disability Management Program in terms of the return on investment attained through lower disability costs, reduced use of employee group benefits, improved employee well-being and health, and increased employee productivity.

DISABILITY MANAGEMENT NURSING SKILLS

When providing disability management nursing best practices, the occupational health nurse must demonstrate a suite of technical specialist (occupational heath nursing) skills, relationship skills, and business skills. These are described in Appendix 1 of Chapter 4, "Integrated Disability Management Program: Stakeholder Roles".

The additional skills that pertain to disability management nursing best practices are:

*   **Clinical assessment skills** — the ability to conduct an objective assessment of an injured/ill worker's situation by integrating and applying clinical, professional, communication, and practical skills for nursing practice.

*   **Critical thinking** — examination of an issue or concept from a number of perspectives with a view to gaining greater understanding. It is the purposeful and reflective judgment about what to believe or what to do.

- **Cultural competence** — the ability to provide quality disability management care and services to a diverse employee population. It encompasses the development of a receptive environment for disability management systemic responses (*e.g.,* organizational policy, procedures, practices, *etc.*) as well as the delivery of individual disability management services. Hence, cultural competence implies a responsibility at both the organizational and individual level.

- **Disability management research** — the use of the "scientific method" to discover, understand, interpret, and develop disability management principles, models, practices, and processes.

- **Legal knowledge** — a working knowledge of the various pieces of legislation relevant to the field of disability management.

- **Liaison** — the position, or responsibility, within an organization for maintaining communication links with external individuals, agencies, or organizations, as well as the internal stakeholders.

- **Coaching** — the process of assisting a supervisor, union leader, employee to effectively participate in a Disability Management Program. It is the act of enabling an individual to successfully undertake a new role/responsibility.

- **Disability management governance** — consistent disability management — that means cohesive policies, processes, and decision-making practices.

- **Disability management stewardship** — personal responsibility for overseeing and guiding an organization's Disability Management Program and its functioning.

Additional to the above skills, the occupational health nurse has the nursing knowledge, process, and expertise to interact with the employee and family, the various players in the health care system, the workplace, the unions, the insurers, and community resources to affect a timely recovery and safe return to work by the employee. Importantly, this professional group is qualified to receive, comprehend, and, interpret medical reports and findings — a unique aspect in the world of disability management. Hence, occupational health nurses can play a pivotal role in assessing ill/injured workers and in coordinating effective return-to-work plans — a true cost-saving for employers and employees.

SUMMARY

This germane work on the disability management nursing best practices, is the result of the expertise of, and contributions made by, the Canadian Occupational Health Nurses in attendance at the National Nurses Conference, May 2009, Vancouver, British Columbia. This work is intended to be the foundation on which additional disability management nursing best practices can be built.

APPENDIX 1
List of Contributors

Thanks are extended to all the Occupational Health Nurses who participated in the development of the Disability Management Nursing Best Practices at the BC WorkSafe OHN Conference, May 13, 2009. Special mention is offered to Jan Beesley, Margaret Smithson, Jocelyne Fidyk, WorkSafeBC, Barbara Roberts, and Mardi Denis for all their time, expertise, and assistance in making this work possible.

Occupational Health Nurse	Occupational Health Nurse
Rupel Amershi	Lois MacDonald
Christine Andersen	Sally MacDonald
Lydia Arnold-Smith	Sheila MacLean
Paulette Baker	Patrick Madden
Shelley Barnard	Ros Maddren
Marla Barnes	Anu Manhas
Susan Bates	L. Marie Marple
Mary Beeksma	Julie Matear
Jan Beesley	Catherine Matte
Kyra Bell	Abha McDonell
Sharon Blaney	Sandra McGuire
Juliana Boratto	Cynthia McKeown
Mary-Anne Brittain	Kim McMahon
Elizabeth Brydon	Joan Meidl
Arvin Cajigas	Candice Moore
Jim Cariaso	June Murray
Barbara Carter	April Negrin
Cordia Chung	Sundeep Nijjar
Eva Clegg	Patricia O'Brien
Barb Curtis	Dee Ogden
Mardi Denis	Nan Ouimet
Sharon Dent	Pearl Pacheco
Bernice Doedel	Heather Palmer
Patricia Doiron	Sheryll Papilla
Manon Ducharme	David Poelzer
Arlene Dyer	Elayne Preston
Kathy Fast	Stacy Purewal
Jo-Anne Finley	Andrea Ram
Barbara Flesh	Usha Reddy
Steve Fur	Nicole Richards
Simone Gardezy	Barb Roberts

Occupational Health Nurse	Occupational Health Nurse
Patricia Garnham	Karin Rolfes-Kubik
Lynda Goodman-Bell	Kathy Romano
Rachelle Grace	Penny Ross
Donna Graham	Bernadette Rudolphi
Diana Grant	Helen Ryan
Heather Grauman	Eva Sadowski
Catherine Guy	Lucy Samuel
Ronda Haley	Tammy Scott
Alison Hannah	Margaret Smithson
Helene Heppner	Melanie Solari
Stephanie Higgins	Susan Stryck
Nicole Hough	Sheila Thiessen
Sharon Hoyle	Aurora To
Alice Hsing	Jacinthe Tremblay
Tess Juliano	Cheryl Walilko
Elise Kobylanski	Sean Woo
Jennifer Kullman	Susan Wood
Iris Lama	Juanita Woodrow
Karen LaRonde	Benita Yan
Suzanne Ledet	Doreen Yanick
Olivia Wei Li	

CHAPTER REFERENCES

F. Ferozali, *The Nursing Process*, available online at: <http://www.porter villecollege.edu/ferozali/folder3/Nursing_Process_online.ppt>.

Institute for Work & Health, "Workplace Disability Benchmarking", available online at: <http://www.iwh.on.ca/wdb>.

Section 2:

Disability Management:
Other Considerations

Chapter 19

Disability Management: Ethical Practice

INTRODUCTION

Disability management is based on relationships and trust. It impacts corporate plans and costs; individual/family well-being, vocational aspirations, and finances; and employee culture and morale. In dealing with such an important topic, ethical considerations must be addressed. The following discussion deals with the key ethical theories and their implications for disability management practitioners.

ETHICAL CONSIDERATIONS

By Bonnie Rogers

Ethics is defined as the science of morals, a system of principles and rules of conduct,[1] the study of standards of right and wrong, or having to do with human character, conduct, moral duty and obligations to the community.[2] It is the moral reasoning that humans possess.

Ethical theories and principles guide us in making ethical decisions. The major ones include the **teleological theory** — **utilitarianism**, which focuses on the consequences of an action and gauges the value of that action by the end results, rather than by the means to achieve the results. It concentrates on providing the greatest good (or the least harm), for the greatest number of people. In this context, policy formation based on cost-benefit analysis, wherein the greatest benefit is achieved by the most, but not all, for the lowest cost, is a good example of utility.

The **deontological theory** deals with action and asserts that "rightness" and "wrongness" are measured by means, rather than by consequences of an action. So, the nature of an action is more important than the outcomes. By way of comparison, the deontologist would assert that confidentiality of employee health information must always be maintained; whereas the utilitarian might hold that if keeping certain kinds of health information secret would cause more harm than good, then confidentiality should be broken.

---

[1] B. Kirkpatrick, ed., *The Cassell Concise English Dictionary* (London, England: Cassell Publishers Ltd., 1989) *s.v.* "ethic".

[2] *Ibid.*

Ethical principles extend from the deontological theory, and the most widely observed principles are autonomy, nonmaleficence, beneficence, and justice. **Autonomy** is a form of personal liberty whereby the individual is regarded as having the right to self-determination. This means that the individual's values and goals must be considered in major decisions that affect his or her welfare, and precludes paternalistic decision-making (when one claims to know what is best for another person), as well as requiring informed consent when decisions are made. Health professionals or others who are making decisions for employees without the employee's input and consent would be in violation of this principle. The inclusion of the employee in making disability care choices is important to upholding the autonomous principles.

The second principle, **nonmaleficence,** is often referred to as the "no harm" principle. It is the foundation of most professional codes of ethics. For example, an employee with a known disability, such as a hearing loss, should not be placed in a job situation that would further compromise his or her hearing. In addition, returning an ill or injured employee to work too soon could compromise his or her continued recovery and potentially harm the employee. Here, the health care professional must guard against having divided loyalties to the employee-organization, and remain an advocate for the employee. Conducting return-to-work examinations is one way to provide protection for the health of the employee, as well as for the well-being of the organization, co-workers, and public at large.

Beneficence, the third principle, requires that health care professionals act in the best interest of the employee. The identification of potential health hazards through routine work site "walk-throughs", the identification of employees at increased risk for illness or injury, and making recommendations for risk reduction, represent a positive occupational health intervention. Positive occupational health intervention is aimed at employee protection thereby preventing a potential disabling event from happening. For example, the development of a back injury prevention program for employees with a previous history of back injury would be a beneficent action. In addition, assuring the disabled employee that he or she will receive quality case management is critical to this principle.

The fourth principle, **justice**, is directed towards treating employees fairly, equally, and without discrimination. This includes providing equal opportunity for disabled persons regarding job availability and promotion; and assuring that individuals are not discriminated against because of a health condition, such as HIV, or another chronic disorder, when they are able to perform the job safely. This concept is embodied in Canadian human rights legislation. Another example is treating employees equally with regard to access to modified/alternate work opportunities within an organization.

In many instances, ethical principles provide us with a guide with which to weigh the risks and benefits with respect to individual health and welfare, and the development of policies and procedures to safeguard individual rights and protect health. It is incumbent upon the Disability Case Manager, in particular occupational health nurses and physicians, to examine the situation with respect to these guiding principles and to assure that the benefits of their actions clearly outweigh the risks.

ETHICS AND CASE MANAGEMENT[3]

By Jane Hall

Professional bodies and organizations establish professional codes of ethics. Occupational health professionals and Disability Case Managers are bound to uphold the codes of the professional disciplines. Professional behaviour will be held accountable to the standards, regardless of feelings, personal beliefs, or views.

In professional practice, particularly when delivering case management services, we speak of "autonomy" or the right of the employee to determine as much as possible the direction of his or her care. Autonomy is critical to keep in mind during problem solving or advocacy, especially if the employee's desires are in conflict with those of the health care providers or employers.

The other ethical principles to consider are truthfulness and justice — that is, what is right versus what is wrong in a given situation. The term **ethical dilemma** comes into play when two apparent truths are in conflict with one another. For example, an ethical dilemma may arise when a legal situation regarding a medical matter is in conflict with a religious belief. A moral wrong may not be illegal, but could be unethical. A clear legal parameter may be at odds with the moral-judgement consensus. Ethics, then, is a philosophical issue rather than a scientific one. In case management, evaluation and weighing of the ethics of a case must be done in an unemotional manner so that decision-making is rational and based on facts rather than the emotional issues attached to the decision at hand.

An everyday definition of ethics would be: *"Doing the right thing, at the right time, for the right person, in the right way and knowing why it is the right thing, at the right time, for the right person, in the right way."*

Common Ethical Case Management Considerations

PERSONAL BELIEFS VERSUS PROFESSIONAL EXPECTATIONS

Culture, experiences, belief systems, and academic persuasions influence Disability Case Managers. As human beings, we react emotionally as well as intellectually to situations. To deny that case management activities are prone to influences from our background and beliefs is to bury your head in the sand.

---

[3] Adapted and reprinted with permission. Copyright © 1999 by OEM Health Information Inc., J. Hall, "Ethics and Case Management" (1999) 13:2 *The OEM Report* 13

What is required is "physician know thyself" imperative. Disability Case Managers must take the time for introspection and examination of their beliefs, values, biases, and prejudices. Only when we have acknowledged to ourselves where we stand on various issues can we put those issues aside and deal with the factual realm, which is the professional case management standard.

CONFIDENTIALITY VERSUS RIGHT TO KNOW

Confidentiality has to do with credibility and with legality. A Disability Case Manager should be clear with employees that theirs is not a legally supported confidential relationship like the relationship between physician and patient, lawyer and client or priest and parishioner. The Disability Case Manager is bound to share information with other stakeholders who need to know about information pertinent to the individual case. It is strongly recommended that the Disability Case Manager have a frank discussion with the employee at the onset of the relationship to disclose what his or her role and responsibility entails. A client who starts a sentence with, "I don't want you to tell", needs to be stopped, counselled about the case management role, and told that depending on what is shared, confidentiality cannot be promised.

On the other hand, it is not ethical for a Disability Case Manager to share information with anyone else who does not need to know the information. Shoptalk is a common breech of confidential employee information. Sharing a dilemma with a supervisor, however, is an appropriate method of communication.

Another example of appropriate sharing of information is when the Disability Case Manager realizes that the employee is non-compliant with treatment. The employee may request that the Disability Case Manager not tell his or her physician. The Disability Case Manager should attempt to determine why the employee is being non-compliant, but cannot agree to the request of non-disclosure to the physician. Such an action may prevent needed adjustments to the treatment regimen.

INDIVIDUAL WISHES VERSUS FAMILY OR LEGAL CONSTRAINTS

Disability case management never occurs in a vacuum. Physicians and other health care providers, claim adjusters, employers, co-workers and family members frequently contribute to the employee's assessment and rehabilitation plans. The manner in which the Disability Case Manager obtains and uses the information must be carefully thought out and planned, keeping in mind the employee's best interests and wishes. The Disability Case Manager should avoid becoming entangled in legal issues. Once again, the guidelines used to effect this should be sought in the standards for case management practice. If a legal decision is rendered, the Disability Case Manager is bound to obey the law. If this presents an ethical dilemma for the Disability Case Manager, then the Disability Case Manager's supervisor and/or lawyer should be consulted. In some cases, a Disability Case Manager may need to withdraw from a case rather than compromise the principles of case management.

Tools for Determining Ethical Case Management Practices

DISCUSSION WITH SUPERVISORS

Also known as the "when in doubt, check it out" philosophy, this method of dealing with ethical issues is recommended as the first step in acknowledging and confronting a problem. It is appropriate because in most situations the supervisor is accountable for the actions of individual Disability Case Managers that they supervise. Presumably, they have attained their supervisory position on the basis of greater knowledge and experience. Also, being more removed from the situation, they may possess more rationality and wisdom in case management practices.

LEGAL COUNSEL

Most organizations have access to legal counsel. In ethical situations related to occupational health, legal counsel is likely to be a labour lawyer. If a Disability Case Manager seeks legal counsel, it is appropriate to remember that there is usually some bias by the attorney(s) towards the organization's position on the situation. The Disability Case Manager should consider the legal opinion as well as any other opinions as representing part of the picture in a specific case.

SELF-APPRAISAL

Self-appraisal is a difficult tool, but by examining our rationale, motives, and emotions as Disability Case Managers we can gain an understanding of what we believe and why we believe what we do. In that way we can gain some self-insight so that we can act on our client's behalf in an informed and non-judgmental manner.

RESOURCES

Seldom is there a situation in which the critical ethical issues have not been raised before. Thus, it is helpful to search for other similar cases and examine them for any pearls of wisdom that may apply.

ETHICAL DECISION-MAKING

By Dianne Dyck

There are numerous ethical conflicts and dilemmas that can arise in today's work environment, including issues such as confidentiality of employee health records, worker notification of "right to know", substance abuse, employee screening for **health indices**,[4] and "whistle-blowing". Ethical dilemmas often arise, such as cost containment versus the quality of health care; conflicting loyalties of the health care professional between the employee and the organization; and returning a worker to a safe work environment.

Ethical Dilemma

An ethical dilemma exists when two core values that the person upholds come into conflict, making it difficult for the person to decide how to move forward. In the fields of occupational health and workers' compensation, ethical issues are more likely to centre on matters of confidentiality of employee medical records, employee "right to know", action regarding potential workplace hazards and human resource issues that conflict with human rights legislation and the duty to accommodate. As well, psychological issues often come to the attention of the Disability Case Manager, and issues of roles and responsibility may arise. Disability Case Managers can easily find themselves in the middle of "hot issues" and may be called upon to advocate for an employer rather than the employee. In such situations, the Disability Case Manager needs to carefully assess the situation and all the issues, both medical and ethical; utilize the available resources and tools; and ultimately make conscious, carefully thought-out decisions before taking any action.[5]

Although there is no magic remedy to resolve ethical dilemmas, there are a number of ethical decision-making models that can be used. The following is a discussion on two such models:

Ethical Fitness™ Model [6]

Developed at the Institute for Global Ethics, this ethical decision-making model assumes that human beings have universal core values that cross religious, cultural, and geographic boundaries. It serves as a decision-making guide, helping the individual to move from ethical dilemma recognition to resolution.

For example, as a Disability Case Manager, you are aware that an employee has multiple sclerosis. She is being considered for a promotion that will include long hours, high service demands, and extensive travel. A couple of months ago, this employee was off work for two weeks due to an exacerbation of her medical condition. She is fine now, but her manager has come to ask you if you know of any reason why this employee should not be considered for this new position within the company. You have a good relationship with this manager and would

---

[4]   **Health indices** are the measures used to establish "normal" or "abnormal" health conditions, such as body temperature, blood pressure, pulse, neurological functioning, *etc.*

[5]   Adapted and reprinted with permission. Copyright © 1999 by OEM Health Information Inc., J. Hall, "Ethics and Case Management" (1999) 13:2 *The OEM Report* 13.

[6]   R.M. Kidder, *How Good People Make Tough Choices: Resolving the Dilemmas of Ethical Living* (New York, NY: Fireside Books, 1995).

like to tell him that you are concerned that the employee will not be able to handle the stress and rigours of this job due to health reasons. However, in your role as Disability Case Manager, you are bound to uphold the medical confidentiality entrusted to you. This is an ethical dilemma for you.

The critical step is recognizing that an ethical dilemma exists, followed by identifying which of the core values are in conflict. Once achieved, the Disability Case Manager, or occupational health nurse, can apply the following steps of the Ethical Fitness™ Model:

a) *Awareness: Determine the moral issue* — First recognize that an ethical dilemma exists.

b) *Actor: Determine the actor* — Decide who is experiencing the conflict in values.

c) *Facts: Get the details* — Gather all the facts and assess what you learn. There may or may not be an actual conflict at hand.

d) *Determine if the moral issue is "right vs. wrong"* — Could this simply be an issue of "right and wrong" and not an ethical dilemma? To determine this, you can use five tests:

(i) The legal test	— Does the action or choice contravene any laws?
(ii) The front page test	— Would this action/decision stand the test of public scrutiny?
(iii) The gut feeling test	— What does your "gut" tell you about this decision: is it right or wrong?
(iv) The role model test	— How would you feel about someone you respect knowing you took this action or made this decision?
(v) The professional standards test	— Would your action/decision align with your professional standards?

e) *Test for "right" by assigning one of the four dilemma paradigms* — With facts in hand and the assurance that an ethical dilemma exists, determine which core values are in conflict and why. The ethical decision-making paradigms are:

Figure 19.1: Ethical Decision-making Paradigms

Ethical Decision-making Paradigms[7]	
Truth versus Loyalty	Disclosure versus Confidentiality
Justice versus Mercy	Fairness versus Compassion
Short-term versus Long-term	Immediate individual needs versus Conservation for future needs
Individual versus Community	Autonomy versus Collective rights of the larger community

f) Apply resolution principles: Ends-based, Rules-based, or Care-based —
Examine the dilemma using the three resolution principles:

   (i) ***Ends-based Principle*** — What is the end result of the action or
   decision made? Which choice would result in the greater good for the
   largest number of people?

   (ii) ***Rules-based Principle*** — What is your obligation here? If you have a
   duty to uphold medical confidentiality, then that is what you must do.

   (iii) ***Care-based Principle*** — This principle is based on the Golden Rule:
   "do unto others as you would have done unto you". In essence, show
   the level of compassion that you would like shown if the roles were
   reversed.

g) *Identify if a third option exists* — Is there another action or decision option
that could be adopted? If so, could it allow the players to reach that "win-win"
plateau that we all strive to attain?

h) *Decide* — Once all the options have been considered, it is time to decide. As
Egdar[8] notes, procrastination can be a decision — the decision to choose not
to decide. Usually, it is not a recommended resolution tactic.

i) *Evaluate the decision* — Looking back on actions taken or decisions made is
worthwhile. It serves to help prepare the Disability Case Manager for future
instances of ethical decision-making.

---

[7] P. Edgar, "Resolving Ethical Dilemmas: Applying the Institute for Global Ethics' Ethical
Fitness™ Model to Occupational and Environmental Health Practice Issues" (2002) 50:1
AAOHN Journal 40.

[8] *Ibid.*

Model for Ethical Decision-Making in a Professional Situation[9]

For health care and disability management professionals, ethical dilemmas abound. This is compounded by being in a position of trust: the person whom you have agreed to help trusts that you will act as their advocate and provide them reasonable guidance during a vulnerable period in their life. According to Parsons, two ethical guidelines for caregivers in a professional situation are:

- the needs of the client come first and foremost; and
- the practitioner must recognize his or her own needs and biases and avoid situations in which these might negatively impact client caregiving.

The steps that Parsons recommends for ethical decision-making are:

a) *Parameters of the situation* — What are the facts and issues in this situation and who are all the players?

b) *Ethical-legal issues* — Identify all the legal issues and then all the ethical ones. By separating them out, it helps to clarify the situation and what action to take.

c) *Would legal guidelines help* — Consult the applicable legal guidelines and determine if they would lead to the resolution of the issue.

d) *Stakeholder rights, responsibilities and welfare* — List the stakeholders, how they are involved, their rights, responsibilities and welfare.

e) *Alternate Decisions/Actions* — Develop a list of alternative decisions possible for each identified issue.

f) *Consequences* — Assess the consequences of making each decision. Evaluate the short-term, ongoing, and long-term consequences of each possible decision.

g) *Assessment* — Present any evidence of the likelihood that the various consequences or potential benefits may occur.

h) *Decision* — Make the decision and monitor the outcome.

Ethical Dilemma: Case Study

The following scenario is designed as an illustration of the above Model for Ethical Decision-making in a professional situation:

Hank is a long-term employee who for years has been "a thorn in management's side". Recently, as a result of a workplace incident in Area B, management took disciplinary action against two fellow employees. This exacerbated Hank's questioning of management's practices. He thinks employees and the union should be far more involved in investigating workplace

---

[9] R.D. Parsons, *The Ethics of Professional Practice* (Needham Heights, MA: Allyn & Bacon, 2001).

incidents. He questions whether management is using these two employees as "scapegoats" for a series of "management system failures". This dialogue along with all the "heated emotions" has gone on for about three months now.

Simultaneously, the area in which Hank works has undergone significant operational changes due to a major labour shortage. Rotation through all functions of the operation is now required. This is a significant change in this company given that many employees choose to work in either Area A or Area B.

Hank who is a qualified tradesperson has for years avoided working in Area B. Now, he is required to do so. Upon hearing of this operational change, Hank said he would not comply given the occurrence of the recent workplace incident in Area B. He claims Area B is unsafe. Management tried to reason with Hank, but he cursed and swore at the Section Manager and left in a "huff".

The next day, Hank called in "sick". The following day, he produced a medical note stating that he is "unfit to work for an undetermined period of time, pending further medical investigation".

Hank was referred to the company's external Disability Management Service Provider. This is a standard practice within this company. All the details of Hank's job (Job Demands Analysis), job performance, and the recent labour-management issues were relayed to them by the internal Disability Management Coordinator.

Upon further medical assessment of Hank's fitness to work, it was determined that Hank was indeed medically unfit to work and that he would require treatment and a lengthy recovery period.

Management questioned the above decision, believing that Hank is "bucking the system" because he does not want to work in Area B. They claim that one of Hank's coworkers just met him at the mall and that Hank told him that he was "unhappy with his current job, but at least will never have to work in Area B". They do not believe that there is anything wrong with Hank other than he does not want to comply with the new operational change. They feel he is "playing the system", and voice strong opposition to Hank being on short-term disability.

Hank's Section Manager and the Human Resources Director approach you, the Disability Management Coordinator. They again state their concerns and want to know what is medically wrong with Hank. They tell you that management has the right to information enabling them to manage the employee and the employment relationship. They also hint that you, being in a management role, are *"one of them"*, and that you can share what you know with them. As well, you have been work colleagues for about 20 years.

You have always had a good working relationship with both parties. You know that Hank can be a difficult person to deal with and that he is often very sarcastic. In fact, on a number of occasions, he has been impertinent to you for no apparent reason.

In discussing the current situation with the external Disability Management Service Provider, you inadvertently find out that Hank is experiencing a severe bout of mental illness compounded with a significant physically illness. This mental breakdown, although it has been coming on for a number of years, is now significant.

Using Parson's Model,

a) *Parameters of the situation* — The facts are that Hank is medically unfit to work and will be for some time to come. There are employee-management distrust and ill feelings. Hank does not want to work in Area B, stating he feels it is unsafe working there. Management and his co-workers, on the other hand, are adamant that Area B is a safe place to work. All the other workers have agreed to the new operational change – they realize Management had to make this move because of a significant labour shortage.

b) *Ethical-legal issues* — The legal issues are:

   • Hank is entitled to short-term disability;
   • Hank is entitled to medical privacy; and
   • Hank has the right to seek work accommodation if and when, he is deemed fit to work.

The ethical dilemma for the Disability Management Coordinator is:

   • Keep Hank's medical information confidential at the risk of losing face with the Section Manager and Human Resources Director;

OR

   • Divulge what you know about Hank's medical status and risk violating your Disability Management Coordinator's Code of Ethic and the applicable terms of the privacy legislation.

c) *Would legal guidelines help* — Upon review of the applicable legal guidelines, the Disability Management Coordinator determines that under the privacy and Duty to Accommodate legislation, it is illegal to disclose what has been learned about Hank's condition. Given Hank is on a medically-substantiated absence, he is eligible for benefit coverage with this company. Likewise, when and if requested, management will likely have to accommodate Hank as per the Canadian Human Rights duty to accommodate legislation.

d) *Stakeholder rights, responsibilities and welfare* — The stakeholders involved are:

   • Hank — A qualified tradesperson who is off on medically leave;
   • his Section Manager — The manager who Hank strongly dislikes and vice versa. He has a large operation to run and has a low tolerance for *"dissention in his ranks*;
   • the Human Resources Director — The support staff member for the Section (Areas A & B) who is charged with assisting the Section Manager to effectively manage employees and their benefits;

- co-workers — Hank's co-workers with whom he has worked for 20 years and who will now have to "pick up the slack" for Hank who is off ill;
- the Disability Management Coordinator — The individual whose role is to coordinate and manage disability situations within the company;
- the External Disability Management Service Provider — The agency contracted to adjudicate and case manage the company's disability claims; and
- the Union who has a legal responsibility to support Hank.

e) *Alternate Decisions/Actions* — The possible decisions are:

- #1 — Explain the privacy legislation, and advise the Section Manager and Human Resources Director that Hank is medically unfit to work and that he is obtaining the appropriate care;

   OR

- #2 — Explain the Duty to Accommodate legislation, and counsel the Section Manager and Human Resources Director that although Hank was insubordinate, right now, he is medically unfit to work and that he is in appropriate care; or

   OR

- #3 — Explain the Duty to Accommodate and privacy legislation, and counsel the Section Manager and Human Resources Director that although Hank was insubordinate, right now he is medically unfit to work and that he is in appropriate care; or

   OR

- #4 — Tell the Section Manager and Human Resources Director what you know about Hank's medical condition since this information is not documented in your information on Hank, and because you trust them to keep the information confidential. Likewise, it may help to quell some of the employee-employer tensions.

f) *Consequences* — Actions #1, #2, and #3 would all work, but #3 is probably the best option. Option #4 is unethical and illegal.

g) *Assessment* — Actions #1, #2, and #3 would all work, but #3 is probably the best option.

h) *Decision* — The decision is to select Action #3..

Although this scenario is fictitious, it is designed to demonstrate how the Disability Management Coordinator can objectively formulate an ethical decision.

DISABILITY MANAGEMENT STAKEHOLDERS: CONFLICTING GOALS

By Dianne Dyck

In any organization, the interests of the various players or stakeholders can be in opposition with each other. The area of disability management is no exception. To explain this issue, two case studies will be presented — one to demonstrate conflict at the individual level; another to illustrate conflict at a management level.

Case Study A — Goal Conflict at the Individual Level

Andrew worked for a large company that was nine months into a major project. Like Andrew, employees from throughout the organization were selected for this top priority project. The project was to last two years, involve intense periods of work, and require total employee dedication. The corporate goal was to have the desired product within two years.

The project leaders were challenged to motivate the team to work as a unit, dedicating 50 to 70 hours per week to a long-term task. For them, the goal was a successful project completed on time and on budget.

Unfortunately, Andrew became very ill and the heavy project demands were believed to be the prime cause. He had a young family and an active community life. The project's extreme time demands became too much and he was unable to cope. However, given that the project was designed to function within a strong team milieu, Andrew continued to struggle. At that point, he did not want to let his team members down and his short-term goal was to survive.

Eventually, the strain became too great and Andrew needed to seek professional help. His desire to be a "team-player", to "pull his weight", and to do a good job could no longer be achieved in this setting. He sought support and guidance from the Employee Assistance Program and occupational health professionals. Their focus centred on getting Andrew the appropriate medical treatment.

Andrew needed time off work to rest, recover, and re-evaluate his situation. The action plan was to put him on short-term disability until he recovered enough to be able to make a rational decision about his future. Family support was deemed critical to a successful recovery. For that reason, some of his family members were enlisted to be part of the case management and treatment processes. At that point, Andrew's wife's goal was to help her husband to regain his health, and be able to work towards putting their family life back together.

After a few weeks of intensive treatment, Andrew recovered. However, the issue of whether or not to return to the environment that contributed to his illness loomed. For career advancement, returning to the current project would have been a wise move. Andrew's support was needed for the project team. He was a key person and the team was missing his expertise and guidance. However, for his personal well-being, Andrew decided that he would be better off to return to his former job outside of the special project. He enjoyed his former job and he could work successfully within that environment.

As an added note, his co-workers were also individually concerned about their respective well-being. They did not know what was wrong with Andrew, and they were concerned that he may have a contagious condition that they would eventually experience. For them, two serious issues existed:

1. A valuable player had been lost to the team and his support was sorely missed.
2. Could they end up like Andrew?

The competing goals in this scenario were as follows (Figure 19.2):

Figure 19.2: Competing Stakeholder Goals and Conflicts

Stakeholder	Goal	Conflict
Company	To attain an important product within two years.	Andrew and his wife's goals and well-being/needs.
Project Leaders	To motivate and guide the team to complete the project as planned.	Corporate goal, team goals, and employee well-being/needs.
Employees	To function successfully within a team environment and do the job expected of them.	Corporate and Project Leader goals.
Co-workers (team)	To function cohesively and do the job expected of them.	Corporate goals, Project Leader goals, and individual goals.
Andrew	To function in a competent manner.	Corporate goals, Project Leader goals, team goals, personal goals, and his wife's goals.
Wife	To have a happy and healthy husband and family	Corporate goals, Project Leader goals, and team goals.

In summary, there can be a number of conflicts within an individual disability case that need to be recognized and managed.

Case Study B — Goal Conflict at the Management Level

Brenda was a long-time employee with a manufacturing firm. She had joined the company early in her career and had remained doing relatively the same job ever since. Her skill sets, although compatible with the original job placement, had not adapted to the radical technological advancements in her area. However, everybody liked working with Brenda.

Brenda's work group experienced significant change during a corporate restructuring. A new manager entered the scene, along with a number of new employees. Brenda, feeling quite threatened by all the changes and by the technical ability of the new people, became sullen and passively aggressive with everyone. This evoked a variety of responses from her co-workers; the older ones supported Brenda while newer employees were quite vocal in their belief that management needed to deal with her. The outcome was a divided, non-productive work group, and a disgruntled employee.

The new manager, being involved in a number of projects, viewed the issue as a "worker problem" and one that the employees would "sort out for themselves". He was quite surprised when the employees came to him requesting that he take immediate action.

After a number of months of group anarchy, Brenda became ill and went on short-term disability. She was clinically depressed — not sleeping, eating or able to concentrate. She came to the occupational health centre a distraught, angry, confused and tearful person. Employee Assistance Program counselling and a medical consultation were arranged.

It took a number of weeks before the root of Brenda's problem could be unearthed. In the meantime, the work group had moved on and was beginning to function as a team. The manager was pleased with the progress and felt that his "laissez-faire" approach had worked well. He also decided that having Brenda out of the group had a positive effect on the group dynamic. His goal was to keep things this way.

Senior management in this company upheld an early-return-to-work policy. So, in the normal course of case management, the occupational health nurse began to work with Brenda and the manager to prepare for a gradual re-entry to the workplace. However, resistance to the idea was encountered with each attempt to initiate the process, resulting in an employee who was even more hurt and confused. Her goal was to get back to "the good old days", and to the working arrangement she knew and enjoyed.

The occupational health nurse began to identify a number of significant barriers to an early return to work for Brenda. Quickly, it became apparent that senior management and line management goals were at odds. One supported early return-to-work actions, while the other was using the employee's absence as a means for dealing with an unpleasant workplace situation.

As time passed, Brenda recovered from her depression and was ready to return to work in a modified work capacity. However, with her manager unwilling to entertain the idea, progress in this direction was impossible.

Having identified the goal conflict, the occupational health nurse adopted a new approach. A meeting was arranged with senior management and the line manager regarding the situation at hand, along with health-related and management issues. The former was being addressed, but the latter issue needed attention.

The occupational health nurse, along with senior management, helped the line manager understand the impact of the management style that had been adopted. The group examined the workplace issues, and explored a variety of ways in which the problem could be resolved. Senior management did not relieve the line manager of his responsibilities; rather they offered guidance and support to address the situation through the company's human resource department.

This is an example of goal conflict at a management level. If unresolved, the absent employee would remain out of the workforce for a protracted period of time and at added cost to the organization.

Conclusion

Case management is essential to manage and resolve goal conflicts at the individual and management level. A highly recommended approach to resolving goal conflicts includes the following steps:

1. identify and understand the underlying issues;
2. hold a case conference with the key players;
3. identify and address the issues as a group;
4. recognize that "competing agendas" exist. Unless there is objective medical rationale supporting a particular agenda, it cannot influence the return-to-work planning;
5. seek feasible solutions to rectify the situation, and using the Disability Management principles, select a suitable approach;
6. implement the plan;
7. monitor the return-to-work plan;
8. evaluate the outcomes; and
9. communicate the outcomes to the interested parties.

SUMMARY

To reiterate, ethics is the science of morals, a system of principles and rules of conduct, the study of standards of right and wrong, or having to do with human character, conduct, moral duty, and obligations to the community. It is the moral reasoning that humans possess.

The ethical principles covered in this chapter provide us with a guide with which to weigh the risks and benefits with respect to individual health and welfare, and the development of policies and procedures to safeguard individual rights and protect health. In case management, evaluation and weighing of the ethics of a case must be done in an unemotional manner so that decision-making is rational and based on facts rather than the emotional issues attached to the decision at hand. In short, it is *"Doing the right thing, at the right time, for the right person, in the right way and knowing why it is the right thing, at the right time, for the right person, in the right way."*

CHAPTER REFERENCES

P. Edgar, "Resolving Ethical Dilemmas: Applying the Institute for Global Ethics' Ethical Fitness™ Model to Occupational and Environmental Health Practice Issues" (2002) 50:1 *AAOHN Journal* 40.

J. Hall, "Ethics and Case Management" (1999) 13:2 *The OEM Report* 13.

R.M. Kidder, *How Good People Make Tough Choices: Resolving the Dilemmas of Ethical Living* (New York, NY: Fireside Books, 1995).

B. Kirkpatrick, ed., *The Cassell Concise English Dictionary* (London, England: Cassell Publishers Ltd., 1989) *s.v.* "ethics".

R.D. Parsons, *The Ethics of Professional Practice* (Needham Heights, MA: Allyn & Bacon, 2001).

Chapter 20

Disability Management:
Legal Aspects

INTRODUCTION

Disability management is a management response to legislation which upholds that:

- disabled employees cannot be discriminated against on the basis of a physical or psychological disability (Canadian human rights legislation, *American Disabilities Act*);
- employers must provide work accommodation for workers recovering from an illness/injury (Workers' Compensation Acts, *Canada Labour Code*, Canadian human rights legislation, *American Disabilities Act*);
- workers must be accommodated up to the point of undue hardship (Canadian human rights legislation); and
- employee personal health information must be respected and kept secure and confidential (Workers' Compensation Acts, privacy legislation).

In this chapter, legislative changes and their impact on disability management efforts; the duty to accommodate; and confidentiality requirements will be discussed.

THE IMPACT OF EVER-CHANGING LEGISLATION ON DISABILITY MANAGEMENT EFFORTS

By Sharon L. Chadwick

All stakeholders in the disability management process must be aware of the relevant legislation that may impact on the disability management processes. Such legislation may include, but is not limited to, occupational health and safety, human rights, Workers' Compensation, employee and labour relations, employment standards, and the freedom of information and protection of privacy legislation. As interpretation and application of the different regulatory requirements is varied and complex, it is also recommended that employers developing Disability Management Programs obtain the advice of a legal consultant.

As legislation varies from province to province and from provincial to federal jurisdiction, it is imperative that stakeholders review the legislation that applies to their specific area. This is imperative now more than *ever before*, as review and revision of these laws occurs more frequently than may have been done in the past.

Workers' Compensation Legislation

Workers' Compensation Boards provide compensation benefits to workers who are injured or become ill through work. Canadian WCB legislation follows the Meredith principles which include: no-fault insurance, collective liability, independent administration, and exclusive jurisdiction. The system exists at arm's-length from the government and is shielded from political influence, allowing only limited powers to the Minister responsible.[1] Each province and territory in Canada has its own exclusive Workers' Compensation Board/Commission (WCB).

A number of Canadian Workers' Compensation Boards (Newfoundland, Manitoba, New Brunswick, Nova Scotia, Ontario, Prince Edward Island, Quebec, and the Yukon) have enacted legislation that outlines employer and worker obligations for return to work and re-employment of ill/injured employees. Details of the specific requirements of each province are outlined on the Association of Workers' Compensation Boards of Canada website under Rehabilitation and Return to Work.[2]

As the specific requirements of each jurisdiction vary and may change, it is most important the stakeholders access the current version of the applicable legislation and/or contact their Workers' Compensation Board.

Occupational Health and Safety Legislation

In Canada, each province has its own occupational health and safety legislation. Organizations under federal jurisdiction are under the *Canada Labour Code, Part II.* Although the specific Acts and regulations vary, the general principles remain the same: employers are responsible for maintaining the health and safety of workers at their work sites. Workers also have a responsibility to work safely and protect the health and safety of themselves, their coworkers, and the general public where applicable. It is imperative that occupational health and safety programs be linked to disability management processes, especially in the area of illness and injury prevention and health and safety hazards.

Areas generally covered in the occupational health and safety legislation include, but are not limited to:

- hazard identification and control;
- investigation and reporting of incidents;
- chemical hazards;
- physical hazards;

---

[1] Association of Workers' Compensation Boards of Canada. *History of Workers' Compensation,* available online at: <http://www.awcbc.org/en/historyofworkerscompensation.asp>.
[2] *Ibid.*

- biological hazards;
- noise;
- general work safety;
- radiation;
- ventilation;
- working alone;
- workplace violence;
- first aid; and
- emergency response.

Within the occupational health and safety legislation, there may be specific requirements for medical examinations and medical surveillance linked to specific hazards and work-related exposures. Requirements for the identification and elimination or control of hazards will be included. Controls include engineering controls; administrative controls, and personal protective equipment. As this legislation is reviewed and updated regularly, employers and occupational health and safety professionals must know the requirements under the current legislation. Legislation for all jurisdictions in Canada is available on the website.

Canadian Human Rights Legislation

Canadian human rights legislation has a major impact on the way employers treat workers, and in particular disability management processes. Although each province is covered by its own human rights legislation, and federal organizations are under federal human rights legislation, the human rights principles expressed in this legislation are fairly consistent.

Under the Canadian human rights legislation, mental and physical disabilities are defined as:

- **Mental disability** *means any mental disorder, developmental disorder or learning disorder, regardless of cause or duration.*[3]

- **Physical disability** *means any degree of physical disability, infirmity, malformation, or disfigurement that is caused by bodily injury, birth defect or illness.*[4]

This legislation does not normally consider temporary or transitory illness such as colds or flu as a physical disability. Having said that, **"perceived disability"** — a situation in which a person is seen as having a disability and is treated accordingly, is covered.[5]

---

[3] Alberta Human Rights and Citizenship Commission, *Obtaining and Responding to Medical Information in the Workplace* (January 2009) at 4, available online at: <http://www.alberta humanrights.ab.ca/publications/bulletins_sheets_booklets/bulletins/1409.asp>.
[4] *Ibid.*
[5] *Ibid.*

The application and interpretation of individual human rights cases is complex and varies depending on the individual circumstances of the case. All cases must be assessed on their own merit, and much of today's awareness and understanding of human rights issues is based on case law. Even so, there is a great deal of variability, and employers are advised to obtain legal counsel when setting up policies and procedures which may have human rights implications, or when assessing difficult cases.

The Canadian Human Rights Commission website[6] provides a section on jurisprudence which presents cases and decisions where the Commission has played a role and/or that established jurisprudence in the area of Canadian human rights.

Generally, the principles of Canadian human rights legislation in relation to disability management include the following:

A)   DISCRIMINATION

Human rights legislation prohibits discrimination in employment practices such as hiring or retaining employees. This applies to all grounds of discrimination covered under the human rights legislation for that jurisdiction which generally includes: race, colour, ancestry, place of origin, religious beliefs, gender, age, physical disability, mental disability, marital status, family status, source of income, and sexual orientation.

This impacts the employer for both pre-placement and return-to-work fitness requirements. Human rights legislation is based on the principle of individual assessment — persons should be evaluated on their *ability*.

The British Columbia Council of Human Rights advises employers to:

- concentrate on a person's capabilities and not disabilities;
- assess persons as individuals, not as members of a group;
- avoid making generalizations about disabilities;
- define specific employment needs according to business priorities;
- clearly state the essential components of the job; and
- establish reasonable standards for evaluating job performance.[7]

B)   DUTY TO ACCOMMODATE

The Supreme Court of Canada has ruled that an employer has a legal duty to take *reasonable* steps in policies or conditions of work, to accommodate an employee's individual needs. This duty applies to all grounds of discrimination.

---

6   Available online at: <http://www.chrc-ccdp.ca/>.
7   British Columbia Council of Human Rights, *Disability and the Human Rights Act* (Victoria, BC: British Columbia Ministry of Labour and Consumer Service, 1998).

However this legal duty does not apply if the only way to resolve the problem will cause the employer undue hardship.[8]

Employers are required to make reasonable accommodation efforts for persons with a physical or mental disability. Duty to accommodate is a tripartite effort with responsibility resting with:

- *The employer* — has the primary duty to originate and implement a solution as he or she is in the best position to assess how the employee can be accommodated without undue interference in the operation of the business.

- *The union* (if applicable) — has a joint responsibility to assist in accommodating disabled employees. Unions must cooperate in the search for and implementation of accommodations as well as considering modifications or waiver of collective agreement provisions if necessary for accommodations of a particular case.

- *The employee* — has a variety of obligations in the process of seeking and sustaining a workable solution to accommodating his or her disability. The employee has the duty to inform the employer of his or her need for accommodation and of the effectiveness of the measures taken to accommodate. The employee is also required to provide to the employer information regarding the expected return-to-work date and any limitations or restrictions. The employee has a duty to take reasonable steps to facilitate the implementation of proposed workplace accommodations.[9]

Employers and unions are required to accommodate employees with disabilities (both physical and mental) to the point of "undue hardship". This includes the return to work of ill or injured employees. Basically, the employer must be able to demonstrate that they have made reasonable attempts to accommodate the employee to the point of undue hardship.

The development of a comprehensive Disability Management Program with clear policies and procedures, as well as clearly defined roles and responsibilities, will ensure that the duty to accommodate is applied consistently for all employees, and will assist stakeholders in demonstrating that appropriate steps have been taken to accommodate disabled employees.

---

[8] Alberta Human Rights and Citizenship Commission, *Employment: Duty to Accommodate Information Sheet* (March 2007), available online at: <http://www.albertahumanrights.ab.ca/publications/bulletins_sheets_booklets/459.asp>.

[9] Centre for Labour-Management Development, "Accommodation Guidelines" (Presented at the Illness and Disability: Claims in the Unionized Workplace Conference, Edmonton, AB, February 1999) [unpublished] at 69.

According to the Centre for Labour-Management Development outlines:

> Where the disability prevents the employee from performing some or all of the functions of a particular position, possible accommodations may include the provision of sedentary, light or modified duties, elimination of physically difficult or hazardous duties, modification of the work environment in a manner which permits the employee to continue to carry out his or her duties, alteration of shift schedules or hours of work, etc.
>
> While the nature of the employment may affect the content of the duty in a particular case, an employer is not relieved of its duty to accommodate simply because the disabled employee is a temporary employee.[10]

C)   UNDUE HARDSHIP

Undue hardship occurs if accommodation would create onerous conditions for an employer such as intolerable financial costs or serious disruption to business. The exact interpretation and determination of "undue hardship" will depend on the individual circumstances of the case. Generally, the concept will include considerations of such factors as:

- financial cost;
- size and resources of the employer or service provider;
- disruption of operations;
- morale problems of other employees brought about by these accommodations;
- substantial interference with the rights of other individuals or groups;
- interchangeability of the workforce and facilities; and
- health and safety concerns.[11]

Regarding safety concerns, the seriousness of risk is assessed considering four factors:

- *The nature of the risk* — What could happen that would be harmful?
- *The severity of the risk* — How serious would the harm be if it occurred?
- *The probability of the risk* — How likely is it that the potential harm will actually occur? Is it a real risk, or merely hypothetical or speculative?
- *The scope of the risk* — Who will be affected by an event if it occurs?[12]

---

[10]   *Ibid.*, at 59.

[11]   *Ibid.*, at 73.

[12]   L. McDowell, *Human Rights in the Workplace: A Practical Guide* (Toronto: Carswell, 1998) at 7-43.

D) BONA FIDE OCCUPATIONAL REQUIREMENTS

The law recognizes that, in certain circumstances, a limitation on individual rights may be reasonable and justifiable. Discrimination or exclusion may be allowed if an employer can show that a discriminatory standard, policy, or rule is a necessary requirement of a job. The onus is on the employer to show that it would be impossible to accommodate the employee without undue hardship.

The *Meiorin* test,[13] based on a 1999 Supreme Court of Canada decision, sets out an analysis to assist employers in determining if particular occupational requirements are reasonable and justifiable The employer must prove that, on a balance of probabilities, the standard:

- was adopted for a purpose that is rationally connected to job performance;
- was adopted in an honest and good faith belief that the standard is necessary for the fulfillment of that legitimate purpose;
- is reasonably necessary to accomplish that legitimate purpose. This requires the employer to demonstrate that it is impossible to accommodate the employee without the employer suffering undue hardship.

The test requires employers to accommodate or consider the capabilities of different members of society before adopting a *bona fide* occupational requirement.[14]

Unions and employees have responsibilities as well. For example, under Alberta human rights legislation unions or union contracts cannot prohibit an accommodation that is considered available, even if that accommodation contravenes a collective bargaining agreement. As well, the employee must consider an accommodation that is deemed reasonable.[15]

The development of a comprehensive Disability Management Program with clear policies and procedures, as well as clearly defined roles and responsibilities, will ensure that the duty to accommodate is applied consistently for all employees, and will assist stakeholders in demonstrating that appropriate steps have been taken to accommodate disabled employees.

---

[13] Canadian Human Rights Commission, *Bona Fide Occupational Requirements and Bona Fide Justifications under the Canadian Human Rights Act: The Implications of Meiorin and Gismer* (March 2007), available online at: <http://www.chrc-ccdp.ca/publications/alphabetical _alphabetique-en.asp>; and Alberta Human Rights and Citizenship Commission, *Employment: Duty to Accommodate Interpretive Bulletin* (May 2002), available online at: <http://www. albertahumanrights.ab.ca/publications/bulletins_sheets_booklets/bulletins/770.asp>.

[14] For more information on the duty to accommodate and its application, refer to *Duty to Accommodate — A PSAC Guide for Local Representatives* (2009 revision), available online at: <http://www.psac.com/what/humanrights/duty_to_accommodate-e.shtml>.

[15] Alberta Human Rights and Citizenship Commission, *Employment: Duty to Accommodate Interpretive Bulletin* (May 2002), available online at: <http://www.albertahumanrights.ab.ca/ publications/bulletins_sheets_booklets/bulletins/770.asp>.

Canadian Human Rights and Substance Abuse Policies

Employers who are considering the development and implementation of workplace substance abuse policies and procedures should be aware of the human rights implications related to these programs. Alcohol and drug addictions are generally accepted as disabilities and employers have a duty to accommodate, the same as they would do for any other physical or mental disability. Employers should reference the human rights legislation and positions in their jurisdictions to access the most current information.

The issue of substance abuse testing remains controversial. In Canada, there is no specific legislation related to drug and alcohol testing in the workplace, and these cases are generally addressed under human rights legislation. Employers considering the implementation of these programs must ensure that they research this area and work closely with legal counsel. It is imperative that these programs are not discriminatory. The need for such a program should be thoroughly researched based on the specific requirements of the company and safety risks involved. Disability management professionals should monitor current court decisions and the position of the human rights authorities for their jurisdiction.

PRIVACY LEGISLATION[16]

By Kristine Robidoux

As with Occupational Health & Safety Acts and human rights legislation, privacy legislation has both provincial and federal statutes that govern the collection, use, and disclosure of personal information. Again, it is important to be familiar with the legislation in the relevant jurisdiction and to know what bodies or organizations are covered under this legislation.

Privacy Legislation

There are a number of pieces of privacy legislation about which disability management professionals/practitioners need to have a working knowledge, namely:

- *Freedom of Information and Protection of Privacy Legislation (FOIP)*

    Public sector bodies are generally bound by provincial Freedom of Information and Protection of Privacy legislation (FOIP). This type of legislation is generally intended to increase government accountability by ensuring that individuals have rights of access to information in the custody or under the control of government or public bodies. FOIP legislation has been developed to grant access to public documents that may be of interest

---

[16]   K. Robidoux, LL.B., Principal, ComplianceWorks (Calgary, AB, November 2005).

to specific groups or individuals, and to protect the privacy and limit the use of individual personal information by public bodies, including medical information.

- ***Personal Information Protection and Electronic Documents Act (PIPEDA)***

In the private sector, there are different statutes that govern British Columbia, Alberta, and Quebec. All have private sector privacy legislation that balance the rights of individuals and employees of organizations to have their personal information protected while ensuring that the needs of private sector organizations to collect, use, and disclose personal information for business purposes are reasonable. Federally-regulated works, undertakings and businesses, as well as private-sector businesses that are outside of British Columbia, Alberta or Quebec, are all subject to the federal statute, the *Personal Information Protection and Electronic Documents Act.*[17] Notably, the federal statute does not apply to the personal information of employees of private sector businesses in jurisdictions without provincial private sector privacy laws, but does apply to employees of federal works, undertakings, or businesses.

This analysis is critical in order to determine whether privacy law applies to the personal information relating to the disability of the employee in question, and if so, which statute in particular. It can be a tricky determination to make.

- ***Personal Information Protection Acts*[18] *(PIPA)***

In 2004, Alberta and British Columbia each enacted largely similar Personal Information Protection Acts[19] ("PIPA"). These two statutes provide that private sector organizations in those provinces may only collect, use and disclose the personal information of individuals and employees for purposes that are reasonable, and to the extent that is reasonable to carry out the purposes. An important exclusion contained in the PIPA statutes allows organizations to collect, use and disclose "personal employee information" without the consent of the individual in some cases: if the information is reasonably required by an organization and is collected, used or disclosed solely for the purpose of establishing, managing or terminating the employment relationship. This exclusion can be important as an organization determines its conduct and strategy in respect to an injured worker.

---

[17] S.C. 2000, c. 5.
[18] S.A. 2003, c. P-6.5 (Alberta); and S.B.C. 2003, c. 63 (British Columbia).
[19] *Ibid.*

As discussed at length in previous chapters of this book, the assurance of confidentiality of medical information is essential in performing effective disability management processes, especially in the area of case management. Health care professionals are bound by professional ethics to maintain confidentiality, but this can be a challenge in the workplace setting, and the health care professional must be extremely stringent in maintaining confidentiality. These obligations are also reiterated in the privacy laws: personal information *must* be safeguarded with security that is appropriate for the relative sensitivity of the information. It must be protected against such risks as unauthorized access, collection, use, disclosure, copying, modification, disposal, or destruction. All stakeholders in the disability management process should be aware of privacy legislation in their jurisdiction and the impact this has on the processes of their programs.

Conclusion

It is important to stress that disability management processes are impacted by a variety of pieces of legislation. This legislation tends to vary from province to province, and from provincial to federal jurisdiction. The most important thing to note is that stakeholders in disability management *must* be:

• aware of the current legislation in their locale; and
• aware that specific acts and regulations are constantly changing and that they should obtain legal counsel to ensure they have the most current and up-to-date case law information when setting up programs or when dealing with specific human rights cases.

Remember — *Ignorance of the law is never a valid excuse!*

PRIVACY LEGISLATION: THE APPLICATION

By Kristine Robidoux and Dianne Dyck

Personal Information Protection and Electronic Documents Act

Canada's federal private sector privacy legislation, the *Personal Information Protection and Electronic Documents Act*[20] (PIPEDA), came into effect on January 1, 2004. This statute governs the collection, use and disclosure of personal information by federal works, undertakings and businesses (such as the federally-regulated banks, telecommunications, airlines, *etc.*), as well as by private sector businesses in provinces of Canada that have not enacted their own legislation that is substantially similar to PIPEDA. Therefore, any province without its own privacy legislation must follow the federal legislation.

---

[20]   S.C. 2000, c. 5.

Personal Information Protection Act

British Columbia, Alberta, and Quebec have enacted provincial private sector privacy legislation that governs the treatment of personal information of individuals and employees of private sector organizations in those provinces. Specifically in British Columbia and Alberta, the *Personal Information Protection Act*[21] (PIPA) provides the requirements for how organizations may collect, use, disclose and protect personal information, which may include personal health information of individuals as well as company employees. Under PIPA, individuals and employees have the right to:

- know why personal information is being collected, used or disclosed;
- expect the organization to collect, use or disclose personal information in a reasonable and appropriate manner;
- know who in the organization is accountable for the organization's compliance with privacy laws and practices;
- expect the organization to use the appropriate security measures to protect the information;
- expect that the information is accurate and complete;
- request corrections if required;
- complain to the organization about how it collects, uses or discloses personal information;
- appeal to the Privacy Commissioner if a dispute over personal health information cannot be resolved using the above measures; and
- access their personal information that is in the custody or under the control of the organization, unless one or more of the exceptions under PIPA apply.

In terms of the field of Disability Management, this legislation:

- requires employers to advise employees about the nature of personal information collected, used and disclosed, along with why, how and when, unless one of the enumerated exceptions applies;
- restricts the amount of personal information that may be collected;
- requires employee consent for the collection, use and disclosure of personal information, unless the personal information is reasonably required by the organization and is collected, used or disclosed solely for the purposes of establishing, managing or terminating the employment relationship;
- limits the free flow of employee personal health information between health care providers and the employers;
- reaffirms the need for "information firewalls" between occupational health personnel and the workplace;
- obligates Disability Management Coordinators to ensure that the employee personal information is accurate and complete; and

---

[21] S.A. 2003, c. P-6.5 (Alberta); and S.B.C. 2003, c. 63 (British Columbia).

- requires employers to ensure that employee personal information is collected, used, retained, disclosed and destroyed in an appropriate manner (for more information refer to the Disability Management Standard of Practice — Confidentiality found in Chapter 11, "Prevention of Workplace Illness and Injury").

Management of Employee Personal Health Information

REQUEST FOR EMPLOYEE PERSONAL INFORMATION

Company representatives who try to obtain employee personal health information without informed consent from the employee act in violation of privacy legislation if it is found that the information was not reasonably required by the organization and collected solely for the purposes of establishing, managing, or terminating the employment relationship. If the personal information does not meet this definition, then the consent of the employee is required.

Since the privacy laws were enacted (in Alberta, the *Health Information Act*[22] in 1998 and the *Personal Information Protection Act* in 2004), employer rights to collect employee personal health information have clearly changed. Before collecting personal information, employers should ask:

- "Is this information reasonably required?"
- "Is it fair?"
- "What will the information be used for?"
- "Is there heightened security around this information?"
- "Is there informed consent?"

To complicate matters, in certain circumstances it may not be proper to ask for consent from an employee to collect, use or disclose his or her personal information. For example, if the company wants to access information that would disclose the presence of a mental health condition, the privacy rights that the employee is being asked to waive are highly protected. The relationship that exists between a manager and employee is a power relationship that can be heavily weighted in favour of the manager. It cannot be assumed that the employee knows his or her rights in this respect. If there was any coercion or duress, or if the impression was given that the employee has no choice but to consent or else face adverse employment action, asking for employee consent may be contrary to the law. Consent must be informed and may not be obtained by providing false or misleading information about the proposed collection, or by using deceptive or unlawful practices.

---

[22]   R.S.A. 2000, c. H-5.

There is a heightened security of personal health information when dealing with a mental health condition versus a physical one. There is far less social stigma attached to a fractured hip than to mental illness. As a result, more vigilance is required to protect this information.

WHAT PERSONAL HEALTH INFORMATION CAN THE EMPLOYER REQUEST?

When requesting medical information related to an employee medical absence, the employer must ensure that the requested information is relevant to the management of the specific disability claim, and/or the operation of the workplace. With most disability situations, the employer requests the following information:

- if the medical absence is work- or non-work-related;
- verification of the presence of a medical disability;
- participation in and compliance with a recommended treatment plan;
- anticipated duration of the medical absence; and
- whether or not work accommodation is warranted.

With a lengthy medical absence, more information may be sought to maintain the employee-employer relationship. For example, continued fitness to work and treatment participation and compliance may be required to continue disability benefits. However, asking about the employee's medical diagnosis or past medical history is generally not acceptable.

Once the employee is fit to return to work in some capacity, the employer may then seek additional information on:

- the employee's fitness to work;
- the employee's work capabilities and limitations;
- the expected duration of the work accommodation; and
- whether or not the employee is undergoing treatment or taking any medication that may affect his or her ability to perform the assigned work duties.

The employer does not have the right to ask all these questions in all situations. Rather, information requests must to be situation-specific. That is, the employer can only seek the information necessary to make business decisions about providing disability leave, accommodating the employee, or assessing if an employee can return to work.

Upon receipt of the employee medical information, the employer may deem the information received to be inadequate. Before taking any action, the employer should review all the information received and identify exactly what additional information is required and why. Only then should the employer proceed by:

- informing the employee in writing, what additional information is needed and why;

- being very clear as to the information needed and in what format it is required;
- reminding the employee that all medical information is held secure and confidential;
- remaining open to any concerns that the employee might have about providing additional information; and
- trying to resolve any of the identified concerns.

As to "who pays" for the additional information requested, the employer pays unless there is a valid case for "undue financial hardship".

Should the employee refuse to provide additional information, and the employer can demonstrate a valid need for the requested information, then a work accommodation can be denied.

If more information is still required to assess the employee's situation, aggressive or more intrusive methods such as an independent medical examination or functional capacity examination may be appropriate. But this is typically a "last ditch" course of action.

The employer **should not**:

- contact the employee's physician by telephone; rather with the employee's consent, the employer should put all requests to the physician in writing;
- request non-employment-related medical information;
- demand a definitive opinion of the employee's continued fitness to work post-recovery from an illness/injury;
- see a medical diagnosis; and /or
- terminate the employee before attempting to accommodate the employee's situation to the point of undue hardship.

PROTECTION OF EMPLOYEE HEALTH INFORMATION

Companies either offer their disability management services "inhouse" or contract the service (external service provision). In the course of their work, the Occupational Health professionals or Disability Management Coordinators (internal or external to the company) have greater access to employee personal health information than does the rest of the company. According to the Canadian human rights legislation:

> Only those designated people receive the information from the employee's doctor and let the employee's supervisor know how long the employee will be absent, or what specific return to work accommodation measures are reasonable.[23]

---

[23]   Alberta Human Rights and Citizenship Commission, *Obtaining and Responding to Medical Information in the Workplace* (January 2009) at 6, available online at: <http://www.alberta humanrights.ab.ca/publications/bulletins_sheets_booklets/bulletins/1409.asp>.

To uphold the privacy and confidentiality of this information, "firewalls" must be in place (Figure 20.1). In essence, there are four privacy firewalls:

• Between the employee, health care providers and the Disability Management Service Provider and the internal employer representatives (the Disability Management Coordinators): the information that can be disclosed is limited to benefit eligibility, fitness to work (FTW), absence duration and work limitations.

• Between the Disability Management Coordinators and Human Resource Managers: there is a smaller amount of information disclosed and it is limited to fitness to work initially, duration of absence (in some instances) and anticipated work limitations with recovery.

• Between the Human Resource Managers and the relevant Operational managers: the disclosed information centres on the modified work details and work limitations.

• Between the relevant Operational manager and the rest of the company: the disclosed information is scaled down to a need-to-know basis.

Figure 20.1: Protection of Employee Health Information

Protection of Employee Health Information

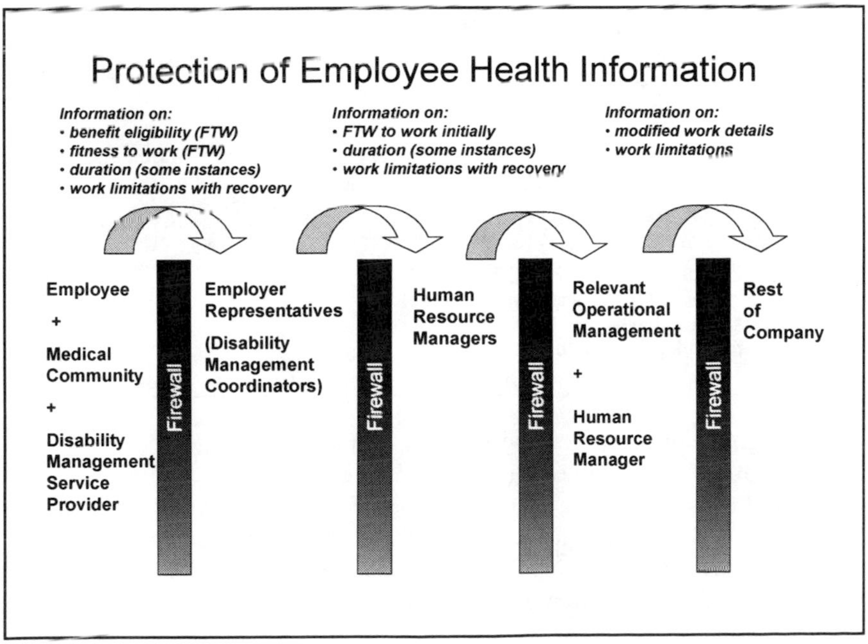

DISCLOSURE OF EMPLOYEE HEALTH INFORMATION

The level of detail that Disability Management Coordinators are allowed to disclose to company managers is limited (Figure 20.2). In the acute phase of the illness/injury absence, only medical information exists, which cannot be provided to company representatives without the employee's informed consent. As a result, the information released is limited to the employee being unfit to work, on a suitable treatment regimen and the nature of the health condition (work-related or non-work-related). This information supports the validity of the claim. In the recovery phase, details on work restrictions can be provided so that return-to-work plans can be made.

Figure 20.2: Stages for the Release of Personal Health Information

Stages for Release of Personal Health Information

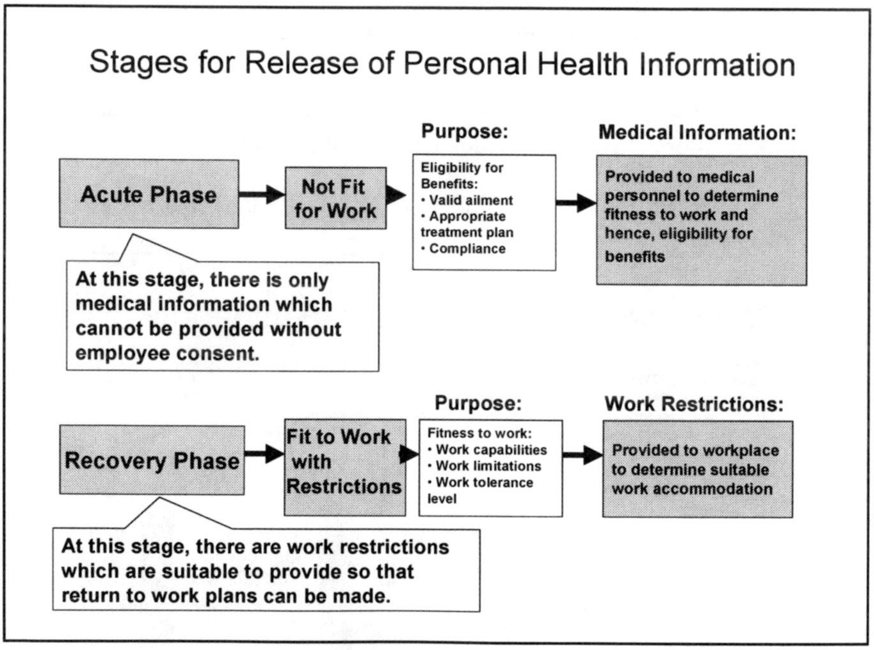

Although employers are advised not to make unnecessary informational demands about the disabled employee and the disability situation,[24] often Disability Management Coordinators are pressured to provide more information. When this occurs, ask the question: "Is this information *reasonably required* for the sole purpose of maintaining the employment relationship?" If an employee is on short-term disability coverage and eligible for benefit coverage as established

---

[24]   *Ibid.*

by the Disability Management Service Provider, asking for specifics about the employee's health condition could be a violation of privacy legislation.

If the Operation Manager claims that the information is *reasonably required* because he or she wants to know what area of practice the physician is engaged in, this may also be an unlawful collection of personal information. Where the nature of the medical practice would, to a reasonable person, reveal the nature of the ailment, the manager would be able to indirectly access information that he or she could not otherwise directly access.

If it is deemed *reasonably required* because the Operational Manager is seeking to take employment action, other aspects of employment law come into play. Employment action cannot generally be taken if the employee is lawfully on medical leave.

The Occupational Health professionals or Disability Management Coordinators are permitted to access some personal health information about the employee's condition in order to assess whether or not the external Disability Management Service Provider is fulfilling its contractual commitments to the company, or to ascertain the company's next steps in the work accommodation and reintegration process. Companies can challenge the external Disability Management Service Provider's findings by requesting an independent medical evaluation (IME). In such instances, company representatives are generally not entitled to medical reports, but rather to knowledge of the general nature of the employee's ailment.

Although privacy legislation is relatively new, recent court decisions are fairly clear that employers are required to ensure that:

- Medical information collected to administer an employee benefit plan is legitimately required.
- The medical information submitted by the employee is held in strictest confidence by qualified medical practitioners (PIPEDA, Case Summary #226).[25]
- Appropriate security safeguards are in place to protect sensitive personal medical information from unauthorized access (PIPEDA, Case Summary #226).
- Employees are aware as to how to submit medical information so that it goes to a qualified medical professional (PIPEDA, Case Summary #226).
- Employee requests to review their personal health information are honoured within 30 days of receipt of the written request (PIPEDA, Case Summary #284);[26] Order P2008-001.[27]

---

[25] Case Summary 226 is available on the website of the Privacy Commissioner of Canada: available online at: <http://www.priv.gc.ca/cf-dc/2003/index2-3_e.cfm?piyear=2003#contenttop>.

[26] Case Summary 284 is available on the website of the Privacy Commissioner of Canada: available online at: <http://www.priv.gc.ca/cf-dc/2004/index2-4_e.cfm?piyear=2004#contenttop>.

[27] Case Summary, Order P2008-001, Case File Number P0423, February 29, 2008, is available online at: <http://www.oipc.ab.ca/ims/client/upload/P2008-001.pdf>.

RESPONSIBLE MANAGEMENT OF EMPLOYEE MEDICAL INFORMATION

When a disability occurs, the employee-employer employment relationship changes. Both parties become vulnerable and must establish a "new employment relationship". As such, employers are advised to address this potential situation "*a priori*" by developing a Disability Management Program which:

- demonstrates respect and compassion for the ill/injured employee;
- clearly explains how medical conditions and return-to-work issues will be managed;
- supports acceptance of employees identifying health conditions before a work absence by the work culture;
- supports the employee before, during and after an illness/injury absence;
- features disability management policies, standards, and procedures that ensure consistency of practice as well as flexibility in the medical management of workplace disabilities;
- provides disability management expertise and resources;
- includes supportive benefits and employee programs;
- supports early intervention;
- features open and honest communication between all parties;
- offers gradual return to work opportunities (work accommodation);
- addresses individual employee needs during the absence, work accommodation and upon return to full-time work;
- provides tools such as medical forms for the collection and management of employee medical information;
- includes security and confidentiality of employee personal health information; and
- includes responsible management of disability data.

This type of management approach will address the employer's duty to accommodate obligations as well as eliminate many potential labour and/or legal pitfalls.

WORK ACCOMMODATION: THE APPLICATION

By Dianne Dyck

Legally defined, "work accommodation" in terms of employee disability, is *"making changes to certain rules, standards, policies, work cultures, and physical environment to ensure that they do not have a negative effect on an employee because of the employee's mental or physical disability, religion, gender or any other protected ground".*[28]

---

[28] Alberta Human Rights and Citizenship Commission, Employment: *Duty to Accommodate Interpretative Bulletin* (May 2002), available online at: <http://www.albertahumanrights.ab.ca/publications/bulletins_sheets_booklets/bulletins/770.asp>.

Operationally defined, **work accommodation** means a work opportunity offered to the recovering employee that allows for re-entry and participation in the workplace, and which is aligned with the employee's rehabilitation goals and the employer's business needs. It involves:

1. consideration of ways in which the employee's job can be modified;
2. consideration of other available appropriate work within the company;
3. the ability to offer rehabilitation and training programs if doing so will enhance the employee's ability for successful re-entry within a reasonable time frame; and
4. the employer taking a lead role in this process.

The duty to accommodate does not mean that companies have to create jobs (*McAlpine v. Econotech Services Ltd.*),[29] or to tolerate excessive innocent absenteeism (*Desormeaux v. Ottawa-Carleton Regional Transit Commission*),[30] or to maintain the employment relationship at any cost (*Coulter v. Purolator Courier Ltd.*[31]).[32] As well, the employer is not expected to instantly provide a perfect accommodation;[33] rather a reasonable accommodation is required. That is, an accommodation that meets the employee's capabilities, work limitations and abilities to perform the job safely.

The most effective work accommodation occurs when management, labour and the employee work collaboratively to meet their respective and collective needs. Work accommodation is not merely a "nice to do" activity; rather, it is the law!

Work Accommodation: Who is Responsible?

The process of determining reasonable and appropriate accommodation is a shared responsibility. The employer, union, and employee each have key roles to play.

A)   THE EMPLOYEE

The employee is responsible for letting the employer know that he or she is fit for some level of work and is seeking work accommodation. The employee must provide the employer with information such as:

- why the accommodation is needed (*e.g.,* due to a disability);

---

[29] [2004] B.C.J. No. 389, 2004 BCCA 111, 32 C.C.E.L. (3d) 165 (B.C.C.A.).

[30] [2004] F.C.J. No. 2172, 2004 FC 1778 (F.C.), revd [2005] F.C.J. No. 1647, 2005 FCA 311 (F.C.A.), leave to appeal refused [2005] S.C.C.A. No. 534 (S.C.C.).

[31] [2004] C.H.R.D. No. 25, 2004 CHRT 37 (C.H.R.T.).

[32] D. Cory, "Duty to Accommodate — Update (2005)" (Presented to the 23rd Annual Labour Arbitration Policy Conference, June 9, 2005, Toronto, ON [unpublished].

[33] *Callan v. Suncor*, [2006] A.J. No. 30, 2006 ABCA 15 (Alta. C.A.).

- documented medical support for the modified work along with work limitations;
- suggested work accommodation measures; and
- anticipated work accommodation duration.[34]

This information is required so that the employer can assign work accommodation duties that are appropriate to the employee's capabilities and work limitations. Failure to provide the needed information could result in the employer having to ask the employee to remain off work. Should the employee choose to not comply with the employer's informational requests, the courts may view this action negatively should legal action be pursued by either party.

Once the employee is offered work that is appropriate to the identified work limitations, he or she must accept that work and endeavour to make it successful. The employee cannot refuse a reasonable accommodation just because it is not what he or she wants to do.

During the work accommodation period, the employee is obligated to provide the employer with feedback on the suitability of the work accommodation as well as his or her tolerance for the work activities and ongoing fitness to work. So as the employee recovers, the graduated return to work activities (work accommodation) should change accordingly.

B)   THE EMPLOYER

The employer is obliged and advised to:

- ask for relevant information about the employee's medical condition and fitness to work. This means getting the appropriate consents to release medical information, respecting the privacy of the employee's medical information and complying with the applicable privacy legislation;[35]
- provide the employee's attending physician(s) with a Job Demands Analysis of the employee's job or a reasonable facsimile;
- respect the dignity and privacy of the employee;
- determine if suitable work accommodations exist;
- obtain, if required, expert advice on the employee's fitness to work;[36]
- be flexible and creative in regards to work accommodation options;[37]
- be willing to take substantial and meaningful work accommodation efforts;[38]
- discuss accommodation options with the employee and union if applicable;[39]

---

[34] Alberta Human Rights and Citizenship Commission, *Obtaining and Responding to Medical Information in the Workplace* (January 2009), available online at: <http://www.alberta humanrights.ab.ca/publications/bulletins_sheets_booklets/bulletins/1409.asp>.
[35] *Ibid.*
[36] *Ibid.*
[37] *Ibid.*
[38] *Ibid.*
[39] *Ibid.*

- respond to the employee's request for work accommodation within a reasonable time frame;
- formally contract with the employee on the selected work accommodation;[40]
- maintain the employee at the same rate of pay unless the work is substantially changed, or if the accommodation poses the employer undue financial hardships;[41]
- document the accommodation process and actions taken;
- protect the employee's right to privacy;
- assume all the related costs;
- monitor the suitability of the work accommodation opportunity, making changes as required; and
- should an offer of work accommodation be deemed impossible, the employer is obligated to explain to the employee why and be prepared to substantiate the decision.[42]

c)   THE UNION

In terms of the union, the duty to accommodate legislation takes precedence over any collective agreement clause that would appear to be discriminatory. The union must be supportive of the work accommodation efforts and facilitate the process up to the point of undue hardship. Hence the union has an equal responsibility to find and support reasonable work accommodation, even if it means crossing union jurisdictions.

By working collaboratively, the employer, employee, and union can effect a successful work accommodation and return to work.

Additional Considerations

Given the complexity of disability situations and the various organizational systems in which they occur, employers/employees/unions face a number of challenges, some of which have been addressed under case law. The following are some important considerations of which disability management professionals/practitioners should be aware:

- *How often can the employer contact the absent employee?*

This is a balance of "the need to obtain information to manage a disability claim" versus "harassment of the employee". The correct answer often depends greatly on the strength of the employee's occupational bond and the level of trust and respect between the employer-employee-union.

---

[40]   *Ibid.*
[41]   *Ibid.*
[42]   *Ibid.*

Many organizations/companies have policies and procedures in place that clearly stipulate what steps the employee must take at the onset of a medical absence, *e.g.,* when to report the work absence; what forms to submit within what timeframes; when and to whom to submit the work absence forms; and/or how the disability management processes operate. This approach helps greatly.

Although early intervention and open communication between all parties is strongly recommended, the employer must take care to not seek so much information that the employee feels harassed.

- *Use of independent medical examinations or functional capacity evaluations*

With prolonged medical absences, or complex situations, the determination of the employee's fitness to work may require detailed information or clarification of conflicting medical opinions. The judicious use of independent medical examinations and functional capacity evaluations can prove valuable. Ideally, the employee and employer agree upon the selected independent examiner and proceed with the examination at the employer's cost. The resulting report is then sent to medical personnel for interpretation and explanation in terms of the employee's fitness to work.

- *Dismissal/Terminations*

When terminating or laying off an employee who is on a medical absence or who has recently returned from a medical absence, the employer must ensure that the grounds for termination are unrelated to a disability. This means having solid performance, behavioural, or business grounds for dismissal/termination. This is definitely an instance when legal counsel should be obtained.

- *Conflicting medical information*

It is common for employers to receive conflicting medical opinions. The "rule of thumb" is that the opinion of a medical specialist takes precedence over that of the general medical practitioner, or some other health care provider.[43] If two specialists of equal medical status provide conflicting opinions, then, the employer is advised to seek the opinion of a third equally qualified specialist to arrive at a suitable answer.

- *Employee misconduct*

Workplace misconduct is typically addressed through disciplinary action. However, if in the course of this management approach, a medical disability is identified, then the employer must review the misconduct situation from the

---

[43]   *United Steelworkers of America, Local 5885 v. Sealy Canada Ltd. (Bender Grievance)*, [2006] A.G.A.A. No. 8.

perspective of an individual experiencing a mental or physical disorder. The duty to accommodate the employee must be explored.[44]

• *Management of questionable work absences*

As part of the management of questionable work absences, the employer often asks the employee to provide documented medical support for those work absences. Should the employee refuse to provide the requested information, then it is best for the employer, employee, and union representative to meet and discuss how to address this identified work issue. By respectfully requesting the information directly from the employee and explaining the importance of the requested information, the employer is often able to initiate a constructive intervention. This approach is discussed in Chapter 9, "Workplace Attendance Support and Assistance".

It is important for the employer to recognize that a refusal to provide medical information does not negate a valid underlying disability. For example, the social stigma associated with a mental disability or the denial of addictions can be the underlying reason for the refusal to provide the employer with medical substantiation for the work absences.

Should the employee remain steadfast about not providing any medical information, the employer can ask the employee to remain off work until such time as the requested information is submitted. Since this step can be the beginning of a grievance or human rights suit, legal counsel is strongly advised and the employer should make very sure that the requested information is indeed required.

Responsible Disability Management

Interestingly, many employers, for business reasons, strongly encourage ill/injured employees to return to work as soon as possible. This situation is somewhat diametrically opposed to the situations typically addressed by human rights legislation, where the employee wants to return to work and the employer is hesitant. However, in their exuberance to intervene early and to lessen the human and financial costs of disability claims, employers must be careful not "*to do more harm than good*".

The basic tenant of disability management is to return the employee in a safe and timely manner to goal-oriented work focused on employee rehabilitation and optimal recovery. The key aspect is that this activity occurs when the employee is medically fit and able to safely perform the assigned tasks. Rushing an employee back to work for the "wrong reasons" can cause an exacerbation of the employee's health condition and potentially, prolong the medical absence. Thus the recommended approach is for the employer to practice *responsible disability management*.

---

[44] *Ibid.*

Responsible disability management means balancing many factors — the employee's needs and capabilities, and the associated legal requirements against the organization's/company's management practices, work climate, and business requirements (Figure 20.3).

Figure 20.3: Responsible Disability Management

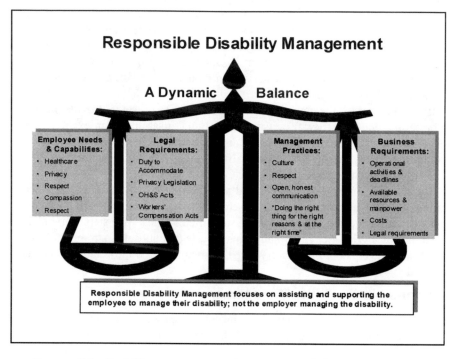

Responsible disability management focuses on assisting and supporting the disabled employee to manage his or her disability condition and situation; not on the employer's management of the disability. It requires the use of strong people skills, respect for the employee, open, honest communication, and treating the employee with compassion. This caring, human approach goes a long way to preventing legal action and suits. The outcome is stakeholder trust; not a lawsuit.

SUMMARY

Disability management is based on principles — it is not on a "recipe book of actions". Each disability situation and claim must be individually dealt with based on the unique circumstances and merits/challenges. Hence, it is imperative for organizations/companies to have a sound Integrated Disability Management Program and qualified disability management professionals/practitioners.

Managing disabilities brings with it many potential pitfalls and legal challenges. Disability management professionals/practitioners and employers need to be well-versed on their legal obligations and need to ensure compliance with the applicable laws. Establishing and following Disability Management Standards can lessen such risks.

CHAPTER REFERENCES

Alberta Human Rights and Citizenship Commission, *Employment: Duty to Accommodate Information Sheet* (March 2007), available online at: <http://www.albertahumanrights.ab.ca/publications/bulletins_sheets_booklets/459.asp>.

Alberta Human Rights and Citizenship Commission, *Employment: Duty to Accommodate Interpretive Bulletin* (May 2002), available online at: <http://www.albertahumanrights.ab.ca/publications/bulletins_sheets_booklets/bulletins/770.asp>.

Alberta Human Rights and Citizenship Commission, *Obtaining and Responding to Medical Information in the Workplace* (January 2009) at 4, available online at: <http://www.albertahumanrights.ab.ca/publications/bulletins_sheets_booklets/bulletins/1409.asp>.

Association of Workers' Compensation Boards of Canada, *History of Workers' Compensation,* available online at: <http://www.awcbc.org/en/historyof workerscompensation.asp>.

British Columbia Council of Human Rights, *Disability and the Human Rights Act* (Victoria, BC: British Columbia Ministry of Labour and Consumer Service, 1998).

Callan v. Suncor Inc., [2006] A.J. No. 30, 2006 ABCA 15 (Alta. C.A.).

Canadian Human Rights Commission, *Bona Fide Occupational Requirements and Bona Fide Justifications under the Canadian Human Rights Act: The Implications of Meiorin and Gismer* (March 2007), available online at: <http://www.chrc-ccdp.ca/publications/alphabetical_alphabetique-en.asp>.

Case Summary 226 is available on the website of the Privacy Commissioner of Canada: available online at: <http://www.priv.gc.ca/cf-dc/2003/index2-3_e.cfm?piyear=2003#contenttop>.

Case Summary 284 is available on the website of the Privacy Commissioner of Canada: available online at: <http://www.priv.gc.ca/cf-dc/2004/index2-4_e.cfm?piyear=2004#contenttop>.

Case Summary, Order P2008-001, Case File Number P0423, February 29, 2008, is available online at: <http://www.oipc.ab.ca/ims/client/upload/P2008-001.pdf>.

Centre for Labour Management, "Accommodation Guidelines" (Presented at the Illness and Disability: Claims in the Unionized Workplace Conference, Edmonton, AB, February 1999) [unpublished].

D. Cory, "Duty to Accommodate – Update (2005)" (Presented to the 23rd Annual Labour Arbitration Policy Conference, June 9, 2005, Toronto, ON) [unpublished].

Coulter v. Purolator Courier Ltd., [2004] C.H.R.D. No. 25, 2004 CHRT 37 (C.H.R.T.).

Desormeaux v. Ottawa-Carleton Regional Transit Commission, [2004] F.C.J. No. 2172, 2004 FC 1778 (F.C.), revd [2005] F.C.J. No. 1647, 2005 FCA 311 (F.C.A.), leave to appeal refused [2005] S.C.C.A. No. 534 (S.C.C.).

Health Information Act, R.S.A. 2000, c. H-5.

L. McDowell, *Human Rights in the Workplace: A Practical Guide* (Toronto: Carswell, 1998).

McAlpine v. Econotech Services Ltd., [2004] B.C.J. No. 389, 2004 BCCA 111, 32 C.C.E.L. (3d) 165 (B.C.C.A.).

Personal Information Protection Act, S.A. 2003, c. P-6.5.

Personal Information Protection Act, S.B.C. 2003, c. 63.

Personal Information Protection and Electronic Documents Act, S.C. 2000, c. 5.

Public Services Alliance of Canada, *Duty to Accommodate — A PSAC Guide for Local Representatives*, (2009 revision), available online at: <http://www.psac.com/what/humanrights/duty_to_accommodate-e.shtml>.

K. Robidoux, LL.B., Principal, ComplianceWorks (Calgary, AB, November 2005).

United Steelworkers of America, Local 5885 v. Sealy Canada Ltd. (Bender Grievance), [2006] A.G.A.A. No. 8.

Chapter 21

Disability Management: Diversity Considerations

INTRODUCTION

"Today's workforce is highly diverse. It ranges from single men and women of varying cultural backgrounds with no dependants, to those married with children and caring for elderly parents."[1] Added to that, we are witnessing increased rates of immigration in Canada and the United States. For example, the current population of two major Canadian cities, Toronto and Vancouver, includes 25 per cent South Asian and Chinese residents.[2] In terms of the cultural mix of these two cities, 42 per cent of the population is represented by one of nine visible minorities — a growing an influential segment.[3]

The relevance of increased population diversity is that each cultural group has unique values, beliefs, needs, and expectations on life and work. By effectively managing diversity, organizations can enhance their competitive advantage in the Canadian labour market.

CULTURE

Culture can be defined as the values, beliefs, customs, behaviours, and structures shared by a group of people.[4] A group may be identified by many criteria such as nationality, religion, geographic origin, language, group history, or life experiences. Although nationality often encompasses several cultures, it is the most commonly used notion of culture.

Culture is not biologically inherited: it is learned and passed on from generation to generation via **enculturation**, the repetitious and systematic inculcation of a shared system of values, beliefs, attitudes, and learned behaviours.[5] All the beliefs, traditions, language, values, customs, rituals,

---

[1] T. Buller, "A Flexible Combination", *Benefits Canada* (November 2004) at 99, available online at: <http://www.benefitscanada.ca>.

[2] Ipsos Reid, "New Research Tool Examines Needs of Ethnic and New Canadians" (April 22, 2009), available online at: <http://www.ipsos-na.com/news/pressrelease.cfm?id=4354>.

[3] *Ibid.*

[4] H.V. Ngo, Cultural Competency: *A Self-Assessment Guide for Human Service Organizations* (Calgary, AB: Cultural Diversity Institute, 2000) at 8.

[5] P.G. Kittler & K.P. Sucher, *Food and Culture*, 3rd ed. (Belmont, CA: Wadsworth/Thomson Learning, 2001); R. Pauly, *Cultural Diversity: Increasing Awareness* (2003), University of Florida, Department

manners of interacting, forms of communication, expectations for behaviours, roles, and relationships commonly shared among members of a particular group are part of that group's culture.

Culture is not static: cultures are constantly evolving and changing in response to new situations, challenges, and opportunities.

Everyone has a culture: it is like gravity, it just "is". So how do we recognize, understand, and effectively live with our culture, and the cultural orientations of others?

Culture is not just the group into which the person is born: people can acquire a new culture. For example, marrying into a different culture, moving to a new country, a change in economic status, or becoming disabled can lead to a cultural change.

Cultures are internally diverse: it is important to note that cultural groups are not homogeneous. There is variability between and among individuals within the same cultural and ethic group. This variability can be the result of:

- age;
- level of education;
- family circumstances;
- rural versus urban living;
- life commitments;
- religious influences;
- level of adherence to traditional customs; and
- the degree of assimilation and acculturation into the major culture.

Culture is not determinative:[6] Individuals within the cultural group respond differently to the same cultural experiences and events. This is why making assumptions about a cultural identity typically fails.

Cultural differences are complicated by differences in status and power between cultures.[7] When a cultural group has most of the power, societal institutions tend to adopt the norms of the dominant culture as being the "right way to do things". For example, our workplaces tend to reflect the norms and values of the two older generations, The Veterans and Baby Boomers (for more details, please refer to Chapter 22, "The Impact of Four Generations in the Workplace on Disability Management Programs").

Culture shapes our life experiences: the way our parents disciplined us as children, the structure of family relationships, the expectations of what it means to be a boy or a girl, the values about health and approaches to healing, our body

---

of Medicine, reported in C. Brannon, Cultural Competency: Values, Traditions and Effective Practice (2007) available online at: <http://www.rd411.com/ce_modules/CUC06.pdf>.

[6] L. Olsen, J. Bhattacharya, & A. Scharf, *Cultural Competency: What It Is and Why It Matters;* California Tomorrow, Lucile Packard Foundation for Children's Health (December 7, 2006), available online at: <http://www.lpfch.org/informed/culturalcompetency.pdf>.

[7] *Ibid.*

language, what types of things that do and do not get said. These learned attributes define the norms, or "how things are supposed to be" for the members of a given culture.[8] Needless to say, culture plays a significant role in the person's expectation of, and response to, the workplace.

OTHER RELEVANT TERMS

Acculturation: Cultural modification of an individual, group, or people by adapting to or borrowing traits from another culture; a merging of cultures as a result of prolonged contact. It should be noted that individuals from culturally diverse groups may desire/seek varying degrees of acculturation into the dominant culture.[9]

Assimilation: The assumption of the cultural traditions of a given people or group.

Cultural awareness: Being cognizant, observant, and conscious of similarities and differences among cultural groups.[10]

Cultural sensitivity: Understanding the needs and emotions of one's culture and the culture of others.[11]

Ethnic: Of, or relating to, large groups of people classed according to common racial, national, tribal, religious, linguistic, or cultural origin or background.

Ethnicity: Ethnic quality or affiliation. Defined by Elliott and Fleras, ethnicity is a "*principle which explains how people are defined, differentiated, organized, and entitled to group membership on the basis of certain physical or cultural characteristics. Ethnicity can also consist of a consciously shared system of beliefs, values, loyalties, and practices that pertain to members of a group who regard themselves as different and apart. The salient feature of ethnicity is the attachment that a person or group has a common cultural heritage.*"[12]

Ethno-cultural minorities: Includes people other than Aboriginal people who belong to cultures not generally considered part of Western society. They are also termed **cultural minorities** or **visible minorities**.[13]

---

[8] *Ibid.*

[9] H.V. Ngo, *Cultural Competency: A Self-Assessment Guide for Human Service Organizations* (Calgary, AB: Cultural Diversity Institute, 2000) at 8.

[10] *Ibid.*

[11] *Ibid.*

[12] J.L. Elliott & A. Fleras, *Unequal Relations: An Introduction to Race and Ethnic Dynamics in Canada* (Scarborough, ON: Prentice-Hall Canada, 1992).

[13] Government of Alberta, Alberta Employment and Immigration, *Employing a Diverse Workforce: Making it Work* (2008). Cat. No. 675126, available online at: <http://alis.alberta.ca/ep/careershop/showproduct.html?DisplayCode=PRODUCT&EntityKey=6388>.

Race: A tribe, people, or nation belonging to the same stock; a division of humankind, possessing traits that are transmissible by descent and sufficient to characterize it as a distinctive human type. Race can also be stated as a social construct used to separate the world's peoples.[14]

CULTURAL DIVERSITY

Diversity refers to "dissimilarity and variance between things and people".[15] **Cultural diversity** is the recognition that people come from a variety of gender, age, ethnic, geographic, economic, and religious backgrounds.[16] Hence, it involves an appreciation of the differences in race, ethnicity, language, nationality, or religion among various groups within a nation, community, or organization. An organization is said to be culturally diverse if its employees include members of different groups.[17]

The main influences on the management of cultural diversity have been:[18]

1) *A Strategic Move To General Diversity Management* — Diversity management, in general, provides an enabling framework with which to address cultural diversity. To be successful at diversity management, the organization must practice openness, good communication, and flexibility. The ultimate benefit for the organization is the attainment of a diverse workforce.

2) *International Business* — Managing business internationally has had a major impact on the Western understanding of culture and how it affects individual and organizational behaviours. Likewise, Western organizations have been influenced by exposure to international management assumptions and business practices. Knowledge and understanding of cultural differences has facilitated and enhanced business negotiations, marketing, sales, and purchasing, among other activities.

---

[14] H.V. Ngo, Cultural Competency: A Self-Assessment Guide for Human Service Organizations (Calgary, AB: Cultural Diversity Institute, 2000) at 8.

[15] C. Brannon, *Cultural Competency: Values, Traditions and Effective Practice* (2009) at 2, Nutrition Dimension, Ashland, OR, available online at <http://www.rd411.com/ce_modules/CUC06.pdf>.

[16] P.G. Kittler & K.P. Sucher, *Food and Culture*, 3rd ed. (Belmont, CA: Wadsworth/Thomson Learning, 2001); R. Pauly, *Cultural Diversity: Increasing Awareness* (2003), University of Florida, Department of Medicine, reported in C. Brannon, *Cultural Competency: Values, Traditions and Effective Practice* (2007) available online at: <http://www.rd411.com/ce_modules/CUC06.pdf>.

[17] H.V. Ngo, *Cultural Competency: A Self-Assessment Guide for Human Service Organizations* (Calgary, AB: Cultural Diversity Institute, 2000) at 8.

[18] D. Crowe & M. Hogan, *Cultural Diversity in the Workplace: Discussion Paper.* (2007). IMI Bizlab on Cultural Diversity, available online at: <http://www.imi.ie/GetAttachment.aspx?id=8a2bff41-a09e-4a9b-9f59-32396d8af825>.

3) ***The Multicultural Marketplace*** — The market segments include ethnic and language minorities; hence there are clear benefits of employing immigrant workers to address the needs of the multicultural marketplace.

4) ***Human Resource Management*** — Employees are now recognized as a source of core competence and competitive advantage. As human resource management increased in value, cultural diversity management along with it as part of its bundle of practices came into vogue. Effective talent management, a Human Resource Management strategy, can play a key role in achieving improved productivity and innovation.

5) ***Globalization*** — The increased ease of mobility and communications for organizations and individuals throughout the world has radically changed the world of work and the emergent workforce.

CULTURAL DIVERSITY: WHAT IS THE ISSUE?

Canadian and American societies are changing demographically. For employers/organizations, cultural diversity is no longer a "nice thing to do". The reality is that the immigration rates in both countries have steadily increased. Why is this happening?

According to Statistics Canada, *"immigration is becoming increasingly important to Canada's economic well-being. Roughly two-thirds of Canada's population growth comes from net international migration. Population projections show that net immigration may become the only source of population growth by about 2030 and could account for virtually all net labour force growth by 2011."*[19] The same situation exists for the United States.[20]

According to the 2006 Canadian Census,[21] there are over 200 ethnic origins in Canada. After being classified as being born in Canada (Canadian), the most frequently reported "origins" were English, French, Scottish, Irish, German, Italian, Chinese, North American Indian, and Ukrainian.[22] The number of individuals identified as part of a visible minority totaled 5,068,100 individuals, or 16.2 per cent of Canada's total population. This was an increase from 13.4 per cent in 2001. Between 2001 and 2006, Canada's visible minority population increased by 27.2 per cent. This increase was five times faster than the 5.4 per cent growth rate of the total Canadian population.[23]

---

[19] Statistics Canada, "Study: Canada's Immigrant Labour Market", *The Daily* (September 10, 2007), available online at: <http://www.statcan.gc.ca/daily-quotidien/070910/dq070910a-eng.htm>.

[20] Wikipedia, *Immigration to the United States* (2009), available online at: <http://en.wikipedia.org/wiki/Immigration_to_the_United_States#Demographics>.

[21] Statistics Canada, *Canada's Ethnocultural Mosaic, 2006 Census: 2006 Census Year* (April 2008), Catalogue no. 97-562-X, at 5, available online at: <http://www12.statcan.gc.ca/english/census06/analysis/ethnicorigin/pdf/97-562-XIE2006001.pdf>.

[22] *Ibid.*, at 5.

[23] *Ibid.*, at 5.

In 2007, the new permanent residents to Canada came from the following countries/areas (Table 21.1):

Table 21.1: Permanent Residents to Canada by Country/Area: 2007[24]

Country/Area	Percentage	Population
Africa & Middle East	20.5%	48,570
Asia & Pacific	47.6%	112,660
South and Central America	10.9%	25,890
Europe & United Kingdom	16.5%	39,070
United States	4.4%	10,450
Unknown Source	0%	118
Total Immigration	**100%**	**236,758**

In the United States, 2006, the total U.S. population was 299 million with the following ethnic distribution (Table 21.2).

Table 21.2: Race Distribution in United States: 2006[25]

Ethnicity	Percentage	Population
White Americans	74%	221.3 million
Hispanic or Latino	14.8%	44.3 million
Black or African Americans	13.5%	40.9 million
Asian	4.4%	13.1 million
American Indian or Alaska Native	0.68%	2 million
Native Hawaiian or other Pacific Islander	0.14%	0.43 million
Two or more races	2%	6.1 million

Note: These figures add up to more than 100 per cent on this list because Hispanic and Latino Americans are distributed among all the races and are also listed as an ethnicity category, resulting in a double count.

Clearly, cultural diversity is here to stay for business and economic reasons. By becoming culturally competent, employers/organizations can appreciate and maximize the strengths of each of the various cultures present in their workplaces. The benefits of having a culturally diverse workforce are to:

- realize greater productivity;
- experience lower staff turnover;
- enhance their understanding of customer needs and wants;
- achieve better access to new markets;

---

[24] Citizenship and Immigration Canada, *Facts and Figures: Immigration Overview — Permanent and Temporary Residents 2007* (2008), Cat. No. C&I-995-07-08E, available online at: <http://www.cic.gc.ca/english/resources/statistics/menu-fact.asp>.

[25] U.S. Census Bureau, *Race — Universe: Total Population, 2006 American Community Survey*, available online at: <http://factfinder.census.gov>.

- benefit from diverse ideas and perspectives; and
- enjoy an enhanced corporate image and reputation.[26]

Beyond the business drivers, there are legislative policies that recognize and promote racial, ethnic, and linguistic diversity. For example, in Canada, the relevant legislation includes:

- *Canadian Charter of Rights and Freedom* — the provision for equity rights, freedom from discrimination, and equal access to participation regardless of race, religion, national or ethnic origin, colour, sex, age, and physical or mental disability.[27]

- *Canada Multiculturalism Act* — aimed at the preservation and enhancement of Canadian multiculturalism, the Act promotes full and equitable participation of individuals and communities of all cultural origins in all aspects of Canadian society. The social, cultural, economic, and political institutions of Canada have to be both respectful and inclusive, and enable meaningful participation by culturally diverse people.[28]

- *Human Rights legislation* — prohibits practices in public services that discriminate on the basis of race, religious beliefs, colour, gender, physical or mental disability, ancestry, place of origin, marital status, source of income, or family status.[29]

- *Employment Equity* — requires federal departments and agencies with 100 employees or more to file an annual statistical profile of the employment equity designated groups. The annual report must compare those designated groups with all other employees, in terms of such dimensions as occupational and salary levels. The principle of this law is that the employer's workforce must reflect the population from which the employer recruits.[30]

TRANSCULTURAL NURSING

Some of the earliest studies in terms of working with different cultures were undertaken in the field of nursing. Leininger[31] defined **transcultural nursing** as:

---

[26] Government of Alberta, Alberta Employment and Immigration, *Employing a Diverse Workforce: Making it Work* (2008) at 9, Cat. No. 675126, available online at: <http://alis.alberta.ca/ep/careershop/showproduct.html?DisplayCode=PRODUCT&EntityKey=6388>.

[27] H.V. Ngo, *Cultural Competency: A Self-Assessment Guide for Human Service Organizations* (Calgary, AB: Cultural Diversity Institute, 2000) at 8.

[28] *Ibid.*

[29] *Ibid.*

[30] *Ibid.*

[31] M. Leininger & M. McFarland, *Culture Care Diversity and Universality: A Worldwide Nursing Theory*, 2nd ed. (Boston, CT: Jones and Bartlett, 2006).

"an essential area of study and practice focused on the cultural care beliefs, values, and life ways of people to help them maintain and/or regain their health, or to face death in meaningful ways."[32]

Transcultural nursing focuses on understanding cultures, their specific health care needs, and how to provide assistance that best fits cultural life ways. This transcultural perspective identifies both diverse and universal cultural variables found among human social groups. Today, transcultural nursing has evolved to include cultural competence — an element of nursing education programs.

CULTURAL COMPETENCE

In regards to the field of disability management, **cultural competence** can be described as having the ability to provide quality disability management care and services to a diverse employee population. It encompasses both systemic responses (*e.g.,* organizational policy, procedures, practices, *etc.*) as well as the delivery of disability management services by skilled and sensitive disability management practitioners/ professionals. Hence, cultural competence implies a responsibility at both the organizational and individual level.

Defined by the Seattle King County Dept of Public Health, 1994:

> **Cultural competency** is the ability of individuals and systems to respond respectfully and effectively to people of all cultures, classes, races, ethnic backgrounds and religions in a manner that recognizes, affirms, and values the cultural differences and similarities, and the worth of individuals, families, and communities and protects and preserves the dignity of each.[33]

Operationalized, cultural competence means that Disability Management practitioners/professionals must be able to identify and challenge their own cultural beliefs. Some call that having the "ability to see the world through different cultural lenses"[34] It translates into the Disability Management practitioner/professional being able to analyze and respond to the cultural beliefs, environments, and events in ways that are meaningful — culturally and psychologically for client and professional alike, and the ability to use that introspection so that it results in the provision of meaningful, satisfying and competent assistance and support.

---

[32] *Ibid.*

[33] Seattle King County Dept. of Public Health (1994), reported in *National Review of Nursing Education — Multicultural Nursing Education*, "5. Australian Nursing Education Today" (2001), on the DEST Commonwealth Department of Education, Science and Technology website, available online at: <http://www.dest.gov.au/archive/HIGHERED/nursing/pubs/multi_cultural/5.htm>.

[34] M. Fitzgerald (1999) reported in *National Review of Nursing Education — Multicultural Nursing Education*, "5. Australian Nursing Education Today" (2001), on the DEST Commonwealth Department of Education, Science and Technology website, available online at: <http://www.dest.gov.au/archive/HIGHERED/nursing/pubs/multi_cultural/5.htm>.

Figure 21.1: Cultural Competency Continuum[35]

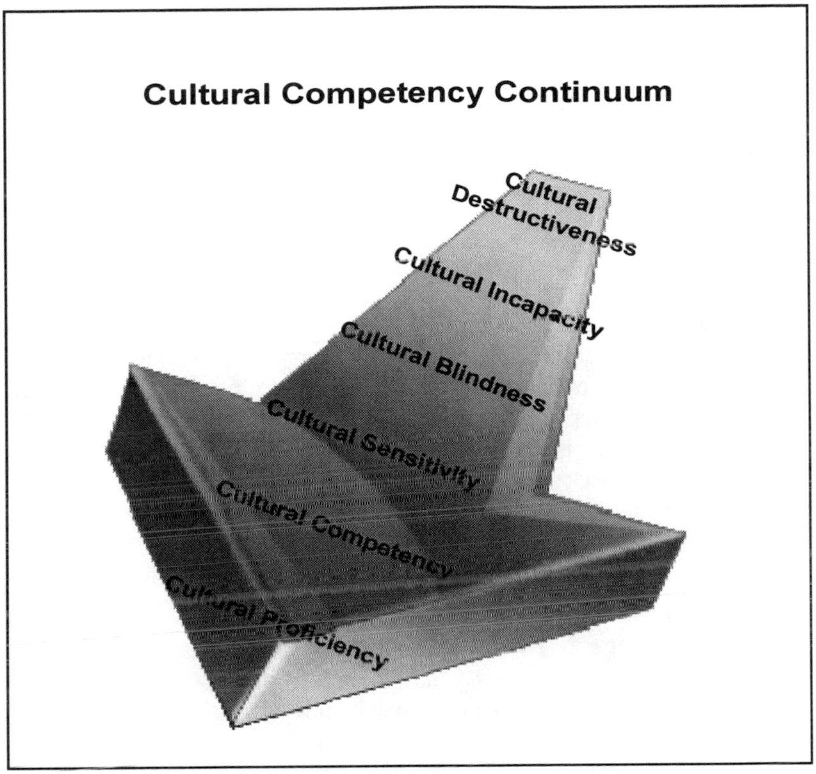

Cultural Competency Continuum

Cultural проflciency occurs along a continuum (Figure 21.1). **Cultural destructiveness** is the stage of intentional denial, rejection, or outlawing of other cultures. **Cultural incapacity** is the stage of acceptance of other cultures, but an inability to work effectively with other cultures. **Cultural blindness** is the stage when people assume that everyone is basically alike and advocate a universal approach and services for all people. **Cultural pre-competence** is the stage of awareness within systems or organizations of their strengths and areas for growth to respond effectively to culturally and linguistically diverse populations. It includes a willingness to learn and understand other cultures.[36]

---

[35] Adapted from T. Cross, B. Bazron, K. Dennis & M. Isaacs, *Towards a Culturally Competent System of Care,* Vol. 1 Washington, DC: CASSP Technical Assistance Center, Center for Child Health and Mental Health Policy, Georgetown University Child Development Center, 1989), available online at <http://www.ncccurricula.info/documents/TheContinuumRevised.doc> and C. Brannon, *Cultural Competency: Values, Traditions and Effective Practice* (2009), at 3, Nutrition Dimension, Ashland, OR, available online at: <http://www.rd411.com/ce_modules/CUC06.pdf>.

[36] T. Cross, B. Bazron, K. Dennis & M. Isaacs, *ibid.*

Cultural competency is the stage when people are able to effectively function in cross-cultural circumstances. It includes the development of standards, policies, practices, and attitudes that value diversity. **Cultural proficiency** is the stage where proactive promotion of cultural diversity occurs and opportunities to improve cultural relationships are sought.

DEVELOPMENT OF CULTURAL COMPETENCE

The development of cultural competence goes through a series of personal and professional growth phases which include the following:

1. **Cultural awareness** — Awareness that enables the disability management practitioner/professional to understand how beliefs, values, and personal or political power are shaped by culture.[37] It starts with acknowledging that cultural differences exist between the Western culture and non-Western cultures. The next step is to recognize that as human beings, we view the world based on our individual culture. In essence, our culture and the socialization into that culture, colours our viewpoints. The key aspect is to realize that our individual culture is but one of many cultures; not the "only and right" culture. By identifying their personal beliefs and social customs, disability management practitioners/professionals can develop a cultural awareness.

2. **Cultural knowledge** — Familiarity with the broad differences, similarities, and inequalities in experience and practice among various societal groupings.[38] Disability management practitioners/professionals can develop cultural knowledge by:

   a) researching a company's profile;
   b) evaluating of the degree to which local health care services meet the needs of these various minority employee groups; and
   c) seeking information on the inequalities in health and health care in relation to class, gender, ethnicity, and age.

3. **Cultural understanding** — Recognition of the problems and issues faced by individuals and groups when their values, beliefs, and practices are compromised by a dominant culture.[39] Disability Management practitioners/professionals can attain cultural understanding by comparing and contrasting the:

   a) lay and professional viewpoints towards minority groups; and

---

[37] P. Lister (1999) reported in *National Review of Nursing Education — Multicultural Nursing Education*, "5. Australian Nursing Education Today" (2001), on the DEST Commonwealth Department of Education, Science and Technology website, available online at: <http://www.dest.gov.au/archive/HIGHERED/nursing/pubs/multi_cultural/5.htm>.

[38] *Ibid.*

[39] *Ibid.*

b) experiences of employee illness/injury and the caregiving relationship. The use of "real experiences" through case studies can be valuable in achieving this end.

4. **Cultural sensitivity** — Regard for the employee's beliefs, values, and practices within a cultural context, and showing awareness of how his or her own cultural background may be influencing professional practice.[40] Disability management practitioners/professionals can become culturally sensitive by evaluating the effectiveness of their Disability Management Program and Services in meeting the needs of various cultures. This translates to internalizing the concept of cultural understanding.

5. **Cultural competence** — Provision or facilitation of services which respect the values, beliefs, and practices of the employee, and which address any disadvantages arising from the employee's position in the company, community, and/or society.[41] Disability management practitioners/professionals demonstrate culture through a combination of knowledge, clinical skills, and behaviours that lead to positive outcomes with culturally diverse populations.

CULTURAL COMPETENCE: ITS IMPORTANCE

Why is cultural competence important? What value does it offer to disability management practitioners/professionals?

Studies have shown that consideration of individual cultures, preferences, and needs in the provision of health care services:

- eliminates health care disparities; [42]
- reduces the misunderstandings between families and health care practitioners; [43]
- reduces non-compliance;
- enhances the cost-effectiveness of health care service provision;[44]
- increases patient/client satisfaction and retention; and
- improves health and recovery outcomes.[45]

---

[40] *Ibid.*

[41] *Ibid.*

[42] Avesis, *Cultural Competency: 2009* (2008 revision, approved January 2009), available online at: <http://avesis.com/Images/Cultural_Competency.pdf>.

[43] L. Olsen, J. Bhattacharya, & A. Scharf, *Cultural Competency: What It Is and Why It Matters'* California Tomorrow, Lucile Packard Foundation for Children's Health (December 7, 2006), available online at: <http://www.lpfch.org/informed/culturalcompetency.pdf>.

[44] Avesis, *Cultural Competency: 2009* (2008 revision, approved January 2009), available online at: <http://avesis.com/Images/Cultural_Competency.pdf>.

[45] American Association of Colleges of Nursing, *Cultural Competency in Baccalaureate Nursing Education* (2008) at 1, available online at: <http://www.aacn.nche.edu/education/pdf/competency.pdf>.

In addition, culture has a profound impact on how people respond to preventive interventions and health care services, as well as in how they experience illness/injury, how they access health care, and how they reach recovery.

The benefits of using a culturally competent approach to disability management include:

- the development of more appropriate return-to-work plans;
- improved quality of disability management case and claims management processes/practices;
- better disability management services and outcomes;
- increased employee acceptance of, and compliance with, return-to-work plans;
- improved employee satisfaction with the Disability Management Program and services;
- enhanced provision of employee and family assistance and support;
- increased sensitivity as to employee/workgroup needs; and
- the ability to work more effectively with diverse employee populations.

Disability management practitioners/professionals must be culturally aware, knowledgeable, understanding, sensitive, and competent. The outcome will be the provision of Integrated Disability Management Programs and services that positively impact the desired business and people outcomes with culturally diverse populations.

CULTURAL COMPETENCE: OTHER CONSIDERATIONS

Cultural competence implies a working knowledge of the various factors that impact a culture. To meet this criteria, disability management practitioners/ professionals must consider the following factors:

- ***Role of Family*** — In traditional cultures, the family plays a major role in decision-making about health issues. Disability management practitioners/professionals should take that into account and involve family members in employee meetings, case conferences, and return-to-work planning.

- ***Role of Economics*** — Poverty brings with it its own cultural aspects. It can be a major determinant in an employee's response to disability management. Economic status can influence the employee's ability to acquire medical supplies and other resources for treatment compliance and rehabilitation. When making decisions about disability management case management and return-to-work planning, disability management practitioners/professionals should consider the different degrees of access to resources.

- ***Role of Religious Beliefs*** — An employee's decision about treatment, rehabilitation, and return-to-work practices can be influenced by religious beliefs. For example, because of their religious faith, employees may want to know what is wrong with them (the diagnosis), but choose not to seek the recommended medical treatment. They may also want to include traditional healing along with the scientific medical treatment modalities. Respecting these beliefs and incorporating them into the employee's care can enhance the ultimate recovery process and health outcome.

- ***Role of Communication Styles*** — Intercultural communication can be challenging for the disability management practitioner/professional as well as for the employee and family. Language barriers are well recognized and must be addressed. In addition, nonverbal communication, or body language is an important part of how people communicate; and there are differences from culture to culture. Hand and arm gestures, touch, and eye contact (or its lack) are a few of the aspects of nonverbal communication that may vary significantly depending upon cultural background.

Facial expressions:

- Smiling is not always an expression of happiness; it can also signify a discussion of something sad or uncomfortable in the Chinese culture.[46]
- Winking can be viewed as a romantic or sexual invitation (in some Latin American cultures); or as a signal to children to leave the room (the Yorubas in Nigeria,); or as rudeness (many Chinese cultures).[47]
- Blinking can be interpreted as sign of disrespect and boredom in Hong Kong.[48]
- Filipinos will point to an object by shifting their eyes toward it or pursing their lips and point with their mouth, rather than using their hands.[49]
- Venezuelans may use their lips to point at something, because pointing with a finger is impolite.[50]
- Crying and a public showing of emotion are culturally determined.

---

[46] D. Morris, *Bodytalk: The Meaning of Human Gestures* (New York: Crown Trade Paperbacks, 1994), reported in *The Provider's Guide to Quality & Culture*, "Topic 9: Non-verbal Communication" (2009), on the Management for Sciences for Health website, available at: <http://erc.msh.org/mainpage.cfm?file=4.6.0.htm&module=provider&language=English>.
[47] *Ibid.*
[48] *Ibid.*
[49] *Ibid.*
[50] *Ibid.*

Head Movements:

- A signal for "yes" may be a nod of the head in Lebanon; the signal for "no" may be pointing the head sharply upward and raising the eyebrows.

- Saudis signal "yes" by swivelling their head from side to side. They may signal "no" by tipping their head backward and clicking their tongue.

Gestures:

- There are a number of gestures commonly used in Canada/United States that may have a different meaning, and/or be offensive, to those from other cultures. One common example is the use of a finger or hand to indicate "come here please". This is the gesture used to beckon dogs in some cultures and is very offensive. Pointing with one finger is also considered to be rude in some cultures; Asians typically use their entire hand to point to something.
- In Japan, the "OK" sign is interpreted as the symbol for money. In Argentina, Belgium, France, Portugal, Italy, Greece, and Zimbabwe, the same sign means "zero" or "nothing". In some Eastern European countries, this is highly offensive as it indicates a bodily orifice.[51]
- Holding up crossed fingers is a gesture wishing one "good luck", while crossed fingers held behind the back negates a stated pledge or thought. In Russia, this is a way of rudely rejecting or denying something. In Argentina and Spain, this same sign is made to ward off bad luck. In China, it signifies the number 10.[52]
- In Iran, the "thumbs-up" gesture is vulgar.[53]
- Tapping the underside of the elbow with the fingers of the other hand indicates that someone is stingy, in Colombia.[54]
- In Latin America, a shrug with the palms facing skyward may be interpreted as a vulgar gesture.[55]

Touch:

- While patting a child's head is considered to be a friendly or affectionate gesture in our culture, it is considered inappropriate by many Asians to touch someone on the head, which is believed to be a sacred part of the body.

---

[51] *Ibid.*
[52] *Ibid.*
[53] *Ibid.*
[54] *Ibid.*
[55] *Ibid.*

- In the Middle East, the left hand is reserved for bodily hygiene and should not be used to touch another or transfer objects. In Muslim cultures, touch between opposite gendered individuals is generally inappropriate.
- Light touching of the arm or a light kiss to the cheek is very common in some cultures, even among people who have just met. People from Latin America and Eastern Europe may be very comfortable with this kind of touching, whereas people from many Asian cultures may prefer less physical contact with acquaintances.[56]
- Physical contact, except for a handshake, early in a relationship may be uncomfortable for some Chinese. This is especially important to remember when dealing with older people or those in positions of authority.[57]
- Men in Egypt tend to be more touch-oriented; a handshake may be accompanied by a gentle touching of the recipient's elbow with the fingers of the left hand.[58]
- A strong, warm handshake is the traditional greeting between men in Latin America. However, because most Latin Americans show affection easily, male friends, like female friends, may embrace. Women may lightly brush their cheeks together.[59]
- A Western woman should not initiate a handshake with a man in India. Many Indian women will shake hands with a foreign woman, but not a foreign man.[60]
- To many Indians, it is considered rather offensive to (even accidentally) step on someone's foot. Apologies should be made immediately.[61]

Eye contact/Gaze:

- In the mainstream Western culture, eye contact is interpreted as attentiveness and honesty; we are taught that we should "look people in the eye" when they are talking to us. In many cultures, however, including Hispanic, Asian, Middle Eastern, and Native American, eye contact is thought to be disrespectful or rude; hence for these cultures, the lack of eye contact does not mean that a person is not paying attention.[62]

---

[56] *Ibid.*
[57] *Ibid.*
[58] *Ibid.*
[59] *Ibid.*
[60] *Ibid.*
[61] *Ibid.*
[62] *Ibid.*

- Women may especially avoid eye contact with men because it can be taken as a sign of sexual interest.[63]
- Many Middle Easterners have what North Americans and Europeans consider "languid eyes". It may appear that the person's eyes are half closed, but this does not express disinterest or disrespect.[64]
- In Ghana, young children are taught not to look adults in the eye because to do so would be considered an act of defiance.[65]
- In Latin America, good eye contact is important in both social and business situations.[66]

Physical Contact:

- It is impolite to show the bottom of the shoe, which is often dirty in many cultures. Therefore, one should not sit with the foot resting on the opposite knee.
- Standing with the hands on the hips suggests anger, or a challenge, in Argentina.[67]
- Slouching or poor posture is considered to be disrespectful. For example, good posture is important in Taiwan, with Taiwanese men usually sitting with both feet firmly fixed to the floor.[68]

Personal Space:

- Difference cultures have difference tolerances for how close people position themselves when communicating. Standing "too close" may be perceived as uncomfortable or rude in some cultures, yet acceptable in others.

- ***Response to Illness/Injury*** — How an employee and the family responds to illness/injury is impacted by their cultural orientation. A better appreciation of the differences can be obtained by comparing the traditional and modern health care systems. Being part of the health maintenance for cultures, **traditional health care systems** have been around forever. They are part of the original culture, having filtered down, generation to generation.

---

[63] J. Ikeda, M.A., R.D.; University of California, Berkley Charles Tidwell Jr. PhD; Andrews University, Berrien Springs, Michigan *Providers Guide to Quality and Culture*: <http://erc.msh.org/mainpage.cfm?file=4.6.0.htm&module=provider&language=English>.

[64] D. Morris, *Bodytalk: The Meaning of Human Gestures* (New York: Crown Trade Paperbacks, 1994), reported in *The Provider's Guide to Quality & Culture*, "Topic 9: Non-verbal Communication" (2009), on the Management for Sciences for Health website, available at: <http://erc.msh.org/mainpage.cfm?file=4.6.0.htm&module=provider&language=English>.

[65] *Ibid.*

[66] *Ibid.*

[67] *Ibid.*

[68] *Ibid.*

Traditional health care is the first resource the individual turns to when ill/injured.[69]

In contrast, the **modern health care systems** are recent social developments and tend to be the last resort when one is ill or injured. They are used when the traditional health care system fails. Hence, this is one reason why some people wait until their disease has reached an advanced stage before seeking physician care.

Other differences are that, in the traditional health care system, the caregiver(s) speak the same language and uphold similar cultural beliefs and attitudes, as well as lifestyles. Community-based, the traditional health care provider, knows and understands the patient's social relationships and can enlist assistance from significant others.

In contrast, the health care providers in the modern health care systems experience professional ethnocentrisms that can negatively affect the health care provider-patient relationship. For example, the belief that the individual's well-being surpasses the well-being of the family can be negatively viewed. Portraying the belief that the "physician knows best", can be offensive. As well, the practice of hastily handing a patient a fact sheet on a disease condition, or treatment modality, can be viewed as rude. The outcome will be non-compliance with the recommended health care regimens.

Lastly, the two health care systems have different focuses. The traditional health care system is ego-focused, taking cures from the client and accepting the client's symptoms at "face value".[70] The modern health care systems, on the other hand, are technically-oriented. An illness/injury tends not to be valid unless sit can be organically defined, or scientifically understood.

- ***Response to Pain*** — Pain is a subjective sensation and the expression of pain is culturally determined. Some cultures promote stoicism, while others accept crying and open expressions of pain and discomfort.[71]

CULTURAL ASSESSMENT

Cultural assessment of the ill/injured employee is required to identify his or her views and beliefs about health and illness. Beliefs about the cause, prevention, and treatment of illness/injury vary among cultures. As already noted, health

---

[69] C.L. Edelman & C.L. Mandle, *Health Promotion Throughout the Lifespan*, 4th ed. (St. Louis, MO: Mosby, 1998).

[70] *Ibid.*

[71] D. Morris, *Bodytalk: The Meaning of Human Gestures* (New York: Crown Trade Paperbacks, 1994), reported in *The Provider's Guide to Quality & Culture*, "Topic 9: Non-verbal Communication" (2009), on the Management for Sciences for Health website, available at: <http://erc.msh.org/mainpage.cfm?file=4.6.0.htm&module=provider&language=English>.

care practices can be traditional (classified as folk, spiritual, or psychic healing practices), and modern (conventional medical practices). A summary of both health care systems is provided in Table 21.3.

Table 21.3: Comparison of Traditional and Modern Health Care Systems[72]

Traditional Health Care System	Aspect	Modern Health Care System
Forever in some format	*When introduced*	Developed within recent memory
Generationally promoted	*How promoted*	Commercially marketed
Initially	*When sought*	When Traditional Health care methods fail
Same language	*Language*	Language differences
Similar	*Cultural beliefs of caregiver(s)*	Different and varied
Home-based, community-based	*Location*	Clinic- or hospital-based
Good	*Knowledge of ill/injured person*	Unknown to limited
Good	*Knowledge of Available Social Supports*	Unknown to limited
On total family	*Focus of care*	On the individual
Ego-focused	*Focus*	Technically-oriented

In addition to the usual disability management data collected, specific cultural information can assist disability management practitioners/professionals to gain a better understanding of the employee and his or her cultural affiliation. Areas for consideration are, the individual's:

- *Place of birth* — to determine the country of origin and country(ies) of residence.

- *Length of time in Canada* — to assess the degree of acculturation to Western society.

- *First language and other languages spoke* — to obtain an understanding of the employee's level of English comprehension and how readily he/she will be able to understand the Disability Management documents, forms, and materials.

---

[72] C.L. Edelman. & C.L. Mandle, *Health Promotion Throughout the Lifespan*, 4th ed. (St. Louis, MO: Mosby, 1998).

- *Available support systems* — to learn who will support the employee and who makes the decision regarding health care.

- *Number and type of dependents* — to determine the magnitude of the employee's family responsibilities.

- *Caregiving responsibilities* — to identify the ill/injured employee's extra duties.

- *Relationships* — to find out if the ill/injured employee wants certain people to be in attendance as part of the disability management case management planning and return to work initiatives.

- *Response to illness/injury* — to ascertain the level of reliance on traditional and modern health care systems. Questions like, "What do you do when you become ill?" "How do you respond?" can be asked.

- *Traditional health care system* — What does that look like for this employee? Questions like, "Do you ever see a native healer or other type of practitioner when you don't feel well?" "Does this healer help?" "Do you ever take any herbs or medicines that are commonly used in your native country or by your cultural/ethnic group?" "If so, what are they, and for what reason(s) do you take them?" can be asked.

- *Health beliefs* - - Some questions to ask the ill/injured employee are:
  - What do you think caused your health problem(s)?
  - Why do you think it started when it did?
  - What does your sickness do to you? How does it affect you and your life?
  - How severe is it? From your opinion, will it last a short or long period of time?
  - What do you fear most about your illness/injury/disorder?
  - What are the chief problems that your illness/injury has caused for you?
  - What kind of treatment do you think you should receive? What are the most important results you hope to receive from that treatment?

There are a number of other factors for the disability management practitioners/professionals to consider. For example, culturally:

- Are individuals comfortable answering personal health questions?
- When the health care provider asks questions, does the person or the family, perceive this inquiry as a "lack of knowledge" on the part of the health care provider?
- Who should be told about the illness/injury?
- Are health care decisions made individually or through family consensus?
- Is the gender of the health care provider an issue?
- Does "more medicine" equal greater severity of illness?
- Does "no medication" prescribed by the physician indicate wellness?

- Does the patient prefer to "feel" the symptoms, or to "mask" them?
- Does the patient prefer ONE solution, or a choice of treatment options?
- Does the patient want to hear about the treatment risks?[73]

A thorough cultural assessment can assist the disability management practitioner/professional to better understand the cultural orientation of the ill/injured employee, and the impact of the employee's cultural orientation has or will have on the employee's response to the current illness/injury, the recovery process, and a safe and timely return to work.

RECOMMENDATIONS FOR WORKING WITH PEOPLE OF DIVERSE CULTURES

Disability management practitioners/professionals are advised to:

- Understand the cultural differences that may exist.
- Be aware of your own cultural beliefs and biases.
- Be sensitive of your positional authority within the company, real or perceived.
- Greet employees in their own language, and/or work with their beliefs. Acknowledge that you care and don't worry about making mistakes. Employees appreciate a sincere effort by the disability management practitioner/professional to understand and work with them in a manner that is comfortable for them.
- Recognize that there are a number of cultural "hot buttons", namely:

  - superstitions and customs;
  - religious beliefs;
  - death and dying practices;
  - individual autonomy;
  - dietary practices;
  - physical space; and
  - body language.[74]

Be aware of the potential for these topics to result in cultural differences and reactions. Seek ways to approach and address them effectively.

- Ask the employee, early in the disability management claim or case management process, to identify any actions deemed as offensive in his or her culture. That indicates respect and caring on the part of the disability management practitioner/professional.

---

[73] A. Kleinman, *Patients and Healers in the Context of Culture* (Berkeley, CA: University of California Press, 1981).

[74] General Healthcare Resources Inc., *Cultural Diversity* (2005) at 6, available online at <http://www.ghresources.com/documents%5CCultral%20Diversity.pdf>.

- Follow the employee's lead: if the employee moves closer or touches you in a casual manner, you may do the same.[75]
- Use hand and arm gestures with great caution. Gestures can mean very different things in different cultures.[76]
- Be careful in interpreting facial expressions. They may lead you to misinterpret the patient's feelings, or to over- or underestimate the employee's level of pain. This is also true of the presence or absence of crying and other expressions of pain, which are closely tied to a person's culture.[77]
- Avoid seeking eye contact from the employee/family: it may be a sign of respect by the employee's culture to not make eye contact.[78]
- Be patient establishing a rapport and the associated trust with employees from different cultures can take more time.
- Thoroughly explain the disability management process and procedures, and their rationale.
- When working with employees who have limited language proficiency, be sure to use a trained interpreter, not merely a family member or friend.
- Understand that there may be some cultural reluctance to discuss certain topics, particularly if the disability management claim or case manager, or interpreter, is gender similar to the employee.
- Communicate effectively. As much as possible, use words (not gestures) to express the message(s). Gestures that are acceptable in our culture may be offensive or meaningless in other cultures.
- Find out how the employee views this illness or injury by asking questions such as:

  - What do you call your problem? What name does it have?
  - What do you think caused your problem?
  - Why do you think it started when it did?
  - What does your sickness do to you? How does it work?
  - How severe is it? Will it have a short or long course?
  - What do you fear most about your condition/disorder?
  - What are the chief problems that your sickness has caused for you?
  - What have you done so far to treat the sickness?
  - What kind of treatment do you think you should receive?

---

[75] D. Morris, *Bodytalk: The Meaning of Human Gestures* (New York: Crown Trade Paperbacks, 1994), reported in *The Provider's Guide to Quality & Culture*, "Topic 9: Non-verbal Communication" (2009), on the Management for Sciences for Health website, available at: <http://erc.msh.org/mainpage.cfm?file=4.6.0.htm&module=provider&language=English>.

[76] *Ibid.*

[77] *Ibid.*

[78] *Ibid.*

- What are the most important results you hope to receive?[79]
- What does this illness/injury mean to you? To your family?
- What is it like to be injured/ill within your culture?

- Identify areas of potential conflict and seek was to address them.
- Compromise: Show respect for the employee's beliefs and be willing to work with the employee/family members to establish acceptable claims and case management plans, and a safe and timely return to work.
- Provide clarity on the Disability Management Program while being respectful of their culture. It is really important for workers and family members to understand the disability management process and what to expect at each stage. They need to understand the way things are done in this particular workplace. If required, they should be given access to a language and "cultural interpreter". The reality is that clinicians can be sensitive, but the whole system will not change to accommodate them. As disability management professionals/practitioners, walk them through the disability management process and explain the available options available. Help them understand their options so that they can make informed consents to treatment and return-to-work options. Advocate for them, remaining within the boundaries of the employer's and health insurance systems.

DIVERSITY TYPES

The first part of this chapter focuses on culture, transcultural nursing, cultural competence, and how to conduct a cultural assessment. At this point, these concepts and terms will be operationalized, beginning with a review of some types of diversity, and then moving towards effective management of cultural diversity in the workplace.

The Older Worker (over aged 60 years)

In 2008, 13.5 per cent of the Canadian workforce were workers aged 55 years and over.[80] Older workers have many work qualities that make them a valuable asset to any workplace. They are described as experienced, loyal, possessing strong work ethics, and willing to try a variety of roles. However, older workers do face a number of challenges, namely:

- Society as a whole tends to be gerontophobic (fear of the aging process) and as such, tends to be prejudiced against older workers. Some of this is

---

[79] A. Kleinman, *Patients and Healers in the Context of Culture* (Berkeley, CA: University of California Press, 1980); D. Lozorik, *Pilot Study to Develop a Tool to Elicit Khmer Beliefs about the Cause of Illness* (Master's Thesis, Boston University School of Medicine, 1984) [unpublished].

[80] Statistics Canada, *Average Hourly Wages of Employees by Selected Characteristics*, available online at: <http://www40.statcan.gc.ca/l01/cst01/labr69a-eng.htm.>.

perpetuated by the media, and some by older workers themselves. For example, many older workers view themselves as being too old to start a new career or to tackle a new business endeavour. Having spent their entire career in one line of work, many believe that they could not do anything else. And some view themselves as being overqualified to do a less demanding job.

• In terms of hiring the older worker, employers question the required training and development investment given that the older worker may not be with the company all that long.

• Some employers hold true to the myths that older workers are physically slower, less physically able, less productive, more set in their ways, unable to adapt to new technology, and more likely to get hurt. These myths should be challenged, as the research shows them to be unfounded. For example, worker strength can improve with age. Add to that, the older work tends to learn to work smarter and not to rely on "bronze" and "brute strength".

In reality, older workers do face a number of health issues that come with the aging process. For example, 23 per cent of Canadian workers experience illness/injuries that negatively impact their ability to function. They also experience visual deficits, slower reaction times, and problems with doing shift work, in the workplace. By age 65, the prevalence of disability increases to 42 per cent.[81] The number of missed workdays does increase with age from an average of 5.9 days for young full-time workers to 11.4 for workers 55-64 years of age.[82]

Occupational injuries, although fewer than what younger workers experience, tend to require more than twice the recovery time for workers over age 58 years.[83] As well, the type of injuries differ: older workers are more susceptible to soft tissue injuries, especially back injuries.[84]

Some health conditions that are associated with aging are hearing loss, increased susceptibility to lengthy absences if injured and increased prevalence of chronic health conditions. However, these human failings can

---

[81] K. Williams, "Returning to Work After Disability: What Goes Wrong?" (Presented at Canadian Human Resource Planners event, May 15, 2003, Calgary, AB) [unpublished].

[82] Statistics Canada, *Work Absence Rates, 2007*, Cat. No. 71-211-XWE (Ottawa: Statistics Canada, May 2008).

[83] Association of Workers' Compensation Boards of Canada, *Key Statistical Measures for 2007* (December 2008), available online at: <http://www.awcbc.org/common/assets/ksms/2007ksms.pdf>; and Alberta Workers' Compensation Board, *Average Severity of a Claim Table, Financial Synopsis, 2008* available online at: <http://cr.wcb.ab.ca/public>.

[84] T. McDonald & H. Harder, "Older Workers and Disability Management" (2004) 3:3 International Journal of Disability, Community & Rehabilitation 1, available online at: <http://www.ijdcr.ca/VOL03_03_CAN/index.shtml>.

be mitigated through the adoption of a supportive lifestyle, and by the employer providing realistic work assignments.

- In terms of work-personal life conflict, older workers are often involved in providing care for an even older, dependant relative. Working and shouldering this type of responsibility can lead to caregiver strain — the stress of caring for an elderly dependant. Older women are particularly susceptible to this phenomenon, especially when this situation is compounded by caregiving responsibilities for grandchildren.

Today, many older workers are holding down a variety of jobs that range from entry-level to key knowledge positions. Employers appreciate the dedication, experience, and expertise that they bring, and therefore, are willing to shoulder any associated risks and costs.

RECOMMENDATIONS FOR DISABILITY MANAGEMENT PROFESSIONALS/PRACTITIONERS

Disability management professionals/practitioners are encouraged to:

- educate management and union leaders on the specific needs of the older worker.
- structure Disability Management Program approaches so that they adequately address the needs of the older worker.
- recommend ergonomic assessments on the jobs held by older workers with a view to preventing unnecessary strains and sprain injuries.
- when accommodating older workers, consider providing ergonomic education to the relevant stakeholders.

Women

Women have played a major role in the workforce for many years; however, they still experience a certain degree of systemic discrimination. For example, although they hold managerial and professional positions, many earn less income than men. Women who are trying to get into, or are employed in male-dominated occupations, continue to face many barriers. Other aspects like different communication styles, relationship styles, primary caregivers' responsibilities, absence of mentoring programs, and the need for flexibility on work assignments, set women apart from men.

In terms of well-being, women over age 40 years experience more stress than men or younger women.[85] This phenomenon is believed to be related to balancing work and family issues. From a work perspective, the higher the amount of work interference with family duties, the greater the amount of stress

---

[85]   L. Duxbury & C. Higgins, *Report Four: Who is at Risk? Predictors of Work-Life Conflict* (Ottawa: Public Health Agency of Canada, 2005) at 7, 9 and 10, available online at: <http://www.phac-aspc.gc.ca/publicat/work-travail/report4/index.html>.

experienced by women. For example, business travel, which requires making alternate childcare and eldercare arrangements, is more stressful for women than for men. From a home perspective, the amount of caregiving that the woman is committed to provide is directly proportional to the amount of strain experienced. Additionally, as women age, they tend to be more involved in additional caregiving activities (aging parents, children, and grandchildren).[86]

Women differ from men in the nature of the disabilities experienced. For example, they are more likely to suffer mobility problems, pain-related disabilities, and vision problems, whereas men tend to have more hearing and speech problems.[87] Some of these conditions tend to worsen with age.

Companies that have a predominantly female workforce are advised to provide family-friendly workplaces. Supportive policies and programs such as flexible work hours, flex days, childcare and eldercare information, daycare, EAP, family days, *etc.*, help women to balance their work and family commitments, thereby enabling them to meet company performance expectations.

RECOMMENDATIONS FOR DISABILITY MANAGEMENT PROFESSIONALS/PRACTITIONERS

Disability management professionals/practitioners are encouraged to:

- educate management and union leaders on the specific needs of the female worker;
- structure Disability Management Program approaches/services so that they adequately address the needs of the female worker;
- seek opportunities for enhancing the work/life balance, especially for women;
- suggest caregiving support be included in the organization's suite of employee group benefits; and
- when accommodating female workers, consider the family responsibilities that may be impacting the worker's recovery and return to work.

Generations

Like age, gender, and ethnic diversity, each generation has it own beliefs, attitudes, values, communication styles, lifestyles, and work styles. Each has a unique set of expectations of management and the work environment. The outcome is that these generational differences can affect everything — employee recruitment, selection and retention practices; leadership; building work teams; managing and motivating employees; and maintaining and increasing productivity. This includes the management of employee disability and the return to work practices.

---

[86] *Ibid.*

[87] Statistics Canada, *A Profile of Disability in Canada, 2001* (Ottawa: Statistics Canada, 2003), available online at: <http://www.statcan.gc.ca/pub/89-577-x/index-eng.htm>.

Generational diversity, like age, gender, and cultural diversity, is a factor to consider in disability management. This topic and the recommendations for disability management professionals/practitioners are covered in detail in Chapter 22, "Impact of Four Generations in the Workplace on Disability Management Programs".

Ethnic Groups

Immigration is on the increase in Canada and the United States. In the past five years, immigration has accounted for 70 per cent of the growth in Canada's labour force.[88] Each ethnic group brings with it a unique set of characteristics that impacts their lives, social interactions, and well-being. To assist disability management practitioners/professionals, summary descriptions of some ethnic groups are provided in Table 21.4.

Table 21.4: Summary Descriptions of a Variety of Ethnic Groups[89]

African Americans	Asians
Religions: Christian and Islam	*Religions*: Buddhism, Christianity, Hinduism, Islam, Sikh, Jain, Parsi, and other traditional faiths
Family Issues: Raising children is traditionally a family/"whole village" affair: Matriarchal households	*Family Issues*: Patriarchal with ancestor reverence
Health Care: Often uncomfortable and mistrustful of the modern health care system. Fear being diagnosed with a terminal disease; or experiencing an invasion of privacy as a result of diagnostic procedures	*Health Care*: Prefer health care practitioner of same sex. Many expect treatment that includes the administration of medication
Economic: Generally members of the lower economic level of society	*Beliefs*: Numbers are important, with the lucky numbers being 3 and 8. The number 3 sounds like the word for "life"; number 8 sounds like the word for prosperity. The number 4 is very unlucky — the word sounds like "death"
Education: Lower levels of formal educational	*Social*: Bowing versus shaking hands is preferable. Impolite to make and hold eye contact with elders or those in positions of power. Smiling masks emotions of anger, frustration, and lack of knowledge or unhappiness
Lifestyle: Poor health status indicators	

---

[88] L. Duxbury, "Managing a Changing Workforce", presented in Calgary, AB (2004) [unpublished].

[89] Adapted from General Healthcare Resources Inc., *Cultural Diversity* (2005) at 3, available online at: <http://www.ghresources.com/documents%5CCultral%20Diversity.pdf>.

Susceptibility to Health Problems:	Susceptibility to Health Problems:
• Higher incidence of high blood pressure, sickle cell anemia, diabetes, obesity, cardiovascular disease, lactose intolerance • Women more likely to have HIV • Cancer death rates are about 35% higher than the regular population • Diseases like prostate and breast cancer progress faster than in the regular population	• For women, the common cancers are lung, breast, colon, stomach and pancreatic cancers • Higher rates of cervical cancer and mortality than in regular population • For Chinese men, common cancers are liver, colon, stomach and nasopharynx cancers • Cambodians tend to get tuberculosis, hepatitis B, and intestinal parasites • Lactose intolerance is common

Eastern Europeans	Hispanics/Latinos
Religions: Orthodox Christianity, Roman Catholicism, Islam and Judaism	*Religion*: Roman Catholicism. The Caribbean peoples have many spiritual traditions, beliefs and practices that originated in the American and African cultures
Social: Moral and physical support provided by relatives	*Social*: • Value eye contact • Friendly physical contact is common • Friendliness and treating others respectfully is valued
Family: Practice extended-family living: Multiple generations live together	*Family*: • Time with family and friends is highly valued • Children are highly valued and loved. • Parental discipline of young is mild
Health Care: Open expression of emotions — can find personal questions uncomfortable. Note-taking by health care providers can be viewed as suspicious. Sick individuals are encouraged to communicate suffering with others. Treatment is not complete with the issuing of a prescription	*Social*: Often workers send money "home" to extended family members
Lifestyle: • Excessive alcohol use is common • Smoking is common among men • Limited awareness of the harmful effects of second-hand smoke • Little awareness of the importance of exercising	*Beliefs*: Education, degrees valued
Diet: • Food is culturally important: Good appetites are admired.	*Diet*: Cakes and sweets are part of the regular diet
Susceptibility to Health Problems: • Higher incidence of digestive system diseases in men • Higher incidence of musculoskeletal	*Susceptibility to Health Problems*: • High rates of diabetes, hypertension, obesity, cervical cancer

problems in women • More smoking and obesity-related conditions	

Western Asia/Middle East	Pacific Islanders
Religions: Islam, Christians, Jews, Bahais, Druze, Parisis, and Zoroastrians	*Religions*: Holistic view of the world. Emphasize the interconnectedness of person, family, environment and spiritual world
Family: When outside, women are secluded from men	*Family*: Tight knit communities. Family, community and church play prominent roles
Health Care: Prefer health care provider to be the same sex as the patient. Treatment expected to include the administration of pills, injections or minor procedures	*Health Care*: Basic distrust of Western approaches to health care and treatment. "Scare tactics" to motivate behaviour rarely works
Diet: Most follow a strict kosher diet. Muslims fast during the holy month with no food or drink between sunrise and sunset. Fasting may include the avoidance of medications or injections. Ill people are exempt.	*Social*: • Respect ancestors and elders • Interpersonal and social behaviour based on mutual respect and sharing
Lifestyle: Muslims do not consume alcohol.	*Economic*: Low income and poverty are risk factors for health status
Susceptibility to Health Problems: • Egyptians have a higher incidence of parasitic diseases, blindness, typhoid fever, streptococcal disease, rheumatic fever and tuberculosis • Prone to obesity, high blood pressure, lower back pain, cardiovascular disease, diabetes, hepatitis A and B, tuberculosis, syphilis, and stomach-intestinal problems	*Susceptibility to Health Problems*: • Hawaiians experience high rates of breast, lung, ovarian and stomach cancer, and leukemia and non-Hodgkin's lymphoma • Hawaiians have high rates of heart disease, high blood pressure, obesity, diabetes, cancer, and stroke

Sub-Saharan Africans	Native Americans /Canadian First Nations People
Religions: Wide variety of religions and languages	*Religions*: Holistic view of the world, life, and health.
Family Issues: Family is composed of people from the village, friends and distinct blood relatives. Some practice polygamy	*Family Issues*: Family and tribal affiliations and obligations are important
Health Care: Males and females are circumcised in most countries	*Health Care*: Integrate physical, social, psychological, and spiritual ways of healing.
Diet: Eat root crops: prefer cooked vegetable to raw ones; season foods with hot peppers	

Lifestyle: Close friends greet each other by shaking hands and asking about the health of the person and their family.	**Economic**: Poverty, poor nutrition, stress and inadequate access to healthcare negatively impacts health status and well-being.
Susceptibility to Health Problems: • High incidence of sickle cell anemia, lactose intolerance, malaria, dental caries, parasite diseases, post-traumatic stress and complications of female genital mutilation	**Susceptibility to Health Problems**: • High rates of diabetes, colon and rectal cancers, and tuberculosis • Poor cervical cancer outcomes • Lactose intolerance

People of all cultures share common needs in terms of personal health. That is, we need to talk about our illnesses or health concerns; we need to get competent health care; we need to be acknowledged, understood, and valued;[90] and we need a social support system.

Based on the above descriptions of the various ethic groups found in our society, disability management practitioners/professionals can gain an appreciation that today's workplaces are composed of multicultural workforces with different views on life and approaches to work and life events. To complete the picture, add to this mix an awareness of one's own culture and cultural biases.

WESTERN CULTURE

As disability management practitioners/professionals we need to recognize and understand our own Western cultural beliefs and practices. In our Western society, we tend to value:

• individualism;
• personal responsibility;[91]
• a sense of personal control;
• the nuclear family as opposed to the extended family;[92]
• direct, open and honest communication;
• the "right to know";
• informality, which is considered akin to friendliness — hence using first names is acceptable;[93]

---

[90] R.A. Levy & J.W. Hawks, "*Multicultural Medicine and Pharmacy*" 7:3 Drug Benefit (1996) Trends 30.

[91] C. Brannon, *Cultural Competency: Values, Traditions and Effective Practice* (2009). Nutrition Dimension Ashland, OR, available online at: <http://www.rd411.com/ce_modules/CUC06.pdf>.

[92] P.G. Kittler & K.P. Sucher, *Food and Culture*, 3rd ed. (Belmont, CA: Wadsworth/Thompson Learning, 2001); G.G. Hall, *Culturally Competent Patient Care: A Guide for Providers and Their Staff* (October 2001), Institute for Health Professions Education, available online at: <www.de.state.az.uz>.

[93] P.G. Kittler & K.P. Sucher, *ibid.* and G.G. Hall, *ibid.*

- a future-orientation — setting short-, medium- and long-term goals is practised;[94]
- the desire to work hard and provide a better future for our offspring;
- promptness and keeping to a set schedule;[95]
- being task-oriented;[96]
- personal accomplishments — they equate to our self-worth;
- our physical appearance — it determines "the first impression" of the person and is linked with self-esteem;[97]
- thinness — it is a societal obsession;[98]
- self-determination — fate is not a determining force;[99]
- monochronistism — we focus on and perform tasks sequentially;[100] and
- women as "partners", if not "equals".

In contrast, the more traditional cultures tend to value:

- the welfare of the extended family over the individual;
- the extended family's involvement in decision-making;[101]
- personal relationships which take precedence over promptness and time schedules;[102]
- their belief in "fate", God or some other supernatural factors to determine a person's health and destiny;
- politeness;

---

[94] C. Brannon, *Cultural Competency: Values, Traditions and Effective Practice* (2009); Nutrition Dimension, Ashland, OR, available online at: <http://www.rd411.com/ce_modules/CUC06.pdf>.

[95] P.G. Kittler & K.P. Sucher, *Food and Culture,* 3rd ed. (Belmont, CA: Wadsworth/Thompson Learning, 2001), CA; G.G. Hall, *Culturally Competent Patient Care: A Guide for Providers and Their Staff* (October 2001).

[96] C. Brannon, *Cultural Competency: Values, Traditions and Effective Practice* (2009), Nutrition Dimension, Ashland, OR, available online at: <http://www.rd411.com/ce_modules/CUC06.pdf>.

[97] *Ibid.*

[98] J. Sobal, "Social and Cultural Influences on Obesity" in P. Björntorp, ed., *International Textbook of Obesity* (London: John Wiley and Sons 2001) 305.

[99] C. Brannon, *Cultural Competency: Values, Traditions and Effective Practice* (2009), Nutrition Dimension, Ashland, OR, available online at: <http://www.rd411.com/ce_modules/CUC06.pdf>.

[100] P.G. Kittler & K.P. Sucher, *Food and Culture*, 3rd ed. (Belmont, CA: Wadsworth/Thompson Learning, 2001); G.G. Hall, *Culturally Competent Patient Care: A Guide for Providers and Their Staff* (October 2001).

[101] C. Brannon, *ibid.* Dimension, Ashland, OR available online at: <http://www.rd411.com/ce_modules/CUC06.pdf>.

[102] C. Brannon, *ibid.*

- polychronistism — being able to do many things are once — multi-tasking;[103] and
- men as typically being the head of the household.[104]

In our Western society, the modern health care system tends to portray Western cultural values. However, one system of health care is not superior to the traditional health care systems — just different. They can operate side by side to the benefit of the individual and the family unit.

CULTURAL VIEWPOINTS: APPROACH TO WORK AND THE WORLD OF WORK

Based on the cultural information provided, it is obvious that it is in the employer's/organization's best interest to be aware of, and to understand, how various ethnic groups approach life and how that cultural orientation impacts their world of work and work practices.

To better explain this phenomenon, a comparison of the three dominant cultures found in Canada is provided (Table 21.5).

---

[103] P.G. Kittler & K.P. Sucher, *Food and Culture*, 3rd ed. (Belmont, CA: Wadsworth/Thompson Learning, 2001); G.G. Hall, *Culturally Competent Patient Care: A Guide for Providers and Their Staff* (October 2001), Institute for Health Professions Education, available online at: <www.de.state.az.uz/dcyf/cmdpe/reports/cultural%20comptenecy%20Guide1.doc>.

[104] P.G. Kittler & K.P. Sucher, *ibid.*, and G.G. Hall, *ibid.*

Table 21.5: Cultural Viewpoints: The Approach to Work

Business Aspect	Western Perspective	First Nations Perspective	Asian Perspective
Meetings	• The focus is on completing tasks and achieving goals. Time considerations are usually a driving force. • Agendas, deadlines, and schedules are specifically set out. • Punctuality is valued.	• Interpersonal relations and affiliations are important when starting a discussion. The outcome is a prolonged discussion with the task being secondary. • Meetings may not be scheduled; dealings and accomplishments are based on need, attendance and consensus. • Punctuality is not expected.	• The desire is to keep the conversation smooth and harmonious. Issues, circumstances, and relationships are as important as the work. • Meetings, agendas, schedules, and punctuality are handled with regard for the individuals involved. In essence, human relations play an important role.
Individual versus Group Importance	• Individual importance is valued over the importance of the group.	• Group importance is valued over individual importance.	• Group importance is valued over individual importance.
Competitiveness	• Competition and confrontation are accepted and individual initiative is valued. • Criticism and confrontation are accepted in order to "get the job done". • Criticism and opposition may be used to expose the full picture.	• Co-operation brings the best results; harmony and personal humility are important in the process. • Personal and group honour and dignity are valued and preserved. • Criticism, disagreements, or unsolicited suggestions are avoided.	• Conversations are harmoniously conducted. This means refraining from open disagreements, asking difficult questions of superiors, publicly embarrassing a person, or saying things that will cause problems. Differences are best worked out quietly.

Business Aspect	Western Perspective	First Nations Perspective	Asian Perspective
Goal Achievement	• Tasks are compartmentalized and considered one at a time. • The facts directly related to the issue are presented with an emphasis on reaching a solution. Clarity is expected. • Rational, logical, linear problem-solving is valued. • Accuracy and perfection are expected. • Timelines and completion expectations are required to achieve the desired goals. • Problems are solved by the leader or when a group vote decides a course of action. • Ruthless measures may be taken to attain results.	• Information and ideas are dealt with in the widest possible context. • Several suggestions may be offered simultaneously and all are considered. This prolongs and enriches the process of problem-solving. • Problem-solving is intuitive, creative, and holistic. • Inaccuracy and error are accepted. • While completion is at times important, time elements are seldom considered. • Group decision-making prevails, conflicts are resolved through consensus after divergent ideas are debated. • Loss of dignity and disharmony is avoided.	• Decisions are made by consensus. • The context of where and how comments are heard can be more important than what was said. Communication is indirect and implicit • Problem-solving is handled with regard for the individuals involved. • Accuracy and perfection are expected. • Timelines and completion expectations are required to achieve the desired goals. • Decisions are made by consensus. • Behaviours are directed primarily to maintaining congenial relations and affiliation within the group.
Directing Work	• Direct orders and instruction are readily given.	• Rather than direct orders, suggestions are better received.	• Direct orders are avoided.

Business Aspect	Western Perspective	First Nations Perspective	Asian Perspective
Performance Feedback	• Aversion to criticism, heeding advice, soliciting feedback may be viewed as a lack of commitment, motivation, confidence, enthusiasm, or knowledge.	• Criticism, advice, confrontation, and emotional outbreaks are viewed as a lack of maturity or respect.	• Self-disclosure and frankness about one's emotions are viewed as inappropriate.
Leadership	• Male dominance presides.	• Women are expected to assume a leadership role in families and are highly regarded in tribes where they often sit as elders.	• Elders are revered.
Knowledge	• Knowledge is for controlling peace and order.	• Knowledge is for the sake of living in harmony with nature.	• Knowledge is for the sake of living in harmony with nature and man.

In essence, *"Cultures are like icebergs; some features are apparent to anyone not in a fog, while others are deeply hidden [and] are so far below the surface that they are hard to recognize."*[105]

CULTURAL DIVERSITY MANAGEMENT

"The development of cultural competency may be best thought of not as arriving as a set of skills and knowledge, but rather as a journey and a way of being."[106]

When addressing how cultural competency can be attained, it is important to view the approach from two perspectives:

1. The Organizational Approach; and
2. The Disability Management Practitioner/Professional Approach

1. The Organizational Approach

Cultural diversity is not enough; organizations must demonstrate inclusiveness.[107] **Inclusiveness** translates to employees recognizing that they are valued and belong.[108] This desired state is attained when an organization and the workplace are respectful, stable, productive, innovative, and energized.[109]

One challenge for employers/organizations is to adopt the "Platinum Rule": *Treat people as they wish to be treated, not like you want to be treated.*[110] This requires a change in mindset, something that many companies struggle to achieve. In essence, it involves looking for the strengths that employees bring to the workplace, not their differences.

There is a definite link between inclusiveness and cultural competency. For organizations, being culturally competent is an ongoing journey — one of intentional and continuous practices aimed at including employees from all cultural orientations in the organization's strategic planning and operations. It involves learning about, and responding to, the various cultural contexts of the community at large and the people it serves. Culturally competent organizations continuously strive to bridge the cultures gaps with a view to addressing the needs of all employees.

---

[105] E. Winters, *Cultural Issues in Communication* (2002) at 2, available online at: <http://www. citehr.com/12441-cross-cultural-issues-communiation.html>.

[106] L. Olsen, J. Bhattacharya, & A. Scharf, *Cultural Competency: What It Is and Why It Matters*, California Tomorrow, Lucile Packard Foundation for Children's Health (December 7, 2006), available online at: <http://www.lpfch.org/informed/culturalcompetency.pdf>.

[107] Government of Alberta, Alberta Employment and Immigration, *Employing a Diverse Workforce: Making it Work* (2008) at 9, Cat. No. 675126, available online at: <http://alis.alberta.ca/ep/careershop/showproduct.html?DisplayCode=PRODUCT&EntityKey=6388>.

[108] *Ibid.*

[109] *Ibid.*

[110] S. Calhoun & P. Strasser, "Generations at Work" (2005) 53:11 American Association of Occupational Health Nurses Journal 469.

The characteristics of culturally competent organizations are as follows:

- valuing diversity, equality and institutionalizing these values in policy;
- being self-reflective on what they have done and what yet needs to be achieved;
- integrating cultural knowledge into the organization's work;
- encouraging and supporting staff to become culturally competent;
- addressing inequities; and
- integrating cultural competence into the organization's programs.

2.   The Disability Management Practitioner/Professional Approach

Given that disability management practitioners/professionals will be providing Disability Management Services and assisting employees with a variety of cultural orientation, they are strongly encouraged to develop cultural competency, and hopefully cultural proficiency.

In the field of disability management, instead of trying to "force fit" employees to adapt to established practices, consider redesigning those practices so that they adopt some of the employees' cultural beliefs/practices. Create a culture of inclusion. Involve workers in the design of the Integrated Disability Management Program and accommodate cultural differences where possible. Listen to the workers and show trust in them by seeking their opinions on the things that matter to them.

When planning an individual employee's return to work, the disability management practitioner/professional should consider factors such as the:

- impact of cultural attitudes towards illness/injury;
- role of the family in the illness, treatment regimen, and recovery process;
- relationship development within the culture;
- preferred communication style;
- cultural aspects that could impact the return-to-work process;
- mechanisms of problem-solving and goal-setting;
- potential for cultural conflicts between the Disability Management Coordinator and worker;
- potential for the worker to freely express concerns or issues about the return-to-work process; and
- presence/absence of language barriers.

Recognize that not all diversity is visible. Be aware that disability brings many diversity issues to light. Seek understanding and offer your respect. Try to look at the situation through the eyes of the ill/injured person, and determine where the challenges for recovery and return to work exist. Most of all, promote employee responsibility for the problems and solutions.

To achieve this end, the disability management practitioner/professional must develop good listening skills and observe without making judgments. It also means developing and practicing empathy, a comfort level with differences, self-awareness, reflectiveness, flexibility, and an appreciation of multiple perspectives.

As already mentioned, cultural competency is a journey. This means that disability management practitioners/professionals should seek ongoing opportunities to learn about cultural competency and to hone their skills. However, the first step is a personal commitment of cultural competency.

If I waited until I knew everything about how to address diversity issues, I would never get started. The learning really begins once you get going!

Julie Edwards[111]

SUMMARY

Cultural competence, in terms of disability management, requires a combination of knowledge, skills, and behaviours that lead to positive return-to-work outcomes for ill/injured employees with ethnically and culturally diverse orientations. Central to cultural competency is the provision of Disability Management Program education, information, and services in a manner that meets the needs of a diverse workforce.

CHAPTER REFERENCES

Alberta Workers' Compensation Board, *Average Severity of a Claim Table, Financial Synopsis, 2008*, available online at: <http://cr.wcb.ab.ca/public>.

American Association of Colleges of Nursing, *Cultural Competency in Baccalaureate Nursing Education* (2008), available online at: <http://www.aacn.nche.edu/education/pdf/competency.pdf>.

Association of Workers' Compensation Boards of Canada, *Key Statistical Measures for 2007* (December 2008), available online at: <http://www.awcbc.org/common/assets/ksms/2007ksms.pdf>.

Avesis, *Cultural Competency: 2009* (2008 revision, approved January 2009), available online at: <http://avesis.com/Images/Cultural_Competency.pdf>.

C. Brannon, *Cultural Competency: Values, Traditions and Effective Practice* (2009). Nutrition Dimension, Ashland, OR, available online at: <http://www.rd411.com/ce_modules/CUC06.pdf>.

T. Buller, "A Flexible Combination", *Benefits Canada* (November 2004) at 99, available online at: <http://www.benefitscanada.ca>.

S. Calhoun & P. Strasser, "Generations at Work" (2005) 53:11 American Association of Occupational Health Nurses Journal 469.

---

[111] J. Edwards, "Looking In, Looking Out: Redefining Early Care and Education in a Diverse Society" (2006), quoted in L. Olsen, J. Bhattacharya & A. Scharf, *Cultural Competency: What It Is and Why It Matters*, California Tomorrow, Lucile Packard Foundation for Children's Health (December 7, 2006), available online at: <http://www.lpfch.org/informed/culturalcompetency.pdf>.

CCOHS, "Stress Higher Among Working Women Over Forty, Study Finds" *CCOHS* (5 September 2005) at 5.

Citizenship and Immigration Canada, *Facts and Figures: Immigration Overview — Permanent and Temporary Residents 2007* (2008), Cat. No. C&I-995-07-08E, available online at: <http://www.cic.gc.ca/english/resources/statistics/menu-fact.asp>.

J. Cowell, "Fitness to Work" (Presented at the Conference on Workers' Compensation, Calgary, 1996) [unpublished].

T. Cross, B. Bazron, K. Dennis & M. Isaacs, *Towards a Culturally Competent System of Care*, Vol. 1, (Washington, DC: CASSP Technical Assistance Center, Center for Child Health and Mental Health Policy, Georgetown University Child Development Center, 1989), available online at: <http://www.nccccurricula.info/documents/TheContinuumRevised.doc>.

D. Crowe & M. Hogan, *Cultural Diversity in the Workplace: Discussion Paper.* (2007). IMI Bizlab on Cultural Diversity, available online at: <http://www.imi.ie/GetAttachment.aspx?id=8a2bff41-a09e-4a9b-9f59-32396d8af825>.

L. Duxbury & C. Higgins, *Report Four: Who is at Risk? Predictors of Work-Life Conflict* (Ottawa: Public Health Agency of Canada, 2005) at 7, 9 and 10, available online at: <http://www.phac-aspc.gc.ca/publicat/work-travail/report4/index.html>.

L. Duxbury, "Managing a Changing Workforce" (Presented in Calgary, AB, 2004) [unpublished].

C.L. Edelman & C.L. Mandle, *Health Promotion Throughout the Lifespan*, 4th ed. (St. Louis, MO: Mosby, 1998).

J. Edwards, "Looking In, Looking Out: Redefining Early Care and Education in a Diverse Society" (2006), quoted in L. Olsen, J. Bhattacharya, & A. Scharf, *Cultural Competency: What It Is and Why It Matters*, California Tomorrow, Lucile Packard Foundation for Children's Health (December 7, 2006), available online at: <http://www.lpfch.org/informed/culturalcompetency.pdf>.

J.L. Elliott & A. Fleras, *Unequal Relations: An Introduction to Race and Ethnic Dynamics in Canada* (Scarborough, ON: Prentice-Hall Canada, 1992).

M. Fitzgerald (1999) reported in *National Review of Nursing Education — Multicultural Nursing Education*, "5. Australian Nursing Education Today" (2001), on the DEST Commonwealth Department of Education, Science and Technology website, available online at: <http://www.dest.gov.au/archive/HIGHERED/nursing/pubs/multi_cultural/5.htm>.

General Healthcare Resources Inc., *Cultural Diversity* (2005), available online at: <http://www.ghresources.com/documents%5CCultral%20Diversity.pdf>.

Government of Alberta, Alberta Employment and Immigration, *Employing a Diverse Workforce: Making it Work* (2008), Cat. No. 675126, available online at: <http://alis.alberta.ca/ep/careershop/showproduct.html?Display Code=PRODUCT&EntityKey=6388>.

G.G. Hall, *Culturally Competent Patient Care: A Guide for Providers and Their Staff* (October 2001), Institute for Health Professions Education, available online at: <www.de.state.az.uz>.

J. Ikeda, M.A., R.D.; University of California, Berkley Charles Tidwell Jr. PhD; Andrews University, Berrien Springs, *Michigan Providers Guide to Quality and Culture*: <http://erc.msh.org/mainpage.cfm?file=4.6.0.htm&module= provider&language=English>.

Ipsos Reid, "New Research Tool Examines Needs of Ethnic and New Canadians" (April 22, 2009), available online at: <http://www.ipsos-na.com/news/pressrelease.cfm?id=4354>.

P.G. Kittler & K.P. Sucher, *Food and Culture,* 3rd ed. (Belmont, CA: Wadsworth/Thompson Learning, 2001).

A. Kleinman, *Patients and Healers in the Context of Culture* (Berkeley, CA: University of California Press, 1981).

M. Leininger & M. McFurland, *Culture Care Diversity and Universality: A Worldwide Nursing Theory* (Boston, CT: Jones and Bartlett, 2006).

R.A. Levy & J.W. Hawks, "Multicultural Medicine and Pharmacy" (1996) 7:3 Drug Benefit Trends 27.

P. Lister (1999) reported in *National Review of Nursing Education — Multicultural Nursing Education*, "5. Australian Nursing Education Today" (2001), on the DEST Commonwealth Department of Education, Science and Technology website, available online at: <http://www.dest.gov.au/ archive/HIGHERED/nursing/pubs/multi_cultural/5.htm>.

M. Wilson, R. Joffe & B. Wilkerson, *The Unheralded Business Crisis in Canada: Depression at Work,* An Information Paper for Business, incorporating "12 Steps to A Business Plan to Defeat Depression" (Toronto: Global Business and Economic Roundtable on Addiction and Mental Health, 2002) at 22, available online at: <http://www.mentalhealthroundtable.ca/aug_round_pdfs/ Roundtable%20report_Jul20.pdf>.

T. McDonald & H. Harder, "Older Workers and Disability Management" (2004) 3:3 International Journal of Disability, Community & Rehabilitation 1, available online at: <http://www.ijdcr.ca/VOL03_03_CAN/index.shtml>.

D. Morris, *Bodytalk: The Meaning of Human Gestures* (New York: Crown Trade Paperbacks, 1994), reported in *The Provider's Guide to Quality & Culture*, "Topic 9: Non-verbal Communication" (2009), on the Management for Sciences for Health website, available at: <http://erc.msh. org/mainpage.cfm?file=4.6.0.htm&module=provider&language=English>.

H.V. Ngo, *Cultural Competency: A Self-Assessment Guide for Human Service Organizations* (Calgary, AB: Cultural Diversity Institute, 2000).

L. Olsen, J. Bhattacharya, & A. Scharf, *Cultural Competency: What It Is and Why It Matters*, California Tomorrow, Lucile Packard Foundation for Children's Health (December 7, 2006), available online at: <http://www.lpfch.org/informed/culturalcompetency.pdf>.

R. Pauly, *Cultural Diversity: Increasing Awareness* (2003), University of Florida, Department of Medicine reported in C. Brannon, *Cultural Competency: Values, Traditions and Effective Practice* (2007), available online at : <http://www.rd411.com/ce_modules.CUC06.pdf>.

Seattle King County Dept of Public Health (1994), reported in *National Review of Nursing Education — Multicultural Nursing Education*, "5. Australian Nursing Education Today" (2001), on the DEST Commonwealth Department of Education, Science and Technology website, available online at: <http://www.dest.gov.au/archive/HIGHERED/nursing/pubs/multi_cultural/5.htm>.

J. Sobal, "Social and Cultural Influences on Obesity", in P. Björntorp, ed., *International Textbook of Obesity* (London: John Wiley and Sons, 2001) 305.

Statistics Canada, *A Profile of Disability in Canada, 2001* (Ottawa: Statistics Canada, 2003), available online at: <http://www.statcan.gc.ca/pub/89-577-x/index-eng.htm>.

Statistics Canada, *Average Hourly Wages of Employees by Selected Characteristics*, available online at: <http://www40.statcan.gc.ca/l01/cst01/labr69a-eng.htm>.

Statistics Canada, *Canada's Ethnocultural Mosaic, 2006 Census: 2006 Census Year* (April 2008), Catalogue no. 97-562-X, available online at: <http://www12.statcan.gc.ca/english/census06/analysis/ethnicorigin/pdf/97-562-XIE2006001.pdf>.

Statistics Canada, "Study: Canada's Immigrant Labour Market", *The Daily* (September 10, 2007), available online at: <http://www.statcan.gc.ca/daily-quotidien/070910/dq070910a-eng.htm>.

Statistics Canada, *Work Absence Rates, 2007*, Cat. No. 71-211-XWE (Ottawa: Statistics Canada, May 2008).

U.S. Census Bureau, *Race — Universe: Total Population, 2006 American Community Survey*, available online at: <http://factfinder.census.gov>.

Wikipedia, *Immigration to the United States* (2009), available online at: <http://en.wikipedia.org/wiki/Immigration_to_the_United_States#Demographics>.

K. Williams, "Returning to Work After Disability: What Goes Wrong?" (Presented at Canadian Human Resource Planners event, May 15, 2003, Calgary, AB) [unpublished].

E. Winters, *Cultural Issues in Communication* (2002), available online at: <http://www.citehr.com/12441-cross-cultural-issues-communiation.html>.

Chapter 22

Impact of Four Generations in the Workplace On Disability Management Programs

INTRODUCTION

For the first time in history, there are four distinct generations working in today's workplaces. According to Howland, 90 per cent of Canadian workplaces employ four generations of workers,[1] and 40 per cent of the surveyed Canadians report that a multi-generational workplace adds challenges to the job.[2]

The issue is that each generation has it own beliefs, attitudes, values, communication styles, and work styles. Each has a unique set of expectations of management and the work environment. The outcome is that these generational differences can affect everything: employee recruitment, selection and retention practices; leadership; building work teams; managing and motivating employees; and maintaining and increasing productivity.

This unique situation of having four generations in the workplace raises questions like:

- What impact will each of these generations have on employer absenteeism and disability management efforts?
- How will the inter-generational differences impact absenteeism and disability rates and processes?

Disability management practitioners/professionals are advised to explore and appreciate the impact that sociological and demographic changes have on employees and the world of work. Rethinking how disability management services are packaged and delivered is recommended.

---

[1] A. Howland, "Multi-Generations Bring Challenge to Workplace", *The Vancouver Province* (May 27, 2007), available online at: <http://www.canada.com/theprovince/news/working/story.html?id=c25b6bfa-f64a-40a5-a7d8-7de807e3ce63>.

[2] *Ibid.*

WHAT IS A GENERATION?

The term, **generation**, was traditionally defined as "the average interval of time between the birth of parents and the birth of their offspring".[3] However, this definition has changed and today, the term **generation** is viewed as a set of people (cohort) born within the same period of time (approximately a 20-year span), and whose lives and viewpoints were shaped by the events within that span of time.[4] As a result, a given generational cohort shares similar unique values, attitudes, and behaviours.

According to Strauss & Howe,[5] the 20th Century generations are:

Table 22.1: The 20th Century Generations

Generation	Other Names	Period of Time
Hero Generation	GI Generation, Greatest Generation[6]	1901-1924
Veteran Generation	Traditionalists, Depression Generation, Silent Generation	1925-1942
Baby Boomers	Boom Generation, Me Generation	1943-1964
Generation X	Baby Busters, 13th Generation, Post-Boomers	1965-1981
Baby Boomlets	Generation Y, Echo Boomers, Nexus, Nexters, Millenial, Generation Me	1982+

Note: *Depending on the country, sociologist, researcher, or author, there is a great deal of variance in terms of the actual dates of the onset and closure of the generations.*

It is important to note that individuals born on the "cusp of a generation" may have a blended set of characteristics of the primary and following generation.[7] Some authors term these individuals who demonstrate the traits of either generation as "cuspers".[8]

For the purposes of this text, the following generational dates will be used:

• Veteran Generation, born 1927-1945.

---

[3] M. McCrindle, *New Generations at Work: Attracting, Recruiting, Retraining & Training Generation Y* (Sydney, NSW, Australia: McCrindle Research, 2006) at 8, available online at <http://www.mccrindle.com.au/resources.htm>.

[4] *Ibid.*

[5] W. Strauss & N. Howe, *Generations: The History of America's Future, 1584 to 2069* (New York: Harper Perennial, 1992) (reprint).

[6] Coined by journalist, Tom Brokaw in his book, T. Brokaw, *The Greatest Generation* (New York: Random House, 1998).

[7] D. McPhail, Corporate Perspectives on Workplace Learning "Four Generations in the Workforce", (May 9, 2006). Presentation made on behalf of TELUS, AB, available online at: <http://www.wln.ualberta.ca/seminar_resources/Generations_May9.ppt>.

[8] A. Stefaniak, *Black Hole or Window of Opportunity? Understanding the Generational Gap in Today's Workplace*, Policy Brief: 04-11-07, Center for Public Policy & Administration, available online at: <http://www.cppa.utah.edu/publications/workforce/Generations.pdf>.

- Baby Boomers, born 1946-1964.
- Generation X, born 1965-1979.
- Baby Boomlet Generation, 1980-2000.

WHAT IS A GENERATION GAP?

By nature, generations tend to be skeptical of the preceding and subsequent generations. The term, **generation gap**, refers to the differences between the members of two different generations.

This phenomenon can also be referred to as the "clash of the generations", with the reasons for the differences deemed as the clash points. A **Clashpoint®**[9] is an aspect of the workplace where generational differences of perspective, attitude, and opinion tend occur. They tend to include career goals, performance feedback, performance rewards, job changes, and retirement.[10]

Generations tend to differ on many of the following:

- the social, political, and economic influencers that they experience;
- family structure and dynamics;
- educational opportunities and format;
- life values;
- attitude toward work;
- work ethics;
- company loyalty;
- preferred leadership styles; [11]
- work styles;
- communication styles;
- need for performance feedback;
- preferred delivery of performance feedback, both in frequency and method of delivery;
- their relationship with technology;
- motivational drivers;
- preferred degree of recognition and type of rewards for good performance;
- job satisfaction criteria;
- career expectations;
- relationship practices;
- spending habits; and
- the preferred balance between work and personal time.

---

[9] L. Lancaster & D. Stillman, *When Generations Collide: Who They Are, Why They Clash, How to Solve the Generational Puzzle at Work* (New York: Harper Collins, 2002).

[10] *Ibid.*

[11] M. McCrindle, *New Generations at Work: Attracting, Recruiting, Retraining & Training Generation Y* (Sydney, NSW, Australia: McCrindle Research, 2006), available online at: <http://www.mccrindle.com.au/resources.htm>.

The differences between the generations affect interpersonal, team, and supervisory interactions and relationships. To put this into perspective, each of the Veterans and Baby Boomer generations have erroneously assumed that the newer generations entering the workforce will measure success like they do and that they will be willing to climb corporate ladders and "pay their dues" to achieve success.[12]

UNDERSTANDING GENERATIONAL DIFFERENCES: THE BENEFITS

Recently, much attention has been paid to the existence of the four generations in the workplace. Is this all "hype", or is it a topic for valid concern? Many folks believe it to be the latter, and that belief, is supported by recent American demographic statistics (Figure 22.1).

Figure 22.1: Percentage of American Workers in the Workplace by Generation: 2006-2011* (projected)[13]

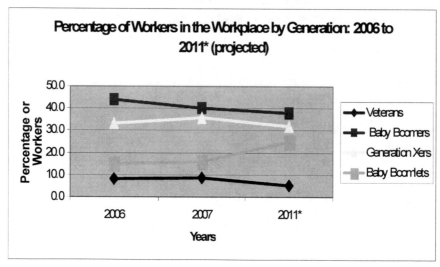

---

[12] C. Marston, *Motivating the "What's in It for Me?" Workforce: Manage Across the Generational Divide and Increase Profits* (Hoboken, N.J.: John Wiley & Sons, 2007).

[13] Data from two sources: 1) AARP, *Leading a Multigenerational Workforce* (Washington, DC: AARP, 2007), available online at: <http://www.aarp.org/money/work/employer_resource_ctr/articles/workforce_publications_for_employers.html>; and 2) T.K. McNamara, "Analysis of the March 1977 and 2007 Current Population Surveys", unpublished raw data (2007), reported in J. Dobbs, P. Healey, K. Kane, D. Mak, & T. K. McNamara, *The Multi-Generational Workplace, Fact Sheet #9* (July 2007), The Center on Aging & Work: Workplace Flexibility, Boston College, available online at: <http://agingandwork.bc.edu/documents/FS09_MultiGenWorkplace_000.pdf>.

As graphically shown, in 2006, the Baby Boomers constituted 44 per cent of the workforce (66 million); Generation Xers made up 33 per cent of the workforce (50 million); Baby Boomlets numbered 15 per cent (22 million); and Veterans, 8 per cent (12.5 million). By 2007, these percentages shifted with more Generation Xers and Baby Boomlets entering the workforce and a slight decrease in the number of the Veterans and Baby Boomers. The projections for 2011 forecast a significant increase in the percentage of the Baby Boomlets that will enter the workforce, with only slight changes in the percentage of Veterans, Baby Boomers, and Generation Xers. Hence, organizations and employers are advised to understand the generational differences with which they will be faced.

The benefits of understanding the generational differences are that this approach:

- *Supports the Corporate Culture*: By educating employees on generational differences, a milieu of acceptance, respect, and productivity can be achieved.[14]

- *Leads to Effective Recruitment, Selection, and Retention*: With many organizations experiencing high retirement rates, there is a need to understand the major generational differences in order to both attract and keep good employees.

- *Supports Real Communication*: It enables more effective communication and hopefully, fewer misunderstandings and relationship issues within the workplace.

- *Enhances Employee Engagement*: It allows for the development and use of more effective motivational approaches and methods with employees, and It promotes teamwork and increased worker productivity.

- *Fortifies the Employer-Employee Relationship*: It enhances employer-employee expectations and hence, their respective perceptions of the work relationship. Here is a need to understand what employees want from a job, what they expect from management, and what they will do if the organization or management fails to meet their expectations.[15]

- *Strengthens Issue Management*: It helps organizations to better manage workplace situations, such as employee absenteeism and disability,

---

[14]   AARP, *Leading a Multigenerational Workforce* (Washington, DC: AARP, 2007) at 4, available online at: <http://www.aarp.org/money/work/employer_resource_ctr/articles/workforce_publications_for_employers.html>.

[15]   D. McPhail, Corporate Perspectives on Workplace Learning, *"Four Generations in the Workforce"*, (May 9, 2006). Presentation made on behalf of TELUS, AB., available online at: <http://www.wln.ualberta.ca/seminar_resources/Generations_May9.ppt>.

- *Enhances Customer Service*: It helps the organization to better understand and address customer preferences and needs across the age spectrum.

Organizations can develop high performance workplaces by:

- understanding each generation — how the generation was shaped, the key influencers, and the resultant impact on the generation's values, attitudes, and behaviours;

- establishing an integrated system of policies, a supportive work environment, and work tools/technologies designed to bridge the generations and to bring out the "best" of each generation;[16] and

- creating a "**generation-neutral**" **workplace** — a workplace that values and utilizes the contributions of all generations.[17]

THE FOUR GENERATIONS: DESCRIPTIONS

Although throughout the centuries generations have been identified, labelled, and described, the focus of this text will be on the four generations currently found in today's workplaces, namely:

1.   Veterans, Traditionalists, or the Depression Generation

Workers born between 1927 and 1945 make up this generation called The Veterans. Veterans believe in duty, honour, and country, and are dedicated workers who value sacrifice, conformity, and patience. Dubbed the "Silent Generation", this generation brings a traditional and realistic attitude to the workplace. Today's business infrastructure was established by the Veterans, and their values and work ethic continue to influence modern business policies and procedures.[18]

Now aged 64-82 years old, Veterans are approaching retirement, or have retired and returned to the workforce. Some Veterans are currently working because of financial reasons, or a desire to remain physically, mentally, and socially active, as well as productive.[19]

---

[16] K. Kirkpatrick, S. Martin & S. Warneke, *Strategies for the Intergenerational Workplace* (July 17, 2008), Gensler, available online at: <http://www.gensler.com/uploads/documents/Intergenerational Workplace_07_17_2008.pdf>.

[17] AARP, *Leading a Multigenerational Workforce* (Washington, DC: AARP, 2007) at 5, available online at: <http://www.aarp.org/money/work/employer_resource_ctr/articles/workforce_publications_for_employers.html>.

[18] *Ibid.*, at 9.

[19] E. Quick, "Disability Management that Works", *Benefits and Compensation Solutions Magazine* (January/February 2007) at 46, available online at: <http://www.bcsolutionsmag.com/disability_management/>.

The issue that employers face with these workers is that they are not sure how to use these very experienced older workers. Although Veterans are reliable workers, possess a wealth of experience, and have a strong work ethic, they are now working in low-end service jobs. Employed in entry-level positions, they tend to make up the "shadow workforce" and absorb the "first jobs" typically held by workers entering the workplace — jobs that set the foundation for the building of work ethics of the generation entering the workplace.

Veterans, having been greatly influenced by the stock market crash and the Hindenberg Tragedy, Great Depression, World War II, VE Day, Winston Churchill, the Atomic Bomb, Korean War, and the Cold War, display traits such as:

- deep patriotic values;
- practicality;
- a prudent approach to life and spending — they tend to save their money to pad their "nest-egg";
- when spending, valuing quality and nationally-made products;
- a willingness to make personal sacrifices for delayed gratification;
- possessing a black and white world view;
- strong family values — great belief in the nuclear family;
- strong religious beliefs and reliance on the church;
- strong company loyalty;
- acceptance of hierarchical leadership;
- respect of authority;
- valuing a command and control approach to management and the chain of command;[20]
- not valuing individualism — believing in working together towards a common good;
- participation in team work provided they lead the team;
- valuing work relationships;
- viewing work performance feedback in terms of "no news is good news";
- believing that men belong in the workplace, women in the home;
- an inability to understand the need for work/life balance — struggling with the concept of leisure and recreation time; and
- a reluctance to exercise.

Having experienced the hardships of life during World War II and the Great Depression, Veterans came into the workplace with an attitude of "head down, onward and forward".[21] Disciplined and respectful of rules and regulations,

---

[20]   J. Duchscher & L. Cowen, "Multigenerational Nurses in the Workplace" (2004) 34:11 Journal of Nursing Administration 493.

[21]   L. Lancaster & D. Stillman, *When Generations Collide: Who They Are, Why They Clash, How to Solve the Generational Puzzle at Work* (New York: Harper Collins, 2002).

Veterans are used to a management style that gives orders and disseminates information on a "need to know" basis. For them, job satisfaction is a "job well-done, and career advancement is seniority-based, with seniority directly associated with "age".

The Veterans' work values include loyalty, dependability, persistence, hard work to get ahead, authoritarian leadership, and wisdom and experience over technical knowledge. The Veterans have been viewed as being adaptive in nature,[22] although today they remain uncomfortable with the blend of technology and age/gender/ethnic diversity in the workplace.[23]

2.   Baby Boomers

Born between 1946 and 1964, these workers are the heart and soul of today's workforce in many countries. This very large generation,[24] which is now between the ages of 45 and 63 years, has shaped the face of the North American work scene for a number of years. They defined "what is good and acceptable".[25]

Influenced by Civil Rights, War on Poverty, Atomic Age, Race to Space, Vietnam War, political turmoil of assassinations (J.F. Kennedy and Martin Luther King), impeachment (Richard Nixon), the Beatles, Woodstock, the death of John Lennon, the sexual revolution,[26] space travel, Dr. Benjamin Spock, and the first heart transplant, this cohort has challenged the existing social institutions, conventions, and assumptions through the use of protests.

Baby Boomers were the first generation in which students were graded on report cards for "works well with others" and "shares materials with classmates".[27] Not surprisingly, Baby Boomers prefer to work collaboratively and in team settings. Some of their contributions are business practices such as participative management, quality circles, employee involvement, and team building.[28]

---

[22]   W. Strauss & N. Howe, *Generations: The History of America's Future, 1584 to 2069* (New York: Harper Perennial, 1992) (reprint).

[23]   K. Kirkpatrick, S. Martin & S. Warneke, *Strategies for the Intergenerational Workplace* (July 17, 2008), Gensler, available online at: <http://www.gensler.com/uploads/documents/Intergenerational Workplace_07_17_2008.pdf>.

[24]   Baby Boomers are estimated to number 80 million in the United States of America; 10 million in Canada; and 5.3 million in Australia.

[25]   A. Stefaniak, *Black Hole or Window of Opportunity? Understanding the Generational Gap in Today's Workplace* at 5, Policy Brief: 04-11-07, Center for Public Policy & Administration, available online at: <http://www.cppa.utah.edu/publications/workforce/Generations.pdf>.

[26]   Office of Institutional Equity, Duke University, *Cross Generational Communication: Implications in the Work Environment* (April 2008), available online at: <http://www.duke.cd4/web/equity/Diversity. htm>.

[27]   AARP, *Leading a Multigenerational Workforce* (Washington, DC: AARP, 2007) at 10, available online at: <http://www.aarp.org/money/work/employer_resource_ctr/articles/workforce_publications_ for_employers.html>.

[28]   *Ibid.*

Boomers seek lots of control in their lives and perceive that they do not have it. Dubbed the "whiners", today, Baby Boomers are viewed as a disenchanted group because "the promise that they bought into" was that by this time in their careers/lives, they would not be working as hard as they are. The result is that many Boomers go to work, but are not really fully engaged.[29]

Having grown up in relative prosperity and safety, child abductions, terrorism, world pollution and pessimism, were not part of the Boomers' world view. Hence, this generation has been described as idealistic and optimistic, believing they could change the world for the better.[30] Boomers chose the workplace as the arena in which they would "prove their worth".[31]

Generalizing, Baby Boomers as a generation:

- are extremely competitive due to the enormous size of the generation;
- crave stability and dislike change;[32]
- are strong consumers;
- buy goods partly because they like them, but mainly to impress others;
- tend to buy foreign goods for prestige reasons;
- are heavily into personal gratification;[33]
- are known as the true "Sandwich Generation" with responsibilities to aging parents and children;
- view religion as a "hobby", although they tend to be spiritual in nature;
- are communitarians;[34]
- prefer leadership by consensus — in fact, they were the originators of consensus-based leadership;[35]
- value participatory leadership and coaching;[36]
- have a "love/hate" relationship with authority;
- value being able to work collaboratively;[37]
- work hard, play hard — they personify the term, "workaholic";

---

[29] J. Jamrog, "The Perfect Storm" (Presented at a CHRP Seminar, Calgary, AB, September 15, 2005) [unpublished].

[30] L. Lancaster & D. Stillman, *When Generations Collide: Who They Are, Why They Clash, How to Solve the Generational Puzzle at Work* (New York: Harper Collins, 2002).

[31] AARP, *Leading a Multigenerational Workforce* (Washington, DC: AARP, 2007) at 10, available online at <http://www.aarp.org/money/work/employer_resource_ctr/articles/workforce_publications_for_employers.html>.

[32] S. Calhoun & P. Strasser, "Generations at Work" (2005) 53:11 American Association of Occupational Health Nurses Journal 469.

[33] K. Kirkpatrick, S. Martin, & S. Warneke, *Strategies for the Intergenerational Workplace* (July 17, 2008), Gensler, available online at: <http://www.gensler.com/uploads/documents/Intergenerational Workplace_07_17_2008.pdf>.

[34] *Ibid.*

[35] *Ibid.*

[36] S. Calhoun & P. Strasser, "Generations at Work" (2005) 53:11 American Association of Occupational Health Nurses Journal 469.

[37] *Ibid.*

- value their reputation;
- tend to lack realistic views of their abilities and stamina;[38]
- value profitability and tend to worry lots about money;
- prefer yearly feedback work performance and with documentation; and
- perceive exercising as a duty.

The Baby Boomers' work values include employer loyalty, an acceptance of long work hours and stress, team-oriented, high regard for title and status symbols, demand respect and sacrifice from subordinates, "live to work", value job security, and seek to have their contributions recognized.

3.   Generation X or the Baby Bust Generation

Deemed the "slackers", Generation Xers were born between 1965 and 1979. Their values differ greatly from those held by the Boomers. They grew up with self-immersed,[39] workaholic parents.[40] Being "latch-key children" who watched their parents being "laid off" after years of hard work and personal sacrifices for "the company", this cohort tends to display great skepticism, independence, resourcefulness, and "street-smarts". In addition, they were impacted by increased technology, personal computers, Bill Gates, video games, Madonna, cultural diversity, homelessness, nuclear threats and disasters (Three-Mile Island and Chernobyl), environmental disasters (Exxon Valdez Oil Spill), rap music, anti-child society, Watergate, the fall of the Berlin Wall, Tiananmen Square Uprising, and AIDS.

A small generation, Generation X views itself as neglected. Mistrustful of institutions and organizations, Generations Xers readily move from job to job seeking the work knowledge and skills that they want. Their loyalties revolve around their friends and family, not their jobs.[41]

Some other characteristics of Generation Xers are that they:

- are skeptical; [42]
- are cynical;
- are pessimistic;
- are pragmatic; [43]
- are nonconformists;

---

[38]   *Ibid.*

[39]   J. Duchscher & L. Cowen, "Multigenerational Nurses in the Workplace" (2004) 34:11 Journal of Nursing Administration 493.

[40]   N. Pekala, "Conquering the Generational Divide" (2001) 66:6 Journal of Property Management 30.

[41]   R. Zemke, "Generations at Work" (2001), CEO Agenda Series, available online at: <http://www. asaecenter.org/PublicationsResources/articledetail.cfm?ItemNumber=13053>.

[42]   K. Kirkpatrick, S. Martin & S. Warneke, *Strategies for the Intergenerational Workplace* (July 17, 2008), Gensler, available online at: <http://www.gensler.com/uploads/documents/Intergenerational Workplace_07_17_2008.pdf>.

[43]   *Ibid.*

- come from divorced, single-parent, and/or blended families; [44]
- value self-empowerment; [45]
- are self-reliant; [46]
- are independent thinkers and actors;
- learned to trust themselves, not institutions [47] — hence, they tend not to be into established community groups like the Lions Club or Rotary, or religion;
- possess an attitude of "I like it and I don't care what you think";
- are reluctant to commit to a relationship: prefer trial marriages/relationships;
- like inner-city living;
- thrive on chaos and change; [48]
- are avid risk-takers; [49]
- value exercise for the well-being of their mental health;
- strongly value work/life balance and they want it *Now*;
- believe work is important [50] — they will work hard provided work does not interfere with their play plans;
- are willing to sacrifice some personal life for career advancement;
- value leader competence;
- are neither unimpressed nor intimidated by authority;
- seek stimulation, balance, and feedback from their work world — they tend to want regular and timely feedback on their work performance;
- are action-oriented; [51]

---

[44] AARP, *Leading a Multigenerational Workforce* (Washington, DC: AARP, 2007) at 12, available online at: <http://www.aarp.org/money/work/employer_resource_ctr/articles/workforce_publications_for_employers.html>.

[45] L. Lancaster & D. Stillman, *When Generations Collide: Who They Are, Why They Clash, How to Solve the Generational Puzzle at Work* (New York: Harper Collins, 2002).

[46] K. Kirkpatrick, S. Martin & S. Warneke, *Strategies for the Intergenerational Workplace* (July 17, 2008), Gensler, available online at: <http://www.gensler.com/uploads/documents/Intergenerational Workplace_07_17_2008.pdf>.

[47] L. Lancaster & D. Stillman, *When Generations Collide: Who They Are, Why They Clash, How to Solve the Generational Puzzle at Work* (New York: Harper Collins, 2002).

[48] AARP, *Leading a Multigenerational Workforce* (Washington, DC: AARP, 2007) at 12, available online at <http://www.aarp.org/money/work/employer_resource_ctr/articles/workforce_publications_for_employers.html> at 12.

[49] K. Kirkpatrick, S. Martin & S. Warneke, *Strategies for the Intergenerational Workplace* (July 17, 2008), Gensler, available online at <http://www.gensler.com/uploads/documents/Intergenerational Workplace_07_17_2008.pdf>.

[50] L. Lancaster & D. Stillman, *When Generations Collide: Who They Are, Why They Clash, How to Solve the Generational Puzzle at Work* (New York: Harper Collins, 2002).

[51] K. Kirkpatrick, S. Martin & S. Warneke, *Strategies for the Intergenerational Workplace* (July 17, 2008), Gensler, available online at: <http://www.gensler.com/uploads/documents/Intergenerational Workplace_07_17_2008.pdf>.

- are results-focused[52] — enjoy achieving measurable results and streamlining systems and processes;[53]
- are techno-savvy;[54]
- prefer informality;[55]
- value recognition for their achievements; and
- are good at saving money.

In terms of work, they are determined to manage their own time. They value minimal supervision, a flexible work schedule, participatory leadership and coaching.[56] Being influenced by sweeping social changes and being "the children of divorce" and familial change, Generation Xers tend to be less trusting,[57] but more adept at accepting and adapting to chaos and change. When faced with meaningful work, leaders, and co-workers they respect, and a work schedule that meets their work-life balance needs, Generation Xers can be very creative and productive.[58]

4. Baby Boomlets (Echo Boomers, Nexus, Nexters, Generation Y and Millennial)

This last generational group, born 1980-2000, is currently nine (9) to 29 years of age. They are in the throws of starting a career and entering the workforce. Baby Boomlets have lived through and been influenced by:

- the Iraq War;
- business/corporate scandals (*i.e.*, Enron);
- multiculturalism and globalism;
- global terrorism, *e.g.*, September 11th;
- rapidly expanding technology (Internet, DVD);
- the death of Princess Diana;
- Rap and Hip Hop music;
- the Oklahoma City bombing;
- the Columbine and other school shootings;

---

[52] *Ibid.*

[53] AARP, *Leading a Multigenerational Workforce* (Washington, DC: AARP, 2007) at 12, available online at: <http://www.aarp.org/money/work/employer_resource_ctr/articles/workforce_publications_for_employers.html>.

[54] K. Kirkpatrick, S. Martin & S. Warneke, *Strategies for the Intergenerational Workplace* (July 17, 2008), Gensler, available online at: <http://www.gensler.com/uploads/documents/Intergenerational Workplace_07_17_2008.pdf>.

[55] *Ibid.*

[56] S. Calhoun & P. Strasser, "Generations at Work" (2005) 53:11 American Association of Occupational Health Nurses Journal 469.

[57] K. Kirkpatrick, S. Martin & S. Warneke, *Strategies for the Intergenerational Workplace* (July 17, 2008), Gensler, available online at: <http://www.gensler.com/uploads/documents/Intergenerational Workplace_07_17_2008.pdf>.

[58] *Ibid.*

- the Dot.Com Crash;
- the proliferation of communication and mobile technologies; and
- the tsunami in Asian Ocean.

Being the largest generation of "have and have nots", this group has been greatly impacted by environmental concerns, violence and bullying, terrorism, and being "wired" to technology. Life without technology is inconceivable to them.

Baby Boomlets are the first generation to grow up without expectations of living within a nuclear family — less than 33 per cent lived in homes with two parents.[59] One estimate is that 25 per cent of the Baby Boomlets are the product of single parent families.[60] Additionally, both parents worked: one estimate is that 75 per cent of Baby Boomlets have working mothers.[61]

Interestingly, despite the breakdown of the nuclear family through divorce and single parenthood, Baby Boomlet families tended to be child-centred, with both parents involved in their children's education and activities.[62] Their parents wanted to give the children the "best".[63] Possibly this is the reason why reportedly, Baby Boomlets have developed close parent-child relationships.[64]

Baby Boomlets were raised or are being raised by parents who involved them in a whirlwind of extra-curricular activities. They were/are the busiest kids ever, with many of them carrying daytimers to track their daily activities.[65] Because their parents did not, and do not, know how to deal with their children's "hyperactivity", Baby Boomlets have the distinction of being the most medicated generation ever.[66] In fact, some socialists feel that these children are growing up with a form of post-traumatic stress disorder.[67]

---

[59] J. Duchscher & L. Cowen, "Multigenerational Nurses in the Workplace" (2004) 34:11 Journal of Nursing Administration 493.

[60] A. Schwartz, *Generations at Work: Understanding and Influencing* (2008), available online at: <http://www.wiziq.com/tutorial/13675-Generations-at-Work-PowerPoint-Content>.

[61] *Ibid.*

[62] *Ibid.*

[63] K. Kirkpatrick, S. Martin & S. Warneke, *Strategies for the Intergenerational Workplace* (July 17, 2008), Gensler, available online at: <http://www.gensler.com/uploads/documents/Intergenerational Workplace_07_17_2008.pdf>.

[64] A. Schwartz, *Generations at Work: Understanding and Influencing* (2008), available online at: <http://www.duke.edu/web/equity/Diversity.htm>.

[65] A reason put forth for this phenomenon of "busy children" is that their parents, the Generation Xers, who got into trouble in their younger years, opted to keep their children too busy to "follow in their footstep". *Source:* A. Stefaniak, *Black Hole or Window of Opportunity? Understanding the Generational Gap in Today's Workplace* at 6, Policy Brief: 04-11-07, Center for Public Policy & Administration available online at: <http://www.cppa.utah.edu/publications/workforce/Generations.pdf>.

[66] J. Jamrog, "The Perfect Storm" (Presented at a CHRP Seminar, Calgary, AB, September 15, 2005) [unpublished].

[67] *Ibid.*

This generation tends to use online technology to forge relationships. Reportedly, 35 per cent of them report having found their "best friends" online.[68] As well, Boomlets rank high in terms of sociability, civic duty, and morality.[69]

As a generation, the specific traits of the Baby Boomlets include:

- optimistic; [70]
- very pragmatic; [71]
- very realistic; [72]
- being less skeptical and angry with life and the world than are the Generation Xers; [73]
- being "Gap" shoppers; [74]
- valuing inclusive relationships;
- desiring flexibility in their daily routine;
- willingness to participate in community endeavours;
- judging institutions by their own merit; [75]
- strongly disliking organized groups like labour unions;
- inability to relate with religion;
- being heavily into playing sports;
- liking living with their parents;
- valuing cultural diversity in the workplace and work well in diverse workgroups; [76]
- possessing a global perspective on world events; [77]
- viewing leadership as "pulling together" for a cause;
- valuing collaboration and relationship-oriented leadership;[78]
- being polite towards authority figures;

---

[68] *Ibid.*

[69] FGI, "One Workplace, Four Generations: Managing the Conflicting Needs", *Working Well for Managers* (September 2004), published by FGI, Thornhill, ON, available online at: <www.mta.ca/hr/managers/workingwell_sept2004.pdf>.

[70] K. Kirkpatrick, S. Martin & S. Warneke, *Strategies for the Intergenerational Workplace* (July 17, 2008), Gensler, available online at: <http://www.gensler.com/uploads/documents/Intergenerational Workplace_07_17_2008.pdf>.

[71] L. Lancaster & D. Stillman, *When Generations Collide: Who They Are, Why They Clash, How to Solve the Generational Puzzle at Work* (New York: Harper Collins, 2002).

[72] *Ibid.*

[73] *Ibid.*

[74] J. Jamrog, "The Perfect Storm" (Presented at a CHRP Seminar, Calgary, AB, September 15, 2005) [unpublished].

[75] L. Lancaster & D. Stillman, *When Generations Collide: Who They Are, Why They Clash, How to Solve the Generational Puzzle at Work* (New York: Harper Collins, 2002).

[76] *Ibid.*

[77] *Ibid.*

[78] S. Calhoun & P. Strasser, "Generations at Work" (2005) 53:11 American Association of Occupational Health Nurses Journal 469.

- being ambitious but not entirely focused; [79]
- looking to the workplace for direction and an avenue for achieving their goals; [80]
- working towards getting good grades in school;
- being extremely techno-savvy; [81]
- seeking and demanding feedback on their work performance — they are used to getting feedback at the touch of a button;
- wanting balance in their lives; and
- valuing the saving of money.

The Baby Boomlet worker is characterized as having a relatively short attention span, expecting things to happen quickly, and seeking variety in life and work. These traits are often misunderstood and negatively viewed. In actuality, Baby Boomlets have a strong sense of self-worth, are ambitious, believe that they can achieve anything, and seek a variety of tasks and work experiences to demonstrate their abilities. Their "can-do" attitude about work tasks leads them to be viewed as over-confident, self-absorbed, and demanding, looking for feedback about how they are doing frequently — even daily. Hence, they have been called "Generation Me" and are viewed as being ready and willing to take on the world. Some researchers believe that they can more than measure up to their "can-do" attitudes. [82]

Unlike other generations, Baby Boomlets have developed work characteristics and tendencies from doting parents, structured lives, and contacts with diverse people. [83] They are used to working in teams and want to make friends with people at work. Baby Boomlets tend to work well with diverse coworkers and value the knowledge possessed by older workers. [84] Their values and worldviews are expected to make significant changes to society, and the work scene.

Given that approximately 75 million Baby Boomlets are preparing to enter the work place or have done so already, it is important to understand how best to

---

[79] A. Stefaniak, *Black Hole or Window of Opportunity? Understanding the Generational Gap in Today's Workplace* at 6, Policy Brief: 04-11-07, Center for Public Policy & Administration, available online at: <http://www.cppa.utah.edu/publications/workforce/Generations.pdf>.

[80] *Ibid.*

[81] L. Lancaster & D. Stillman, *When Generations Collide: Who They Are, Why They Clash, How to Solve the Generational Puzzle at Work* (New York: Harper Collins, 2002).

[82] A. Stefaniak, *Black Hole or Window of Opportunity? Understanding the Generational Gap in Today's Workplace* at 6, Policy Brief: 04-11-07, Center for Public Policy & Administration, available online at: <http://www.cppa.utah.edu/publications/workforce/Generations.pdf>; and S. Heathfield, *Managing Millennials: Eleven Tips for Managing Millennials* (2008), available online at: <http://humanresources.about.com/lr/managing_millennials/220710/1/>.

[83] S. Heathfield, *ibid.*

[84] Go2 Tourism HR Society, *Capitalizing on the Generational Gap in the Workplace* (2008), available online at: <http://www.go2hr.ca/ForbrEmployers/Retention/GenerationsintheWorkplace/tabid/566/Default.aspx>.

manage this generation of workers. According to Heathfield,[85] here are some tips for working with Baby Boomlets:

- provide them structure;
- provide them with leadership and guidance;
- encourage their self-assuredness, "can-do" attitude, and positive self-image;
- take advantage of their comfort level with teams and teamwork by encouraging them to join in;
- listen to them;
- provide them with challenges and ever-changing tasks;
- capitalize on their ability to multi-task;
- take advantage of their computer, telephone, and electronic literacy;
- benefit from their affinity to network with people;
- enable a reasonable work-life balance; and
- provide a fun, employee-centred workplace.

THE FOUR GENERATIONS: PERSONAL AND LIFESTYLE CHARACTERISTICS

Each generation has a unique worldview and approach to life and work. To illustrate this concept, a comparison table of the personal and lifestyle characteristics of the four generations follows (Table 22.1). Bear in mind, this stereotyping is meant to illustrate generational differences, not to be taken as representative of every member of a generational group.

---

[85]   S. Heathfield, *Managing Millennials: Eleven Tips for Managing Millennials* (2008), available online at: <http://humanresources.about.com/lr/managing_millennials/220710/1/>.

Table 22.1   Comparison of the Personal and Lifestyle Characteristics of the Four Generations[86]

Aspect	Veterans (~1927-1945)	Baby Boomers (~1946-1964)	Generation Xers (~1965-1979)	Baby Boomlets (~1980-2000)
Core Values	• Conformer • Discipline • Respect for authority • Sociability	• Optimistic • Involvement	• Skepticism • Fun • Informality	• Realism • Confidence • Extreme fun • Sociability
Outlook on life	• Adaptive	• Optimistic	• Skeptical	• Realistic
Family	• Nuclear family with support of extended family	• Nuclear family with some disintegration occurring • Some working mothers	• "The Children of Divorce" • Single-parent families • Working parents • "Latch-key kids"	• Single-parent families, blended families • Working parents
Education	A "dream"	A birthright	A way to get there	An incredible expense

[86] Adapted from: 1) D. McPhail, Corporate Perspectives on Workplace Learning, "Four Generations in the Workforce" (May 9, 2006). Presentation made on behalf of TELUS, AB, available online at: <http://www.wln.ualberta.ca/seminar_resources/Generations_May9.ppt>; 2) D. Dyck, "Multi-Generational Workplaces: The OH&S Challenge" (Presented at the American Occupational Health Nurses Symposium and Expo, Orlando, FL, April 2007) [unpublished]; 3) M. McCrindle, *New Generations at Work: Attracting, Recruiting, Retraining & Training Generation Y* (Sydney, NSW, Australia: McCrindle Research, 2006), available online at: <http://www.mccrindle.com.au/resources.htm>; 4) G. Hammill, "Mixing and Managing Four Generations of Employees", *FDU Magazine Online*, (Winter/Spring 2005), available online at: <http://www.fdu.edu/newspubs/magazine/05ws/generations.htm>; AARP, 5) *Leading a Multigenerational Workforce* (Washington, DC: AARP, 2007), available online at: <http://www.aarp.org/money/work/employer_resource_ctr/articles/workforce_publications_for_employers.html>; and 6) A. Stefaniak, *Black Hole or Window of Opportunity? Understanding the Generational Gap in Today's Workplace*, Policy Brief: 04-11-07, Center for Public Policy & Administration, available online at: <http://www.cppa.utah.edu/publications/workforce/Generations.pdf>.

Aspect	Veterans (~1927-1945)	Baby Boomers (~1946-1964)	Generation Xers (~1965-1979)	Baby Boomlets (~1980-2000)
Compelling Messages	• "Make do, or go without" • "Stay in line" • "Sacrifice" • "Consider the common good" • "Any job worth doing, is worth doing right"	• "Be anything you want to be" • "Change the world" • "Work well with others" • "Live up to expectations" • "Duck and cover"	• "Don't commit" • "Heroes don't exist" • "Get real!" • "Take care of yourself" • "Always ask, 'Why?'"	• "You are special" • "Leave no one behind" • "Connect 24/7" • "Achieve now!" • "Serve your community"
Communication Media	• Rotary phones • One-on-one talks • Write a memo	• Touch-tone phones • Television • Call me at any time	• Cell phone use • Call me only at work • Email messages	• Internet, email messages, chat lines, blogs • Text messages • Picture phones
Iconic Technology	• Newspaper • Telegraph • Radio	• TV • Audio Cassette • Colour TV • Fax Machines	• VCR • Walkman • Personal Computers	• Laptops • Internet/ • Email/ SMSing • DVD • Play Station/X-Box
Music	• Frank Sinatra • Bing Crosby • Duke Ellington	• Elvis • Beatles • Rolling Stones	• INXS • Nirvana • Madonna	• Eminem • Brittney Spears • Puff Daddy
TV and Movies	• No TV — just movies • Cassablanca • All Quiet on the Western Front • Gone with the Wind	• Easy Rider • The Graduate • Jaws	• ET • Hey Hey Its Saturday • MTV	• Titanic • Pay TV • Reality TV

Aspect	Veterans (~1927-1945)	Baby Boomers (~1946-1964)	Generation Xers (~1965-1979)	Baby Boomlets (~1980-2000)
Popular Culture	• Jazz • Nylon stockings	• Flare jeans • Mini skirts • Barbie • Frisbee	• Rollerblades • Hyper colour • Torn jeans	• Body piercing • Baseball caps • Men's cosmetics
Money Management	• Save for a rainy day • Pay cash	• Focus on long-term needs • Cash • Credit — buy now, pay later	• Focus on medium-term goals • Cautious with money • Conservative spenders • Save, save, save	• Focus on short-term wants • Earn to spend • Credit dependent
Approach to Relationships	• Uncomfortable with personal relationships • Committed to work	• Self-sacrifice	• Reluctant to commit to relationships	• Committed to success
Influencers	• Trial and error	• Evidential experts	• Pragmatic practitioners	• Experiential peers
Decision-making	• Reliant on commands • Individual • Trial and error	• Team-oriented • Collaborative decision-making • Consensus-based decision-making	• Self-reliant • Independent decision-making	• Focus on what is "good for all"
Media Images (images that may not accurately represent reality)	• Tired • Resent Generation X and Baby Boomlets for their entitlement mentality when Traditionalist had to work so hard for what they got in life	• Workaholic • Guilt-ridden • Resent Generation X and Baby Boomlets for frequent job change and for demanding work/life balance	• Tattooed • Slacker • Resent Veterans for resisting change	• Precocious • Resent Baby Boomers for leaving the planet in a mess • Clever • "Techno-kids"

Aspect	Veterans (~1927-1945)	Baby Boomers (~1946-1964)	Generation Xers (~1965-1979)	Baby Boomlets (~1980-2000)
Definition of Technology	• Massive structures, *e.g.*, Hoover Dam	• Anything that makes life easier, *e.g.*, microwave oven	• Can be held in one's hand, *e.g.*, cell phone, personal digital assistant	• Can't define technology — it is just there!
Current Life Challenges	• Dealing with aging parents, adult children and grandchildren • Experiencing own/spousal health issues • Require help with new technologies and workplace changes • Fail to understand the "new" employees of today • Often forgotten/neglected by companies: close to retirement	• Sandwiched between demands of aging parents and children • Need flexible work schedules, especially female workers • Seeking control over own life situation • High desire to excel career-wise, but have little time left to "reach the top" • Some question if they made the right career choices	• Dislike company rules, policies: tend to question authority • Want adequate explanations for why things are done a certain way • Concerned about their "shelf-life" at work — fear obsolescence • Approach life with a fair amount of skepticism	• Don't believe that they have to "pay their dues" and "bide their time" for job advancement • Strong dislike for organized groups (*e.g.*, labour unions) • Will be difficult to retain

THE FOUR GENERATIONS: IMPACT ON THE WORKPLACE

Over the years, the world of work has changed. Company loyalty and commitment to employers has vanished. Being at work on time has decreased in importance. Sick leave abuse is common. Job security and high pay are not the motivators they once were. Why? Young people have watched their parents remain loyal to their employees, only to witness them experience downsizing and layoffs.

Today, young workers are seeking jobs in which they can make a valuable contribution, work at a variety of tasks, and learn new marketable skills. They demand intellectual stimulation, team environments, transferability of work experiences, and salaries that match the rising cost of living. Interestingly, they do not believe they should have to "pay their dues" and bide their time for job advancement. Because they "work to live" and not "live to work", they refuse to be the workaholics that their parents were.

The Veterans and Baby Boomer are working their way towards retirement; however, some, for a variety of reasons, are choosing not to retire as soon as was once predicted. Likewise, some older workers who have retired are back doing entry-level jobs.

To illustrate the breakdown of workers by generation, McNamarra provides the results from the 2007 Current Population Survey, a survey done in the United States of America at Boston College.[87]

Figure 22.1: Percentage of Workers by Generation: March 2007

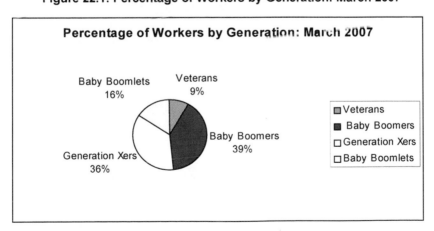

[87] T.K. McNamara, "Analysis of the March 1977 and 2007 Current Population Surveys", unpublished raw data (2007), reported in J. Dobbs, P. Healey, K. Kane, D. Mak, & T. K. McNamara, *The Multi-Generational Workplace, Fact Sheet #9* (July 2007), The Center on Aging & Work: Workplace Flexibility, Boston College, available online at: <http://agingandwork.bc.edu/documents/FS09_Multi GenWorkplace_000.pdf>.

With four generations in the workplace, each with their own beliefs, values, wants and needs, employers face the daunting challenge of trying to meet worker expectations. For example, meetings are viewed by Veterans and Baby Boomers as "busy work". They prefer short meetings, speedy decisions, and only want to meet when there is an urgent need. Generation Xers and Baby Boomlets tend to value the interaction and view meetings as a way to reach a solution to an identified problem.

Veterans and Boomers value rules and regulations. Generation Xers and Baby Boomlets have been known to ignore rules, policies, and chain-of-command. Baby Boomlets live in a world of advanced technology. They are techno-wizards who embrace technology as a normal element of their lives. Veterans and Boomers had to learn to adapt to technology and for some, there remains a healthy "distrust of these new tools".

At work, generational differences can affect everything from recruiting to teamwork, to change management, to motivating workers, and to managing and increasing productivity. To better understand the generations and their impact on the workplace, it is important to first understand the work characteristics of each generation (Table 22.2).

Table 22.2: Comparison of the Work Characteristics of the Four Generations[88]

Aspect	Veterans (~1927-1945)	Baby Boomers (~1946-1964)	Generation Xers (~1965-1979)	Baby Boomlets (~1980-2000)
Work Ethic and Values	• Hard work • Respect authority • Sacrifice • "Duty" before fun • Adhere to rules • A "head down, onward and upward" approach to work	• Workaholics • Work efficiently • Crusading causes • Personal growth and fulfilment • Desire quality • Question authority	• Eliminate the task • Self-reliant • Seek structure and direction • Skeptical	• Action-oriented • Multi-tasker • Tenacious • Entrepreneurial • Tolerant • Goal-oriented
Work is	• a duty or obligation	• an exiting adventure	• a difficult challenge; a contract	• a means to fulfill an end
Attitude towards work	• Glad to have a job — view work as a privilege • Dutiful • Personal attitudes do not factor into the equation	• Live to work • Driven • Dutiful, but focused on personal achievement and advancement	• Work to live • Balanced life • Do not want to be "tied to a desk" or even to one employer • Value achievement	• Work to live • Looking for meaning and relevance in work • Interested in life outside of work • Value achievement

88 Adapted from: 1) D. McPhail, Corporate Perspectives on Workplace Learning "Four Generations in the Workforce" (May 9, 2006). Presentation made on behalf of TELUS, AB, available online at: <http://www.wln.ualberta.ca/seminar_resources/Generations_May 9.ppt>; 2) D. Dyck, "Multi-Generational Workplaces: The OH&S Challenge". Presented at the American Occupational Health Nurses Symposium and Expo, Orlando, FL, April 2007) [unpublished]; 3) M. McCrindle, *New Generations at Work: Attracting, Recruiting, Retraining & Training Generation Y* (Sydney, NSW, Australia: McCrindle Research 2006), available online at: <http://www.mccrindle.com.au/resources.htm>; 4) G. Hammill, Mixing and Managing Four Generations of Employees", *FDU Magazine Online*, (Winter/Spring 2005), available online at: <http://www.fdu.edu/newspubs/magazine/05ws/generations.htm>; 5) AARP, *Leading a Multigenerational Workforce* Washington, DC: AARP, 2007), available online at: <http://www.aarp.org/money/work/employer_resource_ctr/articles/workforce_publications_for_employers.html>.

Aspect	Veterans (~1927-1945)	Baby Boomers (~1946-1964)	Generation Xers (~1965-1979)	Baby Boomlets (~1980-2000)
Preferred Management Style	• Chain of Command (*Command and control*) • Prefer formality • Expect to be told what to do, or to tell others what to do • Seek explanations/logic behind management decisions • Seek job explanations clearly spelled out — dislike "napkin work orders" • Want to be treated fairly, consistently, and with respect	• Consensus-based Command • Value having objectives and results stated in people-centred terms • Prefer to be part of work decisions — work by consensus • Originated the use of performance reviews • Like the democratic approach • Seek to be treated as equals	• Self-command (*Self-direction*) • Respect leaders based on merit, not position or title • Prefer to be told what is to be done and not how to do it • Like multi-tasking and freedom to set own work priorities	• A mix of *Self-command, Consensus* and *Collaboration* • Seek continuous learning opportunities and ability to hone their work skills • Value mentoring from managers and colleagues • Respond to a supportive, positive, and organized work environment • Want to be "coached", not "bossed" or micromanaged • Seek motivational and achievement-oriented managers
Preferred Leaders	Commanders	Thinkers	Doers	Feelers
View of Authority	• Value and respect authority • Time = right to authority	• Love/hate relationship • Time = right to authority	• Skeptical of authority • Constantly testing authority figures	• Ambivalent about authority • Will test authority • Look to authority figures to "Help me achieve my goals"[89]

89   C. Marston, "Four Generations in the Workplace: A Diversity Challenge" (Presentation delivered at Utah Department of Workforce Services: Roads to Success, Salt Lake City, UT, 2003) [unpublished].

Aspect	Veterans (~1927-1945)	Baby Boomers (~1946-1964)	Generation Xers (~1965-1979)	Baby Boomlets (~1980-2000)
Organizational Loyalty	• Dedicated — same company for entire career	• Loyal, but also upwardly mobile — will leave for career advancement	• Cynical about organizational loyalty: tend to direct loyalty to individual supervisors/managers. • Will have a number of jobs	• Loyal to managers when they receive help to achieve self-fulfilling jobs • Mobile, looking for what they need[90]
Sacrifice	Action taken for the "greater good".	Working hard for success.	Forfeiting personal time.	Do not make sacrifices: they pursue what is in their best interest.[91]
Work Assets	• Experienced • Knowledgeable • Dedication • Emotional maturity; stability • Perseverance	• Dedicated • Team player • Experienced • Knowledgeable	• Adaptable • Techno-literate • Independent • Creative • Challenge the system/status quo	• Extremely techno-savvy • Great multi-taskers • Value collaboration and team work • Optimistic
Work Liabilities	• Reluctant to challenge the system • Dislikes conflict • Reticent when they disagree	• Not "budget-minded" • Dislikes conflict • May focus more on the process instead of the outcome	• Skeptical • Distrust authority	• Inexperienced • Few people-management skills • Require supervision and structure

---

90 *Ibid.*

91 C. Marston, "Four Generations in the Workplace". (A presentation delivered at the Planned Parenthood Federation of America, Western Region Conference, Salt Lake City, UT, 2004) [unpublished].

Aspect	Veterans (~1927-1945)	Baby Boomers (~1946-1964)	Generation Xers (~1965-1979)	Baby Boomlets (~1980-2000)
Time at Work	• Punch in and out	• Visibility is important: long work hours (50 hours++ per week)	• Project oriented	• View work as a "gig" — in at 9 AM and out by 5 PM.
Interactive Style	• Individual work	• Collaborative • Team player • Loves to have meetings	• Strong collaborators • Entrepreneur	• Strongest collaborators • Participative
Communication Style	• Prefer formal communication — memos, letters, personal notes	• Personal contact — face-to-face meetings or phone calls	• Direct communica-tion — corridor contact, voice mail Immediate — email, text messages	• Email, blogs, text messages • Voice mail
Use of Technology	• "A struggle"	• " A necessary evil"	• Comfortable with using technology • Enables them to enjoy a flexible work schedule	• "An essential part of life and work"
Feedback	• "No news is good news" • Having a job equals good work performance	• Do not appreciate personal feedback • Prefer an annual, written performance review • Do not want to be viewed as the "problem"	• Seek frequent feedback — "Sorry to interrupt, but how am I doing?"	• Seek frequent feedback — "Whenever I want it, at the push of a button"

Aspect	Veterans (~1927-1945)	Baby Boomers (~1946-1964)	Generation Xers (~1965-1979)	Baby Boomlets (~1980-2000)
Worker Expectations	• The employer will manage the employee's career	• Believe the employee's career path is a joint responsibility — employer and employee	• Aggressive regarding career development and advancement	• Career development and advancement
Messages and Motivators	• "Your experience is respected" • Being told that their actions directly contribute to organizational success	• "You are valued" • "You are needed" • Motivated by goals set by managers, and managers who get them involved and show them how to best contribute • Strive for financial benefits and compensation, title and fame	• "You can do it your way" • "We have few rules around here" • "We have new hardware and software" • Let them do the job done on their own schedule and in their own way • Like "fun", casual dress and flexible work schedules • Flexible work schedules • Freedom to work according to their work style and schedule	• "You will have the chance to work with other bright, creative people" • "You and your co-workers can help turn this company around" • "You can be a hero here" • Work that has meaning • Tangible rewards • Varied work assignments • Team work: fun work places

Aspect	Veterans (~1927-1945)	Baby Boomers (~1946-1964)	Generation Xers (~1965-1979)	Baby Boomlets (~1980-2000)
Rewards	• Recognition is the "pay cheque every 2 weeks" • Prefer subtle recognition • Tangible symbols of loyalty and commitment • Value plaques, certificates, pictures with top executives	• Personal appreciation • Public recognition: recognition is the "corner office with the rug", financial incentives, name in the newsletter or on the parking spot • Value money and bonuses • Promotion	• Free time is the best reward • Top-notch resources/ technology • Growth and development opportunities • A focus on bottom-line results • Certification for skill and knowledge achievement	• Recognition from their "heros" — bosses and grandparents • Making a difference for organization and the community/society
Attitude about Careers	• Up to the employer to manage • One employer, one career	• Views work as a lifetime pursuit[92] • Experienced downsizing, layoffs and early retirement situations	• "Free agent" mentality • Entrepreneurial • Seek work-life balance, mutual respect, and meaningful work	• "Free agent" mentality • Entrepreneurial • Seek work-life balance, mutual respect, and meaningful work

---

92   Research shows that 50% of Baby Boomers envision working until beyond age 70 years; 40% prefer a phased retirement; 67% expect to do paid work after aged 60 years; 67% will work to stay mentally active; and 57% will work to remain physically active.

Aspect	Veterans (~1927-1945)	Baby Boomers (~1946-1964)	Generation Xers (~1965-1979)	Baby Boomlets (~1980-2000)
Training Focus	• Learning new skills benefits the company; not the individual • Prefers demonstrations • Hands-on (on-the-job training)	• Skills needed for success, but not as import as hard work and "face-time"[93] • Prefer technical training • Seek data/evidence-based learning	• The more skills/knowledge the better: enhances the tool kit for future job attainment • Seek practical skills • Prefer case studies/ applications	• Learning is key and will help one cope • Learn for emotional reasons • Prefer stories/ participative learning
Learning Environment	• On-the-job	• Classroom style • Quiet atmosphere	• Round-table style • Relaxed ambience	• Café style • Music • Multi-modal learning
Work Environment	• Seek an office or defined space of their own • Value a workplace that communicates status and accomplishment • Decorated with tangible items or symbols of work accomplishments	• Managers who are bureaucratic, reject input, are brusque, disinterested, practice "one-upmanship" and	• Like open work spaces; prefer closed/secluded places inside/ outside of the workplace to undertake solo work	• Comfortable working anywhere
Irritants	• Managers who are "touchy feely", indecisive, hesitant to make the tough decisions • Vulgar language; slang		• Being micromanaged • Managers who fail to "walk the talk" • Flashy managers: hype • Bureaucratic managers	• Cynicism, sarcasm • Being treated as if they are too young to understand/know • Managers threatened by their techno-savvy

93 C. Marston, "Four Generations in the Workplace: A Diversity Challenge" (Presentation delivered at Utah Department of Workforce Services: Roads to Success, Salt Lake City, UT, 2003) [unpublished].

Aspect	Veterans (~1927-1945)	Baby Boomers (~1946-1964)	Generation Xers (~1965-1979)	Baby Boomlets (~1980-2000)
	• Trendy or experimental management approaches	send out the sage, "It is my way or the highway" • Political incorrectness	• Too much time spent on process and not enough time on outcome	• Condescending managers • Inconsistency; disorganization
Job Change	• Seek cradle to grave experience • Uncomfortable situation • Job loss is stigmatized	• Seek lengthy employment situations • Job loss is a "glitch in their career path"	• Seek career security versus job security • Job change is necessary: part of their career path	• Seek career versus job security • Expect frequent job change • Seek portable work experience that guarantees skills for whatever life offers them
Employee Absenteeism & Disability	• Tend to not miss much work • Work through illness/injury • If seriously injured, tend to be away longer • Can be a challenge to place in modified work • Reluctant to do "lesser jobs" • Technologically challenged • Few cross-transferrable skills	• Seeking control over life and destiny • Unrealistic life and work goals • Predisposed to mental health problems • Tend to deny mental health problems — "struggle on" at work untreated until they "crash"	• More likely to experience sports injuries and reproductive-related absences • Willing to do modified duties • Strong transferable skills	• More likely to experience sports injuries • Willing to do modified duties • Strong transferable skills
Work and Family Life Balance	• In the past, there was no connection between the two lives	• No balance • Workaholics: "Live to work"	• Seek work-life balance • Want work/life balance NOW	• Strongly value work-life balance • Work is not everything • Want flexibility to balance life

Aspect	Veterans (~1927-1945)	Baby Boomers (~1946-1964)	Generation Xers (~1965-1979)	Baby Boomlets (~1980-2000)
	• More comfortable with working than with leisure time • Now, seek help to shift work/life balance	• Now, seek help to balance their work/family life	• Will *temporarily* sacrifice personal time, but only occasionally	• interests and activities • Value travel opportunities
Current Status	• Cautious about the changed workplace • Eager to share the work knowledge they possess	• Want to make an impact and remain relevant • Caught between the desire to succeed and the desire to slow down and enjoy their successes	• Seek balance and meritocracy • Caught between feeling that they must constantly prove themselves and being criticized for being overly ambitious, disrespectful and irreverent	• Starting out in their careers • Want to learn and contribute • Seek to be valued • Very savvy yet socially conscious • Seek to change the world of work

THE FOUR GENERATIONS: IMPLICATIONS FOR THE DISABILITY MANAGEMENT PRACTITIONER/PROFESSIONAL

Disability management practitioners/professionals working with these four generations need to appreciate the individual characteristics of each generation. For example, the Veterans and Boomers, being older workers, tend to be away from work more days per year due to illness or personal reasons than are younger, Generation Xers and Baby Boomlets.[94] If injured, the Veterans and Boomers require much longer time off work than do younger workers to recover. However, the Veterans and Boomers have a strong work ethic and therefore are amenable to a variety of return-to-work options. Unfortunately, many of the Veterans have vocational limitations in terms of their educational background and cross-transferable skills, making some modified work options unfeasible.

Some Baby Boomers are disenchanted with their lot in life and are trying to decide what their "golden years" might look like. They tend to overestimate their abilities and stamina, and are seeking to control their life and destiny. Such unrealistic goals tend to predispose them to an increased incidence of mental health problems. However, they are a generation where admission to having mental/nervous health problems remains "taboo", and therefore they tend to "struggle on" without seeking professional help until they "crash". For them, recovery can be difficult because to seek help, they first have to overcome a number of long-standing values and beliefs.

The younger Generation X and Baby Boomlets, on the other hand, are less likely to succumb to illness, but are more likely to get injured in sport-related incidents or other risk-taking activities. Given that the Generation Xers tend to challenge authority, company rules, and policies, these workers will be looking for adequate explanations of the Disability Management Program and processes. They will be seeking innovative rehabilitation plans and modified work opportunities. They value competence and expect disability management practitioner/professionals to provide quality, competent services.

As for the Baby Boomlets, although they may also experience similar sports-related injuries, they are amenable to getting back into a social milieu. The disability management practitioner/professional can capitalize on this aspect and seek a suitable modified work opportunity. Luckily, these Generation X and Baby Boomlet workers have strong computer skills and technological capabilities that align well with many modified work opportunities.

---

[94] Statistics Canada, *Work Absence Rates, 2007*, Cat. No. 71-211-XWE (Ottawa: Statistics Canada, May 2008).

A) The Organizational Approach

The effective management of multi-generational workplaces can be promoted by the disability management practitioner/professional. How can this be achieved?

Disability management practitioners/professionals can help organizations/ companies to:

- understand that the phenomenon of four generations in the workplace will not "just resolve": it needs to be managed;
- appreciate that events, experiences, and conditions in the formative years helped to shape the various generation personalities;
- take the time to understand each generational group, their characteristics, and why they are the way they are;
- demonstrate respect for each generational cohort;
- seek ways to bridge the gaps between the generations;
- understand the need to clearly communicate the company's expectations of employees;
- demonstrate flexibility;
- give people the benefit of the doubt;
- assist workers to achieve their career goals; and
- develop a "cafeteria approach" to employee group benefits and support programs, such as the Employee Assistance Program, Attendance Support & Assistance Program, Disability Management Program, Occupational Health & Safety Program, Human Resources Program, and Employee Education/Training Programs.

A checklist on the recommended approach to the effective management of four generations in the workplace is provided in Appendix 1.

B) Intergenerational Conflicts

When four groups with different beliefs, attitudes, values, needs, and wants exist in a workplace, misunderstanding and conflict can occur. In the past, workplace policies, programs, and benefits were designed to meet the beliefs, attitudes, values, needs, and wants of the majority. Clearly, that approach of "one size fits all" is no longer effective.

POTENTIAL CLASHPOINTS®

Some potential generational clashpoints® are:

- ***Reaction to Authority***: Veterans and Boomers tend to not question or challenge authority, or the status quo. This may cause confusion and resentment among the Generation Xers and Baby Boomlets who have been taught to respond to their concerns and to ask, "Why?"

- ***Work Styles***: Baby Boomers who like to work collaboratively and in teams, can prove frustrating to Veterans and Generation Xers who prefer independent work and perceive frequent meetings exasperating.

Generation Xers and Baby Boomlets, who have had different life experiences and use different communication styles, may fail to actively listen to Veterans and Boomers thereby missing valuable work information and key opportunities for guidance. Conversely, the older generations may ignore the Baby Boomlets, deeming them too inexperienced for any meaningful contributions.

- *Performance Feedback*: Feedback styles that may appear informative and helpful to one generation might seem formal and "preachy" to another. Feedback a Generation Xer perceives as immediate and honest can seem hasty, or even inappropriate, to Veterans and Baby Boomers. Likewise, some older generations have been told that there is "a time and place" for feedback. The two younger generations may not have received this message, thereby seeking frequent and immediate feedback from colleagues and management.

  Veterans seek "no applause" for their work performance, but appreciate subtle acknowledgement that they have made or are making a difference. Baby Boomers often provide feedback to others but seldom receive the same, especially positive feedback. Hence, they can be uncomfortable being told by a Generation Xer or Baby Boomlet that they are doing a great job.

  Generation Xers need positive feedback to let them know that they are on the "right track". Baby Boomlets, who are used to praise from doting parents and activity coaches, may mistake "silence" for disapproval. They need to know what they are doing right and what they are doing wrong.

- *Advancement*: It appears that Baby Boomers will likely remain in the workplace, especially in supervisory and management roles, longer than originally expected. For the up and coming Generation Xers, this situation creates a sort of "glass ceiling": a frustrating situation for the aspiring Generations Xers who could easily direct their resentment of the situation towards the Baby Boomers.[95]

CHALLENGES FOR DISABILITY MANAGEMENT PRACTITIONER/PROFESSIONALS

For disability management practitioner/professionals, challenges can arise in scenarios like the following:

1. *The Veteran employees working with Generation Xers or Baby Boomlets.*

As noted, Veterans are used to taking orders and hence, giving orders. Information is disseminated on a "need to know" basis. Both of the younger generations want to be included and involved in the work at hand. That

---

[95] M.J. Douglas, *"Generation Clash! Making Generational History"* (2009), available online at: <http://content.monster.ca/7371_en-CA_pf.asp>.

means open communication and the use of a collaborative and inclusive approach. The two views can be in conflict.

Likewise, their communication styles and work styles differ. Veterans prefer formal communication or face-to-face communication; the two other generations use voice mail, email, or text massages — the latter of which the Veteran may have no idea how to receive or respond.

The Veterans' work style is one of individual work or teamwork if they are leading the team. The Generation Xers and Baby Boomlets prefer collaborative work.

The Veteran might also resent the younger generations' demands for work/life balance and ask, "How will all this work get done if you guys aren't willing to put in the extra time to get it done?"[96]

On the other hand, the younger generations may wonder why the Veterans and Baby Boomers have not been able to balance their work and personal time. Waiting until retirement to "play" seems unacceptable — they want work/personal life balance now.[97]

The difficulties noted are substantiated by a recent poll that indicated that Veterans and Baby Boomlets have difficulties working together.[98]

2. *The Baby Boomer supervising the Generation Xers.*

According to a recent poll, 50 per cent of the respondents noted that Generation Xers and Baby Boomlets have the most challenges working with Baby Boomers.[99] Looking at their respective traits, this finding is not surprising. For example, Baby Boomers "live to work". They are dedicated to the job and are prepared to work long hours to achieve success. The concept of having "fun" and "work enjoyment" is not an essential part of this process. Additionally, the Baby Boomer prefers to hold meetings, work in a team, and to reach decisions based on collaboration and consensus.

On the other hand, Generation Xers "work to live". They like to be told what needs to be done, but not how to do it. Generation Xers are independent, entrepreneurial workers. Meetings are not popular. Although they prefer collaborative decision-making, they like to multi-task and to set their own work priorities. Their personal time is valued, so working long hours is not a popular practice. They do not like to be tied to a job, especially a job that fails to challenge them or meet their learning needs. Leaving the organization is always a viable option.

---

[96] L. Panszczyk, "Benefits and Balance in a Four-Generation Workplace", *2004 CCH Unscheduled Absence Survey* (2004), available online at: <http://www.cch.com/absenteeism2004/excerpt.asp>.

[97] *Ibid.*

[98] A. Howland, Multi-Generations Bring Challenge to Workplace, *The Vancouver Province* (May 27, 2007), available online at: <http://www.canada.com/theprovince/news/working/story.html?id=c25b6b fa-f64a-40a5-a7d8-7de807e3ce63>.

[99] *Ibid.*

The outcome is that the work motivators, work styles, and lifestyles are in conflict unless the two players can reach a common position on how they will successfully work together.

3. *The Baby Boomer Human Resource manager counselling a Baby Boomlet employee.*

As already noted, research has indicated that the Baby Boomlets face challenges working with Baby Boomers. In regards to this scenario, the two generations differ on a number of key aspects, namely:

- The Baby Boomer is a "workaholic" seeking advancement and personal achievement; the Baby Boomlet is looking for meaning and relevance in work, but also values work and the social aspects of work. The Baby Boomlet has a life outside of work.

- The Baby Boomer lives to work; the Baby Boomlet works to live, with many social, community and travel interests filling the personal time.

- The Baby Boomer is dutiful, but focused on personal achievement and advancement; whereas the Baby Boomlet values work achievement.

- The Baby Boomer is motivated by goals set by his or her manager; the Baby Boomlet is driven by the search for meaningful work and an enjoyable work environment.

So when the Baby Boomlet comes in and announces to the Baby Boomer human resources manager that a lengthy trip is coming up, and that he or she wants to know if the current job will be available upon return, the manager is caught off guard. The resentment may stem from the fact that this Baby Boomlet has the nerve to ask for a leave that the Baby Boomer never had even thought to request.[100]

4. *The Generation Xer or Baby Boomlet working in a traditional workplace where company loyalty, lines of authority, work rules, vertical career ladders, and linear advancement are strongly valued.*

Given the discrepancies between the employee's values, beliefs, attitudes, expectations and needs, and what this workplace offers, there is a great potential for the employee to either leave, or remain and become dysfunctional or sick.

From the generational descriptions provided, one can imagine any number of conflicts that could arise when four generations are communicating, problem solving, working together, or trying to address differences of opinions. If these

---

[100] L. Panszczyk, "Benefits and Balance in a Four-Generation Workplace", *2004 CCH Unscheduled Absence Survey* (2004), available online at: <http://www.cch.com/absenteeism2004/excerpt.asp>.

conflicts cannot be effectively addressed and resolved, employee casualties can occur. Many "stress-related" illnesses have their origins in unresolved workplace issues, situations, and dysfunctional relationships. These are the most difficult disabilities to manage and successfully resolve. Hence prevention is the key!

C) Motivational and Performance Reward Differences

While no two people are motivated in the same manner, performance motivators tend to be generational-based. This means that managers need greater insight into age-related issues and what motivates workers. For example, Baby Boomers strive for money, title, and the "corner office with the rug". Generation Xers want freedom and job security; whereas the Baby Boomlets want a job that has meaning for them and for society. The Veteran, on the other hand, is baffled as to why these other workers need any more motivation than the pay cheque they get every two weeks.

To motivate Veterans, the manager needs to opt for formality, such as communicating face-to-face or by phone as opposed to communicating through email or voice mail. The message should be: "Your experience is respected."[101] As for recognition, the traditional forms of recognition, such as plaques, certificates, or photos with top executives are appreciated.

Boomers are motivated by goals that have been set by their managers. They value having the objectives established and the desired results stated in people-centred terms. Team participation is important. The motivational message should read as: "You are valued; you are needed."[102] For them, recognition is being mentioned in the company newsletter, having their name on a parking spot, or receiving a promotion and title.

The Generation Xers prefer to be told what needs to be done; not how to do it. They like multiple tasks and the freedom to determine their own work priorities. Frequent and frank feedback is expected. As for their work preferences, they like flexibility, dressing casually, having fun, and enjoying a healthy work/life balance. The motivational message would be: "Do it your way; forget the rules."[103]

Motivating the Baby Boomlets differs. They seek opportunities for continuous learning and enhancement of their work skills. Their managers need to appreciate the Boomlets' personal goals and respond by linking the assigned tasks to these goals. Baby Boomlets respond to a positive work environment and prefer their manager to be more of a coach and less of a boss. For them, informal communication such as casual chats in the hallway, emails, or voice mail, will suffice. For them, the

---

[101] G. Hammill, "Mixing and Managing Four Generations of Employees", *FDU Magazine Online* (Winter/Spring 2005), available online at: <http://www.fdu.edu/newspubs/magazine/05ws/generations. htm>.

[102] *Ibid.*

[103] *Ibid.*

motivational message is: "You will work with other bright creative people." [104] Their preferred form of recognition is to be given bonus days off work.

D) Other Differences

Worker expectations and communication styles vary by generation. The Veterans do not seek much feedback. Their credo is "No news is good news." The Boomers prefer to receive feedback on their work performance once a year and in writing. Both the Generation X and Baby Boomlets want immediate and frequent feedback, only the Boomlets want it daily.

In terms of work/life balance, the Veterans want help to shift the work/life balance. The Boomers seek help to balance their work and family life. Generation Xers want work/life balance now. For the Boomlets, work isn't everything. They want the flexibility to balance their lives and activities. Family life and travel opportunities are highly valued. They are often willing to give up a job to return to school or to travel for extensive periods of time.

The perspectives on job change radically differ. For the Veterans, a job change carries a stigma. The Boomers perceive job change as a "glitch" in their career path. To the Generation Xers, job change is necessary — it is part of their career development and path. The Boomlets feel likewise, but they expect job change to happen many times in their careers.

THE FOUR GENERATIONS: GENERATIONAL INTEGRATION

Successful employers are gearing up to effectively manage the phenomenon of four generations in the workplace through the use of **generational integration** approach — that is, bringing the four generations found in today's workplaces together in such a way that the "best" of each generation is accessed and put into practice to enhance the well-being and performance of the entire workforce. [105] The intent is to enable the four generations to interact, to learn about and from each other, to bridge the gaps between the generations, and to ultimately have them "bond". The goal is to manage, motivate, and retain a multi-generational workforce.

Generational integration begins with identifying key areas of interest or areas of dissonance, such as:

- meaningful work — the opportunity to contribute to the organization and to make a difference;
- collaboration;
- learning and development;

---

[104] *Ibid.*

[105] K. Kirkpatrick, S. Martin & S. Warneke, *Strategies for the Intergenerational Workplace* (July 17, 2008), Gensler, available online at: <http://www.gensler.com/uploads/documents/Intergenerational Workplace_07_17_2008.pdf>.

- use of technology — a divisive force between the generations which can be bridged by engaging workers to help each other use the various technological tools; and
- flexibility. [106]

With generational integration, information flows in all directions. The most enlightened organizational leaders find a way to let every generation hear and be heard. They recognize that no one has all the answers. This appreciation of diversity allows each generational group to contribute and be a part of the growth and development of a department or organization. [107]

THE FOUR GENERATIONS: RECOMMENDATIONS TO DISABILITY MANAGEMENT PRACTITIONERS/ PROFESSIONALS

Disability management practitioners/professionals must continue to use a *holistic approach* when dealing with ill/injured workers. This means understanding the characteristics of these four generations, and adapting disability management services to meet their respective needs. Disability Management Programs, like other employee benefits, need to be "cafeteria style", providing flexibility and variability in the offerings and services.

Disability Management Program *communications* must be designed to appeal to all four generations. Multi-media approaches that include the traditional written documentation (brochures, newsletters, worker packages, *etc.*) should be combined with more interactive media approaches (webpages, electronic message boards, *etc.*). Solicit feedback about the Disability Management Program and its services using a variety of techniques, namely, hardcopy and electronic surveys, focus groups, chat boxes, blogs, *etc.*

Disability Management Program *marketing messages* need to be tailored. The Veterans, who tend to possess strong company loyalty, value money and work relationships, and have strong work ethics, respond well to the message that the Disability Management Program can help them and their coworkers to remain active in the workplace. The Boomers on the other hand, tend to be workaholics. They work and play hard. They also perceive exercise and staying physically fit as their duty. They respond well to the sports analogy that one would never put a recovering athlete back into a game situation before providing rehabilitation and a period of participation in game workouts. Modified work is the same. It provides an opportunity for work hardening aimed at enabling the employee to return to his/her regular job. Additionally, they value money and perceive

---

[106] *Ibid.*

[107] Office of Institutional Equity, Duke University, *Cross Generational Communication: Implications in the Work Environment* (April 2008), available online at: <http://www.duke.edu/web/equity/Diversity. htm>.

modified work as worthwhile if there is a pay differential over being on short-term disability coverage.

With the phenomenon of an aging workforce, the approaches used within the Disability Management Program should *address the challenges faced by aging workers*. For example, aging workers experience changes in muscles, bones, cardiovascular systems, hearing, vision, mental processes, reaction times, and sensory and motor processes. Hence disability management professionals/ practitioners should take this knowledge into account when designing modified or alternate work opportunities. Management education on these factors is recommended. Many work tasks can be readily modified to reduce the wear and tear on the human body. Likewise when counselling the aging worker, the following recommendations can be made in order to enhance the worker's well-being and productivity:

- maintain a healthy lifestyle — exercise and diet;
- get enough sleep;
- exercise the brain and cognitive functions;
- stretch before, during and after work; add weight-bearing activities to their exercising program;
- dress for weather extremes;
- use material handling equipment to reduce lifting;
- minimize awkward postures;
- maintain proper posture;
- make frequent postural changes;
- wear suitable footwear;
- obtain regular vision and hearing tests;
- use prescribed corrective lenses and hearing aids; and
- be aware of drug side-effects when taking medications.

Generation Xers perceive exercise as essential to their well-being. For them, the sports analogy would also work, however they will expect frequent feedback on their recovery progress and recognition for their modified work efforts. The Baby Boomlets are similar on both the above issues, however, they may respond better to the message that modified work is one way of helping their work team to continue to operate through this disability period.

The *choice of modified work duties* is another area for consideration. Boomers, Generation Xers, and Baby Boomlets who are technologically savvy, are well suited for modified duties involving office work, working at home, and alternate job duties. Veterans who work in primarily labour positions pose an interesting challenge. Although knowledgeable and experienced, they may be unwilling to do modified duties that are outside of their comfort zone, or deemed to be lesser jobs than their "own" job.

Worker *response to support services* differs. As already noted, Veterans and Baby Boomers perceive mental/nervous health conditions in a negative manner. To them, the stigma of mental health disorders remains alive and well.

Generation Xers and Baby Boomers are much more tolerant about human frailties. As a result, one would expect younger workers to be more receptive to using Employee Assistance Programs and other company supports. Boomers, Generation Xers, and Baby Boomlets all value exercise and the benefits that participation affords. Physiotherapy and reconditioning efforts would be better received by them than by the Veterans who tend to view exercise only as a "necessary evil".

From a *prevention* point of view, Generation Xers and the Baby Boomlets, who have tended to be sedentary and to consume lots of processed and fast foods, and who have been exposed to more pollution and stress, may be more prone to the development of health problems as they age.[108]

These are but a few of the generational challenges that a disability management practitioner/professional will face. The key recommendations are to:

- *Recognize, support, and build on the work aspects that all the generations seek, namely:*

    - respect from management;[109]
    - open and honest management communication;[110]
    - meaningful work;[111]
    - the ability to self-manage their work — input into work and the management of their own workloads are important to worker well-being;[112]
    - work-life balance — a personal life and "down-time" are critical;[113]
    - interesting work — employees want to be challenged and to feel that they are making a difference in the work that they are doing;[114]

---

[108] FGI, "One Workplace, Four Generations: Managing the Conflicting Needs", *Working Well for Managers* (September 2004), published by FGI, Thornhill, ON, available online at: <www.mta.ca/hr/managers/workingwell_sept2004.pdf>.

[109] Ontario Restaurant Association, "Employees Today want Education, Respect and More" *Ontario Restaurant News* (January 2005), available online at: <http://www.go2hr.ca/ForbrEmployers/Retention/GenerationsintheWorkplace/Employeestodaywanteducationrespectandmore/tabid/1042/Default.aspx>.

[110] *Ibid.*

[111] K. Kirkpatrick, S. Martin & S. Warneke, *Strategies for the Intergenerational Workplace* (July 17, 2008), Gensler, available online at: <http://www.gensler.com/uploads/documents/Intergenerational Workplace_07_17_2008.pdf>.

[112] M. Shain, "Managing Stress at its Source in the Workplace" (Presented at the Health Work and Wellness Conference '98, Whistler BC, September 27-30, 1998) [unpublished]; and D. McPhail, Corporate Perspectives on Workplace Learning, "Four Generations in the Workforce" (May 9, 2006). Presentation made on behalf of TELUS, AB, available online at: <http:www.wln.ualberta.ca/seminar_resources/Generations_May9.ppt>.

[113] D. McPhail, *ibid.*

[114] *Ibid.*

- a good salary with benefits [115] — fair pay leads to better quality of life;[116]
- the ability to learn and grow at work;[117] and
- good performance and recognition.[118]

- *Know your clientele.*
- *Respect their unique differences.*
- *Seek modified work opportunities that not only "fit" the employee's recovery needs, but also take into consideration the generational needs of the parties involved.*
- *Be flexible and innovative in the disability management approaches.*
- *Promote the development of programs designed to support general employee health and enhance employee resilience against life stressors.*
- *Promote "ageless thinking" where employees are equal regardless of age.*[119]

SUMMARY

So, "Yes, there are four generations in today's workplaces." "Generational difference can lead to strength and opportunity, or to stress and conflict.[120] It all depends on how organizations/employers chose to handle the situation. Best practice solutions involve the recognition, appreciation, and respect for the traits of each generation. One option is to develop a **generational strategy** — a method of:

- understanding what makes their "employees tick";
- emphasizing the importance of teamwork;

---

[115] *Ibid.*

[116] Ontario Restaurant Association, "Employees Today want Education, Respect and More", *Ontario Restaurant News* (January 2005), available online at: <http://www.go2hr.ca/ForbrEmployers/Retention/GenerationsintheWorkplace/Employeestodaywanteducationrespectandmore/tabid/1042/Default.aspx>.

[117] D. McPhail, Corporate Perspectives on Workplace Learning "Four Generations in the Workforce" (May 9, 2006). Presentation made on behalf of TELUS, AB, available online at: <http://www.wln.ualberta.ca/seminar_resources/Generations_May9.ppt>; and Ontario Restaurant Association, "Employees Today want Education, Respect and More", *Ontario Restaurant News* available online at: <http://www.go2hr.ca/ForbrEmployers/Retention/GenerationsintheWorkplace/Employeestodaywanteducationrespectandmore/tabid/1042/Default.aspx>.

[118] D. McPhail, *ibid.*

[119] A. Howland, "Multi-generations Bring Challenge to Workplace," *The Vancouver Province* (May 27, 2007), available online at: <http://www.canada.com/theprovince/news/working/story.html?id=c25b6bfa-f64a-40a5-a7d8-7de807e3ce63>.

[120] A. Stefaniak, *Black Hole or Window of Opportunity? Understanding the Generational Gap in Today's Workplace*, Policy Brief: 04-11-07, Center for Public Policy & Administration, available online at: <http://www.cppa.utah.edu/publications/workforce/Generations.pdf>.

- effective communications; and
- adopting "ageless thinking".[121]

However, it is vitally important to not stereotype employees — "the generational concept is simply 'one lens' that can be used to help us understand people".[122] Generational diversity, like gender, racial, and ability diversity, is a factor to consider in managing and positioning an organization, but it is not the "whole show".[123] The answer for employers is to regularly assess the needs of the organization to determine if and how employee needs are changing, and then based on the findings, respond accordingly.

---

[121] A. Howland, "Multi-Generations Bring Challenge to Workplace", *The Vancouver Province* (May 27, 2007), available online at: <http://www.canada.com/theprovince/news/working/story.html?id=c25b6b fa-f64a-40a5-a7d8-7de807e3ce63>.

[122] D. McPhail, Corporate Perspectives on Workplace Learning, "Four Generations in the Workforce", (May 9, 2006). Presentation made on behalf of TELUS, AB, available online at: <http://www.wln.ualberta.ca/seminar_resources/Generations_May9.ppt>.

[123] R. Zemke, "Generations at Work" (2001), *CEO Agenda Series*, available online at: <http://www.asaecenter.org/PublicationsResources/articledetail.cfm?ItemNumber=13053>.

Appendix 1

Multi-Generational Workplaces: Effective Management

Recommended Actions:

☐ Assist the company/organization to understand that this situation will not "just resolve itself": it needs to be managed.

☐ Help the company/organization appreciate that the various events and conditions in the generation cohorts' formative years helped to shape their generation personalities.

☐ Encourage the company/organization to take the time to understand each generational cohort and why they are the way they are.

☐ Encourage the company/organization to demonstrate respect for each generational cohort.

☐ Promote company/organizational interest in seeking ways to bridge the gaps between the four generations

☐ Encourage the company/organization to clearly communicate company/ organizational expectations of employees

☐ Encourage the company/organization to demonstrate flexibility in terms of how the various employee groups are supported and their needs addressed.

☐ Promote the management practice of giving workers the "benefit of the doubt" when issues/conflicts/disputes arise.

☐ Assist workers to achieve their career goals.

CHAPTER REFERENCES

AARP, *Leading a Multigenerational Workforce* (Washington, DC: AARP, 2007), available online at: <http://www.aarp.org/money/work/employer_resource_ctr/articles/workforce_publications_for_employers.html>.

T. Brokaw, *The Greatest Generation* (New York: Random House, 1998) Inc.

S. Calhoun & P. Strasser, "Generations at Work" (2005) 53:11 American Association of Occupational Health Nurses Journal, 469.

M.J. Douglas, "Generation Clash! Making Generational History" (2009), available online at: <http://content.monster.ca/7371_en-CA_pf.asp>

J. Duchscher & L. Cowen, "Multigenerational Nurses in the Workplace" (2004) 34:11 Journal of Nursing Administration 493.

D. Dyck, "Multi-Generational Workplaces: The OH&S Challenge" (Presented at the American Occupational Health Nurses Symposium and Expo, Orlando, FL, April 2007) [unpublished].

FGI, "One Workplace, Four Generations: Managing the Conflicting Needs", *Working Well for Managers* (September 2004), published by FGI, Thornhill, ON, available online at: <www.mta.ca/hr/managers/workingwell_sept2004.pdf>.

Go2 Tourism HR Society, *Capitalizing on the Generational Gap in the Workplace* (2008), available online at: <http://www.go2hr.ca/Forbr Employers/Retention/GenerationsintheWorkplace/tabid/566/Default.aspx>.

G. Hammill, "Mixing and Managing Four Generations of Employees", *FDU Magazine Online* (Winter/Spring 2005), available online at: <http://www.fdu.edu/newspubs/magazine/05ws/generations.htm>.

S. Heathfield, *Managing Millennials: Eleven Tips for Managing Millennials* (2008), available online at: <http://humanresources.about.com/lr/ managing_millennials/220710/1/>.

A. Howland, "Multi-Generations Bring Challenge to Workplace", *The Vancouver Province* (May 27, 2007), available online at: <http://www.canada.com/theprovince/news/working/story.html?id=c25b6bfa-f64a-40a5-a7d8-7de807e3ce63>.

J. Jamrog, "The Perfect Storm". (Presented at a CHRP Seminar, Calgary, AB, September 15, 2005) [unpublished].

K. Kirkpatrick, S. Martin & S. Warneke, *Strategies for the Intergenerational Workplace* (July 17, 2008), Gensler, available online at: <http://www.gensler.com/uploads/documents/IntergenerationalWorkplace_07_17_2008.pdf>.

L. Lancaster & D. Stillman, *When Generations Collide: Who They Are, Why They Clash, How to Solve the Generational Puzzle at Work* (New York: Harper Collins, 2002).

C. Marston, "Four Generations in the Workplace". A presentation delivered at the Planned Parenthood Federation of America, Western Region Conference (Salt Lake City, UT, 2004) [unpublished].

C. Marston, "Four Generations in the Workplace: A Diversity Challenge" Presentation delivered at Utah Department of Workforce Services: Roads to Success (Salt Lake City, UT, 2003) [unpublished].

C. Marston, *Motivating the "What's in It for Me?" Workforce: Manage Across the Generational Divide and Increase Profits* (Hoboken, NJ: John Wiley & Sons, 2007).

M. McCrindle, *New Generations at Work: Attracting, Recruiting, Retraining & Training Generation Y* (Sydney, NSW, Australia: McCrindle Research, 2006), available online at: <http://www.mccrindle.com.au/resources.htm>.

T. K. McNamara, "Analysis of the March 1977 and 2007 Current Population Surveys", unpublished raw data (2007), reported in J. Dobbs, P. Healey, K. Kane, D. Mak, & T.K. McNamara, *The Multi-Generational Workplace, Fact Sheet #9* (July 2007), The Center on Aging & Work: Workplace Flexibility, Boston College, available online at: <http://agingandwork. bc.edu/documents/FS09_MultiGenWorkplace_000.pdf>.

D. McPhail, Corporate Perspectives on Workplace Learning, "Four Generations in the Workforce" (May 9, 2006). Presentation made on behalf of TELUS, AB, available online at: <http://www.wln.ualberta.ca/seminar_resources/ Generations_May9.ppt>.

Office of Institutional Equity, Duke University, *Cross Generational Communication: Implications in the Work Environment* (April 2008), available online at: <http://www.duke.edu/web/equity/Diversity.htm>.

Ontario Restaurant Association, "Employees Today want Education, Respect and More", *Ontario Restaurant News* (January, 2005), available online at: <http://www.go2hr.ca/ForbrEmployers/Retention/GenerationsintheWorkplac e/Employeestodaywanteducationrespectandmore/tabid/1042/Default.aspx>.

L. Panszczyk, "Benefits and Balance in a Four-Generation Workplace", *2004 CCH Unscheduled Absence Survey* (2004), available online at: <http:// www.cch.com/absenteeism2004/excerpt.asp>.

N. Pekala, "Conquering the Generational Divide" (2001) 66:6 Journal of Property Management 30.

E. Quick,"Disability Management that Works", *Benefits and Compensation Solutions Magazine* (January/February 2007) at 46, available online at: <http://www.bcsolutionsmag.com/disability_management/>.

A. Schwartz, *Generations at Work: Understanding and Influencing* (2008), available online at: <http://www.wiziq.com/tutorial/13675-Generations-at-Work-PowerPoint-Content>.

M. Shain, "Managing Stress at its Source in the Workplace" (Presented at the Health Work and Wellness Conference '98 (Whistler, BC, September 27-30, 1998) [unpublished].

Statistics Canada, *Work Absence Rates, 2007*, Cat. No. 71-211-XWE (Ottawa: Statistics Canada, May 2008).

A. Stefaniak, *Black Hole or Window of Opportunity? Understanding the Generational Gap in Today's Workplace,* Policy Brief: 04-11-07, Center for Public Policy & Administration, available online at: <http://www.cppa.utah. edu/publications/workforce/Generations.pdf>.

W. Strauss & N. Howe, *Generations: The History of America's Future, 1584 to 2069* (New York: Harper Perennial, 1992) (Reprint).

R. Zemke, "Generations at Work" (2001), CEO Agenda Series, available online at: <http://www.asaecenter.org/PublicationsResources/articledetail.cfm? ItemNumber=13053>.

Chapter 23

Outsourcing Disability Management Services

INTRODUCTION

Disability management services can be provided to an organization through an in-house occupational health service or through a contract service arrangement with an external service provider. Each option has its advantages and limitations. Organizations must decide which option is best suited to their particular disability management and business needs. Once the decision to use an external service provider is made, the next step is to determine a "best fit" between the organization's Integrated Disability Management Program, business approaches and corporate culture, and the services offered by available external service providers.

In today's marketplace, the plethora of disability management service providers makes determining a "best fit" a difficult task for organizational leaders. Interestingly, a low percentage of Canadian companies (28 per cent) using external disability management services are satisfied with the disability management service provider's abilities and knowledge.[1]

This chapter examines the relevant issues in outsourcing disability management services and how to address them effectively.

WHY OUTSOURCE?

Companies must first decide whether to outsource their disability management services or to keep it in-house. After examining their business practices, many large organizations decide that internal disability management services are not within the scope of their core business practices or competencies. For smaller companies, having an in-house disability management service may be impractical and too costly.

However, before going to the marketplace, an organization should identify and understand their reasons for potentially outsourcing disability management services. It is paramount to know why and how the decision to outsource was made. In this way, attention can be paid to addressing the issues that were originally identified as drivers for outsourcing the disability management services. Without understanding why outsourcing is necessary, service providers

---

[1] M. Vandenhurk & S. Philchuk, "Know Your DMC" (March 2006) 30:3 Benefits Canada 39.

and contracted services can be positioned in a manner that fails to address the reasons for seeking external services in the first place.

Decision-making Process

According to Jane Hall,[2] a comprehensive process is needed to make sure that all aspects of the decision-making process have been considered. The necessary steps are listed below:

1. Identify the desired changes and the reasons behind making those changes.
2. Explore the possibility of alternative service delivery options.
3. Obtain stakeholder input into what they want from a disability management service.
4. Develop a communication strategy to explain the need for change, and to describe the new disability management service that is ultimately selected. According to Hall, "ineffective or inadequate communication of change is a prime reason for implementation failures".[3]
5. Establish value criteria for deciding on a suitable service provider.
6. Define the nature of the desired service provider arrangement. Is the organization seeking service/product delivery, or a partnership arrangement to deliver disability management services?

Some of the reasons organizations choose to outsource disability management services include:

• *Lack of internal expertise* — By the time the reader reaches this chapter in the book, he or she will appreciate that disability management services require a level of expertise lacking in many organizations. Without occupational health support, case management is difficult, if not impossible. Likewise, claims management expertise is required to effectively and efficiently process employee disability claims.

• *Lack of internal resources* — Resources, facilities and funding are needed for a successful internal disability management Program to operate. The type and amount of resources required varies depending on the size of the organization. In general, office space and equipment, file cabinets, support personnel and a budget for rehabilitation services are key to providing efficient internal disability management services.

• *Insignificant demands for services* — If an organization experiences only a few absences per year, having an internal disability management service can be a costly venture. This is often the major reason for outsourcing disability management services on an "as needed" basis.

---

2   J. Hall, "The Decision to Vendor and Vendor Management: A Tool for Occupational Health and Workers' Compensation Management" (1997) 11:5 The OEM Report 44.

3   *Ibid.*, at 45.

- *Desired benefits of economies of scale* — This reason ties into the one provided above. By accessing disability management services from a service provider that works with many other organizations, the organization can benefit from the infrastructure and services already in place. Theoretically, this type of arrangement can provide quality disability management services at a lower unit price than the organization could manage internally. Companies value economies of scale and often seek disability management service arrangements that can offer savings through a contracted service arrangement.

- *Specialty expertise is required to achieve a cultural shift within the organization* — Some organizations desire extensive changes in their service practices over a short period of time. To achieve such an aggressive goal, they need the help of an external service provider. Getting there on their own would take too much time, resources, and money. This is often seen when a shift from a traditional to a more business- and people-oriented approach to disability management is sought.

- *Geographically complex services are required* — In some instances, organizations choose to keep the majority of their disability management services in-house except for those services that are remote and better provided by a local service provider. These mini-contract arrangements are common and usually purchased as "one-off" situations.

- *Seek a method to deal with fluctuating service demands* — disability management service demands can be unpredictable. Theoretically, service providers are better positioned to handle the peaks and valleys of demand.

- *Desire to purchase current skills* — Remaining current in an emerging field like disability management can be difficult, particularly for smaller organizations. By purchasing disability management services from a service provider whose core business is disability management servicing, current disability management service practices and expertise will be obtained.

- *Desire to transfer assets and people to a third party manager* — Organizations that have an in-house occupational health service may *prefer* to outsource the personnel and resources that provide the disability management services. The intent is often to keep only "core" business functions in-house, and to outsource the rest.

For the above reasons, an outsourced disability management service option is often sought. However, to be successful the service provider arrangement must be well planned, implemented, and evaluated.

PREPARATION FOR OUTSOURCING

For organizations to attain a suitable disability management service provider, a number of preparations must be made prior to going to the marketplace. They are discussed below.

Development of an Integrated Disability Management Program

First, develop the type of Disability Management Program that the organization wants to have in place. This important first step can be likened to house shopping. Prior to meeting with a realtor, the purchaser must decide what type of house is required. Will it be a starter home, large family home, or a retirement residence? The same holds true for seeking a disability management service provider. The organization must determine the extent of the disability management services required and the framework within which they are to be delivered.

This is a vital step to a successful service provider arrangement. By having an Integrated Disability Management Program in place that is known to all stakeholders, the participants are aware of their roles and areas of responsibility. As well, there is an established structure within which the service can function. Trying to operate without a framework will result in confusion. Service expectations and perceptions will become divided and poor service quality will result. This is one of the major reasons for disability management service provider failures.

Determination of the Preferred Customer-Service Provider Relationship

The organization must identify the preferred customer-service provider relationship desired. Some options include:

(a) a service that functions independently and is separated from other organizational activities (*i.e.*, service/product delivery only);

(b) a service that is integrated with the rest of the corporate programs and that is expected to provide and receive organizational data relevant to the Integrated Disability Management Program and various prevention strategies (*i.e.*, a partnership); or

(c) a service that is not only integrated, but comprehensive in the approach to disability management (*i.e.*, an enabler arrangement). This includes providing disability management services, and participating in the long-term planning for employee/organizational health and well-being.

In summary, the continuum ranges from a completely outsourced service with minimal involvement by the purchaser, to a service provision that enables the organization to offer a comprehensive Disability Management Program with an internal feel.

Before choosing the desired service provider arrangement, the organization must explore the differences between the following three options:

Option 1: The provision of a service/product is not only the least involvement that a service provider can have with the organization, but it is also the least time-consuming, risky, and costly option for the organization.

Option 2: A partnership arrangement takes more time, energy, and expertise for the service provider to deliver. It involves building relationships, knowing about the organization and its employees, and seeking ways to provide effective and efficient disability management services.

Option 3: An enabling relationship is the most comprehensive in nature. It involves partnering, as well as enabling the organization to move towards illness or injury prevention. To achieve this level of service provision, the service provider must fully understand the organization, its people, the business strategies, service demands, work environment, and challenges. This takes the most time and expertise, and involves risk-taking. In essence, it requires the service provider making a personal investment in the organization and its issues. This is also the most costly of the three options provided.

Service gaps occur when the organization believes the service purchased is a partnership or enabling agreement, and the service provider has contracted for service delivery only. Service gaps can cause an outsourcing disaster.

Determination of the Nature of Services Required

The next step is to decide what parts of the Disability Management Program will be kept internally and which ones will be contracted. A complete Disability Management Program is made up of program management, provision of clinical services, and return-to-work responsibilities. Some organizations design their Disability Management Program so as to keep all the program management and return-to-work activities in-house. In this type of program, only the disability management clinical services are contracted out. Others seek the provision of a complete provision of clinical services from a service provider.

An awareness of the services required, and the ability to articulate them clearly are essential to outsourcing Disability Management Program services. The organization should not only list the desired services, but also clearly describe the nature of the services, desired service quality, required turnaround times and preferred reporting mechanisms for the services provided. Linkages for these services back into the organization have to be outlined; for example, how will the service provider work with the manager for exploring return to work activities? How will they maintain contact? What is the process?

The positioning of the desired client-service provider relationship is also important. Some organizations want their service provider to operate within the confines of the organization and to provide consulting services to employees, work groups and the organization as a whole. Others prefer a completely external service, with an "arm's length" relationship and very little input into the organization's business and operational practices.

Establishment of Service Criteria

Organizations must decide what service criteria of the disability management service provider will be expected. What quality of service, service reliability, proven track record, level of expertise, nature of the service facility, data management and reporting capabilities and cost savings are expected? How will these be assessed and evaluated?

The organization should rate the value placed on each service criterion. For example, the organization should prioritize the value of service quality responsiveness and cost, data management capabilities, comprehensive servicing, provision of integrated services, service provider solvency as a business entity and the features of the service facility. This critical step influences how the bidders' response to the Request for Proposal for service provision will be evaluated.

Establishment of Desired Funding Arrangement

Funding arrangements for the disability management service can vary. The typical arrangements are fee-for-service, capitation, or a fee-for-service arrangement with a per capita retainer for administration services.

Companies that have set budgets and little margin for budgetary overruns often choose the per capita option. It is also the funding option of choice for mature Disability Management Programs with predictable service demands and outcomes.

The fee-for-service option can be suitable for organizations with new or changing Disability Management Programs. Since the organization only pays for the services used, they can establish what yearly costs are incurred and then, if desired, they can establish an appropriate per capita pricing arrangement.

A mixture of fee-for-service and capitation can work well in situations where the corporate services and the care services for the organization are funded under a per capita scheme, while the business units (operational) services are paid on a fee-for-service arrangement. Thus, a combination of funding can meet an organization's various demands.

Establishment of a Desired Payment Arrangement

Once a desired funding arrangement is selected, the next step is to establish a payment arrangement. The options may include a set fee per month or a variable fee based on the services rendered. Again, depending on the organization's needs, available cash flows and budgetary constraints, a suitable funding arrangement can be determined.

Determination of the Desired Performance Criteria and Measurement Techniques

As with any service contract, performance criteria, and measurement techniques for the disability management service provider contract must be set. These should be established in concert with the selected service provider. However, it is critical for the organization to decide on the performance criteria and to document the measurement techniques to be used.

Some typical performance measures are:

- service response time;
- service provision turnaround times;
- satisfied employees or business units;
- compliance with legislative requirements;
- short-term and Workers' Compensation disability durations;
- the percentage of short-term disability cases that progress to long-term disability;
- the percentage of disability cases that include modified work opportunities;
- the average duration of disability cases; and
- the cost-benefit ratio per disability case.

SERVICE PROVIDER MARKET SEARCH

A disability management service provider search is a relatively new approach to determining a suitable organization-service provider match. The key is to find a suitable arrangement that meets all the organization's required criteria.

Steps

STEP 1: DEVELOP A REQUEST FOR PROPOSAL (RFP)

The Request for Proposal (RFP) should describe the organization, its business and people needs, the Disability Management Program, and the services sought. Typically, the approach is to provide background information on the organization, the corporate values and beliefs, and its products or services, size and locations. A description of the organization's Disability Management Program and commitment to employee well-being should be provided. Other available employee support services and how they link with the Disability Management Program also warrant explanation. The current service provision arrangements should be included, along with the reasons for seeking the current request for quotation for services.

The requested disability management plan design must be fully described. What are the services sought? What is the expected standard of service required, and how will these be demonstrated?

RFP questions must be asked in a format that will elicit bidder responses that can be compared. Comparison of bidders is facilitated using a questionnaire. In this way, all bidders are asked the same questions and their responses can be rated according to pre-determined value criteria.

Submission information must also be included in the RFP. It should describe to the bidders the scope of the project, the procedure for the bidder to acknowledge receipt of the RFP, the format for the proposal, the terms for proposal response submission, the terms for proposal response rejection, the length of time for bid acceptance, the potential method for proposal clarification and the confidential manner in which bidder information will be handled. For ease of processing, the required response letters to be used by the bidders should be included, along with a sample service agreement contract. Bidders are asked to document their level of agreement with the contract format and terms.

STEP 2: SELECT SUITABLE SERVICE PROVIDERS

The organization has to decide whether to seek an invited or open bid for services. The invited bid to tender is a request for proposal from a selected number of potential service providers. The open bid is a general invitation for any service provider to respond to the RFP.

For many organizations, an open bid situation is just too cumbersome to conduct and manage. As well, the responding service providers may be unable to meet the organization's needs. More and more, organizations are choosing to pre-screen potential service providers, and then, conduct an in-depth examination of the individual service capabilities of each service provider.

STEP 3: DISTRIBUTE THE RFP

The RFPs should be sent out in enough time to allow the service providers to adequately respond. RFPs can take over two weeks to prepare. As well, time should be allowed for mailing and delivery. A minimum of three weeks is recommended between issuing the RFP and the deadline date for bidder response.

It is important to clearly restate in the accompanying cover letter the preferred method of submission and the closing time and date. As well, bidders should be reminded that any late responses will be considered invalid and returned to the sender unopened. Likewise, it is critical for organizations to abide by this statement.

RFPs should be sent out with a self-addressed, return envelope that ensures that the bid response gets to the appropriate department or person for processing. One tip is to have an identifier of some sort put on the envelope to indicate that a returned bid is enclosed. In this way, the recipient of the RFPs within the organization knows it is a returned bid and refrains from opening it until the RFP response time has elapsed. Then all the bids can be opened at once.

STEP 4: DATA COLLECTION AND COLLATION

Each RFP response is reviewed in its entirety. Then, all the RFPs are dissected in terms of their responses to each of the questions asked. A standard approach is to use a spreadsheet to list the RFP questions and the individual bidder responses to each question. The spreadsheet helps compare the individual bid responses to each question.

STEP 5: ANALYSIS OF THE RFP RESPONSES

The RFP response analysis process can take a number of formats. One is to score each question based on the value for each service criterion established by the organization. For example, if the organization pre-determines that it values quality of service first, service cost second, data management capabilities third, comprehensive servicing fourth and business solvency fifth, then scores of five points would be given to the questions that deal with service quality, four points for service cost questions, three points for data management capabilities, two points for comprehensive servicing and one point for business solvency. In this way, each question can be objectively scored. The outcome is an overall score for each bidder, and in this instance, high scores are good.

A second approach is to decide which of the RFP questions are "show-stoppers" and to rate each bidder response on those questions. The service providers with the best responses to all the critical questions are then identified as candidates for a final presentation.

With any scoring or rating system, it is important to predetermine whether the responses will be rated against each other, or whether an "all or nothing" scoring system for each question will be used. As well, plans should be made for how to deal with instances where all respondents score equally on a question. This allows for a consistent approach to the scoring technique.

Once the questionnaire responses are scored, service costs are addressed. Typically, bidders are asked to provide per capita and fee-for-service price schedules for the services requested. By applying the fee-for-service prices to the disability management utilization rates for a former year, a comparison can be made between the fee-for-service and capitation models quoted for each bidder. Bidders are also compared respecting the services *excluded* from their respective capitation models.

Other areas for in-depth examination are:

- staffing levels;
- staff qualifications;
- service facilities;
- service provider network;
- service capabilities; and
- client references.

STEP 6: SELECTION PROCESS

Once all the responses are analyzed, the findings are reviewed by the organization's decision-makers. In addition to the items noted above, other factors like accessibility, fit with the corporate culture, service responsiveness and service nature (reactive versus proactive, service provider versus partnership arrangement) are discussed. Based on the "fit", the decision-makers then select the service providers that they want to interview.

Finalist presentations are designed to permit the organization to meet the potential service providers and to learn more about their services, philosophies, and plans to provide the disability management services requested. Typically, these are formal presentations in which the service providers describe their business, service capabilities, staff qualifications, provider network, facilities, data management systems, past successes and future plans. Presentations should include discussion of how the provider plans to deliver the requested disability management services, various funding options and the nature of the potential working relationship.

To facilitate the interview, the organization should develop a list of questions for the service providers to answer. This allows for the further exploration of a potential business relationship, as well as adding rigour to the comparison process of the finalist presentation.

The responses to the prepared questions provided by the two or three finalists can be assessed and rated using the decision matrix tool which rates responses in order of merit. Similar rating systems can also be used. It is of prime importance to keep the reasons for originally going to the marketplace, the predetermined value criteria, the desired service outcomes, and the need to find a suitable service provider in mind.

The interview is usually the most revealing part of the selection process. On paper, many service providers sound great. However, in person the match between the organization and service provider tends to become apparent.

STEP 7: RESPONSE TO BIDDERS

Successful and unsuccessful bidders expect a decision regarding the success or failure of their RFP responses. Service providers spend considerable time and resources developing RFP responses and out of professional courtesy, they deserve a response letter, regardless of the bid's success or failure.

SERVICE CONTRACT DEVELOPMENT

The development of the service contract begins at the onset of the project. By knowing the value criteria, services required, desired funding arrangement and duration of the contract, the procurement officer for the organization can begin to craft a service contract document.

Many organizations have standardized service contract templates. These can be used and modified to meet the needs of the proposed disability management service contract. Regardless of the form used, the following elements should be included:

- description of services to be provided;
- expected level of service quality;
- required levels of reporting and communication;

- mutually agreed upon service performance measures;
- responsibilities of each party;
- pricing agreement;
- duration of the contract;
- payment schedule;
- legal compliance;
- hold harmless clause; and
- required business insurance coverage.

VENDOR MANAGEMENT

Vendor management is a key aspect of a successful disability management outsourcing arrangement. Having a comprehensive service agreement contract is only the first step in this process. Other strategies need to be in place to ensure that the outsourced service is in alignment with both organizations' needs and wants.

Recommended Strategies

PARTNERING

Partnering is a method of accomplishing the mutual goals of the organization and the outsourced service in a planned and pre-described way. It involves jointly establishing service goals, objectives, and procedures. The intent is to have open communication and a solid working relationship, which foster the accomplishment of the desired goals.

QUALITY ASSURANCE AND CONTINUOUS IMPROVEMENT

Programs and disability management services are established to address needs. As needs change, so must the programs and services. This can be successfully accomplished by keeping the two concepts of quality assurance and continuous improvement in mind.

Quality assurance involves the determination that the desired quality of service is indeed being attained. There are a number of evaluation techniques that can be used. However, even before any of those can be employed, the contracting organization must establish the standard of disability management servicing that will be expected of the service provider or vendor. These standards should be clear; valid in their rationale and intent; based on research; specific to the area of disability management best practices; and measurable. Chapter 3, "The Supportive Infrastructure for an Integrated Disability Management Program"; Chapter 10, "Disability Management Practice Standards"; and Chapter 17, "Disability Management Best Practices" of this book address some of the possible standards of practice for disability management programs.

A number of quality assurance techniques are provided by Jane Hall,[4] and include:

- *Cat in the Corner* — visiting and observing first-hand the services provided by the service provider to employees. The intent is to evaluate the services offered.
- *The "I Don't Understand" Tool* — asking the service provider to explain a process, or practice of concern.
- *Checking Out the Competition* — scanning the marketplace and comparing the various services and practices available.

Organizations should closely scrutinize the service provider's activities and make sure that the agreed upon service demands and service quality are being met.

PERFORMANCE MEASUREMENT

The development and use of performance standards is recognized as being an effective measure for reducing disability management costs.[5] The service agreement contract should stipulate the expected levels of performance for both the hiring organization and the service provider. Once in place, the onus falls on both parties to monitor the performance levels exhibited. This includes the regular measurement of the service quality and outcomes delivered.

The measurement criteria and the techniques spelled out in the service agreement contract should be followed. A review of the results should involve both parties. Here, the partnership arrangement becomes important. Both parties should be cognizant of the issues or problems and should work together to arrive at feasible solutions.

Performance measurement is an ongoing process — not an event. Regular measurement is key to the success of the outsourced arrangement. It allows for the identification of issues or problems, development of action plans and solutions, establishment of short- and long-term goals, trend analysis, and identification of proactive approaches to illness or injury prevention. Without regular performance measurement and open communication of performance issues, an outsourced service arrangement can fail. This is often the reason for tension between organizations and service providers, which is all too common, and can easily be prevented. As Yogi Berra once stated, "If you don't know where you're going, you'll end up someplace else". In any service arrangement,

---

4   *Ibid.*, at 44-47.

5   Watson Wyatt Worldwide, *Staying@Work: Effective Presence at Work — 2007 Survey Report — Canada* (2007) at 10, available online at: <http://www.easna.org/documents/WatsonWyatt StayingatWorkSurvey.pdf>.

the organization and service provider have to work together. Performance measurement is one tool to enable this to successfully happen.

SERVICE PROVIDER REPORTING

Regular reports on the service provided and the outcomes achieved are another important element to a successful contract arrangement. This feedback should be timely and should address all the requirements stated in the service agreement contract.

COST-CONTAINMENT

The costs associated with the outsourced disability management services require monitoring and cost-containment. Both parties should regularly review the projected costs stated in the service agreement contract. Knowing where cost savings and cost overruns occur will help to deal with the service costs experienced or anticipated. In this way, contingency plans for the disability management service costs can be developed, if required.

REGULAR MEETINGS

Regular meetings between both parties should be held to discuss the successes and limitations of the outsourced servicing. This is one way to promote open communication; to identify problems before they escalate; to determine which services are working well and those that require more attention; to identify any noted service trends; and to build a solid working relationship.

These six strategies are but a few examples of vendor management practices that can be implemented to ensure a successfully operated disability management service. Partnering, open communication, regular monitoring and measurement of performance and continuous service improvement are key aspects of a comprehensive service agreement contract.

CONFUSION REGARDING THE SELECTION OF DISABILITY MANAGEMENT SERVICE PROVIDERS

By Heidi Börner

Disability management was typically offered as part of the duties of the occupational health professionals. However, as interest in the field of disability management grew, many new players became involved, each offering unique disability management services to corporate clients. Confusion reigned. A discussion on informed selection of disability management service Providers follows.

The business world has recognized the potential for personal and economic savings through disability management instead of letting illness/injury situations take their own course. Of late, many disability management service providers have sprung claiming to be able to save companies huge amounts of money. Many of them *can* help companies save money while ensuring that their employees are getting the care they need, but how does an employer-client choose the one that is right for his or her organization? What capabilities and qualities should a disability management service provider demonstrate before a potential employer-client should even consider bringing the provider into the organization?

Rationale for a Disability Management Program

Before choosing a disability management service Provider to deliver disability management services, the employer should have a good idea as to why his or her organization wants to manage disability. Is it to save money? To improve workplace relations with employees or unions? To retain valuable employees? A mixture of reasons? Knowing what is wanted from the disability management service, the employer can determine which disability management service provider would be right for the organization. The beauty of disability management is that "doing it right" *does* result in saved resources for the organization — time, expertise, experience *and* money.

Values, Attitude, and Practices

There are universal characteristics of effective disability management services — ethics, knowledge, motivation, professionalism, respect, trust, confidentiality, communication, diplomacy, understanding of systems, reporting, and record-keeping. In order to handle disabilities effectively, the disability management service provider must have and use all of the skills and possess all of the qualities needed to operate according to the established disability management principles. This is what makes disability management both "a science" and "an art".

An ethical disability management service provider operates honestly, truthfully, and consistently according to professional practice standards and recognized policies and procedures. As well, the provider must strive to create "win-win" situations, that is, a "win" for the organization and a "win" for the injured/ill employee.

Many disability management service providers operate only by creating barriers for the injured/ill employee, believing that money will be saved by blocking employee access to insurance or Workers' Compensation benefits. While that may be true, managing claims in this manner not only creates undue hardship for the injured/ill employee in terms of financial, or medical care resources, but it can also be an illegal practice. Most organizations do not want this type of "win-lose" situation for their employees. They consider employees to be the organization's greatest resource. They have insurance plans in place because they want to assist employees in returning as productive members of the organization. Most organizations want also to be seen as good employers that offer a caring work environment. In choosing a disability management service provider, or hiring one internally, employers must ask the candidates what is their primary motivation for providing disability management services. A good disability management service provider's motivation is aligned with the sponsoring organization's culture and goals.

Disability management service providers' ethical beliefs motivate their disability management service efforts. Are the disability management service providers in business solely to make money? If so, they are not necessarily good disability managers. Good disability managers are in business because they have the expertise to assist both the organization and the employee in getting through the disability period and successfully returning to productive work, or an optimal level of functioning. They are there to help both the organization and the employee. This sound and basic management principle can save resources for the organization. Ask for the disability management service providers' mission statements. If they do not have one, find out what their motivation is to do this type of business. Being knowledgeable about potential service providers will help narrow your search.

Good Communication

Good communication is a key attribute for a disability manager service provider. Communication occurs in several areas — between the disability manager and the employee; the disability manager and employer; the disability manager and community resource agencies; the employee and employer; the employee and co-workers; the disability manager and insurance companies; the employee and health professionals; the employer and unions; and the employee and unions — to name a few. The disability manager must have the ability to recognize what communication is taking place in the course of a claim, and be able to relate effectively with each party.

Proactive communication with all parties in the form of defining roles and responsibilities early in the case allows the disability management process to proceed without confusion. It is important to know how the disability management service provider plans to handle each step of a disability claim. By asking for a disability management process flowchart, the lack of consistent processes would be evident. Endless time and money can be wasted on poor or ineffective communication processes. Therefore, it is important to thoroughly investigate how the potential disability management service provider plans to do both claims and case management.

The ability to communicate with diplomacy, empathy, and understanding to the injured/ill employee and family is critical. Not only should the claims process reflect communication between all parties involved in the claim, it should also demonstrate respect and understanding for the ill/injured employee and his or her family. A therapeutic relationship can only be created when there is mutual understanding, respect, and trust. When interviewing a potential disability management service provider, ask for real and specific examples of how difficult claims are handled; what makes those claims difficult; and what results can be expected.

Past Performance

Effective disability management service providers acknowledge that they have encountered difficult claims, and demonstrates effective problem-solving techniques. What's more, the body language of the prospective disability management service providers usually reflects just how committed they are to the human element. If the prospective disability management service providers appear dismissive and tell you that they have never had a difficult claim, they should be regarded as suspect. A potential disability management service provider who warms to the topic and displays a sense of accomplishment at a successful resolution gets marks for showing appropriate motivation.

Client Satisfaction

Determine if the potential disability management service provider conducts client satisfaction surveys, and ask to see the results. Verify the information obtained from the disability management service provider against the client references supplied. Many disability management service agreement contracts are not renewed due to deficiencies in this area; so be sure to check them out thoroughly before entering into a service agreement.

Qualifications

Disability management service provider qualifications are poorly defined. Occupational health nurses, occupational therapists, physiotherapists, kinesiologists, and physicians, all could have the proper qualifications. However, a good disability management service provider must have connections with both the medical and rehabilitation world. Without these connections, it becomes very difficult to refer ill/injured employees to the appropriate community resources.

Make sure that the disability management service provider can describe an employee's health status and history in medical terms; that the right information is recounted; and that effective rehabilitation plans are developed. Also, knowledge of the terms required for the completion of Workers' Compensation Board and third party insurance forms is essential to ensure that full and appropriate claims information is communicated. Knowledge of human anatomy, physiology, and treatment modalities makes the disability manager a recognized part of a rehabilitation team, rather than an outside challenge or threat to health care providers.

Disability management service providers must adhere to a code of professional ethics, especially around the issue of confidentiality. Each health science professional has a code of ethics and process of confidentiality. Failure to adhere to the specific code of ethics can result in dismissal. Thus, it is important to determine what qualifications the prospective service provider's staff have, especially those handling the initial intake call to the service, and those involved in claims and case management.

Disclosure Practices

Ask the disability management service providers what information they disclose and to whom; what processes they use in obtaining the employee's consent to release medical information; and who has access to their patient records. Employers should only be receiving information from the disability manager who determines the ill or injured employee's fitness to work, and/or work restrictions. Anything more requires a signed consent to release personal health information.

Occupational Health & Safety Knowledge

Education in the field of Occupational Health & Safety is fundamental to the disability management process. Gathering the appropriate information regarding job demands, and translating that information into medical implications of an illness or injury, requires education in toxicology, human anatomy and physiology, environmental hazards and stressors, occupational safety, and business practices. The disability management service provider must be able to demonstrate competence in translating medical terminology into business terms, and work demands into implications for care.

A disability management service provider's list of client references can help to identify his or her level of competence. Ask the service provider's clients if they feel that they know and clearly understand what their returning employees can do upon re-entry to the workplace. Also, establish what information for improving the Occupational Health & Safety practices is communicated to the client-organization.

Data Management and Reporting

An organization's reporting and record-keeping requirements should be decided before interviewing a prospective disability management service provider. Organizations need to be able to quantify both the related disability management costs and savings in order to measure the performance of their Disability Management Program, and to celebrate the success of the program. Justifying the program's existence at budget time becomes that much easier if this information is available. Ask the disability management service provider what kind of reports can be generated; how data is tracked and illness/injury and recovery trends are reported; and how the total costs of a disability management program, as well as the associated return on investment are determined.

Service Performance

Service performance is not just measured in terms of dollars and cents. disability management service providers should reflect the universal disability management principles covered in Chapter 1, "Disability Management: Overview", of this text. Ask the prospective disability management service providers how you will know if they have delivered the services promised. Know what you want them to report to you and within what time frames. Ask how quickly they are able to respond to an employee in crisis; how many "lost time" days they usually save for their clients; how satisfied employees using their program/service are with the service; what rating they get from their clients for their staff being respectful, helpful, friendly and/or appropriate; and what measures they use to maintain client confidentiality. There are many ways to measure service performance. A responsible disability management service provider will work with the organization to set up an evaluation program that meets both the organization's and disability management service provider's needs.

Process

Choosing a disability management service provider should not be a hasty move. It requires introspection, planning, and commitment from all levels of the sponsoring organization. It also requires internal preparation for the management of the activities or functions that the disability management service provider cannot be expected to deliver. Even the best disability management service provider cannot be effective in an organization that has no time, resources, or interest in a Disability Management Program. The sponsoring organization must identify the internal and service provider roles; establish the areas of accountability; set performance measurement standards for each party; clearly define the measurement techniques and schedules; and ensure that the lines of communication remain open. By working together, the disability management service provider and organization can effectively manage employee disability. The payoffs, for each, are definitely worth the effort required.

SUMMARY

Disability Management Programs and services can be outsourced in whole or in part. Regardless of the arrangement, the sponsoring organization must remain actively involved in managing the service agreement contract. Organizations can contract out services, but not liability and accountability, for the provision of those services. This means that they must think strategically and act responsibly: "An organization's decision to outsource or retain a particular service should be a well-thought-out process encompassing all the ramifications of the decision."[6]

---

[6]   J. Hall, "The Decision to Vendor and Vendor Management: A Tool for Occupational Health and Workers' Compensation Management" (1997) 11:5 The OEM Report 44 at 44-47.

CHAPTER REFERENCES

J. Hall, "The Decision to Vendor and Vendor Management: A Tool for Occupational Health and Workers' Compensation Management" (1997) 11:5 The OEM Report 44.

M. Vandenhurk & S. Philchuk, "Know Your DMC" (March 2006) 30:3 Benefits Canada 39.

Watson Wyatt Worldwide, *Staying@Work: Effective Presence at Work — 2007 Survey Report — Canada* (2007) at 10, available online at: <http://www.easna.org/documents/WatsonWyattStayingatWorkSurvey.pdf>.

Chapter 24

Disability Management Practitioners/Professionals: Career Development

INTRODUCTION

Few disability management practitioners/professionals ever conscientiously plan out their career paths. Rather they tend to end up in the field of disability management by happenstance. This chapter provides career planning and development information for disability management practitioners/professionals, along with an appreciation of the importance of position/job descriptions.

CAREER STREAMING: MODEL OF CAREER DEVELOPMENT FOR DISABILITY MANAGEMENT PRACTITIONERS/ PROFESSIONALS[1]

Disability management practitioners/professionals will change the type of work they do, the organizations in which they work and the cities in which they live several times during their work lives. For this reason, they need to examine not only the first profession and job they choose, but also the series of occupations and jobs they will hold over a 50-year period.

The sequence of jobs and occupations is called a career. Hall (1976) describes a **career** as:

> ... an individually perceived sequence of attitudes and behaviours associated with work-related experiences and activities over the span of the person's life.[2]

This sequence of jobs and work pursuits represents what a person does for a living. The basic assumptions underlying this definition are:

---

[1]   Excerpts taken from: D. Dyck & M. Walker, "Career Streaming: A Model of Career Development" (1996) 44:4 *American Association of Occupational Health Nurses Journal* 177 Copyright (1996) the American Association of Occupational Health Nurses, Inc. Used with permission. All rights reserved.

[2]   D.T. Hall, *Careers in Organizations* (Glenview, IL: Scott, Foresman, 1976) at 96.

- A **career** is seen as a lifelong series of events, rather than an evaluation of how successful individuals have been in their life.
- Career success is subjective and based on personal judgment rather than on peer opinions.
- A career is a series of work events made up of the things the individual feels and does over time.
- A career is best viewed as a process of work-related experiences.

A career goes through various stages: "*different points of work responsibility and achievement through which people pass during the course of their work lives*".[3] Schermerhorn (1991) has labelled the stages as career entry, career advancement, career maintenance and career withdrawal, and links these stages to employee performance and age (Figure 24.1).

Figure 24.1: Career Stages, Individual Performance, and Age

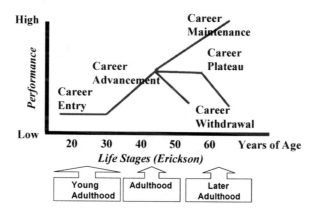

In the **career entry stage** or exploration (Hall, 1976) stage, the individual tries to match individual need, abilities, and skills with organizational requirements. It is that early period when the person tries to answer the question: "*Is this job for me?*"

The **career advancement stage** is characterized by a steep learning curve. The person begins to better understand the work environment and organizational demands, and strives to establish personal worth within the organization. It is a period of growth and acceptance of responsibility.

---

3   J. Schermerhorn, J. Hunt & R. Osborn, *Managing Organizational Behavior*, 4th ed. (New York: John Wiley & Sons, 1991) at 210.

In the **career maintenance stage**, the individual becomes entrenched in the job. Usually, the person has strong identity ties with the organization and job, is financially bound to the position, and is unlikely to leave. It is during this stage that Hall (1976) pointed out a tendency to adopt one of three avenues:

1. continued growth within the organization;
2. career plateauing; or
3. career stagnation.

During this stage, the greatest managerial challenge is to keep the employee stimulated and productive. Failure to do so ends in wasted employee time and energy.

The final stage is **career withdrawal**. Traditionally, this was associated with retirement. Now, formal retirement tends to occur earlier and at a point when some individuals are unready. As a result, they continue to advance their careers informally though self-employment, consulting, or re-employment with another organization.

Career Plateauing

Every career ultimately reaches some sort of plateau — a position from which one is unlikely to advance to a higher level of responsibility in their career.[4] A lack of career growth can occur because of personal choice, limited ability, or lack of opportunity. Today, due to both economic and demographic factors, many persons are reaching a plateau at a relatively early stage in their careers.

When individuals hit a **career plateau**, there is always the danger that they will lack motivation and become apathetic towards work. They may perform poorly, become bitter, blame the organization for their situation, and transfer their bitterness to fellow employees. As a result, general employee morale and performance may suffer. Effectively managing the "career plateaued" employee can be an important contribution to the organization. Employees can be salvaged if the organization gives the message to the individual that he or she is a valued employee, and that what he or she has to offer, is important.[5]

Career Anchors

Since World War II, people have come to expect more from their jobs than merely a paycheque. Among the expectations are a challenging and rewarding career, the ability to grow on the job, an opportunity to satisfy personal needs, advancement, and the chance to influence business decisions and plans. Schein

---

[4] *Ibid.*; and R. Steers, *Introduction to Organizational Behaviors*, 2nd ed. (Glenview, IL: Scott, Foresman, 1984).

[5] B. Moses, *Manager's Guide to Career Development* (Toronto, ON: BBM Human Resource Consultants, 1989).

(1975, 2006) termed the aspects of work that people value or need for fulfillment as **career anchors**.[6] They include:

- **managerial competence** — the driver is the opportunity to manage people;
- **technical/functional competence** — the driver is the opportunity to use various technical abilities and special competencies;
- **security** — the motivation is a need for job security or stability;
- **creativity** — the motivation is a need to create or build;
- **autonomy and independence** — the driver is the opportunity to work independently, without organizational constraints.[7]

Career planning and development activities allow employees to grow in any of these desired directions.

Career Planning and Development

With the entry of the "baby-boomer" generation into management positions, increased occurrence of corporate downsizings, and decreased opportunities for promotion, fewer and fewer career positions are available.[8] To prevent employees from moving on, managers and human resources practitioners/ professionals are challenged to redefine the philosophy, mechanics, and management of employee career growth.[9]

The act of putting the "humanism" back into Human Resources is vitally important. By directing employees in a way that helps them realize their personal career goals, satisfy their personal needs, and be valuable assets to the corporation, managers and human resource practitioners/professionals can facilitate employee retention and reduce one source of employee dissatisfaction.[10]

Career development is the process through which individual employees, with the help of their managers, match up their skills, interests and goals with the opportunities available to them, and develop plans for achieving their goals.[11] This process should be employee-initiated and management-supported. Schermerhorn (1991) defined **career planning** as an organization's development intervention that creates opportunities for employees to achieve long-term congruence between their individual goals and organizational career opportunities. The steps involved in career planning are:

---

[6] E. Stone, *Career Anchors: Self-Assessment*, 3rd ed. (San Francisco, CA: Wiley, 2007).

[7] T. Stone & N. Meltz, *Human Resource Management in Canada*, 2nd ed. (Toronto, ON.: Holt, Rinehart and Winston of Canada, 1988).

[8] *Ibid.*

[9] R. Goddard, "Lateral Moves Enhance Careers" (1990) 35:12 HR Magazine, at 69.

[10] *Ibid.*

[11] B. Moses, *Manager's Guide to Career Development* (Toronto, ON.: BBM Human Resource Consultants, 1989).

- assessing personal strengths and weaknesses;
- analyzing opportunities;
- selecting career objectives;
- selecting and implementing the plan;
- evaluating the results and revising the plan as necessary;
- increased ability to link personal career ambitions with organizational opportunities; and
- a mechanism for dealing with concerns about career plateauing.[12]

Employees and managers benefit from career development. For employees, the process provides:

- emphasis on attaining transferable work skills versus focusing on job titles;
- assistance in making informed career decisions and developing realistic career goals;
- open communications with managers about career plans;
- a mechanism for getting feedback and improving work areas of performance; and/or
- a means of communicating training and improving weak areas of performance.

The managerial benefits include:

- improved communications with employees about their career plans;
- stimulation of employee enthusiasm and job motivation;
- a means for addressing performance problems; and
- a technique for the discovery and use of employee skills, interests and strengths.[13]

Through career development, an organization benefits from enhanced productivity; increased information about employee skills, experience and interests; more productive use of Human Resources; more realistic employee career goals; an image that the company cares about its employees; and better employee adaptation to organizational change.[14]

Career Planning Concepts

Three approaches to career planning will be now discussed. The last one, career streaming, is used to demonstrate a potential model for Occupational Health & Safety and Disability Management practitioners/professionals.

---

[12] J. Schermerhorn, J. Hunt & R. Osborn, *Managing Organizational Behavior*, 4th ed. (New York: John Wiley & Sons, 1991).

[13] *Ibid.*

[14] *Ibid.*

CAREER LADDER

A career ladder is the traditional way of advancing within an organization. The employee enters the company, achieves the necessary skills, and automatically progresses up the corporate ladder. It exemplifies the career path as outlined by Hall (1976), Steers (1984) and Schermerhorn (1991) in their Career Stages Model. This technique is popular with unions and tradespeople. Hospitals find it advantageous because the process ensures selective socialization of the workforce; that is, it maximizes the probability that supervisors and managers will be individuals whose personality, skills, and knowledge align with the institutional character.[15] Promotion from within also increases employee motivation at lower levels because they see that hard work can lead to job advancement. It is a predictable mode of advancement that unfortunately, can be quite rigid in its patterning and scope.

The major problem with this technique is that individuals can be promoted beyond their capabilities. This phenomenon is known as "the Peter Principle",[16] which tends to prove dysfunctional for the company and the work group, and disastrous for the individual. Jacques (1961) theorized that individuals have an accurate, unconscious awareness of the level of work they are capable of doing, the amount and quantity of work produced, and what should be equitable payment for that work.[17] When individuals are promoted beyond their capabilities, their psychological equilibrium becomes jeopardized. The employee feels guilty and tends to behave defensively with coworkers. Ultimately, the work-pay inequity leads to feelings of insecurity and dissatisfaction.

In addition, career ladders tend to be narrow, providing few opportunities for career advancement. This can lead to staff turnover by the more ambitious and assertive employees. Employees who remain in the organization, can feel thwarted and frustrated at being unable to attain their career goals. The usual outcome is reduced organizational effectiveness.

CAREER MODELLING

Career modelling is the development of a framework for attaining various positions in the organization. It is the assessment of the employee's current position and skills needed for that position as compared to other positions within the organization and their respective skill requirements.

This type of career planning is done at an organizational level and is a management tool designed for individual career counselling. It is used to clarify

---

[15] D.A. Gillies, *Nursing Management: A Systems Approach*, 2nd ed. (Philadelphia, PA: W.B. Saunders, 1989).

[16] L.J. Peter & R. Hull, *The Peter Principle* (New York: W. Morrow, 1969).

[17] E. Jacques, *Equitable Payment* (New York, NY: Wiley, 1961).

the rationale for employee development, to spell out expectations involving career growth, to assess training needs, and to establish the expectations for skill development. It communicates the opportunities for career growth within the organization and management's commitment to develop both broadly-skilled managers and technical specialists.

Work force planning and succession planning can be achieved. Career modelling can ensure that candidates with the right skills are available to meet future organizational requirements. Also, clarifying job and skill requirements make recruiting and employee selection easier.

The major problem with career modelling is that it still depends on upward movement to satisfy individual career aspirations. Unfortunately, with flatter organizational structures and fewer opportunities for upward advancement, new ways to keep employees interested in their jobs need to be discovered.[18]

Companies are beginning to address this career development issue in various ways. Some are using parallel career tracks, job rotation, job enrichment, or lateral and downward moves. An alternate approach is **career streaming**.

CAREER STREAMING

Organizations can provide career development for employees within a defined professional field. The challenge is to provide a range of levels of defined skills for each level. As employees progress through the "stream", they attain certain skills, and through experience and new growth opportunities, add to their "skill bank" and scope of operation within the organization.

A large Canadian petro-chemical company developed one such model for occupational health services staff. In this model, for example, the entry-level Occupational Health Advisor I (Occupational Health Nurse) learns crisis-counselling skills to be used with individual employees. The Occupational Health Advisor II, having acquired individual counselling skills, is then exposed to group crisis counselling (such as critical incident stress debriefing). The Senior Occupational Health Specialist, on the other hand, deals with crisis planning at a corporate level as well as debriefing in a multi-workgroup situation. In summary, as one progresses through the "stream", one's skills set increases along with the scope of responsibility and accountability.

Career Streaming: Industry Application

This Career Streaming Model was designed to provide an opportunity for professional and career growth within the specialized area of Occupational Health Services, benefiting both the employee and the organization.

---

[18]   R. Goddard, "Lateral Moves Enhance Careers" (1990) 35:12 HR Magazine, at 69.

The objectives of the model are to:

- Provide a career path within the specialized area of Occupational Health Services.
- Facilitate employee development by identifying key technical and core management/business skills required in each stage of the career stream.
- Provide definitions for the key technical, business, and relationship skills.
- Provide direction for supervisors and employees to plan skill development.
- Assure senior management that professional development within Occupational Health Services is receiving due attention.

CAREER STREAMING PRINCIPLES

Career streaming opportunities are governed by experience, academic qualifications, demonstrated level of performance, skill development and employee aspirations, along with the business needs and available opportunities within the company. For example, occupational health nurses can optimize their contribution to the company if they have a balance of technical specialist, relationship, and business skills (Table 24.1); likewise can disability management practitioners/professionals (Table 24.2).

Table 24.1: Occupational Health Nurse: Technical Specialist, Relationship, and Business Skills[19]

Skill Set	Description	
Technical Specialist Skills	• Fitness-to-work assessments • Health surveillance • Medical monitoring • Emergency care • Hazard/risk assessment • Work site evaluation • Emergency planning and response • Event investigation • Case management • Critical Incident Stress Debriefing (CISD) • Program development • Standard setting • Training program development and delivery	• Professional networking • Regulatory knowledge • Human factors analysis • Technical communication • Quality assurance • Environment/public health management • Social marketing • Strategic issues management • Health promotion • Risk management and communication • Program evaluation • Research

---

[19] Descriptions of these skill sets are provided in Chapter 4, "Disability Management Program: Stakeholder Roles", Appendix 1 — "Required Skill Sets for the Disability Management Coordinator".

Skill Set	Description	
Core Management and Business Skills	• Planning and organization • Decision-making • Problem-solving • Leadership • Financial/Business perspective • Negotiating • Information systems management • Process facilitation • Project management • Computer skills	• DM Governance • DMP Stewardship • Performance management • Employee development • Training • Change management • Presentation • Risk communication • Consulting • Strategic issues management
Relationship/ People Skills	• Interpersonal skills • Communication skills • Team building/Team work • Coaching • Client advocacy • Relationship building • Change management • Preceptorship	• Mentoring • Negotiating • Reputation management • Community relationship management • Mediating • Facilitation

Table 24.2: Disability Management Practitioner: Technical Specialist, Relationship, and Business Skills[20]

Skill Set	Description	
Technical Specialist Skills	• Loss control • Regulatory knowledge • Claims management • Case management • Educational program development and delivery • Communication • Function evaluation • Risk management	• Program development, administration and management • Networking • Regulatory compliance • Technical communication • Quality assurance • Social marketing • Strategic issues management
Core Management and Business Skills	• Planning and organization • Decision-making • Problem-solving • Leadership • Financial/Business perspective	• Performance management • Employee development • Training • Change management • Presentation • Risk communication

---

[20] Descriptions of these skill sets are provided in Chapter 4, "Disability Management Program: Stakeholder Roles", Appendix 1 — "Required Skill Sets for the Disability Management Coordinator".

Skill Set	Description	
	• Negotiating • Information systems management • Data collection and management • Process facilitation • Project management • DM governance	• Consulting • Strategic issues management • Computer skills • Process facilitation • DMP stewardship
Relationship/ People Skills	• Interpersonal skills • Communication skills • Team building/Team work • Preceptorship	• Mentoring • Negotiating • Reputation management • Mediation

Continuing with the industry application, the **technical specialist skills** are unique skills, or combinations of skills, required in each stage. The Occupational Health Nurse Advisor I is expected to enter the company with two to three years basic supervisory and/or management experience. The **core management/ business skills** specific to the company are learned through progressive training and work experience. Health practitioners/professionals bring highly developed communication, interviewing and teaching skills for working with individual clients to the job. New skills are group/team relationship skills.

Not all employees need to progress within their career stream to achieve job satisfaction, and not all have the same career aspirations. This is normal and expected. Also, one must recognize that all employees will eventually reach their ultimate career level as determined by their skills and abilities, and the overall needs of the company.

The Occupational Health Nurse Advisors demonstrate specific skills before they can move to a higher level. Determining achievement of the practice skills remains with supervisors and managers. Progression is not automatic: if skills are developed but are not required by the organization, there is no recognition in job compensation. However, job satisfaction likely will increase because of the contribution to the business.

DEVELOPMENT STAGES

The Career Stream Model has four developmental stages. Descriptions of each developmental stage with a matrix chart to identify the applied skills at each stage are provided for occupational health nurses (OHNs) in Appendix 1, and in Appendix 2 for disability management practitioners/professionals. Skills acquired during an earlier stage are built on in subsequent stage experiences. In several instances, the scope of the skill changes is indicated by the following:

1. **OHN Advisor I** — This is the entry level for OHNs. New entrants must have an appropriate combination of education, occupational health nursing experience (five to seven years), and basic supervisory skills. The primary

purpose of this function is to manage the daily operations of a specific health centre. Development of new specialist skills, cross-functional relationships and understanding of the company's business endeavours is expected to require two (2) to three (3) years in this position.

2. **OHN Advisor II** — At this stage of development, the role of the OHN is to influence the business of a particular operation by regularly bringing occupational health nursing perspectives to management, union and employee business. Strategic occupational health plans are tailored to meet operational requirements, introduced to all parties, and monitored with the effects analyzed and reported. Local issues are worked cooperatively with other functions and management groups through task forces, special projects, and regular contributions to Joint Health and Safety Committees. The daily operational needs of Occupational Health Services are maintained but balanced with operational influence. This influence, which focuses primarily on health, human factors, and loss control, is not always popular with management, unions or employee groups. However, if effective, this unique perspective influences the way business is carried out in an operational setting.

3. **Occupational Health Nurse Specialist** — The role of the OHN at this stage is to influence more than one major business unit by regularly bringing the health, human factors and loss control perspectives to this level of decision-making and key business operations. This position provides few day-to-day, hands-on, technical occupational health services. Rather, the responsibilities extend to the environmental health perspectives by assisting the organization to address public inquiries and concerns related to health. The position takes the strategic direction plan and applies it differently in business units to achieve the same goals. The OHN is expected to identify strategic issues, make recommendations, and participate in developing a corporate approach. Through the use of process management, consulting and facilitation, together with team skills, actions are taken to achieve the desired outcomes.

4. **Senior Occupational Health Nurse Specialist** — The primary purpose of this fourth stage is to:

   • develop and ensure strategic direction for Occupational Health Services for the organization;
   • develop standards, policies and audits;
   • manage issues at the senior management levels, as well as with national unions, government and community groups; and
   • provide general direction and monitor other positions on health and human factor issues.

   This leadership position plans cooperatively with other business groups to best serve the strategic and organizational business plan, paying particular attention to health, environment, human factors, loss control, "due diligence", and functional issues.

Conclusion

The Career Streaming Model has been successfully used in a number of workplace settings and with various occupational health and safety practitioner/professional groups. Industry examples are provided in Appendix 1: "Occupational Health Nurse Career Stream", and in Appendix 2: "Disability Management Professional/Practitioner Career Stream".

JOB DESCRIPTIONS

Many disability management practitioners/professionals function within their jobs without ever having a position or job description to explain and to guide their practice with the organization/company. Position descriptions are important as they clarify what management expects the employee to be responsible and accountable for within a specific position. They facilitate wage and salary administration; provide a basis for manpower planning; assist with recruitment, selection, placement, orientation and evaluation of employees; and enable job evaluation.[21] They also enable an organization to implement its purposes and ensure the efficient use of human capital. Accurate job descriptions make job performance appraisals easier by reducing the influence of subjective factors (*e.g.*, personalities, personal opinions, nature of the employee-supervisor relationship), and by focusing on objective performance measures as stated in the job description and the planned growth and development objectives.

In terms of malpractice issues, company insurance policies tend to cover the disability management practitioner/professional provided the practitioner/professional operates within the scope of his or her position. Without a job description, it would be difficult to legally establish what is the actual scope of the position in question.

A **job description** is a written record of the principal duties and scope of responsibility for a particular job/position. Usually written in a standardized format, it includes the required employee characteristics such as academic qualifications, work experience, skills, and aptitudes. It delineates the appropriate tasks to be performed.

Typically, position descriptions address:

- whether the position level is a management or unionized position;
- if the position is permanent, limited term, part-time or seasonal;
- the position/job title;
- the identity of the immediate supervisor;
- the business unit in which the position resides;

---

[21] D.A. Gillies, *Nursing Management: A Systems Approach*, 2nd ed. (Philadelphia, PA: W.B. Saunders, 1989) at 177-81.

- a position/job identifier (usually a code);
- the date the position was approved and by whom;
- a summary of the purpose of the position;
- the specific functions and responsibilities;
- the educational requirements;
- qualifications;
- the experience, attributes and/or experience necessary;
- the span of authority;
- performance standards;
- the positions to be supervised;
- the reporting structure of the business group; and
- signatures of the position holder and immediate supervisor.

When preparing a position/job position, a good rule of thumb is to write it in enough detail and with so much clarity that an outsider, unfamiliar with the company and the job, can understand it. Use a simple, direct narrative writing style and avoid the use of unfamiliar jargon and complex sentence structures. Begin each statement with an active verb that graphically describes the expected employee behaviour. For example, the position holder "conducts workplace walk-through inspections on a regular basis"; "collects and analyzes incident data monthly"; "distributes incident statistical reports to line management on a monthly basis", *etc*. Samples of disability management practitioner/professional position descriptions are provided in Appendices 3–5.

SUMMARY

A career is an individually perceived sequence of attitudes and behaviours associated with work-related experiences and activities over the span of the individual's life. For disability management practitioners/professionals, the career path can be varied and quite convoluted. For new entrants to the field of disability management, hopefully the contents of this chapter will assist them to plan their careers. For seasoned disability management practitioners/ professionals, this chapter is designed to assist with the management of not only their own careers, but also those of the practitioners/professionals they supervise or mentor.

Appendix 1

Occupational Health Nurse Career Stream

Position	OHN ADVISOR I	OHN ADVISOR II	OHN SPECIALIST	SENIOR OHN SPECIALIST
Qualifications/ Experience	OHN education; entry level; basic computer training; OH&S-related experience	OHN education; case management; ergonomics education; intermediate computer training; 2-3 years OH&S-related experience	OHN education & certification; case management experience; ergonomics education; advanced computer training; 5-7 years OH&S-related experience	Extensive OHN experience & certification; case management expertise; auditor training; ergonomics expertise; computer expertise; business certificate; 8-10 years OH&S-related experience
Position Scope	Narrow			Broad
Position Depth	Shallow			Deep
Application of Skill Types with Advancement	Hi　Lo	Technical/Specialist Skills		Business Skills Relationship Skills

Position	OHN ADVISOR I	OHN ADVISOR II	OHN SPECIALIST	SENIOR OHN SPECIALIST
Technical/ Specialist Skills	• Fitness to Work Assessments • Health Surveillance • Medical Monitoring • Crisis Counselling • Emergency Care • Emergency Response • Work-site Evaluation • Loss Control (operational) • Regulatory Knowledge • Health Promotion • Risk Management (OH) • Professional Networking	• CISD Debriefing (groups) • Human Factors Analysis • Event Investigation • Audit • Case Management • Quality Assurance • Research • Technical Communication (individual) • Social Marketing (individual) • Program Evaluation (individual/projects)	• Standard Setting • Environmental Health Assessments • Environmental/Public Health Risk Management (operational) • Technical Communication (operational) • Social Marketing (operational) • Program Evaluation (operational) • Emergency Planning, Preparedness and Response	• CISD (corporate) • Environmental/Public Health Risk Management (corporate) • Technical Communication (corporate) • Social Marketing (corporate) • Program Evaluation (national focus) • Audit Leadership • DM Governance • DMP Stewardship
Business Skills	• OH Communication (OH advice to individual employees/workgroup, effective oral & written communication skills) • Problem-solving (basic) • Decision-making (basic) • Data Collection and Management (document and retain OH records) • Presentations (OH education sessions)	• OH Communication (OH advice to one Business Line; technical resource to Joint Health & Safety Committees; promote EAP; good written & oral skills) • Problem-solving (intermediate) • Decision-making (intermediate)	• OH Communication (OH advice to multiple business lines; perfect written & oral skills) • Problem-solving (strong) • Decision-making (strong) • Data Collection and Management (establish Disability Management/Occupational Health databases)	• OH Communication (OH advice company-wide; public relations; expert written & oral skills) • Problem-solving (exceptional) • Decision-making (exceptional) • Data Collection and Management (evaluate/enhance OH databases; oversee data

Position	OHN ADVISOR I	OHN ADVISOR II	OHN SPECIALIST	SENIOR OHN SPECIALIST
Business Skills	• Computer Skills (basic) • Consulting (OH resource) • OH performance (basic) • OH Functional Management (basic) • Social Marketing (OH & DM and individually delivered)	• Data Collection and Management (maintain an OH database) • Presentations (business line) • Computer Skills (intermediate) • Project Management (basic) • OH Performance Management (OH practices within workgroups) • OH Functional Management • Issue Management (workgroup) • Social Marketing (employees/workgroups) • Consulting (expert)	• Presentations (multiple business lines/external) • Computer Skills (advanced) • Project Management (intermediate) • OH Performance Management (OH practices within a business line) • Process Facilitation • Issue Management (multiple business lines) • Social Marketing (business lines)	management, channel reports accordingly) • Presentations (executive level/public/external)• Computer Skills (evaluation of computer resources) • Project Management (advanced) • OH Performance Management (within multiple Business Lines and the company, apply TQM principles) • Process Facilitation (corporate) • Issue Management (strategic) • Financial/Business Perspective • Social Marketing (multiple business lines) • OH Stewardship • OH Governance

Position	OHN ADVISOR I	OHN ADVISOR II	OHN SPECIALIST	SENIOR OHN SPECIALIST
Relationship Skills	• Communication Skills • Interpersonal Skills • Coaching (employees) • Team participation • Advocacy (employees; workgroup)	• Communication (business line) • Relationship Skills • Coaching (workgroups, business line) • Team Building (business line) • Negotiating (conflict resolution management re: OH issues in workgroups) • Preceptorship • Change Management (individual & groups)	• Communication (business line) • Community Relationship Management • Coaching (business lines) • Team Building (leadership role with business lines) • Negotiating (conflict resolution management re: safety issues in business lines) • Mediation • Change Management (operational)	• Communication (company/community) • Reputation Management • Mentoring (safety advisors) • Team Building (leadership role for company) • Negotiating (conflict resolution management re: safety issues in company) • Facilitation • Change Management (corporate)

Appendix 2

Disability Management Professional/ Practitioner Career Stream

Position	Disability Claims Administrator	Return to Work Coordinator	Disability Management Coordinator	Disability Management Program Manager
Qualifications/ Experience	Entry-level position. High School Diploma or equivalent education and experience. Completed at least one Workers' Compensation Claims Management course.	Developing position. Completion of, or entry into, a Disability Management instructional program. Working knowledge of company business operations, the various work units, the collective agreements, and the union's role in the return-to-work process.	Performing position. Certification as a Disability Management Coordinator or equivalency, and work experience in the field of Disability Management. Strong working knowledge of company business operations and the various work units, as well as the insurance programs and available community services. Ergonomics training; Basic Occupational Health & Safety education.	Leadership position A degree or equivalent combination of education (diploma or degree in Disability Management) and experience. Ergonomics training. Advanced Occupational Health & Safety education. Risk Communications training. Consulting certificate. Business certificate. Advanced computer training. Demonstrated leadership skills.

Position	Disability Claims Administrator	Return to Work Coordinator	Disability Management Coordinator	Disability Management Program Manager
Qualifications/ Experience	5 years related-industry experience; basic computer skills; problem-solving skills; demonstrated written and verbal communication skills; good interpersonal skills; team player.	2-3 years Disability Management experience; intermediate computer skills; good problem-solving skills; ability to work independently; strong written and verbal communication skills; strong interpersonal skills; team player; organizational and administrative skills; strong appreciation and commitment for workplace safety; valid driver's licence.	4-7 years Disability Management experience; demonstrated strong problem-solving skills; ability to work independently; strong written and verbal communication skills; strong interpersonal skills; team player; organizational and leadership skills; strong appreciation and commitment for workplace safety; valid driver's licence.	8-10 years OH&S experience; demonstrated sound problem-solving skills; self-initiative; exceptional written and verbal communication skills; exceptional interpersonal skills; team leader; sound appreciation and commitment for workplace safety. Strong people and process management skill. Strong project management abilities. Valid driver's licence
Position Scope	*Narrow*			*Broad*
Position Depth	*Shallow*			*Deep*

Position	Disability Claims Administrator	Return to Work Coordinator	Disability Management Coordinator	Disability Management Program Manager
Technical/ Specialist Skills	• **Loss Control** (at an individual level, mitigate injury/illness costs through effective claims management — WCB, self-insured programs and third party insurance programs) • **Regulatory Knowledge** (develop an awareness of the WCB, human rights and privacy legislation as it applies to claims management; monitor worker compliance with the applicable legislation; promote due diligence at a worker level; assist with the interpretation of the applicable pieces of legislation at the worker level)	• **Loss Control** (at a workgroup level, assist workers to return to work in a safe and timely manner) • **Regulatory Knowledge** (develop greater knowledge of the WCB, human rights, privacy and OH&S legislation; monitor workgroup compliance; promote due diligence at a workgroup level; interpret legislation for the workgroup)	• **Loss Control** (at a business line level, oversee the WCB claims management and return-to-work practices; undertake incident analysis and trend analysis of disability management data; evaluate the Disability Management Program; promote injury/illness prevention; promote desired return-to-work practices) • **Regulatory Knowledge** (develop a level of proficiency on WCB, human rights, privacy and OH&S legislation; interpret these pieces of legislation for a business line; regularly monitor the applicable legislation; assist with the development of corporate Disability Management Program standards)	• **Loss Control** (at a company-wide level, direct general disability loss control; direct WCB claims management and rehabilitation; direct injury/illness prevention activities; use disability management outcomes to advise on related management theories and practices) • **Regulatory Knowledge** (possess expertise on WCB, human rights, privacy and OH&S legislation; interpret legislation at a company/ industry level; assist with the provision of disability management governance; promote responsible government/industry disability management standards/ practices)

Position	Disability Claims Administrator	Return to Work Coordinator	Disability Management Coordinator	Disability Management Program Manager
Technical/ Specialist Skills	• **Program Management** (at an individual level, assist with the delivery of the Disability Management Program, especially in the area of claims management) • **Administration** (assist with the documentation and retention of disability management claim records)	• **Program Management** (at a workgroup level, assist with the development and implementation of the Disability Management Program, especially in terms of the Gradual Return-to-work process) • **Leadership & Administration** (promote the Disability Management Program and how it applies to a workgroup; schedule return-to-work educational activities for a workgroup; assist a work group to return recovering workers to the workplace monitor, measure outcomes and seek ways to enhance the Gradual Return-to-work initiatives)	• **Program Management** (at a business line level, oversee the development and delivery of the Disability Management Program; monitor its effectiveness and efficiency; develop and monitor work accommodation and ergonomic solutions for business lines) • **Leadership & Administration** (promote the Disability Management Program and how it applies to a business line; schedule Disability Management Program activities for a business line; coordinate case management activities for the business line; ensure quality Disability Management Program principles are applied; conduct case management	• **Program Development and Management** (at a company level, direct Disability Management Program development and delivery; interpret and report on its effectiveness and efficiency; direct the implemented work accommodation and ergonomic solutions) • **Leadership** (oversee company Disability Management Program activities; ensure quality Disability Management Program principles are applied; conduct Disability Management Program reviews; assume budget responsibilities; assist Director, Human Resources with supervisory duties)

Position	Disability Claims Administrator	Return to Work Coordinator	Disability Management Coordinator	Disability Management Program Manager
Technical/ Specialist Skills	• **Disability Management Program** (at an individual level, assist with Disability Management Program educational sessions; promote sound claims management)	• **Disability Management Program** (at a workgroup level, coordinate Gradual Return-to-work initiatives; assist with development and implementation of various Gradual Return-to-work initiatives; provide appropriate coaching to management and employees on sound disability management principles and practices; monitor and measure Gradual Return-to-work outcomes; learn from and seek ways to enhance the Gradual Return-to-work initiatives)	• **Disability Management Program** (at a business line level, oversee and manage the daily activities of the Disability Management Program; coordinate Disability Management Program educational sessions; promote sound Disability Management Program principles and practices within a business line; monitor, measure and evaluate Disability Management Program outcomes; seek ways to enhance the Disability Management Program) reviews with a view to continuous improvement; provide Disability Management Program leadership to other Disability Management Program team members)	• **Disability Management Program** (at a company level, direct the Disability Management Program and its components; monitor its efficiency and effectiveness; provide an interpretation of the disability management Program outcomes and how they can be improved; maintain codes of practice for the disability management practitioners/professionals; direct the promotion of the Disability Management

Position	Disability Claims Administrator	Return to Work Coordinator	Disability Management Coordinator	Disability Management Program Manager
Technical/ Specialist Skills	• **Education** (at an individual level, assist with conducting Disability Management Program and Gradual Return-to-work training; provide claims initiation education to new employees at orientation sessions; participate in external training opportunities)	• **Education** (at a workgroup level, develop and co-ordinate Gradual Return-to-work training for a work group; provide Gradual Return-to-work education to new employees during orientation sessions; educate and coach line management on sound Gradual Return-to-work practices participate in external training opportunities)	• **Education** (at a business line level, develop and co-ordinate Disability Management Program training for business lines; educate supervisors and line management in their unique roles in the Disability Management Program; participate in external training opportunities; evaluate the Disability Management Program training initiatives; participate in and evaluate new employee orientations as they relate to Disability Management Program education)	Program; seek ways to integrate the Disability Management Program into business strategies and other business functions) • **Education** (at a company level, direct and evaluate the overall Disability Management Program training initiatives)

Position	Disability Claims Administrator	Return to Work Coordinator	Disability Management Coordinator	Disability Management Program Manager
Technical/ Specialist Skills	• **Communication** (at an individual level, promote awareness of the Disability Management Program and Gradual Return-to-work initiatives among workers; explain claims management jargon/terms, requirements and processes; explain sound claims management practices to management and employees with a view to loss control) • **Program Evaluation** (conduct ongoing claims evaluations and assist management/employees	• **Communication** (at an individual level, provide technical Gradual Return-to-work communication to workgroups; relate results of Gradual Return-to-work initiatives to workgroups; present trend analysis reports to work groups; seek ways to continually improve the outcomes of Gradual Return-to-work initiatives) • **Program Evaluation** (at a workgroup level, conduct ongoing evaluation of Gradual Return-to-work	• **Communication** (at a business line level, provide technical Disability Management Program communication; relate Disability Management Program outcomes; present and explain departmental trend analysis reports; describe Disability Management Program audit results; explain rationale for corrective actions; seek ways to continually improve the Disability Management Program) • **Program Evaluation** (at a business line level, conduct ongoing Disability Management Program	• **Communication** (at a company level, design and provide Disability Management Program communication to the Executive Team and Board of Directors; explain and interpret corporate trend analysis reports; present results of Disability Management Program audit results to the company and Executive/Board; explain the purpose of compliance audits and for corrective action follow-up by the company; manage public/media relations in regards to Disability Management Program issues) • **Program Evaluation** (at a company-wide level, provide leadership and interpretation of Disability

Position	Disability Claims Administrator	Return to Work Coordinator	Disability Management Coordinator	Disability Management Program Manager
Technical/ Specialist Skills	with corrective actions; conduct summative claims management evaluations; interpret and communicate the findings) • **Risk Management** (promote effective claims management practices and compliance with the applicable legislative requirements)	initiatives; promote corrective actions; conduct summative Gradual Return-to-work evaluations; interpret and communicate the findings) • **Risk Management** (at a workgroup level, promote risk assessment and management practices in terms of successful Gradual Return-to-work initiatives and compliance with legislative requirements) • **Social Marketing** (of the Gradual Return-to-work initiatives and concepts among management and employees)	evaluation; undertake regular compliance audits and Disability Management Program customer satisfaction surveys; interpret and communicate the findings) • **Risk Management** (at a business line level, promote risk assessment and risk management practices in terms of disability management and the prevention of occupational and non-occupational injury/illness; compliance with legislative requirements) • **Social Marketing** (of the Disability Management Program and concepts at a business line level)	Management Program evaluations; communicate findings; seek ways to link program results with other company business practices and strategies) • **Risk Management** (at a company level, promote and direct sound risk assessment and management practices; direct and communicate risk on Public/Health/ Environment issues (*e.g.,* emerging illness/injuries;) • **Social Marketing** (of the Disability Management Program and concepts within the company and externally to service providers and insurers)

Position	Disability Claims Administrator	Return to Work Coordinator	Disability Management Coordinator	Disability Management Program Manager
Business Skills	• **Communication** (demonstrates basic oral and written communication skills in providing claims management advice to individual managers and employees) • **Problem-solving** (basic level)	• **Communication** (demonstrates strong written and oral communication skills; provides Gradual Return-to-work information and advice to individuals and workgroups; serves as a resource on Gradual Return-to-work initiatives; promotes RTW supports such as WCB On-site Job Demands Assessments or ergonomic assistive devices) • **Problem-solving** (intermediate level)	• **Communication** (demonstrates effective written and oral communication skills; provides Disability Management Program advice at the business line level; serves as a technical resource on related procedure or policy use; promotes Disability Management Program supports such as the EAP, the attendance support programs, ergonomic assistive devices, or OH&S program/practice changes) • **Problem-solving** (strong)	• **Communication** (demonstrates expert written and oral skills, provides advice on the Disability Management Program and its related practices at a company level; serves as a technical resource on Disability Management Program policy or procedure development; promotes integration of company support services, *e.g.*, the Disability Management Program, Attendance Support and Assistance Program, EAP, and Ergonomic Program; undertakes public relations as required) • **Problem-solving** (exceptional)

Position	Disability Claims Administrator	Return to Work Coordinator	Disability Management Coordinator	Disability Management Program Manager
Business Skills	• **Decision-making** (basic level)	• **Decision-making** (intermediate level)	• **Decision-making** (strong)	• **Decision-making** (exceptional)
	• **Data Collection and Management** (document and retain claims management data according to company-set practice standards)	• **Data Collection and Management** (maintain a Gradual Return-to-work database)	• **Data Collection and Management** (establish and maintain the Disability Management Program database)	• **Data Collection and Management** (evaluate and enhance the Disability Management and Gradual Return-to-work databases; direct data management; channel reports accordingly)
	• **Presentations** (at new employee orientations and educational sessions that address claims management)	• **Presentations** (at new employee orientations and educational sessions that address Gradual Return-to-work initiatives; deliver other related presentations at the workgroup level)	• **Presentations** (at new employee orientations and educational sessions that address the Disability Management Program and processes; deliver other related presentations at the business line level)	• **Presentations** (deliver Disability Management Program presentations at the Executive and Board of Director level, to the public and externally)
	• **Computer Skills** (basic level)	• **Computer Skills** (intermediate level of computer skills)	• **Computer Skills** (advanced level of computer skills)	• **Computer Skills** (advanced computer skills; conducts ongoing evaluations of

Position	Disability Claims Administrator	Return to Work Coordinator	Disability Management Coordinator	Disability Management Program Manager
Business Skills	• **Functional Management** (Claims management)	• **Project Management** (basic skills) • **Performance Management** (Gradual Return-to-work practices within workgroups) • **Functional Management** (Gradual Return-to-work initiatives)	• **Project Management** (intermediate skills) • **Performance Management** (Disability Management Program within business lines) • **Process Facilitation** (business line)	Team's computer resources, the direct computer resources, and the Disability Management Program Team's computer skills) • **Project Management** (advanced and directional skills) • **Performance Management** (within the company, direct and apply the Total Quality Management principles to the performance of the Disability Management Program; evaluate Disability Management Program performance and recommend related enhancements) • **Process Facilitation** (company)

Position	Disability Claims Administrator	Return to Work Coordinator	Disability Management Coordinator	Disability Management Program Manager
Business Skills		• **Issue Management** (individual and workgroup) • **Social Marketing** (employee/management/workgroup)	• **Issue Management** (business line) • **Social Marketing** (business lines)	• **Issue Management** (corporate and strategic) • **Social Marketing** (multiple business lines and corporate) • **Financial/Business Perspective** (direct) • **Disability Management Program Stewardship** (direct and align with the company's business strategies and other company functions) • **Disability Management** Governance (direct)
Relationship Skills	• **Communication** (at the individual level; basic communication skills; basic interpersonal skills)	• **Communication** (at the individual and workgroup levels; intermediate communication and interpersonal skills)	• **Communication** (at the business line levels, advanced communication and interpersonal skills)	• **Communication** (at the company, government, industry and community levels; expert communication and interpersonal skills)

Position	Disability Claims Administrator	Return to Work Coordinator	Disability Management Coordinator	Disability Management Program Manager
Relationship Skills	• **Interpersonal Skills** (basic level) • **Coaching** (employees and line management on claims management) • **Team participation** (team player) • **Advocacy** (for employees; a workgroup regarding claims management)	• **Relationship Skills** (developing) • **Coaching** (employees and workgroups on Gradual Return-to-work initiatives) • **Team Building** (participatory and in workgroups) • **Negotiating** (conflict resolution management re: Gradual Return-to-work issues in workgroups)	• **Community Relationship Management** (developing) • **Coaching** (business lines on the Disability Management Program) • **Team Building** (leadership role with business lines) • **Negotiating** (conflict resolution management re: Disability Management Program issues in the business lines) • **Mediation** (at a business line level)	• **Reputation Management** (advanced) • **Mentoring** (Disability Management Team) • **Team Building** (leadership role for company/industry) • **Negotiating** (conflict resolution management re: Disability Management Program and Gradual Return-to-work issues at a corporation level) • **Mediation and Facilitation** (at a corporate level)

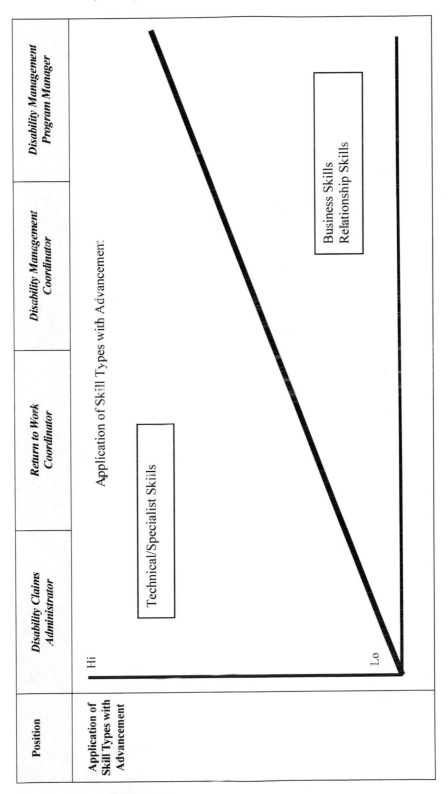

Appendix 3

Position Profile:
Unionized Position

Position Profile for: **Disability Claim Administrator**

Position Reports to: **Disability Management Program Coordinator**

Interfaces with: *Internally*: Line operations, Human Resources Department, and Occupational Health & Safety Department

Externally: Family physician offices, health care provider offices, Employee Assistance Program Service Provider office, third party insurance agencies, and government agencies (WCB)

Purpose: The Disability Claim Administrator is responsible for the administration of the claim function for medical absences, including follow-up procedures of the various employee benefit plans such as short-term disability and long-term disability.

Accountabilities: The Disability Claim Administrator:

- acts as resource and contact person with respect to the claim management for medical absences;
- coordinates all the medical absence claims;
- calculates benefits payable under the long-term disability plan with consideration for any offsets, if applicable;
- prepares cheque requisitions, long-term disability cheques and employee information forms, if required;
- assists in the administration (oral and written) and interpretation of company policies to staff and supervisors;
- coordinates claim follow-up;
- maintains liaison with claimants, departments, insurance agencies, and legal representatives regarding claim management;
- maintains a computerized database of medical absences;
- participates in claim appeals;
- provides clerical support as required;
- assists in special projects assigned by the Disability Management Coordinator;
- prepares monthly long-term disability claim reports for budget and planning purposes; and
- performs related duties as assigned.

Qualifications and Experience:

High School Diploma or equivalent education and experience. Claim management training including at least one Workers' Compensation Claim Management course.

Experience in coordinating activities, working with professionals, and acting as a team member to make claim process judgments; current knowledge of the related disability benefit plans and policies, along with other related employee benefits.

Five years related-industry experience; strong computer skills in word processing, database management, report generation and systems; ability to organize work and time effectively; ability to express ideas clearly in oral and written forms; problem solving skills; good interpersonal skills; team player.

Special Skills and Attributes:

Technical/Specialist Skills:

- **Loss control:** At an individual level, mitigate injury/illness costs through effective claim management — self-insured programs and third party insurance programs
- **Regulatory knowledge:** Develop an awareness of the WCB, human rights and privacy legislation as it applies to claim management; monitor worker compliance with the applicable legislation; promote due diligence at a worker level; assist with the interpretation of the applicable pieces of legislation at the worker level.
- **Program Management:** At an individual level, assist with the delivery of the Disability Management Program, especially in the area of claim management
- **Administration:** Assist with the documentation and retention of Disability Management claim records
- **Disability Management Program:** At an individual level, assist with Disability Management Program educational sessions; promote sound claims management
- **Education:** At an individual level, assist with conducting Disability Management Program and Gradual Return-to-work training; provide claim initiation education to new employees at orientation sessions; participate in external training opportunities
- **Communication:** Promote awareness of the Disability Management Program and gradual return-to-work initiatives among workers; explain claims management jargon/terms, requirements, and processes; explain sound claim management practices to management and employees with a view to loss control
- **Program Evaluation:** Conduct ongoing claim evaluations and assist management/employees with corrective actions; conduct summative claim management evaluations; interpret and communicate the findings
- **Risk Management:** Promote effective claim management practices and compliance with the applicable legislative requirements

Business Skills:

- **Communication:** Demonstrate basic oral and written communication skills in providing claim management advice to individual managers and employees
- **Problem-solving** (basic level)
- **Decision-making** (basic level)
- **Data Collection and Management** (document and retain claim management data according to company-set practice standards)
- **Presentations** (at new employee orientations and educational sessions that address claim management)
- **Computer Skills** (strong)
- **Functional Management** (claim management)

Relationship Skills:

- **Communication** (at the individual level; basic communication skills; basic interpersonal skills)
- **Interpersonal Skills** (basic)
- **Team Participation** (team player)
- **Advocacy** (for employees; for the workgroup regarding claims management)

Date Developed: September 2009

Appendix 4

Position Profile:
Management Professional

Position Profile for:	**Disability Case Manager**
Position Reports to:	**Disability Management Program Coordinator**
Interfaces with:	***Internally*:** Senior management, union leaders, line operations, Human Resources Department, Occupational Health & Safety Department, and Legal Department.
	***Externally*:** Family physicians, health care providers, Employee Assistance Program Service Provider, third party insurance agencies, and government agencies (WCB).
Purpose:	The Disability Case Manager, is an Occupational Health Nursing professional, who practices within an occupational setting to assist ill and injured workers in reaching their maximum health and productivity. The Disability Case Manager is also responsible for the coordination of employee health care services across multiple environmental systems from the onset of injury or illness to a safe return to work or an optimal alternative. The Disability Case Manager is expected to achieve quality care delivered in a cost-effective manner. Using a unique knowledge of employees, their families and the work environment, the Disability Case Manager assesses, plans, implements, coordinates, monitors and evaluates care for clients in the Disability Management Program.
Accountabilities:	The Disability Case Manager:

- assesses the broad spectrum of client needs, including physical and psychosocial factors, using data from employees and families, other health care providers, health records, *etc.*
- identifies client (employee and employer) goals, objectives and actions in a comprehensive case management plan to achieve desired outcomes within designated time frames
- identifies the need for vocational rehabilitation when appropriate
- is accountable for the progression of disability claim cases
- establishes communication plans involving internal and external parties, as appropriate
- implements interventions to achieve client goals and objectives
- identifies qualifications and expectations for, and monitors and evaluates outcomes and quality of services delivered by, health care providers and vendors in the treatment outcomes
- identifies needed community resources and coordinates referrals as appropriate

- assists with the Integrated Disability Management Program evaluation process regarding client satisfaction, processes, outcomes and cost effectiveness
- supports claim processing with insurance and third party representatives
- generates consistent documentation of the case management aspects of the program
- contributes to the assessment of Disability Management Program using company, insurance and other health data
- acts as a professional occupational health resource for the company's management in planning and maintaining the Integrated Disability Management Program
- assists with the development of primary, secondary and tertiary prevention and occupational health promotion strategies to optimize employee health and prevent injuries/illness
- assists with the establishment of criteria to identify employees for inclusion in the Integrated Disability Management Program
- assists with the development of processes for identifying situations that require early intervention to maximize the desired outcomes
- supports the vocational rehabilitation efforts implemented by the Vocational Rehabilitation Specialist
- maintains and safeguards confidentiality of employee personal health, and disability information and records
- develops and conducts educational programs to enhance case management for health care providers, management and employees
- identifies researchable problems and participates in studies and projects according to research skills
- assumes responsibility for his or her own professional development and continuing education

Qualifications and Experience:

The qualifications for the Disability Case Manager depend on the breadth and scope of the position. Typically, a Disability Case Manager should be a Registered Nurse with an Occupational Health Nurse Certificate/Specialist and advanced disability management education.

A valid Registered Nurse licence, some related-industry experience; basic computer skills; problem-solving skills; ability to work under minimal supervision; strong written and verbal communication skills; strong interpersonal skills; team player; strong appreciation and commitment for workplace health and safety; valid driver's licence.

Special Skills and Attributes:

OH Nursing Technical/Specialist Skills:
- **Disability management expertise**
- **Fitness-to-work evaluation**
- **Health surveillance and medical monitoring**

- **Crisis counselling**
- **Emergency care**
- **Emergency response**
- **Worksite evaluation**
- **Loss control** (operational)
- **Regulatory knowledge** (develop an awareness of human rights, OH&S and WCB legislation; monitor worker and company compliance with WCB legislation; promote due diligence at a worker level; assist with the interpretation of legislation at an individual and workgroup level)
- **Health promotion**
- **Risk management** (disability management and occupational health)
- **Professional networking**

Business Skills:

- **Communication** (disability management and occupational health advice to individual employees using effective oral and written communication skills)
- **Problem-solving** (strong)
- **Decision-making** (strong)
- **Data Collection and Management** (document and retain Disability Management Program and Occupational Health Service data)
- **Presentations** (Disability Management Program and occupational health educational sessions)
- **Computer Skills** (strong)
- **Consulting** (Disability Management Program and occupational health resource)

Relationship Skills:

- **Communication** (individual and workgroup level)
- **Interpersonal Skills**
- **Coaching** (employees and line management)
- **Team Participation** (team player)
- **Advocacy** (for employees; workgroup)

Date Developed: September 2009

Appendix 5

Position Profile:
Management Professional

Position Profile for:	**Disability Management Program Coordinator**
Position Reports to:	**Disability Management Program Manager**
Interfaces with:	***Internally*:** Senior management, union leaders, line operations, Employee Training Department, Occupational Health & Safety Service Provider, Employee Assistance Program Service Provider, Human Resources Department, and Legal Department.
	***Externally*:** Family physicians, health care providers, third party insurance agencies, and government agencies (WCB).
Purpose:	• Managing the company's Integrated Disability Management Program and services within designated business line(s)
	• Functioning as a team member to provide high-quality Integrated Disability Management Program services to the various company business lines and their employees — our customers
	• Providing Integrated Disability Management Program advice and assistance for our customers
	• Mentoring and coaching the Disability Claim Advisor, Return-to-Work Coordinator, and Disability Case Manager
	• Providing a strong Integrated Disability Management Program leadership role within the company
Accountabilities:	As a member of the Disability Management Program Team, manage and oversee the development, delivery, and continuous improvement of the company's Integrated Disability Management Program. The specific position duties include:
	• **Regulatory Stewardship and Governance:** Ensure that the company remains in compliance with the applicable legislation and industry standards.
	• **Disability Management Expertise:** Support the designated business line(s) with the development and implementation of the Integrated Disability Management Program and practices.
	• **Issue Management/Negotiating:** Assist the designated business line(s) with Integrated Disability Management Program issue management and resolution.
	• **Disability Management Program Performance Management:** Support the designated business line(s) with its/their Integrated Disability Management Program performance management.
	• **Loss Control:** Assist with the maintenance of the

company's loss control data management system.
- **Presentations:** Provide Disability Management Program presentations in instances such as new employee orientations, management meetings, operational meetings, safety meetings and in public forums.
- **Event Investigation:** Investigate and prepare reports related to occupational and public events.
- **Program Evaluation:** Conduct Integrated Disability Management Program compliance audits and prepares the resulting reports.
- **Risk Communication:** Communicate Integrated Disability Management Program risks in terms that are understandable for the business lines.
- **Risk Management:** Provide Disability Management Program training/educational seminars for employees and external third parties.
- **Program Development:** Develop a customized Integrated Disability Management Program as required.
- **Communication:** Undertake effective Disability Management Program communications that are targeted and customer-focused.
- **Relationship Building:** Build effective business relationships both internally and externally.
- **Professional Growth:** Seek and avail oneself of opportunities for continued education and competency in the field of disability management.

Qualifications and Experience:

Disability management certification or an equivalent Occupational Health Nurse Certificate; incident training and experience; ergonomics training; advanced computer training/skills; auditor training; 8-10 years disability management experience

Special Skills and Attributes:

Disability Management Technical/Specialist Skills:
- **Loss Control** (at a business line level, oversee the WCB claim management and return to work practices; undertake incident analysis and trend analysis of Integrated Disability Management data; evaluate the Disability Management Program; promote injury/illness prevention; promote desired return-to-work practices)
- **Regulatory Knowledge** (develop a level of proficiency on WCB, human rights, privacy and OH&S legislation; interpret these pieces of legislation for a business line; regularly monitor the applicable legislation; assist with the development of corporate Disability Management Program standards)
- **Program Management** (at a business line level, oversee the development and delivery of the Integrated Disability Management Program; monitor its effectiveness and efficiency; develop and monitor work accommodation and

ergonomic solutions for business lines)
- **Leadership and Administration** (promote the Integrated Disability Management Program and how it applies to a business line; schedule Integrated Disability Management Program activities for a business line; coordinate case management activities for the business line; ensure quality Disability Management Program principles are applied; conduct case management reviews with a view to continuous improvement; provide Disability Management Program leadership to other Integrated Disability Management Program team members)
- **Disability Management Program** (at a business line level, oversee and manage the daily activities of the Integrated Disability Management Program; coordinate Disability Management Program educational sessions; promote sound Disability Management Program principles and practices within a business line; monitor, measure and evaluate the Integrated Disability Management Program outcomes; seek ways to enhance the Integrated Disability Management Program)
- **Education** (at a business line level, develop and co-ordinate Integrated Disability Management Program training for business lines; educate supervisors and line management in their unique roles in the Integrated Disability Management Program; participate in external training opportunities; evaluate the Integrated Disability Management Program training initiatives; participate in and evaluate new employee orientations as they relate to Disability Management Program education)
- **Communication** (at a business line level, provide technical Disability Management Program communication; relate the Integrated Disability Management Program outcomes; present and explain departmental trend analysis reports; describe Disability Management Program audit results; explain rationale for corrective actions; seek ways to continually improve the Integrated Disability Management Program
- **Program Evaluation** (at a business line level, conduct ongoing Disability Management Program evaluation; undertake regular compliance audits and Disability Management Program customer satisfaction surveys; interpret and communicate the findings)
- **Risk Management** (at a business line level, promote risk assessment and risk management practices in terms of disability management and the prevention of occupational and non-occupational injury/illness; compliance with legislative requirements)
- **Social Marketing** (of the Integrated Disability Management Program and concepts at a business line level)

Business Skills:
- **Communication** (demonstrates effective written and oral communication skills; provides Disability Management

Program advice at the business line level; serves as a technical resource on related procedure or policy use; promotes the Integrated Disability Management Program supports such as the EAP, the attendance support programs, ergonomic assistive devices, or OH&S program/ practice changes)
- **Problem-solving** (strong skills)
- **Decision-making** (strong skills)
- **Data Collection and Management** (establish the Disability Management Program databases)
- **Presentations** (multiple business lines/external)
- **Computer Skills** (advanced skills)
- **Project Management** (intermediate skills)
- **Disability Management Program Performance Management** (safety practices within a business line)
- **Process Facilitation** (business lines)
- **Issue Management** (multiple business lines)
- **Social Marketing** (business lines)

Relationship Skills:
- **Communication** (at the business line levels; advanced communication skills and interpersoanl skills)
- **Community Relationship Management** (developing)
- **Coaching** (business lines on the Integrated Disability Management Program principles and practices)
- **Team Building** (leadership role within the business lines; team player)
- **Negotiating** (conflict resolution management regarding Disability Management Program issues within business lines)
- **Mediation** (at the business line level)

Date Developed: September 2009

CHAPTER REFERENCES

D. Dyck & M. Walker, "Career Streaming: A Model of Career Development" (1996) 44:4 American Association of Occupational Health Nurses Journal 177.

D.A. Gillies, *Nursing Management: A Systems Approach*, 2nd ed. (Philadelphia, PA: W.B. Saunders, 1989).

R. Goddard, "Lateral Moves Enhance Careers", (1990) 35:12 *HR Magazine* 69.

D.T. Hall, *Careers in Organizations* (Glenview, IL: Scott, Foresman, 1976).

E. Jacques, *Equitable Payment* (New York, NY: Wiley, 1961).

B. Moses, *Manager's Guide to Career Development* (Toronto, ON: BBM Human Resource Consultants, 1989).

L.J. Peter & R. Hull, *The Peter Principle* (New York: W. Morrow, 1969).

J. Schermerhorn, J. Hunt & R. Osborn, *Managing Organizational Behavior*, 4th ed. (New York: John Wiley & Sons, 1991).

R. Steers, *Introduction to Organizational Behaviors*, 2nd ed. (Glenview, IL: Scott, Foresman, 1984).

E. Stone, *Career Anchors: Self-Assessment*, 3rd ed. (San Francisco, CA: Wiley, 2007).

T. Stone & N. Meltz, *Human Resource Management in Canada*, 2nd ed. (Toronto, ON: Holt, Rinehart and Winston of Canada, 1988).

Chapter 25

Internal/External Consulting: Tips for Disability Management Practitioners/Professionals[1]

INTRODUCTION

Consulting is the art of influencing people at their request.[2] In essence, it is a helpful relationship. It means reaching a conclusion of acceptable quality, of maintaining an acceptable commitment to that conclusion, of supporting the client to prevent and/or minimize any detrimental outcomes as a result of the conclusion, and being perceived as being helpful and efficient by the client.[3]

The **Disability Management Consultant** by definition is a practitioner/ professional who provides influence, recommendations, and expertise in the area of disability management, but has no direct power to make changes. Regardless of the degree of involvement, the consultant does not own the problem: the client does.

DISABILITY MANAGEMENT PRACTITIONERS/ PROFESSIONALS AS CONSULTANTS

Disability management practitioners/professionals act as consultants when someone asks them if they have five minutes to discuss a disability management issue; when the disability management practitioner/professional advocates for an employee or champions a new idea; or when the disability management practitioner/professional makes the following statements on behalf of others: "*I'll look into that*", "*I think the real problem is ...*", "*Here is what I think we should do about this situation*".

In these ways, the disability management practitioner/professional functions as either an internal, or as an external, consultant. The irony is that although consulting skills are essential to the practice, they are not skills that disability management practitioners/professionals have been well prepared to implement.

---

[1] D. Dyck "Internal and external consulting: Assisting clients with managing work, health and psychosocial issues" (2002) 50:3 American Association of Occupational Health Nurses Journal, 111. Copyright (2002) the American Association of Occupational Health Nurses, Inc. Used with permission. All rights reserved.

[2] G.M. Weinberg, *The Secrets of Consulting* (New York: Dorset House Publishing, 1985).

[3] Proactive Consultants, *Effective Internal Consulting* (Calgary, AB: Proactive Consultants, 1989).

For the disability management practitioner/professional, this chapter contains information that can be used to evaluate and hone internal or external consulting skills.

The intent of this chapter is to:

- define disability management consulting — internal and external;
- explain how to manage any disability management consulting request or project using a six-phase consulting model;
- explain how to build collaborative and accountable client-consulting relationships;
- learn to negotiate appropriate consulting roles with clients;
- reframe the presenting issues into working issues;
- gather relevant data while building client commitment;
- present relevant information to create the foundation for appropriate recommendations; and
- learn the top 10 secrets of disability management consulting.

While reading, think of some opportunities that might lend to the application of the techniques described, and then look for work situations in which to test them.

CONSULTING: WHAT IS INVOLVED?

As an operational definition, **consulting** is the provision of temporary professional help to assist the client to address current or potential problems or opportunities. It is the ability to:

- help the client discover problems and to facilitate the assessment of the client's needs and willingness to change;
- ensure clarity of roles, responsibilities, and resources through formal and/or informal contracting with the client;
- gather and present facts, observations, opinions and feelings that assist the client to define the problem(s);
- coordinate the implementation of one or more intervention(s) (resource, expert, or process) that successfully and productively address the defined problem(s) in a manner that is fully supported by the client;
- evaluate the effectiveness of the intervention and any further actions required;
- develop self-sufficiency in the client-system so as to minimize dependence on the consultant and to ensure a minimum of stress during disengagement; and
- assume any of the varying roles of a consultant as an advocate, technical specialist, trainer/educator, collaborator in problem-solving, identifier of alternatives, fact-finder, process specialist, or a reflector.

THE CONSULTING RELATIONSHIP: ITS CHARACTERISTICS

Disability management consulting is a voluntary, temporary, and supportive relationship that involves a helper and a help-needing party (the client). It focuses on providing assistance to the client to enable him or her reach a solution to a potential/real problem situation. By helping clients to make use of their own knowledge, products, and services, the consultant facilitates the resolution of a problem by the client.

As Disability Management Consultants, disability management practitioners/ professionals exert influence, but they do not have any power. Their leadership is non-authoritarian in nature. Disability Management Consultants may be involved with the problem, but they remain outsiders. They do not own the problem or the solution. It is the client that owns the problem and makes the final decision.

Consulting requires discipline by both parties to recognize and play their respective roles in reaching a mutually agreed-upon solution. At each phase of the consulting process, the Disability Management Consultant needs to deal with three questions:

1. What do we need to accomplish?
2. What process should we use?
3. What should my role be?

There is a wide range of available consulting roles. Any role negotiated requires use of disability management technical expertise. This expertise will differ from role to role. The main question is: *"Which role will be the most helpful in this particular situation?"* To answer this question, consider:

*   the skills and knowledge required to do the job;
*   the time constraints, if any exist;
*   the client's expectations;
*   the potential for developing the client's capabilities so that he or she can manage a similar issue next time it arises; and
*   any systems that may need to be developed and implemented for success.

The disability management professional's/practitioner's role may change several times throughout an disability management consulting project. Remember: *"Help is never help unless it is perceived to be so by the client."*[4] Be prepared to re-negotiate the necessary role changes with the client.

There are two types of disability management consulting relationships: internal or external. **Internal Disability Management Consulting** is when the consultant is a member of the organization and is assuming a consulting role to assist with the resolution of a problem or the chance to capitalize on an

---

[4]   D. Sousa, "Internal/External Consulting: Ten Tips for Occupational Health Nurses" (Seminar presented at the American Occupational Health Conference, San Francisco, CA, April 2001) [unpublished].

opportunity. The client may be the whole organization for whom the consultant assumes an advocacy role. The internal Disability Management Consultant tends to have better knowledge about the organization — its goals, structure and operations. The internal Disability Management Consultant keeps the organization's "best-interests" in mind. Although acting as a Disability Management Consultant, this type of consultant does retain some power to veto proposed actions.

The **External Disability Management Consultant** is an "outsider" who has access to specialized services not traditionally found within the client organization. This type of consultant tends to have more than one client group, is more likely to be able to bring a wide variety of experiences to the situation, and is better positioned to view the situation more objectively. Unlike the internal disability management consultant, the external Disability Management Consultant has no decision-making power.

Being labelled a "Disability Management Consultant" does not make the disability management practitioner/professional a consultant. Rather, the skills demonstrated by the person, qualifies one to be called a Disability Management Consultant.

THE CONSULTING TOOL KIT

In addition to technical expertise, the Disability Management Consultant requires a number of specialized skills:

- *Interpersonal Skills* — building effective working relationships such as active listening skills, assertiveness skills, conflict management and issue resolution, providing support and reassurance, and giving/receiving feedback;

- *Business Skills* — linking solutions to client needs and business drivers such as strategic planning, project management, project evaluation, and cost/benefit analysis of the solution;

- *Analytical Skills* — gathering and manage the relevant information such as data gathering, data management, data analysis, data interpretation, and reporting skills;

- *Consulting Skills* — managing the consulting process such as the knowledge and ability to use the consulting model/process and adherence to professional ethics; and

- *Technical Specialist Skills* — functioning competently within the field of Disability Management.

In essence, the Disability Management Consultant needs a consulting tool kit (see Figure 25.1 below).

Figure 25.1: Disability Management Consulting Tool Kit[5]

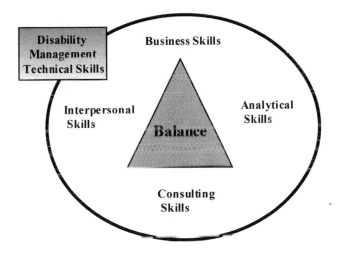

Consulting Tool Kit:

Disability Management Technical Skills

Business Skills

Interpersonal Skills

Balance

Analytical Skills

Consulting Skills

---

5   Adapted from L. Goode, "Consulting Successfully Within Organizations" (Seminar presented at Petro-Canada, Calgary, AB, 1995) [unpublished].

SIX PHASES OF A DISABILITY MANAGEMENT CONSULTING PROJECT

According to Goode (1995), a Disability Management Consulting project has six phases (see Figure 25.2 below).

Figure 25.2 The Disability Management Consulting Process

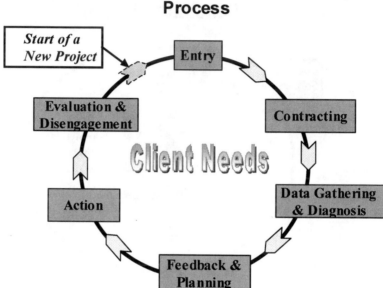

The Disability Management Consulting Process

1. Entry

Entry is the first contact with a client about the concern or project. It is analogous to engaging an employee or manager to work on an issue. The purpose of the Entry Phase is to decide whether or not to work together on the project. This is a critical point: if a contract "sours", 90 per cent of the time it goes awry in either the Entry Phase or the Contracting Phase. Remember that both parties are nervous about this phase. It is up to the Disability Management Consultant to manage these phases.

    The criteria for the "Fit/No fit" decision include an exploration of:

- **The task**

  Exploration of the task is critical during this stage. For example: What is the objective of the work/task? Is it possible to do? What has been done so far? Are there clear expectations for the work and a successful completion? Is it original work or routine work? What about the timing — can it be done in the allotted time frame? Are there political implications that need to be addressed?

- **The client-consultant relationship**

   Who is the real client(s)? Who are the real decision-makers? Who are the end-users? Is there positive chemistry between the client(s) and the consultant? Do their values and ethics align? What is the level of trust like? Can both parties "win" if this project is successful? What level of commitment does the client(s) have to the completion of this project?

- **The disability management professional/practitioner's consulting experience, expertise, and availability**

   What is the disability management professional/practitioner's technical knowledge and skill level? Are the disability management professional/ practitioner's personal values and ethics aligned with those of the client(s)? What are the disability management professional/practitioner's other business priorities and/or demands? Is this a "high-risk" project with low-payoff potential?

   The recommended approach for the Entry Phase is to begin by analyzing the situation. This means clarifying the real versus the presenting problem; identifying the client/consultant wants and expectations; identifying the client's commitment level to the project; and establishing the roles that the Disability Management Consultant and client will assume. Reach a decision point of "Go/No Go" with the disability management consulting assignment.

2. Contracting

A **consulting contract** is an explicit agreement clarifying what the client and consultant can expect from each other and how they will work together. This can be formal or informal in nature, and involves mutual exploration and decision-making about what is to be done and how to work together. While the Entry Phase determines whether the client and consultant will work together, the Contracting Phase determines how the client and consultant will work together.

   Why is contracting necessary? To begin with, it establishes a basis for working together. It is during this period that decisions such as the following are made: Will the relationship be formal or informal? Will the work be done together or independently? Who will have the final say in how things are done?

   Secondly, develop a 50/50 relationship if possible. The reason for this is that the disability management practitioner/professional wants the client to own the problem and the solution, so that when it comes time to exit the consulting relationship, the client will be successfully launched.

   Thirdly, a Disability Management Consultant's maximum leverage occurs at the beginning of the working relationship, just like in a courtship. By clarifying expectations, establishing individual roles, making plans for the project and setting the ground rules at this point, you have the greatest leverage for attaining success in the long run. The key is to set things up right in the first place.

Lastly, most consulting "failures" can be traced back to omissions or errors in the entry and contracting phases. To be successful, the consulting services/products must meet the client's expectations. To achieve this, ensure that the client's expectations are clearly articulated in the Contracting Phase and avoid over-promising on what you can deliver.

The recommended approach is to:

- confirm the client's level of commitment to the project;
- seek a balance of responsibility for the project;
- develop a clear project contract; and
- make sure that the contract is signed.

Depending on the complexity and nature of the concern/project and the client system, some or all of the following items should be clarified in the Contracting Phase:

STATEMENT OF THE WORKING ISSUE AND SCOPE OF THE WORK

- the desired results and products;
- the scope of the project in terms of the boundaries of the consulting process and project content; and
- a definition of success and failure for this project.

CLIENT PROFILE

- identification of the decision-maker(s) for this project;
- identification of all the project stakeholders and their interests/needs/ wants in relation to this project;
- identification of all people/systems affected by the project; and
- identification of who else needs to be involved in the project and consulting arrangement.

STAKEHOLDER ROLES AND RESPONSIBILITIES

- establish the type and degree of involvement of stakeholders in the project; and
- define the consultant role.

CONTRACT BY PHASE OR "ONE-SHOT" APPROACH

- decide on the scope of this project: Will it be treated as one large project, or a project with a number of phases, each perceived as an individual project?

COSTS AND RESOURCES

- agree on the fee structure, charge codes and/or budget approvals for the project; and
- clarify the materials, supplies and/or resources needed.

SCHEDULE

- establish the start time, specific milestones and completion date;
- articulate the "success indicators" and when they will be reached; and
- prepare a timeline and tracking process for the project.

DATA COLLECTION

- determine the acceptable/non-acceptable sources and methods of data collection;
- decide how feedback of data will be obtained (to whom? how? by when?); and
- address the issue of confidentiality.

CONSTRAINTS/POTENTIAL ISSUES

- be aware of ethical, legal and/or political sensitivities that may impact the project; and
- identify the critical steps in the project and have contingency plans in effect.

FEEDBACK TO THE CONSULTANT

- clarify up front, how, by whom and when feedback will be given to the consultant.

As already mentioned, critical to the success of the Contracting Phase (and ultimately, to the success of the project) is the client-consultant relationship. For this reason, it is important to explore some tips for building accountable, collaborative client-consultant relationships. To begin with, start where the client "is at". Clients tend to vary in their readiness to address problems/issues, as well as in their knowledge of the situation.

Support the clients in their results and efforts. The Disability Management Consultant may have strong opinions about the situation at hand, but those will not help the clients reach a successful resolution of their problem(s). Remember that the concern/problem is the client's. They need to own the concern, their part in creating the concern, the desired results, and the solution.

Work towards a partnership: that is, a 50/50 relationship concerning the consulting process. Fully explore and seek to understand the client's situation, concerns, agendas, and motivations before moving into action. Be careful to stay within the client's frame of reference.

As for the interpersonal relationship with the client, there are a few things to note. Before ever challenging the client on any issue, first "earn that right". To do so, be honest, ethical, and dependable. When stating that something will be done for the client, treat it as a promise. A failure to do so can lead to distrust with this client and subsequent clients.

Keep the task, process, and relationship visible. This means regular meetings to keep the lines of communication open, working from an action plan, and paying attention to project successes and failures.

Lastly, the client-consultant relationship requires clear explanations and focused listening to establish a clear understanding of the goals, objectives and expected outcomes for the project. To reach action, it requires honouring specific requests and committed promises.

The core listening skills required involve focusing the entire Disability Management Consultant's attention on the client, deciding what needs to be understood, reflecting on assumptions made, and questioning for understanding. Remember that the more the Disability Management Consultant tries to persuade a person, the less the Disability Management Consultant is attending to the listening aspect of the process. As well, one is not listening when one is waiting for a turn to speak.

3. Data Gathering and Diagnosis

The purpose of data gathering and diagnosis is to develop a clear understanding of the situation by both the client and the consultant, to set the stage for problem solving, and to build a client commitment regarding the problem ownership and resolution. The goal of data gathering is to gain accurate, reliable, and complete information. Performing data gathering activities can result in consciousness raising, creating expectations, and supporting relationship building. If the client disowns or disagrees with the data, he or she will not be committed to the problem resolution and solution.

Data is operationally defined as any form of information that can be collected and is relevant to an individual, group or organization function. Data gathering involves systematic data collection, data analysis and data feedback. Data collection includes devising a method to determine the nature of the problem, the kinds of information required, the number of people involved, the time available to do the project and the cost of the method in question. A comparison of different methods of data collection is provided in Table 25.1.

As Disability Management Consultants, our mental filters affect both our ability to gather data and to analyze the information. Questions are essential information gathering tools. The quality of the data gathered depends on the quality of the questions used. In data gathering, our mental filters influence which questions are asked. Unconsciously, we can ask questions that lead us and our clients down a path to our "preferred solution" instead of to the "best solution".

In terms of an analysis of the problem, Disability Management Consultants can easily jump to conclusions based on our mental filters. Our filters make some aspects of a problem more visible to us than others do. For example, a financial consultant will tend to see the problem as a financial one; a business consultant will attribute the problem to business reasons; and human resources personnel will conclude that the issues are people-oriented. The challenge for the Disability Management Consultant is to be able to see an issue from many perspectives and to identify the root cause, not to focus on the symptoms of the problem.

The secret is to use the right questions in the right order. Begin with open-ended questions to help the client to describe the concern. For example, use questions like: Can you tell me about the issue? In your opinion, what is the issue? Why has this happened? Why do you think the system is this way? The next step is to use content questions. They ask for specific information: the What's, the Where's, the When's, the Who's, and the How's. The last step is use of the binary questions. They confirm understanding and are answered with a "yes" or "no".

During this phase, the data gathering and diagnosing methods must:

- gather the relevant information in an effective and efficient manner;
- be aligned with the client's culture, norms and standards of operation; and
- be appropriate to the desired results for the project.

The recommended approach is to:

- collect the data;
- organize data into manageable issues;
- decide how to use the data;
- develop an assessment of the problem/issues;
- determine the real technical/business problem(s);
- determine the controls in place; and
- assess their effectiveness.

4.   Feedback and Planning

The purpose of the Feedback and Planning Phase is to ensure that the client understands the situation, owns the data/situation, has a plan of action to address the concern, and is committed to taking action. It is at this point that the client needs to move out of an "understanding mode" and into an "action mode".

There are a number of feedback and recommendation issues that need to be addressed and overcome. Next to the Contracting Phase, this stage is often the most difficult to deal with.[6] Clients are often stalled in the action-taking phase. A second issue is that frequently there is an overwhelming amount of data, making the selection and presentation of the most essential data difficult. This data is important to deciding how to move forward.

---

[6]   *Effective Internal Consulting* (Calgary, AB: Proactive Consultants, 1989).

Table 25.1: Comparison of Different Methods of Data Collection[7]

Method	Advantages	Disadvantages
INTERVIEWS	• Builds rapport • Source of broad and deep data • Adaptive — collects data on a range of topics	• Time consuming/expensive • Can result in "interviewer response bias" • Coding/interpretation challenges • Self-reporting bias
FOCUS GROUPS	• Builds rapport • Can reach more people in less time • Works well in combination with other methods	• "Facilitator bias" • Potential for domination by some focus group participants • Can get derailed from investigation process
SURVEYS/ QUESTIONNAIRES	• Useful in describing traits of large populations • Easy to use with large samples • Inexpensive: flexible • Obtains large amount of data • Easier to probe into more sensitive areas/issues • Responses can be easily collated, quantified and summarized	• Takes time and expertise to develop • Questions are predetermined • May appear superficial in coverage of complex topics • Seldom able to deal with the context of social life • Unable to measure social action, only recall past action • Data may be over-interpreted • "Response bias" • Responses may reflect other confounding issues
OBSERVATIONS	• Collects data on behaviour rather than reports on behaviour • "Real-time" data, not retrospective • Can obtain large amounts of data • Good for studying subtle	• Problems coding and interpreting • Sampling is a problem • "Observer bias/reliability" • The impact of observing — the Hawthorne Effect • Difficult to generalize • Costly

7   Adapted from: E. Babbie, *The Practice of Social Research*, 4th ed. (Belmont, CA: Wadsworth Publishing, 1986); H. Checkoway, N. Pearce & D. Crawford-Brown, *Research Methods in Occupational Epidemiology* (Toronto, ON: Oxford University Press, 1989); and Proactive Consultants, *Effective Internal Consulting* (Calgary, AB: Proactive Consultants, 1989).

Method	Advantages	Disadvantages
	nuances of behaviours	
DOCUMENTATION	• Non-reactive — no response bias • High face validity • Easily quantified	• Problems with access/retrieval • Validity problems • Problems coding/interpreting
LABORATORY EXPERIMENTATION	• Can control variables • Better observation • Easier to do	• Validity problems: Does this represent reality? • Results are difficult to generalize • Some situations cannot be replicated in a laboratory

Another quandary is that the Disability Management Consultant, for a number of reasons, may not feed back the difficult realities to the client or may focus only on the problems and fail to adequately support the client. When this happens, the client fails to be able to move into action and successfully solve the problem.

Additionally, the client's representative may not want other clients within the organization to have access to the data or to be involved with the implementation. This can lead to implementation problems in the future.

There may be difficulties with the feedback meeting. For example, the wrong people may be at the meeting; the people present may be unauthorized to make decisions; or there may be no chance for a face-to-face meeting with the client. This can lead to problems such as an inability to make critical decisions, a misinterpretation of the findings and the inability to move forward. Finally, the Disability Management Consultant may prevent the client from creating his or her "own solutions".

To effectively frame the recommendations, the Disability Management Consultant must consider the following:

• As Disability Management Consultants, our role is one of influence, not power. Essentially, the challenge is to influence clients to do things differently. As Disability management practitioners/professionals, we are in the business of helping our clients — we are not in the business of making recommendations that may or may not be used. When consulting, a shift in perspective must occur.

• When making recommendations, Disability Management Consultants need to remember two paradoxical points: (1) they are trying to influence the client to do things differently (to change); and (2) the client is always responsible for making the final decision to change or not to change.

Some key issues concerning the art of influence and change are:

• What are the "drivers" for the client to change?

- What recommendations are logically linked to the analysis of the problem?
- What are the broader implications of the recommendations made? What are the financial, technological, cultural and organizational implications? Remember, the best "technical recommendation" may not be the best recommendation.
- Change requires human energy. Decide how feasible the suggested recommendations are and how much energy is required to implement them.
- Can the client make the changes or will the client need help?
- Is it feasible to hold a face-to-face meeting with the client to openly discuss the analysis and recommendations?
- Can the recommendations be framed in terms of the client's needs and business drivers?

The extent to which clients can hear and accept recommendations often depends on how we have "framed" them. To frame a recommendation, Disability Management Consultants need to understand the impact of their recommendations, the client needs, and the client's business drivers.

The recommended approach is to:

- deliver the message personally;
- plan for reaction and discussion time;
- provide the client with feedback and recommendations in a non-judgmental manner;
- be direct and simple with your explanations (avoid circling the issue(s));
- focus on process versus people issues;
- be specific and timely;
- seek reaction to the message (probe for concerns and/or resistance);
- address any client resistance;
- decide what actions to take;
- confirm that this is what the client wants to do;
- jointly develop goals and action steps for the project;
- seek client commitment;
- offer client support; and
- re-contract as required.

5.   Action

At this stage, someone carries out the proposed action(s). Individual responsibilities and roles have to be clarified and defined. Implementation roles can vary between being client-directed, requiring joint participation and being consultant-directed. Depending upon which way the client chooses to proceed, the Disability Management Consultant can be a bystander, a mentor, or a "pair of hands".

Which role is the most appropriate for the Disability Management Consultant to assume? This depends on the situation, the task, the available internal resources, and the level of expertise of both parties. In general, the greater the role flexibility demonstrated by the Disability Management Consultant, the greater the capability to appropriately and effectively help the client.[8]

6.   Evaluation and Disengagement

This final stage is where the client and Disability Management Consultant "part company". Success is when the client is ready, willing, and able to "go it alone". Some things to consider at closure are:

- Does the client agree that the Disability Management Consultant's work is done?
- Have the client expectations been met?
- Who will carry the project forward?
- Is the documentation adequate?
- What has been learned from the consulting experience?
- What impact has the work had on the business?
- Is the client-consultant relationship strong?
- How can others benefit from what the Disability Management Consultant has learned from this project?

Failure to close brings a cascade of undesirable outcomes, namely:

- the project continues despite the work having been completed;
- the client/consultant relationship is jeopardized;
- consulting fees become jeopardized; and
- questions about the consultant's integrity loom.

To prevent this from happening, successful launching of the client can be accomplished by:

- evaluating the effectiveness of the Action Stage;
- seeking an extension for the project if required and appropriate;
- recycling the consulting process if a new problem emerges;
- disengaging from the project because the original work is done, or the current work cannot be done; and
- keeping the door open for future work.

The six phases of a Disability Management Consulting project and relationship are summarized in terms of their actions, goals, and purpose in Table 25.2.

---

[8]   L. Goode, "Consulting Successfully Within Organizations" (Seminar presented at Petro-Canada, Calgary, AB, 1995) [unpublished].

Table 25.2: The Six Phases of an Disability Management Consulting Project and Relationship: Their Actions, Goals and Purpose

PHASE	ACTION	GOAL	PURPOSE
ENTRY	First contact to mutually determine whether to work together.	A "fit"/"no fit" decision. A reframed issue. An effective working relationship.	That the right people are doing the right work.
CONTRACTING	Mutual exploration about how to work together.	An explicit agreement	To clarify the scope of work and the client-consultant commitments.
DATA GATHERING AND ANALYSIS	Information about the concern is gathered and analyzed.	A clear picture of the situation.	To create client understanding of the issue and foster intelligent action.
FEEDBACK AND RECOMMEND-ATIONS	Information is summarized and plans are created to address the concern.	Client understands the situation and the action plans have been created.	To create action plans that clients can realistically carry out or manage.
IMPLEMENT-ATION	The plan is implemented.	Sustained action by clients.	To create action in the client system because nothing changes until it changes.
CLOSURE	The consultant and client reach closure on the situation.	Clients are ready, willing and able to go it alone.	To foster long-term client success with this project/issue.

DISABILITY MANAGEMENT CONSULTING: ROLE OF THE INTERNAL CONSULTANT

The internal Disability Management Consultant, while encouraging client self-sufficiency, helps to solve problems so that they stay solved. This element of empowerment is crucial for a consulting assignment to be viewed as successful.

There are a number of roles that the internal Disability Management Consultant can play. The Expert Role is where the Disability Management Consultant embodies the message: "*I can tell you how to fix it.*" This scenario is typified by the manager being a passive decision-maker, and the Disability

Management Consultant making the decisions, as well as planning and implementing the main events. The problem with this approach is that the client or the manager does not learn the skills or gain the knowledge to deal with this type of problem in the future. Also, with less involvement, the manager has less commitment to the issue(s).

The Pair of Hands Role is where the Disability Management Consultant approaches the problem with the message: *"I will fix it for you."* Here, the Disability Management Consultant is a passive decision-maker. Decisions are made by the manager who specifies the desired change procedures. The problem with this approach is that the problem analysis is made solely from the manager's perspective, which often results in a lack of innovation and repetition of the same solutions to problems.

The Collaborative Role of *"We need to work together"* is characterized by joint decision-making, planning, implementation, and project evaluation. Although this approach may be viewed as duplicating efforts, it ends up being the most functional approach.

DISABILITY MANAGEMENT CONSULTING: PROJECT RECOMMENDATIONS

As Disability Management Consultants, disability management practitioners/ professionals are expected to produce recommendations for the client to consider. When making recommendations, you should be sure that they are:

- consistent with the data/findings;
- designed to have a positive impact;
- feasible;
- prioritized; and
- aligned with the organization's other business strategies.

CONSULTING DO'S AND DON'TS FOR DISABILITY MANAGEMENT CONSULTANTS

DO:

- Act in ways that promote client trust.
- Be permitted to be influenced, as well as influence.
- Deal with problems collaboratively.
- Communicate effectively: Listen, listen, listen!
- Reframe problems/issues for clarification.
- Remain open-minded and objective.
- Seek to reduce "any threat" that the Disability Management Consultant role may generate.
- Be non-judgmental.
- Remember, help is only help when viewed as help.

DON'T:

- Get trapped into a "telling role".
- Take advantage of the situation to show how bright, knowledgeable and experienced you are.
- Meet defensiveness with pressure and arguments about "the facts".
- Confuse "helping" with "over-praising and unfounded reassurances" regarding the person being helped.

DISABILITY MANAGEMENT CONSULTING: ETHICAL GUIDELINES

Disability Management Consultants should adopt an ethical approach to consulting that includes:

- maintaining a high quality of services;
- maintaining confidentiality about client issues;
- informing the client about confidentiality limits;
- offering *ONLY* what can be competently delivered;
- not misrepresenting credentials/affiliations;
- delivering a high quality of services;
- adhering to professional standards;
- being wary of sacrificing ethics for economic/financial gains; and
- terminating the relationship when the client is no longer benefiting.

CRITERIA FOR SUCCESS IN A CONSULTING SITUATION

As measures of success in a Disability Management Consulting situation, the following are suggested as goals for the Disability Management Consultant to strive towards attaining:

- a result that the client and organization can accept and successfully implement;
- a result that adds business/personal value to the client and the organization;

- an outcome that ends in having a positive (or neutral) effect on the working relationship; and
- the Disability Management Consultant is, and is perceived as, helpful by the client and the organization.

THE TOP 10 TIPS FOR DISABILITY MANAGEMENT CONSULTANTS

- Listen to the client and address his or her concerns
- Understand and work towards the client's objectives — not yours
- Strive to be objective and recognize when you are not
- Treat the relationship as confidential unless otherwise agreed upon
- Work to make the client look good
- Be non-judgmental: accept the client at his or her level
- Whenever possible, give the client credit for the successes realized
- Try to understand the client's organization and the content in which people work
- At disengagement, leave the client as independent and self-reliant as possible
- Practice ethical disability management consulting

FOR EXTERNAL DISABILITY MANAGEMENT CONSULTANTS: SUGGESTIONS FOR BUILDING YOUR BUSINESS

In building any consulting business, there are some basics that need to be upheld. They include the following:

- Understand and meet your client's needs.
- Listen! Listen! Listen!
- Do work that contributes to the bottom line: work that is productive, satisfying and profitable.
- Focus on results.
- "Contract" your services upfront: avoid doing work for free.
- Have project progress meetings with your clients, particularly on large or lengthy projects.
- Use a "contract" to ensure that what was promised gets accomplished and delivered.
- Set performance targets and keep track of the results.
- For standard requests and repetitive work, create efficient and standardized processes.
- Accept advice from other professionals (*e.g.*, legal, financial, business planners) to do your work and to achieve your business goals and targets.
- Use recognized strategic planning practices.

- Be clear about the business principles in use to run your company and live by them. Remember that the characteristics of your disability management business are strongly associated with your reputation.
- Build your business over time, but start now.

For any business, new or established, marketing is crucial. To be effective, marketing must be targeted and focused. It should be informative and geared towards building relationships. Some marketing tips are:

- Market by attraction, rather than promotion.
- Be clear about who you are and what you offer.
- Specialize: "You can't be all things to all people."
- Know what "the competition" is doing.
- Recommend others when the services sought are out of your area of expertise.
- Be visible to decision-makers.
- Spend 5-20 per cent of your time making business contacts and doing marketing.
- Ask clients for references and referrals.
- Consider getting help from marketing professionals.
- Decide what combination of time, money and energy you want to invest for your marketing efforts.

To minimize the "feast or famine phenomenon" associated with building a Disability Management Consultant business, it is recommended that each day, week, month or year, make business contacts and market 5-20 per cent of the time, and prepare and do actual work 80-90 per cent of the time.

Some additional business thoughts for the external Disability Management Consultant are to decide how to finance your business. The options are to either infuse money into your business as needed, or infuse money upfront. There are pros and cons to each approach. Evaluate each approach carefully.

Consider registering your business, doing a business plan, using a commercial bank account, getting a line of credit for the business, and evaluating the need for business insurance. Be open to advice from and make the appropriate legal/contractual arrangements with them. Above all, learn what you are good at and do it. Get help with what you do not do well and refer to colleagues when asked to do work outside your area of expertise. Be clear about your products and services, and then market. For more information on marketing refer to Chapter 13, "Marketing Disability Management Programs and Communicating the Results".

SUMMARY

To reiterate, Disability Management Consulting is the art of influencing people at their request. It means reaching a conclusion of acceptable quality; maintaining an acceptable commitment to that conclusion; supporting the client to prevent and/or minimize any detrimental outcomes as a result of the conclusion; and being perceived as being helpful and efficient by the client.

Disability management practitioners/professionals are involved in a variety of consulting roles along with different types of consulting relationships — internal and external Disability Management Consulting. To consult well, Disability management practitioners/professionals need specialized knowledge and skills. "Top-notch" Disability Management Consultants are not merely born; they work hard at developing the sensitivity and competency to help others, and leave their clients self-sufficient when the project is complete.

CHAPTER REFERENCES

E. Babbie, *The Practice of Social Research*, 4th ed. (Belmont, CA: Wadsworth Publishing, 1986).

H. Checkoway, N. Pearce & D. Crawford-Brown, *Research Methods in Occupational Epidemiology* (Toronto, ON: Oxford University Press, 1989).

D. Dyck, "Internal and External Consulting: Assisting Clients with Managing Work, Health and Psychosocial issues" (2002) 50:3 American Association of Occupational Health Nurses Journal 111.

L. Goode, "Consulting Successfully Within Organizations" (Seminar presented at Petro-Canada, Calgary, AB, 1995).

D. Sousa, "Internal/External Consulting: Ten Tips for Occupational Health Nurses" (Seminar presented at the American Occupational Health Conference, San Francisco, CA, April 2001) [unpublished].

G.M. Weinberg, *The Secrets of Consulting* (New York: Dorset House Publishing, 1985).

Proactive Consultants, *Effective Internal Consulting* (Calgary, AB: Proactive Consultants, 1989).

Chapter 26

Future Challenges in Disability Management

INTRODUCTION

The field of disability management came into vogue in the late 1980s. It was born out of necessity. Organizational leaders realized that employee medical absences were costly, and that disability-related costs involved "after tax" dollars. This meant that organizations had to sell more gas, televisions, cars, goods, and services to cover the cost of employee absenteeism and disability. As organizations became more sophisticated in measuring employee absence and disability costs, they realized the need to manage medical absences and to facilitate early return-to-work opportunities for recovering employees. The adopted approach was to develop Disability Management Programs that assist employees in successfully returning to work.

Disability management professionals/practitioners come from a variety of disciplines and educational backgrounds. Each brings a different perspective to the field of disability management. To become a full-fledged profession, the field of disability management must include specialized education. Currently, confusion reigns s to the various disability management educational offerings, as well as to what exactly the participants will attain upon completion of those educational offerings. Lastly, there is a lack of adequate teaching resources.

Given that disability management was, and still is, an emerging field, confusion continues as to what it is; how it is implemented, and by whom; and what are the best practices. As well, much of what has been learned since the late 1980s has been by "trial and error" as opposed to evidence-based, that is, the result of solid research. This book is an attempt to compile that knowledge. However, there remain a number of challenges yet to be addressed. This chapter is a discussion on some of the future challenges in the field of disability management, namely:

A) Professionalism: How does the Field of Disability Management "Stack-up"?
B) Educational Preparation of Disability Management Practitioners/Professionals
C) The Canadian Approach to Disability Management Advanced Education
D) Disability Management: The International Disability Scene

A)   PROFESSIONALISM: HOW DOES THE FIELD OF DISABILITY MANAGEMENT "STACK-UP"?

A Profession

Taking the term "**profession**" literally, it is an occupation, vocation, or high-status career that usually involves prolonged academic training, formal qualifications, and membership of a professional or regulatory body.[1] The Registered Nurses Association of Ontario (RNAO) defines it as:

An occupation whose core element is work based upon the mastery of a complex body of knowledge and skills. It is a vocation in which knowledge of some department of science or learning or the practice of an art founded upon it is used in the service of others. Its members possess a commitment to competence, integrity, morality, altruism and the promotion of the public good within their domain. These commitments form the basis of a social contract between a profession and society, which in return grants the profession the right to autonomy in practice and the privilege of self-regulation. Professions and their members are accountable to those serviced and to society.[2]

Some examples of professions are lawyers, accountants, engineers, teachers, professors, librarians, priests, pilots, physicians, dentists, nurses, vets, pharmacists, physical therapists, and other specialized technical occupations.

A profession typically involves the application of specialized knowledge of a subject, field, or science to customers or fee-paying clientele. It is usually regulated by a professional body that sets competency examinations, acts as a licensing authority, and enforces adherence to an ethical code of practice. Examining these four elements further:

- *Regulation*:
  A profession differs from a trade group in that it regulates by statute, its members, and their participation.

- *Autonomy*:
  Professions have a high degree of control over their activities and practices.

- *Status and Prestige*:
  Society recognizes and regards professions with respect and prestige.

---

[1]   Oxford University Press, *Oxford English Dictionary*, 2nd ed. (New York: Oxford University Press, 1989).

[2]   Registered Nurses Association of Ontario (RNAO), *Professionalism in Nursing, Healthy Work Environments, Best Practice Guidelines* (Toronto, ON: RNAO, 2007) at 58, available online at: <http://www.rnao.org/Storage/28/2303_BPG_Professionalism.pdf>.

- *Power*:
  Professions have power — power to control their own members, their area(s) of expertise, and their interests. According to Larkin,[3] a profession dominates, polices and protects its area of expertise and the conduct of its members, and exercises significant influence over its field.

Profession Characteristics: How Does the Field of Disability Management Measure Up?

So what are the characteristics of a profession? That is, what are the essential elements that an occupation would have to possess to be deemed a "profession"?

- ☑ *Skill based on theoretical knowledge*: Professionals possess extensive theoretical knowledge and related skills in a certain field or area of expertise.

- ☑ *Individual clients*: Professions have fee-paying clients/patients: payment that is direct or indirect in nature.

- ☑ *Work autonomy*: Professions retain control over their work and their theoretical knowledge. Hence, they are autonomous in their practice and can make independent judgments about their work.

- ☑ *Status and rewards*: Professions are highly respected by society and accordingly, rewarded. The prestige comes from society viewing their work as having a special and valuable nature. All professions possess *professional expertise* — defined as technical, specialized, and highly skilled work/abilities.

- ☑ *Middle-class occupations*: Professionals tend to earn more than do non-professionals.

- ☑ *Public service and altruism*: Professions provide a valued public service and tend to do so in an unselfish way. Some are even viewed less as a profession and more as a "calling", for example the clergy, physicians, nurses, teachers, and others.

- ☑ *Mobility*: Professionals own their knowledge and skills, as well as the authority to practice. Hence, they are mobile in their employment opportunities and the services they provide. This mobility is supported by the standardization of professional education and the related codes of practice.

Examining these seven characteristics only, one could conclude that the field of disability management is meeting some of the tests of a profession as noted

---

[3]   G. Larkin, *Occupational Monopoly and Modern Medicine* (London, UK: Tavistock Publications, 1983).

by the ☑ symbol. However, there are more characteristics that need to be explored, namely:

☑ *Professional association*: Professions have management and administrative functions designed to control the entrance and exit requirements of members, and to promote the status of their membership. In the field of disability management, this is not formalized.

☑ *Code of professional conduct or ethics*: Professions have rules of ethical conduct which the members are required to uphold. There is no control over the practice of disability management in Canada.

☑ *Extensive period of education*: Professions require their members to attain at least three years of formal university education. Again, there are individuals practising in the field of Disability Management without formalized schooling.

☑ *Institutional training*: In addition to formalized schooling, professions usually require a lengthy period of institutional training focused on specific practical experience before being recognized as a full member within the profession.

☑ *Testing of competence*: Professions require potential candidates to successfully complete theory and practice-based examinations, as well as to provide evidence of ongoing practice competence. Disability management practitioners are not required to undergo any competency testing before "setting up shop".

☑ *Offer reassurance*: Society looks to the professions to offer reassurance to clients/patients that things are being properly addressed and moving towards a "normal state". An example is the lawyer who assures his client that the proper steps are being taken to resolve an issue.

☑ *Male-dominated*: Professions have traditionally been male-dominated with the exception of nursing.

☑ *Legitimacy*: Society awards professions, based on their education and competence, legal authority to conduct specific service duties and obligations.

☑ *Indeterminacy of knowledge*: Professions deal with codes and standards of practice, not rules. They are faced with situations/conditions that can only be addressed through a mix of knowledge, skills, and experience, not by following a set of prescribed rules.

A review of these next nine characteristics leaves one more skeptical (**?**). There is no overall system compelling disability management practitioners to meet these acid tests. Some practitioners have undergone an extensive period of education, or institutional training, or even a test of their competence. Some have their practice governed by their professional bodies (*e.g.,* occupational health nurses, occupational physicians, psychologists, occupational therapists, kinesiologists, lawyers, accountants, engineers, *etc.*). But for the most part, this is a "hit and miss" situation.

To avoid pre-mature closure on this issue, let's need to look at the last six characteristics of a profession, namely:

☒ *Self-regulation*: Professions are self-regulated, usually through a professional association that upholds professional standards and codes of practice.

☒ *Licensed practitioners*: Along with self-regulation comes licensure — a legally sanctioned license to practice.

☒ *Exclusion, monopoly, and legal recognition*: To achieve socially sanctioned self-regulation and licensure, a profession must be legally recognized to exclude those who do not meet the entrance criteria and to expel those members who are deemed incompetent.

☒ *Control of remuneration and advertising*: Professions tend to set acceptable fee rates as well as to establish acceptable standards of advertising.

☒ *Ritualistic*: Professions vary in the degree and types of rituals that they uphold, for example the clergy and legal counsels tend to uphold many rituals; physicians, nurses and other scientifically based professions, rely more on research-based practices.

☒ *Inaccessible body of knowledge*: The accessibility of knowledge is usually limited or unavailable to the layperson. These topics tend not to be covered in schools, universities, or libraries; as well, barriers arise from the technical jargon used. Sometimes it is legally sanctioned, for example, medical/legal/ religious information can be deemed privileged information, available for only those qualified to understand the information.

As denoted by the symbol ☒, the field of disability management has not met the terms of these six characteristics.

So back to the question of interest, *Is the field of disability management a "Profession"?* The answer is "no": the field of disability management is made up of a number of currently recognized professions such as:

- occupational health nursing;
- occupational medicine;
- psychologists;
- occupational therapists; and
- kinesiologists, *etc.*

As well, the field of disability management is composed of a number of quasi-professions, such as Disability Case Managers, Disability Claim Managers, claim adjudicators, return-to-Work coordinators, Disability Management Professionals, ergonomists, kinesologists, occupational therapists, rehabilitation therapists, *etc.* Hence, the field of disability management is a "salad of professions and disciplines"; rather than a pure science. As a result, it does not meet the essential conditions of being a profession.

Professionalization

Professionalization is the process by which a profession arises from a trade or occupation. It is described as:

> ... *starting with the establishment of the activity as a full-time occupation, progressing through the establishment of training schools and university links, the formation of a professional organization, and the struggle to gain legal support for exclusion, and culminating with the formation of a formal code of ethics.*[4]

Professionalization involves establishing acceptable qualifications and professional norms. That requires the establishment of a professional association to oversee the conduct of members and to identify the "qualified" from the "unqualified amateurs".[5] This process is termed **occupational closure** — the division between qualified members and unqualified outsiders.[6]

Typically, trade groups/occupations "dream" of attaining the status of being a "profession" — but like the fisherman who dreams of "catching that big fish", are disability management practitioners prepared to "land professionalism"?

---

[4]   J. Roberts & M. Dietrich, "Conceptualizing Professionalism: Why Economics Needs Sociology" (1999) 58:4 The American Journal of Economics and Sociology 977, available online at: <http://findarticles.com/p/articles/mi_m0254/is_4_58/ai_58496769>.

[5]   Wikipedia (2008), "Professionalization", available online at: <http://en.wikipedia.org/wiki/professionalization>.

[6]   S. Cavanagh, "The Gender of Professionalism and Occupational Closure: The Management of Tenure-related Disputes by the 'Federation of Women Teachers' Association of Ontario' 1918-1949" (2003) 15:1 Gender and Education 30.

The Field of Disability Management: Ready or Not?

For the field of disability management to evolve from an occupation to a profession, certain actions must be undertaken, such as:

- *Professional body/association — administration*: Establishment of a legally recognized body/association designed to set professional standards and codes of practice, administer member eligibility, and self-regulate the profession. Although the National Institute of Disability Management and Research (NIDMAR) is moving towards this goal, disability management practitioners/professionals practice outside of any professional association.

- *Professional standards*: Development of practice standards/codes of practice to guide members in acceptable and safe practices. NIDMAR has developed some practice disability management standards, however, they are not widely recognized or used by disability management practitioners/ professionals.

- *Professional licensure*: Establish, administer, and maintain a system to legally sanction license to practice.

- *Educational standards and requirements*: Establish defensible (research-supported) educational standards and requirements for the profession. NIDMAR has undertaken considerable disability management research, but more is needed.

- *Research and development ability*: Establish, promote, and support disability management research and development.

- *Political action ability*: Proactively work with society, industry and the government to promote the profession.

- *Learn from others*: Network with other newly formed professional associations to determine what worked/failed in regards to the move from an occupation to a profession.

The Disability Management Practitioner: Ready or Not?

Aside from the initiatives that a group of disability management practitioners can take to move towards professionalism, individual disability management practitioners must position themselves to be *ready*. Hence, they should possess:

- *Disability management technical/specialist skills*: The unique skills, or combinations of skills, required to competently function in the field of disability management. They include regulatory knowledge; competency in the field of disability management practices; program development; leadership, management and administration of Disability Management Program and services; disability management training and education; Disability Management Program communication and marketing; strategic issues management; program evaluation; and disability management risk management and risk communication skills.[7]

- *Interpersonal skills*: Otherwise known as "people skills", these skills include communication, interpersonal skills, team-building/team-work, mentoring, coaching, negotiating, and reputation management skills.[8]

- *Business skills*: The skills required to effectively manage people and business functions. They include planning and organization, decision-making, problem-solving, leadership, financial/business perspective, negotiating, information systems, internal/external consulting, process facilitation, performance management, employee development, educating, change management, presentation-making, and risk management and communications.[9]

- *Research and development skills*: The skills required to undertake defensible disability management research and development. They involve using recognized research techniques and practices.

---

[7]   See Chapter 24, "Disability Management Practitioners/Professionals: Career Development".
[8]   *Ibid.*
[9]   *Ibid.*

In short, disability management practitioners have to position themselves towards demonstrated professionalism: "Qualities or typical features of a profession or professional. A collection of attitudes and actions; it suggests knowledge and technical skill."[10]

In future, hopefully, the question may no longer be whether the field of disability management is a profession or not: Rather it will be, *"Are you prepared for professionalism?"*

Conclusion

The road ahead towards disability management professionalism may seem unattainable and rocky, but "stay the course" and work collaboratively towards attaining professionalism. The key is to learn from what other professional groups have done or what disability management groups in other countries are doing — there is no need to "re-invent the road to professionalism". Instead move smartly and steadily forward.

B) EDUCATIONAL PREPARATION OF DISABILITY MANAGEMENT PRACTITIONERS/PROFESSIONALS

INTRODUCTION

In Canada, disability management is an emerging field. The growth of disability management practitioners and professionals has mushroomed. However, issues exist with the academic preparation of these practitioners/professionals. Are they adequately prepared to competently practice in the field of disability management? Can they function without *"doing harm"* to stakeholders?

Disability management practitioners/professionals tend to enter the field from the medical, nursing, various health care/rehabilitation, and social work professions, as well as from areas of study/work such as occupational health & safety, human resources, group insurance, Workers' Compensation Boards, and union involvement. The preparation and orientation that each group has towards disability management differs. Hence, standardized preparation for functioning as a disability management practitioner/professional does not exist.

According to Harder, little information exists on what kind of education is required to function as a disability management practitioner/professional, as well as what knowledge/skills Canadian employers expect the disability management practitioner/professional to possess or bring to the workplace.[11] As a result,

---

[10] Registered Nurses Association of Ontario (RNAO), *Professionalism in Nursing, Healthy Work Environments, Best Practice Guidelines* (Toronto, ON: RNAO, 2007) at 58, available online at: <http://www.rnao.org/Storage/28/2303_BPG_Professionalism.pdf>.

[11] H. Harder & D. Voaklander, "Disability Management Career Awareness Survey" (2003) 2:1 *International Journal of Disability, Community & Rehabilitation*, available online at: <http://www.ijdcr.ca/VOL02_01_CAN/articles/harder.shtml>.

many different approaches to the development of academic programs and educational offerings have emerged. The outcome is that there is great confusion among students and employers as to which disability management educational offerings to pursue and to trust.

The purpose of this section is to examine and compare the various disability management educational offerings available in Canada. The methodology used is:

Step 1:   Identify the current disability management educational offerings.
Step 2:   Identify the desired elements of an educational offering.
Step 3:   Identify the gaps between the current and desired disability management educational offerings (*gap analysis*).
Step 4:   Identify the elements of the "ideal" disability management educational offering.

Hopefully, this review and analysis will assist students interested in advanced disability management education to be informed consumers.

Step 1 – Description of the Disability Management Educational Offerings in Canada

A description of a number of Canadian disability management educational offerings will be provided along with a comparison table (Table 26.3 located in Appendix 1).

Of note, participants taking these disability management educational offerings may be eligible for continuing education credits from a number of professional organizations.

A)   NIDMAR: DISABILITY MANAGEMENT PROGRAM

According to the NIDMAR website:

Return to Work Coordinator Program

The RTWC program emphasizes the skills and knowledge required to return to work individuals who have incurred injuries or illnesses and provides an introduction to the competencies that are required to administer disability management programs.

Certified Return to Work Coordinators may work internally within their own organization or externally as providers. Responsibilities include, but are not limited to expediting, coordinating and facilitating the return to work of persons with temporary or permanent injuries, illnesses and disabilities in a range of settings.

The Occupational Standards identify that successful completion of diploma or certificate program training in Disability Management meets the educational component eligibility requirement to sit the certification examination for a Certified Return to Work Coordinator.

Program Overview: Delivery and Assessment

The Return to Work Coordinator Program consists of 25 modules covering the essential skills and competencies required by Return to Work Coordinators, including those who also have some responsibilities for program administration. Each module requires ten to twelve hours of study. Modules focus on such topics as return to work plans, job analysis, workplace modifications, assessment, assistive devices, organizational skills, marketing, information technology, labour relations, rehabilitation, disability-related legislation, program development, and evaluation.

.....

The Return to Work Coordinator program is available online, on site at various educational institutions, or is available for delivery in-house.[12]

Online Return to Work Coordinator Program

The online Return to Work Coordinator Program consists of a series of twenty-five modules designed to provide the skills and competencies essential for Disability Management/Return-to-Work practitioners as they assist workers, who have incurred injuries and illnesses, in returning to the workplace.

The twenty-five modules may be taken as a complete program or as individual modules to develop expertise in specific areas. For those who intend to complete the entire 25-module program, it is strongly recommended that you first complete Module A, Effective Disability Management Programs and Module B, Introduction to Return to Work Coordination, as they provide a foundation for all other modules.

Module activities generally run from Monday to Sunday of a scheduled week although participants will have access to the online course from the previous Friday in order to review course materials and resources prior to the Monday commencement of module activities. All assignments must be submitted by 12:00 a.m. (midnight) Sunday, the last day of weekly module activity.

The estimated time required to complete an online module is ten to twelve hours during the course of the week including readings, self-tests, participation in an online discussion forum, use of other media resources and completion of an assignment.

---

[12] Printed with permission from NIDMAR. NIDMAR website, available online at: <http://www.nidmar.ca/education/education_background/background_information.asp>.

The schedule for the online modules is designed so that the entire program may be completed in one year (September to June or January to December) or over a two-year or longer period. In order to receive a certificate of completion for the entire program, all modules must be completed within a three-year period.

Participants may register in any number of modules at one time and discounts may be available based on the number of modules (please refer to the section on Module Fees). To qualify for a discount, enrollment and payment for all modules must be made prior to course/module commencement.

Those wishing to obtain the certificate of completion for the entire program and who have previous education in a particular module subject area, may apply to obtain an exemption or prior learning assessment credit.[13]

Delivery

Participants must have a computer and Internet access. They can log on to the workshops with their regular Internet browser and complete their study in the time and place that best meets their needs.

Each workshop module includes a 15- to 35-page manual and many modules include other textual materials such as articles and industry examples. There are video clips, self-tests, and links to information and Internet sites of interest. During the week of module activities, participants are provided with discussion scenarios, which through the use of a discussion forum, they analyze with their instructor and fellow participants. At times, the participants work in small groups.

Each module requires the completion of a short assignment designed to provide participants with practical skills and tools that can be used in their own return-to-work practice, or Disability Management Program.

The module activities are expected to take 10 to 12 hours, and in most cases, are completed within a week. The module topics include:

*   Effective disability management programs
*   Introduction to return-to-work coordination
*   Physical impairments, rehabilitation services, and return-to-work
*   Mental health issues, rehabilitation services, and return-to-work
*   The role of assessments
*   Communication skills for Return-to-work Coordinators
*   Communication and helping skills
*   Introduction to group skills
*   Introduction to conflict resolution
*   Disability and diversity in the workplace

---

[13] Printed with permission from NIDMAR. NIDMAR website, available online at: <http://www.nidmar.ca/education/education_online/online_background.asp>.

- Organizational skills for Return-to-work Coordinators
- Legislation and disability management
- Workers' compensation and return-to-work
- Insurance and other benefits
- Disability management in unionized organizations
- Disability management from a human resources perspective
- Managing change
- Job accommodations and assistive technology
- Evaluating the return-to-work process and disability management programs
- Injury prevention and health promotion
- Education and promotion activities
- Information management
- Professional conduct
- Managing the return-to-work process.[14]

Note: These courses are offered according to an established schedule with most modules offered at least twice a year. It is possible for students to start their program in January and finish in December of the same year.

Admission Requirements

- Completion of a high school diploma or equivalent.

Program Fees (as of 2009)

The NIDMAR modules are individually priced, with fee discounts for registering in multiple modules. To qualify for a discount, enrollment and payment for all modules must be made at the same time and prior to course/module commencement.

NIDMAR Fee structure:

- one to five modules: $225 per module;
- six to thirteen modules: $200 per module;
- fourteen to twenty modules: $190 per module;
- twenty-one to twenty five modules: $170 per module.[15]

If students participate in 20-25 of the modules, they automatically qualify for the $170 per module rate, making the total cost for the 25 modules, $4,250, whether they complete the 25 modules in two or three years. It is worthwhile to note, that this cost includes all the required course materials. Students do not have to purchase additional course materials.

---

[14] NIDMAR website, available online at: <http://www.nidmar.ca/education/education_online/online_module_descriptions.asp?progID=1>.

[15] NIDMAR website, available online at: <http://www.nidmar.ca/education/education_online/online_fees.asp>.

B)   MOHAWK COLLEGE OF APPLIED ARTS AND TECHNOLOGY

According to the Mohawk College website,

> In 1995, the National Institute of Disability Management and Research, in a joint labour/management initiative in British Columbia, developed a curriculum to provide practical disability management skills in Canadian workplaces. Now, with a special emphasis on Ontario legislation, this 180-hour Certificate is available through Mohawk College.[16]

Program Description and Delivery

This 180-hour, "in-class" certificate program offers the NIDMAR modules previously mentioned in this section. The benefits of the "in-class offering" are:

- small classes to facilitate interactive learning;
- networking opportunities and socialization with other colleagues and professionals; and
- expert instructors with a wealth of experience, knowledge, and related practical working experience.

A Ministry of Education (Ontario) Certificate from Mohawk College is awarded upon successful completion of the entire program. This is an approved certificate program.[17]

Admission Requirements

- Computer skills to prepare a basic Word document, use email, and the Internet.
- All applicants for whom English is a second language must provide proof of Canadian Language Benchmark 7.

Fee Structure (as of 2009)

The 25 modules are priced according to the number of modules in which the participant registers, for example in 2009, at a cost of $198.50 - $256 per course.

15 courses @ $198.50	$2977.50
10 courses @ $256.00	$2560.00
Total cost	*$5,537.50*

---

[16]   Printed with permission from Mohawk College. Mohawk College website, available online at: <http://www.mohawkcollege.ca/__shared/assets/healthsci2089.pdf>.

[17]   Mohawk College Continuing Education website, available online at: <http://www.mohawkcollege.ca/Discover/CE/health/disability.html>.

C)   GRANT MACEWAN COLLEGE

According to the Grant MacEwan College website:

> Disability Management in the Workplace is a growing professional industry. With a focus on assisting workers who have been injured or ill return to meaningful and productive work, disability management is an important part of any health and safety framework.

> As the economic and human costs of worker injuries and illnesses rise, the demand for controlling those costs increases. Effective disability management in the workplace can decrease these human and financial costs by getting the worker back on the job in a safe manner at the earliest time.

Program Description

Disability Management in the Workplace has been designed for distance delivery (a combination of print and online), offering learners a mix of flexibility and support that allows individuals to work at their own schedule.

Beginning with courses in communications, anatomy and physiology, and interpersonal skills, students gain a basic understanding of the principles and practices of disability management. In the second term, courses in ethics, professionalism and crisis management add to hands-on skills in return-to-work planning. After 30 credits, learners graduate with a certificate in Disability Management in the Workplace and can move right into a career.

For a higher credential, a second year of courses provides advanced skills in business communications as well as program design, delivery and evaluation. Comprehensive courses and a more focused field placement results in the attainment of a diploma with higher earning potential and greater career mobility.

Program Length

The certificate in Disability Management in the Workplace is 10 courses (30 credits) and is usually completed in eight months.

The diploma in Disability Management in the Workplace is achieved through an additional 10 courses (total of 60 credits) and is usually completed with an additional eight months of study.

Practicum

Two directed field placements are included in the program, coming at the end of the second and fourth terms. The field placements are arranged in consultation with the learner to provide a focused practical environment in which to apply their developing skills. Working under the supervision of a certified professional, learners can gain valuable work experience while being exposed to the challenges of the workplace and establishing a network of professional relationships.[18]

Delivery

All Disability Management in the Workplace certificate and diploma courses are credit courses.

1) Disability Management In the Workplace Certificate

The courses include:

- Essential Anatomy and Physiology
- Medical and Pharmaceutical Concepts
- Introduction to Disability Management
- Ethics and Professionalism in Disability Management
- Health, Social and Legislative Foundations
- Conflict and Crisis Management in Return-to-work
- Return-to-work Management
- Communications
- Interpersonal Skills Development
- Field placement

Fee Structure (as of 2009)

Tuition fees = $6,449 (exclusive of material fees)

2) Disability Management in the Workplace Diploma

Year 1 — As described above
Year 2 — The courses are as follows:

- Disability Management Program Design
- Trends and Issues in Disability Management
- Evidence-based Practice in Disability Management
- Health & Safety Issues in Disability Management
- Treatment and Prevention
- Disability Management Program Evaluation
- Introduction to Case Management
- Business Communications
- Elective course
- Field placement

---

[18] © Grant MacEwan College. Used with permission. Grant MacEwan College website, available online at: <http://www.macewan.ca/disabilitymanagement>.

Fee Structure:

Year 1	$ 6,449 (exclusive of material fees)
Year 2	$ 6,488 (exclusive of material fees)
Total	**$12,937** (exclusive of material fees)

Admission Requirements

• For year #1: Applicants must present an Alberta high school diploma or equivalent.
• For Year #2: Successful completion of the Year #1 Program is required.
• Graduates of the diploma program also have the opportunity to move into year three of the Bachelor of Applied Human Service Administration degree from MacEwan.

D)   DALHOUSIE UNIVERSITY: DIPLOMA IN DISABILITY MANAGEMENT

According to the Dalhousie University website:

> The goal of the Diploma Program in Disability Management is to provide professionals in the disability management field with knowledge and skills necessary to standardize and improve the service they provide to their clients. The program will enhance the students' knowledge and skills to facilitate a team-oriented approach to case management; convey an understanding of the health aspects of injury and illness as well as of the impact of injury on work and the individual; and develop decision-making and management skills. Individuals trained in disability management will function as Disability Managers, Case Managers, Return-to-work Facilitators, and Vocational Rehabilitation Consultants.[19]

Program Description

> The Diploma Program in Disability Management (DDM) is a ten-course program built on core competencies of thinking and decision making, communicating, delivering service, working with people, changing and learning, and self-management. Specific courses focus on understanding occupational injury, occupational assessment, return-to-work strategies, and psycho-social issues in disability management.[20]

The DDM Program consists of the following ten courses that address the following topics:

• Introduction to Occupation and Disability Management
• Workers and the Work Environment

---

[19] Printed with permission from Dalhousie University. Dalhousie University website, available online at: <http://disabilitymanagement.distanceeducation.dal.ca/>.

[20] *Ibid.*

- Understanding Occupational Injury and Disability
- Occupational Assessment
- Return to work Planning and Communication
- Referral, Co-ordination and Follow-up
- Return to work
- Strategies for Alternative Work and Prevention
- Psycho-social issues in Disability Management
- Program Evaluation in Disability Management

Delivery

All courses are offered via distance learning technology. The DDM Program uses a web-based courseware package called Blackboard Learning System (BLS). It is necessary to have Internet access, preferably a high-speed connection, to enroll in the DDM Program.

Admission Requirements

- Applicants to the Disability Management Diploma program must be presently working for a Canadian Workers' Compensation Board, or performing similar work with a public or private agency dealing with the return-to-work process for injured workers.
- Students who do not meet these criteria may be eligible for the Diploma in Disability Management Mentorship Program.

Fee Structure (as of 2009)

10 courses at $900 per course	$9,000
10 student fees at $15 per course	$ 150
One-time application fee	$ 45
Total	*$9,195*

E)   UNIVERSITY OF NORTHERN BRITISH COLUMBIA (UNBC)

According to the UNBC website,

> The master's degree in Disability Management at UNBC is the first of its kind in Canada and offers unique opportunities to students from a variety of fields.

> Interdisciplinary by design, the program provides graduates with the knowledge and skills necessary to assist labour, management, insurance providers, and employees with the development of successful "return-to-work strategies" for injured workers and / or workers with disabilities.

> .....

> The program is attractive to students interested in integrating the fields of economics, community health, social work, psychology, education, and business. The combination of course work, research, and the practical

application of knowledge gives students a well-rounded, applied education in the field of Disability Management.

The program is also available at the Prince George campus, either full-time or part-time, or on a part-time basis via distance delivery on the World Wide Web. Please see the information below and our website www,unbc.ca/ disabilitymanagement for details.

.....

Prospective Students

The program is intended to attract students from a diverse range of backgrounds interested in integrating the fields of economics, community health, social work, psychology, education, and business. It will be of interest to professionals currently working in the human resources, occupational therapy, social work and related professions. It offers undergraduate students a graduate program option in which to pursue a new, applied, and interdisciplinary field of study.

Components of the Degree

The MA in Disability Management combines course work, research and the practical application of knowledge to give students a well-rounded, applied education in the field of Disability Management. This degree consists of nine courses, a practical component, and a written project.

The courses listed on-line are:

- Professional Ethics in Health Care Management
- Foundations of Disability Management
- Disability Management: Legislation, Policy & Procedures
- Disability Interventions
- Special Topics — 5 courses (not listed)

Many students will be able to complete the degree in two years of full-time study, but there is a provision for students to pursue the degree on a part-time basis. Part-time studies can be completed on Campus in Prince George or at a distance with the majority of classes taught via the World Wide Web.

Entrance Requirements

Students intending to enroll in the Masters in Arts degree in Disability Management are required to have an undergraduate degree in a related field. The usual requirements for graduate admission apply; see the Graduate Calendar for details."[21]

---

[21] Printed with permission from the University of Northern British Columbia (UNBC), UNBC website available online at: <http://www.unbc.ca/disabilitymanagement/>.

Admission Requirements

- Admission requires a Bachelors degree in a related field with a 3.0 GPA (B). For mature students, a GPA of 2.7 (B-) may be acceptable.
- For individuals with experience in the field of disability management, flexibility regarding their undergraduate degree is extended.

Program Fees (as of 2009)

Full-time Program (2 years) (6 units x $1,681.93)   *$15,875.00*
Part-time Program (2+ years) (12 units x $883.00)   *$10,596.00+*

F)   OTHER DISABILITY MANAGEMENT EDUCATIONAL OFFERINGS

In addition to the above disability management educational offerings, the University of Alberta, British Columbia Institute of Technology, University of Calgary, University of Fredericton, and Ryerson University regularly offer Disability Management courses as part of their Occupational Health & Safety (OH&S) Certificate or Diploma Programs, or Occupational Health Nurses Certificate (Table 26.1).

Table 26.1: Other Disability Management Educational Offerings

University	Course Length	Nature	Cost	Context
University of Alberta[22]	39 hours	4-day compressed course	$495	Part of the OH&S Certificate Program
British Columbia Institute of Technology (BCIT)	36 hours	OCHS 3620 Credit course (3 credits)	$484	• Part of the OH&S Certificate Program[23] • Part of the OH&S Diploma of Technology[24]
	45 hours	NSOH 7400Credit course (3 credits)	$713	Part of the Occupational Health Nurse Certificate[25]

---

[22] University of Alberta website, "OH&S Certificate Program", available online at: <http://www.extension.ualberta.ca/sciences/prog_ohs.aspx>.

[23] British Columbia Institute of Technology (BCIT) website available online at: <http://www.bcit.ca/study/programs/6850cert>.

[24] British Columbia Institute of Technology (BCIT) website available online at: <http://www.bcit.ca/study/programs/6850diplt>.

[25] Printed with permission from BCIT. BCIT website available online at: <http://www.bcit.ca/study/programs/680hascert> and <http://www.bcit.ca/study/programs/680hascert#NSOH 7400>.

University	Course Length	Nature	Cost	Context
University of Calgary[26]	20 hours	3-day compressed course	$450	Part of the Health Safety & Environment Certificate Program
University of Fredericton	2-42 hour courses	Two online full-credit courses		Advanced courses in the Professional Diploma in Occupational Safety, Health & Environmental Management Program[27]
Ryerson University[28]	42 hours	Full-credit course	$478	Part of the OH&S Certificate Program

SUMMARY OF THE REVIEW OF THE CANADIAN DISABILITY MANAGEMENT PROGRAMS

- There are a number of disability management educational offerings that range from individual courses to certificate programs, diploma programs (credit and non-credit), and a masters program.

- *Certificate Programs*: The disability management certificate programs require completion of 9-10 full-term (45-hour) courses (360-450 hours) with the programs patterned according to the NIDMAR program having twenty-five (25) one-week modules (probably equivalent to 25 3-hour classes) that could be equated to 182-250 educational-hours. *Note:* NIDMAR does offer in-class courses which are 6.5 hours in length, thereby increasing the total educational hours.

- *Diploma Programs*: The diploma programs reviewed are composed of 10 to 20 45-hour courses or 450 to 900 educational hours. The two diploma programs reviewed are designed for Workers' Compensation personnel, or professionals and non-professionals in nursing or rehabilitation studies; the admission standards are stringent.

- *Master Program*: The one masters program combines course work with research and the practical application of disability management concepts.

---

[26] University of Calgary website, "HS&E Certificate Program", available online at: <http://conted.ucalgary.ca/public/listCertificate.do?method=load>.

[27] The University of Fredericton offers an online Professional Diploma in Occupational Safety, Health and Environmental Management program, with specializations in Disability Management, Environmental Leadership, and others. This Diploma program is part of an online degree-completion option. Available online at: <http://www.universityfredericton.ca/programs.html>.

[28] Ryerson University's *The G. Raymond Chang School, 2008-2009 Catalogue*, available online at: <http://ce-online.ryerson.ca/ce_2008-2009/calendar/default.asp?section=course&sub=0&mode=course&ccode=COHS%20477>.

Through full-time study, this masters program can be completed in two years.

- ***Educational Offering Outcomes***: Each disability management educational offering focuses on a different outcome. Some offerings are "stand-alone", offering a certificate, diploma, or masters degree when successfully completed. Others are courses that are associated with occupational health & safety certificate/degree programs, or occupational health nursing certificate/diploma programs. Likewise, some educational offerings address Disability Management Program management, and/or clinical case management, while others are designed to cover disability management claims management and return-to-work administration.

- ***Delivery Modes***: The delivery methods vary from classroom delivery, to distance learning via e-learning. Most of the e-learning is accomplished using the Blackboard Learning System (BLS) technology.

- ***Course Schedules***: All the educational offerings have set schedules, with some being offered only once or twice a year.

- ***Study Duration***: The length of study varies according to the program outcomes: for example, disability management courses are 36-45 hours long; disability management certificate programs are 1-2++ years; disability management diploma courses are at least two years in duration; and the disability management masters program is 2++ years.

- ***Costs***: Although the costs of these various educational offerings are difficult to compare, the individual disability management courses cost between $170-$225 for non-credit courses, and between $458-$713 for credit courses. The various certificate programs cost between $4,250-$5,983; the diploma courses cost $9,195-$12,937; and the master program costs $10,595-$15,875 depending on the study options.

- ***Field Work***: Some of the educational offerings involve workplace applications as part of the study program, *e.g.,* many of the NIDMAR modules require the participant to involve actual workplace elements in the assignments; the Grant MacEwan College programs include workplace field experience; and the University of British Columbia masters program includes a strong workplace focus and applied research component.

- ***Target Audience***: The target audiences vary as well — from individuals working in the area of Workers' Compensation, human resource, occupational safety, union, and disability management practitioners to professionals occupied in occupational health nursing, medicine, rehabilitation, or social work.

Step 2 — Desired State for Disability Management Educational Offerings in Canada

Disability management educational offerings should be standardized, as well as the admission criteria to educational offerings. From the viewpoint of a participant (the learner), other attractive features in a disability management educational course/program would likely be:

- ease of access;
- ease of use;
- designed to address learner needs and expectations, as well as employer expectations of a disability management practitioner/professional;
- industry-relevant course content: disability management is a complex discipline in that it requires knowledge of:
  - the workplace and organizational behaviour;
  - the diverse disability insurance schemes (Workers' Compensation insurance, sick leave, weekly indemnity, short term disability plans, long-term disability plans, Employment Insurance), their purpose, how they function, and their respective roles in the management of workplace illness/injury;
  - the etiology of a disability — illness or injury, occupational or non-occupational in nature, essential anatomy and physiology, relevant medical and pharmaceutical concepts;
  - the impact of diverse cultures on human response to illness/injury;
  - the management of workplace illness/injury;
  - the elements of an integrated Disability Management Program;
  - the design of an effective Disability Management Program;
  - the recognized disability management principles, models, key components, processes, and practices;
  - the requisite infrastructure for a Disability Management Program — policies, practice standards, tools, and procedures;
  - the key stakeholders in disability management and their respective roles and responsibilities, including the unions;
  - evidence-based disability management practices;
  - the elements of employee injury/illness treatment and prevention;
  - the difference between an impairment, handicap and disability;
  - terms such as "sick role", "occupational bonding", social capital theory, work accommodation, rehabilitation, gradual return-to-work, work hardening, *etc.*;
  - Disability Claims Management — its importance, standard of practice, and practices for both occupational (WCB) and non-occupational insurance plans;
  - Disability Case Management — its importance, standard of practice, and practices as well as effective management of disabilities with strong psychological overtones;

- the difference between medical and functional information, and work abilities;
- workplace (position/job) assessment and the various work accommodation options;
- the related ethical aspects — professional ethics, dealing with ethical dilemmas, ethical decision-making;
- the related legal aspects — duty to accommodate legislation, Occupational health & safety legislation, WCB legislation, privacy legislation, confidentiality, re-employ provisions;
- the related occupational health & safety issues;
- conflict and crisis management in the return-to-work process;
- effective business communication skills, including report writing and delivery of powerful presentations;
- effective interpersonal communication skills, including interviewing and assessment techniques;
- disability management data management, trend analysis, interpretation, and reporting;
- effective marketing of the Disability Management Program;
- the various illness/injury prevention techniques — primary, secondary and tertiary prevention through the effective management of management theories and practices, of work hazards, of mental health risks, and of physical health risks;
- the components of a Gradual Return-to-work Program and the related techniques — includes workplace assessment, work accommodation, case conference techniques, monitoring of the work accommodation, actions to address "failure to progress";
- the techniques for program evaluation and continuous improvement of the Disability Management Program and Gradual Return-to-work initiatives;
- the role of other workplace programs in a Disability Management Program, *e.g.*, OH&S Program, Employee Assistance Program, Attendance Management Program, Ergonomic Program, Human Resources, *etc.*;
- effective techniques for providing supervisors and workers with Disability Management Program education and training;
- the industry best practices in disability management; and
- effective consulting skills;

- readily available resource materials;
- a reasonable study length — ideally one to two years in duration;
- results that are transferable to higher learning opportunities; and
- reasonably priced program.

Step 3 — Identified Gaps

Currently there are a number of disability management educational offerings available, each designed to address a certain educational market niche. However from observation, some gaps exist, namely:

- *Standardized disability management educational content*: There is no standardization of the disability management educational programs in Canada; hence educational institutions can design a program deemed suitable for a particular educational purpose.

- *Admission criteria*: The admission criteria are "wide-open", hence there is lots of latitude for institutions to set their admission requirements.

- *Ease of* access: Courses are offered online or in classroom settings. Although these delivery modalities appear to address a variety of learner needs, they are delivered according to a set delivery schedule and the learners cannot readily progress at their own pace, or expedite the completion of their individual program.

- *Ease of use*: The methods of program delivery are either in-class delivery or web-based using Blackboard Learning System (BLS). For in-class delivery, participants must live near the educational institution. For e-learning delivery, participants require computer access and ideally, high-speed cable access. Most institutions are using the Blackboard technology; there are newer e-learning delivery systems in the marketplace that are more interactive and user-friendly than the Blackboard technology.

- *Designed to address learner needs and expectations*: There is no recommended standard for program/course content; hence the content offered is according to the discretion of the program planners and institution. Based on this review, the available disability management educational programs appear to be designed to meet an educational agendas that is not well-aligned with what learners will require to use in the workplace.

- *Industry-relevant course content*: Based on this review, the available disability management educational programs appear to be designed to meet agenda that are not well-aligned with what employers might expect from disability management practitioners/professionals, or with the knowledge and skills learners will be required to apply in the workplace.

- *Readily available resource materials*: This gap is believed to be smaller than the rest, but centres around the availability of relevant disability management resource materials and industry-relevant tools that the learners can use in the workplace. NIDMAR and some Canadian authors have produced some valuable resource materials, but more is needed.

- *Reasonable study length*: Educational program/course lengths vary greatly and appear to be designed to meet the institution's needs as opposed to learner needs. The current programs vary in length. Ideally, for industry-sponsored support, a disability management educational offering should be two years or less.

- *Results that are transferable to higher learning opportunities*: Educational offerings vary between credit and non-credit courses. In particular, the NIDMAR program requires a lengthy time commitment, but in the end, there are no academic credits offered. Ideally, the course/program results should be transferable so that learners can progress in the advancement of their disability management education, without having to "redo" some of the courses.

- *A reasonably priced program*: There is a wide variance in the cost of the disability management courses and programs offered. Individual non-credit courses range from $170-$450 depending on the payment options, while the credit courses cost between $484 and $713. The Disability Management Certificate programs cost $4,250-$6,449. The Disability Management Diploma programs are priced between $9,195 and $12,937. The Disability Management Masters program totals between $10,596 and $15,875.

Step 4 — The Elements of the Ideal Disability Management Educational Program

To address the identified gaps, the following elements for a disability management educational program are proposed:

1. **Standardized content for disability management educational offerings**
   In the field of disability management, there are two types of practitioners:

   a) those with medical education, experience and expertise in case management and illness/injury management and who are legally qualified to undertake disability management case management, identification and referral of complications, and return-to-work planning and coordination; and

   b) those with work experience in disability management, occupational health & safety, or human resources who are capable of claims management and the administration of the return-to-work process.

2. **Admission Requirements**
   The applicants should be screened according to their academic background and work experience in the field of disability management. Depending on the nature and focus of the disability management educational program, the admission criteria differ.

   For educational offerings aimed at competent clinical practice — case management, identification and referral of complications, and return-to-work planning and coordination, preference for admission should be given to applicants possessing a nursing or allied health degree.

For educational offerings aimed at claims management and the administration of return-to-work planning and coordination, preference should be given to those with work experience in the field of disability management, and at least a high school diploma.

For disability management educational offerings aimed at program management, the registrants would require business experience as well as experience with disability management. Again, a degree or diploma is preferable.

3. **Course/Program Delivery**
   The educational components/elements should be offered and delivered so that the program/course participants enable the participants to meet their learning needs in an organized and timely manner.

4. **Access to the Educational Offering**
   Instruction should be offered online using a friendly mode of delivery that can be readily accessed using a variety of computer systems and which enables interactive learning.

5. **Course/Program Design**
   Disability management courses/programs should be designed to address learner needs and expectations, as well as industry/employer expectations for a disability management practitioner/professional.

6. **Course/Program Content**
   The disability management content of the educational offering should be industry-focused and industry-relevant, and designed to meet the workplace and stakeholder needs and expectations of a disability management practitioner/professional.

7. **Course/Program Resource Materials**
   Relevant disability management resource materials and industry-relevant tools should be made available for the student participants to use in their respective workplaces.

8. **Course/Program Length**
   For industry-sponsored support, a disability management educational offering should be one to two years in duration, depending on the expected level of expertise required in the field of disability management. The greater the involvement and expertise required, the longer the program.

9. **Course/Program Transferability**
   The disability management educational offering should be transferable so that learners can advance their disability management education without encountering many barriers.

10. Course/Program Price

The disability management educational offering should be priced according to the outcome achieved, not according to its length or some other comparable criteria. That is, programs/courses aimed at program management and/or clinical case management, should be priced higher than programs/courses aimed at teaching claim management and the administration of return-to-work processes.

Conclusion

This review of Canadian disability management educational offerings indicates that academia and the marketplace afford great latitude to the design, offering, and delivery of disability management courses and programs. Without standardized criteria for a disability management course, certificate, diploma, or degree program, academic institutions have the latitude to develop and deliver what they wish. Hence, it is up to the disability management practitioners/ professionals and industry to stipulate what they need and want.

C)   THE CANADIAN APPROACH TO ADVANCED DISABILITY MANAGEMENT EDUCATION

INTRODUCTION

Professional certification, trade certification, or professional designation, often shortened to "certification" or "qualification", is a designation earned by an individual to assure qualification to perform a job or task.

Certifications are earned through a professional association or society, and must be periodically renewed, or may be valid for a specific period of time. Certification renewal typically requires proof of continued learning in the field of endeavour. This is commonly termed, continuing education, or earning continuing education credits. As well, the candidate must provide evidence of professional practice, usually in terms of the hours worked; and responsible and competent practice, in terms of a letter of recommendation by a manager or other qualified person. Submission of certification fees are also part of this renewal process.

Professional Licensure

Professional licensure refers to the granting of a license, which enables individuals to practice in their field of endeavour. The purpose of licensure is that it publically indicates a high level of specialized skill, and is used to regulate activities deemed dangerous or a threat to the person or the public.

Professional licensing tends to be granted through a professional body, or a licensing board, composed of advanced practitioners who oversee the applications for licenses. This often involves accredited training and examinations, but can vary a great deal for different activities, and in different countries. In Canada, some examples of professional licensure are the licenses to practice medicine, law, nursing, engineering, psychology, public accounting, *etc*.

Licensure is similar to professional certification, and these terms are sometimes used synonymously; however, certification is an employment qualification and not a legal requirement for practice in a profession.

The NIDMAR INITIATIVE

In Canada, the National Institute for Disability Management and Research, commonly termed NIDMAR, established a professional certification program for disability management practitioners and professionals and offers eligible candidates the opportunity to sit one of the two certification examinations:

1. Certified Return to Work Coordinator (CRTWC) designation; and
2. Disability Management Coordinator Certification (CDMP) designation.

Before being able to write these professional certification examinations, the candidate must meet the eligibility requirements that include a mix of educational programming and work experience. NIDMAR uses an eligibility qualifications table to determine the amount of work experience required (Table 26.2).

Table 26.2 NIDMAR Eligibility Qualifications Table[29]

Education	Employment*
Masters degree in health-related field AND diploma, certificate, or short course in Disability Management. The licence or certification must have been obtained by passing an examination in field of specialization	600 FTE hours performing roles and responsibilities, preferably with some supervision by a Certified Disability Management Professional or Certified Return To Work Coordinator; can be through mentor support of educator or management representative involved in Disability Management AND letter of attestation from supervisor
Masters degree in health-related field	900 FTE hours performing roles and responsibilities, preferably with some supervision by a Certified Disability Management Professional or Certified Return To Work Coordinator; can be through mentor support of educator or management representative involved in Disability Management AND letter of attestation from supervisor

[29] Reproduced with permission from NIDMAR, "Eligibility Qualifications — Certified Disability Management Professional" (2006). NIDMAR website, available online at: <http://www.nidmar.ca/certification/cdmp/cdmp_eligibility.asp>.

Education	Employment*
Bachelors degree in health-related field AND diploma, certificate or short course in DM. The licence or certification must have been obtained by passing an examination in field of specialization	600 FTE hours performing roles and responsibilities, preferably with some supervision by a Certified Disability Management Professional or Certified Return To Work Coordinator; can be through mentor support of educator or management representative involved in Disability Management AND letter of attestation from supervisor
Diploma or certificate program in DM	1800 FTE hours (approx. 1 year) performing roles and responsibilities with at least 50% or more of time in the delivery of Disability Management services supervised by qualified Disability Management supervisor or management representative AND letter of attestation from supervisor
Other educational experiences, credentials AND short courses in DM program principles and delivery	3600 FTE hours (approx. 2 years) performing roles and responsibilities with at least 50% or more of time in the delivery of Disability Management services supervised by qualified Disability Management supervisor or management representative AND letter of attestation from supervisor

*** Please note:** The NIDMAR Certification Council will only accept full-time paid employment (FTE) or its equivalent as a valid fulfillment of the employment criteria. Roles and responsibilities of employment must have been in the direct provision of disability management/return to work services for workers with disabilities encompassing the domain areas identified.*

The individual is not required to undertake the NIDMAR education program in order to become eligible to write the professional certification examinations. Participants from any disability management education program may be eligible.

The NIDMAR Certification process and examination costs $475. Once the candidate has successfully passed the certification examination, NIDMAR has annual requirements for Certification Maintenance allowing the individual to continue to use the CRTWC or CDMP designation. The maintenance requirements include a renewal application, proof of full-time employment, evidence of continuing education credits, a Statement of Agreement for Ethical Standards and Professional Conduct, and an annual membership fee of $250.[30]

According to the NIDMAR website: "Failure to maintain certification status will require the candidate to repeat the entire certification process by applying to re-

---

[30] For more details refer to "Maintaining Certification", NIDMAR website, available online at: <http://www.nidmar.ca/certification/cdmp/cdmp_maintaining.asp>.

certify, which includes re-writing the examination and paying the certification examination fees.[31]

Related Certifications

In Canada, there are other professional certifications that include disability management knowledge, skills, and expertise as part of the area of specialization, namely:

- **CANADIAN OCCUPATIONAL HEALTH NURSE CERTIFICATION — COHN(C)**

The Canadian Occupational Health Nurse Certification is offered through the Canadian Nurses Association (CNA). As part of the certification process, the occupational health nurse must be competent in the following areas:

A) *Provision of Occupational Health, Safety and Environmental Nursing*
B) *Recognition, Evaluation and Control of Workplace/Environmental health and Safety Hazards*
C) *Health Assessment, Planning, Implementation, Monitoring and Evaluation*
D) **Assessment, Care and Case Management of Injuries and Illness — the OHN is expected to:**
- **apply the nursing process to implement the interventions that will minimize the effects of illness and injury;**
- **use ongoing data gathering activities to evaluate ill/injured employees;**
- **identify fitness for work for a variety of medical conditions;**
- **identify occupational and non-occupational illness/injuries, assess employee limitations and recommend suitable work accommodation;**
- **provide and coordinate ability and/or case management; and**
- **counsel employees on illness/injury prevention.**
E) *Environment, Health, Safety, Wellness Promotion and Education*
F) *Environment, Health, Safety and Wellness Management*[32]

Eligibility for Occupational Health Nursing Certification includes:

Option A:

1. being currently registered as a nurse in Canada;
2. having accumulated a minimum of 5,000 hours of experience as a Registered Nurse (RN) in occupational health within the past five years;
3. having accumulated 75 hours of continuous learning activities during the past five years and submit proof of such; and
4. obtaining and submitting verification of registered nursing experience and endorsement from a supervisor or consultant in the specialty.

---

[31] *Ibid.*
[32] Canadian Nurses Association, "Occupational Health Nursing Certification: Summary", available online at: <http://www.cna-nurses.ca/cna/documents/pdf/publications/CERT_Occup_e.pdf>.

Option B:

1. being currently registered as a nurse in Canada;
2. having completed a nursing degree or post-basic nursing course or a program in Occupational Health of at least 300 hours;
3. having accumulated a minimum of 3,050 hours of experience as a registered nurse (RN) in occupational health within the past 4 years;
4. having accumulated 75 hours of continuous learning activities during the past five years and submit proof of such; and
5. obtaining and submitting verification of registered nursing experience and endorsement from a supervisor or consultant in the specialty.[33]

Recertification is required every five years and necessitates the applicant having to rewrite the certification examination, or submit evidence of 100 continuous learning activity hours and 3,900 active occupational health nursing hours. Re-certification fees apply — $477.75 for CNA members and $677.25 for non-members.[34]

Currently, 21 Canadian university nursing programs recognize Canadian Nurses Association certification in certain specialties for university credit.[35]

- **CANADIAN OCCUPATIONAL HEALTH & SAFETY CERTIFICATION — CRSP**

An Occupational Health & Safety Specialist seeking certification must meet the requirements for registration established by the Board of Canadian Registered Safety Professionals (BCRSP). Eligibility includes:

A) ***An Educational Component***: The successful completion of either a one year college or university certificate or diploma program in occupational health, safety, or environment; or a two-year college or university non-occupational health safety or environment certificate or diploma program.[36]

B) ***Experience***: Immediately prior to making application, three years of continuous Occupational Health Safety & Environment (OHS&E) experience.[37]

C) ***Employment***: Current employment of greater than 50 per cent (minimum 900 hours in a year) in an OHS&E practitioner role.[38]

---

[33] Canadian Nurses Association, "2009 Certification by Examination", available online at: <http://www.cna-nurses.ca/cna/documents/pdf/publications/Certification_guide_2009_e.pdf>.
[34] *Ibid.*
[35] Canadian Nurses Association, "Occupational Health Nursing Certification", in Obtaining CNA Certifications (2009), available online at: <http://www.cna-nurses.ca/CNA/nursing/certification/specialties/default_e.aspx>.
[36] Board of Canadian Registered Safety Professionals (BCRSP) "ANNOUNCEMENT: BCRSP Raises Minimum Formal Education Requirement" (January 2009), available online at: <http://www.bcrsp.ca/pdf/announcement.pdf>.
[37] Board of Canadian Registered Safety Professionals (BCRSP) "Qualifying For Your Professional Designation" (January 2009), available online at: <http://www.bcrsp.ca/designation.html>.
[38] *Ibid.*

The certification process involves applying to sit the examination, studying using the BCRSP Self-Study Guide, and then sitting the examination. Typically this takes at least one year to complete.

The areas of study and examined competence include:

- Accident Theory
- Environmental Practices
- Ergonomics
- Fire Prevention and Protection
- Health Promotion, which addresses Disability Management
- Health, Safety, Environment Auditing
- Law and Ethics
- Occupational Health Safety and Environment Systems
- Occupational Hygiene
- Risk Management
- Safety Techniques and Technology

The CRSP designation is widely recognized as an indication of OHS&E expertise. To maintain this certification, the individual must demonstrate proof of continuing education, employment, and competence.[39]

The cost for the certification process and examination is $446.25, with the annual recertification of $131.25.[40]

CONCLUSION

As presented, there are a number of certification options for practitioners/ professionals practising in the area of disability management. However, many practitioners/professionals continue to conduct business without any formal disability management education or certification. The only players in the field of disability management that hold professional licensure are physicians, nurses, and psychologists.

It is encouraging to know that voluntary certification is being considered as a minimum standard for practising disability management; however, it will take considerable time before this becomes mandatory. Industry and consumer pressure may help drive this initiative forward.

---

[39] For more details, refer to the CRSP Certification Maintenance Program available online at: <http://www.bcrsp.ca/programs.html> and <http://www.bcrsp.ca/pdf/cmpprogram.pdf>.

[40] Board of Canadian Registered Safety Professionals (BCRSP), "Application for the CRSP Designation", available online at: <http://www.bcrsp.ca/application.html>.

D) DISABILITY MANAGEMENT: THE INTERNATIONAL SCENE

INTRODUCTION

Internationally, there are three major players, each with their own focus, in the field of Disability Management:

1)   The International Labor Organization (ILO);
2)   The International Disability Management Standards Council (IDMSC); and
3)   The International Forum on Disability Management.

Each view their role as reducing the human, social, and economic costs of employee disability in the workplace through the development of internationally developed practice standards.

The International Labour Organization

The **International Labour Organization** (ILO) is a specialized agency of the United Nations that focuses on labour issues. The ILO governing body represents governments, employers, and workers.

In terms of disability management, the ILO developed a Disability Management Code of Practice designed to provide practical guidance on the management of disability issues in the workplace with a view to:

*   ensuring equal opportunities in the workplace for people with disabilities;
*   improving employment prospects for persons with disabilities by facilitating recruitment, return to work, job retention and opportunities for advancement;
*   promoting a safe, accessible, and healthy workplace;
*   assuring that the employer costs associated with employee disability are minimized; and
*   maximizing the workplace contributions that employees with disabilities can make.

The *Managing Disability in the Workplace: ILO Code of Practice* was released in 2003 and addresses the general duties of employers and workers' representatives; responsibilities of competent authorities; a framework for the management of disabilities in the workplace; recruitment and promotion of disabled employees; job retention; workplace accommodation; and the confidentiality of personal health information.

The overall belief of the ILO is that effective workplace disability management practices based on evidence, good practice, and experience, enable workers with disabilities to contribute productively to the organization/company and to maintain valuable work expertise. Employers benefit from the employment of people with disabilities — they can make significant contributions to the organization/ company. Through effective disability management, disability-related costs can be reduced or eliminated. The most effective disability management programs occur when stakeholders work collaboratively.

For more information on the ILO's Disability Management Practice Standard refer to: <http://www.ilo.org/skills/what/pubs/lang--en/docName--WCMS_103324/index.htm>.

The International Disability Management Standards Council

The **International Disability Management Standards Council** (IDMSC), founded in 2003, was established by senior representatives of business, labour, government, and other stakeholder groups from around the world. The current IDMSC member countries include Australia, Austria, Belgium, Canada, France, Germany, Hong Kong, Ireland, Luxemburg, Netherlands, New Zealand, Switzerland, and the United Kingdom.

The intent of the IDMSC is to reduce the human, social, and economic costs of employee disability in the workplace through the development of internationally developed practice standards. Viewed as a global advocate of consensus-based disability management, the IDMSC's mission statement reads:

> *To promote, through a system of policy, program and professional certification, the international acceptance, continued development and broad-based implementation of consensus-based, outcome focused Disability Management policies, programs and professional standards. This will be accomplished within an economically and socially balanced framework.*[41]

Operationalized, the scope of the IDMSC is the:

1. oversight of the global certification process of the professional designations: Certified Return to Work Coordinator (CRTWC) and Certified Disability Management Professional (CDMP); and
2. management of the global administration of the Consensus Based Disability Management Audit (CBDMA) and Workplace Disability Management Assessment (WDMA).[42]

The IDMSC Governing Body upholds the role of safeguarding, supporting, and developing the credibility, reliability, and defensibility of its certification systems. This is achieved through Operational Commissions such as the:

- Professional Certification Commission;
- Audit Program/Policy Commission;
- Regulation and Compliance Commission; and

---

[41] International Disability Management Standards Council (IDMSC), Mission Statement available online at: <http://www.idmsc.org/Main.php?do=viewPage&id=430>.

[42] International Disability Management Standards Council (IDMSC), available online through home page links at: <http://www.idmsc.org>.

- Research Commission.

The stated objectives of the IDMSC include:

- To ensure the ongoing development, relevance, and application of the Code of Practice and Occupational Standards as well as the associate international certification systems.
- To promote IDMSC certification.
- To foster continued global research, education, and awareness in the field of disability management.
- To provide leadership in the development of innovative disability management approaches, tools, and processes.
- To offer coordination, current access, and public recognition to organizations and individuals with valid certifications.
- To work together and in association with the International Forum on Disability Management to promote consensus-based disability management and prevention initiatives internationally in order to reduce the socio-economic cost of disability and improve reintegration outcomes for ill and injured workers.
- To govern the regulation and use of trademarks.
- To monitor the effectiveness and impact of the system within each jurisdiction and make recommendations for changes to license agreements or to international strategy.

Some of the achievements of the IDMSC include:

- **Practice Standards:** The adoption of the NIDMAR Occupational Standards in Disability Management (NIDMAR 1999).
- **Certification:** The adoption of the NIDMAR standards for the CRTWC and CDMP professional certifications.
- **Consensus Based Disability Management Audit (CBDMA):** A standardized disability management audit tool designed to be used by organizations/companies as a means to assess the performance of their Disability Management Program.

For more information on the IDMSC refer to: <http://www.idmsc.org>.

The International Forum on Disability Management (IFDM)

The **International Forum on Disability Management** organizes disability management conferences designed to promote global sharing of disability management research, knowledge, industry practices, and experiences. Disability managers from throughout the world come together to exchange "best practices". To view the past and upcoming International Forums on Disability Management refer to:

- **First International Forum on Disability Management, Vancouver, Canada — 2002**

  <http://www.nidmar.ca/news/archives/ifdm.asp>

- **Second International Forum on Disability Management, Maastricht, Netherlands - 2004**

  <http://www.starlingweb.com/adp/as00028e.htm>

- **Third International Forum on Disability Management, Brisbane, Australia — 2006**

  <http://www.ifdm.com.au/docs/IFDM2006-abstracts.pdf>

- **Fourth International Forum on Disability Management, Berlin, Germany — 2008**

  <http://www.disability-manager.de/e/ifdm2008/>

- **The upcoming International Forums on Disability Management — 2010, 2012, 2014**

  <http://www.idmsc.org/Main.php?do=viewPage&id=436>

Conclusion

Disability management professionals/practitioners need to be aware that disability management practice standards are multi-levelled, as depicted in Figure 26.1.

Figure 26.1: Levels of Disability Management Standards

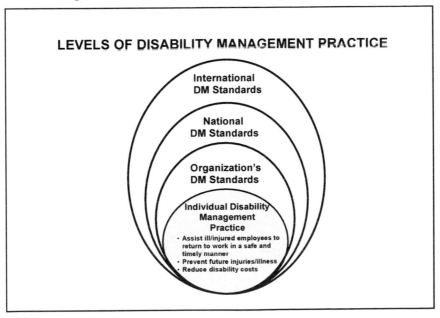

Although the field of disability management began in industry settings, national and global interest in worker illness/injury management ensued. At each level — the individual, organizational, provincial, national, and international levels — disability management practice standards have been prepared to address specific economic, social, and business needs. Disability management professionals/practitioners are advised to be familiar with these standards and to contribute to their development and continuous improvement.

SUMMARY

The field of disability management will continue to be fraught with interesting challenges — all part of its natural evolution. To practice effectively, disability management practitioners/professionals need to be equipped with current knowledge; sound disability case management principles and standards; honest and open communication skills; good relationship building and nurturing skills; and regular practice evaluation techniques. Without these, it is the employee that pays the ultimate cost.

APPENDIX 1

Table 26.3: Current State of Disability Management Programs in Canada — Comparison Table

Comparison Element	NIDMAR	Mohawk College	Grant MacEwan College		Dalhousie University	University of Northern BC
Offering	NIDMAR Certificate of Completion	NIDMAR Certificate of Completion	Certificate	Diploma	Diploma	Masters
Target Group	Non-professionals & Professionals interested in Disability Management	Non-professionals & Professionals interested in Disability Management	Non-professionals & professionals interested in Disability Management	Non-professionals & professionals interested in Disability Management	Applicants must be working for a Canadian Workers' Compensation Board, or performing similar work with a public or private agency	Degree-prepared professionals
Outcome	NIDMAR Certificate of Completion	Certificate of Completion from Mohawk College	Disability Management Certificate	Disability Management Diploma	Diploma in Disability Management	MA in Disability Management

Legend:

Certificate	Diploma	Masters Degree

Table 26.3: Current State of Disability Management Programs in Canada — Comparison Table

Comparison Element	NIDMAR	Mohawk College	MacEwan College	Dalhousie University	University of Northern BC
Delivery Method	Online using Blackboard technology	In-class	Distance learning (combination of print and online using Blackboard technology)	Distance learning (combination of print and online using Blackboard technology)	Online using Blackboard technology	In-class or Online using Blackboard technology
Set Schedule	Flexible	Yes	Yes	Yes	Yes	No
Availability	Readily	Limited to small classes	Must meet academic entrance requirements	Must meet academic entrance requirements	Must meet the academic entrance and program requirements	Limited
Workplace Application	Through course work	Through course work	Field placement at the end	Field placement at the end of years 1 and 2		Industry-applied research required

Legend:

Certificate	Diploma	Masters Degree

Table 26.3: Current State of Disability Management Programs in Canada - Comparison Table

Comparison Element	NIDMAR	Mohawk College	MacEwan College		Dalhousie University	University of Northern BC
Time Required	The time needed to complete 25 modules. This varies between 10 months to 2-3 years depending on the student's timelines	The time needed to complete 25 modules	1 year (8 months) to complete 10, 45-hour courses and a 15-hour field placement	2 years (16 months) to complete 20, 45-hour courses and two 15-hour field placements	The time needed to complete 10 courses	At least 2 years
Fees (as of 2009)	$4,250 This includes all the course materials	$5,537.50	$6,449 (exclusive of material fees)	$12,937 (exclusive of material fees)	$9,195	$10,596 - $15,875

Table 26.3: Current State of Disability Management Programs in Canada - Comparison Table

Comparison Element	NIDMAR	Mohawk College	MacEwan College		Dalhousie University	University of Northern BC
Comments	This is the standard NIDMAR Program delivered online with industry-experienced instructors	This is the standard NIDMAR Program delivered in class	Designed for professionals and nonprofessionals (*e.g.* Human Resources, Occupational Health & Safety)	Designed for professionals and nonprofessionals (*e.g.* Human Resources, Occupational Health & Safety).Graduates have the opportunity to move into year three of the Bachelor of Applied Human Service Administration degree at MacEwan	This is designed for individuals working for a Canadian Workers' Compensation Board, or performing similar work with a public or private agency	The UNBC Disability Management Program is the only post-graduate degree program offered in Canada

Legend:

Certificate	Diploma	Masters Degree

CHAPTER REFERENCES

British Columbia Institute of Technology (BCIT) website available online at: <http://www.bcit.ca/study/programs/6850cert>.

British Columbia Institute of Technology (BCIT) website available online at: <http://www.bcit.ca/study/programs/6850diplt>.

British Columbia Institute of Technology (BCIT), "Occupational Health Nursing Specialty", available online at: <http://www.bcit.ca/study/programs/680hascert> and <http://www.bcit.ca/study/programs/680hascert#NSOH7400>.

Board of Canadian Registered Safety Professionals (BCRSP), "ANNOUNCEMENT: BCRSP Raises Minimum Formal Education Requirement" (January 2009), available online at: <http://www.bcrsp.ca/pdf/announcement.pdf>.

Board of Canadian Registered Safety Professionals (BCRSP), "Application for the CRSP Designation" available online at: <http://www.bcrsp.ca/application.html>.

Board of Canadian Registered Safety Professionals (BCRSP), "Certification Maintenance Program" available online at: <http://www.bcrsp.ca/programs.html> and <http://www.bcrsp.ca/pdf/cmpprogram.pdf>.

Board of Canadian Registered Safety Professionals (BCRSP), "Qualifying For Your Professional Designation" (January 2009), available online at: <http://www.bcrsp.ca/designation.html>.

Canadian Nurses Association, "2009 Certification by Examination", available online at <http://www.cna-nurses.ca/cna/documents/pdf/publications/Certification_guide_2009_e.pdf>.

Canadian Nurses Association, "Occupational Health Nursing Certification", in *Obtaining CNA Certifications* (2009), available online at: <http://www.cna-nurses.ca/CNA/nursing/certification/specialties/default_e.aspx>.

Canadian Nurses Association, "Occupational Health Nursing Certification: Summary", available online at: <http://www.cna-nurses.ca/cna/documents/pdf/publications/CERT_Occup_e.pdf>.

S. Cavanagh, "The Gender of Professionalism and Occupational Closure: The Management of Tenure-related Disputes by the 'Federation of Women Teachers' Association of Ontario' 1918-1949" (2003) 15:1 Gender and Education 30.

Dalhousie University website, available online at: <http://disabilitymanagement.distanceeducation.dal.ca>.

H. Harder & D. Voaklander, "Disability Management Career Awareness Survey" (2003) 2:1 International Journal of Disability, Community & Rehabilitation 1 available online at: <http://www.ijdcr.ca/VOL02_01_CAN/articles/harder.shtml>.

International Disability Management Standards Council (IDMSC), Mission Statement available online at: <http://www.idmsc.org/Main.php?do=view Page&id=430>.

International Forum on Disability Management (IFDM), available online at: <http://www.ifdm.org>.

International Labour Organization (ILO), available online at: <http://www.ilo.org>.

G. Larkin *Occupational Monopoly and Modern Medicine* (London, UK: Tavistock Publications, 1983).

Grant MacEwan College website, available online at: <http://www.macewan.ca/disabilitymanagement>.

Mohawk College website, available online at: <http://www.mohawkcollege.ca/__shared/assets/healthsci2089.pdf>.

Mohawk College Continuing Education website, available online at: <http://www.mohawkcollege.ca/Discover/CE/health/disability.html>.

National Institute for Disability Management and Research (NIDMAR) website, available online at: <http://www.nidmar.ca/education/education_background/background_information.asp>.

National Institute for Disability Management and Research (NIDMAR) website, available online at: <http://www.nidmar.ca/education/education_online/online_background.asp>.

National Institute for Disability Management and Research (NIDMAR) "Maintaining Certification", NIDMAR website, available online at: <http://www.nidmar.ca/certification/cdmp/cdmp_maintaining.asp>.

National Institute for Disability Management and Research (NIDMAR) website, available online at: <http://www.nidmar.ca/education/education_online/online_fees.asp>.

National Institute for Disability Management and Research (NIDMAR), website available online at: <http://www.nidmar.ca/education/education_online/online_module_descriptions.asp?progID=1>.

National Institute for Disability Management and Research (NIDMAR), "Eligibility Qualifications — Certified Disability Management Professional". NIDMAR website, available online at: <http://www.nidmar.ca/certification/cdmp/cdmp_eligibility.asp>.

Oxford University Press, *Oxford English Dictionary*, 2nd ed. (New York: Oxford University Press, 1989).

Registered Nurses Association of Ontario (RNAO), *Professionalism in Nursing, Healthy Work Environments, Best Practice Guidelines* (Toronto, ON: RNAO, 2007) at 58, available online at: <http://www.rnao.org/Storage/28/2303_BPG_Professionalism.pdf>.

J. Roberts & M. Dietrich, "*Conceptualizing Professionalism: Why Economics Needs Sociology*" (1999) 58.4 The American Journal of Economics and Sociology, 977, available online at: <http://findarticles.com/p/articles/mi_m0254/is_4_58/ai_58496769>.

Ryerson University's The G. Raymond Chang School, 2008-2009 Catalogue, available online at: <http://ce-online.ryerson.ca/ce_2008-2009/calendar/default.asp?section=course&sub=0&mode=course&ccode=COHS%20477>.

University of Alberta website, "OH&S Certificate Program", available online at <http://www.extension.ualberta.ca/sciences/prog_ohs.aspx>.

University of Calgary website, "HS&E Certificate Program", available online at: <http://conted.ucalgary.ca/public/listCertificate.do?method=load>.

University of Fredericton website, available online at <http://www.universityfredericton.ca/programs.html>.

University of Northern British Columbia (UNBC) website, available online at: <http://www.unbc.ca/disabilitymanagement/>.

Wikipedia (2008). "Professionalization", available online at: <http://en.wikipedia.org/wiki/professionalization>.

Section 3:

Disability Management:
Glossary

Disability Management: Glossary of Terms and Definitions

Absenteeism — unplanned work absence due to illness, injury or personal reasons, or just failing to come to work.

Accommodation — the process and implementation of changes to a job and/or to the environment in which the job is accomplished which enable a disabled person to perform the job productively.

Acculturation — cultural modification of an individual, group, or people by adapting to, or borrowing traits from, another culture; a merging of cultures as a result of prolonged contact. It should be noted that individuals from culturally diverse groups may desire/seek varying degrees of acculturation into the dominant culture.

Advocacy — the activity associated with pleading or representing an employee's cause to management, or to external individuals or agencies.

Advocate — the role of pleading or representing an employee's cause to management, or to external individuals or agencies.

Alternate work — the change of work duties or time to accommodate the individual currently off because of illness or injury. It is any job, task or function, or combination of functions that a worker who suffers from a diminished capacity may safely perform without risk to self or to others, which would not normally be done by that worker. The key ingredient is that the work be gainful with rehabilitation as the ultimate goal. Alternate work is a permanent placement offered to recovering employees, or those with diminished capacity, when it is medically determined that the employee will not return to their own occupation. It includes:

- changing existing "own" occupation conditions (hours/duties/ responsibilities);
- providing different duties within another occupation/work site; and/or
- providing retraining or job search assistance for movement to a new occupation.

ASAP — Attendance Support & Assistance Program.

Assimilation — the assumption of cultural traditions of a given people or group.

Attendance Support & Assistance Program (ASAP) — proactive approach to promoting and supporting employee attendance at work, and to address and prevent "employee presenteeism".

Auditing — a systematic examination of the Disability Management Program performance for the purposes of evaluating and reporting on company operations and of being compliant with company standards and regulatory requirements. Auditing involves documentation reviews, interviews, and observations to verify the existence and functionality of various programs, policies, and procedures.

Autonomy — a form of personal liberty whereby the individual is regarded as having the right to self-determination. This means that the individual's values and goals must be considered in major decisions that affect his or her welfare, and precludes paternalistic decision-making (when one claims to know what is best for another person), as well as requiring informed consent when decisions are made.

Average Disability Claim Cost — determined by dividing the number of total disability claim costs by the number of claims for a particular period of time.

Benchmarking — continual and collaborative discipline that involves measuring and comparing the results of the key process with "best performers" or with one's own previous achievements.

Beneficence — the ethical principle that requires health care professionals to act in the best interest of the person.

Best practices — a form of benchmarking that result from direct observation of clinical practices.

Black Flags — signify the "*actual*" features of work that can be "real" barriers to a successful return to work.

Blue Flags — the "*perceived*" features of work that are associated with work loss and delayed recovery from injury/illness.

Bona Fide Occupational Requirement (BFOR) — a standard or rule that is integral to carrying out the functions of a specific position. For a standard to be considered a BFOR, an employer has to establish that any accommodation or changes to the standard would create an undue hardship. For example, an airline pilot must have very good eyesight. This standard is integral to carrying out the duties of a pilot's job.

Business skills — include planning, organizing, directing and controlling the business aspects of the organization, as well as the ability to conceptualize — better known as being able to "see the big picture".

Career — a lifelong series of events, rather than an evaluation of how successful individuals have been in their life.

Career advancement stage — characterized by a steep learning curve in which the person begins to better understand the work environment and organizational demands, and strives to establish personal worth within the organization. It is a period of growth and acceptance of responsibility.

Career anchors — the aspects of work that people value or need for fulfillment.

Career development — process through which individual employees, with the help of their managers, match up their skills, interests, and goals with the opportunities available to them and develop plans for achieving their goals.

Career entry stage — an exploration stage in which the individual tries to match individual need, abilities, and skills with organizational requirements.

Career maintenance stage — the individual becomes entrenched in the job.

Career modelling — is the development of a framework for attaining various positions in the organization.

Career plateauing — a position from which individuals are unlikely to advance to a higher level of responsibility in their careers.

Career withdrawal — the stage that was traditionally associated with retirement.

Casual Sick Leave — coverage for a non-occupational absence that typically extends for less than five consecutive workdays.

Case management — a collaborative process for assessing, planning, implementing, coordinating, monitoring, and evaluating the options and services available to meet an individual's health needs through communication and accessible resources to promote quality, cost-effective outcomes.

Change management — the ability to anticipate and to proactively plan for major changes impacting the company's operations.

Chronic fatigue syndrome — a complex disorder marked by incapacitating fatigue of uncertain etiology which results in at least a 50 per cent reduction in activity and is of at least six months in duration.

Claim adjudication — the process of determining whether a claim is eligible under the terms of the benefit contract or plan for benefit coverage.

Claim administration — includes claim submission, claim adjudication, claim appeal if required, and claim termination.

Claim Incidence Rate — determined by dividing the total number of disability claims multiplied by 200,000 by the total number of hours worked. This is also termed the Disability Frequency Rate.

Claim management — the service provided in administering income loss claims through employee benefit plans such as short-term disability, Workers' Compensation or long-term disability.

Claim management action plan — the planned approach for managing a specific claim.

Claim management plans — tools designed to facilitate the disability management claim process by helping key players to focus their actions towards a claim resolution.

Claims per Employee — determined by dividing the total number of claims for a given period of time by the total number of employees for that same period of time.

Clarity — the company members know what is expected of them and why.

Clashpoint® — an aspect of the workplace where generational differences of perspective, attitude, and opinion tend occur. They tend to include career goals, performance feedback, performance rewards, job changes, and retirement.

Client advocacy — the activity associated with pleading or representing an employee or organization's cause.

Client liaison — the position or responsibility within an organization for maintaining communication links with external individuals, agencies or organizations.

Client satisfaction — in terms of disability management, client satisfaction can be defined as the client being aware of receiving care in a timely and responsible manner, and of the many variables in the environment that contribute to his or her successful recovery.

Client satisfaction survey — an assessment tool to ascertain the level of satisfaction a client has with a particular service, product, program, or practice.

Clinical assessment skills — the ability to conduct an objective assessment of an injured/ill worker's situation by integrating and applying clinical, professional, communication, and practical skills for nursing practice.

Coaching — a process of assisting a supervisor, union leader, or employee to effectively participate in a Disability Management Program. It is the act of enabling an individual to successfully undertake a new role/responsibility.

Collection — the act of gathering, acquiring, or obtaining personal information from any source, including third parties, by any means.

Commitment — passionate "buy-in" and ownership of a belief/concept/ practice.

Communication — the ability to convey facts, concepts, or reasoning clearly to others, and to receive and understand the communication of others.

Communication strategy — a plan for designing and distributing information to stakeholders.

Confidentiality — maintenance of trust expressed by an individual verbally, or in writing, and the avoidance of an invasion of privacy through accurate reporting and authorized communication.

Confounding variable — a variable that confuses the relationship between the dependent and independent variables and that needs to be controlled through the design of the evaluation plan or via statistical procedures.

Corporate culture — the system of shared beliefs and values that develops within an organization and guides behaviour of its members. It is the way things are done within an organization. It embodies the learned values, assumptions, and behaviours that convey a sense of identity for employees and management. It acts to encourage employee commitment and organizational stability as desired behaviours.

Consent — the voluntary agreement with what is being done or proposed. Consent can be either expressed or implied. Expressed consent is given explicitly, either orally, or in writing. It is unequivocal and does not require any inference on the part of the organization seeking consent. Implied consent arises where consent may reasonably be inferred from the action or inaction of the individual.

Consulting — the art of influencing people at their request. It is a voluntary, temporary, and supportive relationship that involves a helper and a help-needing party (the client). It focuses on providing assistance to the client to enable him or her reach a solution to a potential/real problem situation. It is the provision of temporary professional help to assist the client to address current or potential problems or opportunities.

Consulting contract — an explicit agreement clarifying what the client and consultant can expect from each other and how they will work together.

Content objective — a specific statement that speaks to the content to be covered in a training session/course. For example: *"At the end of this educational session, the worker will be aware of the legislative requirement for accommodating ill/injured workers back into the workplace."*

Contingent workforce — that portion of the workforce who are contractors, consultants, or workers in part-time positions.

Continuous improvement — the process of enhancing the Disability Management Program to achieve improvements in overall performance in accordance with the organization's policy on disability management.

Control group — a group which is as similar as possible (in observable and unobservable dimensions) to those receiving the intervention (the study group).

Coping — is an attempt to overcome the obstacle by adopting a variety of human behaviours.

Cost benefit — weighing costs of the Disability Management Program against the benefits provided.

Cost-benefit analysis — an analysis technique that weighs the costs of a program/function against the benefits provided.

Cost-benefit projection analysis — establishing the causal relationships between the Disability Management Program and the benefits realized.

Cost containment — refers to keeping costs to a minimum.

Cost effectiveness — demonstrating the results of the Disability Management Program from a financial perspective.

Cost Relief — a reduction in a company's Workers' Compensation (WCB) claim costs as the result of a reassignment of those costs to the other industry members.

Costs per Employee — determined by dividing the total claim costs for a given period of time by the total number of employees for that same period of time,

Counselling — the process of helping employees (clients) manage health and psychosocial problems.

Critical thinking — examination of an issue or concept from a number of perspectives with a view to gaining greater understanding. It is the purposeful and reflective judgment about what to believe or what to do.

Cultural absenteeism — employee absenteeism that is supported and nurtured by the beliefs of the company's work culture.

Cultural awareness — being cognizant, observant, and conscious of similarities and differences among cultural groups. Awareness than enables the disability management practitioner/ professional to understand how beliefs, values, and personal or political power are shaped by culture.

Cultural blindness — the stage on the Cultural Competency Continuum when people assume that everyone is basically alike and advocate a universal approach and services for all people.

Cultural competence — having the ability to provide quality disability management care and services to a diverse employee population. It encompasses both systemic responses (*e.g.,* organizational policy, procedures, practices, *etc.*) as well as the delivery of disability management services by skilled and sensitive disability management practitioners/ professionals. Hence, cultural competence implies a responsibility at both the organizational and individual level.

Cultural competency — the stage on the Cultural Competency Continuum when people are able to effectively function in cross-cultural circumstances. It includes the development of standards, policies, practices, and attitudes that value diversity. Provision or facilitation of services which respect the values, beliefs, and practices of the employee, and which address any disadvantages arising from the employee's position in the company, community, and/or society.

Cultural destructiveness — the stage of intentional denial, rejection, or outlawing of other cultures on the Cultural Competency Continuum.

Cultural diversity — recognition that people come from a variety of gender, age, ethnic, geographic, economic, and religious backgrounds.

Cultural incapacity — the stage of acceptance of other cultures on the Cultural Competency Continuum, but an inability to work effectively with other cultures.

Cultural knowledge — familiarity with the broad differences, similarities, and inequalities in experience and practice among various societal groupings.

Cultural minorities — includes people other than Aboriginal people who belong to cultures not generally considered part of Western society.

Cultural pre-competence — the stage on the Cultural Competency Continuum of awareness within systems or organizations of their strengths and areas for growth to respond effectively to culturally and linguistically diverse populations. It includes a willingness to learn and understand other cultures.

Cultural proficiency — the stage on the Cultural Competency Continuum where proactive promotion of cultural diversity occurs and opportunities to improve cultural relationships are sought.

Cultural sensitivity — understanding the needs and emotions of one's culture and the culture of others; regard for the employee's beliefs, values, and practices within a cultural context, and showing awareness of how their own cultural background may be influencing professional practice.

Cultural understanding — recognition of the problems and issues faced by individuals and groups when their values, beliefs, and practices are compromised by a dominant culture.

Culture — the values, beliefs, customs, behaviours, and structures shared by a group of people.

Data — any form of information that can be collected and is relevant to an individual, group or organization function.

Decision-making — the ability to objectively analyze a range of possible alternatives and to apply judgment in selecting the most appropriate course of action.

Definitive causality — attributing observed changes to the program, while removing confounding factors.

Detection activities — focus on identifying workplace concerns and issues before they become problematic.

Deontological theory — deals with action and asserts that "rightness" and "wrongness" are measured by means, rather than by consequences of an action.

Dependent variable — the outcome variable of interest; the variable that is hypothesized to depend on or be caused by another variable.

Designated Representative — any individual (or organization) to whom an employee gives written authorization to exercise a right to access.

Direct Case Management Model — a disability management model that is characterized by an employee-employer approach to dealing with the employee's reduced work capacity and the employer's business needs and resources to decide the terms of the medical absence and the return-to-work plan.

Direct disability management costs — costs directly identifiable in terms of disability management such as disability claim costs, Workers' Compensation administrative costs, work accommodation costs, replacement worker costs, and the associated Disability Management Program costs.

Disability — the loss or reduction of functional ability and activity consequent to impairment. This is the reduction of the ability to "do things" such as performing movements or tasks.

Disability case management — the planned coordination of activities to maintain, or rehabilitate, an employee to an optimal level of functioning and gainful employment without risk to the health of the employee or fellow workers. Disability case management is a collaborative process for assessing, planning, implementing, coordinating, monitoring, and evaluating the options and services available to meet individual health needs through communication and accessible resources.

Disability Case Manager — an occupational health professional who practices within an occupational setting to assist ill and injured workers in reaching maximum health and productivity; who is responsible for the coordination of employee health care services across multiple environmental systems from the onset of injury or illness to a safe return to work or an optimal alternative; and who achieves quality care delivered in a cost-effective manner

Disability Claim Administrator — is responsible for the administration of the claim adjudication process for medical absences, including follow-up procedures for the various employee benefit plans such as short-term disability, Workers' Compensation, and long-term disability.

Disability claim management — the service provided in administering income loss claims through employee benefit plans such as short-term disability, Workers' Compensation, and long-term disability. This activity includes the determination of eligibility to receive a benefit according to the definition of eligibility contained in the plan contract, the facilitation of income-loss replacement, and the processing of the claim towards a resolution or termination.

Disability Frequency Rate — determined by dividing the total number of disability claims multiplied by 200,000 by the total number of hours worked. This is also termed the Claim Incidence Rate.

Disability management — a systematic, goal-oriented process of actively minimizing the impact of impairment on the individual's capacity to participate competitively in the work environment, and maximizing the health of employees to prevent disability, or reduce the risk of further deterioration when a disability exists.

Disability Management Consultant — a practitioner/professional who provides influence, recommendations, and expertise in the area of disability management, but has no direct power to make changes.

Disability management consulting — a voluntary, temporary, and supportive relationship that involves a helper and a help-needing party (the client).

Disability Management Coordinator — the position accountable for the overall management of all disabilities. This includes acting as a liaison with all stakeholders, including the third party insurers, being an active supporter of the ill or injured employee and family members, and functioning as a catalyst for facilitating the reintegration of the disabled worker back into the workplace.

Disability management education — providing management and workers with the information, concepts, and models to undertake and deliver an effective Integrated Disability Management Program.

Disability management governance — consistent disability management — that means cohesive policies, processes, and decision-making practices.

Disability management implementation strategies — defined methods of assessment, referral points, intervention options, potential job accommodations and alternative jobs.

Disability Management Program — a workplace program designed to facilitate the employment of persons with a disability through a coordinated effort that addresses individual needs, workplace conditions and legal responsibilities.

Disability Management Program Committee — a joint labour-management committee that acts as a steering committee for a Disability Management Program; serves as a foundation for the Disability Management Program; and provides support for the Disability Management Coordinator and the program.

Disability Management Program infrastructure — the system and environment within which a Disability Management Program operates. It encompasses the corporate culture, the disability-related policies and procedures, the benefit plans, and the linkages between the Disability Management Program and other company resources.

Disability management research — the use of the "scientific method" to discover, understand, interpret, and develop disability management principles, models, practices, and processes.

Disability Severity Rate — determined by dividing the total number of disability days lost multiplied by 200,000 by the total number of hours worked.

Disclosure — the act of making employee personal information available to others outside the organization.

Diversity — dissimilarity and variance between things and people.

Downstream activities — in business, the term "downstream" relates to the product/service marketing, retail, transportation, handling, storage, use, and disposal activities. In terms of disability management, it relates to all the activities that occur once an illness/injury has occurred.

Downstream safety performance indicators — See *lagging indicators of safety performance.*

Due diligence — the level of judgment, care, prudence, determination and activity that a person/organization would reasonably be expected to do under particular circumstances.

Early intervention — contacting the ill or injured employee within five days from the onset of a medical absence, and initiating case management if warranted.

Education — instruction on various topics.

Emotional Intelligence (EI) — the ability to motivate oneself and persist despite frustrations; to control impulse and delay gratification; to regulate one's moods; and to empathize and to hope.

Employee presenteeism — the phenomenon of employees being at work, but because of wasted time, failure to concentrate, sleep deprivation, distractions, poor health, and/or lack of training, they may not be working at all.

Ethnic — of, or relating to, large groups of people classed according to common racial, national, tribal, religious, linguistic, or cultural origin or background.

Ethnicity — the principle which explains how people are defined, differentiated, organized, and entitled to group membership on the basis of certain physical or cultural characteristics. Ethnicity can also consist of a consciously shared system of beliefs, values, loyalties, and practices that pertain to members of a group who regard themselves as different and apart. The salient feature of ethnicity is the attachment that a person or group has a common cultural heritage.

Ethno-cultural minorities — includes people other than Aboriginal people who belong to cultures not generally considered part of Western society. They are also termed cultural minorities or visible minorities.

Employee Assistance Program — a company-, union- or association-arranged service that provides confidential, professional counselling and assistance to employees and their families to help them resolve problems affecting their personal lives and, in some cases, their job performance.

Employee development — the ability to define the developmental experiences required to enhance an employee's job performance, and to prepare the employee for future responsibilities.

Employee morale — the employee group's general level of confidence or optimism about the workplace and management theories and practices, especially as it affects discipline and willingness. Employee morale is subject to environment, work, economic factors, and corporate culture.

Employee relations — all the interactions between employees and management in a non-unionized environment.

Enabler — the role of enabling another to persist in self-destructive behaviour (such as substance abuse) by providing excuses or by making it possible to avoid the consequences of such behaviour.

Enculturation — the repetitious and systematic inculcation of a shared system of values, beliefs, attitudes and learned behaviours.

Ergonomics — the study of how people interact with their work environment. This involves people, machinery, and the work organization.

Ergonomist — an individual who has (1) a mastery of ergonomics knowledge; (2) a command of the methodologies used by ergonomists in applying that knowledge to the design of a product, process, or environment; and (3) has applied his or her knowledge to the analysis, design, test, and evaluation of products, processes, and environments

Ethical dilemma — exists when two core values that the person upholds come into conflict, making it difficult for the person to decide how to move forward.

Ethical Fitness™ Model — an ethical decision-making model that assumes human beings have universal core values that cross religious, cultural and geographic boundaries. It serves as a decision-making guide, helping the individual to move from ethical dilemma recognition to resolution.

Ethics — defined as the science of morals, a system of principles and rules of conduct, the study of standards of right and wrong, or having to do with human character, conduct, moral duty, and obligations to the community.

Excessive absenteeism — absenteeism that exceeds either the corporate average for employee absence, or the Canadian national average of 10 days (2007).

Exchange — the actual delivery of the product or service.

Executive Summary — summarizes these findings and conclusions, along with any recommendations, and places them at the beginning of the study.

Expectancy — the belief that ones effort will result in attainment of desired performance goals.

Expectancy violation — occurs when an individual's behaviour does not conform to the expectations of others.

External consultant — an "outsider" who has access to specialized services not traditionally found within the client organization.

External Disability Management Consultant — is an "outsider' who has access to specialized services not traditionally found within the client organization.

Failure Activities — are described as the losses an organization incurs due to breakdowns in the system.

Financial/Business perspective — the ability to understand and to apply basic financial concepts (*i.e.,* profit/loss, loss control, variance, *etc.*) to the management and stewardship of the company's operations, and to understand the relevance of a specific job activity or function to the company operations and objectives as a whole.

Fitness-to-work evaluation — determination of an employee's health in relation to the job demands and the stressors of the work environment.

Focus group — a representative sample of the target workplace population assembled to obtain their feedback on a particular issue or concern. Typically they are asked their opinion on a product, service, concept, or idea. Open-ended questions are asked in an interactive-group setting, thereby encouraging the participants to freely express their thoughts and observations with other group members.

Formal practice/performance standards — documented company expectations, rules, and safe work practices.

Formative evaluation — is designed to validate or ensure that the goals of the program/product/training course are being achieved and to make improvements, if necessary, by means of identification and subsequent remediation of problematic aspects.

Frequency — the rate of occurrence of a loss.

Gap analysis — the approach used to determine how great and how many gaps exist between the two states and what is it going to take to eliminate or reduce those gaps.

Generation — set of people (cohort) born within the same period of time (approximately a 20-year span), and whose lives and viewpoints were shaped by the events within that span of time.

Generation gap — refers to the differences between the members of two different generations.

Generation-neutral workplace — a workplace that values and utilizes the contributions of all generations.

Generational integration — refers to the actions taken to bring the four generations found in today's workplaces together in such a way that the "best" of each generation is accessed and put into practice to enhance the well-being and performance of the entire workforce.

Generational strategy — a method of:
- understanding what makes their "employees tick";
- emphasizing the importance of teamwork;

- effective communications; and
- adopting "ageless thinking".

Gerontophobic — fear of the aging process.

Goal — a broad statement about something you want to accomplish.

Graduated return-to-work opportunity — the offer to return to work in a graduated capacity: reduced duties, hours, responsibilities, *etc.*

Health indices — are the measures used to establish "normal" or "abnormal" health conditions, such as body temperature, blood pressure, pulse, neurological functioning, *etc.*

Health promotion — the process of enabling individuals and groups to control and to improve their health. Health promotion is the science and art of helping people change their lifestyle to move toward a state of optimal health.

Health protection — also termed illness/injury or disease prevention — any behaviour performed by a person, regardless of his or her perceived or actual health status, in order to protect, promote or maintain his or her health, whether or not such behaviour is objectively effective toward that end.

Healthy organization — an organization that achieves a balance between the organization's health practices and the workforce's health practices.

High-status employee — any employee who is well regarded within the organization. High status may derive from an employee's formal position in the hierarchy, from a special level of expertise, or from the employee's social networking skills (*e.g.,* social capital credits).

Human factors analysis — the process of analyzing the relationship between people, technology and organizational systems to optimize organizational goals and human health.

Human Resources and Behavioural Management Theory — focuses on human needs, workgroups and social factors that impact work, and upholds that people are naturally social and self-actualizing.

Impact Evaluation — measures the degree of change in the behaviours/ well-being/attitudes of workers, workgroups, business units, or organizations that can be attributed to a particular disability management initiative, program, or policy. The central impact evaluation question is: *"What would have happened to those receiving the intervention if they had not in fact received the OH&S initiative, program, or policy?"*

Inclusiveness — translates to employees recognizing that they are valued and belong.

Independent Medical Examination (IME) — is a third-party medical examination to determine the employee's level of disability, length of disability, and to make recommendations regarding possible rehabilitation and modified work programs.

Independent variable — the variable that is believed to cause or influence the dependent variable. In a research scenario, it is the variable that is manipulated.

Indirect disability management costs — the "hidden" costs such as the management time and effort to promote workplace safety, worker time to do things properly the first time, data management time and costs, *etc.*

Informal disability management practice/performance standards — "what gets done in the workplace when the worker thinks no one is watching". These are the actual practices/work performances that go on within the field, work sites and offices.

Information systems — the ability to access basic computer systems for daily activities and familiarity with the application of computer technology to disability management functioning.

Informed consent — There is an obligation on the employer to ensure that sufficient information is provided to employees about the nature and consequence of the intended action to allow the employee to reach a reasoned decision. The employee must be mentally competent, and possess the ability to understand and appreciate the nature and consequences of the procedure. The consent must be freely given; not obtained through misrepresentation or fraud. The consent given must be in relation to the specific act contemplated unless the employee's life is immediately endangered and it is impractical to obtain consent. Consent cannot be given to the performance of an illegal procedure.

Integrated Disability Management Program — a planned and coordinated approach to facilitate and manage employee health and productivity. It is a human resource risk management and risk communication approach designed to integrate all organizational/company programs and resources to minimize or reduce the losses and costs associated with employee medical absence regardless of the nature of those disabilities.

Internal consulting — occurs when the consultant is a member of the organization and is assuming a consulting role to assist with the resolution of a problem or the chance to capitalize on an opportunity.

Internal Disability Management Consulting — is when the consultant is a member of the organization and is assuming a consulting role to assist with the resolution of a problem or the chance to capitalize on an opportunity.

International Disability Management Standards Council (IDMSC) — a council established by senior representatives of business, labour, government, and other stakeholder groups from around the world to reduce the human, social, and economic costs of employee disability in the workplace through the development of internationally developed practice standards.

International Forum on Disability Management — organizes disability management conferences designed to promote global sharing of disability management research, knowledge, industry practices, and experiences.

International Labour Organization (ILO) — a specialized agency of the United Nations that focuses on labour issues.

Interpersonal skills — the ability to form and to maintain effective working relationships with individuals or groups.

Job/Position Demand Analysis (JDA/PDA) — is designed to identify all the physical and psychological demands of the job or position.

Job description — a written record of the principle duties and scope of responsibility for a particular job/position.

Job finding — the process of finding suitable alternate employment for the disabled employee.

Job inventory — a listing of the available jobs for employees on an early return-to-work, or modified work program.

Job Matching Model — a disability management model which involves a fitness assessment of the injured or ill employee and an analysis of the physical/psychological demands of the employee's job. The intent is to determine if there is a "match" or "mismatch" in terms of a safe return to work for the employee.

Job modifications — can include adjustments or a redesign of the employee's workstation, use of adaptive devices (*e.g.*, ergonomically designed tools), use of work aids (*e.g.*, enlarged font on the computer for visually impaired employees), and/or telecommuting.

Joint Health and Safety Committee (JHSC) — has the mandate to identify, evaluate, and participate in the resolution of workplace health and safety issues/concerns.

Justice — the ethical principle that addresses treating individuals fairly, equally, and without discrimination.

Labour relations — all the interactions between labour and management in which employees are represented by a trade union.

Lagging indicators of safety performance — the outcome safety performance measures that are used by many companies, such as lost-time injury frequency and severity rates. Also known as upstream safety performance indicators.

Leaders — individuals that have the ability to excite, stimulate, and drive other people to work towards a vision, making it a reality.

Leadership — the ability to influence the activity of another individual, or a group, in an effort to accomplish desired goals and objectives. Leadership is an art that liberates people to do what is required of them in the most effective and humane way possible. Leadership is both about getting results and about how those results are obtained.

Leading indicators of safety performance — an index designed to anticipate or forecast the Safety outcomes of current trends. Also known as downstream safety performance indicators.

Learning objective — a specific statement that speaks to the worker learning. For example: *"At the end of this educational session, the manager will know how to report an employee medical absence."*

Legal Knowledge — a working knowledge of the various pieces of legislation relevant to the field of disability management.

Level I Integration — integration of the disability management of all types of medical disabilities — occupational, non-occupational disability management, as well as the short- and long-term disabilities.

Level II Integration — integration of the Disability Management Program with the organization's Employee Assistance Program, Occupational Health & Safety Program, Attendance Support & Assistance Program, Workplace Wellness Program, and Human Resources Programs.

Liaison — the position, or responsibility, within an organization for maintaining communication links with external individuals, agencies or organizations.

Line management — the management pyramid base — are the individuals who are directly responsible for assigning workers to specific jobs and evaluating their daily work performances.

Long-term disability — insurance plans that provide benefits to employees who are disabled and have exhausted their short-term benefit supports.

Loss control — the minimizing loss due to people, property, process, plant, or profit damages/threats.

Managed Care Model — a disability management model in which the employee's diagnosis is referenced against standardized care plans, procedures and diagnostic testing guidelines to determine if the treatment and the suggested leave duration are appropriate.

Managed Rehabilitative Care — a comprehensive approach towards accommodating ill or injured employees back into the workplace as soon as they are medically fit to function without harm to themselves or others. Goal-oriented and gainful work is offered to eligible employees in the form of modified/alternate work on a temporary basis, or alternate work on a permanent basis.

Management — the achievement of organizational objectives through people and other resources.

Management disclosure — the release of health information to management which is limited to the following:
- report of employee fitness to work;
- determination that a medical condition exists and that the employee is under medical care;
- time that the employee has been or is expected to be off work;

- medical limitations, if any, to carry out work in a safe and timely manner; and/or
- medical restrictions, if any, regarding specific tasks.

Management skills — skills required to effectively manage people and business functions. They include planning and organization, decision-making, problem-solving, leadership, financial/business perspective, negotiating, information systems, internal consulting, process facilitation, performance management, employee development, training, change management, presentation making and risk communications.

Market — the potential customers for whom the product or service has been designed.

Marketing — a social and managerial process through which individuals and groups obtain what they need and want by creating and exchanging products or services and value with others.

Marketing management — involves managing customer demand which, in turn, involves managing customer relationships.

Mental disability — any mental disorder, developmental disorder or learning disorder, regardless of cause or duration.

Mentoring — the process of coaching employees/other disability management professionals/ practitioners to learn a new role.

Middle management — which includes a level of executives such as plant managers, department heads and assistant vice-presidents, is involved in developing detailed operational plans and procedures to implement the business strategies developed by senior management.

Mission statement — describes the labour-management commitment to a program by presenting the high-level program objectives, describing the related values and beliefs held by the workplace, and stating the allocated resources.

Model — an approach created to explain a theory.

Modern Health Care Systems — modern medicine and health care practices; a recent development; technically-oriented; evidence-based health care; used when the traditional health care system fails.

Modified work — the change of work duties or time to accommodate the individual currently off because of illness or injury. It is any job, task or function, or combination of functions that a worker who suffers from a diminished capacity may safely perform without risk to self or to others, which would not normally be done by that worker. The key ingredient is that the work be gainful with rehabilitation as the ultimate goal. Modified work is interim work offered to recovering employees, or those experiencing a diminished capacity when it is medically foreseen that the employee will return to their own occupation. It includes:

- changing the existing "own" occupation conditions (*i.e.*, hours, duties, responsibilities, *etc.*);
- accommodating workplace restrictions (*i.e.*, lifting, sitting, bending, climbing, driving, *etc.*);
- providing transitional work;
- providing different duties within another occupation/work site;
- providing a training opportunity;
- all, or any combination of the above.

Multi-disciplinary interventions — interventions that involve assistance form a number of caregiving disciplines.

Needs assessment — a form of gap analysis — it is the systematic exploration of the way things are (the current state) and the way they should be (the desired state). The intent is to define the need — that is the gap(s) between the current and desired states with a view to reducing or eliminating those identified gaps.

Negotiating — the ability to interact with internal and external parties, with a view to making joint decisions when the involved parties have different preferences.

Nonmaleficence — the "no harm" principle.

Norms — rules of behaviour agreed upon by a particular social group.

Nursing process — a systematic, rational method of planning and providing individualized nursing care. It is the process by which registered nurses deliver nursing care to patients, clients, companies, or workers.

Objectives — the specific aims of a program that state the desired outcomes in a manner that is meaningful, relevant, realistic, actionable, sustainable, useful, measurable and result-oriented. Each objective should be written so that it is:

- specific;
- measures only one thing;
- attainable, but challenging;
- realistic; and
- time-oriented.

Occupational bond — the identity of the employee with the workplace.

Occupational bonding — the mutually beneficial relationship between the employee and the employer.

Occupational closure – the division between qualified members and unqualified outsiders.

OH&S Program — a complete system that ensures high safety standards throughout the company's operations and;

- reflects a strong commitment from management towards workplace health and safety;
- encourages worker commitment towards workplace health and safety;

- helps workers understand their responsibility for preventing workplace incidents;
- provides a work environment that provides the elements required to work safely, namely know how to work safely, able to work safely, equipped to work safely and motivated to work safely; and
- enables program evaluation and continuous improvement.

It is a defined action plan designed to prevent incidents and occupational diseases.

Occupational Injury (OI) — is any "work-related" injury or illness suffered by an employee. It is work-related if an event or exposure in the work environment either caused or contributed to the resulting condition, or aggravated a pre-existing condition.

Open system — a system that is permeable to external influences.

Optimal health — a balance of physical, emotional, spiritual, intellectual, and social (workplace) health.

Organization culture — a pattern of thinking, feeling, and acting that members of an organization pass along to new members as the "correct" way to perceive and behave.

Organizational wellness — managing both business functioning and employee well-being in a manner that allows the organization to be more resistant to environmental pressures.

Outcome evaluation — designed to determine if the OH&S training course/program met the participants' expectations in terms of the pre-stated OH&S training objectives.

Partnering — a method of accomplishing the mutual goals of the organization and the outsourced service in a planned and pre-described way. It involves jointly establishing service goals, objectives, and procedures. The intent is to have open communication and a solid working relationship, which foster the accomplishment of the desired goals.

Payout Ratio — determined by dividing the total dollars saved through the efforts of a Disability Management Program, initiative, gradual return-to-work program by the total dollars paid for the cost of the Disability Management Program, initiative, gradual return-to-work program for that same time period.

Perceived disability — a situation in which a person is seen as having a disability and is treated accordingly.

Perception survey — measurement of worker experience and perception of the quality and effectiveness of a program, function or corporate culture.

Performance management — the ability to plan, monitor and evaluate the individual performance and development of the employees reporting to the position of Disability Management Coordinator.

Performance measurement — a systematic evaluation of performance.

Personal health information — an accumulation of data relevant to the past, present and future health status of an individual that includes all that Occupational Health personnel learn in the exercise of their responsibilities.

Personal problems — physical illness, emotional and stress-related problems, family problems, alcohol or drug abuse or similar related matters which may adversely affect the employee's job performance and/or health.

Personal wellness — involves managing both psychological and physical issues in response to environmental stress, including the work environment.

Physical Capacity Evaluation (PCA) — an assessment of the functional abilities of an individual.

Physical disability — any degree of physical disability, infirmity, malformation, or disfigurement that is caused by bodily injury, birth defect, or illness.

Planning and organization — the ability to set appropriate goals and objectives, to predetermine a realistic course of action, and to negotiate correctly and allocate the resources required to complete a project.

Policy — a guide for employees that is consistent with the company's vison, goals and business strategies, and which is developed to prevent, or help to resolve problems. A policy should be comprehensive in its scope, clear in its intent, fair to all, documented, and readily available.

Post-return absences — employee absenteeism that continues after a disabled employee has returned to work in a temporarily or permanently modified position.

Practice/Performance standards — stated approaches to practice/performance based on recognized and accepted principles of industry practice for planned processes. They form the guidelines and rules for work practices, provide the boundaries for work activities, clarify stakeholder roles and responsibilities, and serve as a benchmark.

Pre-learning assessments — a baseline measure of level of awareness/knowledge/skills/abilities that the participant possesses prior to the educational session. This can be done using checklists, surveys, interviews, or demonstrations.

Premium holiday — is the period of time that a client or employee is not required to pay insurance plan premiums because the plan is over-funded.

Presentation skills — the ability to orally convey facts, concepts and reasoning to a group, and to receive feedback from that group.

Presenteeism — the phenomenon of employees being at work, but because of wasted time, failure to concentrate, sleep deprivation, distractions, poor health, and/or lack of training, they may not be working at all.

Prevention activities — focus on addressing and eliminating the identified concerns and issues so that they do not lead to health problems.

Primary prevention — deals with preventing problems before they exist, such as health education on heart health, smoking cessation, cancer awareness, nutrition, off-the-job safety.

Privacy — the claim of individuals, groups or institutions to determine for themselves when, how, and to what extent information about them is communicated to others.

Problem-solving — the ability to apply rational and creative approaches for analyzing and solving problems.

Procedures — defined actions that serve to standardize the Disability Management Program by providing a basis for stakeholder education, clarifying the disability management process, and facilitating smooth functioning of the Disability Management Program.

Process evaluations — see **formative evaluation**.

Process facilitation — the ability to introduce and steward a process to assist a client or group to achieve the desired results in an effective, collaborative manner.

Products and services — involve anything that can be offered to a market to satisfy a customer need or want.

Profession — an occupation, vocation, or high-status career that usually involves prolonged academic training, formal qualifications, and membership of a professional or regulatory body.

Professional certification — (*trade certification, or professional designation*) a designation earned by an individual to assure qualification to perform a job or task.

Professional licensure — the granting of a licence, which enables individuals to practise in their field of endeavour. The purpose of licensure is that it indicates a high level of specialized skill, and is used to regulate activities deemed dangerous or a threat to the person or the public.

Professional networking — the process of establishing relationships with community professionals to best serve the needs of employees and the organization.

Professionalization — the process by which a profession arises from a trade or occupation.

Program evaluation — the examination of whether a program has met its objectives, of other consequences that have occurred because of the program, and of whether the program's structure and activities are relevant and appropriate in terms of the program, company and government goals and changing conditions. It identifies the gaps between *the current state* and *the desired state* of a program, indicates whether the program goals/objectives are met or not, and enables improvements both along the way and periodically.

Psychosocial — the interaction between the person and his or her social environment, and the influences on the person's behaviour.

Quality assurance — assurance of a high level of excellence in Disability Management Programs and services.

Race — a tribe, people, or nation belonging to the same stock; a division of humankind possessing traits that are transmissible by descent and sufficient to characterize it as a distinctive human type.

Red Flags — factors indicative of medical problems.

Referral points — occur during the case management for a disability management case when the employee is referred for various forms of medical assessment, physical therapy, rehabilitation or vocational assistance.

Regulatory compliance — the process of managing the company's statutory obligations regarding disability management.

Rehabilitation — the process of assisting medically disabled employees to adjust to their disabled condition, and to recognize and maximize their financial, occupational and social goals. It can also be defined as, the restoration of an employee who has been disabled by an injury, disease, or congenital abnormality to an optional level of vocational, medical, social, and psychological functioning. The ultimate goal of rehabilitation is the return of the disabled employee to the workplace with the maximal use of his or her capacities.

Relationship skills ("people skills") — involve the ability to work with and through people to get the work done. They include the ability to communicate, lead and motivate people, as well as the ability to listen, empathize, care for and support employees in a constructive manner.

Reputation management — the process of establishing and maintaining the esteem of the internal and external publics regarding the company's disability management responsibility.

Request for Information (RFI) — a request for needed information prior to issuing a solicitation or request for proposal.

Request for Proposal (RFP) — explains what the customer is interested in procuring and provides instructions regarding how to prepare and submit a proposal for the provision of services/products.

Request for Quotation (RFQ) — explains what a company is seeking when all they are interested in is the price.

Return on Investment (ROI) — a performance measure used to evaluate the efficiency of an investment or program, or to compare the efficiency of a number of different investments or programs. The ROI is a popular metric because of its versatility and simplicity. That is, if an investment/program does not yield a positive ROI, or if there are other opportunities with a higher ROI, then the investment/program should be not be undertaken.

Return-to-Work Coordinator — is accountable for working with the other team members to facilitate the safe and timely return to work by the recovering employee, which includes acting as a liaison between the Disability Management Program team and the workgroups, employee groups, and unions.

Risk communication — the exchange of information among interested parties about the nature, magnitude, significance or control of a risk. Interested parties include individual citizens or communities, unions, scientists, government or industry associations.

Role-playing — an instructional technique used when participants are expected to be able to apply a specific skill.

Secondary prevention — deals with the early detection of disease and the initiation of early treatment programs such as screening for vision disorders, cholesterol, diabetes, tuberculosis, lung disorders.

Selling — the act of promoting a product or concept in such a way as to get another individual to adopt the product or concept.

Senior management — the highest level of management on the management pyramid; it is composed of the president and senior executives or vice-presidents.

Service Gap Analysis — a methodology for measuring client perceptions of service quality.

Service quality — the extent of discrepancy between client expectations, or desires, and their perceptions. Good service quality is meeting or exceeding client expectations of the service. The motto is "under-promise" and "over-deliver".

SERVQUAL instrument — a survey tool used to measure client satisfaction in regards to a service.

Short-term disability — insurance coverage can take on a variety of forms from weekly indemnity (or accumulated sick leave plan) to self-insured short-term disability coverage — all designed to provide income replacement for the employee during a period of non-occupationally related injury or illness.

Short-term elimination period — the time of illness/injury prior to applying for long-term disability benefits. This period of time varies in length depending on the long-term disability plan design. It may be 17 weeks, six months, 12 months, or 24 months.

Sick Leave — income replacement for the employee while recuperating from a non-occupational illness or injury.

Sick role — a societal-sanctioned role that an ill or injured person assumes once they become ill or injured.

Social capital — the goodwill available to individuals through their social networks.

Social capital credits — employees gain access to the goodwill of others when they have worked to establish personal credits. Credits are built by meeting following group norms, being trustworthy, meeting group expectations, and returning favours.

Social capital deficit — occurs when a member of a social group is unable to build enough social capital credits to access the goodwill of the group.

Social Capital Theory — suggests that our willingness to help others is based on the quality of our social relationships and is one way to analyze the impact of workplace disability on social relationships.

Social group/network — any group of people with whom we have social relations. This can be a workplace team, a family, or any other group of individuals who engage in social exchange on a regular basis.

Social marketing — the process of applying organizational analysis, planning and control to problems associated with social change in order to persuade different groups to accept the recommended ideas, concepts and actions.

Social sanctions — any penalty imposed by a social group on a member who violates accepted standards of behaviour.

Specialist skills — the skills required for disability management and encompass counselling, health promotion, professional networking, fitness-to-work evaluation, human factor analysis, work site evaluation, risk assessment, quality assurance, regulatory compliance, technical communication, case management, auditing, program evaluation, social marketing and strategic issues management.

Strategic issues management — Disability Management Strategic Issues Management links major health and safety issues to the corporate strategic business plans.

Summative evaluation — provides information on a program's efficacy, that is, the ability to do what it was designed to do.

Targets — the levels of Disability Management Program performance that the company wishes to attain.

Teaching objective — a specific statement that speaks to what the worker must do to demonstrate what he or she knows or how to apply a learned skill. For example: *"At the end of this educational session, the manager will be able to demonstrate the organization's absence recording practices."*

Team-building — the ability to plan steps designed to gather and analyze data on group functioning and to implement changes to increase group effectiveness.

Teamwork — involves a group of people working together to pool their skills, talents and knowledge to address specific problems and arrive at solutions.

Technical communication — the ability to research, analyze, transform and present technical data into a format understandable by targeted groups.

Technical skills — involve the ability to understand and use the techniques, knowledge and tools specific to the industry or ones area of expertise.

Teleological theory — the ethical theory that focuses on the consequences of an action and gauges the value of that action by the end results, rather than by the means to achieve the results. This theory is also called **utilitarianism.**

Tertiary prevention — deals with the correction of disease and/or prevention of further health deterioration as a result of disease such as rehabilitation and restoration with chronic diseases and conditions (substance abuse).

Theory — a set of ideas or principles that work together to explain a concept or something more tangible.

Traditional health care systems — part of the original culture, having filtered down, generation to generation. Traditional health care is the first resource the individual turns to when ill/injured; person-oriented; family-focused.

Traditional Model — a disability management model in which the care plan, authorized leave and return-to-work process are medically directed. The employer relies on the treating practitioners (primarily the physician) to substantiate the validity of the illness and to help the employee to return to work.

Training — the ability to provide clients with the skills and attitudes required to accomplish a task and to keep current regarding changes.

Transcultural nursing — focuses on understanding cultures, their specific health care needs, and how to provide assistance that best fits cultural life ways

Transformational leadership — inspired leadership that influences the beliefs, values, and goals of followers so that they can perform in an extraordinary manner.

Trend analysis — the concept of collecting information and attempting to spot a pattern, or *trend*, in the information.

Undue hardship — occurs if the accommodation creates onerous conditions for the employer, or union, or other workers.

Upstream activities — in business, the term "upstream" refers to the product/service research, development, production, and refinement activities. In terms of disability management, it refers to all the activities that occur to prevent employee illness/injury.

Upstream safety performance indicators — see **Leading indicators of safety performance.**

Utilitarianism — the ethical theory that focuses on the consequences of an action and gauges the value of that action by the end results, rather than by the means to achieve the results. This theory is also called the Teleological theory.

Value — the client's overall assessment of the utility of a service/product based on perceptions of what is received and what is given.

Vendor management — a key aspect of a successful disability management outsourcing arrangement. It involves establishing an effective working relationship between the organization and the service provider (the vendor).

Visible minorities — includes people other than Aboriginal people who belong to cultures not generally considered part of Western society.

Vocational rehabilitation — the discipline of coordinating rehabilitation efforts across multiple environmental systems.

Vocational Rehabilitation Specialist — coordinates rehabilitation efforts across multiple environmental systems as part of the disability management team and facilitates a return to employability. The Vocational Rehabilitation Specialist assesses plans, implements, coordinates, monitors and evaluates the rehabilitation care for clients in the Disability Management Program.

Weekly indemnity — an insurance arrangement that usually begins payments on the first day of a non-occupational accident or absence requiring hospitalization, and on the fourth or eighth day for other illnesses.

Work accommodation — a work opportunity offered to the recovering employee that allows for re-entry and participation in the workplace, and which is aligned with the employee's rehabilitation goals and the employer's business needs.

Work hardening — a rehabilitation method aimed at improving a person's tolerance to perform a job.

Work sample evaluations — Simulates real jobs or tasks for the purpose of evaluation.

Worker training — providing workers with the information, concepts, and models needed to do the assigned job tasks.

Workers' Compensation Board (WCB) — a third party, government-operated insurance system designed to protect the injured/ill worker and afford the employers litigation protection. It is a no-fault, industry funded insurance that is mandatory for certain industry groups. Employers pay all the premium and claim costs, while employees forfeit their right to take legal action against the employer.

Workers' Compensation Claim Administrator — is responsible for the administration and implementation of the Workers' Compensation claims. The Workers' Compensation Claim Administrator advises the company of the appropriate process and procedure relating to Workers' Compensation; provides interpretation, advice and guidance to employees on how to proceed with Workers' Compensation claims; and is the contact and liaison for Workers' Compensation matters for the employees and departments.

Working model — a graphic depiction of a theory. It must be general in nature and be intuitive to promote understanding.

Workplace wellness — from a personal perspective, workplace wellness can be defined as managing both psychological and physical issues in response to environmental stress, including one's work environment.

Workplace violence — any act in which an employee is abused, threatened, intimidated or assaulted in his/her employment.

Worksite evaluation — assessment of the work site for physical, chemical, biological, safety and psychosocial hazards, along with the related recommend corrective activities.

Yellow Flags — psychosocial barriers — factors that increase the risk of chronicity, disability, and work loss.

Index

S